OPENING THE QUR'AN

OPENING THE QUR'AN

Introducing Islam's Holy Book

WALTER H. WAGNER

University of Notre Dame Press • Notre Dame, Indiana

Manufactured in the United States of America

Reprinted in 2009

Library of Congress Cataloging-in-Publication Data

Wagner, Walter H., 1935–
Opening the Qur'an : introducing Islam's holy book / Walter H. Wagner.
p.   cm.
Includes bibliographical references and index.
ISBN-13: 978-0-268-04415-2 (cloth : alk. paper)
ISBN-10: 0-268-04415-5 (cloth : alk. paper)
1. Koran—Criticism, interpretation, etc.   2. Koran—Hermeneutics.
3. Koran—Reading.   4. Koran—History.   I. Title.
BP130.4.W24   2008
297.1'2261—dc22

2008027221

∞ *The paper in this book meets the guidelines for permanence and
durability of the Committee on Production Guidelines for Book Longevity
of the Council on Library Resources.*

CONTENTS

PART II.   THE QUR'AN OPENED

PART III.   THE EVER-OPEN QUR'AN

ACKNOWLEDGMENTS

Many persons over nearly twenty years have assisted, encouraged, and helped make this study possible. The selected bibliography recognizes the community of scholars whose insights stand behind the text. I am grateful to student and faculty colleagues at Muhlenberg College (1984–93) and the Moravian Theological Seminary (1993 to the present) plus congregational and community members who endured various versions of this work. Their comments and reactions are appreciated.

The editorial staff of the University of Notre Dame Press, especially Charles Van Hof, Rebecca DeBoer, and Sheila Berg, provided more than ink and paper. They have shared insights and assistance. I am particularly indebted to the members of the Islamic Education Center of Pennsylvania, Allentown, especially to Ruhi Subzposh and Ayman Kanan, Arief Subzposh and Eman Elseyyid for their patience, skill, and, above all, witness to God as they shared their understandings with me. Maria Ruby Wagner deserves special thanks for reading and commenting on the manuscript and proposing corrections and nuances. Naturally, I am responsible for any errors and misunderstandings in the book. Even more patient and supportive by living with me, open Qur'ans, and scattered papers has been my wife, Deborah. The book is dedicated to Nathan and Maria. May their ways always be straight and loving.

> To Allah belong the East and the West;
> Withersoever ye turn, there is Allah's countenance.
> For Allah is All-Embracing, All-Knowing.
> Surah 2:115, al-Baqarah, the Cow or Heifer

INTRODUCTION

In the Name of God, Most Gracious, Most Merciful . . .

The words with which the Qur'an begins open us to understanding this holy Book of Islam and through it Islam, Muslims, contemporary situations, and ourselves. The Gambian Muslim scholar Sulayman Nyang advised a group of non-Muslim professors who ventured to teach others about Islam that if we began with and stayed focused on the Qur'an everything would follow naturally.[1] He was absolutely right. The Qur'an is the basis for Islamic piety, politics, social life, mission, and more. It is the daily comfort, guide, resource, liberating power, incentive for hope for over a billion people, and more. For Muslims the Qur'an is al-Furqan, the Criterion, revealed to Muhammad as "an admonition to all creatures . . . sent down by Him Who knows the mystery in the heavens and on the earth."[2]

Still, reading the Qur'an can be a bewildering experience. It is a book, yet more than a book. The word *Qur'an* means "proclamation" and "recitation." Muslims believe that the Speaker of each word and Arranger of its order is the One-Only God. So its words, spoken, chanted, preached, quoted, and written in seventh-century Arabic, are holy and are to be heard, handled, interpreted, and applied with reverence. Al-Qur'an al-Karim (the Noble Qur'an) or al-Qur'an al-Majid (the Glorious Qur'an) is unlike any other book. Expecting something like the Bible's books, chapters, and verses, readers instead encounter 114 sections called surahs, divided into units called ayas. One surah may consist of more than two hundred or fewer than half a dozen ayas. Likewise, ayas are of different lengths, ranging from a few to scores of words. Each surah has a traditional name, some sounding odd to unopened ears, such as Cow (Heifer), Ants, Spider, and Flame, and others that are familiar, such as the Arabic equivalents of Mary, Noah, Abraham, and Jonah. I use the traditional title and number when citing a passage for the first time; thereafter, I use only the number.

Readers who expect historical narratives, stories, logical sequences of ideas, or essays on morals, are puzzled once they pass the beautiful first surah (which I examine in detail) and often are shocked and then bogged down by Surah 2 (the Cow) and even offended by Surah 3's (Family of Imran) strictures against nonbelievers. Those familiar with biblical accounts may be startled by Quranic versions of stories about Abraham, Moses, and Jesus. Instructions to maim thieves, flog adulterers, and slay opponents, along with descriptions of the agonies of Hell and the delights of the eternal Gardens, have been criticized for inculcating cruelty, violence, and lust. At the same time, sections such as the Throne and Light ayas (both of which are considered in detail), Purity of Faith (al-Ikhlas, Surah 112), and portions concerning the beautiful coherence of creation soar with poetic images, express the compassion of God, and challenge all humans to establish justice and peace.

Misunderstandings of the Qur'an by Muslims and non-Muslims alike, especially in the late twentieth and into the twenty-first century, have led to and still generate distortions and hostilities. Concepts such as jihad (struggle), martyrdom, the roles of women, and the treatment of non-Muslims in Muslim-majority societies—all subjects dealt with in the Qur'an and in this book—have fueled fears, rumors, and conflicts. I follow Nyang's advice: my aim here is to engage the Qur'an's spiritual depth and recognize its impetus to foster a devout interethnic community so as to foster an understanding of Islam and, with Muslims, create equitable social orders. This book by a non-Muslim offers other non-Muslims an entry into the Qur'an and ways in which readers may start to understand, assess, and perhaps adapt Quranic aspects to their own situations.

Opening the Qur'an's Procedure

This book offers a step-by-step procedure that makes the Quranic message accessible to students, teachers, clergy, and general readers. Following this introduction is a basic chronology from the birth of Muhammad (ca. 570) to the death of his grandson, Husayn (680). Three parts and three appendices follow. These provide comparative religious, geographic, and historical contexts together with accounts about the Qur'an's origins, structures, contents and issues, and some views of those who reject its claims. The selected bibliography serves as a resource for further reading and study. Woven into the informational material are references to Islamic beliefs and practices. I suggest that readers move straight ahead from start to finish and then return to portions for more thorough examination.

A fuller description of this book will be helpful. Although lengthy and sometimes complex, Part 1, Approaching the Qur'an, is essential to our whole task. Chapters 1 and 2 recognize that Judaism and Christianity as religions and Jews and Christians as individuals and communities were important in the development of Islam and are prominent in the Qur'an. Given concerns about the three religions' claims to God's truths, chapter 1 deals with the risks and opportunities for non-Muslims who attempt to interpret the Qur'an; several approaches to the important and recurring question of whether Jews, Christians, and Muslims believe in the same God; and the Qur'an's place in Muslim worship, practice, and theology. Chapter 1, therefore, raises key questions and issues that are implicit in the rest of the book and reappear explicitly in the final chapter. Chapter 2 continues the comparisons between the three religions by dealing briefly with basic Jewish and Christian beliefs, using the theme of covenants to set the stage for relating and contrasting those beliefs to Islam. The covenant motif is continued in chapter 3's extended discussion about Islam (largely but not exclusively in its Sunni aspect) in the context of God's plan for creation, with a focus on Islam's Pillars and Teachings. Chapters 4 and 5 deal respectively with the geography and people of Arabia, the time of the Revelation, and the man to whom the Qur'an was revealed. A map of the Arabian Peninsula at the beginning of chapter 4 provides a spatial context relevant to current national boundaries. Having set the general context, we get closer to the

Qur'an itself in chapter 6. It discusses the Qur'an's transmission and its transition from an oral proclamation-recitation to a book and some important problematic areas such as the abrogation or cancellation of some passages. That matter is taken up again in seeking to understand advocates of jihad as a violent struggle. Chapter 7 surfaces the necessary topic of interpretation and the freedom and accountability of Muslim and non-Muslim interpreters and scholars. I also explore briefly some types of and options for interpretation and suggest an approach that may be helpful for non-Muslims.

Part II, The Qur'an Opened, enters directly into selected texts and issues. We move from devotional passages to increasingly complex and controversial areas. Chapter 8 highlights four cherished passages. I trace what I call trajectories of themes that recur throughout the Qur'an. From that chapter onward, we step into difficult and provocative subjects: the end of this world and life in the hereafter (chap. 9); women (chap. 10); biblical figures, Jews and Christians (chap. 11); and justice and jihad (chap. 12).

Part III, The Ever-Open Qur'an, cites some challenges from the Qur'an to Muslims and non-Muslims (chap. 13) and challenges to the Qur'an by some critics (chap. 14). Chapter 15, "The Qur'an Opened and Open," returns to issues and questions raised earlier and completes our journey with a coda. The appendices are designed to aid and deepen the reader's involvement with the Qur'an. Appendices A and B chart the surahs' traditional names and order and the Arabic and English names of biblical figures mentioned in the Qur'an; appendix C is a glossary of key names and terms mentioned in this book. The notes often extend discussions begun in the main text; citations include the names of authors and page numbers. Full citations are found in the select bibliography, which also cites works that are not mentioned in this book.

ADDITIONAL INTRODUCTORY MATTERS

SOME TERMINOLOGICAL CLARIFICATIONS

Dating. I use the academic designations BCE (before the common era) in place of BC (before Christ) and CE (common era) instead of AD (Anno

Domini, Year of the Lord). Muslims use a lunar calendar of 354 days, whereas the West uses a 365-day solar calendar. In addition, Muslims calculate their era as beginning with Muhammad's emigration from Mecca to Medina (September, 622 CE). That movement is termed the Hijra (also spelled Hijrah and Hegira). The Muslim abbreviation AH stands for Anno Hijra, that is, after the Hijra. Rendering dates and years is problematic, and formulas have numerous exceptions. Generally I use the solar calendar. Where necessary, I give the combined dates CE/AH, so, for example, Muhammad died in 632/11.

Anglicizing Arabic terms and letters. I render the plurals for *surah, aya,* and *rasul* simply as surahs, ayas, and rasuls rather than in their Arabic forms. Traditions about Muhammad have been gathered in several collections. When referring to these collections as a whole or one in particular I use the words *Hadith* and *Hadiths.* When referring to a statement within a Hadith, I use the singular, lowercase *hadith.* I follow preferred Muslim transliterations: Muhammad (not Mohammad), Qur'an (not Koran), and Muslim (not Moslem). Arabic letters are often difficult to render into English and Roman fonts. Often strict accuracy in these aspects impedes fluid readings and is not always agreed upon. For example, the proper transliteration of the Holy Book is Qur'aan or Qur'ān, and the name of the Messenger is Muḥammad (hard *h*). Arabic contains characters and pronunciations that technically call for transliterations as double vowels such as *aa* and *ii*. Generally, I simplify transliterations with single letters and often omit diacritical marks. In the case of the cube-shaped building in Mecca toward which Muslims face when praying, several spellings are possible. I use *Ka'bah* instead of Ka'aba or Ka'abah, *Mecca* instead of Makki, and *Medina* instead of Madinah.

The Qur'an and translations. The Qur'an is the Qur'an only in the Arabic language of the seventh century and as sanctioned by Muslim authorities. All translations are interpretations, and there is no "New Modern Arabic Version." The Arabic text and its translation discussed here are officially sanctioned and used by most English-speaking Muslims. *The Meaning of the Glorious Qur'an* originally was completed by Abdullah Yusuf Ali, usually cited as Yusuf Ali, (d. 1947). Its English text, notes, and appendices have been revised regularly. Usually I cite it as "Yusuf Ali." At several points I cite the more literal translation by Muhammad Marmaduke Pickthall. The selected bibliography lists a number of other translations.[3] Yusuf Ali often translated the Arabic *rasul* as "apostle." I agree with numerous Muslim scholars that this rendering is too close to the Christian view that an apostle is a proclaimer of Jesus as the Son of God and resurrected Lord. In place of "apostle," I substitute "Messenger" for Muhammad and "messenger" for others designated as rasuls.

Yusuf Ali's translation and my use of it. Translators frequently introduce words for clarification. When Yusuf Ali did so, he enclosed the additional words in parentheses. When I introduce a clarification, for example, in citing the antecedent of a pronoun, I use square brackets[ ]. Words in parentheses and brackets, therefore, are not literally in the Quranic text.

Further, Yusuf Ali arranged the text in lines that resemble blank verse. The results and his punctuation may confuse readers. I have taken the liberty of restructuring the lines and altering the punctuation when necessary. He also capitalized words, sometimes inconsistently. I have retained some capitalizations and adjusted the text to lowercase initial letters to aid readers. His use of *ye* is helpful in distinguishing between the English singular and plural second-person pronouns.

HADITH COLLECTIONS

As the Qur'an is the highest and most revered authority for Muslims, the Hadith is regarded as the second authority. The word *hadith* means "speech," "report," or "account." Specifically applied to Muslim religious matters, hadiths (pl. *ahadith*) connote the sayings and actions of Muhammad. Muhammad is the fullest God-inspired human being who lived the Islamic way. Consequently, his words and deeds are valued as valid interpretations of the Qur'an and he is the living exemplar of what a Muslim is to be and do. In the two centuries after the Messenger's death (632), Muslim scholars collected accounts about him, checking diligently the veracity of those who reported those accounts, comparing versions, and eventually collating the results. Several collections are considered by all Muslims to be purer (*sahih*) than others. The most highly regarded hadith collections are by

Muhammad ibn Isma'il Bukhari (d. 870), referred to as Bukhari; and Abu-l-Husayn Muslim ibn al-Hajjaj (d. 875), referred to as Muslim. Two other sahih collections recognized by Sunni and Shi'ia Muslims to which I will refer are by Abu Dawood as-Sijistani (also known as Dawud; d. 875) and Abu Isa Muhammad al-Tirmidhi (d. 892 or 915).[4]

A clarification about the references to Bukhari and Khan. In 1997 the Muslim World League at Mecca, Kingdom of Saudi Arabia, published a new English translation and edition. The Muslim World League states: "As regards the previous [old] editions of this book (*Sahih Al-Bukhari*) nobody is allowed to reprint or to reproduce it, after this new edition has been published."[5] The translator is Muhammad Muhsin Khan. The Khan edition seeks to be a clearer and more accurate translation than the long-established and widely used other versions, as in the Bukhari contained in the Alim (see the section "English Translations of Hadith Collections" in the bibliography). At various places the Khan numbering of the books, chapters, and items differs from the previous versions. Furthermore, the Khan translation numbers the items serially throughout the entire nine-volume edition, from 1 to 7563. When I cite the Bukhari traditional collection, I use the term "item" for a particular hadith statement. The traditional Bukhari collection numbers the hadith statements (my "item") serially in each book. In that collection, I cite book number first, then the traditional item (hadith) number. "Bukhari 4.819" refers to bk. 4, item 819. To accommodate those who use the Khan translation, when citing Bukhari and when there is a difference, I cite first the Bukhari traditional reference followed by the Khan reference, as follows: Bukhari book number.item number/Khan item number. I also cite the Abu Dawood and Tirmidhi collections contained in the Alim by item (hadith) number, for instance, Tirmidhi 3834.

GOD AND HONORIFICS

Allah is not a name like Zeus or Krishna; it is the Arabic word for the Supreme Being. Christians, Jews, and atheists who speak of God in Arabic use Allah. The Qur'an has one speaking voice, that of God, sometimes in first-person singular and plural and sometimes in third-person singular. Following Yusuf Ali and for clarity, I use the uppercase initial letter for references to God/Allah, for example, I, He, We, and Who. Following suggestions by Muslims and to avoid the implication that Allah is somehow different from God, I retain "Allah" in quotations but use "God" in my discussion.

The Arabic word *ilaha,* often translated into English as "god" (note the lowercase *g*), carries the sense of something or someone worthy of worship. The Arabic language can also be written so that one letter elides from one word into another, and further elisions are common when the written words are spoken. So the vital statement of faith (the Shahadah, discussed in chap. 3) is usually translated as "I testify that there is no god but God (Allah) and I testify that Muhammad is God's (Allah's) Messenger." It would be transliterated as *Ashhadu an la ilaha illa-Llah, wa ashhadu anna Muhammadun rasulu-Llah.* It would be pronounced: *Ashhadu al-la ilaha illa-Llah, wa ashhadu anna Muhammadar-rasulu-Llah.*[6]

A related point about the usage of *God* is the Muslim practice of saying and writing honorific or reverential blessings when saying God/Allah, Muhammad, the names of angels and the names of prophets and messengers. On referring directly to God/Allah, a Muslim often says or writes, "Subhanahu Wa Ta'ala" (abbreviated SA and SAT), that is, "God is purified from having any offspring" or associated ilaha. On saying Muhammad's name, the honorific is "Salla-lahu Alayhi wa-sallam" (abbreviated SAW, or for English speakers, PBUH), that is, "May God's peace and blessings be upon him." The usual reference for angels, prophets, and messengers is A-Salaam (AS), "Peace be to him." While I acknowledge those uses at this point, I do not use them except in direct quotations.

VOICES

When Muslims read the Qur'an, they believe they are hearing the voice of God mediated through the angel Gabriel to Muhammad and written by his followers. Authors have voices too. You will hear me speak in three voices. One is the voice of the teacher-guide who provides information and context. Another voice is my attempt to speak, as best as one can, from within Muslim perspectives and to do so positively. I have listened to believers in person, in recordings, and in print. Now I endeavor to share with you what I have heard in ways that are understandable to non-Muslims. The third conscious voice is my own. When I am aware that I am giving my own position, I identify that voice with the first-person singular pronoun. Usually that voice's tone is that of a questioner, issue raiser, and suggester of interpretations.

CHRONOLOGY, FROM 570 TO 680 CE

623 Muhammad marries Aisha. Confrontations with Meccans.

624 Raid on Nakhlah. Qibla changed from Jerusalem to Ka'bah (February?). Battle of Badr. Plots by Jewish clan, Banu Nadir, retaliation by Muslims.

625 Battle of Uhud. Expulsion of Jewish groups from Medina that conspired against Muslims.

627 "War of the Confederates," Battle of the Trench (Ditch). Destruction of Medinian critics and remaining Jewish groups in Medina area.

628 March: Treaty of Hudaybiyyah concerning Muslims making Hajj to Mecca. King of the Yemen becomes Muslim, revolts against weakened Persians. Muhammad sends heralds to nations. Jewish citadel at Khaybar destroyed.

629 March: Muslims go to Mecca for Hajj. Bilal gives call to prayer at Ka'bah. Muslims battle with Byzantine Christians in northern Arabia.

630 Year of the Deputations. Mecca surrenders to Muslims. Ka'bah cleansed. Bedouin tribes profess Islam and loyalty to Muhammad. Meccans, Muslims, and new converts go with Muhammad to fight in the north.

631 Ali goes as Muhammad's emissary to the Yemen. Non-Muslims refused entry to Mecca at pilgrimage.

632 January: Muhammad's son, Ibrahim, dies. March: Muhammad defends Ali. Farewell Pilgrimage by Muhammad to Mecca, preaches last sermon (March), campaigns, returns to Medina. Muhammad dies on June 8, buried in Medina. Abu Bakr chosen to be caliph. Wars of Apostasy.

633 Southern Mesopotamia (Iraq) conquered.

634 Death of Abu Bakr. Umar (Omar) becomes caliph. Military campaigns expand Dar al-Islam (Realm of Islam), defeating Byzantine Christians.

635 Jews and Christians expelled from Arabia. Syria conquered.

636 Muslims defeat Persians.

637 Umar captures Jerusalem. Clears Temple Mount. Damascus becomes center of Muslim political authority.

640–41	Egypt conquered. Byzantine emperor (Heraclius) dies.
644	Death of Umar. Uthman becomes caliph.
650	Collation of Qur'an under Uthman.
656	Uthman assassinated. Ali acknowledged as caliph. Battle of the Camel.
657	Mu'awiyah attacks Ali. Battle of Siffin. Kharijites defect from Ali.
658	Mu'awiyah recognized by many as caliph.
661	Ali assassinated by a Kharijite. Older son, Hasan, relegates political leadership to Mu'awiyah. Ali entombed in Najaf, Iraq.
661–80	Husayn (Hussein), younger son of Ali and Fatimah, asserts authority as direct descendant of Muhammad. In 680 (10 Muharram), he and his group massacred near Karbala, Iraq. Husayn entombed in Najaf, Iraq. Split between Sunni and Shi'ite Muslims widens.

PART I

APPROACHING THE QUR'AN

Let there be no compulsion in religion. Truth stands out clear from error; whoever rejects evil and believes in Allah hath grasped the most trustworthy hand-hold that never breaks. And Allah heareth and knoweth all things. Allah is the Protector of those who have faith: from the depths of darkness He will lead them forth into light. Of those who reject faith, the patrons are the Evil Ones: from light they will lead them forth into the depths of darkness. They will be companions of the fire to dwell therein (for ever).

Surah 2:256–57

Being introduced to the Qur'an is somewhat like being introduced to another person. One or both may have heard about the other. Each may have expectations, perhaps anxieties, about the meeting and its results. Introductions are often arranged and guided by an intermediary. He or she can serve as an interpreter, mediator, and critic as the persons communicate or fail to communicate with each other. In the ebb and flow of the introduction, the introducer may inform either or both sides more fully about the character, background, and intentions of the other, set the scene for the meeting, and start the initial conversations.

The dynamics of introductions match our preparing to open the Qur'an. Part I is essential to the rest of our study. Chapter 1, "Perspectives," recounts some risks and opportunities for those who engage in religious studies, interfaith relations, and related sociopolitical issues. Questions raised in the chapter are recalled in the last chapter. Because I do not assume that readers are religiously committed or have a deep knowledge of Judaism, Christianity, and Islam even if they include themselves in one of those faith families, chapters 2 and 3 cover those religions' basic beliefs. I present "master narratives" for each in which the major accounts of the religions are told. "Covenant" is cited as a significant motif common to all three. In the instances of Judaism and Christianity, I angle the beliefs toward concerns relevant to Quranic responses. chapter 3's master narrative is long enough to range through God's plan for the cosmos and history from before the world's creation to the Hereafter and broad enough to include Islam's Five Pillars and Teachings.

Part I introduces the writer–interpreter to the reader–meeter, provides basic religious positions that are woven throughout the study and brings us to the point of approaching the Qur'an in its original setting, first listeners, and traditional shape.

> Mankind was one single nation and Allah sent messengers
> with glad tidings and warnings; and with them He sent the
> Book in truth to judge between people in matters wherein
> they differed; but the People of the Book, after the clear
> signs came to them, did not differ among themselves except
> through selfish contumacy. Allah by His grace guided the
> believers to the truth concerning that wherein they differed.
> For Allah guides whom He will to a path that is straight.
>
> *Surah 2:213*

ONE

RISKS, PERSPECTIVES, AND UNDERSTANDINGS

To each is a goal to which Allah turns him; then strive together (as in a race) toward all that is good. Wheresoever ye are, Allah will bring you together. For Allah hath power over all things.

Surah 2:148

Being introduced to and introducing others to a religion involves risks and opportunities. We come with culturally conditioned understandings about ourselves and the faith we are about to consider. Those understandings are confirmed, corrected, adapted, or amended as we engage the other religion and its believers. No matter how "objective" a person may think he is or how committed he feels he is to his own position, the other faith challenges with its questions and causes us to rethink that which we hold and why. As we prepare to open the Qur'an, I mention three sets of general risks and opportunities I have encountered. The key questions are "Do Jews, Christians, and Muslims worship the same God? Is Islam the true religion? Is the Qur'an God inspired? Is Muhammad a genuine prophet?" The several options for answering these questions color how we consider the Qur'an and Islam. The chapter concludes with three Muslim perspectives on the Qur'an.

THREE SETS OF RISKS AND OPPORTUNITIES

The first set is a double confrontation. The Muslim college student from Pakistan was irate. Since I introduced the Qur'an, spoke respectfully of Muhammad, and presented Islam accurately to the class, he assumed that I would convert to Islam. When I remained a Lutheran-style Christian, he reproached me with a Quranic forecast for my fate: "As to those who reject Faith, it is the same to them whether you warn them or do not warn them: they will not believe. Allah has set a seal on their hearts and on their hearing, and on their eyes is a veil. Great is the penalty they (incur)" (Surah 2:6–7). Almost simultaneously, the born-again Christian student from New Jersey demanded that I denounce Islam as blasphemy, Muhammad as a lecherous fraud, and the Qur'an as a satanic ploy to delude the gullible. As an ordained member of the clergy, she said, I was obligated to proclaim Jesus as the only Lord and Savior for, according to John 14:6, Jesus said, "I am the Way and the Truth and the Life. No one comes to the Father except through me."

Each student was convinced that his and her own religion was the only truth and insisted that the introducer respond as each expected. They called for answers that neither equivocated nor took refuge in bland relativism nor feigned "objectivity." Yet within the risks to my academic accountability and personal integrity were opportunities for us to assess our positions through study and dialogue.

The second set of risks and opportunities involves self-examination and the possibility of changing one's views. The testy parishioner intended to argue with the Muslim couple I invited to address the congregation's adult forum. His opposition faltered when the wife-mother-veterinarian spoke of her daily reading of the Qur'an for guidance in raising their children and in her own spiritual life. She shared her worry about the spread of vulgarity and obscenity in the media because she felt the morals of all adults and children were being corrupted. The husband-father-businessman witnessed that he began each day by prostrating himself before the Lord of all and repeated often the opening words of the Qur'an, "In the Name of God, most gracious, most merciful," as he undertook daily routines. He strove to direct his attitudes and actions toward clients and employees in light of the Qur'an's ethical standards. The parishioner started to rethink his earlier hostility to Islam and Muslims, then began to recalibrate at a higher level how his faith could be expressed in his whole life. He realized that in spite of sharp differences, Muslims and non-Muslims shared common concerns and aspirations and might even risk cooperating with each other.

The third set puts the study of religion, specifically Islam, in sociopolitical context. A student in our seminary class on Christian-Muslim relations took a copy of Yusuf Ali's translation to her office. A coworker saw her reading the Qur'an in the company's cafeteria and promptly reported her to the security guards as someone who might blow up their building. Subsequently the personnel director criticized her for causing her fellow workers consternation, advised her to keep "that book" at home, and told her to assure the others that she was a loyal American. Opening the Qur'an is indeed risky.

BASIC PERSPECTIVES

Since we are preparing to open the Qur'an together, it is appropriate at the outset to share some perspectives that are both explicit and implicit in our study. Our endeavor is to understand the Qur'an, not for me either to persuade readers to convert to Islam or to denigrate it. At the same time, we will not ignore areas that are difficult and contentious among Muslims and between Muslims and non-Muslims. Neither will I discuss whether or not Muhammad existed, or question the historicity of Muslim accounts about his life and the developments of the early Muslim community, or make judgments on the validity of the Muslim traditions about how the Qur'an came to be written and collated, or venture opinions about the morality of Quranic principles. Those matters are highly controversial, and when positions contrary to Muslim beliefs are advanced, Muslims deem them largely slanders on the part of Western "Orientalists" and blasphemies proffered by apostates from the Faith.[1] For those interested in the views of several critics and criticisms, I have provided chapter 14. Instead, I deal with the Qur'an as we have it and with respect for Muslim views of it, the Messenger, and the Message. Further, while I recognize and occasionally refer to the serious differences and contrasts between Sunni and Shi'ia Muslims as well as the divisions within those two broad groups, I focus on positions on which they agree. Where that is not possible or relevant, I defer to generally accepted Sunni positions.

The question at hand is, "Do Jews, Christians, and Muslims worship the same God?"

PERSPECTIVES OF PERSONS WHO ARE NEITHER JEWISH NOR CHRISTIAN

Persons who are neither Jewish nor Christian consider the question on at least three grounds. First, if those persons are religious, they implicitly ask if they and Muslims worship the same God in some manner. Islam claims to absorb and fulfill their religions, as well as Judaism and Christianity. To some degree, non-Muslims will open the Qur'an with attention to its resonance with their own belief systems. Second, much of the scholarship in Western languages has been undertaken by Jewish, Christian, and religiously uncommitted scholars. Their methods and conclusions are colored by their responses to the question. All readers need to be sensitive to the perspectives of those who introduce readers to the text. Third, Jews and Christians are mentioned prominently in the Qur'an and in the foundation of the Muslim community. How those Muslims, Christians, and Jews regarded each other and how they are presented as relating to each other is part of the Qur'an's content. For the theistically inclined, Tibetan Buddhism's leader, the Dalai Lama, may provide a general response applicable to the question and its corollaries:

> How are we to resolve this difficulty [that each religion claims to be the one "true" religion]? It is true that from the point of view of the individual practitioner, it is essential to have a single-pointed commitment to one's own faith. It is also true that this depends on the deep conviction that one's own path is the sole mediator of truth. But at the same time, we have to find some means of reconciling this belief with the reality of a multiplicity of similar claims. In practical terms, this involves individual practitioners finding a way at least to accept the va-

lidity of the teachings of other religions while maintaining a whole-hearted commitment to their own. As far as the validity of the meta-physical truth claims of a given religion is concerned, that is of course the internal business of that particular tradition.[2]

THE MUSLIM PERSPECTIVE

Muslims answer the question in the affirmative:

> Say: "We believe in Allah and in what has been revealed to us and what was revealed to Abraham, Isma'il, Isaac, Jacob, and the Tribes, and in (Books) given to Moses, Jesus, and the Prophets from their Lord; we make no distinction between one and another among them and to Allah do we bow our will (in Islam)." (Surah 3:84, al-Imran, Family of Imran)

They insist that Islam is the oldest and most natural of all religions and that it supersedes and draws into itself all other religions. Judaism and Christianity have a special relationship to Islam because they are the religions closest to Islam with regard to prophets, Scriptures, and practices. At the same time, Jews and Christians are considered to have misunderstood, corrupted, and been led astray from the clear truths proclaimed to them through those prophets and Scriptures. Nevertheless, the "People of the Book" (the Quranic term for Christians and Jews) worship Allah, even if mistaken and misguided.

THE TRADITIONAL JEWISH PERSPECTIVE

Although it is difficult for Jews and Muslims to divest themselves of the twentieth and twenty-first centuries' political-military-social developments focused on Israel-Palestine, Jews follow the precedent stated by Maimonides (1135–1204). He conceded, somewhat grudgingly, that Christians and Muslims worship the same God as do Jews:

But it is beyond the human mind to fathom the designs of the Creator, for our ways are not His ways, neither are our thoughts His thoughts. All these matters relating to Jesus of Nazareth and the Ishmaelite (Mohammed) who came after him, only served to clear the way for King Messiah, to prepare the whole world to worship God with one accord, as it is written *For then will I turn to the peoples a pure language, that they may all call upon the name of the Lord to serve Him with one consent* (Zeph. 3:9).[3]

CHRISTIAN PERSPECTIVES

Throughout their history Christians have struggled with their relationships with other religions and the cultures that are part of those religions. Some Christian attitudes have remained constant; others have changed. A substantial body of literature has emerged dealing with those relationships.[4] Since our focus is on the Qur'an and the perspectives through which it is seen and interpreted and not on interfaith relations, the following is intended to provide us with a basic context. The history of Christian–Muslim relationships is fraught with war, conflicting missionary efforts, political-economic domination, and heated rhetoric on both sides. It is also marked by mutual respect, reciprocal cultural enrichment, and humanitarian cooperation. Both Muslims and Christians have made claims about theirs being the only true faith through which a person may have blessed eternal life, and both have traditions that respect the other's religious sincerity, leaving questions of salvation to the mercy and justice of God.[5] How Christians respond to the question and its corollaries clearly influence and sometimes determine what they see and hear when they open the Qur'an. Generally, Christian considerations of the question may be grouped in three perspectives: exclusivist, inclusivist, and pluralist.[6]

The Exclusivist Perspective

The exclusivist perspective is maintained by many conservative Protestant Christians, including Christian missionaries and American evangelicals.

The core position holds not only that there can be no salvation apart from faith in Jesus as Lord and Savior but also that since Jesus' death and, as Christians believe, resurrection, God may be known only through him.[7] That core may be extended to posit that prior to God's revelation in Jesus, Jews were God's covenanted people, but they did not discern the prophecies concerning the coming Messiah-Jesus in the Scriptures God gave them and did not accept him as the Messiah. As a result, such Christians believe, the Jews have forfeited their covenanted role as God's Israel, even though they continue to worship the Creator. Jews and Judaism have been superseded by the Christian community. The Church is now the true Israel. The "New Testament" is the proper interpretation of the earlier Hebrew Scriptures ("Old Testament," as Christians call it), and both Testaments are the inspired word of God. No other writings may be accepted at the same level of inspiration, just as there can be no other person or spiritual being who supersedes, supplements, or corrects the "good news" (gospel) of Jesus. Logically, then, every saving action and prayer is to be in and through Jesus to God the Father.

Exclusivists appeal for support to numerous passages in the New Testament and may cite the writings of past and modern Christian theologians.[8] The core position can be extended to ask, Who or what, then, do believers in religions apart from Judaism and Christianity worship? One response is to claim that the object(s) of that worship are false gods (often termed "idols") and on occasion demons.[9] Applied to the key question and its corollaries, exclusivists are clear: Muslims worship a false god, and neither Islam, nor the Qur'an, nor Muhammad is divinely inspired, and Muslims are in danger of being eternally damned on the Day of Judgment.

Inclusivist Perspectives

The inclusivist position is expressed in three major ways. Each holds that Jews, Christians, and Muslims worship and seek to serve the same God and are in some way included in God's inscrutable saving will—yet the Christian way of worshiping and serving the one God is the clearest and closest to God's revealed truth about Godself. Frequently the expression "Abrahamic Faiths" is used to relate the three monotheistic religions through a common "father."[10] Again, biblical and historical precedents may be cited to support the inclusivist perspective.[11]

Roman Catholicism's Second Vatican Council (1962–65), while definitely affirming that Jews, Christians, and Muslims worship the same God and are embraced in God's plan for salvation, did not address the thornier issues of the Qur'an and Muhammad.[12] At the same time, the Council held that religions other than the form of Christianity as professed by Roman Catholicism are "not on an equal footing with Christianity. These other religions contain many authentic values, although they are mixed with error, and hence need to be purified."[13]

Eastern Orthodox theologians emphasize that God in God's being is unknowable, but humans see the light of God's revelation in terms of God's wisdom and glory throughout creation.[14] Humans are able to do so because they are created in the divine image and likeness. All religions share in testifying to some degree to God's glory-light-wisdom and in their own ways respond to God through worship and service. So Muslims and Jews worship the same God as do Christians. As may be expected, the Orthodox hold that God has revealed the heart and source of God's light and wisdom as the Word made flesh (John 1:14) who is the Light of the world (John 8:12) and the Wisdom of God (1 Cor. 1:24).[15] The Ecumenical Patriarch, Bartholomew I, gave the basic Orthodox position: "Whether we are Christians, Moslems or Jews, we are children of God and our efforts as peacemakers will be blessed and rewarded by the one God whom we share as common Creator."[16] One contemporary Orthodox theologian summed up the Orthodox view as follows: "The salvation of all people, including non-Christians, depends on the great goodness and mercy of the Omniscient and Omnipotent God who desires the salvation of all people. Those who live in faith and virtue, though outside the Church, receive God's loving grace and salvation. Saint Paul reminds us, 'O the depth of the riches and wisdom and knowledge of God! How unsearchable are His judgments and how inscrutable His ways!' (Rom. 11:33)."[17]

Protestant theologians who take the inclusivist approach often do so on grounds that reflect some agreement with Roman Catholic and Orthodox positions, and on their own grounds.[18] A focus on Genesis 1–2 and John 1:1–14 provides others with a creation-based starting point that moves toward an Orthodox-type focus on the unity of humanity under the gracious sovereignty of the one God who is revealed gradually in cultural contexts, yet with Jesus Christ as the fullest revelation of God.[19] Within the circle of inclusivists are theologians who see Islamic monotheism as rigid and requiring Muslims to submit fatalistically to God while Christianity emphasizes divine grace and love.[20] Nevertheless, a number of scholars deeply involved in interreligious dialogue, especially in predominantly Muslim societies, are making significant contributions to deepening understanding of Islam, the Qur'an, and the implications of interfaith cooperation intellectually, socially, and politically. W. Montgomery Watt states his position clearly: "Muhammad was a prophet chosen by God for a particular task and also that God was behind the spread of Islam throughout the world," and "Not all the ideas [of Muhammad] are true and sound, but by God's grace he has been enabled to provide millions of men with a better religion than they had before they testified that there is no god but God and that Muhammad is the Messenger of God."[21] The Anglican bishop Kenneth Cragg holds that Muslims, Jews, and Christians worship the same God, that the Qur'an resonates with the biblical insistence on the oneness of God, and that Muhammad was in some way inspired by God, and he encourages Christians to open and engage the Qur'an.[22]

Pluralist Perspectives

Pluralists agree with inclusivists that the three religions (and often all life-affirming religions) worship the same God, but pluralists do not acknowledge that God has granted Christianity the fullest or truest revelation. In other words, all religions are valid journeys to God. Pluralists often propose understandings of "God" quite different from many other theists, as well as from traditional Jews, Christians, and Muslims.[23] A number of those who hold the perspective have been deeply engaged in "traditional Christianity" but found it too intellectually or emotionally confining and immaturely focused on particular doctrines or ecclesiastical structures.[24] They often move away from a concentration on Christology (doctrines related to the nature and functions of Jesus) as expressed in the traditional creeds and structures of the Christian churches. Instead, holding that they are "theocentric," they examine humanity and the human role in the cosmos. They note that people construe God and the gods differently in different times and cultures but that there is always an awareness of an inner yearning to transcend the self. That inner yearning or consciousness may be the constant rather than an ineffable transcendent being called "God." For the purposes of our study, such pluralists will aver that the inner yearning and experience for transcendence, sometimes called the Ultimate Concern or God beyond God, is present in men and women and that they seek to externalize it though rituals, traditions, accounts, Scriptures, teachings, and so on. "God" is the unity that is behind the fragmentation and heterogeneity of the perceived world and of the individual. Therefore, humans seek the same "God," and the heroic or seminal figures of a religious tradition are persons who have a significant measure of insight into that unity-transcendence that is within and beyond the person.[25]

Other pluralists advocate a theocentric rather than christocentric view of God that is unencumbered by the traditional doctrines and rituals and encourages humans to think and act creatively. They emphasize a broad cosmic theology rather than a particularist formulation centered on Jesus as Savior. Religion is seeking truth, and faith is confidence that humans are free to seek and to come to know that which is beyond them. These pluralists admit that there is a transcendent Being but not one of judgment, wrath, and damnation.[26] In that theocentric light, all religions share the quest, are limited by their times and cultural loci, and ought to understand deeply their accounts about God as expressive of the unifying cosmic theology and not limited "truths." Pluralists answer the question and its corollaries with guarded affirmatives and with the condition that no one religion has a monopoly on knowing God fully, and none is to impose its version of God on others.

THE EXCLUSIVIST PERSPECTIVE answers the basic question and its corollaries with a resounding "No." At the same time the exclusivist view rejects the reasons and conclusions of the inclusivist and pluralist positions. For exclusivists, Islam, the Qur'an, and Muhammad are wrong, even tinged with evil. The proper response by Christians, accordingly, is to expose

Islam's errors, contradictions, and alleged designs to dominate the world, then to seek to convert Muslims to Christianity. As a result, exclusivists who open the Qur'an will be alert to finding in it those errors, contradictions, and designs. Inclusivist Christians answer the question about worshiping and serving the same God with a "Yes" nuanced by holding that the Christian understanding of God takes precedence over Judaism and Islam. An affirmative response to the question, however, raises critical issues for inclusivists: Does saying "Yes" lead logically to the conclusion that Islam is a/the "true" religion; that the Qur'an is divinely inspired and presents God's revelation of truth that might lead to viewing it as scripture; and that Muhammad is a post-Jesus Messenger of God? As inclusivist Christians open the Qur'an, they will enter into a dialogue with themselves about the essentials of Christianity and seek a dialogue with Muslims. Pluralist Christians shift the ground of Christian perspectives from scriptures and Christology to a cosmological theology, proposals to understand God in radically different ways, and address the depths of human experience and aspirations even apart from traditional conceptions of God as a transcendent Being. As pluralists open the Qur'an, they will affirm the universal factors, identify the cultural specifics, and seek to extend universal ethical norms.

To be forthright with readers, I am within the circle of those inclusivist Protestants who answer "Yes" to the question of whether Jews, Christians, and Muslims worship and seek to serve the same God. I hold that in key areas God's ways and truth may be discerned in and through Islam, the Qur'an, and Muhammad's devotion to God. I am still pondering how far and with what reservations and affirmations that response reaches. Therefore, I open the Qur'an as a seeker and listener, inquiring into its message, and asking what that message means personally and for our present and future. Having surveyed some perspectives by non-Muslims, we turn to those who believe that the Qur'an is from God and for the world.

THREE BASIC MUSLIM PERSPECTIVES ON THE QUR'AN

As we study the Qur'an, we will encounter a number of views by Muslims about it, its role in shaping Islam, and its claims on all humanity. Three perspectives are lenses through which Muslims view the Qur'an and even how many believers handle the Book. I offer the perspectives in three long, linked, and layered sentences.

First, the Qur'an is the very word of God transmitted to Muhammad ibn Abd Allah ibn Muttalib by God through the angel Gabriel over the course of twenty-two to twenty-three years (610–32).

Second, Muhammad spoke, recited, proclaimed, and dictated the Revelation in the Arabic language to early Muslims who, in turn, memorized and committed it to writings that were collated into the Book that contains no errors or variants from the original revealed to Muhammad and dictated by him to his Companions and Helpers.

Third, Islam is now the religion of that Book; that is, the Qur'an is both Islam's framework and the content within that framework so that the Quranic Message orders, instructs, guides, consoles, and energizes the Muslim community while also challenging, inviting, warning, and summoning non–Muslims to hear and obey God's will or face the consequences.

The perspectives may be called respectively the Qur'an as Revelation, Book, and Criterion. Although each sentence runs through the Qur'an and our engagement with it, each calls for preliminary comment as we prepare to move forward.

THE QUR'AN AS REVELATION

Islamically considered, Muhammad was neither the founder of a religion nor the author of the Qur'an. God established Islam, and God authored the Qur'an. God established Islam when He created spiritual beings, the cosmos, and humans, endowing everything with the capacity to know and serve Him. The gracious and merciful Lord of all has revealed His existence and will to all peoples through nature, events, prophets, and books from the time of Adam until a night toward the end of the month of Ramadan, 610:[27]

We have indeed revealed the (Message) in the Night of Power. And what will explain to thee what the Night of Power is? The Night of Power is better than ten thousand months. Therein come down the

angels and the Spirit by Allah's permission, on every errand. Peace!
This until the rise of Morn! (Surah 97, al-Qadr, Night of Power)

On that night a heavenly event occurred: God caused the Qur'an to
descend to the Bait al-Izza, the heaven immediately above the earth. Obedient to God's command, Gabriel came to Muhammad, the man whom
God had been preparing to receive the Revelation, and began to impart to
him the content of the Qur'an. The angel commanded the retired merchant to recite, say, and proclaim the Message to his fellow Arabs and to the
world. The one Voice in the Qur'an, therefore, is that of the one God.
Since that night nature and events still point to the one God, but there will
be no further prophets, messengers, or books from God.

Because of his relationship with God through spiritual beings, Muhammad himself became the living model of the totally fulfilled prophet-
messenger. His manner of life, words, and actions all pointed to the one
God, how that God willed to be obeyed and served, and how the community of believers was to relate to God, one another, and nonbelievers: "Ye
have indeed in the Messenger of Allah a beautiful pattern of (conduct) for
anyone whose hope is in Allah, and the Final Day, and who engages much in
the praise of Allah" (Surah 33:21, Al-Ahzab, The Confederates). The term
sunna (also *sunnah*) means literally "custom and usage," and is most often applied to Muhammad. It connotes what he said and did, including "what he
approved, allowed, or condoned when, under prevailing circumstances, he
might well have taken issue with others' actions, decisions or practices; and
what he himself refrained from and disapproved of."[28] Muhammad's sayings,
deeds, and conduct gathered from the remembrances of his followers were
collected and compiled by scholars in books termed *ahadith* (sayings and reports). The Hadiths are important as aids in interpreting the Qur'an and the
Quranic principles that are the basis of Islamic law (Shari'ah). Nevertheless,
the Qur'an remains the chief authority and interpreter by which all others
are judged. Muhammad was given other revelatory words through Gabriel
that are not included in the Qur'an. These sayings, authorized by God, were
to be spoken by Muhammad when and where he thought appropriate.
Those special sayings from God not in the Qur'an are called Hadith Qudsi
(also Hadees-e-Qudsi, that is, Pure or Sacred Hadith).[29]

THE QUR'AN AS Revelation is the Noble or Glorious Book (al-Qur'an al-Karim) of the most authoritative, complete, and never to be surpassed words of God revealed to the most authoritative and final Messenger-Prophet of God.

THE QUR'AN AS BOOK

Traditions about how the Qur'an went from Muhammad's disclosures to his followers to becoming the official and printed text of Islam are taken up in more detail in chapter 6. The present sketch considers the circumstances under which the Qur'an was revealed to Muhammad, its use during his lifetime, and brief mention of its collation into a book.

Hadith references cited in chapter 6 indicate that Muhammad spoke many of the revelations in the presence of believers when he was in a distinct revelatory state that was preceded by painful ringing in his ears and included profuse perspiration and reverent posture. Others could not hear the angel speaking to him but were aware that he was listening to another presence. God assured him and all who read the Qur'an that Muhammad was not deranged: "Thou art not by the grace of thy Lord mad or possessed. Nay, verily for thee is a reward unfailing. And thou (standest) on an exalted standard of character" (Surah 68:2–4, al-Qalam, the Pen or Nun). Because he sometimes spoke rapidly, he was cautioned:

> Move not thy tongue concerning the (Qur'an) to make haste therewith. It is for Us to collect it and to promulgate it: But when We have promulgated it, follow thou its recital (as promulgated): Nay, more it is for Us to explain it (and make it clear). (Surah 75:16–19, al-Qiyamah, the Resurrection)[30]

Those who wrote the Revelation were questioned and tested by Muhammad to determine whether they took down the words exactly. Sometimes Muhammad was alone when the Revelation came, as on the Night of Power. He repeated the words to those who wrote them down and then were tested by him. On other occasions, Muhammad was engaged in a controversy when he received a timely Revelation that was recorded either immediately or later.[31] Several times the community was troubled or he was uncertain about resolving an issue when God spoke clarifying ayas through the angel.[32] Worship provided another occasion for a Revelation, as when he was told to change the direction faced during prayer from Jerusalem to Mecca (Surah 2:142–52). Regardless of the place and conditions under which the Revelation was bestowed and recorded, Muslim traditions generally (yet not unanimously) hold that God also told Muhammad through Gabriel in what order to place the surahs and where in each surah every aya was to be placed. Passages of the Qur'an were recited in public by Muslims during the Messenger's lifetime. He often tested his followers and had them recite portions. He, too, was interrogated and recited the whole that had been revealed to that point each year by Gabriel, except in the year of his death; then the angel required two tests.

Several years after Muhammad's death the accounts that were written on various media and from the hearts of persons were collected and compared with one another, then written and bound in books that had exactly the same text. It is that book which Muslims believe we have now as the Glorious Qur'an. Later scholars added divisions to indicate sections for daily reading. Because Arabic, like Hebrew, is basically consonantal, scholars added vowel and accent indications to assist reading and chanting. The Qur'an, like modern Arabic, may be read without such markings.

THE QUR'AN WAS revealed to one person under circumstances that met the needs of the Muslim community. It went from Muhammad's recitation to being written and eventually put into book form without any errors or variants. The words read today are believed to be the same words that were given by God through Gabriel to the Messenger and the same words that he recited to believers.

THE QUR'AN AS CRITERION

From one angle the Qur'an is the frame around the faith-practice of Islam. Every Muslim is to memorize in Arabic at least twelve ayas, including the first surah, al-Fatihah, the Opener. Al-Fatihah is included in every prayer.

Muslims are encouraged to memorize as much of the Qur'an in Arabic as they are able. Many Muslims gladly memorize whole surahs and sections; others commit the entire text, about 6,400 to 6,600 ayas, to memory.[33] Those who memorize the whole are called *huffaz* (i.e., protectors, preservers, memorizers; sing. *hafiz*). The formal recitation of the Qur'an is a developed science with numerous rules, traditions, and forms.[34] A person who has memorized the text and is recognized as a "reciter" is a *qari* (pl. *qurra*). Qurra often declaim at public events, at celebrations, and on radio and television. In a home, *masjid* (mosque), and *madrassa* (religious school affiliated with a masjid) a Qur'an is often placed on a distinctively carved *rihal* (a stand about eight or ten inches high) and given a prominent, honored place. Often and alternately, the Qur'an is wrapped carefully in a cloth. The Book is to be handled reverently for it is God's word. Readers are not to write across or highlight any of the Arabic text. Abusing, tearing, soiling, or damaging a Qur'an is a serious sin and may provoke punishments.[35] Indeed, one passage seems to discourage non-Muslims from obtaining the Qur'an. The context appears to be a call for Muslims to guard against infidels from desecrating or disparaging the Revelation.[36]

Before opening the Book, devout Muslims wash their hands and prepare themselves spiritually and intellectually to listen to the God who addresses them in their present, and then they pray that they will take refuge in God against the wiles and whisperings of Satan. The reading concludes with a prayer of thanks to God for giving humanity the Qur'an.[37] Some religious leaders provide advice or protocols about handling the Book, such as cleansing one's mouth, as well as one's hands, before reading aloud from the Qur'an; facing the Ka'bah while reading; and not putting other objects on top of the Qur'an.[38] During a devotional reading or while listening to a recitation, Muslims may stop and prostrate themselves as the ayas include references to bowing before God.[39] The devotion and care Muslims show for the Book and its pronunciation and recitation begins to indicate the awe they feel toward the Revelation in all its forms.

From a second angle, the Qur'an contains the substance on which Islam's teachings and Muslim life are based. God's Revelation discloses His mercy and justice, His will for and expectations of humans in this world, and His promises and warnings about the Judgment and Afterlife. The Qur'an combines intense concern for individual, communal, and wider social attitudes and actions in this world with straightforward encouragement for persons and the Islamic community to deepen their devotion and awareness of God's gracious will:

> These are ayat of the Wise Book, Guide and a Mercy to the Doers of Good, those who establish regular prayer and give regular charity and have (in their hearts) the assurance of the Hereafter. These are on (true) guidance from their Lord; and these are the ones who will prosper. (Surah 31:2–5, Luqman)

The Qur'an contains the principles and often specifics regarding family relations, inheritance, divorce, sexual conduct, speech and dress, and personal privacy, along with stipulations about war, treatment of captives and slaves, and punishment of criminals. These are interwoven with exhortations to prayer, care for the poor, acknowledging God's sovereignty, and the divine plan for the cosmos. God calls on the believers to study the Qur'an for knowledge of the nature of the world, history, and the proper functioning of a God-ruled society, and through that study to come to know and be obedient to the God in Whom is genuine freedom. The Qur'an and therefore Islam know no separation between sacred and secular, material and spiritual, reason and revelation, politics and worship. The Qur'an gives directions, at times commands, to believers and, if they will but heed it, to potential believers as well.

THE QUR'AN IS the Furqan, the Criterion: "O ye who believe! If ye fear Allah He will grant you a criterion (to judge between right and wrong) remove from you (all) evil (that may afflict) you and forgive you: for Allah is the Lord of grace unbounded" (Surah 8:29, al-Anfal, the Spoils of War). The Qur'an frames and then gives the content, structure, and standards for living the Islamic life for individuals, the whole Muslim community (*umma*), and relations to other people under the gracious and just rule of God.

Conclusion

Non-Muslims and Muslims open the Qur'an from different perspectives and have different expectations of what they will find there. Non-Muslims approach the Book with attitudes ranging from curiosity and skepticism to possible partial acceptance to outright opposition. Muslims approach the Qur'an as believers eager to hear again and to deepen their understandings of the will of the God who speaks-proclaims life and guidance to them and has given them the pattern for life in Muhammad and the community he established. The one set of readers opens the Qur'an with questions, the other to find answers.

> Among His signs is this: that He created you from dust; and then, Behold! Ye are men scattered (far and wide)! And among His signs is this: that He created for you mates from among yourselves that ye may dwell in tranquility with them, and He has put love and mercy between your (hearts). Verily, in that are signs for those who reflect. And among His Signs is the creation of the heavens and the earth and the variations in your languages and your color. Verily, in that are signs for those who know. (Surah 30:20–22, al-Rum, the Romans)

TWO

BASIC NARRATIVES FOR JUDAISM
AND CHRISTIANITY

Those who believe (in the Qur'an), those who follow
the Jewish (scriptures), and the Sabians and the Christians,
any who believe in Allah and the Last Day and work
righteousness on them shall be no fear, nor shall they grieve.

Surah 5:69, al-Ma'dah, the Repast or Table Spread

Judaism and Christianity occupy special places in the Qur'an. Here I consider Judaism and Christianity through what I call "basic narratives," which furnish an overview of the two religions up to the beginning of the seventh century CE. I tilt the narratives toward issues and references reflected in the Qur'an and early Islam. Along with some biblical accounts, I include nonbiblical references, traditions, legends, and, in the case of Christianity, doctrinal formulations. These were almost certainly known in pre-Islamic Arabia.[1] The Jewish narrative features six selected covenants that were woven together in rabbinical centers during the second through sixth centuries CE to form the basis of what we recognize as Judaism.[2] The covenants express relationships between God and a person or persons often expressed as promises, implicit or explicit responses by humans, and a sign that seals the covenant.

23

Because Judaism contains the covenants that were used, adapted, or altered by Christians and Muslims and because the covenants grew out of Israelite experience, the following general historical categories for Judaism are helpful. We will be involved especially with the first two.

> First Age of Diversity, ca. 500 BCE–70 CE
> Age of Definition, ca. 70–640
> Age of Cogency, ca. 640–1800
> Second Age of Diversity, 1800–present[3]

Two Christian periods relevant to our study are roughly contemporary with the Jewish categories:

> Age of Diversity, ca. 30–325
> Age of Definition, ca. 325–787[4]

When Muhammad began to proclaim the Message of Islam, Judaism and Christianity were in the closing stages of often-contentious efforts to clarify and define their self-understandings, authoritative teachings, relationships within their own ranks, separation from each other, attitudes toward other religions, and interactions with existing political-societal structures.

JUDAISM'S BASIC NARRATIVE

The one and only God created whatever exists—angels and various spirits and all else, from rocks through human beings. Creation is not a hodge-podge but is ordered according to the wisdom of the Creator and is looked upon by God as being "very good" (Gen. 1:31). God made men and women in God's image and likeness, breathed into them life-animating power and ability, gave them the privilege and responsibility to care for the world, and bade them to be fruitful and multiply. Following six days of creational activity, God "rested," setting the precedent for considering the seventh day the Sabbath or day of rest.

THE ADAMIC COVENANT

Adam and Eve, the parents of all subsequent persons, were placed by the Lord in a God-made garden on earth and enjoyed God's presence. Adam and Eve may be said to have been in the initial covenantal relationship with God. God promised to be with them, and they implicitly promised to care for the garden. The Sabbath came to be understood as the covenantal seal.[5] The couple's only restriction was the prohibition against eating from the tree of the knowledge of good and evil. Eve, enticed by a serpent, ate of the fruit and shared it with her mate, thereby violating the covenantal relationship, causing them to be ashamed and to lose direct fellowship with God. The Lord punished them with curses that subjugated the woman to the man, made childbirth painful for her, hardened the ground so that Adam must toil in order to grow food, and expelled them from the Garden. The serpent, too, was cursed, and the Lord decreed enmity between the serpent and humans. Nevertheless, the Lord continued to care for them as they entered the now-damaged world.

The Adamic Covenant was ruptured by human disobedience to God, a disobedience triggered by a creature identified in later legends based on Genesis 6:1–4 as an evil, rebellious angel.[6] The biblical text does not make any reference to humans repenting, asking for forgiveness from God, or inheriting Adam and Eve's original sin.[7] A later Jewish text, probably from the first century CE, claims that when Adam disobeyed God an evil seed germinated in his heart, and since then all humans have been burdened with an evil inclination.[8]

THE NOAHIDE COVENANT

Adam and Eve's descendants deepened humanity's downward spiral from disobedience into murder and immorality. Enoch, an exception to the general decline, was so righteous that God took him into heaven (Gen. 5:18–24). Some later traditions describe him as a sage who shared with his family the secrets of humanity's future as well as the account of the fall of some angels who deceived humanity by distorting God's wisdom into idolatry, violence, lust, and greed.[9] These angels copulated with women to father demons that afflict humans with idolatry, sickness, madness, and false teachings. According to Enochian traditions, God plans to defeat the evil angels and demons and their human supporters in battles preceding a cosmic day of judgment presided over by the most powerful faithful angel. The wicked will be punished in hell, and the blessed righteous will live on an immensely fertile earth. Enoch himself was transformed into an angel in God's presence.

All humanity, except one family, engaged in ever-worsening wickedness until the Lord realized "that every inclination of the thoughts of their hearts was only evil continually. And the Lord was sorry that He had made humankind on the earth, and it grieved Him to His heart" (Gen. 6:5–6). The Creator determined to destroy all persons and animals in a flood. Yet the ever-merciful Lord judged Noah (a direct descendant of Enoch) to be comparatively blameless and warned him to build an ark or boat for himself and his wife, their three sons and their wives, and a representative stock of animals in order to survive the coming disaster. According to nonbiblical Jewish accounts, Noah exhorted his neighbors to change their sinful ways or face God's righteous wrath. They mocked him.[10] And the floods began.

Noah and the occupants of the ark rode out the lethal storm. Once on dry land, the survivors offered sacrifice to God, and God was so pleased with the aroma that He made a covenant with Noah and all subsequent human beings. The terms of the covenant with Noah echo that made with Adam and added a dietary restriction and a juridical condition. Humans were not to consume the blood of any animal, and "Whoever sheds the blood of a human, by a human shall that person's blood be shed; for in his own image God made humankind" (Gen. 9:5–6). The covenant was sealed by the rainbow, the sign that there would be regular seasons and that He would not destroy the earth again by water.[11] God also realized that although, "the inclination of the human heart is evil from youth," women and men were nevertheless responsible for their actions (Gen. 8:21).

Noah planted the first vineyard and was the first to get drunk. Sprawled naked in his tent, he was seen by one of his sons who mocked him.[12] On waking, Noah cursed Canaan, the son of his son who saw him. The account is part of the Israelite disdain for the Canaanites and the claim that the Canaanites were to serve them.[13] Again, no one asked for forgiveness. The reinaugurated world was off to a dismal start. Rabbis later extrapolated seven universally applicable laws from the covenant made with Noah: prohibitions against idolatry, blasphemy, incest, murder, robbery, and cruelty to animals and the injunction to establish law courts to render justice.[14]

THE ADAMIC AND Noahide Covenants are incumbent on all humans. All persons in every place and time have some creation-based knowledge of the one and only God and are aware that they are to honor that God and to keep the terms of the covenants, that is, to care for the world and establish justice. While each person is responsible for his or her actions, an evil inclination darkens but does not excuse human intentions and deeds; all people will be held accountable to the just-merciful God.

THE ABRAHAMIC COVENANT

The Abrahamic Covenant moves the narrative to God's selecting Abraham and his descendants as a special people through whom the Lord would reveal His will and plan for the world. Abraham was promised that his family would become a great nation and be a blessing for all other nations. This covenant is the charter for the people who would later be known as the Jews and whose socioreligious structure is Judaism. In Jewish lore Terah, Abraham's father, was a Babylon-based maker and seller of idols. Abraham, however, reasoned that the idols were lifeless and therefore powerless. Observing the stars and nature, he concluded that there was only one God who created, sustains, and rules the world, and this God is to be worshiped and served. Abraham's conclusion was confirmed by divine revelation. He became thereby simultaneously the first monotheist and the first Jew. He confronted his father and others with that truth, then derided and destroyed the idols. Outraged, Terah and the townspeople hauled Abraham before the city's ruler, who had Abraham cast into a hot furnace. The Lord preserved Abraham, and some believed in the God whom Abraham proclaimed and worshiped.[15]

The biblical account introduced Terah when he moved his clan from Mesopotamia to Syria. Abraham, called by and obedient to God, left Terah and took his family into Canaan. He had a nocturnal vision in which the Lord made a covenantal vow that Abraham would have a son and his vast posterity would possess the land from the Euphrates to the Nile forever (Gen. 15). When Abraham and his wife continued childless, she proposed that he have intercourse with her Egyptian slave, Hagar, in an attempt to have a son. He did, and Hagar bore a son, Ishmael. But Ishmael was not the son promised by the covenant. Another mighty vision expressed the Abrahamic Covenant fully.[16] Abraham and his descendants were to walk in the ways of the Lord and possess the land of Canaan forever; Abraham was promised that Sarah, his wife, would have a son to be named Isaac; and male circumcision was the sign of the covenant. Although God designated Isaac the lineal heir of the covenant, He promised that Ishmael would become a prince with twelve sons. Eventually Sarah conceived and bore Isaac. Accounts about the hostility between Sarah and Hagar culminated with Hagar and Ishmael being left in the wilderness.[17] The Lord intervened, showing her a well that led to their survival. Ishmael became the father of the Arabs. As might be expected, after Abraham's death enmity developed between the offspring of Sarah-Abraham and Hagar-Abraham.

Almost as a codicil to the Abrahamic Covenant and perhaps as chastisement to Abraham for his treatment of Hagar and Ishmael, the Lord ordered him to sacrifice Isaac on Mount Moriah. The act was aborted at the last moment when God provided a ram for the sacrifice.[18] In Jewish traditions, Isaac was twenty-five *and* accepted joyfully the prospect that God desired him to end his earthly life.[19] Mount Moriah is identified in 2 Chronicles 3:1 with the hill in Jerusalem on which Solomon had the temple built.

THE ABRAHAMIC COVENANT sets Jews and Judaism apart from all other peoples, offers the rationale for Abraham's descendants to claim the land of Canaan, establishes circumcision, gives them the purpose of being a blessing to all peoples, and exhorts them to walk in the ways of the Lord. The Adamic and Noahide Covenants are implicitly included in the "ways of the Lord," and link Jews and Judaism to the rest of humanity. The Abrahamic Covenant, however long it is on God's promises, is short on the specifics of what the ways of the Lord might be. The narrative then moves to the next and more detailed covenant.

THE SINAITIC COVENANT

As the Abrahamic Covenant may be regarded as Judaism's charter, the Sinaitic Covenant may be its constitution. The covenant announced through Moses to the fugitives from Egypt came to express Judaism's core beliefs and provided the principles and many of the specifics of Jewish life. The God revealed now as YHWH, the Living One or LORD, promised to be with the people designated the Lord's holy nation and royal priesthood.[20] They responded that they would obey all the terms of the Covenant, knowing that breaches on their part would result in divine punishment.[21] The covenantal sign is the Sabbath (Exod. 31:12–17) and, more broadly, the Torah. (The Hebrew word *Torah* is considered more fully below.) Moses is presented as both telling the people what the Torah is and writing it in a book to be used by future generations. In the present context it is the gracious and just instruction of God, often translated as "Law." In addition to the Ten Commandments, the Torah mandates observing the Sabbath; male circumcision; dietary laws; regulations and exhortations concerning worship, marriage, property rights, criminal sanctions, agricultural procedures, and care for the widowed, the poor, and foreigners; procedures to be followed in making sacrifices and the types of sacrifices to be offered to God. The Torah contains warnings and promises and sets forth the two ways: the way of disobedience to and rejection of God, which leads to death; and the way of obedience to God and acceptance of God's will, which leads to life and prosperity.[22] Throughout the Torah the Lord's people are warned especially against worshiping other gods and are commanded to destroy idols and idolaters.

The Sinaitic Covenant provided the foundation for what later became a determined and vibrant monotheism; that is, there is one and only one God, and this God is not divisible in any manner. The Shema (Deut. 6:4) was the critical text that came to function as the foundational statement of Judaism: *Shema Yisroel, YHWH Elohenu, YHWH echad*. "Echad" could be taken as "only," so that YHWH would be the only God for the covenant people to worship while other peoples may have been given by YHWH to other deities.[23] Then the passage would mean, "Hear, O Israel: The LORD is our God, the LORD alone." Yet, especially during and after the Babylonian exile, the Shema's *echad* came to mean "sole" in the sense that no other gods exist.[24] The absolute authority of God as the sole deity for all that exists, and therefore worthy of worship and service, combined with the absolute indivisibility of God's being to become the bedrock of Judaism.

In the covenant-making scene at the foot of Mount Sinai, the people and the Lord bound themselves to each other through a ritual animal-blood sacrifice.[25] YHWH had already shown faithfulness to them and promised to continue to do so. What now can be called "Israel" vowed to keep the Lord's commandments, precepts, statutes, and instructions or face God's wrath. An essential part of the Sinaitic Covenant was the divine promise that God would be with them as they moved into the land that the Lord had promised to Abraham and his descendants. Their remaining and prospering in the land was contingent on Israel's obedience to the Torah. Disobedience, especially through worshiping other gods and being unjust, would result in Israel's expulsion from the land and the land being given to a worthier people.

The figure of Moses is inseparable from the Sinaitic Covenant and the Torah. In the Bible he is the man with whom God spoke face-to-face as with a friend.[26] Among humans he is brother, husband, father, Israel's chief prophet, general, strategist, lawgiver, judge, organizer, wonder worker, recipient of divine revelations, writer of God's revelations in a book to be read by future leaders, and, on one occasion, murderer. He imposed death penalties and provided food and water under dire circumstances. He opposed polytheist authorities, suffered exile for his faithfulness to God, and supposedly died under strange circumstances. Later Jewish traditions and legends described Moses being taken into heaven by God and/or angels, thereby joining Enoch and Elijah. Subsequently and in the common era, the scribe Ezra was also thought by some to have been taken into heaven.[27]

THE SINAITIC COVENANT transcends the Abrahamic Covenant because it is not tied to a particular land but is incumbent on Jews wherever they may be. Through the Sinaitic Covenant Judaism was able to survive defeats, exiles, and diasporas. The Torah as delivered at Sinai and elaborated in later generations furnishes a consistent framework for Jewish life. At the same time, the one and only God of all creation and time is described as electing Israel to be a special people with a definite holy homeland. The Lord will be with those whom God rescued and will continue to rescue now and forever. YHWH is revealed as merciful and just, present and transcendent. If Abraham was the first Jew, Moses is the most advanced Jew and friend of God.

THE DAVIDIC COVENANT

Judaism's narrative follows the movement of the people Israel into the land originally called Canaan and then Israel. Accounts of the Israelite infiltration and settlement in the land and battles with various peoples lead up to the reign in Jerusalem of the shepherd-soldier-musician, David. A pro-monarchical passage describes a vision to the prophet Nathan in which God made an eternal promise to David and his descendants that has the form of a covenant and resonates with the Abrahamic Covenant:

> And I will appoint a place for my people Israel and will plant them, so that they may live in their own place, and be disturbed no more; and evildoers shall afflict them no more, as formerly, from the time that I appointed judges over my people Israel; and I will give you rest from all your enemies. Moreover the LORD declares to you that the LORD will make you a house. When your days are fulfilled and you lie down with your ancestors, I will raise up your offspring after you, who shall come forth from your body, and I will establish his kingdom. He shall build a house for my name, and I will establish the throne of his kingdom forever. I will be a father to him, and he shall be a son to me. When he commits iniquity, I will punish him with a rod such as mortals use, with blows inflicted by human beings. But I will not take my steadfast love from him, as I took it from Saul, whom I put away from before you. Your house and your kingdom

shall be made sure forever before me; your throne shall be established forever. (2 Sam. 7:8–17)[28]

The promises to David and Abraham assured Jews in later times that they had a special, holy homeland no matter how scattered or how severely punished by God they were. God would still be with the chosen people, leading them not only in terms of the Torah but also toward the establishment of a homeland centered in Jerusalem that would be a refuge for Jews and a center from which God's justice would be seen by the nations. This assurance sustained them throughout their history, from Israel's division into two kingdoms (922 BCE), both being conquered (the northern kingdom in 722 BCE and the southern kingdom in 586 BCE), exile in Babylonia (590s–538 BCE); domination by the Persians (538–332 BCE); Greeks including Greco-Syrians (332–63 BCE), Romans (63 BCE–630s CE), and Muslims (630s–1919); to the League of Nations–United Nations mandates (1919–48) and the establishment of the state of Israel (1948). The Davidic Promise became part of the expectation that one day the Lord would raise up a successor, the Son of David, who would restore the fortunes of the Jewish people, be involved in the punishment of their enemies, and be the harbinger of God's universal rule of justice and peace. Such a person was often called the Messiah, or anointed one. Whether or not the word *messiah* was used, a cluster of expectations took numerous forms that came to be associated with the end of the present age, the resurrection of the dead, an extensive or universal judgment, and a blessed future on a re-created earth or misery in Hell.[29]

Messianic expectations and movements were particularly important when Judaism was threatened by external forces and Jews suffered persecution. Movements that led to rebellions, however, were crushed. The hope lingered and lingers still in Judaism and among Orthodox Jews today.

THE DAVIDIC COVENANT carried the sense of the ultimate vindication of the Jewish people and the establishment of a Jewish homeland ruled by God's will. It was expanded to include expectations of a figure called the Messiah who would save those among the Jewish people who had been faithful to YHWH, defeat evil, and inaugurate a blessed rule of God either in the present or in a future age.

THE NEW COVENANT

In the seventh century BCE, facing a foreign invasion, the prophet Jeremiah presented God promising another covenant:

> The days are surely coming, says the LORD, when I will make a new covenant with the house of Israel and the house of Judah. It will not be like the covenant that I made with their ancestors when I took them by the hand to bring them out of the land of Egypt—a covenant that they broke, though I was their husband, says the LORD. But this is the covenant that I will make with the house of Israel after those days, says the LORD: I will put my law within them, and I will write it on their hearts; and I will be their God, and they shall be my people. No longer shall they teach one another, or say to each other, "Know the LORD," for they shall all know me, from the least of them to the greatest, says the LORD; for I will forgive their iniquity, and remember their sin no more. Thus says the LORD, who gives the sun for light by day and the fixed order of the moon and the stars for light by night, who stirs up the sea so that its waves roar—the LORD of hosts is his name: If this fixed order were ever to cease from my presence, says the LORD, then also the offspring of Israel would cease to be a nation before me forever. Thus says the LORD: If the heavens above can be measured, and the foundations of the earth below can be explored, then I will reject all the offspring of Israel because of all they have done, says the LORD. The days are surely coming, says the LORD, when the city shall be rebuilt for the LORD from the tower of Hananel to the Corner Gate. (Jer. 31:31–38)

Although the New Covenant is meant to replace the often-violated and cleverly circumvented written formulations of the Sinaitic Covenant in favor of heart-written knowledge-devotion to the Lord, the passage reflects the Adamic and Noahide creational covenants. References to the Tower and the Gate, locations in a to-be-rebuilt Jerusalem, may point toward elements in the Davidic Covenant or to the role of Jerusalem anticipated by Micah and Isaiah:

> In days to come the mountain of the LORD's house shall be established as the highest of the mountains, and shall be raised above the hills; all the nations shall stream to it. Many peoples shall come and say, "Come, let us go up to the mountain of the LORD, to the house of the God of Jacob; that he may teach us his ways and that we may walk in his paths." For out of Zion shall go forth instruction, and the word of the LORD from Jerusalem. He shall judge between the nations, and shall arbitrate for many peoples; they shall beat their swords into plowshares, and their spears into pruning hooks; nation shall not lift up sword against nation, neither shall they learn war any more. O house of Jacob, come, let us walk in the light of the LORD! (Isa. 2:2–5)[30]

CLEARLY, THE NEW Covenant presupposed the return to and continued presence of the covenant people in Jerusalem, yet it gave impetus to a creation and humanity-wide perspective. God will bring forth a glorious resolution of hostility among peoples through the Torah. The Torah is for all peoples and is the core for realizing peace among nations and with the Lord. The nation is called to be God's royal priesthood and Jerusalem will be at the center. Yet the hierarchical priesthood will no longer be necessary. References to the days that are surely coming were readily taken as pointers toward the end of the present age and the start of God's reconstitution of creation. Those references were also applicable to messianic expectations.

FROM DIVERSITY TO DEFINITION

Defeats and dispersions contributed substantially to the proliferation of groups among Jews and to their efforts to order beliefs, practices, institutions, and sacred writings. The catalog of defeats inflicted by foreign powers and turmoil created by internal Jewish struggles is formidable.[31] The military-political disasters led to the exile and dispersions of Jews from the land they believed God had given to them and to religious crises. In large measure Jews attempted to cope with their losses and dilemmas in at least two ways, each involving writings that claimed divine authority.

Apocalypticism was one such way. Jews, especially in Palestine, understood their plight as part of God's plan to defeat the demonic challengers and to test the faithfulness of His human creatures. The plan's cosmic dénouement featured dramatic battles, God's victory (sometimes with and sometimes without the leadership of a mighty angelic warrior-messiah), the resurrection of and judgment on some or all of the dead, and the creation of a new world in which the faithful-righteous people will live. The plan and the signs that point to its numerous stages were revealed to special humans either by angels or by God. Sometimes the individual who received the revelations was transported to a vantage point on earth and on other occasions was taken into the heavenly realms for instruction. The recipients were commanded to write books concerning the visions and disclosures shown them and to share these writings with their fellow Jews or to circles of instructed believers. The authors of such works used pseudonyms that credited authorship for the works to past heroes such as Adam, Enoch, Abraham, the sons of Jacob, Moses, Baruch, Daniel, and Ezra.[32] The linked themes of faithfulness to God, patience in times of persecution, keeping the Sinaitic commandments, rejecting idolatry, and avoiding foreign ways run through apocalyptic works. Between ca. 300 BCE and 100 CE numerous works were in wide circulation inside and outside of Palestine. Apparently several sectarian groups collected and used them along with traditional writings.[33]

The apocalyptic writers sought to explain the past, present, and future to the covenant people in terms of their being deceived by devilish spirits into rebelling against God, their just punishment, God's gracious faithfulness to His covenants, the divinely revealed call to loyalty to God, and the coming end of the age in which God would be victorious and His faithful remnant vindicated and rewarded. Apocalypticism emphasized God unleashing wrath on those who followed the ways of the demons and identified foreign nations and culture with evil. Pagan culture, literature, and philosophy, whether Persian, Egyptian, or Greco-Roman, were regarded as instruments used by the fallen angels to seduce Jews into depravity and damnation. Therefore, Jews loyal to the God of the covenants ought to turn toward their own works and strengthen their own communities.

Another and more enduring way Jews used to understand their plight is the way of rabbinic Judaism. The Babylonian exile (590s–530s BCE) and the relatively benign domination of the Persian Empire fostered the growing authority of scribes and teachers along with priests. The destruction of the First Temple (586 BCE) did not terminate Jewish worship, culture, and religious observances. Although the Temple was rebuilt in about 515 BCE, Jews realized that they could be Jews with and without the temple rituals. The biblical accounts of Ezra and Nehemiah indicate that Judaism was being centered on the Torah construed as written and oral as guiding life and practice.

The end of the Babylonian exile did not mean the return of all the descendants of the original deportees. Many continued to live in the former Babylonia and flourished under Persian rule. Although there may have been tensions between the Levitical priesthood and the non-Levitical rabbinate, the emphasis on adherence to the Mosaic Torah and its extended interpretations continued and expanded. The Greco-Macedonian victory over the Persian Empire introduced Hellenistic culture into Palestine-Syria as well as Mesopotamia and Egypt. Traditional Palestinian Jews were moved to define themselves against the Greco-Syrians not only through the Maccabean revolt but also through strengthening their devotion to the Torah. Roman incursions and eventual supremacy furthered the process of gradual religious consolidation until the ill-fated revolts of 66–72 CE. Throughout the postexilic period Jews were confronted by polytheistic powers that dominated them. A determined Jewish response was to insist fervently on the oneness of God to maintain their past identity and future distinctiveness even to the point of martyrdom.[34]

The rise and spread of Christianity complicated efforts by rabbinic leaders to rein in apocalyptic movements and to forestall the erosion of Torah observance. The destruction of the Temple and expulsion from Jerusalem (70 CE) effectively terminated sacrificial worship and the need for a

Levitical priesthood. The sacrificial system was replaced by spiritually attuned ethics, and rabbinic authority took the positions held previously by the Levitical priesthood. While there were residual hopes for the restoration of the Temple, Judaism's future lay with the rabbinic academies in Palestine and Babylonia.

The development of the rabbinate can be traced elsewhere, but three factors are relevant to Judaism and Jews' relationship with Islam and the Qur'an.[35] The first is the collation of biblical, rabbinic, and folkloric materials into collections of writings that were assumed to bear divine authority. By the end of the first century CE the text of the Hebrew Bible seems to have been stabilized. According to an account from the first century wisdom-apocalyptic 2 Esdras, God inspired Ezra to dictate to stenographers the words of the books of the Hebrew Bible and seventy other books to be revealed at a later time.[36] The very letters of the works were of divine origin. In addition, traditions about rabbinic discussions concerning topics addressed by the Torah led to the compilation of a work called the Mishna (ca. 200–250). Within the next century another set of discussions, the Tosephta, was composed as an addendum to the Mishna, and the process continued. By 400 the rabbinate in Palestine combined the Mishna with materials termed Gemara to form the Jerusalem Talmud. The Gemara contained further rabbinic discussions and anecdotal materials often reflecting legends and folklore. By 600 the Babylonian rabbinate produced a Babylonian Talmud. It is a more extensive combination of the Mishna and its version of the Gemara. The written materials composed of divinely dictated scripture and sets of oral traditions committed to writing were widely regarded among Jews as furnishing accounts stretching from the creation through the various covenants to the present seventh century. These works of divine revelation and commentary-extensions formed a special corpus of materials that were considered authoritative for Jewish life and practice, especially in Syria-Palestine and Mesopotamia. Jews and their neighbors in Arabia knew at least some of the texts and accounts in the Hebrew Bible, Mishna, and Talmuds.

Second, the "Torah" and its applications spread throughout Jewish communities from Persia to Rome. "Torah" could be applied specifically to the Pentateuch and considered as written by Moses, then extended through the rest of the works called today the Hebrew Bible and on to the Mishna, Talmuds, and rabbinic decisions claiming to be based on the Torah; even venerated rabbis could be considered living Torahs because they had figuratively ingested its principles as well as texts. Torah could be written (Pentateuch and the other books deemed to be outstandingly holy) and oral (Mishnah-Talmud and rabbinic discussions).[37] Torah could be combed for particular rules of conduct, resulting in a compilation of 365 negative and 248 positive injunctions.[38] Rabbis and scribes were needed to search, study, elucidate, and apply the revelatory texts and principles in guiding fellow Jews under changing circumstances and cultural shifts. A further body of oral and written interpretations of biblical accounts, the midrashim, was widely used. Midrashic accounts sometimes were folkloric, sometimes detailed examinations of texts and accounts. Jacob Neusner recognizes three types of midrashic examinations of portions of the Pentateuch: providing further information not directly in the text, defining problems raised in the accounts, and expressing something new and different from what the text seems to say.[39]

The task was made even more challenging because Jews now lived as a minority, even in Palestine. By 600 the rabbinical academies had developed procedures and standards by which they interpreted the texts and commentaries in meticulous studies of the documents and reached their own conclusions.

Third, the reciprocal rivalries between Judaism and Christianity moved Jews and Christians toward defining themselves to themselves and toward distinguishing one from the other. The parting of the synagogue and the church apparently was gradual and, in the end, a matter of imperial politics as well as ecclesiastical policy.[40] John Chrysostom (ca. 347–407), bishop of Syrian Antioch, delivered eight vituperative discourses against Judaizing Christians (386–87). He denounced Christians who mingled their Christianity with Jewish views and participated in synagogue activities.[41] If the process of separation was sporadic and slow in the Roman Empire and particularly in Syria, it may have been still more gradual in the Persian Empire and Arabia. That may account for the impression given in the Qur'an that Jews and Christians were one people who argued among themselves. Each also shared what appeared to be a common literary corpus and writings that neither would acknowledge to the other as inspired or valid interpretations. Jews regarded the Mishna and Talmuds as authoritative while the Christians rejected these, and the Christians held that they had a "New Testament" that overshadowed the Jewish "Old Testament," which naturally, was rejected by Jews.

But they really did not agree on the literary corpus that they seemed to hold in common. In the early third century BCE Jewish sages, probably first in Alexandria, Egypt, began to translate from Hebrew to Greek works that were already and some eventually considered sacred. The result was the Septuagint (abbreviated LXX), or more accurately different Septuagints. Through the Septuagint Judaism's heritage, especially its ethical monotheism, became well known in the Roman Empire. But there were differences, some minor and others startlingly major, between the Hebrew and Greek versions. Moreover, the Septuagint included "books" that were not in the usual Hebrew works.[42] Jews in the Western Diaspora held that the Septuagint was as fully divinely inspired as the Hebrew version and that the apparently "extra" books were equal to the other works. In essence, the Scriptures used by Jews were written in three languages: Hebrew, Aramaic, and Greek.

Internal Jewish debates over the extent and nature of the sacred text were sharpened by Christian uses of and interpretations based on the Septuagint. Christian missionaries used the Septuagint for preaching to pagans, addressing their fellow believers, proselytizing Jews, and arguing with Jews. Christians quoted Septuagintal passages and interpreted the texts as proving, predicting, and proclaiming Jesus as the promised Messiah of Israel and savior of the world. Such usages of the Scriptures added to the stimulus already under way in the rabbinic academies in Babylonia and Palestine to standardize the Hebrew texts and limit the number of works to those originally written in Hebrew. The account in 2 Esdras 14:37–48 about divinely inspired Ezra dictating in Hebrew to his stenographers meant that no work written after Ezra (ca. 400 BCE) and not in Hebrew could be considered holy. The plurality of languages, differences in texts, and disputes over the extent and contrary interpretations of the Scripture surfaced in the Qur'an and heated Jewish, Christian, and Muslim relations.

JUDAISM'S NARRATIVE STRETCHES from the one and only God creating the world to the present. A series of covenants marks junctures in
the narrative that move from the Lord's covenanting with the whole creation and all humanity to God's electing one people, land, and dynasty to
do God's will to the promise of a new covenant that forecasts a new creation. The narrative includes oral and written traditions, legends and interpretations that range across centuries and use three languages. Shaped
retrospectively by rabbinic authorities in the Persian Empire and Palestine, the narrative testified to the absolute oneness of the only God and
denounced any form of polytheism. A body of literature reflecting the history and present needs of the Jewish people gained varying degrees of authority, resulting in Scripture, Mishna, and Talmuds. Harsh experience with
rebellions and the Christian appropriation of messianism diminished but
did not eliminate apocalyptic currents. On its own merits and as a response
to the loss of the Temple, sages raised the role of the Torah into the multi-
faceted unifying principle of Jewish practice and life. Nevertheless, controversies and diversity were not eliminated, especially in regions beyond
the reach of rabbinic authorities.

CHRISTIANITY'S BASIC NARRATIVE

Jesus is at the heart of the Church's faith, mission, and struggles. In general,
what the Torah is in Judaism, Jesus is in Christianity. I present a core narrative about Jesus, trace its transition into covenantal terms, and conclude with
its transformation into the basic narrative current in the seventh century.

THE CORE NARRATIVE ABOUT JESUS

The New Testament–derived narrative indicates that Jesus was born in
Palestine ca. 7–4 BCE, was raised in Galilee, and was a carpenter. At the
age of about thirty, he left his family of origin in response to the message
of the apocalyptic preacher, John the Baptizer, and was baptized by him
ca. 27–29 CE. He may have been associated with John before engaging in

his own itinerant preaching and teaching. He gathered a group of follow-ers who called him "rabbi." He was known as a teacher-interpreter of the Torah, a wonder-worker, a healer, and an exorcist. Some called him mes-siah, son of David, or son of man. His popularity, interpretations, actions, and confrontational tactics provoked religious and political leaders. The re-ligious leaders concluded that Jesus' teachings were inimical to the emerg-ing consensus concerning Torah interpretation and practice, that his de-nunciations of their authority would further fragment Palestinian Judaism, and that his teachings and his reputation might incite a rebellion against the Roman authorities—and that would lead to a devastating response by the Romans.

In an apparently defiant gesture, Jesus and his entourage entered Jeru-salem shortly before a Passover (ca. 30–32 CE). It was widely believed among apocalyptically minded Jews that the messiah-liberator would appear in Jerusalem during Passover to drive out the oppressor, purify the Temple, and restore Jews to their rightful status and/or inaugurate the Kingdom of God. Toward the end of a particularly acrimonious week, Jesus shared a meal that included wine with his immediate followers. The supper was likened to the Passover and was reported to have used Sinaitic–New Covenantal language with perhaps Adamic and Noahide undertones. He was betrayed to the religious authorities by one of his close followers, taken into custody, and accused by his fellow Jews of blasphemy. The Roman procurator condemned him for rebellion and had him exe-cuted by crucifixion. He was declared dead and was entombed. Within a few days his followers claimed that God raised him from the dead and that they had seen, talked with him, and touched him. There was a claim that some five hundred believers saw him at one time.[43]

The circle of disciples closest to him said that he commanded them and future believers to proclaim the message of the imminent coming of judgment and the beginning of God's kingdom in which he would be revealed as Messiah-Christ-Lord. There were differing reports by several followers that in some manner he was taken into the presence of God and yet promised to be with them as a spiritual guide and that he would re-turn soon as the exalted messiah-son of man to defeat evil and participate in the Day of Judgment.

The core narrative about Jesus treated his relationship to God and humanity in diverse ways. Was he an exemplary human being who was inspired by God and raised to angelic status, or an angel-instructor who came to earth to teach humans the ways of God, or an emanation of the one God? Although first-century Christians wrote of Jesus as being involved in the defeat of evil, achieving forgiveness by God of humans for their sins, and describing the signs of the coming Day of Judgment, they gave mixed directions for living in pagan society until the Day of Judgment and for ways to relate to Jews. In the first century Christians could describe Jesus as the victor who defeated the devil through dying and rising from the dead and as the human version of the lamb sacrificed in order to assuage the justifiable wrath of God for the sins of the community. Within two to four decades of his death and reputed resurrection, some were saying that he was the new Adam, Moses, and David. Common to images used by many Christians in the first century was the insistence that Jesus was a real human being who actually died and was raised physically from the dead. Apparently some in the same period claimed Jesus only appeared or seemed to have a human body, and others ventured that he was an angel among other angels.[44] From its very beginnings, the Christian community's diversities led to factions.[45]

Beginning in about 40 CE Christian leaders wrote to congregations advising them about controversial issues and developing further their understandings of Jesus, while the nascent Christian communities used the Septuagint and apparently a version of Enoch as their scripture, interpreting the texts as predicting and prefiguring the coming of Jesus.[46] At least after 70 CE and perhaps earlier, Christians began to write about Jesus, his mother, his followers, and the spread of the Christian message. Often the accounts about Jesus were called Gospels. By the early fourth century there were numerous Gospels, Acts of various figures, cosmologies, meditations, and tracts. These featured various versions of Jesus' teachings, actions, and death and its aftermath. A number of Gospels described his mother, Mary, and the childhoods of Mary and Jesus. Some were widely popular; others were intended for sectarian Christian communities in the Roman Empire.[47] Most often they were written in Greek and made ample use of Greco-Roman rhetoric. The works were used for instruction, preaching, edification, countering the ideas of other Christians, attracting pagans to Christianity, and defending Christianity from its pagan and Jewish critics.

Some accounts that will appear in the Qur'an included the child Jesus disclosing his divine powers by making clay sparrows that came to life.[48] The Protoevangelium of James reported on the birth and upbringing of Mary. Her elderly parents, Anna and Joachim, were told by angelic messengers that Anna would bear a child. Surprised that the child was the girl, Mary, and not a son, they dedicated her to the Lord by bringing her to the Temple to be raised there. She danced on the altar and readily took to her new life of prayer, and angels fed her. She was watched over by the priest Zachariah until she was betrothed to the elderly carpenter, Joseph.[49] These and similar contributions to the narrative focused on Jesus were known among and beyond Christians. Clearly before and certainly following the suppression of the Jewish revolt in Palestine (72 CE), diverse versions of Christianity emerged and continued to proliferate at the same time rabbinic Judaism was seeking to define Judaism.

THE CORE NARRATIVE INTERPRETED
IN COVENANTAL TERMS

Whoever and whatever Jesus was historically, he was a magnet who attracted and absorbed Christianized versions of the covenants. Covenantal attributions were retrospective interpretations made by Christians seeking to discern scriptural support for their faith that Jesus was and is God's unique revealer to a world that would soon come to an end. They were convinced that in some way Jesus was the one through whom God was fulfilling His plan for the cosmos. On the one hand, they were sure that the Torah, prophets, and writings validated their faith in Jesus and what was yet to come. They therefore appropriated the Scriptures as belonging to the new-true Israel, the Christian Church. On the other hand, on the basis of the contemporary assumption that the most ancient was the authentic version of the truth, they needed to show that their positions were present in the Scriptures and now made clear in and through Jesus.[50] Believers, then, came to what was for them natural, uncontrived conclusions that the Scriptures centered on Jesus.

The New Covenant and Jesus

The New Covenant provided an entry point through which the other covenants could be interpreted in Christian terms. Jeremiah's prediction coupled with passages from Isaiah were lenses through which Christians could comprehend God's promises, human responses, and divine signs. Isaiah 52:7–53:12 was essential in deciphering Jesus' death and resurrection in covenantal terms. The passage opens with praise for the one who comes proclaiming the good news (*evangelion,* "gospel" in the Septuagint) of forgiveness to Jerusalem (i.e., God's faithful remnant). The passage continues with a description of the Lord's servant whose innocent suffering and death will result in God forgiving the servant's offspring and points toward the exaltation of the servant.[51] Christians saw the passage as a prediction of Jesus and as an explanation of his death and the purpose of that death.

The Sinaitic Covenant and Jesus

From the vantage point of the New Covenant, the Sinaitic Covenant could be understood as predicting Jesus and the Christian community. The slaves who escaped from Egypt survived the night on which the firstborn Egyptian males died because a lamb was slain and its blood smeared on the lintel of the escapees' doors; the angel of death passed over their dwellings. This lamb could be regarded as a liberation lamb. At Sinai an animal was sacrificed and its blood splashed on the people and the altar as a sign that YHWH and His people were united in a covenant of the Lord's protection and the people's obedience. The sacrificed animal was a sign of the special relationship of God and His elect. Among the Levitical directions believed to have been given at Sinai was the ritual signaling the people's repentance and God's forgiveness. One animal was symbolically heaped with the sins of the people and driven into the wilderness as a ransom to the malevolent spirits who infested the wilderness. Another animal was sacrificed and its blood was thought to cover the sins of the people before God.[52] Christians saw the liberation, community-creating, and sin-offering sacrifices fulfilled by Jesus and constitutive of the Christian community. Even in the first century CE Christians elided the Passover and Yom Kippur lambs into their understandings of the last meal Jesus shared with his disciples before his death.

The Davidic Covenant and Jesus

The Davidic Covenant was also seen as a precursor to and completed in Jesus. The titles "Son of David" and "Messiah" (in Greek, Christ) were royal titles bestowed on a ruler designated especially to do God's will. The diverse themes about the messiah in several biblical and intertestamental apocalyptic writings were readily blended and even connected with the angelic Son of Man as well as with a human. Christians searched the Scriptures and constructed a genealogy for Jesus that connected him to the Davidic line even before the birth stories and genealogies in Matthew and Luke.[53]

The Abrahamic Covenant and Jesus

The New Covenant perspective on the Abrahamic Covenant raised problems as well as opportunities. The chief problems involved the covenantal sign (circumcision) and the firmness of God's promise of the land. Must males who seek to become Christians be circumcised? Could the Christian message be extended outside of the Holy Land (especially Jerusalem) and what the Oral-Written Torah mandated for that land? Struggles to answer those problems are reflected in the New Testament's Acts of the Apostles and letters of Paul. In a historical sense, the problems were resolved by the success of the mission to the Gentiles that did not insist on circumcision and by the destruction of Jerusalem in 70. Nevertheless, Judaism's emphasis on the Abrahamic Covenant had to be shifted to apply to Jesus. The shift centered on Isaac's and Abraham's "offspring."

The binding and attempted sacrifice of Isaac (Gen. 22) was readily interpreted as a foreshadowing of Jesus' death on the cross at the will of the Father. Jesus was seen as the true Isaac, the child of promise. The apostle

Paul's argument with Christians who understood Christianity as a Torah-observant and fulfilled Judaism used the singular "offspring" to refer to Jesus and not to a multitude of subsequent Gentile converts. He maintained that since the Genesis passage containing God's promise to Abraham about Abraham's offspring came before the command to circumcise physically the males in his family, the message about Jesus could be proclaimed to the Gentiles without requiring male Gentiles to be circumcised physically. Through Jesus, claimed Paul, all converts received the spiritual circumcision of faith in the heart.[54] A passage in the Gospel of John reported Jesus as saying that Abraham rejoiced to see the incarnational coming of Jesus (John 8:39–58).

The Noahide and Adamic Covenants and Jesus

The Noahide and Adamic Covenants were with all humanity. In their Christianized versions, they furnished powerful incentives for Christians to bring the message about Jesus to all people. The flood was interpreted as a predictive-allegorical analogue to the Christian rite, baptism.[55] The Noahide Covenant also gave Christians a way to reach behind the Oral-Written Torah's regulations for Gentile converts regarding purity rituals, dietary regulations, and Sabbath procedures. Jesus was for all persons in all nations through whom God was offering salvation in prospect of the coming judgment.

The Adamic Covenant was reconfigured to regard Jesus as the new Adam, the new beginning for humanity and creation. Humanity had lost its fellowship with God through the First Adam, but that closeness was restored and even greater joy promised through the New Adam. Christians were new creatures because they were incorporated into the life of the risen Jesus. Again, the message was for the world. The Kingdom is coming, creation will be redone, and Jesus is the first fruit from the dead and Lord.[56]

JESUS AND THE accounts about him began in an apocalyptic Palestinian-Jewish milieu, then spread westward through the Roman Empire and, to a lesser degree, eastward into the Persian Empire and possibly filtered into

Arabia. Jesus' preaching and actions centered on the coming Kingdom of God. Those who expected the Kingdom anticipated terrific battles between the representatives of God and the forces of evil, God's victory led by a glorious, divinely empowered figure, the resurrection of the dead, a day or time of judgment, and then the re-creation of the world in which the saved would live in eternal fellowship with each other and God while the wicked were to be damned to eternal punishment. Christians believed that Jesus had decisive roles in that apocalyptic drama. He proclaimed the nearness of the Kingdom and the need for persons to repent and believe in the coming victory of God, and that he would return to be the empowered figure in the last days of this world. Three factors were common amid the different positions that emerged within the first hundred years after Jesus' departure.

First, Jesus was God's unique revealer-messenger. No future revealer-messenger would ever have the same stature as Jesus and would only expand the revelation given through Jesus. Second, Jesus and his message-actions were believed to have been predicted and prepared for in Judaism's scriptures. Jesus was fulfilling what God had started from the beginning of creation and included in obscure forms in those scriptures. Christians, through Jesus, now understood the real meanings of God's actions and scriptures. That understanding involved transposing the Jewish covenants into the core narrative, giving that core further depth and meaning. Jesus was the true subject and substance of the covenants. The original covenants, however, were not uniform; that is, they addressed different circumstances, used different images, and anticipated different results. Consequently, already diverse, even contradictory views of Jesus were carried into subsequent generations. Such differences were often argued over within the first hundred years of the Christian movement. As long as there was a vibrant expectation that the present age would end soon, many of the diversities could be endured under the principle that all would be made clear when Jesus returned. Given that Christians wielded no secular power and that ecclesial authority structures were only emerging, various versions could be debated. Since there was no Christianity-wide authority to define doctrines and enforce discipline on believers, factions formed. Third, once Christians began to write to each other and a broader public, they produced a multitude of letters, treatises, Gospels, Acts, apocalyptics, defenses, and moral manuals. How were these to be regarded, evaluated, and used? What standards might be employed to make judgments about them? What was the relationship between any of these to the existing scriptures retained from Judaism? As the Christian movement entered its second and subsequent centuries, Christianity was developing conflicting narratives and risked being fragmented into mutually contradictory sects.

FROM DIVERSITIES TO DEFINITIONS: THE CORE TRANSFORMED INTO THE BASIC NARRATIVE

The second and third centuries were periods of struggle, controversy, and expansion for the Christian movement. Throughout the fourth century and into the last decades of the eighth century Christianity developed, at least officially, those doctrinal formulations and ecclesial structures that still characterize it. In the process of defining teachings and evolving patterns for worship and establishing authoritative offices, Christians sorted out from the many writings that circulated among them a body of scripture to be used in conjunction with the scriptures taken over from Judaism. Christians called a number of their distinctive works the "New Testament" or "New Covenant" and the earlier Jewish works (in Septuagintal form translated into several languages) the "Old Testament." For our Quranically focused purposes, five areas deserve attention.

HUMAN NATURE

Did humans have the ability to will and do what God requires? In other words, are humans able to merit God's approval and so be granted eternal blessedness?[57] Much within the "Old Testament" answers "Yes," often with conditions, such as humans need guidance, correction, and prodding. Often sin is regarded chiefly as transgression, debt, and offense that can be rectified by reparation, sacrifice, and sincere repentance. Adam and Eve may have set a poor precedent, but they did not so damage the human will and intellect as to render their posterity inherently sinful and unclean. God's grace and mercy is expressed in accepting human intentions and deeds to restore fellowship with God and fellow humans.

Some passages in the "Old Testament," however, respond, "No." People are sinners because something has gone dreadfully wrong within their wills.[58] One explanation noted in our discussion on the Jewish view of the Adamic Covenant laid the blame on Adam and Eve. Sin, then, is chiefly an internal pollution, sickness, and spirit of rebellious disobedience. Transgressions, debts, and offenses are the evidences of the perverted human will. Even good deeds are tainted by the inner corruption. Humans are guilty before God and cannot merit His forgiveness. If there is to be any forgiveness and reconciliation, the initiative comes from divine intervention in the form of at least a mighty angelic figure or from God Himself.

The New Testament did not resolve the tension between the two positions. Most Christians veered from one position to another or settled somewhere between them. By the late fourth century many Christians came to answer that humans did not have full free will because Adam and Eve's "original sin" was inherited by all born of Adam. The rite of baptism moved from being a ritual for converts to enter the community on their confession of faith to a ritual to be administered to infants so as either to drown the old Adam in them or to begin the process of healing their wills. Often Christians fixed blame on Eve and from her on all her daughters, that is, every subsequent woman, except Mary.[59]

JESUS

As indicated earlier, Christians were Christians because they understood Jesus as the Christ or Messiah of God. What that meant, however, was a matter of significant disagreement. Three christologies may be seen within the first centuries: the adoptionist, angelic, and manifestation of the supreme God. How Christians conceived of who Jesus was and is was influenced greatly by their views of human nature. Those who were convinced that humans could will and do what the Lord requires tended toward the adoptionist position. For them, Jesus was the exemplary human empowered by

God and raised to divine-angelic status. He is the supreme model whom humans should follow in life and into eternal life. Those who regarded Jesus as an angelic revealer regarded humans as deeply flawed but still educable. They realized that humans needed not a mere model but a divine guide, loving disciplinarian, and teacher of holy knowledge.[60] Those who came to increasingly negative conclusions about human nature held that only massive divine intervention was able to rehabilitate or renovate humanity; that is, only God Himself would have to enter human experience to defeat the devil's grasp over humans and to accept the just punishment for sinning against God. Jesus was the Passover, Sinai Wilderness, and Yom Kippur sacrifices, the true Isaac given up by his Father, the suffering servant who died for the sins of others and through whom men and women could be forgiven. Jesus was indeed the bread for the salvation of the world, and believers could unite themselves with God through his ritual of sharing bread and wine. He was the New Adam, and his followers could go into all the world to proclaim him as the one through whom they could be saved from hellfire and for life in the new creation.

Over the second through fourth centuries the political and social situations within the Roman Empire worsened and a pessimism about human endeavors deepened. Although the angelic and adoptionist christologies survived, there was a decided shift toward the view that Jesus was a manifestation of the supreme God. After contentious debates and even public disorders, that position was affirmed by a council of bishops held at Nicea in 325 and reaffirmed at the First Council of Constantinople in 381. The Council of Nicea held that Jesus was fully God of God and, as totally fully divine, had no beginning but always was and therefore had the same essence or being with the Creator and yet was fully human.[61] Not all accepted the Niceno-Constantinopolitan definition. Sometimes nonacceptance became a theological factor in civil conflicts and political intrigues. The controversies and imperial political power turned dissenters into resentful citizens and some into refugees beyond the reach of the Roman Empire. At least theoretically that empire became Christian in the fourth century. But the definition raised further questions about whether or not Christians believed in one God.

GOD

On top of consternation over the identity of Jesus, Christians faced further debates about the biblical term *Spirit,* that is, reference to God's Spirit. Was the Spirit of God the spiritual presence of Jesus? Was the Spirit different from the Creator-Father and the Son-Jesus? Did the Spirit reveal new teachings? How did speculations about the Spirit influence thinking about the Creator and the Son? Again, diversity led to controversies and finally to more imperially authorized councils of bishops. The definitions or statements of those councils were the results of complex and often arcane discussions, relying on rhetorical nuances that were understood in different ways in Latin-speaking and Greek-speaking Christianity or not all among average believers. The upshot was a pair of umbrella-like formulations of what is called the Trinity, the three-in-oneness of God. The Western version held that Christians believe God is one in essence (in Godself) and is manifested simultaneously in three distinct but indivisible "faces." The Latin word *persona* originally referred not to an individual but to the mask an actor wore onstage to indicate the character he was portraying. For Christians, then, the One God revealed God's essence simultaneously in three ways: Creator-Provider, Redeemer-Savior, and Spirit-Sanctifier. The Eastern form preferred to consider the Trinity a mystery to be experienced. God may be described as one in the sense of a circle, that is, one as unity instead of as a single point. Within that circle God is Father, Son, and Spirit, with the Father-Creator having functional priority. In both formulations, Father, Son, and Spirit are coequal in Godness, coeternal in scope, and one to be worshiped and served.

If the discussions and arguments over the Trinity were opaque to average believers, continued debates about Jesus were scarcely clearer. Through the fifth century and culminating in the Council of Chalcedon (451), with after-tremors into the seventh century, the christological issues concerned whether Jesus had only a divine will or only a human will, and whether he has only a divine nature or only a human nature. Naturally, imperial political issues were mingled with ecclesiastical political concerns as the theological points were argued. The Chalcedonian formulation held that Jesus was fully God and fully human so that his divinity and humanity could not be separated or confused because of a divinely given union. Again, imperial power was used to enforce conformity. And again there were resentful citizens and refugees. A number of these refugees, followers of the Syrian theologian–bishop Nestorius, settled in the Persian Empire. Others found their way into southern Egypt, Nubia, Ethiopia, and probably Arabia.

SCRIPTURES

The Bible of the first Christians was the Septuagint. As noted earlier, there were sharp differences between the Septuagint and what emerged as the Hebrew Bible. From the end of the first century CE onward rabbinic authorities led most Jews to rely on the books written in Hebrew. Christians continued to use the Septuagint. Among the differences between the Hebrew and Greek versions were significant variants in the respective texts, and the Septuagint included seven works that the rabbis rejected as holy. Christians also used some of the popular intertestamental works that were used by some Jews, such as versions of Enoch, Jubilees, 2 Esdras, the Testament of the Twelve Patriarchs, and legendary materials. Not only did Jews and Christians clash over the extent, content, and interpretation of any writings they used in common, but scores of manuscripts with literally thousands of variant texts were in circulation. Compounding all the foregoing for Christians was the production of Gospels, epistles, Acts, treatises, and apocalyptics that claimed to be testimonies to Jesus, for example, the Gospels of Thomas, Philip, Egyptians, Hebrews, and Truth. Well into the second century and up to the fourth century the treatise Shepherd of Hermas, 1 and 2 Clement, six letters by Bishop Ignatius of Syrian Antioch, and a letter supposedly written by Paul's sometime partner, Barnabas, were widely used, often on par with letters attributed to Paul, Peter, and others. Already mentioned are various Acts and apocalypses. By the end of the second century four Gospels were commended for use in the churches to the exclusion of other Gospels. The four were attributed (inaccurately) to the disciples Matthew, John, and Mark, and Luke, reputed to be companions of apostles.

The process of determining which works were to be used in the churches was gradual and dependent on the authority of church leaders to recommend and enforce their views on subordinate clergy and their congregations. The chief factors appear to have been resonance with the Christian interpretations of the Old Testament, agreement with the received traditions about Jesus and his message, possibilities that disciples and apostles may have been the authors, and, especially, continual usefulness and relevance to the Christian communities. Several lists of books considered canonical or standard were drawn up in the third and fourth centuries.[62] The two most influential were those of the historian bishop Eusebius (ca. 260–339) and the theologian-bishop Athanasius (ca. 300–373).[63] In his festal or Easter letter to his clergy, the latter lists the forty-six books of the Septuagintal version of the Old Testament and twenty-seven works of the New Testament.[64] These became the standard canon for Christians through the sixteenth century, when Protestants reverted to the canon of the Hebrew Bible along with the twenty-seven books of the New Testament. Although the canonical works themselves were written in three languages (Hebrew, Aramaic, and Greek) over the course of more than a thousand years by known and unknown figures and although there are literally thousands of manuscript variations, in essence, church authorities determined what books were to be considered the Bible for Christians. Those officials attempted to bring coherence into previously decidedly diverse practices. More than three centuries had elapsed after Jesus was physically with his disciples before most Christians came to practice a common canon—until the Protestant Reformation.

CHURCH AND EMPIRE

Jesus had circles of followers. The inner circle was composed of twelve men; the middle circle included men and women who apparently traveled with him constantly; and the outer circle was composed of those who attached themselves to him temporarily.[65] Within the inner circle, three disciples were particularly close to Jesus, and Peter was especially important as a leader and missionary. Christian tradition held that he was an early if not the first bishop of the congregation in Rome. Later Western Christians looked to the bishop of Rome as a leading authority in matters of doctrinal and ecclesiastical polity. Apparently distinctions and responsibilities as well as offices emerged quickly following Jesus' departure.[66]

Even before the emperor Constantine (ca. 285–337) initiated policies that put Christianity and the Church on equal footing with other licit religions and gradually favored Christianity over those other religions (beginning 313), the Church had developed hierarchical structures that included bishops, priests, deacons, and other offices. Constantine developed a new imperial capital on the site of the smaller city of Byzantium in 324. It was officially the New Rome but was popularly called Constantinople (Constantine's City). The patriarch (chief bishop) of Constantinople was widely regarded as the central figure for official Christianity in the eastern Mediterranean and into the Arabian Peninsula.[67]

The Church and many of its leaders prospered from the donations of the laity and its connections to the imperial court. Monasticism was one reaction against the growing luxury and worldliness of the higher clergy. The monks were ascetics who decried corruption and sought to imitate the poverty and simplicity of Jesus and the apostles. Sometime before the reign of the emperor Justinian I (527–65) the Eastern Church forbade ordained deacons and priests to marry but allowed the ordination of already married men. During Justinian's reign, bishops were required to be celibate.[68] The Eastern Church, often locked into controversies with the Rome-based Western Church, and the Byzantine imperial establishment sought to develop a harmonious relationship so that Church and state complemented each other as divinely guided institutions, and Constantinople was seen as a holy, God-protected city. Some emperors were skilled theologians who involved themselves in making doctrinal decisions, and some patriarchs were active politicians. Working together, Church and government sought to maintain order, define God's truth, suppress schismatics and heretics, and defend the holy land, Palestine. By the seventh century that task was especially difficult. Pressures from marauding tribes on the empire's northern borders, persistent hostilities from the Persians in the east, and revolts in the Balkans, combined with fiscal crises, a series of unstable emperors, and tensions with the never-docile political and religious leaders in the west, weakened both the Church and the state.

THE CORE NARRATIVE about Jesus changed dramatically on its way to becoming the basic Christian narrative by the seventh century. The elements that motivated that change were present from the beginning, and the diversities remained even when the theological definitions were supported by a powerful church and the imperial government. The official basic narrative understood the oneness of God to be a unity in Trinity of Father, Son, and Spirit. Jesus, the second person of that Trinity, was seen to have been preexistent from all eternity. The fully God person became a fully human person through the incarnation by means of the Spirit and the Virgin Mary. He was truly killed by crucifixion and was truly resurrected from the dead and ascended to heaven. He was expected to return to begin the judgment of all humans who ever existed and then rule with his Father and the Spirit over the eternal Kingdom of God.

Views of human nature ranged from an affirmation that people could know and do the will of God and thereby merit salvation to the denial of humans being able to do God's will because they are distorted by "original sin." The tendency toward the latter position grew from the third century onward. The variable anthropologies influenced significantly the Christian views of Jesus and the purposes of his becoming human. The "work," or mission, of Jesus was accomplished through his incarnation, death, and resurrection through which he defeated demonic forces, ransomed humans from the devil, was sacrificed to assuage the justice of the Father-Judge, served as the moral example of true humanity, revealed the truth of God in his teachings, and reconstituted humanity as the New Adam. Jesus was the one and only one through whom sins could be forgiven. Now believers could become part of his body, the Church, through the rituals of baptism and the meal of bread and wine. Judaism's covenants were radically reinterpreted and transformed so as to support Christian convictions about Jesus.

The basic narrative regarded the Christian Church as the community through which God drew women and men into fellowship with God and to be part of the process of ordering the cosmos so that it would be fulfilled in a new creation. The Church was arranged in a hierarchy that was in concord with what was now regarded as the God-blessed imperial government that enforced theological decisions. A body of divinely inspired scripture included a version of what was termed the Old Testament and works written by Christians. Various manuscripts contained minor and major differences in the texts, and numerous other works continued to be considered important by those on the fringes of official teachings.

The basic narrative was not the only narrative. Theological refugees who settled in the Persian Empire, Ethiopia, Nubia, and Arabia differed in matters related to the Trinity and the nature of Jesus. Movements called collectively "gnostic" regarded Jesus as a supreme angel who was not crucified and who revealed heavenly secrets to those initiated into such saving knowledge. A dwindling number held that Jesus was fully human and then was empowered by God to teach divine ways and ultimately taken into heaven. Stories about Jesus and his mother that were not part of the official narrative continued to circulate as part of popular piety.

CONCLUSION

Muslims claim that the Qur'an corrects both the Jewish and the Christian narratives, replacing them with God's final revelation and the revealer of God's truth.

> Say: "O People of the Book! Exceed not in your religion the bounds (of what is proper), trespassing beyond the truth, nor follow the vain desires of people who went wrong in times gone by—who misled many, and strayed (themselves) from the even Way. Curses were pronounced on those among the Children of Israel who rejected Faith by the tongue of David and of Jesus, the son of Mary, because they disobeyed and persisted in excesses." (Surah 5:77–78)

THREE

ISLAM'S BASIC NARRATIVE
AND CORE POSITIONS

Whatever is in the heavens and on earth let it declare the
praises and glory of Allah: for He is the Exalted in Might,
the Wise. To Him belongs the dominion of the heavens
and the earth; it is He Who gives life and death; and He
has power over all things. He is the First and the Last,
the [Outer] and the [Inner], and He has full knowledge
of all things. He it is Who created the heavens and the
earth in six days and is moreover firmly established on the
Throne (of authority). He knows what enters within the
earth and what comes forth out of it, what comes down
from heaven, and what mounts up to it. And He is with you
wheresoever ye may be. And Allah sees well all that ye do.
To Him belongs the dominion of the heavens and the earth:
and all affairs are referred back to Allah. He merges night
into day and He merges day into night; and He has full
knowledge of the secrets of (all) hearts.

Surah 57:1–6, al-Hadid, Iron

This chapter introduces Islam through a narrative developed around seven
covenants and comments on the Five Pillars and Five Teachings. Its aim
is first to present the essential positions in Islam, set up some key issues

that we will encounter in the Qur'an, and prepare us to move ahead; and, second, to begin listening to the Qur'an speak through references and quotations. Quranic rhetoric, even in translation, is distinctive. I open with a prologue, move to the narrative, and conclude with the core positions.

PROLOGUE

Islam means to submit, surrender, obey fully the One-Only God. God is al-Awaal (the First) and al-Akhir (the Last), az-Zahir (the Outer) and al-Batin (the Inner). Allah is as-Samad (the Eternal) and al-Muta'ali (the Self-Exalted). God is always al-Achad (the One-Only).[1] God is supremely transcendent, yet sees and knows all things and thoughts. He is above the seven heavens, yet closer to us than our own jugular veins.[2] God in Godself is absolutely unknowable and beyond any name such as YHWH or Isis. Humans can know only what God reveals of Himself. On that basis, Muslims say that God has ninety-nine names; that is, He reveals His One-Only-ness in ninety-nine manners, some of which are indicated above. The Outer-Inner revelations complement each other. The Outer Revelation is *wahy* and *tanzil*. This is the direct revelatory action of God that comes from beyond a human by God's inspiration (wahy) and handing down the revelation's content (tanzil). God prepares persons and then discloses what is to be known. The summit of the Outer Revelation is the Qur'an, and Muhammad was the person specially prepared to receive it. Others who have been prepared and who received earlier revelations and books are the prophets and messengers. The Inner Revelation is *ilham,* the intuitive awakening, awareness, spiritual hearing, and insight God gives to persons.[3]

Islam is God's *din* (also transliterated as *deen*). Often translated as "religion," din has four interlocking meanings: sovereignty or supreme authority; obedience-submission-devotion to that authority; the system, rituals, teachings, and structures established by that authority; and retributions and rewards meted out to those who reject and to those who obey that authority.[4] So, "Who can be better in religion [din] than one who submits his whole self to Allah, does good, and follows the way of Abraham, the true in faith? For Allah did take Abraham for a friend. . . . But to Allah belong all things in the heavens and on earth: and He it is that encompasseth all things" (Surah 3:124, 126, al-Imran, Family of Imran).

Islam provides the Siraatal mustaqiim, the Straight Path, for all that exists from creation's beginning to its ultimate goal (Surah 1:6). God made the world by nature and inclination to be in "islam" to Him; that is, all beings are created to be in harmonious obedience to God. From galaxies to microbes, from the least to the greatest event, everything points to the One-Only God Who is merciful and just. Humans who seek and walk in the Straight Path obey God and in that obedience are truly free. They are not subservient to any lesser being, ideology, desire, or object. Islam, then, is the oldest din because it has been from the beginning. It has been proclaimed to all peoples throughout history by God's prophets and messengers. Through Muhammad, Islam is proclaimed clearly and finally as the true and saving din.

Islam's covenants track creation's and humanity's history from its beginnings to the Day of Judgment. Among the Quranic words expressing the nuances and types of covenant the most frequently used are 'ahd and its infinitive 'ahida (29 and 11 times respectively) and mithaq (25 times).[5] A third term, bara'a, is used twice (Surahs 9:1; 54:43) in the sense of a disavowal of a covenant or treaty.[6] 'Ahd and mithaq can apply to civil and political agreements as well as to covenants between God and humans, and sometimes they are interchangeable.[7] 'Ahd and 'ahida appear in ayas revealed mostly in Mecca shortly before Muhammad migrated to Medina (622), and mithaq is used most often in the Medinian period. 'Ahd carries the sense of covenant as commitment, obligation, and pledge, while 'ahida is to entrust, empower, and obligate. Mithaq means covenant as agreement, compact, and contract. It is based on wathiqa, to place confidence in, depend on, and trust in, and wathuqa, to be firm, solid. God is called the guarantor (mawthiq) of His covenant or pledge to Jacob, and the Qur'an is regarded as the Mithaq al-Kitab, the covenant of the Book. God can deny or cancel His promise ('ahd) to those within a covenant community who repeatedly and defiantly break the covenant.[8] We turn now to the narrative and the covenants.

Then praise be to Allah, the Lord of the heavens and the earth—the Lord and Cherisher of all the worlds! To Him be glory throughout the heavens and on the earth. And He is exalted in power, full of wisdom. (Surah 45:36–37, al-Jathiyah, Kneeling Down)

ISLAM'S BASIC NARRATIVE

Believe in Allah and His Messenger and spend (in charity) out of the (substance) whereof He has made you heirs. For those of you who believe and spend (in charity) for them is a great reward. What cause have ye, why ye should not believe in Allah? And the Messenger invites you to believe in your Lord and has indeed taken your Covenant if ye are men of faith. He is the One Who Sends to His servants manifest signs that He may lead you from the depths of darkness into the light. And verily Allah is to you Most Kind and Merciful.

Surah 57:7–9

THE CREATION OF THE WORLDS: THE FIRST COVENANT

The One-Only God created the earth and seven heavens out of nothing over the course of six days.[9] Although God can simply command "Be" and what He commands comes into existence, the Qur'an indicates that the cosmos below the heavens was made in two days and the seven heavens in another two days. It seems that in the course of another two days, God arranged the heavens in their proper order and brought these and the earth into harmony. Both the earthly and celestial worlds stated their willing obedience to their Maker:

Say: Is it that ye [Meccan unbelievers] deny Him Who created the earth in two days? And do ye join equals with Him? He is the Lord of (all) the Worlds. He set on the (earth) mountains standing firm high above it and bestowed blessings on the earth and measured therein all things to give them nourishment in due proportion in four days in accordance with (the needs of) those who seek (sustenance). Moreover He comprehended in His design the sky and it had been (as) smoke: He said to it and to the earth: "Come ye together willingly or unwillingly." They said: "We do come (together) in willing obedience." So He completed them as seven firmaments in two days and He assigned to each heaven its duty and command. And We adorned the lower heaven with lights and (provided it) with guard. Such is the decree of (Him) the Exalted in Might, Full of Knowledge. (Surah 41:9–12, al-Fussilat, the Expounded, and Ha Mim)[10]

From the heaven that is closest to the earth God dispenses that which plants and animals need in order to flourish and sends deserved punishments and judgments—plagues, stones—on disobedient persons and peoples. Moreover, it is the storehouse for the revelations that the angels will give to prophets and messengers as God commands and the location of the primordial Garden. Surah 41:9–12 signals the first covenant—that with the whole creation. The entire cosmos, heavens and earth, have agreed to come together "in willing obedience" to God. In other words, whatever exists is naturally in a state of "islam" with God, and whatever exists testifies to, are pointers (ayas) to, the One-Only God:

> Do they [i.e., unbelievers] not look at Allah's creation (even) among (inanimate) things how their (very) shadows turn round from the right and the left prostrating themselves to Allah and that in the humblest manner? And to Allah doth obeisance all that is in the heavens and on earth whether moving (living) creatures or the angels: for none are arrogant (before their Lord). They all revere their Lord high above them and they do all that they are commanded. (Surah 16:48–50, al-Nahl, Bees)

The narrative stage having been set, the Author introduces angels, spiritual beings, and the initial human, Adam.[11] Islam has a highly developed angelology. Angels do not have the ability to disobey God, but the *jinn* do. Jinn (sing. *jinni*) are spiritual beings ranked below angels and were made from "the fire of a scorching wind" (Surah 15:27).[12] God announced to the celestial host that He created all things for humanity and was about to create the first human who along with his descendants would be His *khalifah* (caliphs) on earth.[13] The angels asked for clarification: will God place on earth a creature who will "make mischief therein and shed blood"? The question disclosed concerns about where humans fit into the beautiful world and what God's intentions were. The angels may have been satisfied with the answer that God knows what they do not know, but some jinn entertained doubts.

ADAM, SPIRITUAL BEINGS, AND THE SECOND COVENANT

God created Adam from lifeless clay and mud, then breathed into him some of His own breath.[14] Taking Adam aside, the Creator instructed him in knowledge that included the names and ranks of the angels. God presented Adam to the celestial beings, commanding them to prostrate themselves before him. To prove Adam's superiority, at least in knowledge, God had him disclose to the angels their names and ranks. After he did so, the angels "prostrated themselves, all of them together" (Surah 15:29–30). But a leader among the jinn, Iblis (also known as Shaytan), refused, thereby defying and disobeying God. The Quranic reports of the encounter between the Divine One and Iblis feature God's blunt questioning of Iblis as to why he refused, giving the jinni and his supporters the opportunity to return to obedience. The exchange between Iblis and God forecast the rest of the basic narrative and world history:

> (Allah) said: "What prevented thee from bowing down when I commanded thee?" He said: "I am better than he: Thou didst create me from fire and him from clay." (Allah) said: "Get thee down from this: it is not for thee to be arrogant here: get out for thou art of the meanest (of creatures)." He said: "Give me respite till the day they are raised

up." (Allah) said: "Be thou among those who have respite." He said: "Because Thou hast thrown me out of the way, lo! I will lie in wait for them on Thy straight way. Then will I assault them from before them and behind them, from their right and their left: nor wilt Thou find in most of them gratitude (for Thy mercies)." (Allah) said: "Get out from this [heaven] disgraced and expelled. If any of them follow thee, Hell will I fill with you all. (Surah 7:12–18)[15]

Adam and his wife (there is no account of her creation, nor is she named), placed in the heavenly Garden, were encouraged to enjoy everything, with the exception of the Tree of Eternity, which they were not to approach (Surah 20:120).[16] God and Adam entered into a covenant, possibly at the time the primal human couple took up residence in the Garden. Implicitly the terms are for Adam to be God's deputy on earth, a position that required him to be faithful, worship only and be obedient to the one God, and care for the world in which he lived.[17] God warned them that Iblis-Shaytan was their enemy and would seek to deceive them. The Garden, promised God, would have sufficient food and clothing so that they would be neither hungry nor thirsty nor naked nor harmed by the sun's heat (Surah 20:118–19). As might be expected, Iblis did deceive them, promising them eternity and a kingdom that never decays (Surah 20:120–21). After both ate from the tree, they realized that they were naked and had disobeyed God.[18] Sorrowful, Adam turned to God, but he had no words to ask for forgiveness. God graciously taught him the words and accepted Adam's willingly offered repentance (e.g., Surah 2:37). According to later commentators, the sin in the Garden was *dhanb*, that is, an infraction, error, or transgression. Its remedy is correction and discipline.[19]

Islam rejects the idea that the sin of Adam was transmitted to his descendants or that the woman was to be blamed for their transgression. Humans have free will to obey and to disobey God. If they choose to disobey, they also have the God-given words and the ability to turn to the Ever-Merciful Lord and be forgiven. Contrary to Genesis 2–3, the earth is not cursed, nor are women subjected by God to their husbands; nor is there any reference that women henceforth will bear children in pain as punishment.

The incident in the Garden resulted in God ordering both humans and Iblis-Shaytan (and his supporting jinn) to leave the heavenly Garden and descend to the earth. Earth will be their dwelling place and where they will earn their livelihood "for a time" (Surah 2:36), that is, until the Day of Judgment. As the human couple left, God assured them, "And if, as is sure, there comes to you guidance from Me, whosoever follows My guidance, on them shall be no fear nor shall they grieve. But those who reject Faith and belie Our signs, they shall be companions of the fire; they shall abide therein" (Surah 2:38–39).[20] He also commented that Adam had forgotten the covenant, "and We found on his part no firm resolve" (Surah 20:115).

A NARRATIVE PAUSE

The Quranic accounts about the creation of all things and God's purposes, the disobedience of the jinn, the deception of Adam and his wife and their repentance, and the scene shifting from the heavens to this world (al-Dunya) deserve brief comments. First, the Qur'an indicates and later becomes more explicit that God always had a plan for the cosmos's history. God is not only all-knowing but also the determiner of events and the Best of Planners. It also underscores the transcendence and omnipotence of the One-Only God. Second, the plan discloses the high value God puts on humans: the whole of creation exists for the sake of people, people are to be God's deputy-servants in the world, and people are responsible for as well as capable of knowing God's oneness and His command that they are to worship the One-Only God. Yet humans are capable not only of islam—that is, general worshipful obedience—but also of rejecting and turning away from God. Forgetful Adam and his descendants may be deceived by Iblis and receive deserved damnation from the God who is both merciful and just. The Oft-Returning and Most Gracious One generates the terms for and accepts genuine repentance.

Third, Iblis did not lie totally. He promised them immortality and an imperishable kingdom. Without God's intervening forgiveness, those who heed the Whisperer and do not repent but follow him will share with him a horrific eternity in the imperishable realm of hell. Fourth, God did not intend Adam and his wife to live permanently in the heavenly Garden. The divine plan entailed the human couple taking up their caliphate on earth. The time in the Garden was meant to prepare them with further knowledge and with the skills for their earthly tasks. Humans are to pursue knowledge and to relate it to serving-worshiping God as they fulfill their covenant with God. Fifth, the plan, shaped by the Merciful-Just Lord, provided for God to give instruction and guidance to humans so that they would be able to be faithfully obedient to Him, mindful of their roles and grateful to their Master. How that guidance was given to Adam's descendants and what they did with it brings us back to the basic narrative.

HUMANITY AND THE THIRD COVENANT

The human caliphate began when the first couple and the disobedient jinn descended to earth. The souls of the children of Adam and his wife, that is, all subsequent persons, are questioned by God before their birth as to whether they confessed that God was the Lord Who gave them life. The souls, apparently invariably, confessed and thereby entered into a general covenant with their Creator: "When thy Lord drew forth from the children of Adam from their loins their descendants and made them testify concerning themselves (saying): 'Am I not your Lord (who cherishes and sustains you)?' They said: 'Yea! We do testify!' (This) lest ye should say on the Day of Judgment: 'Of this we were never mindful'" (Surah 7:172).

Every individual in every time and place, therefore, is oriented and accountable to the One-Only God. In other words, humans are naturally disposed toward islam. They have an innate awareness of and inclination to worship and serve God. That is, we are by nature proto-Muslims, but nurture, in the form of parental and cultural influences, leads some of us into other religious commitments. When a woman or a man hears and understands the Message, she or he has the ability to accept or reject the covenant that her or his soul made before birth. In brief, one does not so much convert to Islam as revert to what one is made as and agreed to be: Muslims.

Since all existence is a network of covenantal entities pointing to the One-Only God, everyone is being constantly directed to and called to confess and obey the Lord of all.[21]

THE NARRATIVE DARKENS

Adam and his spouse were deceived rather than defiant. Because they did not intentionally defy God, they merited correction. When one of their sons murdered his brother, however, a more serious type of sin was introduced, *ithum*. Ithum is a willful, deliberate act, an intentional deed that is knowingly against God's will. Such a sin requires devout repentance and earnest seeking of God's forgiveness:[22]

> Yea to Allah belongs all that is in the heavens and on earth; so that He rewards those who do evil according to their deeds and He rewards those who do good with what is best. Those who avoid great sins and shameful deeds, only (falling into) small faults—verily thy Lord is ample in forgiveness. He knows you well when He brings you out of the earth and when ye are hidden in your mother's wombs, therefore justify not yourselves. He knows best who it is that guards against evil. (Surah 53:31–32, al-Najm, the Star)

The murderer (neither brother is named) formed his plan and carried it out even though the victim warned him of the consequences:

> Recite to them the truth of the story of the two sons of Adam. Behold! They each presented a sacrifice (to Allah): it was accepted from one but not from the other. Said the latter: "Be sure I will slay thee." "Surely" said the former, "Allah doth accept of the sacrifice of those who are righteous. If thou dost stretch thy hand against me to slay me, it is not for me to stretch my hand against thee to slay thee: for I do fear Allah, the Cherisher of the worlds. For me, I intend to let thee draw on thyself my sin as well as thine for thou wilt be among the companions of the fire and that is the reward of those who do wrong." (Surah 5:27–31)

While the Qur'an holds that humanity is shaped and instructed by and covenantally related to God, it also notes weaknesses and flaws in the human character. These are exploited by Iblis, and most persons collude in their own ithum-sin. If persons do not repent, asking for God's forgiveness and compensating for sin with good intentions and deeds, they secure for themselves places in Hell. Among the human fallibilities are ingratitude, haste, impatience, argumentativeness, heedlessness, and willful proneness to being deceived.[23] As we will see, the most heinous and even unforgivable ithum sin is to give God sons, daughters, or other associates. This is the sin of *shirk,* idolatry: the denial that God is Achad, the One-Only God.

The Qur'an speaks of persons who in spite of their creaturely weaknesses see the divine pointer-signs in nature and event, follow their God-given reason, listen to God-sent messengers, and seek to worship the One-Only Lord. God guides such persons on His Straight Path. The Qur'an speaks of others as having diseased hearts that turn them, willingly and willfully, away from God. They wander from the Straight Path through ingratitude, injustice, immorality, murder, and, worst of all, shirk. Knowingly or not, these unbelievers and hypocrites ally themselves with Iblis, the Whisperer-Deceiver.[24] Although most people are led astray from the Straight Path at some points in their lives, in the Most-Compassionate and Oft-Returning Lord's plan, He sends admonitions, judgments, messages, and messengers to warn, command, and promise people about His mercy and His justice.

COVENANTED PEOPLES AND PROPHETS-MESSENGERS

Although the entire creation, the first human couple and every soul, is covenanted to acknowledge, worship, and obey the One-Only God, the gracious Lord goes further to reveal Himself and the Straight Path. Because it would be anachronistic and misleading to use the term *nations,* I will use *peoples* and *communities* when referring to ethnically or geographically discernible groups and *tribes* and *clans* in their more restricted senses. God establishes covenants with peoples and key individuals. Through these covenants, God engages and confronts human communities in their particular circumstances and settings. Put another way, the previous covenants deal with nature and human origins, whereas while the next covenants concern human history. The covenants with communities are inseparable from those with prophets-messengers, yet we will consider the latter separately.

Covenants with Peoples

The Qur'an apparently describes God undertaking covenants with all human communities so that no one human group might claim on the Day of Judgment that it had not known of the One-Only Lord and His will. The Qur'an mentions specifically three "people covenants." The first two are with the "People of the Book," that is, Jews and Christians. The Qur'an regards Jews and Christians as one group split into two squabbling factions. The third covenanted people are the Qurayshi, the powerful Arabian tribe of which Muhammad and his clan (the Hashemites) are members. These three groups are especially blessed by God and have been given clearer revelations than other peoples, and, therefore, they are subject to more scrutiny and higher standards of obedience by God.

The Covenant with Israel and Jews

> Allah did aforetime take a Covenant from the Children
> of Israel and We appointed twelve captains among them,
> and Allah said: "I am with you: if ye (but) establish regular
> prayers, practice regular charity, believe in My messengers,
> honor and assist them, and loan to Allah a beautiful loan;
> verily I will wipe out from you your evils and admit you to
> gardens with rivers flowing beneath; but if any of you after
> this resisteth faith he hath truly wandered from the path of
> rectitude." But, because of their breach of their Covenant, We
> cursed them and made their hearts grow hard: they change
> the words from their (right) places and forget a good part of
> the Message that was sent them nor wilt thou [Muhammad]
> cease to find them barring a few ever bent on (new) deceits:

but forgive them and overlook (their misdeeds): for Allah
loveth those who are kind.

Surah 5:12–13

The Qur'an uses "Israel," "Children of Israel," and "Jews" interchangeably.
Israel entered its covenant with God at "the mountain" (presumably Mount
Sinai) to which Moses led them on their departure from Egypt (Surah
5:12). Surah 2:83–84 describes the covenant's content:

> And remember We took a covenant from the children of Israel (to this
> effect): worship none but Allah; treat with kindness your parents and
> kindred and orphans and those in need; speak fair to the people; be
> steadfast in prayer; and practice regular charity. Then did ye turn back
> except a few among you and ye backslide (even now). And remember
> We took your Covenant (to this effect): shed no blood amongst you
> nor turn out your own people from your homes; and this ye solemnly
> ratified and to this ye can bear witness.

The Jews accepted the privilege and duties involved in knowing, worshiping, and obeying the One-Only God. God gave them revelations that
apparently had not yet been shared to the same extent with other peoples.
In brief, if the Jews fulfilled their portion of the covenant, they would become Muslims.[25] In the context of the Medinian Jews' opposition to Muhammad and the Muslims, Surah 5:12–13 castigates the Children of Israel
for resisting the Messenger and thereby breaking their covenant with God.
The passage also indicates that they corrupted the revealed Book given to
Moses by God. Other passages in the Qur'an (discussed in due course) state
that they placed burdensome restrictions on themselves, claiming these
came from God, and considered themselves and their land superior to all
other peoples and lands and engaged in shirk. In sum, Israel has broken the
covenant they made with God. If they persist in following that course,
they will answer on the Day of Judgment.

The Covenant with Christians

From those too who call themselves Christians We did take a Covenant but they forgot a good part of the Message that was sent them: so We estranged them with enmity and hatred between the one and the other [the Jews] to the Day of Judgment. And soon will Allah show them what it is they have done.

Surah 5:14 al-Ma'idah, the Repast or Table Laid

God's covenant with Christians extended the covenant with the Jews through Jesus' revelation to Israel that the final Messenger was yet to come. Most Jews rejected Jesus' message, but his disciples accepted it:

And remember Jesus, the son of Mary, said: "O Children of Israel! I am the messenger of Allah (sent) to you confirming the Law (which came) before me and giving Glad Tidings of a Messenger to come after me whose name shall be Ahmad." But when he came to them with Clear Signs they said: "This is evident sorcery!" Who doth greater wrong than one who invents falsehood against Allah even as he is being invited to Islam? And Allah guides not those who do wrong. . . . O ye who believe! Be ye helpers of Allah: as said Jesus the son of Mary to the Disciples: "Who will be my helpers to (the work of) Allah?" Said the disciples: "We are Allah's helpers!" Then a portion of the Children of Israel believed and a portion disbelieved: but We gave power to those who believed against their enemies and they became the ones that prevailed. (Surah 61:6, 14, al-Saff, Battle Array)

Ahmad, the Praised One, is a revered title given Muhammad. The root of the name *Muhammad* is *hamid,* "praise." Christians are Jews who believed Jesus' testimony to the One-Only God and should accept Muhammad, the Ahmad. The earlier prophets raised up among the Children of

Israel and the rabbis were entrusted with preserving the revealed Book bestowed on Moses. That Book proclaimed the truth of the One-Only God, gave instructions on living the godly life, and forecast the coming of the Qur'an and the Messenger. Then:

> And in their footsteps We sent Jesus, the son of Mary, confirming the Law that had come before him. We sent him the Gospel [Ingil]. Therein was guidance and light and confirmation of the Law that had come before him: a guidance and an admonition to those who fear Allah. Let the people of the Gospel judge by what Allah hath revealed therein. If any do fail to judge by (the light of) what Allah hath revealed, they are (no better than) those who rebel. (Surah 5:46–47)

Christian leaders, nevertheless, misunderstood, distorted, and corrupted Jesus' revelatory message by falsifying the gospel so that Jesus is presented as the son of God and God is made into a Trinity. In so doing, the Christian leaders broke their covenant and turned Jesus' followers from the Straight Path. In the process Jews and Christians disputed among themselves, compounding and complicating their deviations from the revealed truth: "The Jews say: 'The Christians have naught (to stand) upon'; and the Christians say: 'The Jews have naught (to stand) upon.' Yet they (profess to) study the (same) Book. Like unto their word is what those say who know not, but Allah will judge between them in their quarrel on the Day of Judgment" (Surah 2:113).

The Covenant with the Quraysh Tribe

The Quraysh tribe controlled the city of Mecca. From ancient times Mecca was a major commercial and caravan center, and the most important religious focal point for those living settled and nomadic lives in the central Arabian Peninsula. Pre-Islamic traditions may have associated Adam and his family with the region. Quranic references seem to assume that the polytheistic populace was well acquainted with accounts that Abraham and Ishmael constructed the cube-shaped Ka'bah and established Mecca. In any event, pre-Islamic Arabs undertook annual pilgrimages to Mecca and its environs, circumambulated the Ka'bah, and offered sacrifices there and at other nearby places. The tribes came not only to pray but also to buy and sell goods, pack animals, and slaves while they worshiped the many gods and enjoyed themselves. The Quraysh profited from the pilgrimages politically and economically. Tradition held that the High God commanded that during the sacred month of Ramadan the tribes were not to raid one another's territory or attack their caravans. In addition, He covenanted with the Quraysh that he would protect their caravans on their journeys and the city as long as they ensured that His true worship was maintained in the holy city and at the Ka'bah:

> For the covenants (of security and safeguard enjoyed) by the Quraysh, their covenants (covering) journeys by winter and summer, let them adore the Lord of this House Who provides them with food against hunger and with security against fear (of danger). (Surah 106, Quraysh)

The Ka'bah was not simply another shrine among others; it was the God-designated first and foremost house of worship:

> The first House (of worship) appointed for men was that at Bakka full of blessing and of guidance for all kinds of beings: In it are signs manifest; (for example) the Station of Abraham; whoever enters it attains security; pilgrimage thereto is a duty men owe to Allah—those who can afford the journey; but, if any deny faith, Allah stands not in need of any of his creatures. (Surah 3:96–97)[26]

But the tribe violated its covenant. Islamic tradition holds that representations of some 360 gods were present in the Ka'bah. The Quraysh committed the gross sin of shirk and grew wealthy and powerful through it. To reduce the many gods to the One-Only Lord of all would have meant political trouble with the other tribes and economic collapse. The creation's testimony to God and each individual's birth covenant should have been sufficient to exhort and admonish the leaders and the people of Mecca about their breach of the general covenants. But any change in the Qurayshi persistence in maintaining, advancing, and profiting from polytheism would need clear, definite, and mighty divine intervention. As yet the Arabs had not received their own revelatory prophet. That Prophet-Messenger came to them and for the world.

Covenants with Prophets and Messengers

Behold! Allah took the covenant of the prophets saying:
"I give you a Book and Wisdom; then comes to you a
Messenger confirming what is with you; do ye believe him
and render him help." Allah said: "Do ye agree and take this
My Covenant as binding on you?" They said: "We agree."
He said: "Then bear witness and I am with you among the
witnesses." If any turn back after this they are perverted
transgressors. Do they seek for other than the Religion
of Allah? While all creatures in the heavens and on earth
have willing or unwilling bowed to His Will (accepted Islam)
and to Him shall they all be brought back. Say: "We believe
in Allah and in what has been revealed to us and what was
revealed to Abraham, Isma'il, Isaac, Jacob, and the Tribes
and in (Books) given to Moses, Jesus, and the Prophets from
their Lord; we make no distinction between one and another
among them and to Allah do we bow our will (in Islam)."
If anyone desires a religion other than Islam (submission
to Allah) never will it be accepted of him; and in the
Hereafter he will be in the ranks of those who have lost
(all spiritual good).

Surah 3:81–85

Ar-Rashid, God the Guide, knows that humans are stubborn and easily led astray. His plan includes humans who are especially prepared to receive the revelations that other persons and peoples need in order to journey to the Day of Judgment. The overall term *prophet* includes both messengers and prophets. A prophet (*nabi*) in the specific sense is a person "whose mission lies within the framework of an existing religion" and who seeks to call people to worship and obey the One-Only God through the language and culture of that religion.[27] He may warn and admonish those people about their conduct and their religious commitments. The other type of prophet-in-general is the *rasul,* or messenger. Rasuls bring new revelations that often break the molds of the existing religions and social structures so that they actually introduce clearer and fuller insights and commands that lead to fulfillment in Islam. On the whole, God may give a rasul a book such as the Tawrah for Moses and the Ingil (Gospel) for Jesus. Revelation through the books has been progressive; that is, it fit the stage and state of the people to whom it was sent: "We did send messengers before thee [Muhammad] and appointed for them wives and children: and it was never the part of a messenger to bring a Sign except as Allah permitted (or commanded). For each period is a Book (revealed)" (Surah 13:38, al-Ra'd, Thunder).

The Qur'an insists:

> The worshipers of false gods say: "If Allah had so willed we should not have worshiped aught but Him, neither we nor our fathers. Nor should we have prescribed prohibitions other than His." So did those who went before them. But what is the mission of messengers but to preach the Clear Message? For We assuredly sent amongst every people a messenger (with the command) "Serve Allah and eschew evil." Of the people were some whom Allah guided and some on whom error became inevitably (established). So travel through the earth and see what was the end of those who denied (the Truth). (Surah 16:35–36)

The prophets-messengers agree with one another in their essential proclamations and they are called to keep the covenant into which they have been called:

> O ye messengers! Enjoy (all) things good and pure and work righteousness: for I am well-acquainted with (all) that ye do. And verily

this brotherhood of yours is a single brotherhood, and I am your Lord and Cherisher: therefore fear Me (and no other). (Surah 23:51–52)

God has sent countless numbers of prophets-messengers to all peoples in all times and places: "To every people (was sent) a messenger. When their messenger comes (before them) the matter will be judged between them with justice and they will not be wronged" (Surah 10:48, Yunus, Jonah).[28] Together and individually, messengers-prophets are the custodians of God's truth, are endowed with different gifts by God, and will be held accountable on the Day of Judgment for carrying out their missions faithfully. Uniformly, they will be insulted, opposed, mocked, rejected, persecuted, and even killed, yet God will vindicate them, and woe to those who reject or harm them.[29]

As the whole creation is a covenanted set of ayas pointing to the One-Only God and His plan for the cosmos, the Islamic basic narrative depicts God sending His prophets and messengers to prepare for the coming of the ultimate revelation to be given through the final Messenger, Muhammad, the bearer of the consummate Book, the Qur'an. He is the prophet-messenger to the Arabs and to all peoples for all times until the Day of Judgment:

Alif Lam Ra. A Book which We have revealed unto thee [Muhammad] in order that thou mightest lead mankind out of the depths of darkness into light by the leave of their Lord to the Way of (Him) Exalted in Power, Worthy of all Praise! Of Allah to Whom do belong all things in the heavens and on earth! But alas for the Unbelievers for a terrible penalty (their unfaith will bring them)! Those who love the life of this world more than the Hereafter, who hinder (men) from the Path of Allah and seek therein something crooked, they are astray by a long distance. We sent a messenger except (to teach) in the language of his (own) people in order to make (things) clear to them. Now Allah leaves straying those whom He pleases and guides whom He pleases: and He is Exalted in Power, Full of Wisdom. (Surah 14:1–4)

The narrative has reached its revelatory climax: the appearance of the final Messenger and the final Book.

THE END AND THE BEGINNING

> The (Day) of noise and clamor: What is the (Day) of noise and clamor? And what will explain to thee what the (day) of noise and clamor is? (It is) a day whereon men will be like moths scattered about, and the mountains will be like carded wool. Then he whose balance (of good deeds) will be (found) heavy will be in a life of good pleasure and satisfaction. But he whose balance (of good deeds) will be (found) light will have his home in a (bottomless) pit. And what will explain to thee what this is? (It is) a fire blazing fiercely!
>
> *Surah 101, al-Qari'ah, the Great Calamity*

History from the time God gave the Revelation to Muhammad to the Day of Judgment is the story of humanity's responses to that Message and Messenger. The Straight Path has been disclosed, and women and men are accountable for their responses to following it. The Qur'an is guidance, and Muhammad is the Guide. The Book provides the deep text to be studied-enacted, and the Messenger is the living model for individuals and communities to emulate. God's plan calls for the germination, growth, and flourishing of a worshiping-serving-proclaiming umma that will bring justice, mercy, and peace through the world. Yet God knows that Iblis is at work, deluding humans who will be dragged with him into eternal punishment. Those who are faithful and whose good deeds merit eternal blessedness are promised everlasting life in God's newly created Gardens. Recalling din's several meanings is helpful: sovereignty or supreme authority (God); obedience-submission-devotion to that authority (living the Islamic Way); the system, rituals, teachings and structures established by that authority (the Pillars and Teachings); and retributions and rewards meted out to those who reject and to those who obey that authority (the end of this world-time, al-Dunya; the Day of Judgment, Yawm Din; and the Hereafter, al-Akhira).

The generations between the initial revelation on the Night of Power and the Dawn of the Last Day have been and will be fraught with struggles, conflicts, opportunities, and successes. Muhammad and those who became Muslims experienced opposition, fought battles, established the core umma, and began the mission to the rest of Arabia and then the world. God's plan included the culminating war with Iblis and his spiritual and human allies. The world—heavens and earth—will die. Then the Yawm Din, the Day of Judgment, will begin with the resurrection of and judgment on all human and spiritual beings:

> Has the story reached thee of the Overwhelming (Event)? Some faces that Day will be humiliated, laboring (hard) weary, the while they enter the Blazing Fire, the while they are given to drink of a boiling hot spring. No food will there be for them but a bitter *dhari* which will neither nourish nor satisfy hunger. (Other) faces that Day will be joyful, pleased with their striving. [They will be] in a Garden on high where they shall hear no (word) of vanity. Therein will be a bubbling spring. Therein will be thrones (of dignity) raised on high, goblets placed (ready), and cushions set in rows, and rich carpets (all) spread out. Do they not look at the camels how they are made? And at the sky how it is raised high? And at the mountains how they are fixed firm? And at the earth how it is spread out? Therefore do thou [Muhammad] give admonition for thou art one to admonish. Thou art not one to manage (men's) affairs. But if any turn away and reject Allah, Allah will punish him with a mighty punishment. For to Us will be their return; then it will be for Us to call them to account. (Surah 88, al-Ghashiyah, the Overwhelming Event)[30]

THE WHOLE CREATION has been made for the sake of humanity, and throughout its history women and men have been summoned to be God's caliphs in caring for the world. The task will be finished and the account books opened and audited. The coming of the Last Day is certain and inescapable. Yet the Judge is also Most Gracious, Most Merciful. He has revealed enough of His plan and established the covenants to carry it out for all persons to know and respond to it.

> Those who believe (in the Qur'an), and those who follow the Jewish (Scriptures), and the Christians, and the Sabians, and who believe in Allah, and the last day, and work righteousness shall have their reward with their Lord. On them shall be no fear nor shall they grieve. (Surah 2:62)

ISLAM'S CORE POSITIONS

> It is not righteousness that ye turn your faces toward East
> or West; but it is righteousness to believe in Allah and the
> Last Day and the angels and the Book and the messengers;
> to spend of your substance out of love for Him for your kin
> for orphans for the needy for the wayfarer for those who
> ask and for the ransom of slaves; to be steadfast in prayer
> and practice regular charity; to fulfill the contracts which ye
> have made; and to be firm and patient in pain (or suffering)
> and adversity and throughout all periods of panic. Such are
> the people of truth the Allah-fearing.
>
> *Surah 2:177*

Islam's leading positions, epitomized in the Five Pillars and Five Teachings are presented succinctly, clearly, and practically. Persons whose mental acuity can range from basic understanding to genius are able to comprehend and apply those positions to most if not all issues in daily life. Yet

Islam is also complex and intellectually challenging. God encourages believers to delve deeper into the structures, meanings, and nuances of the world, events, revelations, and, especially, the Qur'an.

THE FIVE PILLARS STATED

1. SHAHADAH: [I bear witness that] there is no god but God. Muhammad is the Messenger of God.[31]
2. SALAT: Five daily obligatory prayers said facing the Ka'bah.
3. ZAKAT: Obligatory annual alms-giving.
4. SAWM RAMADAN: Obligatory fasting from dawn to dark in the month of Ramadan.
5. HAJJ: Obligatory pilgrimage to Mecca during the month of Dhu l-Hijjah.

COMMENTS ON THE FIVE PILLARS

The Pillars are the minimal acts of worship (*'ibadat*) and form a continuum that engages the individual with the worldwide umma. The Pillars support personal and corporate worship, express the unity of the spiritual (Salat, for example) with the material (such as Zakat), link personal discipline to fellowship (fasting in Ramadan), and concretize verbal and devotional confession (Shahadah) with ritualized pilgrimage (Hajj). These obligations are eminently doable. By participating in the activities, persons obey the God who understands their intentions and develop solidarity with the umma. The Pillars also provide a time-space framework and a direction for an individual's life and for all Muslims' lives. The Shahadah may be repeated often each day and is included in each obligatory Salat prayer. The Salat prayers create a rhythm for daily life from dawn to night, and the direction of prayer toward Mecca gives an orderly spatial orientation for devotion. Sawm in Ramadan and Zakat occur with annual regularity wherever believers may be. The Hajj is at least a once-in-a-lifetime undertaking that brings the whole Islamic experience to a consummation that gives continuing impetus to the believer's dedication of body, mind, and heart to God while enhancing the umma.

The Shahadah

"I confess (testify) that there is no god but God. Muhammad is His Messenger," is central to Islam. Traditionally, a parent whispers it and the call to prayer in the ears of the newborn, and on dying, a person says it or hears it said as virtually the last words heard in this life. Saying the Shahadah with sincerity and devotion is the key act by which one accepts Islam formally. The Shahadah may be likened to the Shema; each major term is open to devout study and fruitful consideration. God has created everything to be in a state of obedience to and peace with Himself. So the Shahadah's first portion testifies to the creation-based universal relationship between God and all worlds. The revelation of the Qur'an to and through Muhammad activated the second portion of the Shahadah. The Qur'an is the Message and is implied in the testimony to the Messenger.

Salat

Islam is a religion of prayer combined with purity and action. Every Muslim who has reached puberty or the age of fifteen is obligated to engage in the formal Salat prayers. Other prayers are offered in different circumstances (such as when starting a journey) and in private devotion. Because through the Salat prayers the individual Muslim and the umma keep divinely commanded appointments with God, it is only fitting that the person be prepared for the meeting. The initial physical step involves the believer ritually purifying her or his body through appropriate ablutions. Prayer is offered while the believer engages in a set of prescribed gestures that indicate he or she comes into the presence of the Almighty King of all. The gestures include bowing and full prostration with the forehead touching the floor. A Muslim may engage in the Salat prayers almost anywhere. Muslims are fond of saying that the whole world is a prayer mat, that is, a place for prayer to the Creator-Lord. The word *mosque* (masjid) simply means "a place of prostration." The ground or floor is to be clean and not tainted with anything that is prohibited, such as animal droppings. A piece of carpet may be used for the ritual. Homes, offices, schools, and public areas may have designated areas for prayer. In addition to using the same set of gestures as other Muslims, believers are enjoined to weave passages from the Qur'an and the Shahadah in Arabic into their prayers. The first surah, al-Fatihah, in Arabic, is part of every Salat and devotional prayer. While praying, believers face toward the Ka'bah. The direction is called the *qiblah*. In spaces designated for prayer the qiblah may be marked by an indentation (*mihrab*) in the wall facing Mecca. Because Salat prayers often are public, they have a communal as well as an individual dimension. The signal for the required prayers is given by a call to worship. In Islamic societies and communities that permit it, the call (*adhan*) is usually given over loudspeakers by a *muzzein* from the towerlike minaret. The adhan summons the faithful with reminders of their obligations, promises about God's grace, and blessings that result from obeying-worshiping God. The five obligatory prayers cover the whole day and night, allowing for some variation in performance. If the person misses a time, she or he can make up for it on another occasion.[32]

The individual is always an individual at prayer even when with hundreds of others at a crowded mosque at Friday noon prayers or if far from home. Nevertheless, she or he is always part of a wider community. In a cosmic sense, all that exists is called to prayer. The highest angels through the various beings, including animals, turn toward God in obedience and devotion—or at least are summoned to be. Through prayer the individual is united with a billion other believers in directing the Salat prayers toward the Ka'bah and thence to God. Given the spacing of the prayers over a twenty-four-hour period and different time zones, in every moment of every day prayers are raised to God by those who are expressing their obedience, placing themselves under His protection and earning merit in the same language, using the same gestures and including the same passages of the Qur'an. Every moment of every day can be a time of contact with fellow believers in a community that shares the same basic values and commitment to establish a just Islamic society. For those Muslims who face difficulties, problems of integrity, oppression, and tests of resolve, such a sense of solidarity can be enormously strengthening and inspiring. When Salat prayers are offered in the company of others, the believer has an immediate sense of unity with those around him and her.

Zakat

Zakat is the obligatory annual tax or mandatory alms to be paid by all mature Muslims who have an income from any source. It is calculated on the value of the person's property and may vary from 10 percent of the value of first fruit crops and animals to $2\frac{1}{2}$ percent of the end-of-the-year value of merchandise, cash, and so on. In some Muslim countries, the government collects and distributes the Zakat to the poor. There are other opportunities for giving alms, and these also are registered as merits in the account of good deeds. Where the government is not the collector, the individual may give the funds to the leaders of the mosque or a recognized Muslim charity or allocate it to the needy as he or she sees fit.[33] The usual priorities are poor Muslims in the local area; persons who are experiencing temporary hardship through no fault of their own (e.g. illness, unemployment); Muslim prisoners of war or incarcerated believers, especially those detained for their faith; new converts to Islam who need assistance if their conversions alienated them from families or others; and poor persons regardless of background or religious affiliation.

Contributions usually are made during the month of Ramadan as part of a thoughtful thanksgiving to God and in light of the beginning of the divine gift of the Qur'an's disclosure to Muhammad in the last days of that month. Through the Zakat, the umma has a God-directed and regular means to aid needy believers while preserving their dignity (e.g., Surah 2:177).

Sawm Ramadan

As Salat prayers are geared to the times of the day, so, too, longer time cycles are important in Islam. Many Muslims considered the ninth month, Ramadan, a time to refrain from combat if possible. The term *sawm* means "fasting." Fasting in Ramadan differs from other fasts. First, it is incumbent on all Muslims who are past puberty or fifteen years of age, except for those menstruating, pregnant, nursing an infant, traveling long distances, or frail or ill. It extends from the time in the morning a person is able to distinguish between white and black threads until sunset. During the day portion, the believer neither eats nor drinks and abstains from swallowing medication (unless treatment requires it), kissing, all forms of sexual enjoyment, frivolity, loud laughter, and listening to music. While persons go about their daily activities, they are to do so with a special awareness of God's closeness. After the sunset (Maghrib) prayer, Muslims gather in family and friendship groups first for a light repast and then for a more substantial meal. The daytime restrictions are eased but with the understanding that Ramadan nights are not to be spent gorging on food or engaging in sexual excesses.

Second, Sawm Ramadan is a time for reflective thanksgiving. Every fast is grounded in the sense of limitation. At Ramadan believers acknowledge their creaturely limitations, God's generosity toward creation and humanity, and God's closeness through bestowing the revelation of the Qur'an through Muhammad. The exact evening on which the angel Gabriel embraced Muhammad and began the revelation of the Message is unknown, but it occurred on one of the closing days of the month. The last ten days of Ramadan, therefore, are considered particularly holy, and the presence of God is felt with greater intensity. Often Muslims will gather in mosques on those evenings for prayers and Qur'an reading. During Sawm Ramadan, Muslims thank God for the revelation of mercy and justice generally, then to and through Muhammad specifically. They lift their minds and attentions from daily activities so as to expand their knowledge of God as revealed in the Qur'an. Since charitable contributions and Zakat are often given during Ramadan, their experience of hunger and other limitations develops awareness of and solidarity with the poor. The first days of the next month (Shawwal) are marked by the second most important Muslim festival, Id l-Fitra. Large outdoor prayer meetings are held, Zakat is paid, and grain is distributed to the needy. Sawm Ramadan, thereby, points toward the establishment of the just society willed by God and testified to in the Qur'an (e.g., Surah 2:185).

The Hajj

Pilgrimages are transformational journeys. The pilgrim moves from a common state of being into a special status when he or she reaches the goal, then returns to "normal" life a changed person. Today Mecca and Medina are so holy that they are off limits to non-Muslims. The Hajj takes place during the month of Dhu l-Hijjah. The Ka'bah was (and still is) the shrine on which the pilgrimage focuses. The structure had an ancient foundation, but the upper portion had been knocked down and burned in the past. A black stone, within reach of the pilgrims, is associated with Abraham and Ishmael. Tradition holds that Hagar lived adjacent to the Ka'bah. A well called Zamzam was the water source that the then-baby Ishmael uncovered with his heel to save his mother and himself from dying of thirst while Abraham was away. The triumph of Islam was signaled by the "cleansing" of the Ka'bah in 630 CE/8 AH. All idols and representations of the various divinities were removed, and the building's interior remains empty to the present. Today the Ka'bah stands in the Great Mosque, and thousands circle it together. A heavy black cloth called the *kiswah* covers the cube-shaped building. Quranic ayas in gold embroidery adorn the upper portion of the kiswah, which is replaced annually. The old kiswah is cut into strips and distributed to pilgrims at the end of the Hajj.[34]

Muslims are obligated, if at all possible, to make the Great Hajj, the pilgrimage from Dhu l-Hijjah 8 AH to 10. It is traditional to extend the pilgrim status three days longer. During the Hajj, males do not cut their beards or hair, and all pilgrims vow to abstain from sexual activity, undertake some fasting and not kill animals, avoid anger and deception, and refrain from commercial activities. On arriving at one of several designated points in Saudi Arabia, men change to a simple two-piece white garment (*ihram*) resembling a burial shroud, and women wear modest versions of their national dress. They may ride, run, or walk to Mecca, chanting "Allahu akbar" (God is Greater!) and "Allah, we are here." Prayers and chanted passages from the Qur'an rise from the thousands who move toward the Grand Mosque. They circumambulate the Ka'bah, drink from Zamzam, run between Safa and Marwah (two hills said to be the points that Hagar traversed looking for water), stand in the daytime on the Plain of Arafat, cast stones at the idols at Mina, sacrifice an animal, and break the fast in the most important Muslim feast, the Id-al-Adha. In a formal sense, the Id-al-Adha marks the end of the Hajj. Many also travel to Medina to visit the graves of Muhammad and other holy persons. When successfully completed, many pilgrims prefix Hajj (males) or Hajja (females) to their names.

Through the Hajj, Muslims of many nations and races come together in an outpouring of unity, in which rich and poor are on an equal footing. The shroudlike ihram garment is for princes, millionaires, beggars, and shopkeepers alike. While the pilgrim is on Hajj, the members of the mosque and family at home face the Ka'bah (as they normally would), pray for the pilgrims, and contribute funds and food to the needy in the local Muslim umma. Should a person die while going to or from or during the Hajj, he or she is thought to be granted a place in paradise (e.g. Surah 2:197–98).

THE FIVE BASIC TEACHINGS

1. Belief in Oneness and Transcendence of God;
2. Belief in Angels and Other Supernatural Beings;
3. Belief in the Prophets and Scriptures;
4. Belief in the Final Judgment; and
5. Belief in the Divine Decree and Predestinations.

As the Pillars are the minimal acts of faith, the Teachings are the basic positions or teachings of *iman*—faith as both a commitment and a set of teachings. The Pillars and Teachings relate to each other as practice reflects principle. The Teachings move from one to another to form a coherent theological statement that emphasizes the omnipotence of the one God and the necessity for all creation to be in islam-salaam with God. Other teachings have been generated and expanded throughout Islam's history. Islam's umma has diverse groups that often contend with one another as vigorously as do some Christian denominations. Parenthetically, many Muslims arrange the Teachings into six points by considering Scriptures separate from Prophets.

Belief in the Unity-Oneness and Transcendence of God

Tawhid is the most important teaching. The word means to "make one" or to "declare and acknowledge oneness." The unique singularity and oneness of God is the core of Islam and the subject of intense devotion and speculation.[35] Surah 112 (Purity of Faith), one-third of the Qur'an, states the position plainly: "Say: 'He is Allah, the One and Only; Allah, the Eternal, Absolute; He begetteth not, nor is He begotten; And there is none like unto Him.'" Islam forbids any form of polytheism or divisions within the Godhead. Neither can there be a hint of an association of any other being with God, such as a son or daughter or spouse. Shirk, idolatry, is the only unforgivable sin a person can commit (Surah 4:36–48). Shirk is not only establishing and worshiping idols or other deities but also giving God a "companion." Tawhid, however, ranges far beyond divine numerical oneness. Seen in relation to the one-only-ness of the Creator, the entire cosmos is absolutely contingent and dependent on the will of God. Every creature and thing knows in its basic structure Who made it, that it is to be thankfully obedient to and serve its Maker, and that God has given it a place in the divine plan that reaches from the beginning through eternity. Obedience-service is due to God Who is the Measurer or Setter of Boundaries of all that exists. Repeatedly the Qur'an states that humans are not to break out of or to exceed their proper limits. The Qur'an is the Criterion (Furqan, Surah 25:1–4) for human conduct. Tawhid, then, is the foundation of ethics, politics, and economics, just as it is the source of freedom and justice. The person or community that gives the One its sole and supreme loyalty is truly free to act boldly and resolutely to do God's will. Such a person or community is not subservient to lesser authorities that would compromise or contravene obedience-service to the One.

Belief in Angels and Other Supernatural Beings

Belief in celestial entities is an integral part of the affirmation of tawhid and the resulting Muslim cosmology. The structures of existence, celestial beings, humanity, and the Qur'an are closely connected. God is supremely transcendent and never to be confused with any being that has been created.

He is even shrouded from the gaze of the highest angels and the jinn. The Messenger's Sunna (tradition, custom) contains accounts about and Surah 17 alludes to his Night Journey to Jerusalem (the "Farthest Mosque"), ascent through the seven heavens, and return to Mecca. During the journey, he was accompanied by the angel Gabriel and encountered other angels in his visions of the heavens, but he did not see God directly.[36]

While the basic function of angels is to be Allah's messengers to humans, some are also assigned to specific tasks such as the angels who bear the throne of God (Surah 40:7), nourish human bodies and souls, and record human doings. Under the Lord's scrutiny and command, they are in charge of death, paradise, and the torture of the damned. Each person has two guardian angels who record the individual's deeds in anticipation of the accounting that will be made on the Day of Judgment. Among the major angels, Gabriel the revelatory celestial being, calls for special attention. He is the angel of light and "a most honorable messenger, endued with power, with rank before the Lord of the Throne with authority there, (and) faithful to his trust" (Surah 81:19–21), and by tradition the messenger who announced to Mary that she would bear a son, Jesus (Surah 19:17–21). Gabriel, together with Michael, is highly placed among the Faithful and is the angel who bestowed the revelation on Muhammad:

> Say: "Whoever is an enemy to Gabriel—for he brings down the revelation to thy heart by Allah's will, a confirmation of what went before. And guidance and glad tidings to those who believe—Whoever is an enemy to Allah and His angels and prophets, to Gabriel and Michael—Lo! Allah is an enemy to those who reject Faith. We have sent down to thee manifest signs (*ayat*) and none reject them but those who are perverse." (Surah 2:97–98)

Belief in the Prophets and Scriptures

The books given the messengers contain revelations of God's truth. Unfortunately, people have misunderstood, perverted, corrupted, and distorted the books and divided into various hostile groups (e.g., Surah 21:7–8, al-Anbiya, the Prophets). Obviously, those who reject and oppose the message and messengers will pay for their opposition in eternity (Surahs 13:32; 21:7–8). At the same time the Qur'an insists that messengers and prophets are not to be given divine characteristics or worshiped.

The Qur'an indicates Moses' Tawrah is not the Jewish Torah or Hebrew Bible, nor is Jesus' Ingil the four Gospels or the New Testament. According to the Qur'an, Jews and Christians misinterpreted and perverted the books brought by Moses and Jesus. So it is not that Muslims, Jews, and Christians have different accounts; the People of the Book are wrong and have been deceived by their leaders, who in turn are deceived by the deceiver, Iblis. The Qur'an calls on the People of the Book to forsake these errors and, since the true Book has been revealed, to accept and live by the Qur'an and the message given through Muhammad (Surah 7:157). Reflecting on the disagreements and mutual animosities between Jews and Christians as well as the Israelites' frequent lapses into idolatry and falsification of the written Tawrah, God said:

> But because of their [Jews'] breach of their Covenant, We cursed them, and made their hearts grow hard: they change the words from their (right) places and forget a good part of the Message that was sent them, nor wilt thou [Muhammad] cease to find them—barring a few—ever bent on (new) deceits. But forgive them, and overlook (their misdeeds): for Allah loveth those who are kind. From those, too, who call themselves Christians, we did take a Covenant. But they forgot a good part of the Message that was sent them: so We estranged them with enmity and hatred between one and the other, to the Day of Judgment, and soon will Allah show them what it is they have done. O People of the Book! There hath come to you Our Messenger, revealing to you much that ye used to hide in the Book, and passing over much (that is now necessary): There hath come to you from Allah a (new) and perspicuous Book—wherewith Allah guideth all who seek His good pleasure to ways of peace and safety, and leadeth them out of Darkness, by His will unto the light—guideth them to a Path that is Straight. (Surah 5:13–16)

The Qur'an speaks to four major groups that resisted the Revelation and the Messenger. The first is the polytheists, especially in Mecca, who opposed Muhammad and the Message. Once the hijra to Medina took place, the Qur'an also addressed Jews, Christians, and Medinian "hypocrites"—all of whom sought to undermine the Messenger and those with him. Naturally, the Qur'an criticized them, as in a stricture against Christians and Jews: "Ye [the faithful Muslims] are the best of all peoples, evolved for mankind, enjoining what is right, forbidding what is wrong, and believing in Allah. If only the People of the Book had faith, it were best for them: among them are some who have faith, but most of them are perverted transgressors" (Surah 3:110b).

Prophets and messengers are inspired by God (Surah 40:15, al-Mumin, the Believer). They have been prepared (wahy) and given the content of their revelations (tanzil). In Islamic tradition, Muhammad is without sin (ithum), and his speaking the revelation of God is considered infallible as well as inspired by God. Any hint, let alone a statement, that Muhammad erred or compromised the revelation he received is considered sacrilegious.[37] The prophets' and messengers' revelations were couched in the language and culture of the audience for whom it was intended, yet was without error because of its celestial origin. The Qur'an, surpassing and fulfilling all prior revelations and books, is God's infallible and inerrant gift—and warning to humanity. From its revelation through Muhammad to the Day of Judgment, it and he are inextricably linked, and are to be heard and obeyed if the person and the world are to obey and be at peace with God (Surah 17:85–88).

Belief in the Final Judgment

The Teachings that began with tawhid and moved to supernatural beings and then to inspired prophets and scriptures carried forward to the climax of creation: the Final Judgment, Resurrection, Hell, and the Gardens. Before the rise of Islam almost all Arabs denied any form of life after or post-death reckonings involving rewards and punishments. Polytheists focused on life now and placating their gods. Muhammad's message ran counter especially to the interests of the Qurayshi. The Qur'an's insistence on justice in society, mercy toward others, integrity in fulfilling contracts, and angels documenting the good and evil deeds of all persons was directed toward the final accountability of jinn and humans to the God who marked out the Straight Path. That Path led to the culmination of creation's space and time on the Day of Judgment. The Fourth Doctrine's points are not so much in details and speculations but in the principles that God is just and merciful, that humans and jinn are accountable, and that the Lord's will reaches through eternity. The Doctrine of Final Judgment places all human activities and institutions under the scrutiny and law of God. No deed or organization will escape His inspection and decision, and all constructions, from the family to international coalitions, are temporary and responsible to God.

Belief in the Divine Decree and Predestination

Monotheistic religions are challenged to deal with the questions of theodicy (providence) and predestination. Does God's foreknowledge of what will happen determine what happens? Do disasters just happen, or does God let them occur? The issue was a matter of controversy among Muhammad's followers. The hadith collection *Sahih Muslim* opens with traditions about Qad-Taqdir, the Divine Decree, and in a hadith collection dependent on *Muslim* Allah's Messenger is reported to have said: "Allah prescribed the Decrees of all creatures 50,000 years before He created the heavens and the earth. . . . Everything has been decreed even the imprudence and shrewdness."[38] Logically, Qad-Taqdir completes the flow of the Teachings and return to the absolute power and glory of the one God. But is the Qur'an as definite as the hadiths? Certainly there are Quranic statements that support the position that all is determined by God's will, for example, "Whatever is in the heavens and on earth—let it declare the praises and glory of Allah: for He is the exalted in might, the wise. To Him belongs the dominion of the heavens and the earth: it is He who gives life and death, and He has power over all things" (Surah 57:1–2). Beyond being all-powerful and all-knowing, Allah might be heard as saying, He chooses not to guide some of the unbelievers to the Straight Path (Surah

6:35–39). Nevertheless, throughout the Qur'an all are said to have the opportunity to hear and respond to the message, to do good works, to worship properly, and to become Muslims (e.g., Surah 7:30). Except when Allah tests a person's faith, as in Job's case (Surahs 21:83–84; 38:41–43), the Qur'an maintains that humans are responsible for bringing disasters on themselves: "Whatever misfortune happens to you is because of the things your hands have wrought, and for many (of them) He grants forgiveness" (Surah 42:30). In the matter of a time appointed for a person's death, the Qur'an states, "To every people is a term appointed: when their term is reached, not an hour can they cause delay, nor (an hour) advance it in anticipation" (Surah 7:35).

Claims especially by many non-Muslim scholars that Islam holds a fatalistic form of the Divine Decree have been based on later developments in Muslim theology, developments that have led to confusion and condemnations.[39] The Shi'ite sage, Imam Ja'far al-Sadiq (d. 756), concluded, "It [the Divine Decree and Predestination] is a deep sea, venture not into it. . . . It is an obscure path, walk not along it. . . . It is one of Allah's secrets, do not talk about it."[40]

CONCLUSION

The basic narrative and the core positions prepare us for the next step in opening the Qur'an and understanding Islam and Muslims. Next we approach the land in which it was revealed, the Messenger to whom it was given, and its shape.

And He is Allah:
There is no god but He.
To Him be praise at the first and at the last:
From Him is the command, and to Him shall ye (all) be brought back.
(Surah 28:70, al-Qasas, the Narration)

FOUR

THE SETTING:
REFLECTIONS ON ARABIA

Thus have We sent by inspiration to thee an Arabic Qur'an:
That thou mayest warn the Mother of Cities and all around her—
And warn (them) of the Day of Assembly, of which there is no doubt:
(When) some will be in the Garden, and some in the Blazing Fire.

Surah 42:7, al-Shura, the Consultation

Islam claims that God created all that exists and that the entire creation testifies to and is covenantally related to al-Khaliq, the Creator:

Whatever is in the heavens and on earth doth declare the Praises and Glory of Allah: to Him belongs Dominion and to Him belongs Praise: and He has power over all things. It is He Who has created you; and of you are some that are Unbelievers and some that are Believers: and Allah sees well all that ye do. He has created the heavens and the earth in just proportions and has given you shape and made your shapes beautiful: and to Him is the final Goal. He knows what is in the heavens and on earth: and He knows what ye conceal and what ye reveal: yes Allah knows well the (secrets) of (all) hearts. (Surah 64:1–4, al-Taghabun, Mutual Loss and Gain)

Nevertheless, Islam centers on Arabia, the people who live there, and the language they speak. Arabia is the supremely sacred space, and within it is the supremely sacred city, and within that city is the supremely sacred structure.

> Remember Abraham said: "O my Lord! Make this city one of peace and security, and preserve me and my sons from worshipping idols. O my Lord! They have indeed led astray many among mankind, He then who follows my (ways) is of me and he that disobeys me but thou art indeed Oft-Forgiving, Most Merciful. O our Lord! I have made some of my offspring to dwell in a valley without cultivation by thy Sacred House in order, O our Lord, that they may establish regular prayer, so fill the hearts of some among men with love towards them, and feed them with fruits so that they may give thanks. O our Lord! Truly Thou dost know what we conceal and what we reveal: for nothing whatever is hidden from Allah whether on earth or in heaven." (Surah 14:35–38)

THE GEOGRAPHY OF ARABIA

> Remember We made the House [the Kaʻbah] a place
> of assembly for men and a place of safety; and take ye
> the station of Abraham as a place of prayer; and We
> covenanted with Abraham and Ismaʻil that they should
> sanctify My House for those who compass it round or
> use it as a retreat or bow or prostrate themselves (therein
> in prayer). And remember Abraham said: "My Lord, make
> this a City of Peace and feed its people with fruits such
> of them as believe in Allah and the Last Day." He said:
> "(Yea) and such as reject faith for a while will I grant
> them their pleasure but will soon drive them to the
> torment of fire an evil destination (indeed)!"
>
> *Surah 2:125–26*

Arabia is a rectangular-shaped peninsula roughly one-third the size of the United States. Its northern or topmost section may be likened to a hinge attached to the eastern frontier of the present-day kingdom of Jordan. To the peninsula's west is the Red Sea, across which are the coasts of Egypt, Sudan, and Eritrea. On its eastern flank, is the Persian Gulf, across which are Iraq and Iran. To the south or bottom of the peninsula is the Gulf of Aden and the Arabian Sea. Today the peninsula is divided politically into United Arab Emirates, Qatar, Bahrain, Kuwait, Yemen, Oman, and Saudi Arabia. Its southern coast stands in stark contrast to the rest of the peninsula. For about 200 miles inland from the 1,300-mile base and extending approximately 100 miles up the eastern and western sides of the peninsula, rainfall is sufficient to maintain an agricultural base. Crops, including figs, dates, melons, and grains, were supplemented by a distinctive coffee known by the name of the city near which it was grown, Mocha. High-quality local cotton met demands for textiles. Substantial income was derived from frankincense and myrrh made from trees native to the region. The Romans rightly called the area *Arabia aromatica.*

Once beyond the green fringe, the coasts on both sides of the peninsula have short and arid coastal plains. Hills and mountains come close to the shore, and the land rises steeply to a plateau often 4,000 feet above sea level and broken only by mountain chains whose peaks reach from 9,000 to 12,000 feet above sea level. Given the topography and prevailing winds, little rain reaches the interior. Except for flash floods, the average rainfall in the interior and northern portion of the peninsula can be as low as three inches per year. There are scattered oases but no permanent rivers or lakes. Wadis (dry riverbeds) used by travelers as roads are deadly when unexpected violent storms send cascades of water through them. Drifting sand and sandstorms generate granular rivers that may be hundreds of yards wide. Sand dunes, frequently over 600 feet high and 30 miles long, characterize one of the half-dozen distinct desert sand systems. The Rub' al-Khali just north of the southern green fringe extends for 250,000 square miles and is the largest sand desert on earth. Between the Rub' and the flourishing south are barren salt flats. In a classic understatement, the Arabs call the interior, "The Difficult Place."

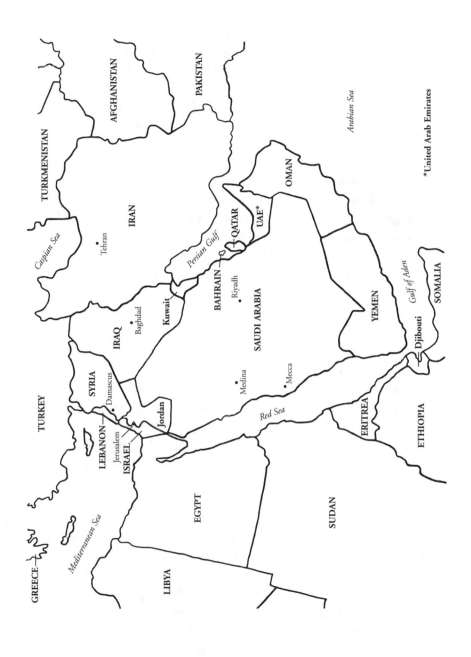

THE PEOPLES OF ARABIA

Why were there not among the generations before you
persons possessed of balanced good sense prohibiting (men)
from mischief in the earth except a few among them whom
We saved (from harm)? But the wrongdoers pursued the
enjoyment of the good things of life which were given them
and persisted in sin. Nor would thy Lord be the One to
destroy communities for a single wrongdoing if its members
were likely to mend. If thy Lord had so willed, He could have
made mankind one people: but they will not cease to dispute,
except those on whom He hath bestowed His mercy: and
for this did He create them: and the Word of thy Lord shall
be fulfilled: "I will fill Hell with jinn and men all together."
All that We relate to thee of the stories of the messengers
with it We make firm thy heart: in them there cometh to
thee the Truth as well as an exhortation and a message of
remembrance to those who believe. Say to those who do not
believe: "Do whatever ye can: we shall do our part; and wait
ye! We too shall wait." To Allah do belong the unseen (secrets)
of the heavens and the earth and to Him goeth back every
affair (for decision): then worship Him and put thy trust in
Him: and thy Lord is not unmindful of aught that ye do.

Surah 11:116–23, Hud

Arabia had long been peopled by a mix of settled and nomadic communities without a peninsula-wide central government.[1] The Qur'an refers
to tribes or communities—among them the Ad, Thamud, and Maydan—
that apparently ceased to exist perhaps before the assumed time of Abraham. To each of these God sent messengers and prophets, Hud, Salih, and
Shu'aib, respectively. Each of these peoples rejected the divine message and
those who proclaimed it. As a result the rejecters were destroyed.[2] Another

people assumed to be from Arabia, the Sabians, traditionally identified as subjects of the queen of Sheba, followed her into submitting to the One-Only God after she was brought to the Faith through Solomon.[3]

The populace in the sixth and seventh centuries may be differentiated by the regions in which they lived, the religions they practiced, and the foreign powers that sought to dominate them. Commerce, however, was the bond that linked them, sometimes as rivals and sometimes as collaborators. Sixth- and seventh-century Arabia was a crossroads for the exchange of commodities and ideas. The southern coasts were open to ships from India and China. From harbors in present-day Yemen and Oman, goods continued by water to the Christian kingdom of Ethiopia (then not landlocked) and, via the Red Sea, to Egypt. On Arabia's eastern shore, boats crisscrossed the Persian Gulf from Persia (Iraq and Iran). Spices and other articles arriving at the southern Arabian docks of ancient Yemen were loaded on camels for the northward caravan journey through Taif, Nakhla, Mecca, and Yathrib (later known as Medina, i.e., Medinat an-Nabi, City of the Prophet). Goods then went overland to Jerusalem, Damascus, Antioch, Constantinople, and Europe or could move up the Red Sea to the port, Qudayd, and then to Egyptian markets or across the Mediterranean.

Jews and Christians had been in Arabia for centuries. Caravans traveling through the region stopped in Jerusalem and other towns in Palestine and Syria where merchants and drivers learned of Judaism and Christianity and their writings and oral traditions. Accounts about Adam and Eve, Enoch, Noah, the patriarchs and their families, Moses, Israelite kings, and prophets, Zechariah and John the Baptist, as well as Mary and Jesus, were well known. Abraham, Hagar, and Ishmael were said to have lived in Arabia. The Idumeans, an Arab people forced to become Jews by the Maccabees, had natural and long-standing relationships with the tribes of northern Arabia. The Roman suppressions of Jewish revolts in the 60–70s and 130s CE added more Jews to the Arabian mix. Later contacts between Arabian Jewish communities and rabbinic academies in both Palestine and Persia were strong. An influx of Jews dislodged by the repressive policies of the Christian Byzantine emperor Justinian I after 527 increased the existing Jewish settlements around Medina. The reign of Jewish converts in Himyar (present-day Yemen) led to close contact with the rabbinical academy in Tiberias and Persian support.[4] Substantial numbers of Christians resided throughout the peninsula. Contemporaries reported the existence of a Christian cemetery in Mecca, and Mesopotamian bishops apparently supervised Christian clergy and churches in portions of Arabia. The massacre of Christians at Najran and Mocha (523), ordered by the Himyarite ruler, Joseph Dhu Nuwas, led directly to the reprisal invasion of southern Arabia by the Ethiopians and the establishment of a Christian enclave under Abrahah. Abrahah attempted to subjugate the peninsula and attacked Mecca, vowing to destroy the Ka'bah. Meccans attributed his ignominious retreat to droves of birds that pelted the invaders with fiery pebbles. The Qur'an cites this event as an intervention by God (Surah 105, al-Fil, the Elephant). Muslim tradition dates the event to 570, the year of the Messenger's birth. Abrahah was killed by Persian invaders who conquered Yemen in 575 and controlled the area for nearly four decades.[5]

What kind of Christians lived in Arabia is not clear. The post-Constantinian Roman Empire and the Church it supported engaged in serious, frequently arcane theological battles within their own ranks. Second- and third-century conflicts concerning gnosticism were superseded by the fourth- through seventh-century Christological and Trinitarian controversies. In the process, authority structures such as bishops and patriarchs, a scriptural canon, and the state's coercive power to enforce creedal conformity generated refugees who crossed into the Persian Empire and Arabia. Some Christians considered as scriptural or important apocryphal Christian writings similar to the Proto-Evangelium of James and at least one gospel about the childhood of Jesus and something like the Dialogue with the Savior.[6] In addition to Christian merchants, evidently from the 400s onward Christian missionaries were successful in Arabia. Shrines and monasteries in Palestine on the caravan routes served as centers to spread the Christian message and to strengthen those travelers who already were Christians. Later Islamic traditions report that representations of Jesus and Mary were among the images in the pre-Islamic Ka'bah.[7]

Clearly, Muhammad and his fellow Muslims knew and had commercial as well as social relationships with Jews and Christians. Indeed, one of Muhammad's closest in-laws and a concubine were Christians, and a wife was Jewish.

SOUTHERN ARABIAN PEOPLES

In the south, the population was more ethnically mixed than in the rest of Arabia. Ready proximity to the African coast and openness to maritime travel attracted traders who settled among and adapted to the indigenous peoples. Blood and family ties yielded to commercial interests. While that decreased the probability of blood feuds between families, it also weakened allegiances to the basic kinship units that could endure economic disruptions, political shifts, and military threats. Religion appears to have played a moderate role in the south. Some interest in the cult of a mono-theistic deity named Rahman (the Merciful or Compassionate) in the early first century CE faded, and veneration of the traditional triad of two male gods (sun and moon) and a female star god was reasserted. To be sure, there were strong influences from Persian dualisms both Zoroastrian and Mani-chaean, as well as from Greek and Roman religions.[8] Alexander the Great captured the imagination of many Egyptian and Mesopotamian poets, art-ists, and pious persons. He might be reflected in the shadowy figure, Dhu al-Qarnayn, in Surah 18:83–101.

The Jewish Himyarites earned the enmity of the Byzantines when the former barred the latter from the ports and markets of their realm. This economic-political act stimulated a temporary Byzantine-Ethiopian alliance against the Jewish state and also engaged Persian attention. The ensuing pressures and conflicts weakened southern Arabian political and military might as both the Byzantines and Persians turned to fighting each other in Syria-Palestine and Mesopotamia. Southern Arabian vulnerabilities were exposed when the Messenger and the Faithful began their successful efforts to unify Arabia.

ARABS OF THE CENTRAL AND NORTHERN REGIONS

Originally "Arab" referred to nomads or bedouin who lived in tents rather than settled in villages and oases-towns. Gradually "Arab" came to en-compass both nomadic and sedentary populations who shared a com-mon language in several dialects and certain cultural values as well as the acknowledgment of numerous deities and spirits. The sedentary Arabs considered the bedouin untrustworthy and opportunistic:

> The Arabs of the desert are the worst in unbelief and hypocrisy and most fitted to be in ignorance of the command which Allah hath sent down to his apostle: but Allah is All-Knowing, All-Wise. Some of the desert Arabs look upon their payments [Zakat, obligatory alms] as a fine, and watch for disasters for you. On them be the disaster of evil: for Allah is He that heareth and knoweth (all things). But some of the desert Arabs believe in Allah and the Last Day and look on their payments as pious gifts bringing them nearer to Allah and obtaining the prayers of the Messenger. Aye indeed, they bring them nearer (to Him). Soon will Allah admit them to His Mercy: for Allah is Oft-Forgiving, Most Merciful. (Surah 9:97–99, al-Tawbah, Repentance, or Bara'ah, Disavowal)[9]

Both types of Arabs emphasized personal honor, courage, and generosity (*'ird* and *muruwa,* or manliness). Both also engaged in periodic raids (sing. *ghazwah,* pl. *maghazi*) on caravans or settlements to capture booty such as camels, sheep, slaves, and women. Raiders were credited for clever stratagems and well-laid ambushes. In pre-Islamic Arabia the month Dhu l-Hijjah was the time for pilgrimages to the Ka'bah in Mecca. Fighting, raiding and bloodshed were prohibited during the month and for the months prior to and following Dhu l-Hijjah (Dhu l-Qa'dah and Muharram) as well as the seventh month, Rahjab (the Revered Month). A special revelation to Muhammad permitted him to breach the custom in 624 for a skirmish at Nakhlah (Surah 2:217). Polygyny was common, and perhaps the number of women a man could marry was unrestricted.

Religion was important to the inhabitants of the interior and the north. Although individuals called *hunafa* (sing. *hanif*) moved from polytheism toward a more clearly articulated monotheism, almost all others were polytheists and regarded their world as suffused with many spirits. At the top of the divine scale was a shadowy overseer who seemed to have little concern or contact with the world, the God (Allah). Below Him was a panoply of many ilahas, both male and female. Among these subdeities were three females who were called at times the daughters or wives of God: al-Lat (associated with Taif), al-Uzza (associated with Nakhlah), and Manat (associated with Qudayd).[10] Hubal, the moon god, was the Qurayshi patron god at Mecca. Pilgrimages to the Qurayshi-dominated Meccan area during Dhu l-Hijjah included circumambulating the Ka'bah and visiting the marketplaces at Mina. Representations of the ilahas were erected at Mina where pilgrims could offer sacrifices to them.

As the Qur'an indicates at numerous points, during the pre-Islamic time Arabs rejected as ridiculous any notion of divine judgment, resurrection, life after death, or the destruction of the world:

> Man says: "What! When I am dead shall I then be raised up alive?" But does not man call to mind that We created him before out of nothing? So by thy Lord without doubt, We shall gather them together and (also) the Evil Ones (with them); then shall We bring them forth on their knees round about Hell; Then shall We certainly drag out from every sect all those who were worst in obstinate rebellion against (Allah), Most Gracious. And certainly We know best those who are most worthy of being burned therein. Not one of you but will pass over it: this is with thy Lord a decree which must be accomplished. But We shall save those who guarded against evil, and We shall leave the wrongdoers therein (humbled) to their knees. When Our clear signs are rehearsed to them the unbelievers say to those who believe: "Which of the two sides is best in point of position? Which makes the best show in council?" But how many (countless) generations before them have We destroyed who were even better in equipment and in glitter to the eye? Say: "If any men go astray (Allah) Most Gracious extends (the rope) to them. Until when they see the warning of Allah (being fulfilled) either in punishment or in (the approach of) the Hour, they will at length realize who is worst in position and (who) weakest in forces!" And Allah doth advance in guidance those who seek guidance; and the things that endure. Good deeds are best in the sight of thy Lord as rewards and best in respect of (their) eventual returns." (Surah 19:66–76)

The tribes of central and northern Arabia subdivided into closely related clans that provided spheres of allegiance for members and frequent conflicts with competitors. Some cities attracted merchants, adventurers, travelers, herders, and artisans. Mecca provided more: it was the commercial-religious hub for much of Arabia. The Quraysh was the leading and most powerful Meccan tribe, and the Banu Hashem was a minor Quraysh clan. One of the less promising members of the clan was Muhammad ibn Abd Allah ibn Muttalib, the orphan whom God chose to be His ultimate Messenger:

> Say: "O ye men! If ye are in doubt as to my Religion (behold!), I worship not what ye worship other than Allah. But I worship Allah Who will take your souls (at death). I am commanded to be (in the ranks) of the Believers." And further (thus): "Set thy face towards Religion with true piety and never in anywise be of the Unbelievers; nor call on any other than Allah, such will neither profit thee nor hurt thee. If thou dost, Behold! Thou shalt certainly be of those who do wrong. If Allah do touch thee with hurt, there is none can remove it but He. If He do design some benefit for thee, there is none can keep back His favor. He causeth it to reach whomsoever of His servants He pleaseth. And He is the Oft-Forgiving, Most Merciful." Say: "O ye men! Now Truth hath reached you from your Lord! Those who receive guidance do so for the good of their own souls; those who stray do so to their own loss: and I am not (set) over you to arrange your affairs." Follow thou the inspiration sent unto thee and be patient and constant till Allah doth decide: for He is the Best to decide. (Surah 10:104–9)

THE HOLY LAND

The Creator of all lands sent prophets and messengers to all peoples, except the Arabs. Now their time to receive a revelation had come. But theirs would be the Revelation for all peoples in all future times and places. When that Revelation came, God Himself spoke it, thereby making Arabic the singularly holy language. The land had already been prepared for its place in the plan through Abraham, Isma'il, and the Ka'bah. The plan provided for the establishment of an umma that would obey-live the Message and extend it to all peoples from Arabia. Not only did God prepare for the holy language; He prepared the one who would hear it, proclaim it, and be its model for all time. Taken together, Arabia became the aya, the holy land, testifying to the One-Only God and now the Messenger to the Arabs and to all humanity:

> So We have made the (Qur'an) easy in thine own tongue, that with it thou mayest give glad tidings to the righteous, and warnings to people given to contention. But how many (countless) generations before them have We destroyed? Canst thou find a single one of them (now) or hear so much of a whisper of them? (Surah 19:97–98, Maryam, Mary)

FIVE

TIMES AND THE MESSENGER

By (the token of) Time through the ages, verily Man is in loss,
except such as have Faith and do righteous deeds, and (join together)
in the mutual teaching of Truth, and of Patience, and Constancy.

Surah 103, al-'Asr, Time through the Ages

The time had come. Millennia of preparatory revelations, exhortations and
warnings by prophets and messengers were over. God readied one individual to receive, proclaim, and live the final Revelation and to form the
community that would lead the world into a new time until the Day of
Judgment. Muslims use the term *al-Jahiliyyah,* or the Time of Ignorance,
for the period before the final Revelation. The chapter begins with comments on Jahiliyyah times from 500 to the 630s, then provides a Muslim
view of Jahiliyyah conditions among the Arabs. In "The Narrative about
Muhammad" we consider the Revelatory Time, from Muhammad's origins
to his death. The chapter concludes with a foreshadowing of the Qur'an's
transition from an oral proclamation to its collation as the Book as part
of what I term the Testing Times, from Muhammad's death to the Day of
Judgment.

By the Night as it conceals (the light); by the Day as it appears in
glory; by (the mystery of) the creation of male and female, verily (the

ends) ye strive for are diverse. So he who gives (in charity) and fears (Allah), and (in all sincerity) testifies to the Best, We will indeed make smooth for him the path to Bliss. But he who is a greedy miser and thinks himself self-sufficient, and gives the lie to the Best, We will indeed make smooth for him the Path to Misery; nor will his wealth profit him when he falls headlong (into the Pit). Verily, We take upon Ourselves to guide. And verily unto Us (belong) the End and the Beginning. Therefore do I warn you of a Fire blazing fiercely; none shall reach it but those most unfortunate ones who give the lie to Truth and turn their backs. But those most devoted to Allah shall be removed far from it: those who spend their wealth for increase in self-purification and have in their minds no favor from anyone for which a reward is expected in return, but only the desire to seek for the countenance of their Lord Most High. And soon will they attain (complete) satisfaction. (Surah 92, al-Layl, the Night)

Jahiliyyah Time

Al-Jahiliyyah was not a time of ignorance due to a lack of awareness of God or knowledge of the Way He willed His humans to follow. God's moral law pervaded all existence, so no one could avoid responsibility for what he or she did or failed to do. Countless prophets and messengers brought admonitions and encouragements to individuals and communities to abandon Iblis's deceptions, which resulted in idolatry and consequent wickedness. Islam and the Qur'an are clear: Women and men are to generate and advance justice and mercy in human communities. They cannot retreat into ascetic seclusion from the realities of living in God's time and in God's world. All humans are summoned to join the umma and challenged to use the time God allots them before the Day. Few heeded; most mocked, rejected, threatened, and even killed the revealers.[1] Their books were misinterpreted, ignored, distorted, and falsified. Jahiliyyah ignorance is instead willful disobedience of, ingratitude toward, and defiance of God. Even during Jahiliyyah time God destroyed especially sinful communities that ignored what would be inevitable:

Follow (O men!) the revelation given unto you from your Lord, and follow not as friends or protectors other than Him. Little it is ye remember of admonition. How many towns have We destroyed (for their sins)? Our punishment took them on a sudden by night or while they slept for their afternoon rest. When (thus) our punishment took them, no cry did they utter but this "indeed we did wrong." Then shall We question those to whom Our message was sent and those by whom We sent it. And verily, We shall recount their whole story with knowledge for We were never absent (at any time or place). The balance that day will be true (to a nicety): those whose scale (of good) will be heavy will prosper. Those whose scale will be light will find their souls in perdition for that they wrongfully treated our signs. It is We who have placed you with authority on earth and provided you therein with means for the fulfillment of your life: small are the thanks that ye give! (Surah 7:3–10, al-Araf, the Heights)

THE BYZANTINE AND PERSIAN EMPIRES, CA. 500–630S

The Roman Empire has been defeated in a land close by;
but they (even) after (this) defeat of theirs will soon be
victorious within a few years. With Allah is the decision in
the past and in the future: on that Day shall the Believers
rejoice with the help of Allah. He helps whom He will and
He is Exalted in Might, Most Merciful. (It is) the promise
of Allah. Never does Allah depart from His promise: but
most men understand not. They know but the outer (things)
in the life of this world: but of the End of things they are
heedless. Do they not reflect in their own minds? Not but
for just ends and for a term appointed did Allah create
the heavens and the earth and all between them: yet are
there truly many among men who deny the meeting
with their Lord (at the Resurrection)! Do they not travel
through the earth and see what was the end of those before

them? They were superior to them in strength: they tilled
the soil and populated it in greater numbers than these
have done: there came to them their messengers with
Clear (Signs) (which they rejected to their own destruction).
It was not Allah Who wronged them but they wronged their
own souls. In the long run evil in the extreme will be the
end of those who do evil; for that they rejected the Signs
of Allah and held them up to ridicule.

Surah 30:2–10, al-Rum, the Romans

The Roman (Byzantine) and Persian (Sassanid) Empires went through periods of weakness and recovery as they sought to respond to attacks from various Slavic and Germanic tribes (in Byzantium) and Hunnish peoples (in both empires), internal intrigues, civil revolts, and extended wars with each other. Peace agreements were short-lived, indemnities agreed on were not paid, military pacts with assorted allies died on battlefields, and, in 540, bubonic plague ravaged Mesopotamia and the Mediterranean.[2] The Sassanids developed a sphere of influence and presence in southern Arabia when Joseph Dhu Nuwas converted to Judaism. Ethiopian Christians attacked and failed in their assault on Mecca. Entreated by the Himyarites, the Sassanid ruler, Khosrau I (also known as Chorosis I, r. 531–79), intervened and drove the Ethiopians out of Yemen-Himyar. He established Persian bases in southern Arabia (ca. 570–75). Later, after a failed attempt by the Himyarites to renounce allegiance to the Sassanids, Khosrau II (r. 590–628) annexed southern Arabia to the Persian Empire (598).

   In spite of Byzantium's near–economic collapse, constant intraempire turmoil (especially in Constantinople), incursions by invading tribes, wars with Persia, and plague, Justinian I (r. 527–65) managed to recover much of Roman North Africa, Italy, and portions of the Balkans. For a time he paid Khosrau I to maintain fortifications intended to stop tribal raids and infiltration. The "Eternal Peace" between Justinian I and Khosrau I,

agreed on in 532, lasted until 540 when the Persians invaded Syria. Justin II
(r. 565–78) failed to regain Roman Mesopotamia. Persian victories in western Asia and southern Arabia added to the Persian plundering of Syria and
unhinged Justin I's mind. Until 610, his successors lost territory and political stability.[3]

Heraclius began his lengthy reign (610–41) in the aftermath of the
civil war that terminated Phocas's rule. During his first two decades, Heraclius lost most of Justinian's gains. His counterpart, Khosrau II, likewise
overcame internal disunity, then launched a successful attack on Byzantine
Anatolia and Syria. The Persians captured Damascus (614) and Jerusalem
(615) and occupied Egypt. Many Jews in Persia and Palestine expected the
Sassanids to rebuild the Jerusalem Temple and reinstate the Levitical priesthood. The Qurayshi rejoiced because their commercial interests led them
to favor the Persians over the Byzantines. These victories served as the immediate context for Surah 30, a warning that the Persian victory would
soon be turned into a rout. The Sassanid armies, working in conjunction
with the Slavs and Avars, began a siege of Constantinople. In 626 Heraclius's bold counterstroke into the Persian heartland made the Persians retreat, and their European allies lifted the siege of Constantinople. The Byzantines were convinced God had protected the New Rome and would
ever do so. As the Roman Empire's armies advanced, the Persians pulled
back from Egypt and Syria-Palestine. In 627, near Ninevah, the Sassanids
suffered a major defeat, and the Byzantines advanced into Georgia and Ar-
menia. In 628 the beleaguered and morose Khosrau II, the triumphant
Heraclius, the restored Byzantine governor of Egypt, the Christian ruler
of Ethiopia, and several polytheistic southern Arabian rulers received a
proclamation sent by couriers from the Arabian oasis, Medina. Muhammad had announced the Revelation and command of God. According to
Muslim tradition, Heraclius (and the others with adaptations relevant to
them) read:

> In the name of Allah the Beneficent, the Merciful. (This letter is)
> from Muhammad, the slave of Allah and His Messenger, to Heraclius,
> the ruler of Byzantine. Peace be upon him who follows the right path.

Furthermore I invite you to Islam, and if you become a Muslim you will be safe, and Allah will double your reward. And if you reject this invitation of Islam you will be committing a sin by misguiding your Arisiyin (peasants). (And I recite to you Allah's Statement:) [from Surah 3:64]

> "O people of the scripture! Come to a word common to you and us that we worship none but Allah and that we associate nothing in worship with Him, and that none of us shall take others as Lords beside Allah. Then, if they turn away, say: Bear witness that we are Muslims (those who have surrendered to Allah)."[4]

According to Ibn Ishaq, some recipients were baffled, the southern Arabians realized that the invitation was an ultimatum, Heraclius supposedly almost converted to Islam, and Khosrau II tore up the message. By the end of the year the Persian "King of Kings" was murdered by his own officers. Christians, Jews, Zoroastrians, and polytheists were put on notice: the days of the Jahiliyyah outside of Arabia were over. God had been preparing the region for the end of one time and the start of another. The empires were exhausted. The errors and distortions that twisted the earlier revelations were to be corrected and fulfilled. The times were changing.

> Now what is the matter with the unbelievers that they rush madly before thee, from the right and from the left in crowds? Does every man of them long to enter the Garden of Bliss? By no means! For We have created them out of the (base matter) they know! Now I do call to witness the Lord of all points in the East and the West that We can certainly substitute for them better (men) than they; and We are not to be defeated (in Our Plan). So leave them to plunge in vain talk and play about until they encounter that Day of theirs which they have been promised! The Day whereon they will issue from their sepulchers in sudden haste as if they were rushing to a goal-post (fixed for them), their eyes lowered in dejection, ignominy covering them (all over)! Such is the Day the which they are promised! (Surah 70:36–44, al-Ma'ariij, the Ways of Ascent)

ARABIA

I do call to witness this City, and thou art a freeman of
this City, and (the mystic ties of) parent and child. Verily,
We have created man into toil and struggle. Thinketh he
that none hath power over him? He may say (boastfully):
"Wealth have I squandered in abundance!" Thinketh he
that none beholdeth him? Have We not made for him a pair
of eyes and a tongue, and a pair of lips, and shown him the
two highways? But he hath made no haste on the path that
is steep. And what will explain to thee the path that is steep?
(It is) freeing the bondman or the giving of food in a day
of privation to the orphan with claims of relationship, or
to the indigent (down) in the dust. Then will he be of
those who believe and enjoin patience (constancy and
self-restraint) and enjoin deeds of kindness and compassion.
Such are the Companions of the Right Hand. But those who
reject Our Signs they are the (unhappy) companions of the
Left Hand. On them will be Fire vaulted over (all round).

Surah 90, al-Balad, the City

From Purity to Idolatry

In addition to being Arabia's center for the gods and their human worshipers, Mecca was the largest and richest city in the peninsula. The annual pilgrimage for the veneration of the ilahas and their connections to
the Ka'bah focused power and authority on the tribe that ruled Mecca and
was the custodian of the Ka'bah. Again, according to tradition, when the
custodial tribe became corrupt, it lost its place and another assumed the
holy privilege and ruled Mecca.[5] The tribe that held those positions also
was the most powerful Arab tribe in the region.

But polytheism and idolatry were not always dominant in Mecca. Abraham and Isma'il were the Ka'bah's builders and the city's founders. They established both in obedience to the One-Only God and for His worship and service:

> Remember We made the house a place of assembly for men and a place of safety; and take ye the station of Abraham as a place of prayer; and We covenanted with Abraham and Isma'il that they should sanctify My House for those who compass it round or use it as a retreat or bow or prostrate themselves (therein in prayer). And remember Abraham said: "My Lord, make this a City of Peace and feed its people with fruits such of them as believe in Allah and the Last Day." He [Allah] said: "(Yea) and such as reject faith for a while will I grant them their pleasure but will soon drive them to the torment of fire, an evil destination (indeed)!" And remember Abraham and Isma'il raised the foundations of the House (with this prayer): "Our Lord! Accept (this service) from us for Thou art the All-Hearing, the All-Knowing. Our Lord! Make of us Muslims bowing to Thy (Will) and of our progeny a people Muslim bowing to Thy (Will), and show us our places for the celebration of (due) rites; and turn unto us (in mercy); for Thou art the Oft-Returning, Most-Merciful." (Surah 2:125–28)

Over time, however, later custodians introduced idols into the Ka'bah and polytheism into Mecca, leading to moral degradation and injustice. Ibn Ishaq reported the corruption of Abraham's and Ishmael's pure worship through the raising of stone idols in and around the Ka'bah and the city, then the construction of temples to patron ilahas for the other cities and settlements and the placement of idols in each home.[6] Yet a semblance, a residual memory of Abrahamic purity, remained:

> Thus as generations passed, they forgot their primitive faith and adopted another religion for that of Abraham and Ishmael. They worshiped idols and adopted the same errors as the peoples before them. Yet they retained and held fast practices going back to the time of Abraham.[7]

Before the corrupt and unjust Jurhum and Khuza'a tribes controlled Mecca and the Ka'bah, "Mecca did not tolerate injustice and wrong within its borders and if anyone did wrong therein it expelled him; therefore it was called 'the Scorcher,' and any king who came to profane its sanctity died on the spot. It is said that it was called Bakka because it used to break the necks of tyrants when they introduced innovations therein."[8] Under the Jurham and Khuza'a the moral climate worsened. Pilgrims were abused and exploited, as the Meccan oligarchy became greedy and arrogant. It was time for a change.

The Qurayshi

Qusayy bin Kilab united the Quraysh tribe and, after verbal confrontations with the Khuza'a and several battles, accepted arbitration of their respective claims. The decision favored Qusayy, thereby ending the Khuza'a's grip on Mecca and the Ka'bah. He then defeated his brother-rival to become the leader of the city and chief custodian of the Ka'bah. Qusayy was concerned about the plight of indigent pilgrims. They had been gouged fiscally and humiliated by the previous tribal rulers. Qusayy set up a pattern whereby the Qurayshi were duty bound to provide for the food and welfare of pilgrims to the Ka'bah. He argued that the Quraysh were "God's neighbors, the people of His temple and sanctuary. The pilgrims are God's guests and the visitors to His temple and have the highest claim on your generosity; so provide food and drink for them during the pilgrimage until they depart out of your territory."[9] Qusayy, however, established Hubal, the ilaha connected to the moon, as the patron of Mecca and put his statue in the middle of the Ka'bah. After Qusayy's death, the Qurayshi consolidated their authority, making neighboring tribes commercially and militarily dependent on Mecca.

Capable warriors and astute merchants, the Quraysh tribe strengthened its influence on and hold over the north–south caravan trade. Hashim ibn Abdu Manaf, leader of the Quraysh clan that bore his name, strengthened the system that cared for pilgrims, even spending from his own resources. His wife was from Yathrib. Five generations later and from a lineage known for honesty and liberality, Muhammad the Messenger was born.

Mecca and the Ka'bah

Abraham and Ishmael prayed that the Ka'bah and Mecca would always be in submission to and at peace with the One-Only God, a refuge for the needy, and a sign of God's will. But Jahiliyyah times were rife with idolatry, and injustice had overtaken the Holy Land, the Holy City, and the Holy Place.

The Qur'an's language and frequent references to finances, trade, auditing, contracts, and debts fit the Meccan-Medinian context. Meccan fixations on ill-gotten profit, wealth, and luxury were, according to Muslims, the results of idolatry and the wholesale spiritual and moral corruption rooted in Iblis's deceptions. The Qurayshi appear to have had a monopoly on the provisioning of caravans that passed through the tribe's territories and were enriched by their own summer and winter caravans. A significant portion of their revenues came from the annual pilgrimage and the business transacted at that time. The Qur'an's exhortations and warnings about greed, dishonesty, honoring contracts, making and fulfilling written commitments, and using legitimate weights and measures, as well as it comments about maritime trade and the quality of products, indicate that the merchant classes' shrewdness verged on avarice and fraud. Judging by the subjects addressed and the strictures stated in the Qur'an, conditions among the poorer Quraysh clans, other tribal groups, Jews, and Christians resident in Mecca seem to have been fraught with injustice and poverty. The vulnerable were being exploited and cheated. God warned that on the Day of Judgment the greedy and dishonest would receive their damnable reward, while the righteous would be welcomed to eternal blessedness (Surah 89:15–30, al-Fajr, Dawn).

The Qur'an often couches its concern for orphans in terms that warn guardians not to embezzle funds from their wards' inheritance or speculate with those funds in risky ventures, or take advantage of them for sexual purposes, or marry them in order to acquire their funds.[10] Apparently the Meccans also practiced female infanticide:

When news is brought to one of them of (the birth of) a female (child) his face darkens, and he is filled with inward grief! With shame does he hide himself from his people because of the bad news he has had! Shall he retain it on (sufferance and) contempt or bury it in the dust? Ah! What an evil (choice) they decide on! To those who believe not in the Hereafter applies the similitude of evil: to Allah applies the highest similitude: for He is the Exalted in Power, Full of Wisdom. (Surah 16:58–60)

The Qur'an singles out such murderers for special mention on the Day of Judgment:

When the sun (with its spacious light) is folded up; When the stars fall losing their luster; When the mountains vanish (like a mirage); When the she-camels ten months with young are left untended; When the wild beasts are herded together (in human habitations); When the oceans boil over with a swell; When the souls are sorted out (being joined like with like); When the female (infant) buried alive is questioned for what crime she was killed; When the Scrolls are laid open; When the World on High is unveiled: When the Blazing Fire is kindled to fierce heat; And when the Garden is brought near, (then) shall each soul know what it has put forward. (Surah 81:1–14)

Relations between husbands and wives, divorce, and inheritance were addressed directly when the umma was taking shape in Medina. The prescriptions and advice in those passages may indicate reactions to common Arabian practices as well as the customs observed in Mecca. Apparently men could marry as many women as they wanted, divorce was frequent and easy, and widows and orphans were relegated to inferior status or made destitute by more powerful and affluent men. (See chapter 11.)

Even if Jahiliyyah conditions in Mecca and other cities were not as dire as Muslim sources describe, there were significant issues of economic and social injustice, corrupt business practices, and individual degradation suffered by the vulnerable, while considerable wealth was garnered by the Qurayshi oligarchy and their supporters. All that happened within the holy city was abetted by the religious observances centered on the Ka'bah. Some scholars theorize that with the rise of hanif-monotheists and the political-economic disruptions caused by the Persian and Byzantine wars the city and north-central Arabia were sliding into or were already caught in crises on the eve of the Revelation's disclosure.[11] The time had come for God to send to the Arabs their messenger, the Messenger for all times and people with the Revelation in their own language:

> He knows what (appears to His creatures as) before or after or behind them, but they shall not compass it with their knowledge. (All) faces shall be humbled before (Him), the Living, the Self-Subsisting Eternal. Hopeless indeed will be the man that carries iniquity (on his back). But he who works deeds of righteousness and has faith will have no fear of harm nor of any curtailment (of what is his due). Thus have we sent this down an Arabic Qur'an and explained therein in detail some of the warnings in order that they may fear Allah or that it may cause their remembrance (of Him). High above all is Allah, the King, the Truth! Be not in haste with the Qur'an before its revelation to thee is completed but say "O my Lord! Advance me in knowledge." (Surah 20:110–14)

THE REVELATORY TIME AND THE MESSENGER

> A revelation from (Allah), Most Gracious, Most Merciful:
> A Book whereof the verses are explained in detail, a Qur'an
> in Arabic for people who understand, giving Good News
> and Admonition. Yet most of them turn away and so they
> hear not. They say: "Our hearts are under veils (concealed)
> from that to which thou dost invite us, and in ours ears
> [is] a deafness, and between us and thee is a screen. So do
> thou (what thou wilt); for us, we shall do (what we will!)."
> Say thou: "I am but a man like you: it is revealed to me
> by inspiration that your Allah is One Allah: so stand true
> to Him and ask for His forgiveness." And woe to those

who join gods with Allah, those who practice not regular charity, and who even deny the Hereafter. For those who believe and work deeds of righteousness is a reward that will never fail.

Surah 41:2–8

While the Revelatory Time is more than the biography of one person, the life of Muhammad and the Revelatory Time are inseparable. Muhammad is the one person who, by the gracious Plan of God, lived that Message and organized the God-centered community that seeks to be guided on the Sirataal Mustiqiim, the Straight Path. Guidance is given by the Qur'an, the testimony of the previous prophets and messengers, and, most sublimely, Muhammad's sunna. The period 610–32 is the holiest and clearest Revelatory Time. All that came before was preparation for that Time, and all that followed is lived in light of that Time. In that period more than ever before or since God disclosed most clearly and authoritatively His Plan for the cosmos and His creatures. In that time God caused His proclamation to be spoken through the prepared man and to be preserved without error for the Arabs and then all humanity. In that period God gave the wholesome principles and instructions for the formation of the umma that is called to live and share those principles and instructions for the well-being of all beings until the Day of Judgment. Many Muslims view the Revelatory Time and Muhammad's way of life as the paradigm or model to be emulated by individual Muslims and non-Muslims, Islamic societies, and the world community if we truly desire and strive for justice and peace.[12] Nevertheless, as important as Muhammad was and is, he was neither divine in origin nor raised to divine status after his death: "Say: 'I am but a man like yourselves (but) the inspiration has come to me that your Allah is one Allah: whoever expects to meet his Lord, let him work righteousness and in the worship of his Lord admit no one as partner'" (Surah 18:100, al-Kahf, the Cave). Still, to understand the Qur'an, its structure, Message, and the umma it shaped and shapes, we turn to the Messenger. In telling "The

Narrative about Muhammad" I use some accounts in the hadith collections and Ibn Ishaq's biography of Muhammad.

THE NARRATIVE ABOUT MUHAMMAD: HIS EARLY TIME

Ye have indeed in the Messenger of Allah a beautiful pattern
of (conduct) for anyone whose hope is in Allah and the
Final Day and who engages much in the praise of Allah.

Surah 33:21, al-Ahzab, the Confederates

He was the son of Abd Allah (Abdullah), who was the son of Abd al-Muttalib, who was a descendant of Hasham, founder of the Hashimite clan of the Quraysh tribe. The patrilineal tradition traces the family to Ishmael and through Ishmael to Abraham. Muhammad's mother, Aminah, was a daughter of Wahb bin Abd-Manaf. Shortly before Muhammad was born, his father died. Following Meccan custom, he was given to a bedouin wet nurse, Halimah, to be raised for his initial years.[13] One account reports that when he was about two years old two men (obviously angels) opened his torso and removed his heart from which they plucked a black drop. They then washed his heart and internal parts with snow from a golden basin that they carried and closed him again.[14] The account expresses God's preparation (wahy) of Muhammad to receive (tanzil) the Revelation. As all prophets and messengers were free from ithum sin, the angelic action purified Muhammad very early in life from any taint of sin, yet he would always be responsible for his choices and actions. On the death of his mother, when he was six years old, the child became a ward of his grandfather, Abd al-Muttalib. Muhammad knew what it was to be an orphan, and although his grandfather was an honest man who did not abuse his ward's trust, Muhammad observed the plight of orphans whose guardians squandered their legacies. Two years later al-Muttalib died, and the child went to live with his paternal uncle, Abu Talib, a merchant-caravaneer.

Abu Talib took his nephew-ward on a caravan trip to Syria. During the trip, a Christian monk blessed with visions recognized that Muhammad had the "seal of the prophets" between his shoulders and was destined to be a great, yet endangered servant of God.[15] Ibn Ishaq reported that the monk urged Abu Talib to protect the youth from idolatry, sin, and Jews for God planned to have him be the best person in character, truthfulness, and other desirable virtues. Muhammad earned the respect of the Qurayshi and other men of commerce in Mecca for his honesty, integrity and diligence. Almost as an aside, Ibn Ishaq mentioned a "Sacrilegious War" ca. 590. The belligerents battled during one of the sacred months when fighting was prohibited. Another violation of that prohibition was to occur in 624.

On the surface Muhammad, now twenty-five years old, had limited prospects socially and financially, but others recognized his ability and competence. According to Ibn Ishaq, a wealthy widow, Khadijah bint Khuwaylid, learned about the young man. Both for profit and as a test, she hired him to take a caravan to Syria and sent one of her servants to observe him. During the trip, the servant witnessed another Christian monk identify Muhammad as a prophet and, later, two angels protecting him from the blazing sun. On learning how Muhammad handled her business and of the two spiritual events, she offered to marry him. Her biblically informed Christian cousin, Waraqa ibn Naufal, predicted that Muhammad was the prophet God promised to send to the Arabs. Their marriage, ca. 595, was mutually happy and productive. Together they had two sons, Qasim and Abd Allah, and four daughters, Zaynab, Ruqayyah, Fatimah, and Umm Kulthum. The boys died in infancy. Another of Khadijah's relatives, a boy named Ali, and a slave, Zaid (or Zayd) ibn al-Harith, (d. 630) were part of the household. Zaid refused to be ransomed by his father, electing to stay with Muhammad. In return Muhammad adopted him as a son. That adoption was to prove problematic. Fatimah married her cousin, Ali, and their sons were Hasan and Husayn. All four are revered especially by Shi'ites. Fatimah, his favorite child, died six months after her father.

Muhammad was so respected by the Meccans that in 603, at the rebuilding of the Ka'bah, he settled a dispute over the placement of the Black Stone. The contending parties deferred to his judgment. He engaged all the leaders in placing the stone, and, by popular consent, he put it in the structure.[16] Apparently Muhammad was religiously sensitive from childhood. Conditions in the city and the Ka'bah seem to have disturbed him. He and others knew that the custodians of the Sacred House would be turned out if they perverted worship and ethics. Although his grandfather, uncle, and most people he knew were polytheists, Muhammad also knew Jews and Christians and traveled in Byzantine-held Palestine-Syria. He may always have been a hanif; soon his life would be transformed by revelatory evidence that there was only one God and that he was the Messenger of God. Financially secure and his family content, yet spiritually troubled, Muhammad retired from the day-to-day management of his and Khadijah's business (ca. 609). The first of three life-changing vision-experiences was about to begin.

THE NARRATIVE ABOUT MUHAMMAD: THE REVELATION STARTS

Proclaim! (or Read!) in the name of thy Lord and
Cherisher Who created, created man out of a (mere)
clot of congealed blood: Proclaim! And thy Lord is
Most Bountiful. He Who taught (the use of) the Pen
taught man that which he knew not.

   Surah 96:1–4, Iqra', Read! also al-'Alaq, the Clinging Clot

---

Mecca sits in a narrow, arid valley amid hills and mountains. Mount Hira, pocked by caves, is three miles north of the city. Muhammad frequented a cave facing Mecca near the summit, contemplating and praying to the one God. In 610, on an evening near the end of Ramadan,[17]

[t]he angel came to him and asked him to read [or "recite"]. The Prophet replied, "I do not know how to read [*ummi*]." The Prophet

added, "The angel caught me (forcefully) and pressed me so hard that I could not bear it anymore. He then released me and again asked me to read and I replied, 'I do not know how to read.' Thereupon he caught me again and pressed me a second time till I could not bear it anymore. He then released me and again asked me to read but again I replied, 'I do not know how to read (or what shall I read?).' Thereupon he caught me for the third time and pressed me, and then released me and said, 'Read in the name of your Lord, who has created (all that exists) has created man from a clot. Read! And your Lord is the Most Generous.'"[18]

The Revelation had begun and would continue until shortly before Muhammad's death in 632. I want to make three points before returning to the narrative. First, elsewhere the revelatory angel is identified as Gabriel (Jibreel). Second, mainstream Muslim tradition holds that Muhammad's use of *ummi* means that he was totally illiterate, thereby enhancing the miracle of the Qur'an's eloquence and role as the Book.[19] That view will be emphasized in order to say that the Messenger was not influenced by the Bible or other Jewish and Christian writings because he could not read. Since he was an experienced merchant, I think it likely that he had the ability to handle figures, money, and orders for transmitting goods, so that *ummi* in this context means "without formal education." Third, the Mount Hira experience was the first of the three life-transforming revelatory visions that validated his and the umma's message and mission. It is the equivalent of a prophetic "call" experience that sets the person apart from others and starts him on a divine mission with the Message given by God. We will encounter the other two events shortly.

The Qur'an "descended" on what has come to be called the Night of Power (Laylat al-Qadar), the most beautiful night, the night that began the Transcendent Time. Ever since, Mount Hira has been called al-Jabal al-Nur, the Mountain of Light.

We have indeed revealed this (Message) in the Night of Power. And what will explain to thee what the Night of Power is? The Night of

Power is better than a thousand months. Therein come down the angels and the Spirit by Allah's permission, on every errand: Peace! This until the rise of morn! (Surah 97, al-Qadr, the Night of Power or Night of Honor)

Traditionally Muslims hold that the Qur'an or its source descended first from God to the heaven just above the earth. As indicated in chapter 3, the heaven closest to the earth is the repository of revelations from which they were to be "sent down" to the prophets and messengers. Gabriel, at the command of God, then descended with the initial ayas and gave the first ayas to the Messenger.

Muhammad left Mount Hira terror-stricken by the experience. He had Khadijah cover him until he was calm enough to recount the event. She brought him to her elderly Christian relative, Waraqa. Waraqa confirmed the validity of the event. He and Khadijah were the first to believe that Muhammad was God's long-awaited messenger to the Arabs and that the Message he was receiving was valid.[20] Soon Zaid, Ali, and Fatimah joined the fledgling umma in Muhammad and Khadijah's house. The first believers, then, were a matronly woman, an elderly Christian, a slave, a boy, and a girl.

Initially assured that his experience was genuine, when nothing further occurred, Muhammad worried that he was losing his mind. The next Revelation came about eighteen months later. The Fatra, or pause, as the period of silence is called, ended with a revelation that was a portion of Surah 68 or Surah 74:1–5, al-Muddaththir (the One Wrapped Up). The former is God's assurance to Muhammad that he is not insane or of deluded mind, or leading others astray; he is to continue the mission:

By the Pen and by the (Record) which (men) write thou art not by the grace of thy Lord mad or possessed. Nay, verily, for thee is a reward unfailing: And thou (standest) on an exalted standard of character. Soon wilt thou see and they will see which of you is afflicted with madness. Verily, it is thy Lord that knoweth best which (among men) hath strayed from His Path: and He knoweth best those who receive

(True) Guidance. So hearken not to those who deny (the Truth).
(Surah 68:1–8)

Bukhari, quoting one of Muhammad's "helpers" in Medina, holds
that the Fatra was broken by Surah 74:1–5 and that it was accompanied
by the second of the great visions. The Prophet told Jabir bin Abdullah
al-Ansari:

> While I was walking, all of a sudden I heard a voice from the sky. I
> looked up and saw the same angel who had visited me at the cave of
> Hira, sitting on a chair between the sky and the earth. I got scared of
> him and came home and said, "Wrap me (in blankets)." And then
> Allah revealed the following Holy Verses (of the Qur'an):
> O thou wrapped up (in a mantle)! Arise and deliver thy warn-
> ing! And thy Lord do thou magnify! And thy garments keep free
> from stain! And all [ilahas] shun!

After this, the revelations started coming strongly and frequently.[21] The
Qur'an describes a significant and empowering vision of Gabriel at Surahs
81:19–25 and 53:2–18 that may refer to or elide Bukhari's report into
the third vision.[22]

Gabriel became a frequent presence in Muhammad's mission. The
second transformative vision triggered the same reaction as the first, terror and escape. It commanded and encouraged Muhammad to live purely,
avoid idolatry, and deliver the message that glorifies God and calls his fellow Meccans—and through them all humans—to prepare for the Judgment. From this point on, the revelations increased in intensity and became
more public. The second vision gave Muhammad an empowering energy
and widened as well as deepened his receptivity to further and fuller revelations. One of its imports was to push him to proclaim the One-Only God
to the people and leaders of Mecca no matter how they might respond.
Still, Muhammad kept relatively quiet about his insights and experiences.
During that time, however, word about the Message spread among limited
numbers of his fellow Meccans, and some gave themselves to the Message
and the Messenger.

THE NARRATIVE ABOUT MUHAMMAD:
THE PROCLAMATION IN MECCA

Glorify the name of thy Guardian-Lord Most High Who
hath created and further given order and proportion;
Who hath ordained laws. And granted guidance; And
Who bringeth out the (green and luscious) pasture. And
then doth make it (but) swarthy stubble. By degrees shall
We teach thee to declare (the Message) so thou shalt not
forget Except as Allah wills: For He knoweth what is
manifest and what is hidden. And We will make it easy
for thee (to follow) the simple (Path) Therefore give
admonition in case the admonition profits (the hearer).
The admonition will be received by those who fear (Allah):
But it will be avoided by those most unfortunate ones.
Who will enter the Great Fire in which they will then
neither die nor live. But those will prosper who purify
themselves. And glorify the name of their Guardian-Lord
and (lift their hearts) in Prayer. Nay (behold) ye prefer the
life of this world; But the Hereafter is better and more
enduring. And this is in the Books of the earliest
(Revelations) The Books of Abraham and Moses.

Surah 87, al-A'la, the Most High

In 613 Muhammad and his followers began to speak and teach publicly.
The Qurayshi leaders reacted sharply against the thoroughgoing monotheism and its socioeconomic implications. The Message Muhammad
received and which he sought to enact demanded a total revision of religious thinking and practice, with accompanying changes in individual piety,
family life, commercial relations, and communal organization. While some
residual forms remained from the traditional ways, such as the Ka'bah
and the pilgrimage to Mecca, their content and intent were transformed.

Islam demands uncompromising monotheism, and that entailed the total elimination of the previous ilahas and a fundamentally different understanding of the once-vague Allah. Among the earliest converts was the wealthy Abu Bakr (also Bekr); the tall Ethiopian slave, Bilal; and a number of young men. From its very start the umma included women, the aged, the young, slaves, free persons, the poor, the wealthy, and at least one Christian. The spectrum of believers foreshadows Islam's openness to all people. Faith in the One-Only God, His Messenger, and the Qur'an bound the umma together and gave it the impetus to embrace others.

Mounting Qurayshi opposition became increasing violent, as well as subtle. Muhammad's insistence on religious and moral change was not only economically and socially objectionable. His way entailed breaking with the traditions of the ancestors and risking the wrath of the ilahas. After a number of followers were assaulted, eighty Muslims left to take refuge with the Christian king of Ethiopia (615). Among the refugees were Muhammad's daughter, Ruqayyah, and her husband, Uthman. The Meccan surahs reflect the conflicts and Muhammad's need to be reassured that he was speaking God's word of hope and judgment. Between 616 and 618 the Qurayshi authorities tried to silence Muhammad by penalizing the Hashim clan, banning them from some commercial activity.

Ibn Ishaq reported an account that Muslims consider a blasphemous lie.[23] In essence, the story is that the Qurayshi promised to convert to Islam if Muhammad gave some sort of recognition to the three ilahas termed the "daughters of Allah." The Messenger was eager for his kinfolk and fellow Meccans to be saved on the Day of Judgment by becoming Muslims. The story continues that under an apparent inspiration, he provided several ayas that seemed to approve veneration of the "daughters." The Muslims were shocked when they heard what happened because the ayas clearly breached the strict monotheism Muhammad had been proclaiming. Soon, however, Gabriel revealed to him that the ayas were due to Shaytan. These are the so-called Satanic Verses. Having been given the proper inspiration, Muhammad proclaimed:

Have ye seen al-Lat and Uzza and another, the third (goddess), Manat? What! For you the male sex and for Him the female? Behold such would be indeed a division most unfair! These are nothing but names which ye have devised ye and your fathers for which Allah has sent down no authority (whatever). They follow nothing but conjecture and what their own souls desire! Even though there has already come to them Guidance from their Lord! Nay, shall man have (just) anything he hankers after? But it is to Allah that the End and the Beginning (of all things) belong. (Surah 53:19–25)

The Qurayshi now intensified their opposition to Muhammad even as the Message of Islam spread to other settlements and among the bedouin. The next Qurayshi step was to isolate, then attempt to kill Muhammad.

THE NARRATIVE ABOUT MUHAMMAD:
THE YEAR OF SADNESS

The aptly named Year of Sadness, 619, was a time of spiritual, personal, and communal crises for Muhammad. Muhammad's uncle Abu Talib, respected head of the Hashim clan, was someone other Qurayshi dared not attack directly. Although he never became a Muslim, he protected Muhammad as much as possible even when the clan suffered a Qurashi-generated economic boycott. But in 619 the old man died. Muhammad not only lost his shield; he also lost one of the last relatives of his family of origin. As he sought to recover from grief, his beloved Khadijah died. She had supported him unstintingly throughout the dangerous time since 610. Now Muhammad was orphaned, widowed, and vulnerable. His and the lives of the Meccan Muslims were in danger. Clearly, he and the umma had to leave their city. Yet he knew that the Meccan authorities would attack them if they left openly. He thought Taif, a city southeast of Mecca, might receive him and the umma. Buoyed by such hopes, Muhammad journeyed there to arrange for refuge. But Taif was a shrine center for the ilah al-Lat. Muhammad was scorned and pelted out of town.

On the return from Taif, he camped overnight and took comfort by reciting the Qur'an. According to Muslim tradition this was the occasion for the revelation of Surah 72:

Say: It has been revealed to me that a company of Jinn listened (to the Qur'an). They say "We have really heard a wonderful Recital! It gives guidance to the Right and we have believed therein: We shall not join (in worship) any (gods) with our Lord. And exalted is the majesty of our Lord: He has taken neither a wife nor a son. There were some foolish ones among us who used to utter extravagant lies against Allah; But we do think that no man or spirit should say aught that is untrue against Allah. True there were persons among mankind who took shelter with persons among the Jinn but they increased them in folly. And they (came to) think as ye thought that Allah would not raise up anyone (to Judgment). And we pried into the secrets of heaven; but we found it filled with stern guards and flaming fires. We used indeed to sit there in (hidden) stations to (steal) a hearing; but any who listens now will find a flaming fire watching him in ambush. And we understand not whether ill is intended to those on earth or whether their Lord (really) intends to guide them to right conduct. There are among us some that are righteous and some the contrary: we follow divergent paths. But we think that we can by no means frustrate Allah throughout the earth nor can we frustrate Him by flight. And as for us since we have listened to the Guidance we have accepted it: and any who believes in his Lord has no fear either of a short (account) or of any injustice. Amongst us are some that submit their wills (to Allah) and some that swerve from justice." Now those who submit their wills, they have sought out (the path) of right conduct: But those who swerve, they are (but) fuel for Hell Fire. (Surah 72:1–15, al-Jinn, the Jinn)

In the midst of sorrow, rejection by humans, and danger from his own tribe, Muhammad retained his faith in God and God's mission for him. Even the lower spiritual beings responded to the new revelation of the Qur'an. They had pried into and failed to understand the will of God, yet somehow this human was the recipient and speaker of the True Guidance for angels and humans. On returning to Mecca and sleeping near the Ka'bah one night, Muhammad had the third transforming vision-experience, the Night Journey to al-Masjid al-Aqsa, the Farthest Mosque, and the Ascent to Heaven:

Glory to (Allah) Who did take His Servant for Journey by night from
the Sacred Mosque to the Farthest Mosque whose precincts We did
bless in order that We might show him some of Our Signs: for He is
the one Who heareth and seeth (all things). (Surah 17:1)

According to the hadiths, the Night Journey and Ascent to Heaven
(al-Isra wa-al-Mi'raj) began with Gabriel awakening Muhammad and
mounting him on the special steed, Buraq.[24] At the Farthest Mosque, traditionally identified with the ruins of Solomon's Temple in Jerusalem, Muhammad and Gabriel ascended through the seven heavens into the closest
proximity to God yet achieved by any human and every celestial creature
except Gabriel. On the way he was greeted by the heavenly gatekeepers: Adam, Jesus, John the Baptist, Joseph, Enoch, Aaron, Abraham, and
Moses. After receiving detailed instructions about prayer and other matters, he returned to Mecca—all this in the same instant.

The jinn and journey experiences were crucial to his mission. Rejected, despised and threatened, grieving and vulnerable, his recitation of
the Qur'an brought willing spiritual beings into an obedient and joyful relationship with God and exposed rebellious jinn as deceivers who would
be damned. The journey-ascent vision-experience had a threefold effect.
The first involved the place of the ascent and the figures he met as he ascended. The Temple Mount (al-Haram ash-Sharif) had been the locus of
worship for Canaanites, Israelites-Jews, Greeks, Romans, and Christians.
When Muhammad arrived, ascended, and returned from the presence of
the One-Only God, all the previous religions were corrected by, fulfilled
through, and subsumed into Islam; the Scriptures of those faiths were now
to be properly understood and purified by the being-revealed Qur'an;
and all the previous prophets and messengers of those religious systems
were fulfilled and surpassed in Muhammad. Second, Muhammad's close
approach to God and the instruction he received, according to the hadith,
provided the basis for the Pillars and the Teachings. He had received confirmation and extensions of that which he had started to proclaim and which
he would put into action for the umma. Third, the vision-experience clarified and extended his mission. Up to that point he had been called to
receive and proclaim the Revelation and then to carry it to the Arabs,

especially the Meccans. The Night Journey and Ascent authorized and empowered him to take the Message of the truly first and ultimate din to all humanity. He could leave idol-polluted Mecca confident that the One-Only God would triumph.

The Year of Sadness was changing. Mecca's commercial rival, the city of Yathrib, was in turmoil. Located some two hundred miles north of Mecca, Yathrib was a key center on the caravan route. Civil strife had broken out among Yathrib's two major tribes, the Aws and Khazraj. Large Jewish tribes or communal groups (the Nadir, Qaynuqa, and Qurayzah) in the city and nearby area also were involved in the often-violent struggles. Clearly no single group would be able to dominate the others. One option was to hand authority to an outsider. During the Hajj in 619, six members of Yathrib's Khazraj tribe met Muhammad in Mecca and professed Islam.

THE NARRATIVE ABOUT MUHAMMAD:
HIJRA AND THE BEGINNING OF THE MUSLIM ERA

In the course of 621 and 622 relations with Yathrib developed through two treaties, whereupon Muhammad and his followers were invited to settle in Yathrib and Muhammad was given the authority to resolve its civil differences. In effect, whether or not the parties to the treaties intended it, Muhammad was to become the city's head. At least one Qurayshi-devised assassination attempt was thwarted by divine intervention, and Muhammad made plans for the umma and himself to leave Mecca. About seventy Muslims gradually left Mecca for Yathrib. Beginning on the night of July 15, 622, Muhammad, Ali, and Abu Bakr undertook the journey, which involved hiding in a cave to outwit their pursuers. The Messenger arrived in Yathrib in September. The Hijra, or Migration, had taken place.

The Hijra is crucial: the Muslim era and calendar date from it, and it marks the beginning of the umma as a religious-political entity. Yathrib soon came to be known as Medina al-Nabi, the City of the Prophet. Many of its Aws and Khazraj as well as Jews and Christians thought they could use the Messenger for their own goals once he restored some semblance of order to their city. Those who gave lip service to Islam but worked behind the scenes to oppose him and Islam are called Hypocrites in the Qur'an (e.g., Surah 2:8–18). Residents in Yathrib-Medina who were sincere converts to Islam and supported Muhammad were called Helpers (*ansari*), while those who emigrated from Mecca are Emigrants (*muhajirun*); and his close Meccan collaborators are Companions (sing. *sahib*, pl. *ashab*). Because Mecca was the holy city and the Ka'bah the holy place, Muhammad always intended to return to Mecca—but in triumph even if that meant combat. His actions flushed the Hypocrites from among the true Helpers, making the dissemblers vulnerable to often-fatal punishments. Initially, he thought the Jews and Christians in Medina would accept Islam as the true faith, the Qur'an as the final revelation, and himself as the last prophet-messenger. Some did, but most remained aloof, or argued with him, or plotted against him.

Muhammad steadily, yet carefully, advanced his program for societal transformation and personal devotion to the One-Only God in Medina. Gradually he put into action the Quranically revealed prohibitions against alcohol consumption, gambling, usurious interest rates, spousal abuse, and mistreatment of orphans. He introduced the Zakat for caring for the poor, limited the number of wives a man might marry, and established conditions for the fair treatment of wives. At first he and the Muslims joined the Jews (and possibly the Christians) in facing Jerusalem when praying. That was to change under God's direction. He urged all Medinans to become Muslims and apparently eliminated any idols in the city. The obligatory prayers were established. Bilal, the tall Ethiopian, was called the Living Minaret because he was the one who usually gave the call to the salat prayers.

In terms of Muhammad's personal life, Ali and Fatimah were also by his side, along with faithful Abu Bakr. Shortly after the Hijra, Muhammad married Aisha, Abu Bakr's young daughter. She and his other wives, called the Mothers of the Faithful, are considered in more detail in chapter 11. Whatever friends or critics may have thought of his religious experiences and civic leadership, Muhammad was highly regarded as an honorable man, a person of impeccable character and sincere humility. His policies, faith, and courage would soon be tested, as would the entire Muslim din.

THE NARRATIVE ABOUT MUHAMMAD:
THE UMMA STRUGGLES, 624–630

Muhammad knew that the Meccans would not allow Medina to harbor the man who opposed them on deeply religious and political grounds. Hostilities were inevitable. Muhammad opted to strike first. In 624 CE/ 2 AH, in violation of a traditional "peace month" and perhaps because of a miscalculation by a commander of a Muslim patrol, a Meccan caravan was attacked and several Meccans killed near the settlement of Nakhlah. After some initial consternation on the part of the Messenger and the Muslims involved, God disclosed that the assault and others like it were permissible:

> They ask thee concerning fighting in the Prohibited Month. Say: "Fighting therein is a grave (offence); but graver is it in the sight of Allah to prevent access to the path of Allah to deny Him to prevent access to the Sacred Mosque and drive out its members. Tumult and oppression are worse than slaughter. Nor will they cease fighting you until they turn you back from your faith if they can. And if any of you turn back from their faith and die in unbelief their works will bear no fruit in this life and in the Hereafter; they will be Companions of the Fire and will abide therein. Those who believed and those who suffered exile and fought (and strove and struggled) in the path of Allah they have the hope of the Mercy of Allah; and Allah is Oft-Forgiving Most Merciful. (Surah 2:217–18)

In short, if the Faith and umma were endangered or blocked from expressing their faith, then ordinary prohibitions may be lifted. The raid also served notice on the Meccans that Muhammad would no longer abide by their traditions and that they could expect further actions that would endanger Meccan prosperity. The Medinans who opposed Muhammad were acutely aware that other Arabs far outnumbered them and would retaliate by attacking their city. An engagement at Badr Springs (March 623, about ninety miles south of Medina) began as a Medinan raid on a Meccan caravan but escalated into a full-scale battle. Promised victory in a dream that a thousand angels would fight with the Faithful, Muhammad devised his battle plan. Outnumbered by nearly 1,000 Meccans and their allies, the 305-man Medinan-Muslim force won a resounding victory that was seen as a sign of God's favor and an endorsement of Muhammad's leadership:

> Say to those who reject Faith: "Soon will ye be vanquished and gathered together to hell an evil bed indeed (to lie on). There has already been for you a sign in the two armies that met (in combat): one was fighting in the cause of Allah, the other resisting Allah; these saw with their own eyes twice their number. But Allah doth support with His aid whom He pleaseth. In this is a warning for such as have eyes to see." (Surah 3:12–13)[25]

Several notorious Meccan prisoners were executed and others ransomed. Because Medinian opponents plus some Jewish and Christians worked against Muhammad and his supporters prior to and during the battle, the Messenger-General-Ruler contemplated their punishment and, under inspiration, changed the qiblah from Jerusalem to Mecca. That act indicated that he stopped expecting large-scale Jewish and Christian conversions to Islam. Instead, he would focus on returning to Mecca, making it the center for God's restored religion (Surah 2:142–52). The change in the orientation while praying is also a political-military statement: Muhammad will return, and he will, with God's help, purify the Ka'bah and restore it to what Abraham promised it would be: the center for true religion.

As a result of the victory at Badr, Muhammad also was given a revelation about the "spoils of war." Surah 8:1–4, 41–44, mandated that such booty belongs to God. The Messenger and the widows and near-relatives of the fallen and their orphans are to receive 20 percent, and the balance is to be shared equitably among God's victorious soldiers and noncombatants who stayed in the city to maintain order.[26] Plunder was never to be a cause for war.

The next engagement, on the slopes and plain of Mount Uhud (625), had a different outcome. Enthusiasm and greed among those who disobeyed the strict discipline demanded by and the strategy developed by Muhammad rather than the evident treachery and double-dealing of supposed allies led to the defeat of the Muslim troops. A lust for plunder and blatant disobedience of Muhammad's orders almost led to the destruction of all the Medinan forces and nearly the death of the Messenger. The Meccans, however, were unable to pursue and destroy the Muslim forces: Muhammad himself was wounded in the conflict (Surah 3:121–29).

The Meccans, emboldened by their tactical victory at Uhud, determined to finish the conflict. To that end they entered into a series of alliances with other tribes. The result was the so-called War of the Confederates. In May 627 the Meccans and their allies amassed an army of nine thousand men. Further, they engaged in secret negotiations with several bedouin tribes, the Jewish tribes of Nadir (settled in nearby Khaybar), and the Qurayzah. Most of Surah 33, Al Ahzab (the Confederates), comments on the ensuing engagement. Prior to the twenty-four- to twenty-seven-day conflict, three hundred Medinans refused to fight for the Muslim cause because their leaders disagreed with the Messenger's strategy. The Muslims, however, shrewdly sowed discord among the Qurayshi and the Qurayzah. The Messenger accepted the Persian tactic of surrounding the defensive position with a deep trench or moat, then a torrential three-day rainstorm saved the Muslims from defeat. The resulting Battle of the Trench, or Ditch, was a protracted struggle in which the Meccans and their allies, worn down by discouragement, retreated. That retreat meant a Muslim victory. The aftermath was catastrophic for the Jewish communities. According to Muslim tradition, the angel Gabriel commanded Muhammad to attack the Qurayzah. As was the standard military custom, the surviving men were massacred and the women and children sold into slavery. The Nadir Jewish settlement at Khaybar was destroyed in 628. In both instances their property was confiscated and added to the umma's expanding treasury. All Hypocrites and People of the Book were duly warned of the consequences of betraying God's cause and the Messenger (Surah 33:25–27).

Events following the Battle of the Trench moved quickly. The Meccans recognized that they could not defeat Muhammad and were unable to sustain the conflict economically. Numerous desert tribes proclaimed their loyalty to Muhammad and professed Islam. He even sent troops to the northern border with Byzantine Palestine. Soon the rest of Arabia would accept the Message or at any rate the Messenger. The Meccans and their allies negotiated an accommodation with the Messenger. In March 628 the Treaty of Hudaybiyyah was concluded by emissaries of both sides whereby the Muslims were given access to Mecca for the next year's Hajj, and a truce was declared between the Medinans and the Confederates. The Meccans agreed to withdraw from the city to nearby hills while the Believers completed their pilgrimage. Almost at the same time, God's Messenger sent his messengers to the rulers of Persia, Byzantium, Ethiopia, Egypt, and Yemen. In seven years Muhammad and the umma went from Hijra to Hajj to issuing international communiqués.

THE NARRATIVE ABOUT MUHAMMAD: VICTORY AND DEATH

In 629, under the conditions of the treaty and absent the Messenger, the Muslims entered Mecca for the Hajj. The Meccans retired to the nearby hills to avoid hostile incidents. They saw the Faithful circumambulate the Ka'bah and, for the first time, heard the call to prayer proclaimed from the Ka'bah. Muhammad, aware of his mission to spread the Message as well as the Byzantine refusal to pay heed to his ultimatum, sent an expedition northward into present-day Jordan. The enemy surprised the Muslims and drove them back at Mu'tah. The Muslim commander, Muhammad's close friend, Zayd ibn al-Harith, was killed. He was replaced by Khalid bin Walid, the leader whom the Messenger called the "Sword of Allah," a title that he fulfilled in later campaigns. The foray into Jordan had two effects: it alerted the Byzantines that there was an aggressive force on their southeastern flank; and it made the outlying desert bedouin tribes realize that Muhammad and his troops intended to unify and control the peninsula. The bedouin could either join the Muslims or meet the Sword of Allah.

Toward the end of 629 a series of skirmishes between bedouin affiliated with the Meccans and Medinans gave the Messenger the opportunity to declare that the Treaty of Hudaybiyyah's truce had been breached.

His soldiers moved against the city. On 20 Ramadan AH 8 (January 630), the Muslims captured Mecca after little resistance. Following Muhammad's orders, there were few reprisals, and many inhabitants converted. The Faithful purified the Ka'bah, casting out the idols. Khalid, under the Messenger's orders, destroyed the shrines of the goddesses Manat and al-Uzza. The Messenger himself led a successful expedition against Taif, the city that had humiliated him, and saw to the destruction of the shrines. The leveling of the ilahah's holy places and the purging of the Ka'bah signaled to many Arab tribes that the One-Only God of Islam was victorious over all other beings. Consequently many converted to the new faith. They sent representatives to Mecca in 630 (now 9 AH) to register their acceptance; therefore 9 AH is termed the Year of the Deputations. But to what did they convert? Was it to obedience to God or loyalty to Muhammad? In April when the tribes were visited by Muslim Zakat tax collectors, the tribesmen realized that they literally had to pay a price for their new religion.

From October through December 630 Muhammad led an expedition across the desert to Tabuk near the Gulf of Aqaba in Palestine in order to drive the Byzantines from the region. Either his informants erred about the presence of a large Christian army or the imperial troops withdrew, for there was no battle. The northern tribes again experienced the new authority of the aging Messenger. He concluded some treaties with Christian and pagan chieftains in the area. On his return he discovered that some critics had established a mosque without his permission. Their persistence indicates that the movement centered on the Messenger was not monolithic. He and especially his successors would be challenged.

Soon polytheists who had remained loyal to their religions while collaborating with Muhammad faced a harsh reality. In 631 they were prohibited from participating in the Hajj. God gave them four months' notice from the last day of the Hajj: become Muslims, or fight, or leave the land:

> O ye who believe! Truly the pagans are unclean; so let them not after this year of theirs approach the Sacred Mosque. And if ye fear poverty, soon will Allah enrich you if He wills out of his bounty for Allah is All-Knowing, All-Wise. Fight those who believe not in Allah nor the Last Day nor hold that forbidden which hath been forbidden by

Allah and His apostle nor acknowledge the religion of truth (even if they are) of the People of the Book until they pay the Jizya with willing submission and feel themselves subdued. (Surah 9: 28–29)

Attitudes were hardening against non-Muslims as Muhammad and his fellow Muslims consolidated their authority and power in Arabia. The jizya, or poll tax, enabled the People of the Book to live under Muslim governments provided they did not spread their religions or criticize Islam. This became the policy in the lands brought into the Muslim orbit, but because of Arabia's place as the supremely holy land, all non-Muslims were expelled from Arabia in 635.

The last year of the Messenger's life, 632, was marked by success and tragedy. In January his only surviving son, Ibrahim, died. In March the sixty-two-year-old former merchant returned to Mecca for his first Hajj in a decade—and it proved to be his last. On the ninth day of Dhu l-Hijjah, the Great Day, and at the plain of Arafat, while on what is now called the Mount of Compassion, he received the last Quranic revelation, and through him God said:

This day have those who reject Faith given up all hope of your religion. Yet fear them not but fear Me. This day have I perfected your religion for you, completed My favor upon you, and have chosen for you Islam as your religion. But if any is forced by hunger, with no inclination to transgression, Allah is indeed Oft-Forgiving, Most Merciful. (Surah 5:3)

In his last sermon, cherished by Muslims then and now, he said:

O People, listen to me in earnest, worship Allah, say your five daily prayers, fast during the month of Ramadan, and give your wealth in Zakat. Perform Hajj if you can afford to. You know that every Muslim is the brother of another Muslim. You are all equal. Nobody has superiority over another except by piety and good action. Remember, one day you will appear before Allah and answer for your deeds. So beware, do not go astray from the path of righteousness after I am gone. O People, no prophet or Messenger will come after me and no new faith will be born. Reason well, therefore, O People, and understand my words which I convey to you. I leave behind me two things, the Qur'an and my example, the Sunna, and if you follow these you will never go astray. All those who listen to me shall pass on my words to others and those to others again; and may the last ones understand my words better than those who listen to me directly. Be my witness, O Allah, that I have conveyed your message to your people.[27]

A week later, at Ghadir Khum, he met with a Muslim army commanded by Ali. The force was returning from an encounter with the Yemenis in the course of which Ali was criticized for his harshness. Muhammad defended his son-in-law in terms that suggested to many that Ali had been designated the next leader of the umma. The exhausted Bearer of the Revelation returned to Medina, where he died in the arms of his wife, Aisha, on June 8, 632 (12 Rabi al-Awad, AH 11). Almost immediately rivalries about the next leader surfaced. Although his friend-Companion and the father of Aisha, Abu Bakr, was acclaimed khalifah, or successor, a party favoring Ali (*shi'at-Ali*) formed.

AN APPRECIATION

Beginning with the Night of Power, the final Messenger was filled with the Qur'an. He and the community gathered about him provided the model for the great umma that would change the world until the dawning of the Last Day. They lived in the Time that transcended all times before and since. Muhammad is the man who was prepared for the ultimate Revelation and on him and only him did it descend. The Qur'an is inseparable from the man from Mecca and from the time and style of his life. Quranic and subsequent Islamic views of inspiration mandate that although Muhammad was a human who did not become divine, he was no mere channel through which the words of Allah passed. Instead, Muhammad, the hero of the Faith, is the model beyond all models for humanity; he is the living evidence and pattern for Quranically shaped life. Not only when he was in a revelatory mode but also in all his words, gestures, actions, and relationships, Muhammad is the human epitome of Islam: "Ye have indeed in the Messenger of Allah a beautiful pattern (of conduct) for any whose hope is in Allah and the Final Day, and who engages much in the praise of Allah" (Surah 33:21). So from the Qur'an and the Messenger's last sermon, Muslims—indeed, all persons—are to study and emulate his Sunna, that is, his example, words, and deeds. These transcend time to guide, encourage, and validate the claim that obedience to God through the Qur'an is incumbent on everyone.

Muhammad was the human for all humans. The time from 610 to 632 serves as the archetype for all subsequent time, personal devotion, and communities. It seemed that all that remained until the Day of Judgment is to recite, hear, interpret, and live the Qur'an's gracious message.

THE TESTING TIME

Although the Testing Time is not formally part of Quranic time, it is important for being the period when the proclaimed Qur'an became a written document. The initial months and years after the Messenger's death were fraught with tensions, conflicts, and, finally, the collation of the Qur'an. Abu Bakr had to contend with both establishing his authority within the umma and rebels, apostates, and claimants to prophethood in Arabia. Several bedouin tribes refused to pay taxes to Medina, claiming their allegiance was to Muhammad and not to his successors. A number of tribes also repudiated Islam. At the same time other prophets, chiefly a man named Maslamah, became prominent. They announced that they were the true messengers of God. A number of bloody battles were fought before Maslamah's adherents were smashed by a Khalid-led army (633) and the rival prophet himself slain at Aqrabah. The butcher's bill for the battle included seven hundred Companions, a number of whom were closely associated with the Messenger.[28] This drastic reduction in the number of those who had heard him recite the Qur'an helped to spur the realization that an official version of the Revelation needed to be compiled.[29] These so-called Wars of Apostasy spread to Oman and Yemen but ended in Muslim victories by 635. Undeterred by struggles in Arabia, Abu Bakr obeyed Muhammad's instruction to launch campaigns against the Byzantines and Persians. The summons delivered to the nations in 628 was more than fulfilled by 650: the Believers took all of Palestine and Syria, began the conquest of Egypt, ruled most of southern Mesopotamia, and unified the Arabian Peninsula under their rule. God seemed to be preparing the way for the spread of Islam. The Byzantine emperor Heraclius died, Byzantium declined, and Persia was in disarray. Given access to the sea and caravan routes and commercial centers in Syria, Arab-led Islam expanded through trade as well as conquest.

Success and expansion did not ensure harmony and unity among the Faithful. Before his death from natural causes in 634, Abu Bakr designated Umar (Omar) the next caliph. Ali and his supporters were disappointed but raised no significant opposition. After the Muslim conquest of Jerusalem in 637, Umar put Ali in charge of Medina and went to Jerusalem. He cleared the Temple Mount, the sacred space that dated to Canaanite and Abrahamic as well as Solomonic times, where Jesus taught and Muhammad ascended through the heavens. Almost a decade later, in 644, Umar was assassinated, but Uthman, rather than Ali, was chosen by the umma's leaders to be caliph. The number of Companions and Helpers who knew and heard the Messenger dwindled further, and rumors of different citations of the Revelation, especially among Ali's supporters in Persia, circulated. Uthman convened the core group that brought together the memories and items on which the Revelation was written. The result of their work was the written Qur'an, ca. 650. The story of its collation is traced in chapter 6.

THE TIME CAME and went. The final and fullest Revelation started with the Night of Power and ended with the death of Muhammad. Since the true Faith has been given in its perfect form, now the Message requires application and interpretation in the circumstances and societies in which people live. Application and interpretation rely first and foremost on the Qur'an interpreting itself, then through examining the Sunna of the Messenger and the first umma. That process led to the development of Islamic law. While the term *Shari'ah* does not appear in the Qur'an, it embraces the intellectual examination, the jurisprudential reasoning by analogies and precedents, the consensus of recognized pious scholars (the *ulamah*), and the lives of men and women in the believing community (umma).

The period from Muhammad's death through the present and into the future looks back to the twenty-two years of revelation, the Messenger's Sunna, and the shape of the umma he established. Believers look forward to the Day of Judgment. Devout Muslims seek to structure their lives, families, and wider communities so as to gain a place in the heaven promised by God. At the same time, because time is running out, the Qur'an and Muhammad's Sunna impel believers to extend the realm of belief throughout God's world. We now approach the Qur'an itself.

By the (winds) sent forth one after another (to man's profit): which then blow violently in tempestuous gusts, and scatter things far and wide; then separate them one from another, then spread abroad a Message whether of justification or of warning—assuredly, what ye are promised must come to pass. Then when the stars become dim; when the heaven is cleft asunder; when the mountains are scattered (to the winds) as dust; and when the messengers are (all) appointed a time (to collect)—for what Day are these (portents) deferred? For the Day of Sorting Out. Ah, woe that day to the rejecters of Truth! Did We not destroy the men of old (for their evil)? So shall we make later (generations) follow them. Thus do We deal with men of sin. Ah woe, that day to the rejecters of truth! (Surah 77:1–19, al-Muralat, Those Sent Forth)

SIX

THE ORIGIN, TRANSMISSION, AND STRUCTURES OF THE QUR'AN

This Qur'an is not such as can be produced by other than
Allah; On the contrary, it is a confirmation of (revelations)
that went before it, and a fuller explanation of the Book—
wherein there is no doubt—from the Lord of the Worlds.
Or do they say, "He forged it"? Say [Muhammad]: "Bring
then a surah like unto it, and call (to your aid) anyone you
can, besides Allah, if it be ye speak the Truth!"

Surah 10:37–38

What is the Qur'an? The answers to this question range from an expression
of a celestial tablet disclosed by an angel to an account of an individual
displaying signs of psychological excitations or of virtually official memorizers or scribes writing on dry bones to the consensus of an editorial committee. All have their place, but no one reply covers the whole. What the
Qur'an is can only be approached with a willingness to engage it on different levels and then to listen to it. Answering the question is an opportunity for the devout to express their faith, earn merit toward salvation, and
be inspired to do God's will. When the question is posed to unbelievers,
the Qur'an itself points them to self-examination and consideration of
their fates on the Day of Judgment. Throughout the chapter, the question

is asked in order to lead us to yet further answers and to explore the Qur'an's structure.

THE LENGTH AND BREADTH OF THE QUR'AN

The Qur'an contains 114 surahs of uneven lengths that are divided into ayat, also of uneven lengths. Each surah has a traditional title. The Qur'an is about 80 percent of the length of the New Testament and substantially shorter than the Hebrew Bible.

> These are ayat of the Qur'an, a Book that makes (things) clear; a Guide; and Glad Tidings for the Believers, those who establish regular prayers, and give in regular charity, and also have (full) assurance of the Hereafter. As to those who believe not in the Hereafter, We have made their deeds pleasing in their eyes; and so they wander about in distraction. Such are they for whom a grievous Penalty is (waiting): and, in the Hereafter, theirs will be the greatest loss. As to thee, the Qur'an is bestowed upon thee from the presence of One Who is Wise and All-Knowing. (Surah 27:1–6, al-Namal, the Ants)

The word *surah* is linked to progress and is used in the Qur'an at several points to indicate its content (e.g., Surahs 2:23; 10:38; 11:13; 52:34).[1] Surahs are characterized by the frequent use of rhymed prose and occasional refrains. In Surah 55, for example, the refrain "Then which of the favors of your Lord will ye deny?" appears thirty-one times in seventy-eight ayas. Because *aya* can mean "sign" or "pointer" the words of the Qur'an are more than words in a surah. Each aya is a sign pointing to God's One-Only-ness and purposes, and each surah is a step toward coming to know, surrender to, and do God's will. Each surah, with the exception of Surah 9, begins with the Basmillah, "In the Name of God, Most Gracious, Most Merciful."[2] The current and most widely used text of the Qur'an is the 1925 Cairo edition. After Surah 1, al-Fatihah, it does not count the Basmillah as a separate aya. The Cairo edition has 6,240 ayas, but several editions have more and some have fewer.[3]

Surahs 2–79 have been divided into sections, each called a *ruku'*. Surah 2, for example, has the most (40 ruku's), and Surahs 1 and 80–114 have none. The latter surahs are associated chiefly with Mecca, whereas Surahs 2–79 are linked to Medina, as well as to Mecca. The scholar-interpreters who made the ruku' divisions apparently recognized that subjects shifted from one portion to another. Nevertheless, ayas in a ruku' are considered related to each other, and all ruku's in the surah are viewed as forming a whole.[4]

PORTIONS TO FACILITATE READING AND LISTENING

Muslim dedication to the Qur'an has led to facilitating its reading and recitation by distinguishing portions to be read at certain times. These portions are the result of scholarly efforts and are not part of the Qur'an itself. Marginal markings often indicate where one portion starts and stops. The most common portion is the *juz* (part, pl. *ajza*). A juz is one-thirtieth of the Quranic text. It is recommended that Muslims read or hear the entire Qur'an in the course of thirty days and then begin it again. Especially during the month of Ramadan, the devout read a juz each day. Because the ajza are all the same length, a juz may end in the midst of an account, in which case reader-listener resumes the next day. Two other, larger designated portions are the *hizb* (pl. *ahzab*) and the *manzil* (pl. *manazil*). The former constitutes one-fourth and the latter one-seventh of the Qur'an.[5] Some Muslim scholars see the surahs in pairs; that is, each pair helps to interpret the other in the context of the whole Qur'an. In addition, frequently each surah is seen as having a central point or axis that serves as the key to interpreting the whole surah.[6]

HIGHLIGHTED SURAHS AND AYAS

Many Muslims posit that since the Qur'an is the Word of God from start to finish, each word carries the same authority, and it is not necessary to interpret passages in the context of when they were revealed (called "occasions of revelation"). We return to the matter of context in chapter 7. Some surahs and ayas are regarded as especially meaningful. Al-Fatihah, the first surah, is perhaps the most important from the standpoint of daily practice and worship. It is to be memorized in Arabic and included in every prayer. A Muslim who prays the obligatory Salat prayers says al-Fatihah seventeen times a day. Al-Fatihah is often called the Essence of the Qur'an. The comprehensive Surah 2, al-Baqarah, is the Outline of Qur'an. Surah 12, Yusuf, is "the most beautiful story" (12:3). Surah 36, Ya Sin, the Heart of the Qur'an, is particularly meaningful for persons who are in danger because of their faith or are near death. Surah 112, al-Ikhlas, is called one-third of the Qur'an on the basis of a charming tradition.[7]

TWO PUZZLES

Among numerous subjects that draw attention and speculation, two are especially noteworthy, the Abbreviated, or Disunited, Letters (al-Muqatt'at) and the Seven Mathani. Twenty-nine surahs, most of them associated with Muhammad's time in Mecca, open with one or more letters of the Arabic alphabet, and several (20, 36, 38, 41, 50) surahs are named for those letters.[8] Speculations about the Muqatt'at assume that every letter and word in the Qur'an is part of God's divine revelation. Yusuf Ali reflects the general consensus that the letters have a mystical meaning and purpose that will be disclosed eventually by God, for the "whole Book is a record for all time. It must necessarily contain truths that only gradually unfold themselves to humanity."[9] The Muqatt'at provide significant material for esoteric considerations, especially among mystically oriented individuals and groups.

The Seven Mathani passage in Surah 15, al-Hijr, presents another puzzle:

And We have bestowed upon thee the Seven Oft-Repeated *mathani* and the Grand Qur'an. Strain not thine eyes (wistfully) at what We have bestowed on certain classes of them nor grieve over them: but lower thy wing (in gentleness) to the Believers. And say: "I am indeed he that warneth openly and without ambiguity." (Of just such wrath)

as We sent down on those who divided (Scripture into arbitrary parts).
(So also on such) as have made the Qur'an into shreds (as they please).
(15:87—91)

Yusuf Ali renders *mathani* as *ayat*. The word, however, means side-by-side,
two-by-two, and repetition. What are mathani? As may be anticipated, there
are numerous views.[10] Most feel that the seven special and repeated items
are the seven ayas of al-Fatihah. Others suggest they are the seven longest
surahs, or the supposed seven parts of the Qur'an, or the seven scrolls on
which the Qur'an was said to have been written, or the seven "books" disclosed by previous messengers (Adam, Noah, Abraham, Moses, David, Jesus,
and Hud), or the whole Qur'an (because the number seven signifies com-
pleteness), or seven punishment stories recounted in the Qur'an.[11] Other
proposals are that the mathani are seven Quranic themes (command, inter-
dict, proclamation of good tidings, warning, striking similitudes, God's blessings, and accounts of previous generations), or Surahs 20—26 (called collectively *al-Mufassal*). As with the Abbreviated Letters, the mathani remain
a mystery and a source of devout consideration and mystical contemplation.

PLACES OF REVELATION

All surahs are connected with either Mecca or Medina, although hadith
traditions hold that some ayas were revealed elsewhere, such as during
the Messenger's return from Taif. Some surahs and passages reflect clearly
where and when they were revealed. For example, Surah 3:13 refers to the
Battle of Badr, and Surah 90 addresses Mecca's leaders when Muhammad
was still in the city. Modern non-Muslim scholars have attempted to identify some of the Meccan surahs as being revealed early in the Messenger's
activity, or in a "middle period," or late in his pre-Hijra efforts.[12] In many
instances, however, the surahs have Meccan and Medinan ayas woven into
them, so that one must be careful not to make generalizations about an entire surah being from one location or another. Eighty-eight surahs are
linked to Mecca. They usually reflect the Message's warning to the people
of the city and the call to worship-obey the One-Only God and forecast

the coming Day of Judgment. The Medinan surahs often deal with events, issues, and regulations concerning the development of the umma, battles fought against enemies and Hypocrites, relations with Jews and Christians as well as bedouin tribes, and rules about worship, family life, hospitality, communal law, and governance. Instead of focusing on the differences, it is advisable to see continuities within a surah and among surahs.

What Is the Qur'an?
Earthly and Heavenly Answers

THE EARTHLY ANSWER

In its earthly form, the Qur'an is a recital or proclamation, a Message spoken by God through an angel-presence and delivered into the heart of a specially prepared Messenger. The Qur'an is a divine revelation that was infused into one person's being and, by God's command to proclaim-recite it, was spoken (to followers) and announced (to appropriate audiences) before it became a mushaf and a kitab. The Qur'an is to be recited and heard in seventh-century Arabic, according to Muslims, so that its power, claims, and convincing beauty may be fully offered to and comprehended by listeners. Closely related to this aspect of the "what" inquiry is, when was the Qur'an revealed? Again, the obvious answer is, Gradually from 610 to 632, that is, from the Night of Power on Mount Hira to the last sermon on the Mount of Compassion.

The revelations did not take place on a schedule. During the Fatra, rumors spread that Muhammad was mentally unbalanced. Surah 68:51–52 warns those who mock the Messenger that they risk damnation at the same time that it confirms Muhammad's mission to the world.

The "when" question involves controversies over the stabilization of the written Arabic language and whether the Qur'an is to be interpreted on the basis of the Syrio-Aramaic language is addressed in chapter 14. It also raises the issue of the seeming timeliness of a number of the revelations. Did Muhammad make up revelations so as to handle certain situations, such as the divine permission to retain Aisha as a wife in

spite of the suspicion that she and a Companion may have been indis-
creet when they were alone on the desert and God granting him more
than four wives?[13] We return to those two specific matters when dealing
with the "abrogated" passages. From the believer's point of view, such questions are impertinent, perhaps blasphemous. God knows what will happen
and is happening at all times, and God chooses when to hand down the
revelation.

THE HEAVENLY ANSWER

> Say: "The (Qur'an) was sent down by Him Who knows the
> Mystery (that is) in the heavens and the earth: verily He is
> Oft-Forgiving, Most Merciful." And they say: "What sort
> of a messenger is this who eats food and walks through the
> streets? Why has not an angel been sent down to him to
> give admonition with him?" Or "(Why) has not a treasure
> been bestowed on him," or "Why has he (not) a garden for
> enjoyment?" The wicked say: "Ye follow none other than a
> man bewitched." See what kinds of companions they make
> for thee! But they have gone astray and never a way will they
> be able to find!
>
> *Surah 25:6*

The questions of what and when, therefore, involve, Where is the Qur'an?
Islam, like other faiths and philosophies, accepts the existence of heavenly
paradigms and documents.[14] The Qur'an revealed to Muhammad originated with God and is said to be contained in or is a reflection of the heavenly "Mother of the Book," the Umm al-Kitab, or as it is sometimes called
the "Guarded Tablet" and the "Tablet Preserved."[15] The term *umm* is rich
with related meanings. It does indeed mean "mother." It also connotes that

which embraces others, a totality that includes related things, ideas, or persons and a comprehensive principle.[16] The word *kitab* can be translated as "book," "law," or "established decree." As such, a kitab is a volume wielding considerable authority over individuals and communities. Muslim commentators usually have been circumspect about a heavenly book always being in God's presence. Would that compromise the One-Only-ness of God? In addition, it is not clear if and how the Qur'an bestowed on Muhammad by Gabriel differs from the Umm al-Kitab.[17] Speculations about such an entity existing prior to the creation of the worlds or that it was created after this world's origin and therefore in time have triggered a controversy and an inquisition and still marks a major difference between Sunni and Shi'ia Islam.[18]

Abu Ameenah Bilal Philips noting some hadith with admittedly weak *isnads* (narrative chains in the Hadiths) explains: "Allaah caused the Qur'aan to descend from the Protected Tablet . . . on which it was written to the lowest heaven. In this revelation all of the Qur'aan was sent down at one time to a station in the lowest heaven referred to as '*Bayt al-Izzah*' (the House of Honor or Power). The blessed night on which this descent took place is called '*Laylatul-Qadr*' (Night of Decree), one of the odd numbered nights in the last ten days of Ramadaan."[19] Whenever the Mother of the Book came into existence, it is the source for the books given the messengers in pre-Islamic times that were superseded by the fullest revelation from God given to and through Muhammad. Another way to express the same point is that the Mother of the Book contains all the books or teachings revealed by earlier prophets and messengers in their uncorrupted forms, as well as the Qur'an revealed to Muhammad. The Qur'an is in full agreement and harmony with the other books. The Mother of the Book may differ in that it includes the hidden meanings that are not explained in the disclosure to Muhammad or the others. The final aya of that disclosure announced during Muhammad's last sermon is, now God has completed and brought to its consummation the religion that He had been manifesting since the beginning of creation (Surah 5:3–16).

The Qur'an contains images and passages that God intended to be unclear and not of humanly well established meaning. The meanings of those passages were known to God and are inscribed in the Umm al-Kitab (Surah 3:7).

> He it is Who has sent down to thee the Book. In it are verses basic or fundamental (of established meaning); they are the foundation of the Book. Others are allegorical. But those in whose hearts is perversity follow the part thereof that is allegorical, seeking discord and search-ing for its hidden meanings but no one knows its hidden meanings except Allah. And those who are firmly grounded in knowledge say: "We believe in the Book; the whole of it is from our Lord"; and none will grasp the Message except men of understanding.

The entire earthly revealed Qur'an is from God, and its truest, most complete meanings are in God's Umm al-Kitab.[20] The Tablet is the source of the inner content, intention, and power of God's law and will. What is not understood now will be unveiled by God through the Umm al-Kitab in the future, either before the Day of Judgment or in the Hereafter. Present-day faithful, disciplined interpreters, guided by the Messenger's Sunna, provide insights and render decisions concerning applications of God's will. Clearly, anyone who seeks to explain the Qur'an must be cautious and reverent.

WHAT IS THE QUR'AN?
FROM PROCLAMATION TO BOOK

We move next to the Revelation's transition from being proclaimed to and bestowed on a uniquely prepared human to that person's recitals of the Message to his Companions and Helpers and their remembering and documenting what he declared. Many ancient and modern religious groups believe that transcendent powers can possess individuals so that those powers can speak and act through the "possessed."[21] The largely Jew-ish first-century CE work 2 Esdras (4 Esdras in the Latin translation) de-scribes Esdras drinking a God-provided potion that opened him to the divine revelation that he dictated to stenographers, so the very letters and words originate with God and are inspirationally transmitted by the reciter to the scribes.[22] Descriptions of Esdras's self-awareness, enhanced energy, and spiritual illumination indicate transformed physical and mental states of acute concentration and endurance. Physiological signs are also common such as changed tone of voice; experience of voices; sounds, and visions; agitation, trancelike passivity; and postrevelation anxiety or exhaustion. Obviously, there are analogues in accounts of Muhammad.

REVELATION AND INSPIRATION

Surah 42:51 describes three means through which divine revelation is made known to a person: by inspiration, from behind a veil, or by sending a Messenger to reveal God's will. The first means is understood as enlightenment in the heart of someone who has been prepared to receive an understanding of God's disclosure. The veil mode probably refers to the angel Gabriel. He is described in the hadith as being manifested as translucent veil-like light through which the presence of God may be sensed. Both Gabriel and Muhammad may be understood in terms of the Messenger mode. In several hadiths the Messenger's followers say that they saw a person speaking with him whom he subsequently identified as Gabriel. In other instances, Muhammad mentioned that Gabriel was among them, but the others present were unable to see him.

According to Aisha, Muhammad said he had been prepared for the great disclosure on the Night of Power through dream-visions. Several hadiths report that sometimes when Muhammad was in a revelatory state his forehead perspired, he heard a painful bell-like ringing, an angel spoke to him, and he felt burdened while his face changed color and he stooped forward.[23] He spoke slowly after receiving the revelation as he dictated its content to his scribes.[24] They wrote the Message on materials available at the time, such as the shoulder bone of an animal, split palm fronds, parchment, flat stones, and clay tablets. Muhammad tested their memories to ensure they had heard and written correctly. Muhammad said that Gabriel tested his memory of the Qur'an annually and twice in the past year.[25]

MUHAMMAD ON VARIATIONS

The Messenger realized that variations in pronunciation, understanding, and perhaps the text would creep in during his lifetime and afterward. On several occasions a Companion who heard Muhammad's recitation or were taught it by him objected vehemently to another Companion's version. Muhammad responded that there were seven different *ahruf* to reciting a passage.[26] Shi'ia and Sunni Muslims area divided over the meanings of *ahruf.*[27] Sunnis hold that the Qur'an was revealed in the seven dialects current in seventh-century Arabia and suggest that there were also seven scripts used to write the Revelation. Shi'ites reject that position, holding that God has provided for continuing revelatory interpretation of the Qur'an through the family of Ali up to the Twelfth Imam. Early and perhaps some contemporary Shi'ites claimed that the dominant Sunni collators of the Qur'an omitted up to one-third of its text and altered or expunged positive references to Ali and the continuation of leadership through Ali. Shi'ites reject the reasons for the collation under Uthman, countering that Muhammad carried on the collation in his lifetime and arranged the surahs and ayas as directed by God through Gabriel. They argue further that there were fifteen persons who recorded the revelations in the Messenger's lifetime. Shi'ites, therefore, reject the view that the seven ahruf refer to dialects and look elsewhere for an explanation. So the ahruf issue discloses a profound difference between Sunni and Shi'ia on the recitation, transmission, and recording of the Qur'an. Most Shi'ites agree that the Qur'an used today is the revealed and most authoritative text. Muhammad handled the potentially divisive matter with skill but did not provide a means to resolve disputes in the future: "The Prophet said, 'Recite (and study) the Qur'an as long as you agree about its interpretation, but when you have any difference of opinion (as regards its interpretation and meaning) then you should stop reciting it (for the time being).'"[28]

TO THIS POINT, the answer to the question, What is the Qur'an? begins with the belief that it is a revelation-recitation originated by God from beyond the seventh heaven that derives from and expresses the celestial Umm al-Kitab. The answer continues that God disclosed the Qur'an through the angel Gabriel to the God-prepared Messenger, Muhammad, who repeated it to his Companions and Helpers. He and they memorized the Revelation. The next portion of the answer moves to those who, having heard the Message, wrote it on various media and had their memories and writings approved by Muhammad. In the process of transmission, he was tested by Gabriel to ensure that the Words of God were heard and recorded without error. The next dimension of the question, What is the Qur'an? concerns its being written and compiled as a mushaf.

THE QUR'AN COLLATED

The Qur'an refers to itself as a kitab, or book. God wills the Revelation to retain its proclamational dimension through ongoing recitation and use in worship and at the same time to have the Qur'an be the ultimate authoritative written guide for the umma as well as for the world:

> These are verses of the Wise Book, a Guide and a Mercy to the Doers of Good, those who establish regular prayer and give regular charity and have (in their hearts) the assurance of the Hereafter. These are on (true) Guidance from their Lord; and these are the ones who will prosper. But there are among men those who purchase idle tales without knowledge (or meaning) to mislead (men) from the Path of Allah and throw ridicule (on the Path). For such there will be a humiliating Penalty. (Surah 31:2–6)

But before it could become a kitab, the Qur'an had to be a mushaf, that is, written on parchment sheaves.[29] As indicated earlier, Sunnis hold that portions of the Qur'an were put into written form after 632, whereas Shi'ites insist that it was written in its entirety before the Messenger's death. Zaid ibn Thabit (also written as Zayd, d. ca. 665), Muhammad's major secretary, wrote numerous Quranic passages revealed and dictated to him by Muhammad. He is reported to have said that when Muhammad felt a revelatory time approaching, Muhammad summoned him to record the recitation.[30] On at least one occasion Zaid wrote the statement (now Surah 4:95) on the shoulder blade of an animal.[31] Muhammad also taught many of the Companions and Helpers portions of the Qur'an along with various prayers.[32] The tradition holds that Zaid corroborated reports that Muhammad said God determined the order of surahs and ayas. Although the matter is hotly disputed by Shi'ites, Sunnis claim that the sheaves were not gathered in a canonical order and arranged until after Muhammad's death.[33]

The move from memories and writings on various media was prompted by the prospect, if not the reality, of variations in recitation, memory, and inscription. Four mushaf traditions associated with Companions and certain Helpers emerged: the Hijazi (Medinan-Meccan), Kufan (southern Iraqi), Basran (also southern Iraqi), and Syrian (Damascus based).[34] Muslims tread carefully when discussing the divine origin and preservation of the Qur'an. According to the main Sunni view of the collection of the Qur'an and one of several nearly identical hadith from Bukhari, the deaths of many Qur'an reciters and memorizers in the Wars of Apostasy and other conflicts raised serious concerns. Abu Bakr and Umar ordered Zaid ibn Thabit to collect the Quranic statements. Eventually persuaded to comply, Zaid undertook the collection, compiled a mushaf, and gave it to Hafsa, a daughter of Abu Bakr and one of Muhammad's widows.[35]

Zaid relied heavily on the memory of those who heard and memorized the Message. Some traditions hold that by the time of Muhammad's death there were fifteen men who had committed the entire Qur'an to their "chests."[36] Shi'ites hold that there were at least three other complete collections and that these stressed the charismatic roles of Muhammad's family, especially through Ali.[37] Because Zaid was not a Qurayshi and was not involved in the struggles for the caliphate, he was free from the taint of Meccan family entanglements. Moreover, he was held in high repute and known to be present when Muhammad spoke in both human and divinely inspired modes.

By 650 CE Uthman took the decisive step. He was persuaded that the spread of Islam into Persia, Syria, and Africa required writing and distributing "perfect copies" of the Qur'an for use by teachers in the newly won territories. Leaders were wary that variant versions would lead to textual wrangling like that among the People of the Book. On retrieving the mushaf from Hafsa, Zaid and three Qurayshi men collated what they had gathered, made numerous exact copies, and burned the variants. The one "perfect" text became the standard.[38]

WHAT IS THE QUR'AN?
"FORGOTTEN" AND "ABROGATED" PASSAGES

Was it possible that some material was lost or forgotten? And what of the statements in the Qur'an that Allah "abrogated" one revelation and substituted another for it?

"FORGOTTEN PASSAGES"

Few topics have provoked more debate within Islam and among those outside of the umma than the issue that portions of the Qur'an may have been forgotten. The debates have brought about distinctions and categories that are also reflected in the Hadiths. For example, Surahs 87 and 2 show that forgotten revelations are part of God's plan:

By degrees shall We teach thee to declare (the Message) so thou shalt not forget, except as Allah wills: For He knoweth what is manifest and what is hidden. (Surah 87:6–7)	None of Our ayat do We abrogate or cause to be forgotten but We substitute something better or similar; knowest thou not that Allah hath power over all things? (Surah 2:106)

Muslim tradition notes two other passages from the Qur'an that address the issue of forgotten text. When Surah 20:113–14 (Ta Ha) was revealed, Muhammad was in the early stages of receiving the Revelation and needed to develop his abilities to retain what Gabriel disclosed:

Thus have We sent this down an Arabic Qur'an and explained therein in detail some of the warnings in order that they may fear Allah or that it may cause their remembrance (of Him). High above all is Allah, the King, the Truth! Be not in haste with the Qur'an before its revelation to thee is completed but say "O my Lord! Advance me in knowledge."

Surah 75:16–19 states:

Move not thy tongue concerning the (Qur'an) to make haste therewith. It is for Us to collect it and to promulgate it. But when We have promulgated it, follow thou its recital (as promulgated). Nay, more it is for Us to explain it (and make it clear).

Several hadiths indicate that there may have been occasional lapses of the Messenger's memory but that others recalled the passages to him, and in due time he recovered them all.[39] Because the Messenger realized that the Qur'an was to be made known especially through its recital, he advised, "It is a bad thing that some of you say, 'I have forgotten such-and-such verse of the Qur'an,' for indeed, he has been caused (by Allah) to forget it. So you must keep on reciting the Qur'an because it escapes from the hearts of men faster than camels do when they are released from their tying ropes."[40] Abu Huraira, a frequent listener, was credited with remembering many of the Messenger's divine disclosures and comments. His extraordinary mental abilities were due to a garment bestowed on him by the Messenger.[41]

ABROGATED PASSAGES

With one exception, the abrogated passages are in a different category from possible forgotten portions.[42] Muslim scholars have never agreed on the number of abrogated passages. Some hold that only about five constitute the whole, but others count 225.[43]

Abrogated, withdrawn, changed, and even canceled passages or positions are not unique to the Qur'an or to Islam. Exodus 20:5−6 threatens to punish to the fourth generation the children of any Israelite who dared to worship a graven image, but Ezekiel 18:2f. presents God as saying that the children shall not be punished for the sins of their forebears. Similar "abrogations" can be cited in the Deuteronomic curses that the Israelites will be expelled from the Promised Land, but the prophets Isaiah, Jeremiah, and Ezekiel proclaim forgiveness and restoration. Shifts in contexts may account for the changes. That is, a regulation that was appropriate at one time in a community's situation could be canceled or changed in a different setting.

Generally, Muslim legal experts hold that the Qur'an expresses absolute or definitive statements without the casuistic or "if . . . then" pattern of case law. One type of abrogation introduces a factor intended to modify the sweep of the initial statement. The earlier of the passages involved in an abrogation, then, states the abiding principle; the later revelation introduces an adjustment. One example is the often-cited Surah 2:256: "Let there be no compulsion in religion. Truth stands out clear from error; whoever rejects evil and believes in Allah hath grasped the most trustworthy hand-hold that never breaks. And Allah heareth and knoweth all things." Numerous ayas could be cited in support of that principle. The Muslim experience of alleged treachery by Muhammad's opponents in Medina who sought to remain polytheists and the Jews and Christians who collaborated with the Meccans brought a change in the basic principle of avoiding compulsion in matters of religion, for example: "Fighting is prescribed for you and ye dislike it. But it is possible that ye dislike a thing which is good for you and that ye love a thing which is bad for you. But Allah knoweth and ye know not" (Surah 2:216; see also Surahs 9:5 and 29).

How those passages are interpreted has been and continues to be critically important for the relationships between Muslims and non-Muslims, including Jews and Christians.[44] If the context of consorting with the enemies of Islam on the eve of battle is kept in mind, then the passages that abrogate 2:256 and others like it are understood as extraordinary actions to safeguard Islam's survival. On the other hand, if the passages are considered as replacing 2:256 regardless of circumstances, then some will find justification for unremitting warfare with non-Muslims.[45]

Fighting in Prohibited Months

The prohibition of fighting during the sacred months was abrogated through a revelation following the action at Nakhlah.[46] The disclosure held that fighting during the sacred months was permissible when it was a "graver" offense to allow a violation of God's path and to defend the Ka'bah (Surah 2:217). In other words, practices given by God for Arabia in the Jahiliyyah were to be obeyed after the advent of Islam, except when the Faith was threatened or the expansion of Islam would be thwarted or tumult and disorder would occur.

Abrogation and Muhammad

Another instance of the abrogation of a long-held custom concerned the practice of granting divorces if there was even a hint of impropriety in the relationship of a married woman and a man who was not her husband. If a man and another person's wife were alone together and unobserved, it was suspected that they were having a sexual relationship. Once, Muhammad's wife, Aisha, was separated from the main body of travelers and was alone with a single man.[47] Ali advised Muhammad to divorce her, causing a rift between Ali and Aisha. In that circumstance Surah 24:11–26 was revealed, which required four witnesses to prove adultery (apart from the confession of one of the parties). The effect was to protect the innocent from slander and preserve the umma's integrity. In so doing, God abrogated a practice in pre-Islamic Arabia.

A clearer abrogation was directed to Muhammad alone. Surah 4:3 (al-Nisa', the Women) limited the number of wives a Muslim may have to four and requires that the husbands "deal justly" with each. Because of the increasing number of widows among the Believers due to battlefield casualties and illness and because the Messenger was a model of virtue and self-control, God made an exception in his case so that it became lawful for him to have an unspecified number of wives and for them to be more closely related to him than the Qur'an normally allowed (Surah 33:50–52).

The Punishment for Adultery

The Uthmanic recension of the Qur'an differs from hadiths that state the Qur'an originally had another reading. Surah 24:2 (al-Nur, the Light) deals with punishment for adultery and fornication: "The woman and the man guilty of adultery or fornication: flog each of them with a hundred stripes. Let not compassion move you in their case in a matter prescribed by Allah if ye believe in Allah and the Last Day: and let a party of the Believers witness their punishment." Several hadiths hold otherwise. A lengthy and repeated hadith tradition contradicts Surah 24, stating that Muhammad said that under Quranic divine inspiration the guilty persons were to be stoned to death. Accordingly, Umar insisted that the Messenger said it and had people executed. Aya Ar-Rajm (the stoning verse) was interpreted to apply to married persons. If the adulterers were married, both were flogged with 100 stripes and then stoned. A pregnant adulteress was permitted to give birth and then had to surrender the baby to another woman to be nursed, after which she was to be stoned to death. Unmarried persons who fornicated were flogged and exiled for a year. Slave adulteresses received 40 lashes for the first offense and 80 for the second. Though the stoning aya was not in the Qur'an, Umar enforced it.[48]

Muslims reject the question of whether other passages were omitted. The Qur'an they have is the Qur'an God revealed and wills humanity to have for its guidance to salvation and for guidance in daily life.

WHAT IS THE QUR'AN?
STRUCTURE AND ARRANGEMENT

Had We sent down this Qur'an on a mountain, verily thou would have seen it humble itself and cleave asunder for fear of Allah, such are the similitudes which We propound to men that they may reflect. Allah is He than whom there is

no other god, Who knows (all things) both secret and open;
He Most Gracious, Most Merciful.

Surah 59:21–22, al-Hashr, the Mustering

The first time a non-Muslim opens or listens to the Qur'an he or she usually is bewildered by its seeming to shift subjects, interject stories, segue into rules, and then reach poetic heights. Some suggest that first-time readers should begin at the end of the Qur'an and then proceed to its beginning, but, as helpful as that may be, it misses the practical timeliness of the Revelation and only postpones the question of arrangement.[49] Still, how and why is the Qur'an arranged in the way we encounter it? Does that arrangement help us to understand the content? Listener-readers are best advised to take time, expend patience, and reread the Qur'an to discern the multiple structures and let these lead to an understanding of the content— and its challenges. The Sufi poet Jalal al-Din Rumi (1207–73) provided an apt image for the Qur'an, a brocaded tapestry: "Every man stirs from his own place. The Koran is a double-sided brocade. Some enjoy one side, and some the other. Both are true, inasmuch as God Most High desires that both peoples should derive benefit from it."[50]

Kenneth Cragg used the brocade image in a manner relevant to this study.[51] When seen from the reverse side, a tapestry's threads crisscross one another and are of varying lengths and widths. Knots are visible, and colors mingle. Yet viewers have only a hint of the patterns and design. When viewers move to the front of the tapestry, the patterns and designs make sense in detail and as a whole. To continue the tapestry image, so far we have been assembling the threads and setting up the loom. When seen from its reverse side, the Qur'an may appear to be a mélange of themes and textures, even a jumble of topics. Many non-Muslims, especially those with a literalist predisposition, are apt to see what is difficult to understand, unpalatable to their cultural tastes, and foreign to their senses of spirituality. Although Muslims hold that God revealed the words and placed these in surahs composed of ayas, the Qur'an does not tell us what its design is.

That silence encourages persons to discern patterns within the parameters of the current order. Of several orders that might be devised, I offer three for our consideration.

> We sent down the (Qur'an) in Truth and in Truth has it descended: and We sent thee but to give Glad Tidings and to warn (sinners). (It is) a Qur'an which We have divided (into parts from time to time) in order that thou mightest recite it to men at intervals: We have revealed it by stages. Say: "Whether ye believe in it or not, it is true that those who were given knowledge beforehand when it is recited to them fall down on their faces in humble prostration" And say: "Glory to our Lord! Truly has the promise of our Lord been fulfilled!" (Surah 17:105–8)

THE RELEVANT REVELATION STRUCTURE

By "relevant revelation," I mean that the present structure answers the situations, needs, and opportunities first of the Messenger and the umma as the Revelatory Time was coming to a conclusion and then of the ongoing lives of individuals and the umma. Surah 1 is the timeless Opener. Surah 2 addresses chiefly the immediate Medinan umma's context, which gives it a critically important place for it outlines the rest of the Qur'an and speaks to the immediate concerns Muslims faced: their identity, the risks posed by Hypocrites, the challenges of the People of the Book, and the vestiges of opposition from the polytheists. Muslims live every day in continuity with Surah 2.

The surahs whose ayas were revealed chiefly after the Hijra need to be heard and read first for they disclose the Messenger's and umma's God-given responsibilities, legitimacy, and assurances, as well as the types of opposition the Muslims will face. The post-Hijra surahs lay the foundation for the umma's ethics and relations with believers and nonbelievers. The surahs provide the historical-revelational framework of prophets and messengers that preceded the final Message and Messenger. So the accounts that stretch from the covenants made with Adam through the Abrahamic patriarchs, continued into the Family of Imran (Moses, Aaron, Mary, and

Jesus) are to be heard and responses of faith and devotion evoked as the content of the umma's God-willed way of life is presented. In that presentation God uses the Medinan surahs to underscore His divine Plan and His will to protect Muhammad and the umma. Therefore, references to the victories at Badr and the Trench, the defeat at Uhud, and the principles for family life, worship, and justice are aptly placed early in the Book.

Later believers and nonbelievers who open the Qur'an will be informed thereby of what Islam is and what Muslims are to be individually and communally for themselves and the world. The Meccan material is not discounted or relegated to a lower place. On the contrary, the Meccan surahs disclose where living Islamically or refusing to live Islamically leads. Although revealed earlier, the basically Meccan surahs point to the end in terms of the Day of Judgment and the fulfillment of God's Plan. The present structure of the Qur'an, then, is not only traditional; it is logical and appropriate. God knew what He was doing when He revealed it as He did.

YUSUF ALI'S PROPOSED STRUCTURE:
COMPREHENSIVE SHAPE

Yusuf Ali advised readers not to complicate their approaches by trying to rearrange the Book in either a chronological or a thematic order. He felt that knowing when and under what circumstances a surah or an aya was revealed is only marginally helpful. Writing as a devout Muslim, he held that the whole Qur'an is set in the framework of God's merciful and just purposes for humanity—the humanity for which He created the world and for which He will bring the Day of Judgment and its cosmic results. He understood the Qur'an to have a comprehensive "scheme" or shape, that is, the "building up [of] the new umma or Brotherhood and its spiritual implications."[52] Behind that scheme is God's One-Only-ness. The One-Only God seeks unity for the creation and humanity.[53] Since God arranged the surahs' order, it is inadvisable for readers to skip around in the Book but to take the Qur'an as a whole from al-Fatihah to al-Nas. Yusuf Ali discerned a natural flow in the Revelation. The Qur'an's structure has movement that ranges from reflections on that which is heavenly to the details of an individual's thoughts and deeds to cascades into God's will for the community of Islam. Laced throughout these movements are exhortations, admonitions, promises, and reflections on rejecting and accepting Islam. There is an antiphonal quality to the Qur'an in which heaven and earth, humanity and God, nature and history and human responses speak to and answer one another. The whole composition points to God's purpose to create the new umma, the Islamic community. In the course of introducing the surahs in his translation, Yusuf Ali provided comments from which I extrapolated an outline of his view of the Qur'an's structure.

Surahs 1–7	Spiritual history of humanity to the formation of the Islamic umma.
Surahs 8–16	Formation of the Islamic umma, with reflections on human communities.
Surahs 17–29	Journeys of individuals from the heavens to earth.
Surahs 30–33	Present realities leading to future final times.
Surahs 34–39	On the spiritual world, endurance, faithfulness, and patience.
Surahs 40–46	The Ha Mim series, which features pairs: Faith/Unfaith, Revelation/Rejection, Goodness/Evil, Truth/Falsehoods.
Surahs 47–49	Organization of the Islamic umma, defense against foes, and the promotion of internal relations.
Surahs 50–56	Revelation through nature, history, and the prophets pointing to the Judgment and Hereafter.
Surahs 57–66	Concern with specific issues of the Islamic umma.
Surahs 67–94	Reflections, revelations, exhortations, and warnings on spiritual life.
Surahs 95–114	Pronouncements on nature and history, human degradation and dignity, revelation and warnings about evil.

Yusuf Ali's pattern indicates the steps or progress of the Revelation as God arranged it, thereby providing Muslims and non-Muslims alike with a context that may be used to interpret particular surahs and ayas while maintaining the "scheme" for the umma at all times and in all places so that humanity may be guided to and through the Day of Judgment.

A ROAD AND JOURNEY STRUCTURE

My approach, which complements the others, uses the metaphor of road and journey. Often the Qur'an describes the Message proclaimed by all prophets and messengers at all times and to all persons in terms of a "Way" or "Path."

The first reference to the Straight Path (Siraatal mustaqiim) occurs in the first and most beloved surah, al-Fatihah. We will consider al-Fatihah further in chapter 8, but for present purposes, I juxtapose it to Surah 114, al-Nas, Mankind. The resonance between the initial and final surahs acts as an energizing force that propels reader-listeners—and the umma—first through Surahs 2–113, then cycles them back to the beginning. Between these two surahs God set forth the entire Way in the present and into the future. By placing these surahs side-by-side, we begin to see how they may be read devotionally so as to disclose the nature of God; God's relationships to space, time, and creatures celestial and terrestrial; the call to worship and obey God; the menace of evil; and the coming Judgment. In other words, here is the essence of both road and journey.

al-Fatihah	al-Nas
In the name of Allah,	In the name of Allah,
Most Gracious, Most Merciful.	Most Gracious, Most Merciful.
Praise be to Allah the Cherisher	Say: I seek refuge with the Lord and
and Sustainer of the Worlds.	Cherisher of Mankind
Most Gracious Most Merciful.	The King (or Ruler) of Mankind
Master of the Day of Judgment.	The Allah (or Judge) of Mankind
Thee do we worship	From the mischief of the Whisperer (of
and Thine aid we seek.	Evil) who withdraws (after his whisper)
Show us the Straight Way.	(The same) who whispers into the
The way of those on whom	hearts of mankind
Thou hast bestowed Thy Grace,	Among Jinn and among Men.
Those whose (portion) is not wrath	
and who go not astray.	

Al-Fatihah is a prayer given by God for the individual and for the umma. Surahs 2–113 are God's answer to that prayer, and al-Nas is a statement of faithful obedience through which the Muslim places himself or herself and the whole umma under the care and protection of God. The titles given God in one surah correspond to those of the other surah. In the Opener, the believer states his or her intentions and praise and grows in heartfelt and mind-enlightened understanding of Who God is, who those are who have obeyed and rejected what God requires, and what the outcome of faith and unfaith will be. By the time the pious reader-listener reaches Surah 114, he or she has advanced in the process of being at peace-obedience (salaam-islam) with God, is eager to practice the ibadat with greater intensity, and is motivated to share the Faith with others as well as to defend it and the umma from detractors and enemies. In both surahs the believers are made conscious that insidious powers attempt to thwart God by turning believers into damnable rejecters. Al-Nas is a resolute yet humble *Ameen* to what was affirmed and begun with the al-Fatihah. Keeping these two surahs in mind, we return to understanding the Qur'an as a road and journey.

The Two Roads

Islam sees two "ways," or roads, by which individuals and the world journey to the Day of Judgment and the Hereafter. The Straight Path laid out by God goes through the landscape of tests, problems and anxieties, obligations and commandments—and blessings, truth, and joy. The other path is the crooked, sometimes seemingly easy road that leads to hellfire (Surah 90:3–20).

God has always shown the Straight Path to human beings. Now the Qur'an has been revealed as the essential and final guiding light and Muhammad the essential and final guide to the destination as well as the basic explanation of all existence and actions (Surah 42:51–53).

The Road's Four Dimensions

Both ways assume the Quranic teaching that God has brought the worlds into existence for the sake of humanity and that humans are God's agents on earth. The Creator starts each person on the Straight Way, yet at every moment that person may exercise her or his free will to step off that path to take the route to perdition. By means of the road journey metaphor for the structure of the Qur'an, we can imagine the terrain over which the journey is undertaken as having four interlocked dimensions, each present in the essence of the Qur'an, al-Fatihah.

The Cosmic-Creation Dimension

By stating that God is the Cherisher and Sustainer (Rabb) of worlds, the Qur'an indicates that the current home for humanity is not the only realm of existence. Nevertheless, all that has ever been and is now and will ever be is on the journey to the consummation of God's merciful and just plan: "It is Allah Who begins (the process of) creation; then repeats it; then shall ye be brought back to Him" (Surah 30:11). In an enumeration of His signs (ayas), God continued: "And among His Signs is this that heaven and earth stand by His Command. Then when He calls you by a single call from the earth behold ye (straightway) come forth. To Him belongs every being that is in the heavens and on earth: all are devoutly obedient to Him" (Surah 30:25–26). The cosmos's obedience involves all its parts following God's will by obeying His physical laws and being signs (ayas) that testify to humans Who the Creator is, what He wills, and what awaits those who do and do not do His will (Surah 10:6–10).

The theme of the aya-filled cosmos runs through the Qur'an, returning with renewed intensity in the fourth dimension. God cherishes as well as sustains what He creates. In terms of the road-journey metaphor, the cosmos-creation is an abundant array of signs showing and testifying to God's authority and power, providential care, and purposefulness, as well as His mercy and justice. The Qur'an does not need a stated creation account because its Message is one of exhortation and warning. The worlds are important illustrations and eloquent witnesses of Who God is and what God has set forth for humans to follow and foreshadow what is in store for those who tread the Straight Way and those who turn aside (Surah 31:27–28).

The Human History Dimension

From the first Garden to the Gardens of Bliss, human beings have been and still are on the two ways. Groups and individuals who have been on the trek earlier serve as paradigms to emulate or from whom to flee. Whether it be the Ad, Thamud, or Egyptian, or People of the Book or any others, God has always been active in human affairs to reveal the Straight Way of divine tawhid and the obligation of all persons in every society to obey Him. Past human events and cultures are a vital dynamic in the Qur'an's structure. Al-Fatihah does not mention the revelation of the Book or Muhammad, but in every prayer believers petition the Lord of All to guide them to walk in the way of those—past and present—who have received God's grace. On that basis the Qur'an offers paradigmatic figures who are on the way to the Gardens and others who are on the way to eternal condemnation. Moreover, past humans, especially prophets and messengers, are lifted up to Muhammad in order to encourage him to continue proclaiming the Message (Surah 11:120–23).

The Personal-Communal Dimension

The third dimension focuses on present personal and communal responses to God's Revelation and the Messenger. The Qur'an anticipates a harmonious reciprocity between Mecca and Medina, so we may see the Way beginning in Mecca, moving to Medina, then after a period of "road construction" widening between the two cities, then moving from them into the rest of the world. If the seventh-century roles of Mecca and Medina in the origins of the Way are finished, the Way's connection to the cities remains relevant to and vital for the umma and humanity. One consequence of the unique and ongoing roles of the two cities in the Way is that they are to be sacred communities witnessing to the One-Only God and the umma. To enter these places, a person must be committed to walk the Sirataal mustaqiim fully, that is, as a Muslim (Surah 9:17–24).

God's revelations to Muhammad and his experiences in Mecca and Medina ensure that those centers will retain their importance for Muslims and the Islamic mission in the world. The divine disclosures given Muhammad in Medina are mirror images of the Meccan rebuff of the Message and hostility to the Messenger and his followers. Whatever was reprehensible and wrong in Mecca is corrected and reconstituted in Medina. So orphans are cared for and their inheritance rights protected, and marriage and divorce regulations are stated clearly and fairly relative to the Jahiliyyah. Economics and political relations, the conduct of war and steps toward peace were structured into the Straight Way of God. Above all, religious obligations, practices, and intentions center on God's tawhid and the ibadat due Him. Once Islam triumphed, many Muslims returned to Mecca. Put in terms of models and paradigms, the Medinan revelations provide the political, social, juridical, economic, and military foundations for the umma and include ways in which Muslims are to relate to non-Muslims. In addition, those surahs also serve as reference points for the manners and actions established by the divinely guided Muhammad for personal, family, and communal ethics in the context of worship and obedience to God.

The Ethical-Eschatological Dimension

The fourth dimension may be considered the Straight Way's roadbed. The Way leads to the Day of Judgment and beyond. God is the Master of the Day of Judgment. He is merciful and gracious, but He will also deal justly with those who go astray. The Day looms as the gateway to the final goal: the Gardens or Hell. The Qur'an describes how and why humans earn entry to both destinations. In the course of pointing out the Way's ethical-eschatological dimensions, God made plain that if He delivered the Qur'an without examples and similitudes, the creation would have been destroyed in awed reverence (Surah 59:21–23).

The end of the Journey is forecast in the Opener and is present throughout the Qur'an as warning and encouragement. The whole creation points toward the Day, and the span of history provides paradigms for those still on the Way of what happened to peoples and persons who either gave themselves to God's Straight Way or rejected it. Al-Nas may seem to end the Qur'an on a negative note. I think, instead, that it is a realistic caution. It repeats al-Fatihah's recognition of God as Lord, Ruler, and Judge and then reminds reader–listeners that Iblis and his evil forces are loose in the world. The warnings of Surah 114 make the reader–listener and the umma wary of the "envious one" as he practices his damning ways among humans up to the Day of Judgment. Given the structure and use of the Qur'an, those who give their hearts to it and their lives to the Master of the Day of Judgment return to al-Fatihah to renew their openness to be shown the Straight Path—and their determination to continue the journey.

CONCLUSION

The Qur'an is a complex, yet clear work. Muslims expend care, reverence, devotion, and scholarly acumen in engaging its text. It may be approached from start to finish in different manners such as the Relevant Revelation, Yusuf Ali's Comprehensive Shape, or my Road and Journey Structure. How the Qur'an has been and may be interpreted is our next step.

> The revelation of this Book is from Allah, the Exalted in Power, Full of Wisdom. Verily, it is We Who have revealed the Book to thee in Truth. So serve Allah offering Him sincere devotion. (Surah 39:1–2)

SEVEN

INTERPRETING THE QUR'AN

A revelation from (Allah) Most Gracious, Most Merciful,
A Book whereof the verses are explained in detail, a Qur'an
in Arabic for people who understand, giving Good News
and Admonition: yet most of them turn away and so they
hear not. They say: "Our hearts are under veils (concealed)
from that to which thou dost invite us and in ours ears in
a deafness and between us and thee is a screen: so do thou
(what thou wilt); for us we shall do (what we will!)."

Surah 41:1–5, Ha Mim

Our study opened with references to the risks involved in opening the Qur'an and raised questions about who can interpret the Qur'an. To this point, we have located the Qur'an in the context of Islamic faith and its geographic and historical settings, introduced the Messenger, and gained basic information about the Qur'an's content and structure. Along the way, we have heard numerous translated passages that provide some idea of the Book's rhetoric and intensity. In this chapter, we return to and build on the issue of interpretation. Major concerns cluster first around Christian and Jewish interpretations past and present and on the freedom and responsibilities of interpreters.[1] Because Muslim interpretations of the Qur'an were and are influenced by Jewish and Christian interpretations of their

Scriptures, I make some generalizations on the course of Jewish and Christian interpretation with an eye toward how the People of the Book's handling of their sacred books could be used and also rejected by Muslims. Second, I deal with interpreting the Qur'an with regard to issues in and types of Quranic interpretation. Third, I suggest a procedure that non-Muslims may find helpful for interpreting the Qur'an.

Westerners and Muslims often do not understand each other's views of freedom and responsibility in matters of interpretation, conduct, and expression. Put simply, the question is, Are there differences between the Western and Islamic approaches to the freedom and accountability of interpretation?[2] The short answer is "Yes." The freedoms of religion, speech, expression, and association are construed differently in the West than in the Islamic World. Those differences have a substantial impact on interpreters and their interpretations.

Interpreters seek to provide, in comprehensible and accurate ways, the meanings of a written or oral text. The interpreter participates in making sense of the materials. Who the interpreters are, what their cultural, historical, social, and religious contexts and views are, sometimes implicitly and sometimes explicitly influence their renderings of and comments on texts. Even the sparest interpretation is a commentary on the meaning of the material. These observations raise the issue of responsibility: To whom or what are interpreters accountable? What are the constraints, if any, on their freedom and autonomy in arriving at and then stating their results? The responses with regard to the Bible and the Qur'an are shaped by history.

WESTERN VIEWS OF THE INTERPRETER'S FREEDOM AND RESPONSIBILITY

Always aware of the many exceptions to generalizations, I think it is helpful to consider the topic of Western views of interpreter's freedom and responsibility first in terms of a pre-Renaissance Christian perspective and Jewish perspectives during the Ages of Definition and Cogency. Next we move to Renaissance-modern Western perspectives (not specifically Christian) and then Jewish perspectives in the Second Age of Diversity.

THE PRE-RENAISSANCE BACKGROUND:
A WESTERN CHRISTIAN PERSPECTIVE

Pre-Renaissance Westerners almost uniformly assumed the divine origin, continuity, and harmony of the Bible, the teachings of the Church, and the social-political structure. From the fourth through fourteenth centuries CE, the mutual support and frequent animosity between church and state was widely accepted.[3] Nevertheless, the political governing authorities and the ecclesiastical authorities understood themselves as bound to scriptural-doctrinal norms for the sake of salvation and the good order of society. Except in the views of schismatic and heretical groups, the church was the custodian of the Bible and its interpretations and the guardian of Christian doctrines. The Bible and doctrines were studied and discussed within limits determined by interpretations of the canonical books of the Bible, creeds, concilliar decisions, and the hierarchy's teaching offices. Those who flagrantly and persistently transgressed the boundaries were liable to punishment by both state and church. Given the context, earlier and revered commentators' works were valued. From 800 to the mid-1300s significant analytical scholarship was carried on in monasteries and universities, usually by members of the clergy who were committed to the received teachings and texts of the church.

Biblical scholars assumed and interpreted the Old and New Testaments as divinely inspired documents that were in agreement with each other. They used and sometimes developed hermeneutical techniques that assigned meanings to passages on literal, allegorical, and heavenly levels.[4] Convinced that the Old Testament testified to Jesus, the Trinity, the sacraments, the end of the age, and other doctrinal points, scholars read it to discover what they believed God had put there, albeit in veiled forms to be discerned through the Spirit by Christians.

Scholars also focused on Jesus as the main subject of both Testaments. The Old Testament was regarded as predicting, prefiguring, and testifying to Jesus. The New Testament was believed to be the fulfillment of the Old Testament and to disclose the divine-human ministry of the Savior and forecast the coming Kingdom of God. Recognizing different literary forms, interpreters assumed there were no errors or contradictions in the

Bible, particularly the New Testament, because the texts were inspired, perhaps dictated by the Holy Spirit. Perhaps the Ezra account served as a precedent for Christians as they considered the inspiration of their texts. Differences in accounts of Jesus' ministry were viewed as the same events recounted from different angles, or it was thought that the differences were in fact reports of different incidents that resembled one another. Teachers and commentators developed "harmonies" of the Gospels, that is, versions that brought the canonical materials into a sustained and unified narrative.[5] Again, the Scripture testified to and upheld the church's teachings.

Biblical scholars were accountable to their immediate superiors, whether these were abbots, bishops, or university officials, and through them political authorities. Faculty members and students within and between schools engaged in debates and defenses of positions, yet the result was assumed to be in agreement with the church's interpretations of the creeds and doctrines.

JEWISH PERSPECTIVES IN THE AGES OF DEFINITION AND COGENCY

Among Jews, what was designated earlier as the Ages of Definition and Cogency led to a focus on rabbinic authority in interpretation.[6] The Hebrew Bible's text, even its letters, was considered given by God. The Dual Torah was believed to have been revealed by God to Moses. Moses transmitted the oral form to key leaders, and it was passed on through successive rabbis. The written form constituted the first five books of the Hebrew Bible. The Mishna, Talmud, and midrashim were authoritative interpretations that provided insights and color to the scriptural accounts. In written and oral forms the interpretations and commentaries were added to the store of rabbinic lore and teaching.

Midrash can be taken as a broad rabbinic term as well as a set of literary documents. It can connote either exegetical or eisegetical commentaries. The former means reading out of the text what it is in the passage. It is comparable to squeezing the juice out of an orange; that is, the meaning is already present and the scholar needs to get to it by careful analysis of grammar, context, literary form, and so on. Eisegesis is reading meanings into a text. The analogy here is that of a bucket. The interpreter-commentator pours or puts meanings into the text that come from outside it. All interpretation and commentary involves both exegesis and eisegesis.

The highly influential rabbi, Rashi Shlomo ben Yitzak (1040–1105), used the term *midrash* in two contrasting yet complementary manners. As *peshit,* the exegetical dimension, midrash entailed detailed analysis of the text's spelling, frequency of word usage, grammar, etymologies, context, and literal meanings and sermonic uses. *Derash,* the eisegetical dimension, allowed for extended philosophical, theological, folkloric, speculative, and question-raising analysis and promoted applications and references to new situations. Later generations of scholars used Rashi's commentaries and those of his contemporaries for further oral and written discussions. Jewish interpreters carried on conversations about commentaries across centuries by adding their marginal notes to certain passages to the marginal notes of Rashi and others.[7] The peshit and derash precedents carried over into Quranic interpretations and commentaries.

Jewish interpreters were acutely aware of the work and political-social power of Christian interpreter-commentators on the Hebrew Bible, Talmud, and midrashim. Because Christians assumed that they had the true interpretations and often demanded public debates, the rabbis were cautious and determined to avoid giving any openings to Christians to gain eisegetical entry points into Jewish interpretations. Publicly, therefore, rabbis emphasized the peshit style of midrashic commentary. Biblical interpretation for Jews, thereby, became an important defense of Judaism to outsiders and an important means to define and unite Jewish community and individuals. The defensive-definitional aspects of interpretation will also be present in Islam.

The rabbis regarded the Dual Torah as divinely given and as the highest authority, yet open to discussion and study. The Talmud, midrashim, and other texts were resources for carrying on a continual conversation that included past as well as present figures. Absent a centralizing interpretive authority such as the Christian papal theologians and the debating forums of universities and monasteries, the Jewish interpreter was accountable to the Jewish community, his disciple-students, and circles of rabbis. The Jewish interpreter-commentator was free to teach and write in the context of the broadly received Jewish narrative rooted in the Hebrew Bible, Talmud, and midrashim. We will encounter similar traits among Muslim interpreters of the Qur'an.

IN THE PRE-RENAISSANCE period Jews and Christians shared the conviction that their Scriptures were God-given, error-free, and intended to be interpreted for the faith community's life and worship. Both groups regarded earlier commentators and interpreters as valid and cherished guides for later times. Both showed a holy awe and high regard for the biblical texts. They disagreed over the extent of the Scripture, the results of interpretations, and the way in which an interpreter was related to the faith community. Christians, moreover, had a hermeneutic centered on Jesus and assumed that interpretations and interpreters would be in accord with the doctrines of the church.

RENAISSANCE AND POST-RENAISSANCE WESTERN DEVELOPMENTS

Desacralization and Secularization

By "desacralization," I mean the process whereby many people no longer regarded rituals, texts, teachings, and institutions as divine or as to be approached with sacred awe. The materials were to be analyzed just as any other document or action. "Secularization" refers to the process of bringing those desacralized items into the purview and grasp of humans. In other words, the "supernatural" was brought into the realm of the "natural." Neither desacralization nor secularization needs to eliminate religion, Scriptures, or God. Instead, these are subjects for human investigation, analysis, criticism, and revision. Desacralization and secularization were and still are attitudes and processes that developed over decades at different rates in different regions with different results.

Since the mid-fourteenth century the West has been undergoing changes that included, sometimes deliberately, the desacralization and secularization of attitudes, intellectual endeavors, activities, institutions, and texts previously regarded as sacred. The resurgence of interest in and study of the Greek and Roman past involved an attempt to return to the sources of philosophy, rhetoric, reason, religion, and social structures in order to move forward to meet the challenges and opportunities of the present and the future.

While this is not the place to discuss the rise of Renaissance humanism, I want to note that among the ongoing concerns during the Renaissance and then the Reformation were the rhetoric of the Bible; emphasis on the Latin, Greek, and Hebrew languages; examination of classical, biblical, and patristic manuscripts; and questioning of Christian doctrines and ecclesiastical structures. Two key figures may be cited as setting the tone for "modern" biblical scholarship. The first is Lorenzo Valla (1407–57). In writings published during his lifetime and in a crucial posthumous work, he used philological and historical analysis to show that a key document used to bolster papal political claims was a forgery and that the Latin translation of the New Testament sanctioned by the church contained grammatical errors and rhetorical infelicities.[8] His posthumously published *Annotations on the Latin of the New Testament* (published in 1505 by Desiderius Erasmus) was a critically important work, for it showed manuscript and textual problems that were addressed in new renditions of the Greek New Testament. Erasmus's Greek edition of the New Testament was essential in the development of the Reformation. Valla and other scholars, while claiming to be devout and orthodox believers, scrutinized sacred texts in the same ways they would scrutinize secular documents and found the biblical materials wanting. That humans could examine, evaluate, and judge negatively the external form and implicitly the content and authority of what was traditionally considered the holy written word of God evidences the emergence of an understanding of freedom markedly different from the West's pre-Renaissance past and nearly diametrically contrary to that of the Islamic world.

The major Protestant Reformers such as Martin Luther (1483–1546), Ulrich Zwingli (1484–1531), and John Calvin (1509–64) retained a holy awe of the biblical texts, but they also were willing to raise questions about the stated authorship of some of its books, developed canons within the canon, challenged traditional interpretations, and formulated positions that sometimes encouraged average believers to come to their own conclusions as to the meaning of texts and teachings. The "received texts" of the Bible actually were composites of what appeared to be the best readings of the multitude of variant readings. Vernacular translations proliferated, as did Protestant groups that based their distinctive practices and theologies on their readings of the Bible.

The second person who contributed substantially to the development of modern Western biblical scholarship is Benedict (Baruch) Spinoza (1632–77).[9] Expelled from the Amsterdam Jewish community, Spinoza followed his own Enlightenment agenda in his anonymously published *Theological and Political Treatise* (1670). After a presumably rational examination of the Hebrew Bible, he explicitly attacked traditional Jewish views of the Bible, traditions, and practices. Logically, his criticisms and methodology applied to standard Christian biblical interpretations and doctrines as well. Spinoza's secularizing rational approach to the texts and teaching of the synagogue and the church concluded that revealed religion contained contradictions, inadequacies, and errors. He understood Jesus as a prophet among other prophets and then took the prophets as preachers of morality. He rejected miracles, resurrection, apocalyptic predictions about the end of the world, and the roles of the government (implicitly rabbinic and ecclesiastical authorities as well) from interfering with, controlling, or punishing any individual for his or her religious views as long as those views accorded with general morality and civil order. Religious views, he insisted, are the province of individual consciences and are not to be rewarded or penalized by external authorities. For Spinoza and those who thought along the same lines, desacralization and secularization also included making religious views matters of personal conviction and devotion. Spinoza, like others in his time, was not a traditional believer but nevertheless interpreted the Scriptures. The Bible was a public work and open to interpretation by anyone.

The Western development of the tolerance for a plurality of religious groups within the same society was another consequence. Regarding religious choices as matters of individual options or preferences rather than as mandates by religious or governmental authorities was spurred by wars and disorders that claimed to be at least partially in the name of religious confessionalism. As long as the adherents and their critics were law-abiding, governing authorities and even dominant religious institutions, grudgingly to be sure, came to tolerate diverse teachings and critiques. Gradually, over the course of the eighteenth and nineteenth centuries in many Western countries, the need to submit manuscripts for the approval of governmental censors was dropped. Toleration entailed gradually increasing freedoms of speech, expression, and publication of views by nonbelievers and believers.

These post-Renaissance developments have influenced Western scholarship generally and biblical-theological research in particular.

The Present Situation

Most Western biblical scholars approach the Bible as they would any text. The work of earlier interpreters and theologians—whether from late antiquity, the Middle Ages, or the past several decades—is often regarded as passé. Admittedly, significant insights and interpretations have resulted from modern scholarship. Also admittedly, many Western scholars engage in arguments that frequently are independent of and question the faith community's traditions. The scholar does not need to be a member of a faith community. Indeed, such a commitment may render the person's interpretations suspect as doctrinal bias. The proliferation of Lives of Jesus in the nineteen century, often unrelated to the canonical Gospels or the general Christian tradition, has resumed and increased since the last quarter of the twentieth century.[10] Noted and widely published theologians have rejected the Christian position that Jesus was resurrected from the dead or that he had a special consciousness of a divine power in him that was not in others. The discovery of Gnostic manuscripts has led to further critiques of Jesus and the authority of the church.[11]

Much of twentieth-century Western biblical scholarship examines biblical texts analytically, seeing smaller units of tradition; differences in author-

ship, editors, or redactors; shifts in audiences addressed; and literary forms.
The conclusions have often challenged the received understandings of the
materials and their roles in shaping the church's teachings and practices.
To be sure, there have been and are efforts to see the wholeness of texts
and the overall unity of theological motifs in the Bible. Sometimes these
efforts are undertaken by conservative and literalist interpreters, sometimes
by those who appreciate the modern approaches yet use these to understand the unities more fully.[12]

THE MODERN WEST'S worldview includes a desacralized and secularized understanding of nature and institutions, science and morality, humanity and freedom. The traditional understandings of the Bible and the
teachings of the Church are analyzed without granting them a presump-
tion of divine authority per se. Freedom in the Western sense is largely freedom to think, express in various media, interpret, and publish as one sees
fit and as the marketplace will bear—all within the limits allowed by secular law. The validity or authority of religious views and teaching are generally relegated to the individual's intellectual and devotional life. While
some ecclesiastical bodies may discipline clergy for doctrinal aberrations,
such procedures are rare and unpopular.

JEWISH PERSPECTIVES IN THE SECOND AGE OF DIVERSITY

In Judaism's Second Age of Diversity the Hebrew Bible and rabbinic authorities of the past are still highly regarded but with different degrees of
emphasis and importance. The Jewish Enlightenment (Haskalah) of the
eighteenth century and the initial yet limited Emancipation of Jews from
ghetto restrictions beginning in the nineteenth century brought many
Jews into the Western mainstream, but the Haskalah and Emancipation
also fragmented Judaism into distinct bodies with sharply different versions of interpreting and using the Bible and the revered sacred traditions.
    Initially numerous German Jews welcomed the Western and Jewish
Enlightenments as opportunities to move beyond what they perceived as

stultifying ghetto mentalities and interpretations. Spinoza's criticisms were answered by some acceptance of the techniques and methods of Western biblical analysis, rejecting, for example, Mosaic authorship of the written Torah, a moralizing interpretation of the Hebrew Bible, jettisoning much of the traditional Jewish halakah (rule or way of acting, e.g., dietary regulations), views of a personal messiah, and resurrection from the dead. The traditional rabbinic commentaries, Talmud, midrashim, and portions of synagogue rituals were minimized or repudiated. The intended result was a reforming modern version of Judaism that emphasized the mission of the Jewish people to illumine the world with justice and reason rather than the particularity of Jews as a chosen people with claims to a holy land. Along the spectrum of variations and historical developments, these developments led to the formation of the Reform movement within Judaism.[13]

The modern Orthodox movement originated in a sharp reaction to the Reform movement. Orthodox leaders such as Moses Sofer (1762–1839), Samuel David Luzzato (1800–1865), Samson Raphael Hirsch (1810–88), and Heinrich Graetz (1817–91) felt that the Reform movement went too far in dropping distinctive Jewish elements and had moved perilously close to Christianity and secularized deistic humanism. Modern Orthodoxy adheres closely to the attitudes and principles of Judaism's Ages of Definition and Cogency. The Conservative movement seeks to walk between the traditionalism of Orthodoxy and the modernism of Reform. It adapts and selects methods from the modern Western perspective such as linguistic and historical findings. The Conservative movement affirms that the Hebrew Bible and other Jewish writings contain truths given by God but says that humans have transmitted these truths in terms of their cultures and contexts. Therefore, the Hebrew Bible and the other Jewish documents contain human elements. The halakah is to be adapted to modern circumstances.[14] A fourth approach, Reconstructionism, is in a state of transition from the views of its founder, Mordecai Kaplan (1881–1983), to a more theistic understanding of the transcendent. Kaplan, sounding almost like Spinoza, rejected the supernaturalism of the Bible, including miracles such as the parting of the Red Sea and God speaking to people. Holding that religion is the projection of sublimated human desires, the God of Judaism is the power of social regeneration, the projection of all the factors and re-lationships in the universe that lead to unity, creativity, and worthwhile-ness in human life.[15]

DESACRALIZATION AND SECULARIZATION, welcomed initially by some Jewish scholars, has been part of the fragmentation and diversifica-tion of contemporary Judaism. The adaptation of Western methods of interpretation has contributed to Reform Judaism's significant changes in Jewish practice and identity. Kaplan's original principles for Reconstruc-tionism may stand as the logical result of a thoroughgoing Jewish accept-ance of Western perspectives and influences: the distinctive character of the Hebrew Bible and rabbinic discourses and their relationship to a tran-scendent personal God are weakened, even canceled.

WESTERN PERSPECTIVES ON freedom and interpretation have em-phasized the examination of biblical and other religious texts in the same manner as secular texts. The methodology employed has disclosed multiple authorship of materials once regarded as written by the divinely inspired heroes of the Bible and disclosed that the Scriptures evolved over time and contain contrasts and contradictions that cannot be harmonized by reason. The application of reason to accounts such as miracles, ancient and classi-cal cosmologies, and linguistics seriously challenged assumptions about the acceptability of the biblical narratives for modern believers and non-believers. The relegation of faith to individual and group piety, rather than the broad structures of society, grounded ethical principles not on divinely given laws but on human authorities. Among Jews the adaptation by many Western approaches contributed to the refragmentation of Judaism into diverse groups that have continued to search for common ground within the Scripture and rabbinic traditions. There have been, of course, many Christians and Jews who resist the results of secularization and desacraliza-tion of biblical materials and have held their interpreters and commentators accountable to their communities. On the whole, however, the Western in-terpreters have become accountable instead to their academic communities and especially to the marketplace of popular opinion. Muslims observe these developments carefully and warily.

ISLAMIC VIEWS OF FREEDOM AND RESPONSIBILITY

The Islamic views of freedom with regard to interpreting the Qur'an and the role of interpreters differ markedly from modern Western views regarding the Bible. Initially, Islamic views of freedom appear similar to pre-Renaissance Western European-Christian positions. Put succinctly, freedom in Islam is expressed within the limits and conventions of the umma, which regards the Qur'an as divinely revealed to Muhammad and therefore beyond question, doubt, emendation, addition, or subtraction. The basic principle underlying the Muslim view of freedom is that the One-Only God revealed Islam as the primal and final, original and ultimate, specific and all-encompassing Way for the whole of His creation to blessed eternal peace. The principle's corollary is that the Qur'an as bestowed on Muhammad and collated by the Companions in what can be called the Uthmanic recension is the authentic and infallible Revelation of Islam. How the principle and its corollary influence interpretations and the freedom interpreters have is an ongoing issue among Muslims.

BASIC PERSPECTIVES, PURPOSE, AND CONDITIONS

The umma's freedom grows from its obedience to God's will. That obedience involves the umma's mission to be the faithful community that seeks to live in the revealed Islamic Way through establishing a just social order in the present based on the Qur'an and its Messenger. To do so, the umma is called to enlarge the realm of Islam in the present and move toward the destination God promises to those who obey Him.

Specifically, the Meccan-Medinan community that gathered around the Messenger and gave itself to the Message is the nucleus of the umma that extends from seventh-century Arabia to the present and on to the Day of Judgment. The Qur'an was revealed through an individual (Muhammad) to a community, and now that community reveals the Quranic Message and Way to the rest of humankind. The umma, then, has significant responsibilities and duties in using, extending, and understanding the Qur'an—and defending the integrity and reverence due to the Book. From Muhammad's Companions to today's teachers, authority to interpret the Qur'an for the umma rises from deep, recognizable personal piety inseparable from thorough knowledge of the Qur'an, the science of its interpretation-understanding, hadith collections, and Islamic law, philosophy, and literature. Bundled into those qualifications is a profound knowledge of and appreciation for earlier commentators and collections of understandings. Islamic freedom for interpreters also entails an insightful recognition of and heavy sense of accountability to the umma. Together and individually, the members of the umma depend on right guidance-understanding to travel the Straight Path in this life as preparation for the Judgment and the Hereafter. Two modern Muslim scholars provide perspectives different in tone but with a common basis.

Faruq Sherif wrote that the purpose of the Qur'an is

> to count God's favors to mankind; to teach wisdom; to bring good news of salvation to believers and the virtuous, and warning of eternal torment to infidels and evildoers; to emphasize that there is only one God and that He has neither associate, consort or offspring, and that both the visible and invisible worlds are in His power and dominion; to explain all mysteries, to prescribe a code of imperative commandments for believers and to condemn those who do not obey them as infidels; to warn against the promptings of Satan, to such an extent that the Prophet himself is commanded to either a formula for taking refuge with God against Satan at the beginnings of all recitations of the Qur'an (XVI.100). Especial emphasis is laid, in the course of numerous verses, on the condition of the Blest in Paradise and the Doomed in Hell.[16]

Ahmad von Denffer, writing for young Muslims living in the United Kingdom, cited ten basic conditions for a sound interpretation (tafsir) by an interpreter (mufassir). The conditions serve as a conservative Muslim template for interpretation, and according to von Denffer, "Any tafsir which disregards these principles must be viewed with great caution, if not rejected altogether." A comparison of von Denffer's conditions and my present Western perspectives discloses some sharp differences, notably items 1, 5, 7, 8, and 9. The mufassir must

1. Be sound in belief [be a devout Muslim]
2. Be well grounded in the Arabic language and grammar
3. Be well grounded in *'ulum al-Qur'an* (Quranic sciences)
4. Have the ability for precise comprehension
5. Abstain from the use of mere [personal] opinion
6. Begin the tafsir of the Qur'an with the Qur'an
7. Seek guidance from the words and explanations of Muhammad
8. Refer to the reports of his Companions (sahaba)
9. Consider the reports of the disciples (*tabi'un*) of the Companions
10. Consult the opinions of other eminent scholars.[17]

From the Islamic perspective, the Western understanding of freedom is often individualistic and irresponsible, verging into license and, ultimately, blasphemy. Attempts by non–Muslims and Muslims to use Western techniques of interpretation when studying the Qur'an are met largely with suspicion and opposition. These are concerns that Western methods may undermine Islam and lead to revision of the Qur'an. Nevertheless, Muslim interpreters have engaged in animated debates and disagreements that range across centuries.

SHARI'AH, FIQH, AND INTERPRETATION

Islam is a religion of obedience to God and achieving freedom by keeping to the Straight Path. In the Muslim framework, the Way is expressed as guidance and law. Quranic interpretation is inseparable from Islamic law because the Qur'an is the highest and fullest guide to obeying God. Key terms are *shari'ah, fiqh,* and *usul al-fiqh.* Muslim interpreters are deeply engaged in interpreting shari'ah (God's law as a whole) and fiqh (jurisprudence, or specific laws), and are expected to have thorough knowledge of usul al-fiqh (the science of the roots of law).[18] Among Sunnis four major schools of law emerged; among Shi'ia three schools are especially prominent.[19] Often Quranic interpretations are undertaken to clarify or apply Quranic guidance to a particular case or issue arising from Muslim law or rules of conduct. In those instances the interpreter is within the umma and is accountable to the umma for the interpretations. Such legal decisions can be based on finding a clear equation between the Quranic text or precedent and the issue at hand. Three other legal hermeneutical factors are (1) *qiyas,* drawing a close analogy between the Qur'an and the issue at hand; (2) *ijma,* drawing on the consensus of the umma's traditional understanding of the Quranic meaning and the issue at hand; and (3) *ijtihad,* drawing on the effort or reasoning of the interpreter on the basis of analogy, consensus, and context.[20]

The role and propriety of itjihad have long been debated among Muslims and is a factor that differentiates Shi'ia from Sunni Islam.[21] Ijtihad is not simply "personal opinion" (*ra'y*) but has come to mean independent reasoning to be used in matters where the Qur'an and Sunnah are silent and, according to many Muslim scholars, where ijma has not been reached. Formally, itjihad is "to be practiced by means of analogical or syllogistic reasoning (qiyas). Its results may not contradict the Quran."[22] Renewing itjihad and applying it to modern contexts is a feature that characterizes Muslim scholars sometimes designated as "reformers" or "progressives" or "New Islamists."[23]

ISLAMIC PERSPECTIVES ON the interpreter's freedom and responsibility to the umma are strikingly different from the freedom of Western interpreters of the Bible and their responsibilities to the Jewish and Christian communities. Muslim scholars stand within the umma and are accountable to the Muslim community. They carry on their efforts within parameters such as devout acceptance of the Qur'an's divine origin and arrangement, the revelatory authority of its words and language, their roles to be interpreters whose efforts may be used in decisions regarding the practices of the Faithful through law, and their being part of a centuries-old succession of interpreters. The results of Western techniques that desacralized and secularized scriptural texts and the non-necessity of Western interpreters to be part of their faith communities warn Muslims to be wary that such perspectives and attitudes do not gain ground within the umma.

BASIC POINTS IN INTERPRETING THE QUR'AN

Generally, Muslim scholars employ two types of Quranic interpretation: *tafsir* and *ta'wil*. All conscientious Quranic scholars engage, at least in a preliminary manner, with tafsir. Tafsir is exegetical interpretation within the parameters discussed above. The meanings derived from tafsir interpretation are open (exoteric, public) to all persons. Tafsir-style interpretation is wedded to rhetorical-grammatical-linguistic analysis, the meaning and placement of words, the examination of Quranic themes, and the reiterations of passages in different settings. In a sense Muslim tafsir interpretations resemble Jewish peshita and Christian literal interpretations. Whether the historical context and occasion of a passage's revelation are considered is a matter of debate among Muslim scholars. Very conservative and literalist interpreters regard the context and occasion of passages largely irrelevant to the God-given meaning. They regard Muhammad, the Companions, the Companions' followers (*tabi'un*), the sahih hadith collections, and past revered commentators as providing the necessary contexts and possibilities for applying the meaning of passages to the present. A growing number of reform-minded and "progressive" Muslim scholars insist on examining the contexts, then relating the contexts to passages in order to discern a passage's meaning in the past and how that meaning may or may not apply in the present. Ta'wil interpretation is similar to the Jewish midrash and Christian allegorical-heavenly meanings. It is regarded as giving the "inner" or spiritual meanings of the Qur'an. These meanings can rise to mystic and esoteric heights that are kept within the circle of communities such as Sufi brotherhoods. For our purposes, I have been using tafsir-style interpretation, with a special concern to make the Qur'an understandable chiefly to non-Muslims.

DEFINITIONS AND COMMENTATORS

Usul al-tafsir (also *Usuool al-tafseer*) literally means the "fundamental principles of Quranic interpretation."[24] Muslim scholars cherish, know in detail, and avail themselves of hadith collections and commentaries that reach back to Muhammad, his Companions, and their tabi'un. There are over one hundred branches of the Quranic sciences (ilm al-Qur'an).[25] We will limit ourselves to some forms of tafsir. Schools of tafsir developed in Iraq, Persia, and Syria, as well as in Mecca and Medina, after the Messenger's death. Several Companions accompanied the spread of Islam and served as references for teaching and promulgating the Faith and its Book. The Companions bequeathed their versions of Muhammad's interpretations to their tabi'un. Sunnis see the line of authoritative interpretative succession in the first generation as Muhammad at the head, then the Companions, and then the tabi'un. Sunnis gathered a number of tafsir collections after the generation of the tabi'un. The latter and their successors apparently absorbed some Jewish Talmudic accounts and Christian legends through converts from those religions to Islam. Ithna Ashri Shi'ites (popularly called Twelvers) hold that the rightful interpreter-commentators are Muhammad, Ali and Fatimah, Hasan, Husayn, and the line of their offspring up to and including the occulted Twelfth Imam.

Priority of Authorities

Ibn Taymiyah (1263–1328) provided a hierarchy of authorities for interpreting the Qur'an.[26] First and foremost, the Qur'an is its own best interpreter. That is, the reader is to study the ways in which words and themes are used in different places and contexts in the Qur'an to understand their meaning. Second, Muhammad often provided explanations, and these may be found in his Sunna as recorded especially in the authentic hadith collections. These two authorities are paramount for interpretation. If neither seems to apply to a passage or issue, the interpreter may turn then to the traditions of the Companions. And should nothing rise to the level needed, then the interpreter seeks explanations from the Companions' tabi'un.

Obviously, the validity of interpretations based on these authorities presumes the infallible transmission of the Qur'an and Muhammad's proclaiming of it and the reliability of the narrators who recorded what he said and did.

Comments on Some Key Interpreters

Three early and three modern interpreters deserve brief comment. Each in his own way interpreted the Qur'an so that the tafsir sought both to interpret the text and to apply it to the political and social situations in which each lived.

Ibn Jarir al-Tabari (d. 928) made significant use of ijtihad while simultaneously basing his interpretations on the text, the Messenger, the Companions, and the tabi'un. He admitted that in some places one could not be certain as to the meanings, yet such uncertainty is not harmful. Al-Tabari included some interpretations later called *Isra'iliyat,* that is, from Jewish sources. When such material is confirmed by traditions related by Muhammad, it is acceptable. Obviously, when it is rejected by Muhammad, it is to be rejected as false by Muslims.[27]

Ibn Taymiyah stands in contrast to al-Tabari. Engaged in controversies throughout his life because of his literalist interpretations of the Qur'an, he was imprisoned numerous times and died while in confinement. He took literally references to God having arms, legs, hands, and face, opening himself to the charge of anthropomorphizing God as did the polytheists. At the same time he opposed what he perceived as innovation (*bidah*), such as easy divorces and veneration of the graves of holy persons. His views brought him into conflict with political and religious authorities. The Wahhabi and Salafi movements are especially attracted to his tafsir and other writings.

Ibn Kathir (d. 1301–72) studied with Ibn Taymiyah and shared his conservative views but not his confrontational style. His tafsir is widely regarded as the most authoritative of the early interpreters.[28] He rejected Isra'iliyat materials that were reflected among some tabi'un. Ibn Kathir was meticulous in checking the narrations and reliability of the Companions and the hadith materials. Like Ibn Taymiyah's, his writings are influential among conservative Muslims.

Muhammad Rashid Rida (1865–1935), Syrian born and active in Egypt, was deeply influenced by the reformist, modernizing views of Muhammad Abduh (1849–1905) and Jamal al-Din al-Afghani (1839–97). Both of Rida's mentors sought a pan-Islamic unity that brought them into conflict with pan-Arab political movements in the late nineteenth and twentieth century. Rida published a journal, *al-Manar*, in which he serialized the first twelve of the thirty juz; therefore it is called generally Tafsir al-Manar. Rida, like al-Afghani and Abduh, sought to move Islam into a wholesome relationship with modern scientific and social developments. Refusing to assimilate or to absorb Western methods, they claimed that Islam was already a modern religion for the whole world. They blamed literalist Muslim interpreters and inept political leaders for allowing colonial powers to gain effective control over Muslim areas and the Ottoman Empire. Rida, Abduh, and al-Afghani advocated thorough economic and political reform from within Islam as the best way to counteract Western domination. Rida was attracted to the early form of the Salafiyyah movement because it advocated emulation of past virtuous leaders. After World War I Rida grew increasingly anti-Western and intransigent. He was a significant influence on Hasan al-Banna, a founder of the Egyptian Muslim Brethren (al-Ikhwan al-Muslimun).

Sayyid Qutb's (1906–66) tafsir, *In the Shade of the Qur'an,* and his *Social Justice in Islam* and *Milestones* (sometimes translated as *Guideposts*) are among the most important and influential commentaries on the Qur'an. While he was intensely critical of the West (especially the United States) and denounced the state of Israel, his insights into the Qur'an and its sociopolitical applications are eloquent. He called for the steady development of what he considered truly Islamic societies. At the same time he did not advocate a return to the seventh century. He regarded the Revelatory Time as providing paradigms for what should be in the future. He insisted that the present constituted a second Jahiliyya, a time of immorality, paganism, injustice, and decadence, that was even worse than that of pre-Islamic Arabia. Only a recovery of Islamic principles and actions could change the situation for Muslims and the rest of humanity. Considered in his lifetime the intellectual light of the Muslim Brotherhood, he is highly regarded across a range of Muslims, from militants to reformers.

Abul A'la Maududi (1903–79) was in some ways the Indian-Pakistani counterpart of the Egyptian Qutb without the latter's fate. A political activist who participated eventually in the establishment of Pakistan as an Islamic state, he advocated Quranically based education, laws, and social rules. Though at times rejected and imprisoned, he was widely revered for his scholarship and multivolume tafsir. Unlike Qutb's obviously political comments in the course of interpreting a passage, Mawdudi was more conservative and subtle. He also built relations with Shi'ia scholars, including the Ayatollah Khomeini.

THIS BRIEF SURVEY of six interpreters indicates variety and engagement. These scholars and many others have engaged with one another over centuries and continents within the parameters of Islamic understandings of freedom. At the same time they are intensely involved with the umma and with the sociopolitical issues of their times. Because Islam is a religion that embraces all aspects of life, the Qur'an is regarded as addressing all aspects of life within Islam and to the world.

AN APPROACH TO THE LITERARY FORMS OF THE QUR'AN

Bilal Philips observed that Quranic tafsir is grounded in understanding God's aim in the Qur'an as giving guidance to humans in three spheres: our relationships with God, within our own selves, and with the society in which we live. His brief explication of four of the basic literary forms in the Qur'an sheds light on the workings of the tafsir tradition and its scholars.[29]

The first is among the most common forms, *mathal*: simile, proverb, metaphor, and ideal. The category is divided into three groups: mathal that are clearly stated or obvious, that are inferred, and those that are formless or brief lessons.[30] The second significant literary form is the oath. Fully seventy-four ayas consist wholly of oaths, and seven others are partial oath utterances.[31] God swears by what He has created, but humans swear only by God if they are to avoid shirk, or idolatry. Surah 91:1–10 is a series of oaths involving the sun, moon, day, night, firmament, earth, and souls.[32] The third literary form is the debate or argument. Sometimes God's argument takes the form of denunciations of humans for rejecting Him and His prophets and messengers and for sins and injustice. At points Muhammad is instructed to argue with polytheists, Jews, Christians, and hypocrites. The fourth and final form for consideration is narratives. Surah 12 is a single narrative or story, while Abraham, Lot, Hud, Jonah, Salih, Moses, Aaron, Jesus, and Noah are subjects of prophet narratives, and Saul (Israel's king), David, Goliath, Mary, Korah, and the Companions of the Cave (Surah 18) are mentioned briefly. Another narrative type concerns events in Muhammad's time such as the Year of the Elephant, the battles of Badr, Uhud, and the Trench, and an oblique reference to the Night Journey (Surah 17). Interpreters recognize that some narratives and mathal as well as ayas are repeated verbatim or nearly so. The Qur'an's response is that the repetition is deliberate and lead the reader-listener to a fuller understanding of God's will (e.g., Surah 39:23).

OPTIONS TO TRADITIONAL TAFSIR

Interpretation is ongoing. Islam has a rich history of interpretation, other writings, sermons, and discussions. Muslim interpretation is far from monolithic. Given the challenges to Islam from the West and from within its own communities, new concerns are raised for interpreters. I conclude this chapter with the example of a feminist option posed by a controversial Muslim scholar, a seminal comment by a Muslim scholar who was influential especially in the West, and my adaptation of his pattern. I propose to use that pattern in seeking to aid non-Muslims to open the Qur'an with increased understanding.

A Feminist Option: Amina Wadud

Female Muslim scholars and their supporters are offering interpretive perspectives that raise questions among traditional teacher-interpreters.[33] Amina Wadud, an African American convert to Islam, proposed that the

Qur'an's major purpose was to provide moral guidance for men and women as they seek to live on God's Straight Path.[34] She holds that although the Qur'an spoke directly to the conditions in seventh-century Arabia, it provides basic principles for all times. In other words, she distinguishes between the conditions of the Transcendent Time and its ever-relevant principles. Wadud builds on the point that the Qur'an and Islam seek to carry out God's will by creating a just and equitable society. She observes that a society's values and expression of those values, in particular, the relationships of men and women, evolve over time. Conditions and contexts change but not the Quranic principles. As societies evolve the Quranic principles are applied to new circumstances. She proposes that the specifics of seventh-century Arabia in terms of the social status of women are not Quranically mandated but are culturally conditioned and open to change in accord with the Quranic principles. How that may be implemented is not clear. In March 2005 she took the preannounced step of leading Muslim men and women in prayer during which she both preached and performed the prayer ritual in front of the mixed assembly. Her reasoning was that the segregation of women and men at prayer and the prohibition of women leading men in prayer were culturally conditioned and no longer relevant among Muslims living in the West. The service was not held in a mosque but on the premises of the Episcopal Cathedral of St. John the Divine in New York City.

Toward New Patterns

Fazlur Rahman pointed toward a new pattern for interpretation and a reorientation of Islam in the mid-twentieth and twenty-first century. He wrote:

> Yet the real solution [to a fourteenth century interpretive trend in which legal opinions were taking precedence over the Qur'an's text] lay only in understanding the Quranic injunctions strictly in their context and background and trying to extrapolate the principles or values that lay behind the injunctions of the Qur'an and the Prophetic Sunna. . . . The basic élan of the Qur'an—the stress on socio-economic

justice and essential human egalitarianism—is quite clear from its very early passages. Now all that follows by way of Quranic legislation in the field of public and private life, even the "Five Pillars" of Islam that are held to be religion par excellence, has social justice and the building of an egalitarian community as its end. . . . *In the building of any genuine or viable Islamic set of laws and institutions, there has to be a twofold movement: First one must move from the concrete case treatments of the Qur'an— taking the necessary and relevant social conditions of that time into account— to the general principles upon which the entire teaching converges. Second, from this general level there must be a movement back to specific legislation, taking into account the necessary and social conditions now obtaining.*[35]

A Proposed Hermeneutical Approach

On the basis of Rahman's statement, I suggest the following pattern that may help non-Muslims who seek an initial understanding of the Qur'an.

I.   First Step: Seek to interpret Quranic texts on the basis of the Qur'an's underlying unity.
   A.   The oneness of God;
   B.   The need for, ability of, and responsibility of all humans to respond to God through obedience and peace.
      1.   Dimension A: the individual is able to respond in mind, heart, and deed.
      2.   Dimension B: the establishment of a just and equitable society in accordance with God's will.
      3.   Dimension C: the responsibility of all cultures and people to obey God and to pursue justice, which entails spreading Islam to where it is not present and deepening adherence to Islam where Islam is dominant or well established.
   C.   The Judgment of God over individuals and over peoples, societies, and religions.
   D.   The blessedness of the Faithful in the peace of God and the dismal fate of the disobedient.

II. Second Step: Two Pairs of Interpretative Techniques
  A. First Pair
    1. Move from the Quranic text to the situations of the Messenger, umma, and wider community and world.
    2. Move from the past situation to the Quranic text.
  B. Second Pair
    1. Analyze the situation faced now. Address the present in terms of personal, familial, social, institutional, political, national, international, economic, and environmental contexts. Ask what the issues and trends are in these arenas.
    2. Turn to the Quranic passage. Let the Qur'an's underlying unity speak to, illuminate, analyze, advise, correct, admonish, and exhort the situation and the people involved. Listen to the foundational message, then move through its principles and experiences to understand how Quranic principles, laws, and insights address current and future prospects and circumstances.
III. Third Step: Understand what the Qur'an said then and act on what it says now.

CONCLUSION

Interpreting the Qur'an is a complex task with a lengthy history that features erudite scholars debating meanings from the beginning of the Revelation. Perspectives on the interpreter's freedom and responsibility differ significantly between the present West and Islam.

Up to this point we have set the scene, considered basic positions, and approached the Qur'an. Now, using my adaptation of Rahman's model and Muslim sources, we start to open the Book.

(Here is) a Book which We have sent down unto thee full of blessings that they may meditate on its Signs and that men of understanding may receive admonition. (Surah 38:29, Sad)

PART II

THE QUR'AN OPENED

So We have made the (Qur'an) easy in thine own tongue,
that with it thou mayest give Glad Tidings to the
righteous, and warnings to people given to contention.

Surah 19:97

To this point we have been introduced to Islam and approached its holy
Book. Now we will open the Qur'an and engage its content through some
important topics, moving from those that are relatively "safe" to those that
are increasingly controversial. Because it is neither feasible nor fruitful to
examine every passage on these subjects, I selected surahs and ayas with
references from hadith materials that I think present Quranic-Islamic positions accurately and understandably to non-Muslims. It is likely that Muslims would increase the references from the hadiths and traditional interpreters. Interested readers may consult the selected bibliography for further
readings.

When thou dost read the Qur'an seek Allah's protection from Satan,
the rejected one.

No authority has he over those who believe and put their trust
in their Lord.

His authority is over those only who take him as patron and who
join partners with Allah. (Surah 16:98–100)

EIGHT

FOUR CHERISHED PASSAGES

The seven heavens and the earth, and all beings therein declare His glory:
There is not a thing but celebrates His praise.
And yet ye understand not how they declare His glory!
Verily, He is Oft-Forbearing, Most Forgiving!

Surah 17:44

Some scriptural passages have continual significance for believers and even for those who are not in the faith community. Psalm 23 in the Hebrew Bible and 1 Corinthians 13 in the Christian New Testament are such passages. The Qur'an, too, contains surahs and ayas that hold distinctive places in Muslim life. In this chapter we consider four such passages: al-Fatihah, the Opener (Surah 1); the Throne Aya, 2:255; the Light Aya, 24:35; and Ya Sin (Surah 36). I include the translated text of Ya Sin in the body of the chapter. Because al-Fatihah is special, I examine its ayas in some detail. We begin at the beginning.[1]

AL-FATIHAH, THE OPENER

English Translation	Arabic Phonetic Transliteration
1. In the name of Allah, Most Gracious, Most Merciful.	1. Bismillaahir-Rahmaanir-Rahim.

2. Praise be to Allah the Cherisher and Sustainer of the Worlds.

3. Most Gracious, Most Merciful.

4. Master of the Day of Judgment.

5. Thee do we worship and Thine aid we seek.

6. Show us the Straight Way.

7. The way of those on whom Thou hast bestowed Thy Grace, those whose (portion) is not wrath and who go not astray.

2. Al-Hamdu lillaahi Rabbil-'Aalamiin;[2]

3. Ar-Rahmaanir-Rahiim;

4. Maaliki Yawmid-Diin.

5. Iyyaaka na'-budu wa iyyaaka nasta-'iin.

6. Ihdinas-Siraatal Mustaqiim.

7. Siraatal-laziina an-amta 'alay-him Gayrilmagzuubi 'alay-him. wa laz-zaaalliin.

PRELIMINARY COMMENTS

Al-Fatihah centers as well as starts the Book. Muhammad's Companions and their students called it the Mother of the Book (Umm al-Kitab), the Praise, the Prayer, the Remedy, and the Cure.[3] Al-Fatihah is the Mother of the Book in the sense of Umm as the comprehensive principle, the embracer of a number of ideas, persons, and documents.[4] More than any other Quranic passage, al-Fatihah shapes the believer's life. Since it is included in each Salat prayer, a devout Muslim says it seventeen times a day in Arabic.[5] When Muslims complete the final juz portion of their Quranic readings, they return to the Opener to begin their hearing-obeying once more and at a more committed level than the last time.

God begins the Qur'an with the prayer that He wills to be used by all who obey Him. He included how they are to pray to Him and for what they are to pray before they ask for anything else or bring any other matter before Him. Through the Opener, God reveals the qualities or attributes by which His creatures are to approach Him. As in all Muslim prayers, God and the believer enter a direct personal and intense engagement. In this surah the Muslim speaks to God by accepting and offering God's own words, yet expresses his or her intention to obey-serve God and then commits himself or herself to live that for which he or she asked.

In transcendent theological terms, God answers the prayer by guiding the Muslim on the Straight Way and giving such divine aid as the believer needs. In devotional-ethical terms, the believer receives the guidance and aid so as to live Islamically. In revelatory-literary terms, the answer to al-Fatihah is in the hands of, is set before the eyes of, and is heard through the ears of believers: the Qur'an is the answer to this and every prayer. Between the Opener and al-Nas is the Message grounded in the One-Only-ness and will of God, human obedience and divine protection, meritorious and deleterious conduct, personal responsibility and societal norms, and communion with God and other humans. Between al-Fatihah and al-Nas stretches the Straight Path through temporal life to eternal blessedness. Again in al-Nas, Allah gives Muhammad and the umma words to say and live by in all times and places. As believers come to the end of the thirtieth juz, they complete a meritorious obligation and are inspired to live as Muslims. The same God with Whom they began the pilgrimage in life using the Qur'an as their guide is still with them as they fulfill His will. And they then continue the journey by praying al-Fatihah again.

RELATION TO THE QUR'AN'S UNDERLYING UNITY

God is beyond all descriptions and language. What we know rightly of God, then, is given by God as God determines how we are to know who God is and what God wants. We can only speak properly of God as God has shown Himself to be—not more and not less. In and through that revelation, He has shown Himself to be what He always has been, what He proclaims Himself to be now and forever in the Basmillah, and what His will has been and is now in the Qur'an. Muhammad and the obeying-serving umma carry that revelation among themselves and into God's world. In light of that, al-Fatihah is God's gift to all creation. Through it God presents the irreducible kernel of how He wants all creatures to know Him, relate to Him, and live in His world. The Opener is a prayer, a confession of submission to and peace with God, and a commitment to serve in His world. Taken together, then, the underlying unity of the al-Fatihah grows out of the divine One-Only-ness, posits human responsibility, and anticipates the establishment of societies in which God's style of justice is pursued—all to be manifested on the Day of Judgment. We turn next to al-Fatihah's structure.

Invocation, 1:1–4

The invocation states the central Islamic understanding of God through the use of the attributes God discloses about Himself. Muslims have identified ninety-nine beautiful names or qualities or attributes that God applies to Himself in the Qur'an.[6] That Allah opens the Message with four such terms indicates that He wants all reader-listeners to encounter Him first and foremost in and through these names. These names are Most Gracious (Rahman) and Most Merciful (Rahim)—stated twice in al-Fatihah—then Rabb of the worlds, and Master of the Day of Judgment. Humans are told from the start that the God who has made them and all that exists and who controls the destiny of the cosmos and each moment is to be approached primarily as beyond every creaturely concept of compassion, love, and mercy. The Opener is a lens through which the Qur'an's restrictions, threats, and punishments are to be seen. It is as if God wrote in the largest and boldest letters that humans are always to know Him through this prayer and to repeat constantly that they give themselves to the One who is Most Gracious, Most Merciful. They repeat that name after they confess Him as Lord and before they praise Him as Master of the Yawm Din. God's sovereign power and awesome verdicts are consistent with His benevolent intentions and compassion. The Basmillah, the Qur'an's first aya, is so essential that it opens every surah, except Surah 9.[7]

Rabb's themes of benevolence, care, and love accompany the more generic meaning of sovereignty. To call God the Rabb of the worlds gives focus and application to His graciousness and mercy. The term *worlds* (al-Alamiin) refers to the world of angels and spirits through the seven heavens and to our cosmos, that is, whatever has been, is now, and will be created, cared for, and responsible to God. Further, no time or place has ever been God-forsaken. This view points to the conviction that God has sent His messengers and prophets to all peoples. Simply, God rules. That leads to the third name: Master of the Day of Judgment.

The name Master of the Day of Judgment points to two factors. One is implicit at this point: humans are agents, engaged in action. For there to be a divine judgment, there must be human volition. The other factor is the assertion that the present world will come to an end. That end will be in God's time and as God wills. Other portions of al-Fatihah bring forward the promise of grace for those who obey God and of punishment for those who reject Him. The cosmic Judge and the beneficent Lord is One and the Same. The One-Only God is at peace-oneness with Himself and wills peace in His creation and among His creatures. His mercy and justice, love and wrath, blessings and condemnations are neither poles between which God oscillates nor contradictions within Him. Islam rejects expressions such as those in the Hebrew Bible that depict God as changing His mind (Gen. 6:5–7), anguishing over punishing the covenant people (Hosea 11:1–12:6), or creating evil (Isa. 44:7). Likewise, Islam finds incomprehensible the assertion by some Christians that God's work and perhaps God's Being can be divided into fearsome "alien" work and gracious "proper" work.[8] The Master of the Yawm Din judges because He is merciful and shows mercy because He is Judge. Humans have the ability and responsibility to come before the Rabb, who sustains, cherishes, and fulfills His worlds. Those who know and submit to Him offer Him praise and obedience by seeking to carry out His will. Whether they realize it or care, every human is in God's presence and under the scrutiny of His angels in preparation for the last day of this world. Those who strive to be faithful present themselves before God and grasp al-Fatihah as they use the words He gave them to ask for His grace and guidance.

Petition, 1:5–6

"Thee do we worship and Thine aid we seek" opens the petition section. Worship precedes all requests for aid. The word *and* may be seen as the pivot between recognizing-submitting-serving God and recognizing of human limitation and need for God. The lives of individuals and the umma are elided through prayer, specifically this prayer, and in reading-hearing the Qur'an. The individual believer and the believing umma join in living the Straight Path. What and how persons worship determines how they act and structure their communities. Worship, then, is preparation for salvation—or condemnation. To know and entrust oneself to God as the gracious and just Rabb carries with it awesome responsibilities. Believers are not only the receivers of the Revelation about and from God; they are to be consistent and sincere praisers of the One and are to employ that praise in how they live their lives. Furthermore, they are to share that Message with fellow humans so as to bring them to the decision about becoming Muslims or remaining apart from the umma. So worship includes and leads to prayers for divine aid.

God expects humans to appeal to Him for aid. Such appeals are signs of the petitioners' faithful reliance on God. Individuals and the umma praying al-Fatihah ask its Author for guidance to and for the journey on the God-given Straight Path. One aspect of al-Fatihah's genius is that its supplication is broad enough to include whatever needs believers may have while sufficiently focused to recognize that God establishes, maintains, and watches over the Straight Path. The Straight Path aya is elegantly lucid and directed toward motivating believers to live in obedience-peace with God. Moreover, the Straight Path is not sets of platitudes or vague principles. It is presented in substantial and even stark detail in the 113 surahs that follow al-Fatihah. To walk in the Straight Way involves more than living an individual pious life. The Way engages the umma, how it is organized and what it does, in order to fulfill God's purposes for humanity.

MUHAMMAD'S CONTEXT

In Muslim tradition, the Opener was the fifth revelation given to Muhammad and the first complete surah. The earlier four revelations were ayas incorporated into the more extensive Surahs 96, 68, 73, and 74. Al-Fatihah was given to Muhammad in Mecca between 612 and 613 as the Messenger began his public ministry. Rising tensions and new opportunities marked the situation in his life and the earliest umma. Word was spreading in Mecca that during meetings Muhammad and Khadijah were holding in their home, Muhammad spoke of the One-Only God and the revelations granted him over the previous two years. Rumors circulated about Muhammad's statements about the consequences of those revelations for himself, his family, the growing circle of believers, and, ultimately, the city. Qurayshi opposition was developing, for the Message threatened Mecca's traditional religion, economic prosperity, and political stability. At the same time those who responded to Muhammad needed further guidance and assurance. The three revelations after the Night of Power exhorted Muhammad to have courage in the face of deepening hostility.[9] The prayer met the umma's need then and subsequently. From the brief description of the situation in Muhammad's time, we turn to its final aya, Momentum for Continual Relevance.

MOMENTUM FOR CONTINUAL RELEVANCE, 1:7

All creation and creatures are moving toward the Day of Judgment. The final aya looks to the past, present, and future with promise and warning. Others have been on two ways to the Day and will receive their due rewards. God always reveals His will through faithful persons, especially prophets and messengers. Among the paradigms for those who went astray and merited God's wrath, Muhammad could have looked to biblical villains as well as the Ad of Arabia and the Byzantine Greeks. Whether Muhammad knew any Arab hanifs in his own time is beyond the evidence available; he certainly had close contacts with those he could deem were headed to hell.

Since the Revelation Muslims have been able to look for encouragement and guidance to the examples of holy women and men from the past 1,400 years. Naturally, Muhammad is the distinctive and unique pattern for one on the Straight Path. Al-Fatihah's concluding words are solemn: a time of judgment is coming. On that Day those who walked the Straight Way will be blessed, but those who defied God will receive His wrath.

THE "ESSENCE OF THE QUR'AN"'S hopeful-somber last aya serves as the bridge to the rest of the Qur'an, beginning with the "Outline of the Qur'an," Surah 2. The Cow or Heifer (al-Baqarah) begins the answer to the Opener's praise of and prayer to Allah: "This is the Book; in it is guidance

sure without doubt to those who fear Allah, Who believe in the Unseen
are steadfast in prayer and spend out of what We have provided for them.
And who believe in the Revelation sent to thee and sent before thy time
and (in their hearts) have the assurance of the Hereafter. They are on (true)
guidance from their Lord and it is these who will prosper. As to those who
reject Faith it is the same to them whether thou warn them or do not
warn them; they will not believe. Allah hath set a seal on their hearts and on
their hearing and on their eyes is a veil; great is the penalty they (incur)"
(Surah 2:1–7).

THE THRONE AYA, AYA AL-KURSI: 2:255

Allah! There is no god but He, the living, the Self-subsisting,
Eternal. No slumber can seize him nor sleep. His are all things
in the heavens and on earth. Who is there can intercede in
His presence except as He permitteth? He knoweth what
(appeareth to His creatures as) before or after or behind them.
Nor shall they compass aught of His knowledge except as
He willeth. His throne doth extend over the heavens and the
earth and He feeleth no fatigue in guarding and preserving
them. For He is the Most High, the Supreme (in glory).

PRELIMINARY COMMENTS

The Qur'an tirelessly proclaims facets of God's oneness, omnipotence, and
omniscience. Muslims believe that even Satan honors the Throne Aya, for
the Throne expresses the all-sovereign power and authority of God. It has
courage-generating power for believers who seek refuge from foes and divine aid in desperate situations.[10] Muhammad is remembered as advising
the believer who sought protection to recite, in addition to the Throne
Aya, all of Surah 23, al-Mu'min, and to continue to Surah 24:42.[11] Accord-

ing to Tirmidhi, Muhammad also said that believers would benefit from saying the Throne Aya and the "end of surat al-Baqarah [Surah 2] for it is one of the treasures of Allah's mercy from under His throne, which He gave to these people, and there is no good in this world and the next which it does not include."[12] The extension into Surah 24 plus the connections to Surahs 2 and 23 illustrate the complex relationships in the Qur'an, prompting me to discern a "throne theme" in the design of the Qur'an.

RELATION TO THE QUR'AN'S UNDERLYING UNITY

The first sentence—"There is no god but He, the living, the Self-subsisting Eternal"—and the last sentence—"His throne ... the Supreme (in glory)"—frame the aya's exuberant praise of God's tawhid and the aya's specific content. The aya is a divinely crafted refutation of all forms of polytheism and more. It implicitly criticizes the Genesis-based notion that God rested after creating the world. The aya's mention of intercessors might refer to practices in Christianity that presented Jesus and those holy persons Christians called "saints" as interceding with the Creator on behalf of sinners. It could also be used to refute the claims of heretical Christian groups that the creator of the physical world was a harsh bungler and that humans were not free to respond to the Most High God.

Al-Kursi's central section challenges humans: How are we to live under the shadow and in the light of the One-Only God who is enthroned over the heavens and earth? By the time reader-listeners reach Surah 2:255, they have traversed a body of ethical, societal, political, legal, familial, and religious directives from God. These form the basic principles and many of the specific duties that are expanded in the balance of the Qur'an. As lofty as the aya's language may be, it is intensely practical, personal, and communal. Proclaiming God to be the only Reality from whom all else comes into existence and to whom all is accountable, the first sentence leads to the body of the aya. Here the aya informs, warns, and comforts humans about God's interest in, oversight of, and coming judgment on them and the world. The Judge and Lord sees and hears; none can obscure their thoughts and ways from the God of non-Muslims and Muslims. The Muslim already knows on the basis of al-Fatihah and the Basmillah that opens al-Baqarah that God is oft-forgiving and gracious to those who return to Him and who counter their sins with acceptable deeds. Non-Muslims who hear-read the Throne Aya are, therefore, encouraged to offer themselves to Him in obedience and to enter His umma. The aya's closing lines move those who hear and read it to the closing portion of the surah, the portion to which Muhammad directed his followers:

> To Allah belongeth all that is in the heavens and on earth. Whether ye show what is in your minds or conceal it Allah calleth you to account for it. He forgiveth whom He pleaseth and punisheth whom He pleaseth. For Allah hath power over all things.

> The Messenger believeth in what hath been revealed to him from his Lord as do the men of faith. Each one (of them) believeth in Allah, His angels, His books and His messengers. "We make no distinction (they say) between one and another of His messengers." And they say: "We hear and we obey; (We seek) Thy forgiveness Our Lord and to Thee is the end of all journeys. On no soul doth Allah place a burden greater than it can bear. It gets every good that it earns and it suffers every ill that it earns. (Pray): "Our Lord! Condemn us not if we forget or fall into error; our Lord! Lay not on us a burden like that which Thou didst lay on those before us; Our Lord! Lay not on us a burden greater than we have strength to bear. Blot out our sins and grant us forgiveness. Have mercy on us. Thou art our Protector; help us against those who stand against faith." (Surah 2:284–86)

MUHAMMAD'S CONTEXT

Surah 2 is Allah's gift to a leader in need of authoritative guidance as well as a blueprint for the God-willed umma. Surah 2 is "open" in that its ayas were disclosed and arranged by God over an extended period. Muslim tradition places al-Kursi soon after the Hijra and before the defeat at Uhud (625), perhaps before the battle of Badr Springs and the change of the qiblah from Jerusalem to Mecca (624). Its eventual placement toward the end of the surah is significant. God, Muslims agree, put it after the legislative directions, family law, various rules that structured the umma, comments about and strictures against Jews and Christians, polemics about what they did to their Scriptures, and the supercessionist theology of revelation. The aya also appears after the surah's presentation of what became the Five Pillars and the Basic Teachings.

If, however, the Throne Aya was revealed prior to a substantial quantity of Surah 2, how did it speak to Muhammad and those with him when they first heard it? To set that context, I place the Throne Aya in the middle of preceding and following ayas. Aya 2:254 advises believers to depend on God's bounty in supporting one another in difficult times. It assures them that God will provide for them, so they are not to become indebted to nonbelievers. Ayas 256–57 command Muslims not to compel anyone in religious matters, for God's truth will shine forth clearly. The sovereignty of God assures the guidance of the Faithful: "Allah is the Protector of those who have Faith. From the depths of darkness, He will lead them forth into light" (Surah 2:257).

The Throne Aya addresses the changed situation of the Messenger and the Muslim umma. The people of Yathrib had legitimate questions. Who were these refugees from rival Mecca? Would the Meccans turn their commercial competition into military action? What religion did the Emigrants and their leader profess? Would the traditional gods react against the city because it opened itself to these people? What conspiracies were at work among the warring factions that signed the covenant to make Muhammad the judge-leader among them? The Jews and Christians in the city and its outlying areas had learned to get along in a polytheistic environment, yet the Message had elements that sounded familiar, even attractive to them. Still, the centrality of a man who claimed to be the recipient of the ultimate revelations from God and who heard angels speak to him raised danger signals for them.

For their part, the Emigrants who arrived in Yathrib had to find their places in a city that welcomed them outwardly, yet harbored inner reservations tinged with suspicion. In Mecca they knew who they were and were developing their understanding of the God Muhammad proclaimed, but now they were displaced persons. They had to give themselves to being reshaped into a coherent community that had greater public visibility and responsibility. Theirs was an ambiguous situation. They might claim authority and privilege by virtue of their association with the Messenger, but they had to be careful about their words and actions so as not to jeopardize his leadership and policies. Soon the Messenger, and the Companions developed a circle of Yathriban associates who made the confession of faith and became sincere Helpers. Others appeared to favor the Muslims, but, hypocritically, worked against Muhammad. And then there were the Jews and Christians. Could they be trusted? Would they enter Islam? Would they balk, perhaps betray the Muslim cause? Had the Muslims gone from the Meccan frying pan into the Yathriban fire?

In this setting God spoke. The God who had started His work in Mecca is the only God. He was their refuge and guide wherever they were and in whatever conditions they lived. The Companions and Helpers were to live in obedience-peace with each other and those around them. Muslims were not to alienate the people who gave them refuge but were to share what they had, to set the example of what Allah's umma could be, and to avail themselves of the protection of the sovereign and only God. Moreover, they were to be careful in selecting those with whom they would associate. The Muslim witness to their own integrity would be demonstrated by their maintaining a distance between themselves and those whom they suspected of hypocrisy and by refusing to compromise on the moral standards revealed to and taught by Muhammad.

Muhammad, too, needed assurance. He had suffered the loss of his wife, his sons, his uncle, and his home. He was forced to exile himself from the city he loved and the Ka'bah he helped to restore. He knew that false friends, open enemies, doubters, and cynics lurked in Yathrib waiting to shove him aside so as to pursue their own ambitions. He realized that the Meccans would not rest until either he or they were defeated. The dual tasks of caring for and organizing the Companions and Helpers into a God-pleasing umma and placating and then reconciling the mutually hostile factions in the city seemed enormous. Where could he turn? What resources were available to a retired caravaneer? Through the Throne Aya the Messenger is told once more that his Protector is the never-sleeping

Lord. God watches over the creation, and He gives strength and security to His Messengers. Muhammad's refuge is not in any city but in the One Who is over all.

The words following the Throne Aya point to a strategy as well as a witness to God's One-Only-ness: "Let there be no compulsion in religion."[13] Muhammad was determined to bring others into Islam before the Day of Judgment. He knew the power polytheism exerted over most of the people of the Arabian Peninsula. Still, he had to move slowly, using the themes familiar to them in order to turn them toward the true God. Mostly, he and the Muslims would demonstrate the truth of Islam by living the Straight Path. Now, however, Muhammad was brought for the first time into sustained contact with Jews and Christians. He observed their internal arguments and divisions, and he listened to them denounce one another. He saw the ways in which they twisted their Scriptures and distorted the revelations brought by the earlier prophets and messengers. Yet at this early juncture he needed them to help solidify the Muslim position. He could state the Message as he received it, even cite the Qur'an in discussions. Still, only God could lead persons to change their hearts and minds. No one should be compelled to mouth beliefs or be forced into practices against her or his conscience. God would make His truth stand out in the midst of error. No matter how friendly discussions and hot arguments might turn out, Muslims could be assured that they relied on the One who is Light and Truth. Those who continued to reject and despise God would find out soon enough who ruled from the throne.

MOMENTUM FOR CONTINUAL RELEVANCE

Revelations about Allah's throne appear in eighteen surahs, in addition to Surah 2.[14] Recalling Cragg's image of the Damascus brocade, I see references to the throne as a pattern woven throughout the Qur'an. Further, when we start to see the outlines of the throne theme and trace them to their first appearance, we are able to understand more fully the grounds for some Muslims to regard al-Kursi as the greatest aya in the Qur'an. Yusuf Ali regularly supplied the parenthetical expression "of authority" to most references to God's throne. I find this more an interpretation than a clarification and omit it in the following discussion.

The subsequent, or subthrone ayas, cover the range of God's authority and engagement with the creation from the world's beginning to the Day of Judgment. The consistent theme in almost all the throne references is that God is the Creator. The points repeated in the creation references are that God is firmly established on His throne—no one can dislodge Him—and that the Creator is the ever-vigilant and eternal Ruler of all He created. Humans, therefore, are exhorted and warned that they are to worship and serve Him. For example, in Surah 7:54–56 the harmony of night, day, stars, sun, and moon testifies to God. As a result of their obedience to God, humans are to call on God with humility and pious fear, yet with a thankful attitude that includes doing good. God is close to those who know and serve Him.

Creation and judgment are of one piece, and in between humans are to act for or against their blessed eternal lives. Other subthrone ayas introduce the Qur'an revealed to the Muhammad as the place from where humans can know the truth that will save them and on the basis of which they would have realized the falsity of polytheism (e.g., Surah 17:41–52). Muhammad and Muslims who proclaim the Quranic Message revealed to him could find assurance in passages such as Surah 10:2–10, in which God states that He wills the Message to be given through a human being, even if his critics accuse him of sorcery. God is the Lord, Creator, Judge, and Master even of Hell. Judgment will be rendered on the basis of works and faithfulness—or the absence thereof. Indeed, the Message given to Muhammad is of cosmic significance and will be shown to be true on the Last Day, so he is to be heard and accepted, if the listeners seek the Gardens rather than the Fire (Surah 81:1–29).

THE THRONE IS the sign pointing to God's all-sovereign will and transcendent presence over the creation He called into existence. The aya provides assurance to Muhammad and all followers of the Straight Path that God protects them in the present and is their refuge in troubled times.

Through it, God strengthens Muslims with the confidence that the Noble Book that gives them guidance individually and as an umma came from the One who rules all. The throne aya points forward to the Last Day on which God will render judgment and mercy. The throne theme embraces virtually the entire scope of Quranic teaching and expresses the certainty of God's transcendent involvement with the Messenger, the umma, and the God-urged movement toward the end of the age and the start of the eternal time. The next cherished passage continues the throne theme with a powerful image in a very earthly setting.

THE LIGHT AYA, SURAH 24:35

> Allah is the Light of the heavens and the earth. The parable
> of His Light is as if there were a niche and within it a lamp:
> the Lamp enclosed in glass: the glass as it were a brilliant star:
> lit from a blessed Tree, an olive neither of the East nor of
> the West, whose oil is well-nigh luminous though fire scarce
> touched it: Light upon Light! Allah doth guide whom He
> will to His Light. Allah doth set forth parables for men: and
> Allah doth know all things.

Enigmatic and evocative, the Light Aya reflects images and ideas common to Zoroastrian, Jewish, and Christian uses of light. The Qur'an makes clear that the aya offers a *mathal,* which can mean parable, aphorism, similitude, allegory, figure of speech, enigma, or riddle. Regardless of the meaning used, the mathal is not direct or univocal speech; God is not to be identified as light or as a star. Given the contexts of Arabian polytheism, vestigial Greco-Roman paganism, and Persian Zoroastrianism, the distinction between univocal speech and mathal speech is important. In addition, we may expect imaginative creativity in the aya and its interpretations. Not all details match neatly and logically. The aya invites reader-listeners to enter its expressions repeatedly. Each time those who accept the invitation gain further insight about God and themselves.

Among Muslim commentators and mystics, the renowned Abu Hamid Muhammad al-Ghazzali (1058−1111) wrote the classic text that verges on making esoteric disclosures to the initiated. He also considered the "Veil Traditions,"[15] ending his treatise, "For 'tis a hazardous thing to plunge into the fathomless sea of the divine mysteries; and hard, hard it is to essay the discovery of the Lights Supernal that are beyond the Veil."[16] His *Mishkat al-Anwar* and other tafsirs provide insights for my interpretation.[17] Al-Ghazzali took the ruku' 24:35−40 as a unit:

35 Allah is the Light of the heavens and the earth. The parable of His Light is as if there were a niche and within it a lamp: the Lamp enclosed in glass: the glass as it were a brilliant star: lit from a blessed Tree, an olive neither of the East nor of the West, whose oil is well-nigh luminous though fire scarce touched it: Light upon Light! Allah doth guide whom He will to His Light. Allah doth set forth parables for men: and Allah doth know all things.

36 (Lit is such a Light) in houses which Allah hath permitted to be raised to honour; for the celebration in them, of His name. In them He is glorified in the mornings and in the evenings (again and again) 37 by men who neither traffic nor merchandise can divert from the Remembrance of Allah, nor from regular Prayer, nor from the practice of regular charity. Their only fear is for the Day when hearts and eyes will be transformed (in a world wholly new) 38 that Allah may reward them according to the best of their deeds, and add even more for them out of His grace. For Allah doth provide for those whom He will without measure. 39 But the Unbelievers, their deeds are like a mirage in sandy deserts, which the man parched with thirst mistakes for water until he comes up to it, he finds it to be nothing. But he finds Allah ever with him, and Allah will pay him his account. And Allah is swift in taking account.

40 Or (the Unbelievers' state) is like the depths of darkness in a vast deep ocean, overwhelmed with billow topped by billow, topped by (dark) clouds. Depths of darkness, one above another. If a man stretches out his hand, he can hardly see it! For any to whom Allah giveth not light, there is no light!

To extract the Light-Darkness ruku' from the rest of Surah 24 detracts from both the section's meaning and God's expressed command. Maududi, with the basic agreement of Pickthall and Shakir, is more accurate than Yusuf Ali in translating 24:1 as, "This is a Surah which We have sent down and We have made it mandatory, and We have sent down clear Commandments in it so that you may learn lessons."[18] The entire surah is so important to the umma that it is to be read-heard as a whole.[19] In addition, as mentioned earlier, Surah 24 is to be read in conjunction with Surah 23 to gain protection and refuge with God. Throne and Light express the transcendent ineffability of the One-Only God while simultaneously declaring Allah's intense involvement in the world He created. I discuss the passage with reference chiefly to Surah 24.

RELATION TO THE QUR'AN'S UNDERLYING UNITY

Al-Nur, Light, is the traditional title for Surah 24, and, indeed, light is the entire surah's theme, rising to a crescendo in 24:35–40. The balance of al-Nur plays out the tones introduced in the opening ayas and is concluded in its final aya: "Be quite sure that to Allah doth belong whatever is in the heavens and on earth. Well doth He know what ye are intent upon: and one day they will be brought back to Him and He will tell them the truth of what they did: for Allah doth know all things" (24:64).

Surah 24 opens with and fills in important points extending some of the topics mentioned in Surah 2. God's light probes all areas of individual, family, and communal life. Prohibitions against adultery and other forms of illicit sexual activity, slanderous accusations, and disagreements between spouses, together with mandates to aid members of the extended family, are all part of the just and equitable society God wills. The commands and instructions are edged with admonitions expressed in punishments such as floggings by the community and damnation on Judgment Day.

God's throne, situated over the seven heavens and earth, expresses His power, authority, knowledge, of and supervision over all existence. The Light Aya opens with God being the Light in all places and times. Apart from God, there can be no existence and no light. The Quranic aya addresses the very being of God in mathal terms: Light. Whatever lights may be seen in the world have God as their source and goal.[20] The Light mathal takes us from God's throne into the houses raised in His honor (mosques) to a room in a home.[21] We see no candles, candelabra, or lanterns on the floor or furniture. The only light comes from a lamp in a *mishkat,* a niche, high in the wall near the ceiling. But what a Light it is!

The Central Image

The Divine Light itself, rather than the lamp and the olive oil, is the aya's central image. Its piercing luminosity is compared to that which is utterly unearthly: a star. This star-light is different from other Quranic references to stars.[22] Likening God-Light to sparkling starlight is an apt figure of speech when we think of the dazzling sharpness of a distant yet bright star on a desert night. A star is a lamp (Surah 67:5, al-Mulk, the Dominion) in a sky-niche, giving light to space and the earth below. The aya's Light is as clear as it is brilliant, and unlike actual starlight, this Light does not twinkle. Its absolute constant clarity is due to its transcendent total purity. God-Light is eternally steady; it neither flickers with time nor fluctuates in intensity as if dependent on a fuel supply. As is the clear or seemingly white-bright starlight, the God-Light is colorless. Color in light indicates an impurity in its fuel or the possibility of its being spread or divided into sections through a prism. Since Allah is indivisibly One, the Light is indivisibly one. In itself, the Light is unapproachable yet seen by all, and by means of it, all can be seen. "Light upon Light! Allah doth guide whom He will to His Light."

We move from the Light to the lamp, the glass in which the lamp is placed, and the olive oil. Neither is the Light, nor can either be said to hold the Light. The Light makes use of the lamp, glass, and oil. The Light uses the lamp and glass in a manner comparable to describing the way light uses a lamp and a lens: that is, the light sends its beams through the lamp and the lens. A comment on glass may be helpful.

High-quality glass was always precious in antiquity. To make even translucent glass depended on the artisan's skill and the purity of the available materials. Arabian glass was often tinged with a greenish hue due to the presence of iron in the sand. How the molten material was heated, handled, and cooled was crucial in avoiding ripples and bubbles, as well as in obtaining the desired thickness and durability of the final product. I picture the similitude of the lamp as a large flawless diamond. The lamp-diamond's inner recess or core lacks a wick floating in the reservoir of the pure olive oil. Nevertheless, spectacular Light at the center of the reservoir sends beams through the lamp and the glass, making them glow with supernal brightness into the darkness of the room.

According to Muslim commentators, oil from olives grown on a plain and therefore constantly and evenly in sunlight is clearer and burns brighter than oil from trees that are in the shade of a cliff or of taller surrounding trees.[23] Surah 23:20 refers to another olive tree: "Also a tree springing out of Mount Sinai which produces oil and relish for those who use it for food." In addition, the olive tree, fig, Mount Sinai, and Mecca are Muslim and perhaps pre-Muslim sacred symbols.[24] The Light Aya's locating or, more precisely, not locating the tree on earth points to frequent references in the Qur'an and other Muslim sources such as Hadith collections to mystic and heavenly trees, and at least one in Hell.[25] The tree from which the oil is taken is, then, not earthly or subject to the changes characteristic of space and time. The placement of the Lamp-Light in a niche high on the wall indicates that the Light discloses all that is in the room. It seems obvious that the room can be likened to the world, a community, and the heart, as well as the mind of an individual. The Light discloses all that happens outwardly and inwardly. The aya also states that the Light guides humans on what we recognize as the Straight Way.

Light and Darkness

Surah 24:36–40 carries the Light image further. One element (24:36–38) has influenced mosque architecture, that is, placing lights as globes or lanterns close to the ceilings of places where Muslims pray. In many masjids a beautiful, often-clear crystal chandelier is suspended from the inside roof, encouraging the faithful at prayer and during the reading of the Qur'an to realize that God is present. The passage affirms the rewards on the Yawm Din that will be given to those who pray and act with sincerity. Surah 24:39–40, included in the above quotation, makes the transition to the other side of the Light theme: the Darkness Ayas.

Unbelievers are described as wandering in deserts and being submerged in the depths of darkness bereft of God's guidance. They will not be given the Light they refused to see and by which they had the chance to be guided. The Darkness Ayas are replete with the hopeless despair of those who reject God and the Straight Way. The Light Aya and its following passage reflects the unity of the Qur'an's proclamation of God's tawhid, rule of the world, call to obedience and right worship, giving of Zakat, and rewards and punishments on the Last Day.

MUHAMMAD'S CONTEXT

Mystic heights and mathal speech are but a short distance from the opportunistic machinations of Medinan Hypocrites. When was the surah revealed? Was it disclosed before or after Surah 33? If it was disclosed after, and, therefore, after the Battle of the Trench (627), then the general seclusion and veiling of Muslim women was in effect. Surah 33 also mentioned what the close associates of the Messenger already knew: there was occasional bickering among his wives. He had to find or be shown ways to rectify the home situation in ways that were to be models for the rest of the umma. Muhammad's marriage to Zaynab is cited in Surah 33. The rudeness of some guests at the wedding feast prompted the revelation about respecting Muhammad's residence and, by extension, the residences of other persons. In spite of Aisha's sometimes scrambled chronological references in the hadith traditions, it is entirely possible that Surah 24 is to be read in light of Surah 33 and not the reverse. On the other hand, Surah 24 might have temporal priority. In that case, the veiling of women would have been gaining ground but would not yet have been mandatory. The crisis with the Medinan Hypocrites would then still have been building and the leader of that contingent (Abdullah ibn Ubbai) not completely discredited in Medina. If the surah was handed down before the Battle of the Trench, Muhammad was on uncertain ground with the people of the city that had given him refuge. If revealed afterward, he had a series of challenges developing from his victory, such as ensuring that the umma remained disciplined and that no sexual scandal would subvert the battlefield victory and the opportunity to subdue the Meccans by negotiation. In either dating, the Messenger faced hard decisions and the need for divine guidance.

The Light Shines in the Darkness of Slander and Gossip

The presenting cause of Surah 24's revelation was the incident involving Aisha and the Companion, Safwan. The rumors and gossip about Aisha were exploited by Medinan Hypocrites. The surah's light exposed their attempt to undermine the Messenger and the Muslim umma. Treacherous character assassins were exposed and duly flogged.[26] The slander against Aisha, her subsequent vindication by Allah, and her restoration to the Messenger's full trust and love occasioned God to expand what He started in Surah 2, that is, issues related to hospitality, privacy, male and female modesty, and the place of women. Light, that is, God, brought the truth into the open by handing down the surah and continued to build up the umma's moral order. Al-Nur, as noted, is commanded to be read and recited not only because it contains the Light Aya but also because it concerns procedures dealing with those accused of violating the unity of the umma through adultery, illicit sexual activity, and slanderous speech in general. Scandalmongers will be punished in this life and in the Hereafter (Surah 24:15–20). Innuendo and gossip were threats as serious to the integrity and survival of the umma as was actual immoral conduct. An attack on Aisha would grieve the Messenger and brand him as a cuckold, thereby diminishing his claims to be rightly guided and knowledgeable about divine ways. Another result would be to weaken the umma by casting suspicion on one of the Companions. Any sexual advance toward the Messenger's wives would be seen as reprehensible by the other Companions and the Helpers. Suspicion could lead to tensions and disunity at a time when the Muslim community needed cohesion. A third serious ramification of the incident could have been the loss of reputation of the Muslims among still-wary Medinans. The umma could ill afford a scandal, especially as it needed the support of the Medinans in the approaching conflicts with hostile Meccans. Al-Nur, however, goes further. The surah lays bare the human tendency to undercut another individual, especially someone who is well placed. Aisha's vindication occasioned the promulgation of procedures governing all future charges brought against persons for adultery and for what would be their futures after the guilty were punished. Following a severe flogging, offenders would be permitted to marry only in the limited circle of other adulterers (Surah 24:2, 26). In one sense they would be regarded as unfit for marriage into "respectable" families lest they spread their lust and unfaithfulness in the community. On the other hand, they were given the opportunity to repent with their own kind and find forgiveness. Both men and women were punished for adultery, but women bore a heavier burden than men in seeking to clear their names.[27] Both men and women were to be chaste before marriage and faithful to their spouses in marriage.[28]

Light Illumines What Ought Not Be Seen

After disposing of matters related to adultery, Surah 24 moves to the treatment of members of the extended family. Again, Muhammad's situation served as the occasion for the discourse on the family. Whether or not Surah 24 is before or after Surah 33 is a factor in dealing with the specifics of asking permission to enter a person's house. Due modesty is a factor linking both surahs. According to one hadith, even Muhammad was spied on.[29] No one should look upon the affairs of others surreptitiously or even accidentally. Nor should any person in her or his home be subject to uninvited intruders, for those in the house may not be attired to receive guests.

As the revelation nears the Light Aya, the faithful are admonished about the direction in which they should look for inspiration and discipline—toward God in order to attain bliss (Surah 24:30–31).

MOMENTUM FOR CONTINUAL RELEVANCE

Text and context make the Light Aya both continually cherished and relevant for believers and those outside the Muslim umma. Quranic speech by God and visions by Islamic mystics are inseparable from the daily lives of Muslims and their expectations for the future. The transcendent mathal tells reader-listeners about the ineffable Rabb of all existence while bringing Allah into the often-unseemly dynamics of human life. The God Who is the Light that illumines all projects the practical rules and norms for God-committed communities. There may be, as al-Ghazzali suggests, 70,000 veils preventing humans from seeing Allah directly, but nothing prevents Allah-Light from seeing into the recesses of human minds and hearts. Muslims affirm that such all-seeing and all-knowing extends from seventh-century Arabia to all peoples now and even throughout the universe. The Light Aya and its Darkness counterpart are intimate parts of Islam's insistence on justice, truth, and submission to God.

The placement of the Light Aya in the middle of al-Nur is neither happenstance nor coincidence. After the Basmillah, the next thirty-four ayas ascend to the Light Aya so that the stipulations about accusations, punishments, scandalmongering, privacy, modesty, and chastity are not meant to repress believers. Instead, they are set between the statements that God is the merciful-gracious Guide to the Straight Path and that God is the Light Who sees and knows human strengths and failings. The twice-repeated refrain between the Basmillah and the Light Aya (24:10 and 20) carries believers away from rigidity to trusting the God Who seeks to establish His umma on the basis of mutual respect among humans and obedience to Himself: "If it were not for Allah's grace and mercy on you, and that Allah is Oft-Returning, Full of Wisdom (ye would be ruined indeed)." The Light cast from 24:35 is not cruel and arbitrary but purposeful and life-enhancing. Likewise from 24:35 to the surah's conclusion, the subjects may deal with chastity and modesty, yet the basic themes are proper worship, prayer, caring for the needy, deepening faith in God and the Quranic Revelation, following the Messenger, and strengthening the umma. The Light now illumines the Straight Path to the Light ("Light upon Light! Allah will guide whom He will to His light") in the present and into the future. Those who refuse the Light and God's way will reap the grim penalties of darkness.

SURAH 36: YA SIN

Following the Basmillah, the surah's opening aya consists of two letters of the Arabic alphabet. Ya Sin is one of the surahs that begins with the abbreviated letters mentioned earlier. I have indicated the surah's five sections (ruku's) with my brief descriptive headings.

1. Ya Sin.

The Qur'an, Muhammad, and God's Sovereignty, 36:2–12
2 By the Qur'an full of Wisdom, 3 thou [Muhammad] art indeed one of the Messengers 4 on a Straight Way. 5 It is a Revelation sent down by (Him) the Exalted in Might, Most Merciful, 6 in order that thou mayest admonish a people whose fathers had received no admonition and who therefore remain heedless (of the Signs of Allah). 7 The Word is proved true against the greater part of them; for they do not believe. 8 We have put yokes round their necks right up to their chins so that their heads are forced up (and they cannot see). 9 And We have put a bar in front of them and a bar behind them, and, further, We have covered them up so that they cannot see. 10 The same is it to them whether thou admonish them or thou do not admonish them: they will not believe. 11 Thou canst but admonish. Such a one as follows the Message and fears the (Lord) Most Gracious unseen, give such a one therefore good tidings of forgiveness and a reward most generous. 12 Verily, We shall give life to the dead, and We record that which they sent before and that which they leave behind, and of all things have We taken account in a clear Book (of evidence).

Parable of the Rebellious City, Warners, and Judgment, 36:13–32

13 Set forth to them by way of a parable the (story of) the Companions of the City. Behold there came messengers to it. 14 When We (first) sent to them two messengers, they rejected them: but We strengthened them with a third. They [messengers] said, "Truly, we have been sent on a mission to you." 15 The (people) said: "Ye are only men like ourselves; and (Allah) Most Gracious sends no sort of revelation. Ye do nothing but lie." 16 They said: "Our Lord doth know that we have been sent on a mission to you: 17 And Our duty is only to proclaim the clear Message." 18 The (people) said: "For us, we augur an evil omen from you. If ye desist not we will certainly stone you, and a grievous punishment indeed will be inflicted on you by us." 19 They said: "Your evil omens are with yourselves: (deem ye this an evil omen), if ye are admonished? Nay, but ye are a people transgressing all bounds!"

20 Then there came running from the farthest part of the city a man saying, "O my people! Obey the messengers. 21 Obey those who ask no reward of you (for themselves), and who have themselves received Guidance. 22 It would not be reasonable in me if I did not serve Him Who created me and to Whom ye shall (all) be brought back. 23 Shall I take (other) gods besides Him? If (Allah) Most Gracious should intend some adversity for me of no use whatever will be their intercession for me nor can they deliver me. 24 I would indeed if I were to do so be in manifest error. 25 For me I have faith in the Lord of you (all). Listen then to me!" 26 It was said: "Enter thou the Garden." He said "Ah, me! Would that my people knew (what I know)! 27 For that my Lord has granted me forgiveness and has enrolled me among those held in honor!" 28 "And We sent not down against his people after him any hosts from heaven nor was it needful for Us so to do. 29 It was no more than a single mighty Blast and behold! They were (like ashes) quenched and silent. 30 Ah! Alas for (My) servants! There comes not a messenger to them but they mock Him!"

Creation's Joyful Obedience as Signs for Humans to Submit to God: 36:33–50

33 A sign for them is the earth that is dead; We do give it life and produce grain therefrom of which ye do eat. 34 And We produce therein orchards with date-palms and vines and We cause springs to gush forth therein,

35 that they may enjoy the fruits of this (artistry). It was not their hands that made this. Will they not then give thanks? 36 Glory to Allah Who created in pairs all things that the earth produces as well as their own (human) kind and (other) things of which they have no knowledge.

37 And a sign for them is the Night: We withdraw therefrom the Day and behold they are plunged in darkness; 38 And the sun runs his course for a period determined for him: that is the decree of (Him) the Exalted in Might, the All-Knowing. 39 And the moon, We have measured for her mansions (to traverse) till she returns like the old (and withered) lower part of date-stalk. 40 It is not permitted to the sun to catch up the moon, nor can the night outstrip the day: each (just) swims along in (its own) orbit (according to Law). 41 And a sign for them [humans] is that We bore their race (through the flood) in the loaded ark; 42 And We have created for them similar (vessels) on which they ride. 43 If it were Our Will We could drown them; then would there be no helper (to hear their cry) nor could they be delivered, 44 except by way of mercy from Us and by way of (worldly) convenience (to serve them) for a time. 45 When they are told, "Fear ye that which is before you and that which will be after you in order that ye may receive mercy," (they turn back). 46 Not a sign comes to them from among the signs of their Lord but they turn away therefrom. 47 And when they are told "Spend ye of (the bounties) with which Allah has provided you," you Unbelievers say to those who believe: "Shall we then feed those whom, if Allah had so willed, He would have fed (himself)?" Ye are in nothing but manifest error. 48 Further, they say "When will this promise (come to pass), if what ye say is true?" 49 They will not (have to) wait for aught but a single Blast. It will seize them while they are yet disputing among themselves!

Promise and Threat of Judgment, Gardens and Fire: 36:51–67
51 The trumpet shall be sounded when, Behold! From the sepulchers (men) will rush forth to their Lord! 52 They will say: "Ah! Woe unto us! Who hath raised us up from our beds of repose?" (A voice will say:) "This is what (Allah), Most Gracious, had promised, and true was the word of the messengers!" 53 It will be no more than a single blast when Lo!

They will all be brought up before Us! 54 Then on that Day not a soul will be wronged in the least, and ye shall but be repaid the meeds of your past deeds.

55 Verily, the Companions of the Garden shall that Day have joy in all that they do; 56 They and their associates will be in groves of (cool) shade, reclining on thrones (of dignity). 57(Every) fruit (enjoyment) will be there for them; they shall have whatever they call for. 58 "Peace!" A Word (of salutation) from a Lord Most Merciful!

59 And O ye in sin! Get ye apart this Day! 60 Did I not enjoin on you, O ye children of Adam, that ye should not worship Satan; for that he was to you an enemy avowed? 61 And that ye should worship Me (for that) this was the Straight Way? 62 But he did lead astray a great multitude of you. Did ye not then understand? 63 This is the Hell of which ye were (repeatedly) warned! 64 Embrace ye the (Fire) this Day for that ye (persistently) rejected (Truth). 65 That Day shall We set a seal on their mouths. But their hands will speak to Us and their feet bear witness to all that they did. 66 If it had been Our Will, We could surely have blotted out their eyes; then should they have run about groping for the Path, but how could they have seen? 67 And if it had been Our Will, We could have transformed them (to remain) in their places: then should they have been unable to move about nor could they have returned (after error).

Deepening the Opening Theme, Call to Faithfulness, and Resurrection: 36:68–83
68 If We grant long life to any, We cause him to be reversed in nature: will they not then understand? 69 We have not instructed the (Prophet) in poetry nor is it meet for him. This is no less than a Message and a Qur'an making things clear 70 that it may give admonition to any (who are) alive, and that the charge may be proved against those who reject (Truth). 71 See they not that it is We Who have created for them among the things which Our hands have fashioned cattle which are under their dominion? 72 And that We have subjected them to their (use)? Of them, some do carry them, and some they eat: 73 And they have (other) profits from them (besides), and they get (milk) to drink. Will they not then be grateful? 74 Yet they take (for worship) gods other than Allah (hoping) that they might be

helped! 75 They [the gods] have not the power to help them: but they will be brought up (before Our Judgment-Seat) as a troop (to be condemned). 76 Let not their speech then grieve thee. Verily, We know what they hide as well as what they disclose.

77 Doth not man see that it is We Who created him from sperm? Yet behold! He [Man] (stands forth) as an open adversary! 78 And he makes comparisons for us and forgets his own (origin and) creation. He says, "Who can give life to (dry) bones and decomposed ones (at that)?" 79 Say "He will give them life Who created them for the first time! For He is well-versed in every kind of creation!" 80 The same Who produces for you fire out of the green tree when behold! Ye kindle therewith (your own fires)! 81 Is not He Who created the heavens and the earth able to create the like thereof? Yea, indeed! For He is the Creator, Supreme of skill and knowledge (infinite)! 82 Verily, when He intends a thing His command is "Be" and it is! 83 So glory to Him in Whose hands is the dominion of all things; and to Him will ye be all brought back.

PRELIMINARY COMMENTS

Ya Sin has a balanced structure through which themes of the One-Only God's sovereign power exercised in mercy and justice are intertwined with the divine plan revealed in the Message and messengers, and the coming Day of Judgment that opens to the Hereafter. One of the surah's tones assures and strengthens Muhammad and the believers with him; another warns those who reject the Message and messengers that they are defying the Lord of all and will be held accountable for their willful disobedience. Each ruku' is a unity that advances the surah's content with Surahs 36:1–6 and 82–83, and they balance and inform each other as they serve to embrace the whole.

Muhammad is reported to have called Ya Sin the "Heart of the Qur'an." He advised believers to repeat it when they faced doubt, danger, and death, for he realized that it could strengthen the resolve and confidence of Muslims in difficult times and be of comfort to the dying.[30] Read and reread, recited and rerecited even in translation, one may see, hear, and feel the Qur'an's and Islam's powerful appeal to serve God, rejoice in the created world, endure hardships and opposition, and merit God's speaking "Peace! Salaam!" to His people.

RELATION TO THE QUR'AN'S UNDERLYING UNITY

Ya Sin is placed in a series that begins with Surah 34 and ends with Surah 39 (al-Zumar, Crowds). Although the set is not in the chronological order of revelation, I regard Ya Sin as the fulcrum for the series. Surahs 34 and 35 build up to Ya Sin. Surah 34 opens with a paean to God's One-Only-ness in words reminiscent of the Throne and Light Ayas. Surah 35 (al-Fatir, the Originator of Creation) calls on celestial beings as witnesses of God's power over all and summons humans to shun Shaytan's snares and be ready for the Yawm Din. Surah 35:1–7 names God as the One full of Wisdom and Exalted in Power, the Creator who sustains and nourishes all, then warns reader-listeners about the Deceiver-Satan and the danger of reject-ing God's latest and final Messenger, for the Day of Judgment is coming. Given their placement in the Qur'an's order, these surahs lead to God's reiterated endorsement of Muhammad and the coming vindication of the Message and the Messenger. Surahs 37–39 look forward to the defeat and punishment of Shaytan and his minions and humans who reject the Straight Way. The picture of crowds of damned persons being herded into Hell by the angels of punishment are matched by descriptions of the joy of those on their way to the Garden of Bliss singing, "Praise be to Allah, the Lord of the Worlds!" (Surah 39:71–75).

Ya Sin is the center for the series. The series' earlier surahs point to signs in creation and history, to the ultimate revelation in the Qur'an and Muhammad. From Surah 36 onward the revelatory action forecasts judg-ment and the Hereafter. God's guidance of and revelations to Muhammad in and through Ya Sin are crucial. Muhammad has been prepared to be the Messenger, is receiving the Qur'an, proclaims it in spite of ridicule and en-mity, gathers believers, and lives the Qur'an. As would anyone, he will feel inadequate for the task, will be wounded by his opponents' barbs, and will be troubled over the fate of those who seem hell-bent for Hell. Ya Sin ad-

dresses him and, subsequently, all who have him as their model. Strengthened by Ya Sin, he carried on his mission with such dedication and obedience to God that one of his honorific names is Ya Sin.

Ya Sin's five sections are in a progressive order that forms a whole.
The sections especially emphasize the Qur'an's underlying unity and draw
in Muhammad's role in proclaiming it to the world.

The Qur'an, Muhammad, and God's Sovereignty, 36:2–12

God's One-Only-ness is the heart of the "Heart of the Qur'an." The first
ruku' is virtually an abstract of the surah and even the Qur'an. God's en-
dorsements of the Qur'an and Muhammad open Ya Sin. Muhammad
is placed immediately in the ranks of the earlier messengers who have
been shown God's grace and who guide others on the Straight Way. The
Qur'an, introduced in Aya 2, is the often implicit and sometimes explicit continuo theme of Ya Sin. Its purposes and Message are sounded
throughout the role given Muhammad. He is the Message's God-authorized
speaker-proclaimer: "It is a Revelation sent down by (Him) the Exalted in
Might, Most Merciful, in order that thou [Muhammad] mayest admonish
a people whose fathers had received no admonition and who therefore
remain heedless (of the Signs of Allah)" (36:5–6). The passage discloses
that God had not yet sent a messenger to the Arab people. Muhammad's preaching-teaching-leading roles directed to the Arabs is crucial for
their specific guidance on the Straight Way. Their eternal fates depend
on their responses to Muhammad and the Message he proclaims. The
ruku' ends with the assurance that God will resurrect the dead for a time
of judgment.

The Parable of the Rebellious City, Warners, and Judgment, 36:13–32

The second ruku', 36:13–32, provides a relevant mathal. It depicts a city that
Allah is giving a last chance to change its ignorant and sinful ways by obeying three messenger-warners sent by God to admonish the inhabitants
to turn toward Allah before they are destroyed.[31] Here the unity of the

Qur'an addresses not only the city dwellers' relationship to God but also the apparently unjust conditions in the city. The audience's reaction is predictable. They sneer that surely a great God would not have entrusted such a message to nondescript folk. The city dwellers denounced the messengers as evil, then prepared to stone them. As the situation turned ugly, a man running from the farthest edge of the city warned that they should obey the messengers. He testified to the one God in spite of opposition and danger. The theme of judgment with rewards as well as punishments was sounded even as the runner-announcer lamented the fate of his fellow citizens if they persisted in opposing God and His messengers. Again the city dwellers refused. There was no need to detail the city's gory end; it was blasted into ashes (36:28–32). An added element is the emphasis given to the reactions accorded the messengers: few will accept and many will reject the message. The messengers, however, should not be deterred or discouraged; God's will shall be done.

Creation's Joyful Obedience as Signs for Humans to Submit to God: 36:33–50

As familiar as it may have been to listener-readers then and may be now, the third ruku' reiterates the role of the created world as ayas pointing to the One-Only God and His will. Bridging the mathal about the city that disobeyed to its death, the Revealer indicated that he brings life out of the dead earth by nourishing vegetation as a sign of raising life from that which has no life except by His will. The oft-stated theme of human ingratitude for the care and bounty God gives through nature is coupled with references to the orderly obedience to God shown by night and day, sun and moon. A deft retransition takes the witness of nature through water and rain to the flood and God saving humanity in the ark. Again, humans showed themselves to be stubborn and disobedient, greedy and uncaring about the needs of others. Rejection of God as God and as the source of justice and compassion will result in the destruction of defiant unbelievers even as they squabble about how and what to feed the needy among them.

Promise and Threat of Judgment, Gardens and Fire: 36:51–67

The beginning of the surah having set the stage for and given clear fore-casts of the coming judgment on the world, Ya Sin becomes specific about the Day of Judgment and the resurrection of the dead. The despised mes-sengers will be vindicated on that Day. More important, the unbelievers-sinners who rejected God and mocked the Message and those who obeyed and served the One-Only God will realize the truth that was proclaimed. The willingly Satan-deceived rejecters will confess and mourn their errors, but it will be too late for them to change the righteous judgment they have brought on themselves. The believers, on the other hand, will be welcomed into the peace God graciously promised them and which they have earned. Themes announced in al-Fatihah about worship, divine aid, the Siraatal Mustiqiim, the ways of believers and the dismal ways of the disobedient reappear for both the righteous and the damned.

Deepening the Opening Theme, Call to Faithfulness, and Resurrection: 36:68–83

The final ruku' begins where the surah opened: with the Qur'an and Mu-hammad. The denial that Muhammad was a poet is apt. Poets were held to concoct their song-stories and to embroider traditional songs with fan-ciful accounts and claims. Surah 26:221–24 links the poets to demons who deceive and mislead persons into sin and unbelief:

> Shall I inform you (O people!) on whom it is that the evil ones de-scend? They descend on every lying wicked (into whose ears) they pour hearsay vanities and most of them are liars. And the Poets it is those straying in evil who follow them: Seest thou not that they wan-der distracted in every valley? And that they say what they practice not? Except those who believe, work righteousness, engage much in the remembrance of Allah, and defend themselves only after they are unjustly attacked. And soon will the unjust assailants know what vi-cissitudes their affairs will take!

Muhammad is one of God's messengers, and the Qur'an is the clear and certain Revelation. Believers, including the Messenger, are not to be discouraged—a theme derived from the mathal about the city—when opposed by idolaters. The opponents will be shamed in this life and certainly in the judgment. Ya Sin's last aya is a baleful admonition to mocking unbelievers and joyful comfort to the faithful: "So glory to Him in Whose hands is the dominion of all things; and to Him will ye be all brought back."

MUHAMMAD'S CONTEXT

Ya Sin relates to Muhammad's immediate situation and overall mission. Muslim tradition considers the surah to have been revealed in Mecca between about 615 and 622. Muhammad was deeply troubled not only by the opposition to him personally but also at the prospect of his fellow Meccans, Qurayshi tribespeople, and Hashem relatives being damned eternally for their polytheistic idolatry, societal inequities, personal iniquities, and refusal to accept God's revelation. Those who now mocked him were once his clansmen, friends, neighbors, and business associates. Convinced of the Message's truth and saddened by the disrupted relationships, as well as the prospect of God's justified wrath that could be visited on the city even before the great calamity of the End Time, Muhammad may even have considered toning down Allah's rhetoric or being open to a gradualist accommodation until the Qurayshi oligarchy was ready to accept the full force of God's One-Only-ness. Ya Sin clarified his mission, strengthened his adherence to God's purposes, and stiffened his resolve not to be distracted by either misplaced compassion or doubt-producing invective from his Meccan critics. Speaking through Gabriel, God assured him that he was one of the messengers of the Straight Way. As the other messengers were opposed, so would he (36:2–7). His task was not to make converts; Allah and those who heard the Message would be engaged in that effort. Muhammad was not to count success or failure in terms of "making" Muslims as an artisan would make a product or a merchant makes a sale. His mission in Mecca was to proclaim the Quranic truth of the only God and His will for individuals, the city, and the world (Surah 36:10–11).

The context of the "Heart of the Qur'an" expanded to Medina. Muhammad's Meccan opponents continued their polemics, open assaults, and subversive activities with Medinan Hypocrites, Jews, and Christians. In Medina Muhammad was not only a warner but also the Messenger-Leader. If Adam was created to be God's vicegerent in the earthly world, Muhammad could be likened to Allah's deputy with the opportunity and challenge to establish the just society whose principles and rules were still being revealed through the Qur'an. As Ya Sin encouraged and emboldened him in Mecca, it was to inspire and strengthen him in Medina. The signs in creation and human events together with the success of the Hijra pointed to the only God and the commission to do what He commanded. Surah 36 included references to sharing the wealth, bounty, and food provided by God with the needy and hungry (36:47). Allah's humans were to remember that He gave them the grains, fruits, and precious water that met their daily and communal needs. The proper response, whether in Mecca or in Medina, was to acknowledge God's mercy and power through generous giving to others. The rebirth of nature, the growth of date palms and orchards, testify to the power and will of God, yet humans still did not see the signs and give glory to God (Surah 36:33–36). While in Medina, the umma faced the creaturely fact of death. Here again Ya Sin applied. Tirmidhi reported (Hadith 2178) and Abu Dawood (Hadith 2113) concurred: "The Prophet (peace be upon him) said, 'If anyone recites Ya Sin out of a desire for Allah's favor, his past sins will be forgiven him, so recite it over those of you who are dying.'"

MOMENTUM FOR CONTINUAL RELEVANCE

The above leads into the third area of understanding Ya Sin: its continuing importance. While the Qur'an's views of death and the Hereafter are taken up in chapter 9, here I note that Ya Sin is especially important when a person is dying. On the surface, Ya Sin seems to spend little time on death. It is a joyful, although stern, affirmation of God's authority and power.

Nothing can thwart God and His will to protect, guide, and vindicate those who follow His way. Those who confess their faith and who obey the Messenger are assured that on the Last Day the One Who created all by the Voice of Command will resurrect the decomposed bones and disclose what is hidden so that believers can have confident hope and anticipate justification before their detractors. They will rejoice in the justice of God, saying, "Peace! [Salaam!] A Word (of salutation) from a Lord Most Merciful! (Surah 36:51–58). But those who reject God, defy the Messenger, and fail to accumulate good deeds will not hear the Master of the Day of Judgment salute them with "Salaam!" Instead, God will tell them to embrace the fire of Hell because they persistently rejected truth (Surah 36:59–64).

Surah 36 calls on members of all societies and especially those that claim to be Muslim to listen to and implement the Qur'an's social principles and instructions. The society may be a small group of believers living under diaspora conditions in the West or in countries that are legally Islamic. In the midst of opposition and misunderstanding, those who are instructed in the Revelation and who follow the Messenger's sunna are called to persevere in their efforts to establish and maintain a just society.

Ya-Sin was addressed to an individual who then gathered a small group of Companions. Although Muhammad was a unique person who was specially prepared to receive the Revelation, he is still the pattern and model for Muslim believers and leaders. Ya Sin is God's word to him to go against the grain of societal and political forces and to risk his life and those of others in order to do God's will. His Meccan mission was to warn, and his Medinan responsibilities called on him to struggle, organize, and rule under God's guidance. Again, the same positive and negative possibilities just mentioned emerge when dedicated individuals gather and lead clusters of like-minded believers to actualize what they understand to be God's will for the umma and the world.

CONCLUSION

These four cherished passages disclose the essence, greatness, and heart of the Qur'an and prepare us to consider the destination of the Straight Way in the Hereafter. The interpretive pattern suggested by Rahman may serve as a way for non-Muslims to gain some understanding of Islam's fullness as a direction in life now for individuals, communities, and the wider society all under the sovereignty of the Most Gracious, Most Merciful, Lord and Master of the Day of Judgment.

> "Is not He Who created the heavens and the earth able to create the like thereof?" Yea indeed! For He is the Creator Supreme of skill and knowledge (infinite)! Verily when He intends a thing, His command is "Be" and it is! So glory to Him in Whose hands is the dominion of all things; and to Him will ye be all brought back. (Surah 36:81–83)

NINE

THE QUR'AN ON THE END OF THIS WORLD AND LIFE IN THE HEREAFTER

We created the heavens and the earth and all between them
in six days, nor did any sense of weariness touch Us. Bear then
with patience all that they say. And celebrate the praises of
thy Lord before the rising of the sun, and before (its) setting,
and during part of the night. (Also) celebrate His praises and
(so likewise) after the postures of adoration. And listen for the
Day when the Caller will call out from a place quite near;
the Day when they will hear a (mighty) Blast. In (very) truth,
that will be the Day of Resurrection. Verily, it is We Who give
Life and Death; and to Us is the Final Goal—the Day when
the Earth will be rent asunder from (men) hurrying out.
That will be a gathering together quite easy for Us. We know
best what they say; and thou art not one to ever awe them by
force. So admonish with the Qur'an such as fear My Warning!

Surah 50:38–45, Qaf

Many religions have revelations, teachings, traditions, and expectations about
the connections between life in the present, death, life after death, the end
of the current world, and what may happen next. The often puzzling and
sometimes lurid descriptions about the end of a person's and the cosmos's

existence usually influence an individual's ethics, a community's sociopolitical structures and values, and views of divine intentions and powers. How literally or figuratively passages and images are to be taken is a matter of serious concern among believers and nonbelievers.

Muslims debate "end-time" issues raised in the Qur'an and the Hadith. The debates escalate when non-Muslims open the Qur'an seeking information about Muslim understandings. Here we venture into this controversial territory. The chapter begins with the Qur'an's summons to humanity in light of the imminent deaths of humans and the world and descriptions of life in the Hereafter, then turns to Quranic descriptions of an individual's death. The third section deals with the end of this world (al-Dunya), and the fourth focuses on life in the Hereafter (al-Akhira). In addition, we examine several Hadith collections that provide details and images concerning death, the end of this physical world, and the Hereafter.

It is Allah Who has sent down the Book in truth and the Balance (by which to weigh conduct). And what will make thee realize that perhaps the Hour is close at hand? Only those wish to hasten it who believe not in it. Those who believe hold it in awe and know that it is the Truth. Behold, verily those that dispute concerning the Hour are far astray. Gracious is Allah to His servants. He gives sustenance to whom He pleases, and He has Power, and can carry out His Will. (Surah 42:17–19)

THE QUR'AN'S SUMMONS

Praise be to Allah Who created (out of nothing) the heavens and the earth, Who made the angels messengers with wings two or three or four (pairs). He adds to Creation as He pleases, for Allah has power over all things. What Allah out of His Mercy doth bestow on mankind there is none can withhold; what He doth withhold there is none can grant apart from Him. And He is the Exalted in Power, Full of Wisdom. O men! Call to mind the grace of Allah unto you! Is there a Creator other than Allah to give you sustenance

from heaven or earth? There is no god but He. How then
are ye deluded away from the Truth? And if they reject thee
[Muhammad], so were messengers rejected before thee.
To Allah go back for decision all affairs. O men! Certainly
the promise of Allah is true. Let not then this present life
deceive you nor let the Chief Deceiver deceive you about
Allah. Verily, Satan is an enemy to you; so treat him as an
enemy. He only invites his adherents that they may become
Companions of the Blazing Fire. For those who reject Allah
is a terrible Penalty: but for those who believe and work
righteous deeds is Forgiveness and a magnificent Reward.

Surah 35:1–7

Everything and everyone in this world is hastening to the Overwhelming Event when all but God will be torn asunder. The Hereafter's eternal
blessed Garden (al-Jannah) and everlasting Hell (Jahannam) will be revealed
as resurrected men and women come to the awesome judgment of God.[1]

When the sky is rent asunder and hearkens to (the Command of) its
Lord—and it must needs (do so)—and when the earth is flattened
out and casts forth what is within it and becomes (clean) empty, and
hearkens to (the Command of) its Lord—and it must needs (do so),
(then will come Home the full Reality). O thou man! Verily, thou art
ever toiling on towards the Lord, painfully toiling, but thou shalt
meet Him. Then he who is given his Record in his right hand soon
will his account be taken by an easy reckoning, and he will turn to his
people rejoicing! But he who is given his Record behind his back,
soon will he cry for Perdition, and he will enter a Blazing Fire. Truly
did he go about among his people rejoicing! Truly did he think that he
would not have to return (to Us)! Nay, nay! For his Lord was (ever)
watchful of him! So I do call to witness the ruddy glow of sunset; the
night and its homing; and the moon in her fullness; ye shall surely

travel from stage to stage. What then is the matter with them that they believe not? And when the Qur'an is read to them, they fall not prostrate. But on the contrary the Unbelievers reject (it). But Allah has full knowledge of what they secret (in their breasts). So announce to them a Penalty grievous, except to those who believe and work righteous deeds: for them is a Reward that will never fail. (Surah 84, al-Inshiqaq, Rending Asunder)

God is the Master of the Yawm Din (Surah 1:4). As noted in chapter 3, *din* has four interlocking meanings: supreme authority; obedience, submission, and devotion to that authority; the system, rituals, teachings, and structures established by that authority; and the retributions and rewards meted out to individuals by that authority. The Day of Judgment is the time when Din's meanings will be brought together so that every person will be accountable for how he and she responded to God's Din. Because the whole of human existence can be embraced within worship as expressed in confessing-serving the One-Only God, establishing prayer, and caring for the poor, every human—Muslim and non-Muslim—will have to answer for faithfulness. The Qur'an, earlier books, and proclamations of previous prophets-messengers disclosed God's will for the ways that humans were told to arrange and live in their communities, from families to empires, that Day will include social and political deeds.[2]

Nature and events prior to the disclosures to Muhammad and the declarations made by the earlier messengers-prophets informed people in those times of the One-Only God and His will. The Qur'an expresses the content of those signs and proclamations, fulfilling the Message in the final disclosure. On the Awesome Day every person's intentions and deeds will be exposed and weighed in the balance on the basis of the God-given Criterion, the Qur'an.

Say: "Shall I seek for judge other than Allah? When He it is Who hath sent unto you the Book explained in detail." They know full well to whom We have given the Book that it hath been sent down from thy Lord in truth. Never be then of those who doubt. The Word of thy Lord doth find its fulfillment in truth and in justice: none can change

His Words, for He is the one who heareth and knoweth all. Wert thou to follow the common run of those on earth they will lead thee away from the Way of Allah. They follow nothing but conjecture: they do nothing but lie. Thy Lord knoweth best who strayeth from His Way. He knoweth best who they are that receive His guidance. (Surah 6:114–17, al-An'am, Cattle)

Moreover, after the Time of the Final Revelation, humanity has a divinely prepared, still human paradigm for living the Straight Path: the Messenger Muhammad. Prepared from childhood and tested by God, Muhammad proved faithful to the One-Only God, seeking to know and do God's will, and steadfast even to the point of near-assassination. He became the human leader on the Straight Path, carrying out the personal, social, political, and military principles and instructions mandated in the Qur'an. He is the one and only person who lived fully and freely the meaning of the Qur'an. God proclaimed him the "beautiful pattern for anyone whose hope is in Allah and the Final Day and who engages much in praise of Allah" (Surah 33:21) and who is of "an exalted standard of character" (Surah 68:4). Responses to Muhammad as God's Messenger is one of the factors in the judgment determining a person's eternal destination:

"And if any believe not in Allah and His Messenger, We have prepared for those who reject Allah a Blazing Fire!" (Surah 48:13, al-Fath, Victory)

O ye who believe! Shall I lead you to a bargain that will save you from a grievous Penalty? That ye believe in Allah and His Messenger and that ye strive (your utmost) in the Cause of Allah with your property and your persons: that will be best for you if ye but knew! He will forgive you your sins and admit you to Gardens beneath which rivers flow and to beautiful mansions in Gardens of Eternity. That is indeed the supreme Achievement. (Surah 61:10–12)[3]

One of Muhammad's roles is to warn all persons about the Day so that they will turn to the One-Only God, worshiping only Him through obedience and service. For them to do otherwise is to forfeit their own souls' blessedness in the Hereafter. Muhammad is commanded to tell the Meccans and through them all people:

Say: "Travel through the earth and see what was the end of those who rejected truth."

Say: "To whom belongeth all that is in the heavens and on earth?"

Say: "To Allah. He hath inscribed for Himself (the rule of) Mercy that He will gather you together for the Day of Judgment there is no doubt whatever. It is they who have lost their own souls that will not believe. "To Him belongeth all that dwelleth (or lurketh) in the night and the day. For He is the One Who heareth and knoweth all things."

Say: "Shall I take for my protector any other than Allah, the Maker of the heavens and the earth? And He is that feedeth but is not fed."

Say: "Nay! But I am commanded to be the first of those who bow to Allah (in Islam) and be not thou of the company of those who join gods with Allah."

Say: "I would if I disobeyed my Lord indeed have fear of the penalty of a Mighty Day. On that day if the penalty is averted from any it is due to Allah's Mercy; and that would be (Salvation), the obvious fulfillment of all desire. If Allah touch thee with affliction none can remove it but He; if He touch thee with happiness He hath power over all things. He is the Irresistible (watching) from above over His worshippers; and He is the Wise acquainted with all things."

Say: "What thing is most weighty in evidence?"

Say: "Allah is Witness between me and you: this Qur'an hath been revealed to me by inspiration that I may warn you and all whom it reaches. Can ye possibly bear witness that besides Allah there is another god?"

Say: "Nay! I cannot bear witness!"

Say: "But in truth He is the One Allah, and I truly am innocent of (your blasphemy of) joining others with Him. Those to whom We have given the Book know this as they know their own sons. Those who have lost their own souls refuse therefore to believe." (Surah 6:11–20)

The Qur'an frequently depicts life in the present as God testing humans—how do they respond to prosperity and poverty, success and failure, obedience to and rejection of the Message. The events of an individual's life and of communities are part of God's plan, yet within the range of human abilities to make choices. Those who endure God's tests and who reject Iblis's deceptions will gain the blessed reward in the Hereafter. Those, however, who turn from God when tested, who are ungrateful to their Lord, and who disobey the Quranic injunctions for justice will find on the Last Day that their deficits in faithfulness and good works will consign them to the Blazing Fire.[4]

Obviously, humans die before the arrival of the cosmic Last Day. According to God's plan, death is a foretaste of the Judgment:

Man We did create from a quintessence (of clay); Then We placed him as (a drop of) sperm in a place of rest firmly fixed; Then We made the sperm into a clot of congealed blood; then of that clot We made a (foetus) lump; then We made out of that lump bones and clothed the bones with flesh; then We developed out of it another creature: so blessed be Allah the Best to create! After that at length ye will die. Again, on the Day of Judgment will ye be raised up. (Surah 23:12–16)

DEATH AND THE GRAVE

It is Allah that takes the souls (of men) at death: and those that die not (He takes) during their sleep. Those on whom He has passed the decree of death He keeps back (from returning to life) but the rest He sends (to their bodies) for a term appointed. Verily in this are signs for those who reflect.

Surah 39:42

God's plan for all existence involves a network of covenants. One depicts each soul entering into a covenant of faithfulness with God before being born into this world. This world itself is a set of covenanted signs pointing all persons and communities to the One-Only God. Every person and society knows about, is called to worship, is able to obey, and is accountable to God. Compounding human responsibility is God sending prophets and messengers to announce to every society the One-Only God's will and the coming of the End. No one, therefore, can claim ignorance of God's will. That will, according to the Qur'an, clearly points to the certainty of resurrection and judgment. Quranically, nature points toward God's plan through the cycle of growth, apparent death, and revival. The waxing, waning, and rewaxing of the moon also signals the pattern of life, death, and resurrection. Sleep, too, is a sign of death, judgment, resurrection, and the Hereafter.[5] God's plan for each person and every community includes His setting a definite term or limit in which He decrees the moment for their deaths (Surah 56:60, al Waqi'ah, the Inevitable). The decree cannot be avoided; wherever a person may be, death will find him or her. During sleep, God takes all souls out of their bodies, returning some to awaken from sleep and others, whose decreed time had come, into death (Surah 4:78–79).

How the soul leaves the body, that is, how the person dies, foreshadows its eternal fate. The deaths of sinners and rejecters of Islam are described as a horror and that of the faithful as a blessing. When a person's allotted term has run out, God sends the angels of death to take the person's soul.[6] The angels of death gently draw the souls of the righteous from their bodies (Surah 79:1, al-Nazi'at, Those Who Tear Out). The souls of those who will be condemned on the Last Day suffer mightily. The angels of death rip their souls from their bodies, then scourge those souls as foretastes of the punishments to come on the Day: "If thou couldst see when the angels take the souls of the unbelievers (at death), (how) they smite their faces and their backs (saying): 'Taste the penalty of the blazing fire. Because of (the deeds) which your (own) hands sent forth: for Allah is never unjust to His servants'" (Surah 8:50–51). Because Islam emphasizes the coordination of faith, religious observance, and righteous deeds, deathbed repentances are of no value. Some plead to be sent back to their bodies and to this world so that they might do the deeds and offer the worship that they had refused to do. But there is a barrier between the grave and the realm of those who live in this world (Surah 23:99–100):

> Allah accepts the repentance of those who do evil in ignorance and repent soon afterwards; to them will Allah turn in mercy; for Allah is full of knowledge and wisdom. Of no effect is the repentance of those who continue to do evil until death faces one of them and he says "Now have I repented indeed"; nor of those who die rejecting faith. For them have We prepared a punishment most grievous. (Surah 4:17–18)

The Quranic point is clear: life in the present world is serious, complete in and of itself, filled with plenty of opportunities to walk in the Straight Way of the merciful and just God. While persons are alive, angels record every thought, word, and deed. Once a person dies, the record is sealed until the Day of Judgment. There will be no surprises, for each person will know what he or she has earned (Surah 29:56–64):

> Every soul shall have a taste of death: and only on the Day of Judgment shall you be paid your full recompense. Only he who is saved far from the fire and admitted to the garden will have attained the object (of life): for the life of this world is but goods and chattels of deception. (Surah 3:185)

THE END OF THIS WORLD

> By the Mount (of Revelation); by a Decree inscribed in
> a Scroll unfolded; by the much-frequented House [the
> Ka'bah]; by the Canopy raised high; and by the ocean
> filled with swell; Verily, the Doom of thy Lord will indeed
> come to pass. There is none can avert it. On the Day when
> the firmament will be in dreadful commotion, and the
> mountain will fly hither and thither, then woe that Day

to those that treat (truth) as falsehood, that play (and paddle) in shallow trifles.

Surah 52:1–12, al-Tur, the Mount,

The Qur'an does not establish a timetable for the destruction of this world for, given room for hyperbole, one of God's days could be as long as a thousand human years.[7] Throughout his revelatory activity Muhammad also declined to give the time when the End would come:

They ask thee about the (final) hour, when will be its appointed time? Say: "The knowledge thereof is with my Lord (alone). None but He can reveal as to when it will occur. Heavy were its burden through the heavens and the earth. Only all of a sudden will it come to you." They ask thee as if thou wert eager in search thereof: Say: "The knowledge thereof is with Allah (alone) but most men know not." Say: "I have no power over any good or harm to myself except as Allah willeth. If I had knowledge of the unseen, I should have multiplied all good, and no evil should have touched me. I am but a warner and a bringer of glad tidings to those who have faith." (Surah 7:187–88)

Although the Qur'an is modest and understated in its descriptions of the end of this world, at least in comparison to the hadiths and passages in the New Testament such as the Revelation to John, it makes clear that this world will end with convulsions in the cosmos and among humans. An initial reading of the Qur'an gives the impression that the end of the present space-time of this world leads immediately to the Hereafter's first stages of the resurrection of all humans so that their souls and bodies will be reunited. A closer reading indicates a more extended and violent process. There will be signs that the end is approaching. Muslim scholars differ on the number and the sequence of these signs.[8] While it is possible for some Muslims to interpret the signs symbolically and allegorically, most understand these as happenings that will occur in the future. Muslim scholars generally discourage speculations that label different groups as instruments of Iblis attacking the faithful before the end of this world and generating apocalyptic calendars. A growing number of Muslims, however, are developing apocalyptic scenarios with contemporary political emphases.[9]

Two major signs amplified in the hadiths require comment. First is Gog and Magog (Yajuj and Majuj). Mentioned by the Hebrew prophet Ezekiel (chaps. 38 and 39) as the ruler of the land of Magog, Gog is predicted to lead an international army of heavily armed and terrifying troops from Mesopotamia and Ethiopia against regions as far-flung as Tarshish (Spain). The Quranic account both resembles and differs from that of Ezekiel 38. Surah 18:83 (al-Kahf, the Cave) introduces Dhu al-Qarnayn, identified sometimes as Alexander the Great. Made powerful by God, he traveled extensively to discover where the sun sets and from where it rises (in a spring of murky water). He arrived at a land between two mountains where a people threatened by Gog and Magog lived. He built a barrier made of iron, rock, and molten lead that filled a mountain pass that separated the hapless people from their foes. But, according to God's plan, in the calamities leading up to the end Gog and Magog will breach the barrier and their armies will pour out on the world.[10] Terrible battles reminiscent of Ezekiel 38 will be fought before God destroys Gog and Magog, and the wild beasts will fatten on the unburied corpses. But the respite will come to its end, and this world will careen to its destruction.

The second sign is ad-Dajjal and the return of Jesus. The word *dajjal* (sometimes *dajaal* or *dajjall*) means "to cover" or "to conceal." It evolved to mean deception and evil persons and beings who present wickedness as good and idolatry as true religion. Finally, the term became the name of a monstrous human who claimed to be God and who would appear almost at the end of this world. The Dajjal is not mentioned directly in the Qur'an, but Muslim interpreters discern references to him through well-attested hadiths, especially by Imam Muslim.[11] He is sometimes called *al-massich ad-Dajjal,* that is, the messiah of Dajjal (deception) and the Antichrist.

The appearance of the Dajjal will be the worst *fitna,* or excruciating trial, that humans would ever face. Instead of confronting him directly, Muhammad advised believers to flee from him. The Dajjal is a hairy, squat, grotesquely deformed human being who is loathsome, sterile, immensely powerful, and able to perform miracles. Between his eyes are the Arabic letters *KFR,* the consonants for *kafir,* misbeliever. Chained in a cave somewhere in the east, he will be released according to God's plan and will march forth with his terrible armies, looting and killing as he goes. He will appear suddenly and in different places and enter all areas of the world, except for the holy cities of Mecca and Medina. Claiming to be God, he will demand that people worship him or die. God's enemies will join his ranks, and many deceived Muslims will follow him. A core group of Muslims will retreat to Jerusalem. Al-Mahdi, the guiding one, will appear to lead them.[12] Al-Mahdi, a member of Muhammad's family, will lead the faithful in fervent prayer as the forces of the Dajjal mass outside of Jerusalem for the final assault on Islam. God's plan then calls for Jesus to descend from his heavenly place to Damascus and proceed in the company of warrior angels to Jerusalem. Deferring to the Mahdi's leadership in prayer, Jesus will open the gates of Jerusalem to confront, then kill the Dajjal. The deceiver's armies will also perish.

One of Imam Muslim's hadiths continues that the Mahdi will establish a seven-year period of justice and equity,[13] during which people will live without rancor. After that God will send a cold wind from the direction of Syria. None of those who have a speck of good or faith in God in them will live. During that time, Jesus will reach the age of forty and die because all humans are intended to experience death and the grave:

> Even if some among you were to enter the innermost part of the mountain, this wind would reach that place also and cause your death. I heard Allah's Messenger (peace be upon him) as saying: Only the wicked people will survive and they will be as careless as birds with the characteristics of beasts. They will never appreciate good nor condemn evil. Then Satan will come to them, in human form, and would say: Don't you respond? They will say: What do you order us to do? He will command them to worship the idols but, in spite of this, they will have an abundance of sustenance and lead comfortable lives. Then the trumpet will be blown and he who hears it will bend his neck to one side and raise it from the other side. The first one to hear that

trumpet will be the person who is busy in setting right the cistern meant for supplying water to the camels. He will faint and the other people will also faint.

After a time of gross immorality, the archangel Israfil will blow the first apocalyptic trumpet blast. All will die, and everything will be obliterated (Surah 69:13–16, al-Haqqah, the Sure Reality). Only God will live (Surah 55:26–27, al-Rahman, the Most Gracious). Al-Dunya, this physical world, will be no more. Al-Akhira, the Hereafter, begins:

The Day that He assembles you (all) for a day of Assembly that will be a day of mutual loss and gain (among you). And those who believe in Allah and work righteousness He will remove from them their ills and He will admit them to gardens beneath which rivers flow to dwell therein forever: that will be the Supreme Achievement. But those who reject Faith and treat Our Signs as falsehoods they will be Companions of the Fire to dwell therein for aye: and evil is that Goal. (Surah 64:9–10)

THE HEREAFTER

The (Day) of Noise and Clamor! What is the (Day) of
Noise and Clamor? And what will explain to thee what the
(Day) of Noise and Clamor is? (It is) a Day whereon Men
will be like moths scattered about, and the mountains will
be like carded wool. Then he whose balance (of good deeds)
will be (found) heavy will be in a life of good pleasure and
satisfaction. But he whose balance (of good deeds) will be
(found) light [He] will have his home in a (bottomless) pit.
And what will explain to thee what this is? (It is) a Fire
Blazing fiercely!

Surah 101

THE DAY OF JUDGMENT

Day of Judgment, Sorting Out, Scattering, Dawn, Victory, Noise and Clamor, Resurrection, Great Event, Overwhelming Event, Great News, often simply the Day or even the Hour are Quranic terms for the inaugural act of al-Akhira. As before the beginning, there is only God. Although the Qur'an does not describe it, in his sovereignty God calls into existence those angels whom He wills to exist again or anew. In accord with His eternal plan the sovereign Lord summons Hell and the Gardens into existence, along with something resembling a flat plain on which all humans and jinn will stand for the Judgment. The Qur'an and Muslim tradition speak of "Garden" and "Gardens." The former includes dwellings for all who are welcomed into eternal blessedness; the latter indicates four types of dwellings closer to God for those who have shown exemplary faithfulness to God. In like manner, the Qur'an and Muslim tradition denote seven levels of Hell. As the Hour begins the Last Day, according to Surah 69:17, eight angels will bear the throne of God to the place of judgment. Israfil obeys the command to sound the trumpet blast that calls the dead from their graves—and the Day begins. The Day may even be fifty thousand human years long (Surah 70:1–4).

Meccans and other Arabs mocked Muhammad and the believers for claiming that the dead would be raised on the Last Day: "The Unbelievers say 'Never to us will come the hour' . . ." (Surah 34:3) and "they (sometimes) say: 'There is nothing except our life on this earth and never shall we be raised up again'" (Surah 6:29). God retorts by asserting that His creative power has not waned and that His plan moves swiftly to completion. Surah 7:5–7 repeats points from Surah 7:187–88; God has made humans from dust, sperm, and blood, concluding, "And, verily, the Hour will come. There can be no doubt about it or about (the fact) that Allah will raise up all who are in the graves" (Surah 7:7).

On that Day souls and bodies will be united so that the person will feel the intensity of the Hereafter physically and spiritually. All the dead will be raised from their graves or from wherever their remains may have been scattered. Those who persisted in worshiping anything or anyone other than the One-Only God and scorned God's signs and revelations about the resurrection as well as His commands to live obediently and justly in God's sight will be stunned as they realize their terrible error and horrible fate. Those who were assured of God's mercy when their souls were separated from their bodies will be awed by God's graciousness and mercy. Except for those who died as martyrs for the faith, everyone will be raised as naked as when born, and males, therefore, will be uncircumcised. All will march toward the throne. As they go, each will receive from his or her recording angel the scroll on which is written the record of the individual's faith, intentions, and deeds. Those who will be admitted to the Gardens will be given the scroll by an angel facing them. If the scroll is given from behind, they will know that they are among the damned. Recording and witnessing angels will denounce the condemned for their unbelief, misbelief, hypocrisy, evil deeds, and, worst of all, idolatry:

> And the Trumpet shall be blown: that will be the Day whereof warning (had been given). And there will come forth every soul. With each will be an (angel) to drive and an (angel) to bear witness. (It will be said) "Thou wast heedless of this; now have We removed thy veil and sharp is thy sight this Day!" And his companion will say: "Here is (his record) ready with me!" (The sentence will be) "Throw, throw into Hell every contumacious rejector (of Allah)! Who forbade what was good transgressed all bounds cast doubts and suspicions; Who set up another god besides Allah: throw him into a severe Penalty." His companion will say: "Our Lord! I did not make him transgress, but he was (himself) far astray." He will say: "Dispute not with each other in My Presence: I had already in advance sent you Warning. The Word changes not before Me, and I do not the least injustice to My Servants." (Surah 50:20–29)

The faces of persons who will be blessed will shine brightly, light will issue from them, and their angels will escort them with praises and joy to the Judgment. The others will be raised dirty, with horror-distorted faces. They will be chained together, their bodies covered with flammable tar, and their faces already on fire (14:49–50). Their angels will curse them and begin torturing them with the punishments of Hell:

> One day the Earth will be changed to a different Earth and so will be the Heavens and (men) will be marshaled forth before Allah the One the Irresistible; And thou wilt see the Sinners that day bound together in fetters. Their garments of liquid pitch and their faces covered with Fire; That Allah may requite each soul according to its deserts; and verily Allah is swift in calling account. Here is a Message for mankind: let them take warning therefrom and let them know that He is (no other than) One Allah: let men of understanding take heed. (Surah 14:49–52)

God will summon the prophets and messengers, inquire of them what they had said, and what humans did with the messages entrusted to His revealers. Christians will find out that they were wrong to ascribe divinity to Jesus. Specifically, He will ask Jesus about the message he proclaimed:

> And behold! Allah will say: "O Jesus the son of Mary! Didst thou say unto men 'Worship me and my mother as gods in derogation of Allah'"? He will say: "Glory to Thee! Never could I say what I had no right (to say). Had I said such a thing Thou wouldst indeed have known it. Thou knowest what is in my heart though I know not what is in Thine. For Thou knowest in full all that is hidden. "Never said I to them aught except what Thou didst command me to say to wit 'Worship Allah my Lord and your Lord'; and I was a witness over them whilst I dwelt amongst them; when Thou didst take me up, thou wast the Watcher over them and Thou art a Witness to all things. If Thou dost punish them they are Thy servants: if Thou dost forgive them Thou art the Exalted the Wise." (Surah 5:116–18)

Just as criminals often turn on each other when brought before a judge, those soon-to-be condemned will attempt to shift the blame for their plight onto one another but to no avail. They will appeal to the false gods they substituted for Allah and to the Iblis-based jinn who deceived them into mocking Allah and His messengers and into greed and cruelty. Then, to save themselves, they will be willing to sacrifice others to save their own selves from the impending doom:

> The Day that the sky will be like molten brass. And the mountains will be like wool. And no friend will ask after a friend though they will be put in sight of each other. The sinner's desire will be: would that he could redeem himself from the Penalty of that Day by (sacrificing) his children, his wife and his brother, his kindred who sheltered him, and all, all that is on earth so it could deliver him: By no means! For it would be the Fire of Hell! Plucking out (his being) right to the skull! (Surah 70:8–16)

Believers, on the other hand, will be guided on the way to the throne and from it to their Gardens so that they will lose all vestigial anger and pride. They will be compassionate and eager to show mercy and justice. Before the throne, they will be divided into three groups. The Companions of the Right Hand are composed of two sets.[14] The foremost will be those who will spend the Hereafter in a Garden of Bliss closest to God. They are Muhammad, his Companions and Helpers, the martyrs, and extraordinary believers. The second set of Companions of the Right Hand are the other believers who have been shown Allah's grace and have met the tests of faith and works. They will be admitted to the other Gardens. The Companions of the Left Hand are the condemned. Once before the throne and as their scrolls are weighed in the balances of justice, each will be asked first about his or her adherence to the One-Only God, then the details of his or her intentions and deeds. Those whose scrolls are heavy with goodness and whose answers are confirmed as faithful and true are assured of God's mercy and will continue on the Straight Path to the bridge that leads to the Gardens. The condemned will scream in anguish, but they have earned their fate. They will be dragged face down through flames to a razor-thin and razor-sharp bridge. They have no chance to complete the journey, and they fall into the abyss of flames and eternal punishment.[15]

HELL

Verily, the Day of Sorting Out is a thing appointed. The
Day that the Trumpet shall be sounded and ye shall come
forth in crowds. And the heavens shall be opened as if
there were doors. And the mountains shall vanish as if they
were a mirage. Truly Hell is as a place of ambush, for the
transgressors a place of destination: They will dwell therein
for ages. Nothing cool shall they taste therein nor any drink
save a boiling fluid and a fluid dark murky intensely cold.
A fitting recompense (for them). For that they used not to
fear any account (for their deeds) But they (impudently)
treated Our Signs as false. And all things have We preserved
on record. So taste ye (the fruits of your deeds); for no
increase shall We grant you except in Punishment.

Surah 78:17–30, al-Naba', the Great News

Hell is described in graphic terms. It will be so painful that the damned
will beg Malik, the angel in charge of punishments, and his nineteen angelic guards to extinguish their lives.[16] The Qur'an has been read to indicate that Hell has seven layers, each with its own type of fire and torture.[17] Hell sounds like an intensified, nightmarish Arabian desert. The
searing heat makes the condemned beg for drink, but they are forced to
drink a stench-smelling concoction from the cursed tree Zaqqum that
grows at the base of Hell.[18] It is boiling, thorn-filled water that cuts their
bowels to pieces. In the meantime their skin will be peeled from their bodies, only to grow again to be peeled again in perpetuity.[19] Among those
punished in Hell are Iblis, the demons, and the wicked jinn. They and the
condemned persons will confess that indeed they had been warned, but because they misused their intelligence, they deserve their dreadful fate (Surah
67:6–14)

THE GARDENS

Verily for the righteous there will be a fulfillment of
(the Heart's) desires; Gardens enclosed and Grape-vines;
Companions of Equal Age; And a Cup full (to the Brim).
No Vanity shall they hear therein nor Untruth. Recompense
from thy Lord a Gift (amply) sufficient (from) the Lord of
the heavens and the earth and all between. (Allah) Most
Gracious: none shall have power to argue with Him. The
Day that the Spirit and the angels will stand forth in ranks
none shall speak except any who is permitted by (Allah)
Most Gracious and he will say what is right. That Day
will be the sure Reality: therefore whoso will let him take
a (straight) Return to his Lord! Verily We have warned you
of a Penalty near the Day when man will see (the Deeds)
which his hands have sent forth and the Unbeliever will
say "Woe unto me! Would that I were (mere) dust!"

Surah 78:31–39

If Hell is the desert dwellers' nightmare, the Gardens are their heaven.
The Qur'an is remarkably subdued in its description of the places and
lives of those who are judged worthy of eternal blessedness. In general
the word for *garden* (al-Janna) refers to an oasis-like enclosed area where
fruit trees and water abound. Surah 55:46–51 mentions four eternal Gardens without going into specific details about them. Characteristics common to the Quranic references are that the Gardens are lush and green
and that beneath them flow never-diminishing rivers.[20] The subterranean
rivers reflect the aquifers that make oases in the Arabian desert. Water
from the rivers bubbles upward, forming springs that delight the residents
of the Garden(s). Because the best in the physical world is a similitude for
the Hereafter, fruits on the Garden's trees are the same as those enjoyed

in the previous creation: "But give glad tidings to those who believe and work righteousness that their portion is Gardens beneath which rivers flow. Every time they are fed with fruits therefrom they say: 'Why this is what we were fed with before' for they are given things in similitude; and they have therein companions (pure and holy); and they abide therein (for ever)" (Surah 2:25). Lovely aromas and tranquility provide the atmosphere for life in the Garden(s). The first half of Surah 47:15 describes other types of rivers:

> (Here is) a Parable of the Garden which the righteous are promised: in it are rivers of water incorruptible: rivers of milk of which the taste never changes; rivers of wine a joy to those who drink; and rivers of honey pure and clear. In it there are for them all kinds of fruits and Grace from their Lord.

The wine, however, neither inebriates nor leaves those who drink it with a hangover. Among the trees in the Garden, or a higher place for the especially meritorious called the Garden of the Abode, is the sacred Lote Tree (Surah 53:14).[21] No one can pass beyond it into the closest presence of Allah. The heavenly Lote Tree balances the Tree of Zaqqum and the tree in the Garden of Eden. According to the Qur'an, those who live in the Garden will exist at different levels of blessed nearness to God. An individual's place will be determined by her or his faith and deeds. There will be mansions, perhaps built on tiers, one above the other (Surah 39:20). Yet what of life in the Gardens?

Again, the Quranic revelation opts for understatement, while the hadiths are much more expansive. Two related passages are important. The first is 55:46–78, which omits the seventeen repetitions of "Then which of the favors of your Lord will ye deny?":

> [T]here will be two Gardens containing all kinds (of trees and delights). In them (each) will be two springs flowing (free); in them will be fruits of every kind two and two. They will recline on carpets whose inner linings will be of rich brocade: the fruit of the Gardens

will be near (and easy of reach). In them will be (maidens), chaste, re-straining their glances, whom no man or jinn before them has touched, like unto rubies and coral. Is there any reward for good other than good? And besides these two there are two other Gardens, dark green in color (from plentiful watering). In them (each) will be two springs pouring forth water in continuous abundance: In them will be fruits and dates and pomegranates. In them will be fair (companions) good beautiful, companions restrained (as to their glances) in (goodly) pa-vilions whom no man or jinn before them has touched, reclining on green cushions and rich carpets of beauty. Blessed be the name of thy Lord full of Majesty, Bounty and Honor.

The second is Surah 56:10–38:

And those foremost (in Faith) will be foremost (in the Hereafter). These will be those nearest to Allah in Gardens of Bliss: a number of people from those of old and a few from those of later times. (They will be) on thrones encrusted (with gold and precious stones), reclining on them facing each other. Round about them will (serve) youths of perpetual (freshness) with goblets, (shining) beakers and cups (filled) out of clear-flowing fountains: No after-ache will they receive there-from nor will they suffer intoxication: And with fruits any that they may select; and the flesh of fowls any that they may desire. And (there will be) Companions with beautiful big and lustrous eyes—like unto pearls well-guarded; A reward for the deeds of their past (life). No fri-volity will they hear therein nor any taint of ill, only the saying "Peace! Peace." The Companions of the Right Hand, what will be the Com-panions of the Right Hand? (They will be) among lote trees without thorns, among talh trees with flowers (or fruits) piled one above an-other in shade long-extended by water flowing constantly, and fruit in abundance whose season is not limited nor (supply) forbidden, and on thrones (of dignity) raised high. We have created (their Companions) of special creation. And made them virgin-pure (and undefiled), beloved (by nature), equal in age, the companions of the Right Hand.[22]

The passages describe the joy and serenity promised to the "foremost in Faith," who include the prophets and messengers, Muhammad, his Companions and Helpers, other exemplary holy persons before and after the Revelation, and those who are martyred while struggling in the Way of God, that is, in a jihad. Whether "average" believers are given the same hope may be implied. Interpreters understand the passage literally or as one of the Qur'an's symbolic images. In either instance, the picture is immensely reassuring regarding God's goodness and mercy toward His foremost Muslims. They have endured misunderstanding, suffering, rejection, and ridicule. Some have died for their obedient loyalty to God and the Message. The Qur'an has also noted that those believers who were afflicted with poverty in the physical world, sacrificed their own ambitions for the Faith, gave generously of the substance (such as they had) to help others, did good deeds, and—above all—had right intentions and prayed regularly would be given special rewards in the Hereafter. The passage promises that they will be accorded royal status in the Garden. There will be no hunger, thirst, loneliness, opposition, poverty, or fear. The persons who, in the physical world, were God's servants will be nobles forever in their Lord's presence. The descriptions of their food and drink, luxurious garments, and throne-couches show the goodness, mercy, and sovereignty of the God who bestows His riches on His servants who are now His friends.

We turn now to the "Companions with beautiful big and lustrous eyes," the houris. This passage, like most of the Qur'an, addresses men. It does not depict life in the Garden(s) as a never-ending orgy. There is no hint of sexual activity between the specially created beautiful spiritual virginal beings and the Companions of the Right Hand. Indeed, the text indicates that sexual desire has been transcended: "No frivolity will they hear therein, nor any taint of ill—only the saying 'Peace! Peace.'" I venture that what is promised males among the "foremost" will have its complement among the foremost women. The passages and thoughtful Muslim understandings of life in the Hereafter's Garden are based in the goodness, mercy, and justice of God as indicated in al-Fatihah and stated throughout the Qur'an.

Houris are mentioned four other times in the Qur'an.[23] Smith and Haddad propose that they are the wives of the believing men to whom they were married in this world.[24] Whatever the case may be, they agree that life in the Garden does not include sensuality in the same manner as in the physical world. That leaves open the possibility of an Edenlike relationship between women and men being restored in the new Gardens. Although the Qur'an says little about women (and children) in the Hereafter, Surah 4:124 states: "If any do deeds of righteousness be they male or female and have faith they will enter heaven and not the least injustice will be done to them."

At the risk of blurring our focus on the Qur'an, I cite some Hadith expansions about life in the Garden. Bukhari transmitted a saying by Muhammad concerning a houri: "And if a houri from Paradise appeared to the people of the earth, she would fill the space between Heaven and the Earth with light and pleasant scent and her head cover is better than the world and whatever is in it"[25] Another saying recorded by Tirmidhi has given rise to further details about the reward of martyrs in the Garden. Critics of Islam and perhaps some literalist adherents may refer to ideas such as might be given by a superficial reading of passages like that of Tirmidhi:

> The martyr receives six good things from Allah: he is forgiven at the first shedding of his blood; he is shown his abode in Paradise; he is preserved from the punishment in the grave; he is kept safe from the greatest terror; he has placed on his head the crown of honour, a ruby of which is better than the world and what it contains; he is married to seventy-two wives of the maidens with large dark eyes; and is made intercessor for seventy of his relatives.[26]

Imam Muslim's hadiths give some interesting details about the Gardens that might be testimonials to the power and generosity of God. For example, in Paradise there is a grand tree whose shadow is so great that a rider on a swift horse would travel for a hundred years before emerging from under it; Friday prayers in Paradise will be prefaced by a breeze that will enhance the beauty of the worshipers to the joy of their families; and the faces of believers will be as bright as stars and each would have two wives. "They would neither pass water, nor void excrement, nor will they suffer from catarrh, nor will they spit, and their combs will be made of gold, and their sweat will be musk, the fuel for their braziers will be aloes and their wives will be large eyed maidens, and their form will be as one single person after the form of their father (Adam), sixty cubits tall." In addition, there will be no disagreements or arguing among them. They will spend their time in unity of heart, glorifying Allah day and night. They will eat and drink but belch only to show contentment.[27] Life in the Gardens is good.

> As to the Righteous they shall be amidst (cool) shades and springs (of water). And (they shall have) fruits all they desire. Eat ye and drink ye to your heart's content: for that ye worked (Righteousness)." Thus do We certainly reward the Doers of Good. (Surah 77:41–45)

CONCLUSION

Even before the beginning, the One-Only God had a cosmic plan that expressed His tawhid-sovereignty, mercy, and justice. From the heavens through this physical world and into Hell and the Gardens, God wills righteousness and compassion, obedience and responsibility from His creatures. They came from Him, and to Him they will return. The revelations about life in this world and in the Hereafter are warnings, encouragements, and corrections. All humans are being summoned to the Straight Path and the guidance given by messengers in the past, and now to the Messenger with the final Book.

> O My servants who believe! Truly spacious is My Earth: therefore serve ye Me (and Me alone)! Every soul shall have a taste of death. In the end to Us shall ye be brought back. But those who believe and work deeds of righteousness to them shall We give a Home in Heaven lofty mansions beneath which flow rivers—to dwell therein for aye; an excellent reward for those who do (good)! Those who persevere in patience and put their trust in their Lord and Cherisher. (Surah 29:56–59)

TEN

THE QUR'AN ON WOMAN AND WOMEN

For Muslim men and women, for believing men and
women, for devout men and women, for true men and
women, for men and women who are patient and constant,
for men and women who humble themselves, for men and
women who give in charity, for men and women who fast
(and deny themselves), for men and women who guard their
chastity, and for men and women who engage much in
Allah's praise, for them has Allah prepared forgiveness and
great reward.

Surah 33:35

Is the female, whether as an abstract principle or as a living woman, a
threat to men and to themselves? It would seem so, according to numerous Greco-Roman, Jewish, and Christian traditions throughout North
Africa, the Syrian-Palestinian corridor, and Asia Minor.[1] The message was
clear: woman/women are dangerous, somehow connected to evil forces,
death, sexual immorality, and deception. Logically, then, females are to be
subjugated to men for their own sakes as well as for all humanity. Islam
contains elements and themes that agree with and also contradict those
views. Today Muslims engage in searching debates about the status and

roles of women in the umma and Muslim-majority societies. The Qur'an has a central place in the understandings and misunderstandings about woman/women, yet powerful cultural traditions with thin or no connections to Islamic beliefs are often attributed to Islam. Often these are localized tribal or societal actions such as female circumcision, or clitoridectomy, that have been taken up by some Muslims.[2] Although the Qur'an has preeminent authority, Hadith collections influence Muslim practice. Here I refer to the hadiths while maintaining the focus on the Qur'an.

WORDS GENERIC AND SPECIFIC

By the Book that makes things clear; We have made it
a Qur'an in Arabic that ye may be able to understand
(and learn wisdom).

Surah 43:2–3

Arabic nouns are either male or female. As is the case in English, the word for "man" (*insan*) can be used of male humans and for humans generally, as in "mankind" and "humankind," thereby including woman and women as in "He who obeys the Messenger obeys Allah" (Surah 4:80a). *Zawj* (pl. *azwaj*) is grammatically masculine, yet means mate, spouse, or one of a pair whether male or female. *Imra'ah* (pl. *nisa*) designates an adult woman and wife. *Nafs* (pl. *anfus*) is grammatically feminine and means soul, self, or person and can be used of the soul of a man as well as a woman. *Ruh*, spirit, is feminine, even when applied to God.[3] The Qur'an frequently addresses all humans without specifying whether it intends men or women, such as in a general *ye* (pl. you), they, believers, unbelievers, People of the Book, and related terms. In some contexts, however, it is clear that only men are being addressed, as in "O ye who believe! Ye are forbidden to inherit women against their will" (Surah 4:19a). However, Surah 4:170 is not simply for males: "O mankind! The Messenger hath come to you in truth from Allah: believe in him; it is best for you" and a gender-adjusted Surah 3:14a can apply to all persons whether male or female: "Fair in the eyes of men is the love of things they covet: women and sons; heaped-up hoards of gold and silver." The reader-listener needs to decide about the context in which the terms are used, then test the passages as to whether they fit all humans or only one gender.

> O Mankind! Reverence your Guardian-Lord Who created you from a single person [soul, *nafs*], created of like nature his mate, and from them twain scattered (like seeds) countless men and women. Reverence Allah through Whom ye demand your mutual (rights) and (reverence) the wombs (that bore you): for Allah ever watches over you. (Surah 4:1)

WOMAN IN THE QUR'AN

> It is He Who maketh the stars (as beacons) for you that
> ye may guide yourselves with their help through the dark
> spaces of land and sea: We detail Our Signs for people
> who know. It is He who hath produced you from a single
> person [*nafs*]: here is a place of sojourn and a place of
> departure.
>
> *Surah 6:97–98*

The Qur'an holds that woman and man are spiritual equals before God. Four times in the Revelation God said that all humans are created from the same nafs, or person or soul.[4] As I note in chapter 12, the one *nafs* for all persons who have ever lived and will live is a Quranic basis for justice.

For present purposes, the passages concerning the singular *nafs* for all humankind probably reflects the biblical accounts in Genesis about the creation of humans.[5] The God-determined pattern or form for humanity is beautiful and made to carry out God's purposes: "We have indeed created man in the best of moulds" (taking "man" as including woman; Surah 95:4, Fig). God is the only singular, that is, in this respect the only unpaired reality. He has determined that His One-Only-ness is unique and unapproachable, and He creates all else in pairs:

> With the power and skill did We construct the firmament: for it is We Who create the vastness of space. And We have spread out the (spacious) earth. How excellently We do spread out! And of everything We have created pairs that ye may receive instruction. (Surah 51:48–49, al-Dhariyat, Winds That Scatter)

Couples or pairs such as sun and moon and male and female complement each other. In terms of plants and animals, this matching accounts for fruits and offspring being of the same kind as their progenitors (Surah 36:36). Women and men have the same spiritual essence and status before God. In Islam, any differences between male and female humans, then, are due to their carrying out different God-willed functions in the community and this world. Obviously, one of woman's God-given and blessed roles is to give birth to children in whom men and women rejoice and for whom they thank God. The primal Man and Woman are united, as God wills, and from them, with the exception of Jesus, all other humans are derived. Every subsequent human, including Jesus, has a woman parent:

> It is He who created you from a single person (*nafs*) and made his mate of like nature in order that he might dwell with her (in love). When they are united she bears a light burden and carries it about (unnoticed). When she grows heavy, they both pray to Allah their Lord (saying): "If Thou givest us a goodly child, we vow we shall (ever) be grateful." (Surah 7:189)

Woman's equal status with man entails her carrying out religious responsibilities. As God's creation, woman, as is man, is intended for mutual goodness, companionship, and purpose to be shared with man in obedience to God. Women and men are equal in and accountable for engaging in the obligatory forms of worship and ethical conduct.[6] She will be welcomed into the Gardens or condemned to Hell on the basis of her own worship, words, and actions (see Surah 16:97):

> O my people! This life of the present is nothing but (temporary) convenience: it is the Hereafter that is the home that will last. He that works evil will not be requited but by the like thereof: and he that works a righteous deed whether man or woman and is a believer such will enter the Garden (of Bliss): therein will they have abundance without measure. (Surah 40:39–40)

As indicated previously, neither Adam's wife nor her female descendants were cursed or punished because she was deceived by Iblis. God forgave Adam and the woman and brought them to earth to be His caliphs, promising to give them guidance, just as He planned for the course of this world to prepare humanity for the Hereafter. Genesis 3:16–19 held that the world was cursed, human labor was toilsome, woman was to be ruled by man, and both woman and man would be returned to dust with no mention of an afterlife. The Qur'an, however, describes the earth as bountiful and eager to be fruitful because the first couple were forgiven and promised resurrection and their children were responsible for their own faithfulness or faithlessness (Surah 7:26–31).

The God-willed relationship between woman and man is not one of female servility to male domination. On the contrary, "And among His Signs is this that He created for you mates from among yourselves that ye may dwell in tranquility with them, and He has put love and mercy between your (hearts); verily in that are Signs for those who reflect" (Surah 30:21). In addition, "And Allah has made for you mates (and companions) of your own nature. And made for you out of them sons, and daughters, and grandchildren, and provided for you sustenance of the best.

Will they then believe in vain things and be ungrateful for Allah's favors? (Surah 16:72).

In matters of sexuality and procreation, the Quranic principle is that sexual activity within marriage is natural and, except for specified periods of menstruation, fasting, or under the conditions of temporary vows, to be engaged in joyfully. The condition "within marriage" is binding on men as well as women, as noted below. The Qur'an reflects the common cultural view that sexual intercourse during a woman's menstrual period is forbidden and that she is ritually "unclean":

> They ask thee concerning women's courses. Say: "They are a hurt and a pollution; so keep away from women in their courses and do not approach them until they are clean. But when they have purified themselves, ye may approach them in any manner time or place ordained for you by Allah." For Allah loves those who turn to Him constantly, and He loves those who keep themselves pure and clean. Your wives are as a tilth unto you; so approach your tilth when or how ye will. But do some good act for your souls beforehand; and fear Allah and know that ye are to meet Him (in the Hereafter) and give (these) good tidings to those who believe. (Surah 2: 222–23)

Harsul, the term translated as "tilth," means a field in the sense of a fertile place where seed is sown. Although it is used in other contexts in the Qur'an, it can be an obvious sexual image.[7] In the Quranic context, however, it is not a depiction of intercourse forced on a woman. Women and men are "garments" for each other, that is, protectors and partners. For example, the always understanding God allows intercourse during the nights of fasting (Surah 2:187).

The Qur'an reflects the biological tradition that fertility resides in the male rather than in the union of sperm and ova. As cited in chapter 9, the Qur'an presents the human seed for all future generations (again, except for Jesus) as being in Adam's and then subsequent males' backs. The context for such passages usually is the Day of Judgment and stresses the sovereignty of God (see Surah 86, at-Tariq, the Night Visitant). In the context of male-female relationships the effect is to put sexuality in the perspective of God's plan and human dependency on God for life in all its stages now and in the Hereafter (Surah 22:5).

As noted in the covenant with all souls at birth, the seed-humans in Adam vow to testify to the One-Only God and to be held accountable for that witness on the Day of Judgment (Surah 7:172–74). Jesus' virginal conception is further evidence that God can generate human life as God wills to do (Surah 3:47).

WOMEN FEATURED IN THE QUR'AN

> For those who give in charity, men and women, and loan to
> Allah a Beautiful Loan it shall be increased manifold (to their
> credit), and they shall have (besides) a liberal reward. And
> those who believe in Allah and His messengers, they are
> the sincere (lovers of truth) and the witnesses (who testify)
> in the eyes of their Lord: they shall have their reward and
> their light but those who reject Allah and deny Our signs
> they are the Companions of Hell-Fire.
>
> *Surah 57:18–19*

The "Beautiful Loan" is more than paying the annual Zakat. Women and men are to give themselves to God in return for His giving them life, His care in the present, and His promise of everlasting blessedness in the Gardens. Testifying to the truth and the God Who gives that truth through His messengers results in their shining with the Light from Allah on the journey to judgment and reward. But for those women and men who spurn God and His signs, the way is dark and the Reward dreadful. The Qur'an cites particular women as well as men who are models for pursuing life and death. While the Revelation names only Mary, Jesus' mother, at least thirteen other women are mentioned and several of these, in my view, are featured:[8]

Adam's wife	Moses' sister
Noah's wife	Pharaoh's wife
Abraham's barren wife	Maidens Moses meets, marries one
Lot's wife	Queen of Saba [Sheba]
Joseph's accuser	Mary, mother of Jesus
Moses' mother	Abu Lahab's wife
	The Complainant

Muslim tradition cites four women as perfect for their time: Khadijah, Fatimah, Mary, and Pharaoh's wife (traditionally named Asiyah).[9] They are the women who have shown their faith in Allah and His messengers in exemplary ways and in the face of opposition. Because we have already considered the wife of Adam, I move to the others.

THE WIVES OF NOAH, LOT, AND ABU LAHAB

The wives of Noah and Lot (Lut, in the Qur'an) are destroyed in this world and are doomed to Hell apparently for their lack of faith in Allah and resistance to their prophet-husbands.[10] These women are paradigmatic warnings of the fate of those who disbelieve God and His warners (Surah 66:10). God promises that the wife of Abu Labab (Muhammad's uncle), known by her husband's nickname, Father of Flame, will share his damnable fate. The couple's hostility toward Muhammad and Islam heightened in 619, the Year of Sadness. She is a lurid example of what will happen to those who mocked Muhammad and sought to harm him while he was still vulnerable in Mecca. Tradition holds that she went out at night to strew thorns and splintery braided ropes on the walkways along which the usually barefoot Messenger would walk in the early morning darkness.[11] Abu Lahab died a painful and messy death from boils a week after the Muslim victory at Badr. Surah 111 describes what Allah will do to the couple in the Hereafter:

Perish the hands of the Father of Flame! Perish he! No profit to him from all his wealth and all his gains! Burnt soon will he be in a Fire of blazing Flame! His wife shall carry the (crackling) wood as fuel! A twisted rope of palm-leaf fibre round her (own) neck!" (Surah 111, al-Masad (the Plaited Rope) or al-Lahab (the Flame)

ABRAHAM'S BARREN WIFE

In the Quran and Genesis accounts, Abraham's barren wife is Isaac's mother. According to the latter, she seems to have laughs derisively when she overheard the Gomorrah-bound angels tell Abraham that she would bear a child. The Quranic wife laughs for joy and in wonder at the glad tidings, showing her willing acceptance of God's will (Surah 11:69–73).

JOSEPH'S ACCUSER

The wife of the otherwise anonymous Egyptian chief minister in the "most beautiful story" of the Qur'an (Surah 12) became obsessed with Joseph's beauty and assaulted him. As Joseph ran from her to the door as she clutched his garment from behind, her husband entered the room. Her defense crumbled when she was forced to admit her designs on the God-protected youth. Joseph forgave her, but when her friends also became infatuated with him, Joseph volunteered to be imprisoned. Before emerging from jail to interpret the Pharaoh's dreams, Joseph insisted that the true story be told to the Pharaoh. The wife and her friends confessed their lust and testified to his innocence in front of the Pharaoh. As she did, the official's wife also confessed that she was now a worshiper of the One-Only God (Surah 12:51–53). She became a repentant sinner and made a public profession of her faith. As a non-Arab, she may also be considered a forerunner of Islam's worldwide mission and Egypt's future adherence to Islam.

THE WOMEN ASSOCIATED WITH MOSES

Four women are associated with Moses: his mother, his sister, Pharaoh's wife, and the shy shepherdess who became his wife. (Moses and the roles of Pharaoh's wife and his own spouse are considered in more detail in chapter 11.) The account about Moses' birth and rescue is tender, showing that a woman receives divine revelations and that God cares for her anxieties about her newborn son. The Quranic version discloses plainly that Moses' survival and rescue were part of God's plan and that Moses' mother and sister trusted and did God's will unquestioningly (Surah 28:7–13).

The third woman, Pharaoh's wife, suggested to her husband that they adopt Moses as their son, thereby saving the infant's life. Disgusted with her husband's and his courtier's cruelty and defiance of the One-Only God, she became a believer (Surah 66:11). After killing an Egyptian and his flight from Egypt, a repentant Moses sought a smooth and straight way from Allah. That Way led him to the bashful shepherd's daughter whom he later married. Each woman risked rescuing a messenger of God at critical junctures in his life and were part of God's plan to bring warning and hope to humanity.

THE QUEEN OF SABA [SHEBA]

The biblical accounts of the queen of Saba's visit to King Solomon are sparse when compared to the Quranic revelation.[12] The account in Surah 27 shows affinities with the biblical and later legendary view of Solomon. Contrary to the biblical narrative of a late-life idolater, the Quranic Solomon is always a devout Muslim. Coupled with the traditions about his immense wealth and reputation for wisdom are those that he understood the languages and commanded the obedience of creatures great and small, including insects and some jinn. The Qur'an reports that at a muster of his birds, Solomon learned about the queen who was deluded by Shaytan. Summoned to come to him by one of his avian ambassadors, she arrived at his palace to learn about the true God. After a series of incidents, including the jinni-arranged transport of her unique throne to Solomon's palace, she became a believer. Although the Qur'an focuses on Solomon, it also shows that no one seemed to question that a woman could rule an empire and that she was able to think and decide for herself in matters dealing with both politics and faith.

MARY

Mary is the only woman named in the Qur'an and also its preeminent woman. Surah 19 is named for her. Jesus is regularly identified as "the son of Mary," thereby stressing her special status and his humanity. Mary is placed in the context of the Family of Imran (the traditional title of Surah 3). At one point she is referred to as the sister of Aaron, giving the initial impression that the Qur'an confuses her with Miriam, the sister of the biblical Moses and Aaron.[13] Amran and Jochebed are the biblical names for the parents of Moses, Aaron, and Miriam (Exod. 6:20). From the perspective of the Qur'an, Imran is not Mary's biological father but the patriarch of the highly honored family so that she, Jesus, John (the Baptist), and his parents are all of the priestly line (Surah 3:33−34).

The revelation about her includes elements that would be familiar to Christians from the Gospel According to Luke and, less familiarly, the Proto-Evangelium of James.[14] The Quranic account starts with a "woman of Imran" petitioning God for a child and vowing to dedicate it to God's special service (Surah 3:35). When the baby is born, the mother is surprised that she has given birth to a girl, yet acknowledges that God knows best and commends the child, named Mary, to God's protection from the Evil One and those whom God has rejected (Surah 3:36). Consequently, the new mother gives her child into the care of Zakariya, a priest in the [Jerusalem] Temple. There she is fed by angels (Surah 3:35−37).

Zakariya, in turn, seems encouraged to pray for a child to be born to himself and his elderly wife, thereby accounting for the eventual birth of John (known to Christians as John the Baptist).[15] The annunciation to Mary that she would conceive Jesus is told at Surah 3:42−49:[16]

> Behold! the angels said: "O Mary! Allah hath chosen thee and puri-
> fied thee; chosen thee above the women of all nations. O Mary! Wor-
> ship thy Lord devoutly; prostrate thyself and bow down (in prayer)
> with those who bow down." This is part of the tidings of the things
> unseen which We reveal unto thee (O Messenger!) by inspiration.
> Thou wast not with them when they cast lots with arrows as to which
> of them should be charged with the care of Mary; nor wast thou with

them when they disputed (the point). Behold! The angels said "O Mary! Allah giveth thee glad tidings of a Word from Him: his name will be Christ Jesus the son of Mary held in honor in this world and the Hereafter and of (the company of) those nearest to Allah. He shall speak to the people in childhood and in maturity and he shall be (of the company) of the righteous." She said: "O my Lord! How shall I have a son when no man hath touched me?" He said: "Even so: Allah createth what He willeth; when He hath decreed a plan He but saith to it 'Be' and it is! And Allah will teach him the Book and Wisdom the Law and the Gospel. And (appoint him) a Messenger to the Children of Israel (with this message): 'I have come to you with a sign from your Lord in that I make for you out of clay as it were the figure of a bird and breathe into it and it becomes a bird by Allah's leave; and I heal those born blind and the lepers and I quicken the dead by Allah's leave; and I declare to you what ye eat and what ye store in your houses. Surely therein is a Sign for you if ye did believe.'"

The account of Mary giving birth and return to her family emphasizes her trusting obedience to God:

Relate in the Book (the story of) Mary when she withdrew from her family to a place in the East. She placed a screen (to screen herself) from them: then We sent to her Our angel, and he appeared before her as a man in all respects. She said: "I seek refuge from thee to (Allah), Most Gracious: (come not near) if thou dost fear Allah." He said: "Nay I am only a messenger from thy Lord (to announce) to thee the gift of a holy son." She said: "How shall I have a son seeing that no man has touched me and I am not unchaste?" He said: "So (it will be): thy Lord saith 'That is easy for Me: and (We wish) to appoint him as a Sign unto men and a Mercy from Us': it is a matter (so) decreed." So she conceived him and she retired with him to a remote place. And the pains of childbirth drove her to the trunk of a palm-tree: she cried (in her anguish): "Ah! Would that I had died before this! Would that I had been a thing forgotten and out of sight!" But (a voice) cried to her from beneath the (palm-tree): "Grieve not! For thy Lord hath pro-

vided a rivulet beneath thee; and shake towards thyself the trunk of
the palm-tree: it will let fall fresh ripe dates upon thee.[17] So eat and
drink and cool (thine) eye. And if thou dost see any man say 'I have
vowed a fast to (Allah) Most Gracious and this day will I enter into
no talk with any human being.'"

At length she brought the (babe) to her people carrying him (in her
arms). They said: "O Mary! Truly an amazing thing hast thou brought!
"O sister of Aaron! Thy father was not a man of evil nor thy mother
a woman unchaste!" But she pointed to the babe. They said: "How can
we talk to one who is a child in the cradle?" He said: "I am indeed a
servant of Allah: He hath given me revelation and made me a prophet;
and He hath made me blessed wheresoever I be and hath enjoined on
me Prayer and Charity as long as I live; (He) hath made me kind to
my mother and not overbearing or miserable; So Peace is on me the
day I was born, the day that I die, and the Day that I shall be raised up
to life (again)!" (Surah 19:16–21)

The newborn Jesus' testimony to God exonerates Mary and proclaims
him as a messenger of Allah (Surah 19:28–33). Plainly, she is extraordinary, from her conception to giving birth to the messenger-messiah who
preceded Muhammad. God's plan called for the special preparation and
birth of this woman, cared for her, nourished her, raised up protectors,
strengthened and relieved her in her pain, and vindicated her in the face
of critics. God understood and responded to her needs—and she gave Him
glory and service. Mary is another model for humanity as a whole and
women in particular.

THE COMPLAINANT

One aya presents a woman whom many wives in Mecca and Medina
would understand:

Allah has indeed heard (and accepted) the statement of the woman who
pleads with thee concerning her husband and carries her complaint

(in prayer) to Allah: and Allah (always) hears the arguments between both sides among you: for Allah hears and sees (all things). (Surah 58:1, al-Mujadilah, the Woman Who Pleads)

The opening leads to revelations concerning procedures on divorce and marital disruptions. God provides a context for understanding marital discord. God's creative will pairs men and women and is a sign of His One-Only sovereignty. He has put into humans the capacities to love one another, show mercy, and live tranquilly with their mates (Surah 30:20–21).

The case of the Woman Who Pleads cracks the stereotypical view that women in Islam have no voice in marital matters. Hadith traditions are mixed regarding her situation.[18] The context and the Hadiths suggest the pre-Islamic practice of Zihar. Zihar involved a husband who tired of his wife and denied her conjugal right and thereby her legitimate place in the family. He did so by declaring, "Thou art to me as the back of my mother." That is, he would no longer treat her as a wife and would not have sexual intercourse with her but did not divorce her. The wife, unable to remarry, may have been disgraced in public and a virtual household servant. Given that pre-Islamic Arabs were polygamous, the men were free to contract any number of other marriages they desired. Islam hedged on the practice by making it costly to rescind the declaration of Zihar, making it an expensive tool for a husband to dominate his wife. Whatever the woman's complaint was, she couched her plea as a prayer, and God "hears the arguments between both sides":

Allah has indeed heard (and accepted) the statement of the woman who pleads with thee concerning her husband and carries her complaint (in prayer) to Allah: and Allah (always) hears the arguments between both sides among you: for Allah hears and sees (all things). If any men among you divorce their wives by Zihar (calling them mothers) they cannot be their mothers: none can be their mothers except those who gave them birth. And in fact they use words (both) iniquitous and false: but truly Allah is one that blots out (sins) and forgives (again and again). But those who divorce their wives by Zihar then wish to go back on the words they uttered (it is ordained that such a one) should free a slave before they touch each other: this are ye admonished to perform: and Allah is well-acquainted with (all) that ye do. And if any has not (the wherewithal) he should fast for two months consecutively before they touch each other. But if any is unable to do so he should feed sixty indigent ones. This that ye may show your faith in Allah and His Messenger. Those are limits (set by) Allah. For those who Reject (Him) there is a grievous Penalty. (Surah 58:1–4)

THOSE WOMEN FEATURED in the Qur'an are as equal as men before the sovereign God. They are liable to punishment now and in the Hereafter for their deeds and misdeeds but may be forgiven and restored to the Straight Way through repentance and creditable deeds. Women may receive God's special revelations though angels, oppose their husbands for the sake of being faithful to Allah and Islam, and can save the lives of God's messengers. Women receive God's care and nurture, are able to exercise authority in their proper domains, and can be confident that Allah will hear their prayers and respond:

He created you (all) from a single person: then created of like nature his mate; and He sent down for you eight head of cattle in pairs: He makes you in the wombs of your mothers in stages one after another in three veils of darkness. Such is Allah your Lord and Cherisher: to Him belongs (all) dominion. There is no god but He: then how are ye turned away (from your true Center)? If ye reject (Allah), truly Allah has no need of you; but He liketh not ingratitude from His servants: if ye are grateful He is pleased with you. No bearer of burdens can bear the burden of another. In the end to your Lord is your return when He will tell you the truth of all that ye did (in this life). For He knoweth well all that is in (men's) hearts. (Surah 39:6–7)

WOMEN IN THE MESSENGER'S HOUSEHOLD

The Prophet is closer to the Believers than their own selves,
and his wives are their mothers. Blood relations among each

other have closer personal ties in the Decree of Allah than
(the Brotherhood of) Believers and Muhajirs: nevertheless
do ye what is just to your closest friends: such is the writing
in the Decree (of Allah).

Surah 33:6

MUHAMMAD'S TWO FAMILIES

Muhammad had two families, one Meccan and the other Medinan. Each
has a special role in the Qur'an and Islam. His first family, the core of
the earliest umma, consisted of himself, Khadijah, four daughters, and at
least two male relatives. The four daughters were Zaynab (or Zanaib, a
name also of two of his later wives and a daughter of Ali and Fatimah),
Ruqayyah, Umm Kulthum, and Fatimah.[19] Umm Kulthum and Ruqayyah
predeceased Muhammad, and Fatimah died within six months of his
death. The males in the Meccan household were Ali ibn Abi Talib and
Zayd.[20]

Muhammad's wives are called the Mothers of the Faithful (Umm al-
Mu'minin). Khadijah, the first person to have heard about and then believe the truth of the Revelation and Muhammad's role as the ultimate
Messenger, is foremost among the wives.[21] Her unwavering courage in
the face of Qurayshi opposition encouraged her husband, providing the
security and support he needed in the dire circumstances the umma faced
in Mecca. Muhammad always held Khadijah as chief in his heart and es-
teem. He described a wonderful palace that was awaiting her in the Hereafter.[22] The daughters all became Muslims and wound up in Medina.

A crucial event distinguished Ali and Fatimah and their two sons
(Hasan and Hussein) from all the others and the Medinan family. According to Muslim tradition, Muhammad and some Christians engaged in a
debate about Jesus around 630. The relevant Quranic passage is 3:61: "If
anyone disputes in this matter with thee now after (full) knowledge hath
come to thee say: "Come! Let us gather together our sons and your sons,

our women and your women, ourselves and yourselves,: then let us earnestly pray and invoke the curse of Allah on those who lie!"

The hadiths vary, but the gist is the same. When asked who would be "gathered" as his group, Muhammad spread his cloak to bring under it only Fatimah and Ali and their sons. The group is called the ahl al-Kisa, the People of the Cloak. Shi'ite Muslims take the event as one major proof that the "Holy Family" is designated to lead the umma after Muhammad's death. Shi'ites have an amplified tradition about the event.[23] Among Shi'ites the term ahl-Bayt (lit., "people of the house") means the divinely favored household composed of Muhammad and Fatimah and Ali and their two sons. Fatimah, for Sunni and Shi'ia Muslims, is a holy individual who was cherished by her father and sometimes silenced her husband. A hadith reflecting a struggle within the ahl al-Bayt mentions that once Ali sought to take a second wife, but Fatimah objected and informed her father. He stopped the process cold. Ali was told that Fatimah was part of Muhammad and he would not countenance her being caused any sadness or turmoil through a second wife or a divorce.[24]

The second, or Medinan, family came into existence only after the death of Khadijah. Muhammad had ten wives and two concubines in Medina. Together with Khadijah, the wives are called the Consorts (Partners, Mates) of Purity and Mothers of the Faithful. The Medinan Consorts and their ages and status at the time they married Muhammad are as follows:

Name	Age	Status	Date
Sauda bint Zamaa	35	widow	619
Aisha bint Abu Bakr	9	virgin	623
Hafsa bint Umar	18	widow	624
Zaynab bint Khuzaima	?	widow	625
Hind bint al-Mughira, Umm Salamah	40 + ?	widow	625
Zaynab bint Jahsh	40	divorcee	625/6
Juwayriyyah bint Harith	30 + ?	widow	628
Ramlah bint Abi Sofyan, Umm Habibah	30 + ?	widow	628
Safiyyah bint Huyai	17	widow	628
Maimoona bint Abbas	?	widow	629

The two concubines were Rayhana bint Amir and Maryam. Rayhana was a captive from the Jewish Qurayzah tribe and became a Muslim.
Maryam (also Maryah), a Coptic Christian, was a "gift" from the Christian Byzantine governor in Egypt. She was the mother of Muhammad's
son, Ibrahim, who died before he was two years old. All of the wives, with
the exceptions of Aisha and Zaynab bint Jahsh, were widowed when they
married Muhammad. Information about the Consorts is found in various hadith collections and studies of Muhammad and Islam.[25] Zaynab bint
Khuzaima, the widow of one of the heroes killed at Badr who herself
died soon after her marriage to Muhammad, had the reputation and set the
precedent for being a generous helper and was called Umm al-Masakin,
Mother of the Poor. Safiyyah was a survivor of the destruction of the Jews
of Khaybar and widow of its chieftain. She became a willing convert to
Islam and a joyful wife to the Messenger. When not campaigning, Muhammad spent most of his time in and around the Medinan mosque. His
wives lived in separate, small dwellings that seem to have had an entry section that could be screened off from the rest of the home. He developed
a schedule whereby he spent a period of time with each wife. The Consorts were involved in the life of Medina and in regular worship. They also
had to get along with each other.

Naturally, there were some uncomfortable personal dynamics, usually involving Aisha. She and Fatimah appear to have had strained relations, undoubtedly aggravated by Ali urging Muhammad to divorce
Aisha in the aftermath of the incident with Safwan. Muhammad was especially indulgent to his child bride. On an occasion when he was criticized for spending more nights with her than the other wives, he responded that he loved her the most and then smiled as she spoke harshly
with another wife.[26] The daughters and Consorts were the persons closest to the inspired and chosen human who was closest to Allah. They
therefore had most access to the inspired Messenger and were to be models of the Islamic way of life and womanhood to the umma and the world.
Given that access and function, the Qur'an addresses them directly and
all women indirectly. Surah 33 contains one of several passages that speak
to and of the women in Muhammad's household. Muslim men were per-

mitted to have four wives at one time, but an exception was made for Muhammad:

> O prophet! We have made lawful to thee thy wives to whom thou hast paid their dowers; and those whom thy right hand possesses out of the prisoners of war whom Allah has assigned to thee; and daughters of thy paternal uncles and aunts and daughters of thy maternal uncles and aunts who migrated (from Mecca) with thee; and any believing woman who dedicates her soul to the Prophet if the Prophet wishes to wed her this only for thee and not for the Believers (at large); We know what We have appointed for them as to their wives and the captives whom their right hands possess in order that there should be no difficulty for Thee. And Allah is Oft-Forgiving Most Merciful. Thou mayest defer (the turn of) any of them that thou pleasest and thou mayest receive any thou pleasest: and there is no blame on thee if thou invite one whose (turn) thou hadst set aside. This were nigher to the cooling of their eyes the prevention of their grief and their satisfaction—that of all of them—with that which thou hast to give them: and Allah knows (all) that is in your hearts: and Allah is All-Knowing, Most Forbearing. It is not lawful for thee (to marry more) women after this nor to change them for (other) wives even though their beauty attract thee except any thy right hand should possess (as handmaidens): and Allah doth watch over all things. (Surah 33:50–52)

The Ayas of Choice (Ayat al-Tahir)

> O Prophet! Say to thy Consorts: "If it be that ye desire the
> life of this world and its glitter then come! I will provide
> for your enjoyment and set you free in a handsome manner.
> But if ye seek Allah and His Messenger and the Home of
> the Hereafter, verily Allah has prepared for the well-doers
> amongst you a great reward. O Consorts of the Prophet!
> If any of you were guilty of evident unseemly conduct the

punishment would be doubled to her and that is easy for
Allah. But any of you that is devout in the service of Allah
and His Messenger and works righteousness to her shall
We grant her reward twice: and We have prepared for her
a generous sustenance."

Surah 33:28–31

The Ayas of Choice offer the Consorts, present and future, the option of
ending their marriages with Muhammad or staying under God's conditions. Most or all of Surah 33 was revealed after the Battle of the Trench
in 626/627. Muslims and the non-Muslim Medinans who fought with
them were enriched by their victories over the enemy confederation.[27] In
that setting the surah warns male and female believers against ostentatious
wealth, spending on luxuries while others are needy, a lust for plunder,
and a hankering after glory. Some men intruded on the residences where
the Messenger was staying in order to present their cases to him or to ask
for advice. A few may have wanted just to catch sight of the wives. Given
their roles, the Consorts were to be the patterns for the attitudes and conduct for Muslim women in the Messenger's time. They were advised by
God to be careful so as not to arouse inappropriate desires within men
but to stay quietly in their homes, be modest, to be observant of prayer,
to give Zakat, and generally to be "pure and spotless" and obedient to the
Messenger:

O Consorts of the Prophet! Ye are not like any of the (other) women:
if ye do fear (Allah) be not too complaisant of speech lest one in
whose heart is a disease should be moved with desire: but speak ye
a speech (that is) just. And stay quietly in your houses and make not
a dazzling display like that of the former Times of Ignorance; and establish regular Prayer and give regular Charity; and obey Allah and
His Messenger. And Allah only wishes to remove all abomination from
you, ye Members of the Family, and to make you pure and spotless.

And recite what is rehearsed to you in your homes of the Signs of
Allah and His Wisdom: for Allah understands the finest mysteries and
is well-acquainted (with them). (Surah 33:32–34)

But were all the conditions applicable for all Muslim women in all
places and all times? The mini-community of the Consorts demonstrated
the practicality of the Quranic-Muslim way and would lead to personal,
familial, and communal harmony and peace. Yet other aspects became general and often restrictive as well as legalistic demands in some Muslim
societies from seventh-century Medina to the present. Does "stay quietly
in your homes" apply only to the Consorts, or is it still to be followed regardless of socioeconomic conditions? Does it foreclose the possibility of
women being educated outside the home? Does it stop women from participating in various professions as well as politics? Does the element of
"quietly at home" serve as the precedent for the seclusion of women in
certain areas of a residence? Or a means to control them?

Privacy and Dress

Surah 33 also provided for the privacy of the Messenger and the Consorts. The revelation concerning privacy was given in the context of the
feast on the occasion of his marriage to Zaynab bint Jahsh. A number of
male guests overstayed their welcome. The revelation continued into what
is called the Aya al-Hijab, the Verse of the Veil.[28] It covers conversations
with the Consorts and the prohibition of their remarriage after Muhammad's death plus the screen, or *hijab:*

O ye who Believe! Enter not the Prophet's houses until leave is given
you for a meal (and then) not (so early as) to wait for its preparation.
But when ye are invited enter; and, when ye have taken your meal,
disperse without seeking familiar talk. Such (behavior) annoys the
Prophet: He is ashamed to dismiss you, but Allah is not ashamed (to
tell you) the truth. And when ye ask (his ladies) for anything ye want,
ask them from before a screen [*hijab*] that makes for greater purity
for your hearts and for theirs. Nor is it right for you that ye should

annoy Allah's Messenger or that ye should marry his widows after him at any time. Truly such a thing is in Allah's sight an enormity. (Surah 33:55)

The first portion of the aya is plain and has served as the part of the general Muslim respect for the privacy of a person's home. Where, however, was the "screen"? It may have been a literal screen or curtain that separated the entryway of the residence from the general living quarters. The visitor is not to barge in on the privacy of the residents but is to stop at the screen and speak with the woman or women in the household. However, the hijab originally could have been or was soon understood to be an article of clothing that could cover the hair and head and have openings for the woman to see and a mesh for her mouth and nose or from just below the eyes to the chin. In the home and among relatives, a more relaxed atmosphere could be observed:

> Whether ye reveal anything or conceal it, verily Allah has full knowledge of all things. There is no blame (on these ladies if they appear) before their fathers or their sons, their brothers or their brothers' sons, or their sisters' sons, or their women, or the (slaves) whom their right hands possess. And (ladies) fear Allah: for Allah is Witness to all things. (Surah 33:54–55)

Another aya went further and applied to both the Consorts and all Muslim women: "O prophet! Tell thy wives and daughters and the believing women that they should cast their outer garments over their persons (when abroad): that is most convenient that they should be known (as such) and not molested: and Allah is Oft-Forgiving, Most Merciful" (Surah 33:59).

The *jibab* (pl. *jalabib*) is a loose-fitting garment that covers at least the neck and bosom or can be extended to cover the whole body.[29] The Quranic purpose was to prevent women from being molested outside the home by lascivious men and to preserve their modesty. By 627 the Consorts appear to have been wearing the hijab and the jibab.[30] A hadith concerning Aisha's sister indicates that even within the home a female who has reached puberty should be almost completely covered: "Asma, daughter of Abu Bakr, entered upon the Messenger of Allah (peace be upon him) wearing thin clothes. The Messenger of Allah (peace be upon him) turned his attention from her. He said: 'O Asma, when a woman reaches the age of menstruation, it does not suit her that she displays her parts of body except this and this,' and he pointed to her face and hands."[31] The matters of seclusion and dress have been and still are contentious among Muslims in different national and cultural contexts. Can Quranic social stipulations be interpreted as being sensitive to seventh-century Arab conditions but open to change in later times and circumstances?

Discord and Discipline

In spite of their unique position, the Consorts argued with Muhammad and jockeyed with one another for his favor. Surah 66 reflects at least one significant issue that disrupted the household and led to rumors of a mass divorce:

> O Prophet! Why holdest thou to be forbidden that which Allah has made lawful to thee? Thou seekest to please thy consorts. But Allah is Oft-Forgiving, Most Merciful. Allah has already ordained for you (O men) the dissolution of your oaths (in some cases): and Allah is your Protector and He is full of Knowledge and Wisdom. (Surah 66:1–2)

God criticized Muhammad for deferring to the Consorts on a particular issue instead of asserting his right, perhaps duty, to act. One suggestion is that the issue concerned his relations with Maryam and the other wives objecting to her presence among them.[32] Apparently the offense to Muhammad rose to the level that he was freed from his oaths or vows on an undisclosed issue or perhaps divorcing his wives. Either the same incident or another domestic problem occasioned a further revelation:

When the Prophet disclosed a matter in confidence to one of his consorts and she then divulged it (to another) and Allah made it known to him, he confirmed part thereof and repudiated a part. Then when he told her thereof she said: "Who told thee this?" He said: "He told me who knows and is well-acquainted (with all things). If ye two turn in repentance to him, your hearts are indeed so inclined; but if ye back up each other against him, truly Allah is his Protector and Gabriel and (every) righteous one among those who believe and furthermore the angels will back (him) up. (Surah 66:3–5)

Various hadiths may clarify the situation or at least the dynamics operative in the household. Again, there may be one situation involving a violated confidence and another involving argumentative wives. The gist is that the normally quiet and submissive Qurayshi women who made the Hijra learned from their Medinan counterparts to argue with and disobey their husbands. This created problems for the Muslim husbands who expected obedient spouses. The retorting and arguing spread to the Consorts. Umar's wife shouted back at him (after he shouted at her) and claimed that the Consorts did the same with the Messenger, and some even refused to talk to him all day and night. Hafsa and Aisha appear to be the chief culprits. Umar and, as the Qur'an indicates, God remonstrated with the women. God added: "It may be if he divorced you (all), that Allah will give him in exchange Consorts better than you who submit (their wills), who believe, who are devout, who turn to Allah in repentance, who worship (in humility), who travel (for faith) and fast, previously married or virgins" (Surah 66:5).

Umar warned the women that their husband might divorce all of them in a single act. Then Muhammad disciplined the Consorts not with a mass divorce but by withdrawing from them, thereby throwing the umma into turmoil. The Consorts repented, and Umar and others pressed Muhammad to relent. He accepted their repentance and resumed relations with them after a twenty-nine-day hiatus.[33] The temporary suspension of marital contacts and relations indicates that Muhammad asserted his authority without the use of physical punishment. The precedent was given for husbands to act with patience and discretion before resorting to corporeal punishment and divorce.

THE QUR'AN PRESENTS the women in Muhammad's families as persons who are quite human, yet agree to be models of Islamic faith and practice for the umma and the world. They were to exemplify not servility but that type of obedience that will lead women and men to continue on the Straight Way and to be rewarded in the Hereafter. The strengths, questions, and ambiguities reflected in the position of the Consorts have passed into the daily life of Muslim women in general.

> But to Allah belong all things in the heavens and on earth:
> and He it is that encompasseth all things. (Surah 4:126)

QURANIC VIEWS OF WOMEN'S ROLES IN THE FAMILY

> Allah has bestowed His gifts of sustenance more freely on
> some of you than on others; those more favored are not
> going to throw back their gifts to those whom their right
> hands possess so as to be equal in that respect. Will they then
> deny the favors of Allah? And Allah has made for you mates
> (and companions) of your own nature. And made for you
> out of them sons and daughters and grandchildren and
> provided for you sustenance of the best: will they then
> believe in vain things and be ungrateful for Allah's favors?
>
> *Surah 61:71–72*

If one side of the Muslim position on woman and women is that the female human is the spiritual equal of the male, then the other side is that women and men have different yet complementary roles in the arrangements and institutions of this world. The role differences are restricted to this world and its time. In the Hereafter there will be no gender-based differences between men and women. Since this world is a fleeting moment compared to the everlasting Gardens and Hell, the distinctions in the present are important only for this world and may be borne in faithfulness to God and patience with one another. The differences in roles are due to biology and physiology. Women and men may be matched as mates one to the other by Allah's plan, but men do not bear babies and women usually do not have the physical strength of men.

Quranic revelations concerning the Consorts have been expanded to encompass Muslim women specifically and Muslim society generally. Does the distinction between roles hold in the twenty-first century? Obviously, some Muslim societies are determined to interpret the Qur'an strictly, while others seek to elucidate core Quranic principles that allow significant adjustments. What a woman wears and does, where she goes and with whom, vary widely in the Muslim world and even among Muslim societies. Tunisia, Indonesia, and Turkey are quite different from Iran, Qatar, and Sudan. In the land of Muhammad and the two holiest places, the Wahhabi religious establishment, the state-sponsored form of Islam in the Kingdom of Saudi Arabia, issued a religious decree (*fatwa*) in 2002 that is a significant liberalization of Saudi policy. The policy states: "A woman should not specialize in a field that is outside of her realm. She has the opportunity to pursue many fields that are suitable to her, like Islamic Studies, or the Arabic Language. Fields such as Chemistry, Engineering, Architecture, Astronomy and Geography do not suit her. A woman should choose what benefits her and that which benefits society. Furthermore, men need to establish institutions for women that will prepare them for those fields that they need to study, Gynecology and pre-natal care being important examples."[34] The "liberalization" is that Saudi women are allowed to study in institutions of higher education, but these must be all-female institutions. Yet what does the Qur'an say about women's roles in general relationships with men, marriage and family life, and society?

WOMEN AND MEN TOGETHER

The believers, men and women, are protectors one of
another: they enjoin what is just and forbid what is evil:
they observe regular prayers, practice regular charity, and
obey Allah and His Messenger. On them will Allah pour
His mercy: for Allah is Exalted in Power, Wise. Allah hath
promised to believers, men and women, gardens under
which rivers flow to dwell therein and beautiful mansions
in gardens of everlasting bliss. But the greatest bliss in the
Good Pleasure of Allah: that is the supreme felicity.

Surah 9:71–72

God decrees more than that the basic human relationship of women and
men is mutual support in their respective roles. They are partners in seeking
to shape a just and equitable society and to squelch evil. Surah 9:71–72's
repetition of Salat, Zakat, and obedience shows men and women are to
strengthen and advance one another's faith and practice. If one person fal-
ters, drifts, or becomes careless, then others can intervene and encourage
the person to regain his or her footing on the Straight Way. If an individual, group, or family undergoes opposition, hardship, distress, danger, or
loss, then other members of the umma—including members of the opposite sex—may be called on to render appropriate assistance and prayer.
While the rewards in the Hereafter await believers, nevertheless the real incentive for humans to act as protectors of each other is the blessed peace
that comes from serving God. Mutual protection in this world leads to the
ways that protection is given, that is, to the normal roles and relationships
the Qur'an prescribes for women and men.

How are men and women to act when they are not married to each
other, yet are in contact one with the other? The basic Quranic advice, already begun with the Consorts, is modesty, honor, respect, and self-respect.

Homes are private spaces, so visitors need permission to enter. When a man enters a home in which women live, both women and men are to keep their gazes lowered and be modest in word and gesture:

> O ye who believe! Enter not houses other than your own until ye have asked permission and saluted those in them: that is best for you in order that ye may heed (what is seemly). If ye find no one in the house, enter not until permission is given to you: if ye are asked to go back go back: that makes for greater purity for yourselves: and Allah knows well all that ye do. It is no fault on your part to enter houses not used for living in which serve some (other) use for you: and Allah has knowledge of what ye reveal and what ye conceal. Say [Muhammad] to the believing men that they should lower their gaze and guard their modesty: that will make for greater purity for them: and Allah is well acquainted with all that they do. And say to the believing women that they should lower their gaze and guard their modesty; that they should not display their beauty and ornaments except what (must ordinarily) appear thereof; that they should draw their veils over their bosoms and not display their beauty except to their husbands their fathers their husbands' fathers their sons their husbands' sons their brothers or their brothers' sons or their sisters' sons or their women or the slaves whom their right hands possess or male servants free of physical needs or small children who have no sense of the shame of sex; and that they should not strike their feet in order to draw attention to their hidden ornaments. And O ye Believers! Turn ye all together towards Allah that ye may attain Bliss. (Surah 24:27–31)

This passage agrees with the revelation about the Consorts and expands on the "in-the-family members" who may see the "beauty" of women and then of men.[35] In Muslim tradition a man's "beauty" extends from the navel to the knees, and he is to keep this area covered. A man may strip off his shirt and wear baggy, somewhat long shorts to work or be part of an athletic contest, but he is not to expose himself further in public. The extent of a woman's beauty is, as we have seen with the Consorts, still a question. It seems clear from 24:27–33 that when speaking with those outside the family circle, a woman is to have her head and bosom covered and perhaps wear a veil. She (and men) are to keep their gazes modestly on the ground. Depending on its "quality," staring can be a challenge, an insult, a lewd once-over, or an invitation for further contact. Depending on the culture, averting one's glance may be taken as subservience to a superior, shifty dissembling, or modesty. The Islamic choice is modesty, and it applies to both males and females. The passage also mandates the sanctity and privacy of the home. The home is for the extended family and is not part of the marketplace. Modesty, self-respect, and privacy belong together for the sake of harmony in the umma.

MARRIAGE AND FAMILY

It is He Who has created man from water: then has
He established relationships of lineage and marriage:
for thy Lord has power (over all things).

Surah 25:54

Loyalties and priority commitments are expressed through lineage and marriage, which are structured by God into humans and their societies. Because family ties and bloodlines result from marriage, it is a matter of deep concern for the honor as well as for the continuation of families. In light of Surah 9:71–72 lineage and marriage are crucial for providing the Islamic network of supporting persons and institutions. In the Qur'an and Islam heterosexual marriage is assumed and a virtual mandate.[36] Sexual activity is restricted to those who are married to each other; permanent or long-term abstinence from sexual relations with one's spouse is forbidden. Because the Qur'an addresses numerous and complex issues, we will examine several areas: eligibility, discipline, divorce, inheritance, orphans and polygamy.

Eligibility

And marry not women whom your fathers married except
what is past: it was shameful and odious an abominable
custom indeed. Prohibited to you (for marriage) are: your
mothers, daughters, sisters, father's sisters, mother's sisters;
brother's daughters, sister's daughters, foster-mothers (who
gave you suck), foster-sisters; your wives' mothers; your step-
daughters under your guardianship born of your wives to
whom ye have gone in—no prohibition if ye have not gone
in; (those who have been) wives of your sons proceeding
from your loins; and two sisters in wedlock at one and the
same time except for what is past; for Allah is Oft-Forgiving,
Most Merciful. Also (prohibited are) women already married
except those whom your right hands possess. Thus hath
Allah ordained (prohibitions) against you. Except for these,
all others are lawful provided ye seek (them in marriage)
with gifts from your property, desiring chastity not lust.
Seeing that ye derive benefit from them, give them their
dowers (at least) as prescribed; but if after a dower is
prescribed ye agree mutually (to vary it) there is no blame
on you and Allah is All-Knowing, All-Wise.

Surah 4:22–24

On the whole the table of prohibited degrees of relationship is like that
in Leviticus 18:6–20 and 20:14–21. Strictures against incest or inbreed-
ing are clear. The foster mother or milk mother and milk sibling restrictions are based on the fact that they have imbibed the same person's body
fluids and are related, if not by blood, then by milk. Sociologically, the milk
siblings have been raised together for several years and are like a family.
Consideration is expressed for sisters being married to the same man.
Married women who have been captured or otherwise enslaved and who

are not widowed and have no prospect of being returned to their first husbands are eligible for marriage to a Muslim man, but they could attain only
the status of a concubine. Eligibility also involved belief:

> If any of you have not the means wherewith to wed free believing
> women, they may wed believing girls from among those whom your
> right hands possess: and Allah hath full knowledge about your faith.
> Ye are one from another: wed them with the leave of their owners, and
> give them their dowers according to what is reasonable: they should
> be chaste not lustful, nor taking paramours: when they are taken in
> wedlock if they fall into shame, their punishment is half that for free
> women. This (permission) is for those among you who fear sin; but it is
> better for you that ye practice self-restraint: and Allah is Oft-Forgiving,
> Most Merciful. (Surah 4:25)

If a man could not afford the regular financial settlement for a free
woman, it was better to marry a Muslim slave than to risk being tempted
into nonmarital sex. Marriages to non-Muslims are to be limited in scope
and gender:

> Do not marry unbelieving women (idolaters) until they believe. A
> slave woman who believes is better than an unbelieving woman even
> though she allure you. Nor marry (your girls) to unbelievers until
> they believe. A man-slave who believes is better than an unbeliever,
> even though he allure you. Unbelievers do (but) beckon you to the
> Fire. But Allah beckons by His grace to the Garden (of Bliss) and for-
> giveness and makes His signs clear to mankind: that they may cele-
> brate His praise. (Surah 2:221)

In brief, Muslim daughters are not to marry non-Muslim men. It is
better for those women to marry believing slaves, no matter how attractive the offer an unbelieving suitor may be. If, however, the man decides
to become a Muslim, the marriage may be contracted. As the closing line
of the aya indicates, this is not only a matter of family but of Judgment
Day. There is, however, an exception to the prohibition of Muslim men

marrying *al-mushrikat,* idolatresses. In the final Quranic revelation given Muhammad, God said:

> This day are (all) things good and pure made lawful unto you. The food of the People of the Book is lawful unto you, and yours is lawful unto them. (Lawful unto you in marriage) are (not only) chaste women who are believers but chaste women among the People of the Book revealed before your time when ye give them their due dowers and desire chastity not lewdness nor secret intrigues. If anyone rejects faith fruitless is his work and in the Hereafter he will be in the ranks of those who have lost (all spiritual good). (Surah 5:5)

Because of the special relationship between the People of the Book and Muslims, Christians and Jews are not idolaters in the Jahiliyyah sense. It is licit, therefore, for a Muslim man to marry a Christian or Jewish woman. She would be encouraged to accept Islam, but she could remain Jewish or Christian. Muslim women, however, are not to marry Christians or Jews.

The Qur'an does not indicate a minimum age for a marriage contract to be drawn up for the male and female. In the instance of Muhammad and Aisha, she was six years old when betrothed to him and nine when they consummated the marriage sexually. Given the views of lineage and marriage, the betrothal-marriage contracts also united two families in a blood relationship. The Qur'an and hadiths provide that a woman cannot be married without her consent. That consent, however, is given in the presence of male family members, and her silence is accepted as her agreement to be married.

Discipline

> Your wives are as a tilth unto you; so approach your tilth when or how ye will. But do some good act for your souls beforehand; and fear Allah and know that ye are to meet Him (in the Hereafter) and give (these) good tidings to those who believe.
>
> *Surah 2:223*

In marriage, the husband has clear and binding responsibilities to care for his wife, provide for her well-being and that of any children, and ensure that the tilth-spouse is neither exploited nor neglected by him and others. Marriages are not matters of convenience but of faithfulness and love. Still, relationships falter and discord occurs. The Qur'an assumes that the husband has the major responsibility to restore order and, as we see in the following passage, when the discord is caused by the wife the husband attempts to correct her so as to restore their harmonious relationship. (I have supplied brackets to clarify the antecedants of the pronouns; parenthetical text has been supplied by Yusuf Ali. His rendering, minus the parenthetical text, agrees with most other translations and is as accurate as one may get in English.)

> Men are the protectors and maintainers of women because Allah has given the one more (strength) than the other, and because they [the men] support them [the women] from their means. Therefore the righteous women are devoutly obedient and guard in (the husband's) absence what Allah would have them guard. As to those women on whose part ye fear disloyalty and ill-conduct admonish them (first), (next) refuse to share their beds, (and last) beat them (lightly); but if they return to obedience seek not against them means (of annoyance): for Allah is Most High Great (above you all). (Surah 4:34)[37]

A fair reading of 4:34 shows that it is not a Quranic license for wife-beating. Having established that men and women are partners before God and in this world, the Qur'an indicates that they have different roles in the context of protecting one another and being mutually supportive in matters of faith and society. A married couple, under the sovereign, merciful, and just God, are to love and be faithful to each other, respecting each other's rights and conjugal needs. The normal relationship is expressed in the aya's first two sentences: men are the protectors and maintainers of women on the basis of biology and physiology; the wife, in turn, carries out her domestic duties in obedience to God and her husband. The husband's partnership is expressed at least partially in his taking the lead in going into the marketplace, fields, battlefield, and other quotidian settings to provide food, funds, and security for his wife and family. She and the children can count on him wherever he has to go, whether on a lengthy caravan journey or to the home workshop. It is her place to maintain the home, care for the children, and protect their possessions and domestic honor. The aya does not seem to anticipate that the wife will work outside the home. Muhammad Ali suggests that the "unseen" she "guards" is her husband's rights and reputation.[38] And God guards the couple.

The second part of the aya concerns severely troubled marriages. Arguments and destructive conduct seem to be involved. Obviously, the aya is weighted against women and assumes that men are correct. We may recall, however, that God listens to the Woman Who Complains and asserts that He hears both sides. Suspecting his wife of not guarding the "unseen," of working against him and the welfare of the family, and perhaps that she is planning to desert him, the husband is given a set of instructions to follow in order to restore domestic tranquillity. The initial step is admonition. If the situation changes and concord is reestablished, then both are to move ahead without rancor, giving thanks to God. The orderly process moves from admonition to the second step, suspension of marital relations. This suspension of relations may be expected to last for twenty-nine days, about the length of a menstrual cycle; a duration of three cycles may be used in divorce procedures. If the situation is unchanged or worsens, as a last resort to settle the problems within the household, the husband may beat his wife to restore the balance in their partnership. The following aya appears to offer a procedure for circumstances in which the "in-house" steps failed to reconcile the couple. They move toward mediation:

> If ye fear a breach between them twain appoint (two) arbiters one from his family and the other from hers; if they wish for peace Allah will cause their reconciliation: for Allah hath full knowledge and is acquainted with all things. (Surah 4:35)

The larger family and clan are available to bring pressure on the parties to settle their differences. Families are vital in the beginning of the marriage and in protecting it, for "the Prophet is closer to the Believers than their own selves and his wives are their mothers. Blood-relations among each other have closer personal ties in the Decree of Allah than (the Brother-hood of) Believers and Muhajirs: nevertheless do ye what is just to your closest friends: such is the writing in the Decree (of Allah)" (Surah 33:6).

Divorce

For divorced women maintenance (should be provided)
on a reasonable (scale). This is a duty on the righteous.

Surah 2:241

God and the Messenger hated divorce.[39] Nevertheless, the Qur'an recognizes that some marriages will end in divorce. *Talaq,* used in the Qur'an to mean divorce, is literally "repudiation." The most common form of divorce involves the husband repudiating the marriage contract and therefore the marriage. In its earliest days, only a man could end a marriage through talaq.[40] The procedure was not simply repeating "I divorce you" three times. The Quranic-Muslim procedure takes account of the fact that words spoken in anger and frustration may be overhasty. The man can retract the words and their impact. In the event of a separation either in the home or if the wife returned to her parents' home, both parties may agree to reconcile, resume sexual relations, and live together once more. The Qur'an also insists that no divorce is final until it is clear that the wife is not pregnant. Obviously, she is not to have sexual intercourse with another man during this time.

Given the process of attempting to hold marriages together and to reconcile spouses, most talaq divorces ought be formal actions of last resort. Yet talaq divorces do not have to go through all those steps. One procedure is to state "I divorce you" once, intending it as a warning and as the initial statement. The husband would then neither have sexual relations with the woman nor sleep in the same room for the duration of her menstrual cycle (*iddah*). If there has been no change in the situation, then a second iddah, then a third iddah:

> And make not Allah's (name) an excuse in your oaths against doing good or acting rightly or making peace between persons; for Allah is one who heareth and knoweth all things. Allah will not call you to account for thoughtlessness in your oaths but for the intention in your hearts; and He is Oft-Forgiving, Most Forbearing. For those who take an oath for abstention from their wives a waiting for four months is ordained; if then they return Allah is Oft-Forgiving, Most Merciful. But if their intention is firm for divorce, Allah heareth and knoweth all things. Divorced women shall wait concerning themselves for three monthly periods nor is it lawful for them to hide what Allah hath created in their wombs if they have faith in Allah and the Last Day. And their husbands have the better right to take them back in that period if they wish for reconciliation. And women shall have rights similar to the rights against them according to what is equitable; but men have a degree (of advantage) over them, and Allah is Exalted in Power, Wise. (Surah 2:226–27)

During the waiting period, the husband is to support his wife at the same level and in the same style prior to his initiation of the talaq. In the event that she is pregnant, there can be no divorce until after she has given birth and nursed the baby for two years after its birth. Throughout that time and afterward, the husband is responsible for child support. Generally but not Quranically, the mother has custody of the children until they reach puberty. It is most likely that a woman will return to her family of origin following the divorce.

Another way to terminate the marriage is by mutual consent (*khul'*):

> A divorce is only permissible twice: after that the parties should either hold together on equitable terms or separate with kindness. It is not lawful for you (men) to take back any of your gifts (from your wives) except when both parties fear that they would be unable to

keep the limits ordained by Allah. If ye (judges) do indeed fear that they would be unable to keep the limits ordained by Allah there is no blame on either of them if she give something for her freedom. These are the limits ordained by Allah; so do not transgress them. If any do transgress the limits ordained by Allah such persons wrong (themselves as well as others). (Surah 2:229)

Note, however, that khul' depends on the husband's agreement. A significant condition is that neither party ought to put the other in a poor light in their respective families or in the umma. In addition to 2:229, Surah 4:128–30 deals with the wife who fears her husband's cruelty or his intention to desert her:

If a wife fears cruelty or desertion on her husband's part there is no blame on them if they arrange an amicable settlement between themselves; and such settlement is best; even though men's souls are swayed by greed. But if ye do good and practice self-restraint, Allah is well-acquainted with all that ye do. Ye are never able to be fair and just as between women even if it is your ardent desire: but turn not away (from a woman) altogether so as to leave her (as it were) hanging (in the air). If ye come to a friendly understanding and practice self-restraint, Allah is Oft-Forgiving, Most Merciful. But if they disagree (and must part), Allah will provide abundance for all from His all-reaching bounty: for Allah is He that careth for all and is Wise.

They are advised to come to an "amicable settlement" in the context of God knowing their intentions as well as legal commitments. Both parties are free to remarry after the final iddah (unless she is pregnant, as indicated). There are times, apparently frequent enough for God to address the practice in the Qur'an, when a divorced couple will remarry. If they divorce a second time, they may remarry a second time. If there is a third divorce, they cannot marry again directly. She will have to marry another man, then be divorced from him in order to marry the first husband for the third time:

A divorce is only permissible twice: after that the parties should either hold together on equitable terms or separate with kindness. It is not lawful for you (men) to take back any of your gifts (from your wives) except when both parties fear that they would be unable to keep the limits ordained by Allah. If ye (judges) do indeed fear that they would be unable to keep the limits ordained by Allah, there is no blame on either of them if she give something for her freedom. These are the limits ordained by Allah; so do not transgress them. If any do transgress the limits ordained by Allah such persons wrong (themselves as well as others). So if a husband divorces his wife (irrevocably) he cannot after that remarry her until after she has married another husband and he has divorced her. In that case there is no blame on either of them if they reunite provided they feel that they can keep the limits ordained by Allah. Such are the limits ordained by Allah which He makes plain to those who understand. When ye divorce women and they fulfill the term of their ('Iddat) either take them back on equitable terms or set them free on equitable terms; but do not take them back to injure them or to take undue advantage; if anyone does that He wrongs his own soul. Do not treat Allah's Signs as a jest but solemnly rehearse Allah's favors on you and the fact that He sent down to you the Book and Wisdom for your instruction. And fear Allah and know that Allah is well acquainted with all things. (Surah 2:229–31)

There is, of course, another way in which a marriage may be terminated: death.

Inheritance

It is prescribed when death approaches any of you, if he leave any goods that he make a bequest to parents and next of kin according to reasonable usage; this is due from the Allah-fearing.

Surah 2:180

Pre-Islamic inheritance traditions in Arabia are not clearly known, but Muslim scholars believe that the whole of what we would call the estate went to the eldest son. That leaves out surviving parents, wife, children, and various dependents. Such a procedure might have been uncomplicated, but it brought hardship, humiliation, and desperation to the other survivors. Islam seeks to establish a just and peaceful society, and that includes avoiding tensions and even violence within family circles concerning the deceased's property (including slaves) and fiscal resources. In addition, because of the precarious nature of caravan trade, there probably were a substantial number of men who died or disappeared on the road or in the deserts. Clearly, women and children were the most vulnerable persons in the society. The Qur'an addresses the situation of women and inheritance at several points. First, the wife is to receive maintenance and the right to live in the home for the year immediately following the husband's death (Surah 2:240). Leaving the residence may have involved a remarriage or return to her parents' home. Following that year, apparently, the Qur'an presents a complex distribution pattern that includes women:

> From what is left by parents and those nearest related, there is a share for men and a share for women whether the property be small or large, a determinate share. But if at the time of division other relatives of orphans or poor are present feed them out of the (property) and speak to them words of kindness, and let those (disposing of an estate) have the same fear in their minds as they would have for their own if they had left a helpless family behind: let them fear Allah and speak words of appropriate (comfort). (Surah 4:7–9)

Honesty and sincerity are required by those family and community members responsible for distributing the assets of the deceased. The Qur'an assumes that the male members of the late husband's family ought to receive the bulk of the post–debt payment residual funds:

> Allah (thus) directs you as regards your children's (inheritance): to the male a portion equal to that of two females: if only daughters two or more their share is two-thirds of the inheritance; if only one her share

is a half. For parents a sixth share of the inheritance to each if the deceased left children; if no children and the parents are the (only) heirs the mother has a third; if the deceased left brothers (or sisters) the mother has a sixth. (The distribution in all cases is) after the payment of legacies and debts. Ye know not whether your parents or your children are nearest to you in benefit. These are settled portions ordained by Allah, and Allah is All-Knowing, All-Wise (Surah 4:11)

The basic rule is that male heirs receive twice as much as their female counterparts. The rationale for such an arrangement is grounded in the man's responsibility to protect the women in the family by spending from his resources, so male heirs need more from the estate than women, who will probably marry or live with their parents. Surah 4:12 continues the distribution, adding the permutation of the wife predeceasing her husband (if there are no children, he received one-half and the children one-fourth):

If it is a man that dies leaving a sister but no child she shall have half the inheritance: if (such a deceased was) a woman who left no child her brother takes her inheritance: if there are two sisters they shall have two-thirds of the inheritance (between them): if there are brothers and sisters (they share) the male having twice the share of the female. Thus doth Allah make clear to you (His law), lest ye err. And Allah hath knowledge of all things. (Surah 4:176)

Orphans and Polygamy

If ye fear that ye shall not be able to deal justly with the orphans, marry women of your choice two or three or four; but if ye fear that ye shall not be able to deal justly (with them) then only one or (a captive) that your right hands possess. That will be more suitable to prevent you from doing injustice.

Surah 4:3

The traditional arguments for polygamy involve a surplus of women in the society as a result of higher female than male birthrates, male-killing war, the need to protect widows and orphaned girls from being exploited, and the need to prevent "unattached" women from becoming prostitutes. Another purported reason is gratifying the male libido while preserving the community's order. Polygamy was traditional in Arabia, and Muslim scholars maintain that in the Jahiliyyah there was no limit on the number of wives or any restrictions on how a man would treat them. But the Qur'an deals with polygamy differently. The only clear and relevant Quranic passage is the already cited Surah 4:3.

The occasion of the aya's revelation is the aftermath of the Battle of Uhud (625). Muslim casualties were high, generating significant numbers of widows and orphans. An examination of the aya indicates that at best polygamy is a concession to the existing customs, the umma's needs, and the plight of the widows and orphans. Surah 4:3 is couched in terms of just actions. Having a plurality of wives was not an obligation then or now. Framed by justice, Islamic polygamy aims at preserving and creating an equitable society in which the lives of the most vulnerable persons are protected and advanced.

Orphans are the aya's starting point. Islam mandates a totally different attitude toward orphans than existed in the Jahiliyyah. As an orphan, Muhammad was keenly aware of the dishonesty of numerous Meccans who were the guardians of orphan wards. The orphans' inheritances frequently were depleted by their guardians' failed business ventures, a great sin condemned by God (Surah 4:2). Further, female orphans seem to have been exploited sexually by their guardians who may have reduced them to virtual concubines or arranged marriages to inappropriate husbands in order to rid themselves of the responsibility. The polygamy aya (4:3) warns that if a guardian is attracted sexually to a female orphan or someone under his authority, he may marry her instead of forcing her into concubinage. Yet there is another condition: he must treat all his wives justly. He might love one more than another (as Muhammad did with Aisha), but he cannot neglect any of his wives. Seen in light of the revealed context and the Qur'an itself, men who marry more than one woman are commanded to protect and provide and care for them justly and lovingly.

Whoever recommends and helps a good cause becomes a partner therein: and whoever recommends and helps an evil cause shares in its burden: and Allah hath power over all things. (Surah 4:85)

Conclusion

Spiritual equals before God, responsible creatures created to care for and be Allah's representatives on earth, companions on the Straight Way that leads to the Hereafter, partners in mutual support and protection, witnesses to the Faith, and made beautiful and complete by God to fulfill their complementary roles in this world—these are some of the Quranic factors that bring and keep women and men together. Yet women are not subsumed under the authority or power of men. The Qur'an speaks of women who took responsibility for their lives, rescued messengers, ruled a kingdom, received revelations through angels, and had their prayers heard by God and Muhammad. And some women resisted and paid for opposing Allah and His warners. Some Muslim practices in the past and present may repress women. The Qur'an, however, sheds light on woman and women that may be seen within and beyond Islam. Whether or not, how and to what extent, when and where changes and adjustments to customs may be made are questions awaiting decisions.

Follow thou the inspiration sent unto thee, and be patient and constant, till Allah doth decide; for He is the Best to decide. (Surah 10:109)

ELEVEN

THE QUR'AN ON BIBLICAL FIGURES, JEWS AND CHRISTIANS

Say: "O people of the Book! Come to common terms
as between us and you: that we worship none but Allah;
that we associate no partners with Him; that we erect not
from among ourselves lords and patrons other than Allah."
If then they turn back, say: "Bear witness that we (at least)
are Muslims (bowing to Allah's will).

Surah 3:64

Islam, the Qur'an, and the Messenger constantly engage the Bible, Jews, and Christians. Historically, the presence of significant Jewish and Christian communities in Arabia challenged Muhammad and the Message while providing a pool of potential converts and possible allies. This chapter opens with Islamic-Quranic perspectives on the Bible, then examines the four messengers who appear in the Bible and the Qur'an in terms of the Qur'an's accounts about them, their relevance for Muhammad and the first umma, and what I suggest may be their relevance for present-day Muslims and non-Muslims.[1] It then develops Quranic views of the People of the Book, that is, Jews and Christians, their relevance for Muhammad and the first umma, and my perspective on the relevance Quranic treatment may have for the present.

QURANIC PERSPECTIVES ON THE BIBLE

Ye people of the Book! Why dispute ye about Abraham
when the Law and the Gospel were not revealed till after
him? Have ye no understanding? Ah! Ye are those who
fell to disputing (even) in matters of which ye had some
knowledge! But why dispute ye in matters of which ye have
no knowledge? It is Allah Who knows, and ye who know
not! Abraham was not a Jew nor yet a Christian, but he was
true in faith and bowed his will to Allah's (which is Islam)
and he joined not gods with Allah. Without doubt among
men the nearest of kin to Abraham are those who follow
him, as are also this Messenger [Muhammad] and those who
believe; and Allah is the Protector of those who have faith.
It is the wish of a section of the People of the Book to lead
you [Muhammad] astray. But they shall lead astray (not you)
but themselves and they do not perceive! Ye People of the
Book! Why reject ye the signs of Allah of which ye are
(yourselves) witnesses? Ye People of the Book! Why do ye
clothe truth with falsehood and conceal the truth while
ye have knowledge?

Surah 3:64–71

Surah 3:64–71 epitomizes the Quranic view of the Bible, Jews, and
Christians. Muslim traditions hold that the passage is part of the Muslim–
Christian encounter that concerned those gathered under Muhammad's
cloak. Three factors are singled out to be understood Islamically: worship
only the God who reveals His ultimate Message through the final Messenger, Muhammad; do not place anyone or anything on par with this
One-Only God; and do not make any human or divine being an interces-
sor between the believer and God. Although Jews were not present when
Surah 3:64–71 was revealed, they could later step gingerly on a common

monotheistic ground but would find that other steps would to lead to their conversion to Islam. Christians would balk at even a first step. The passage entails renunciations of the Trinity, of the meditorial-salvational role of Jesus, and of the veneration of saints as well as the authority of their clergy. In later settings, however, the threefold basis appealed to Christians disaffected by the imperially sponsored church and its increasingly complicated theology, squabbling clergy, and hostile treatment of dissenters.

THE ISLAMIC POINT OF DEPARTURE
FOR UNDERSTANDING THE BIBLE

Muslim understandings of the Bible are framed by the conviction that God's revelatory activity among all cultures manifests His One-Only-ness (tawhid) in many forms, specifically here in the disclosure of His plan for creation and humanity. The plan unfolds in a covenantal, consistent, and developmental manner through His messengers and prophets with revelatory books sent to particular peoples addressed to them in their languages and cultures. The message's core was God's One-Only-ness and His will for men and women to tread the Straight Path through right worship and justice. Each messenger was misunderstood, opposed, rejected, and endangered by the people to whom he was sent. Moses and Jesus, two of several prophets and messengers who came to the Jews, gave them respectively the Tawrah (Law) and the Ingil (Gospel).[2] Not only were Moses and Jesus opposed and resisted, but their books were distorted, corrupted, and made the cause of hostile divisiveness and blasphemy:

> If only the people of the Book had believed and been righteous, We should indeed have blotted out their iniquities and admitted them to gardens of Bliss. If only they had stood fast by the Law, the Gospel and all the revelation that was sent to them from their Lord, they would have enjoyed happiness from every side. There is from among them a party on the right course; but many of them follow a course that is evil. O Messenger! Proclaim the (Message) which hath been sent to thee from thy Lord. If thou didst not, thou wouldst not have

fulfilled and proclaimed His mission: and Allah will defend thee from men (who mean mischief). For Allah guideth not those who reject faith. Say: "O People of the Book! Ye have no ground to stand upon unless ye stand fast by the Law, the Gospel and all the revelation that has come to you from your Lord." It is the revelation that cometh to thee from thy Lord that increaseth in most of them their obstinate rebellion and blasphemy. But sorrow thou not over (these) people without Faith. Those who believe (in the Qur'an) those who follow the Jewish (Scriptures) and the Sabians and the Christians, any who believe in Allah and the Last Day and work righteousness on them shall be no fear nor shall they grieve. (Surah 5:65–69)

CONTRASTS BETWEEN THE BIBLE AND THE QUR'AN

The contrasts between the Bible and the Qur'an are often stark and unbridgeable. From the Muslim side, where the biblical materials diverge from the words and intent of the Qur'an, the Qur'an is the final and authoritative correction for it is the uncorrupted revealed will and word of God. The Qur'an is the infallible guide to all humanity. It sets forth the Straight Way for all persons to the goal of the coming judgment and the certainty of the Hereafter. The One Voice of the Qur'an summons humans and jinn to obedience to God, proper worship, and the establishment of just relationships. In addition to Jews and Christians not agreeing on what is to be called "Scriptures," the languages in which the documents are written and debates among Christians about which books are to be included, as well as the integrity of the biblical texts, the Bible is simply different in style and content from the Revelation given Muhammad.

Unlike the Qur'an, the Bible contains narratives, histories, genealogies, songs to be used in worship, details about sacrificing animals, humans complaining to and petitioning God for various purposes, and even two books that do not mention God at all (Song of Solomon and the Hebrew text of Esther). The Christian "New Testament" has not one but four Gospels, then letters written by various persons about congregational matters. Compared to the Qur'an, the Bible is a mélange of styles, literary forms, authors, ideas, claims, and messages. On occasion the Bible presents God speaking directly, and throughout its pages are accounts about specific persons and events. The Torah texts do have the Lord addressing matters such as worship, morals, military tactics, political policies, communal governance, repentance, punishments, and rewards. Writings by or attributed to prophets and sages do denounce immoral and unjust behavior, cruelty among the nations, and, rarely, the coming judgment on the world. But there are "buts."

First, as quoted in and described by the Torah, prophets, and writings, God is frequently erratic, confusing, and cruel. He repents of creating humanity (Gen. 6:5−7); is bent on destroying the helpless and innocent simply because they get in the way of His allegedly chosen people and without giving them a chance to respond to His will (e.g. Deut. 7:1−26; Josh. 6:15−27); tricks David into taking take a census and then punishes the people for David's obedience (2 Sam. 24:1−25); has a lying spirit deceive prophets (1 Kings 22:19−23); commands a prophet to marry a whore (Hos. 1:2−5); claims that He created evil as well as good (Isa. 45:6); and wagered with Satan about hapless Job, thereby condemning Job's children and servants to their deaths (Job 1−2). Perhaps more telling against the biblical testimony to God is the Jewish assertion that the Lord chose them as His personal treasure.

Second, the Bible presents God's heroic figures in scandalous and reprehensible lights. Certainly, some committed errors, but they would never have sunk to the depths depicted in the Bible. Noah is reported to have made wine, become drunk, and perhaps become involved in a homosexual act; Abraham and Isaac lie about their wives in order to save their own lives; Lot is seduced by his daughters while in a drunken stupor; Jacob is a swindling deceiver and is deceived by his own sons; Joseph withholds food from famine-stricken Egyptians until they become Pharaoh's slaves; Saul is a madman who consorts with a witch; David is an adulterer and murderer; and Solomon ends as a lascivious idolater.

Third, the Christian version of the revelation in the Scripture is no better than that of the Jews. Except for the Gospels, the Qur'an does not directly reflect New Testament materials, although some of its imagery of the end of this world is similar to that of the Revelation to John. Jesus' claims that he is the Son of God, has a divine origin, and is one with the Creator-Father are blasphemous. That Jesus changed water into wine, drank wine, and told his followers to remember him by imbibing wine must be a direct lie. And that Jesus was crucified and then resurrected is a total misperception of what actually happened.

Fourth, the Bible is incomplete in that it omits important parts of accounts, thereby leaving unanswered questions. An example is the account of the murder of one of Adam's sons by his brother. The Genesis version makes God sound arbitrary in accepting the sacrifices of one but not the other brother (4:1–16) The Quranic version provides essential elements that make the conflict a struggle over righteousness and obedience to God (Surah 5:27–32).

The Muslim judgment is that the Bible as it stands cannot be God's fullest revelation, that it has been distorted and corrupted by Jewish and Christian leaders. The Qur'an, then, is the true and infallible corrective. Now the Qur'an replaces the Bible as instructing humans on establishing just societies and guiding them into their everlasting futures:

> O People of the Book! There hath come to you Our Messenger revealing to you much that ye used to hide in the Book and passing over much (that is now unnecessary). There hath come to you from Allah a (new) Light and a perspicuous Book. Wherewith Allah guideth all who seek His good pleasure to ways of peace and safety and leadeth them out of darkness by His Will unto the light guideth them to a Path that is Straight. (Surah 5:15–16)

THE QUR'AN ON FOUR COVENANTAL MESSENGERS

> Say: "I am no bringer of new-fangled doctrine among
> the messengers nor do I know what will be done with me
> or with you. I follow but that which is revealed to me by
> inspiration: I am but a Warner open and clear." Say: "See ye?

If (this teaching) be from Allah and ye reject it and a witness
from among the Children of Israel testifies to its similarity
(with earlier scriptures) and has believed while ye are arrogant
(how unjust ye are!), truly Allah guides not a people unjust."
The Unbelievers say of those who believe: "If (this Message)
were a good thing (such men) would not have gone to it
first before us!" and seeing that they guide not themselves
thereby they will say "This is an (old) old falsehood!" And
before this was the Book of Moses as a guide and a mercy;
and this Book confirms (it) in the Arabic tongue; to
admonish the unjust and as Glad Tidings to those who
do right. Verily those who say "Our Lord is Allah" and
remain firm (on that Path) on them shall be no fear nor
shall they grieve.

Surah 46:9–13, al-Ahqaf, the Winding Sand Tracts

Thirty men, two angels, and one woman named in the Bible are also named
in the Qur'an. Six surahs bear the names of biblical persons.[3] Zachariah
and his son John the Baptist, in addition to Mary and her son Jesus, are the
only New Testament humans identified by name in the Qur'an. Unnamed
other figures range through the Revelation's biblically resonating accounts.
These include Noah's family and neighbors, the men of Sodom, Joseph's
brothers, Pharaoh's magicians, the children of Israel, and Jesus' disciples.
Other passages of the Qur'an record unfamiliar, perhaps new individuals
and groups related to mentioned persons in the Bible. These include Abraham's neighbors; Moses' servant who lost track of a tunneling fish; an enigmatic sage who humbled Moses; the nonbiblical Jewish tradition that Ezra
was taken Enochlike into heaven; and traditions included in pre-Islamic
noncanonical Christian writings such as Mary being raised in the Jerusalem Temple where she was fed by angels, Jesus' turning clay sparrows
into living birds, and his not being crucified.[4] I selected four especially

important and expressly covenanted figures for examination: Noah, Abraham, Moses, and Jesus.

All that We relate to thee [Muhammad] of the stories of the messengers—with it We make firm in thy heart. In them there cometh to thee the Truth, as well as exhortation and a message of remembrance to those who believe. Say to those who do not believe: "Do whatever ye can: We shall do our part; and wait ye! We too shall wait." (Surah 11:120–22)

NOAH (NUH)

We sent Noah to his People (with the Command): "Do thou warn thy people before there comes to them a grievous Penalty." He said: "O my People! I am to you a Warner clear and open: That ye should worship Allah, fear Him and obey me so He may forgive you your sins and give you respite for a stated Term. For when the Term given by Allah is accomplished, it cannot be put forward. If ye only knew."

Surah 71:1–4

The Quranic Noah is mentioned frequently, and Surah 71, traditionally named for him, offers a picture of this early messenger.[5]

Noah in the Qur'an

The Speaker assumes that listener-readers know about Noah and the horrendous flood.[6] God made Noah a clear and forceful spokesperson who lived among his polytheistic people for 950 years before he summoned his neighbors to worship the one true God:

> We (once) sent Noah to his people and he tarried among them a thou-
> sand years less fifty: but the Deluge overwhelmed them while they
> (persisted in) sin. But We saved him and the Companions of the Ark,
> and We made the (Ark) a Sign for all Peoples! (Surah 29:14–15)

Noah told them God "will send rain to you in abundance; give you
increase in wealth and sons; and bestow on you Gardens and bestow on
you Rivers (of flowing water)" (Surah 71:11–12). He continued that if
they persisted in worshiping their ancestral gods after hearing Allah's clear
word, they would be destroyed. The leaders accused him of being deluded
and insane (Surah 7:59–60).[7] Denying the charge, he persisted in claiming that he, a mere human and a member of their own community, had
received a revelation from the only God. They agreed spitefully that he
and the few who joined him were from their midst but held a lowly status among them.[8] The leaders suspected that Noah was out to grab power
from them by usurping their authority through the scare tactic of a message of doom. Others thought that if they waited his insanity would become evident and he would be discredited, while a number rejected him
for being a mere human (Surah 21:24–25). The leaders sneered that if he
was so right and confident about the coming Day of Judgment, why did
he not bring it upon them? Noah's response left the timing of the disaster
to God (Surah 7:32–34), but he anguished over the doom his people faced.
Rumors reached him that the leaders were conspiring to stone him (Surah
26:106–16). He turned to God for strength (Surah 23:26), but as their
threats increased Noah prayed that God would wipe them off the face of
the earth so they would not mislead potential believers (Surah 71:5–20).[9]
Enduring the mockery of his people but obedient to God, he built the
ark.[10] He collected the animals, and as the deluge began God commanded
him to enter the ark with those few who believed. His wife and one of
his sons drowned after they decided not to join him.[11] Distraught, Noah
was told that his true family was not identified by blood relationships but
by those who submitted to God's will (Surah 11:40–49).

The Revealer recounted the story of Noah and the flood for several
general reasons. One concerned the role of Noah as an exemplar for the
power of a righteous person's prayer and deeds done in obedience to God

(Surah 37:75–82, al-Saffat, Those Ranged in Ranks). Second, the account is meant to be a sign and warning for all people to heed God's messengers or face the consequences. For the faithful, the account is an encouragement to stand firm for God's ways because those who persevere will be welcomed in the Hereafter. Those consequences would not be long in coming, for the Noah narrative foreshadows the Day of Judgment and the prospect of everlasting punishment for those who spurn God and His will (Surah 69:11–17).[12] Third, God has revealed His justice and mercy through the messenger and the message. Muslims insist that the true story of Noah, the proclaimer of the One-Only God and the Straight Path is in the Qur'an and certainly not in the Bible (Surah 54:17–22).

Noah's Relevance for Muhammad and the First Umma

The ayas dealing with Noah are regarded as being revealed in Mecca. Clearly, Muhammad fits the Noachian pattern. The message to Qurayshi leaders was the same as that proclaimed by Noah: Muhammad came with a mission; the Meccan elite accused him of madness and delusion, deriding his claims and saying he only sought power. Frustrated and angry at his persistence and success at making converts, they plotted to kill him. Muhammad's activities also were consonant with Noah's: he was relentless in speaking and teaching, stated repeatedly that the signs of God's Oneness and will were evident throughout nature, engaged in private as well as public witness, showed deep concern for the fate of those who rejected the Message, regarded those who responded to the Revelation as closer to him than his family or clan, turned to God in prayer for strength and guidance, relied on God to accomplish His plan for the world rather than give specific dates for the end of this world, and witnessed to all humanity as well as to his own people. What Noah was in a preliminary way, Muhammad is in the fullest and final sense. The Noah story's immediate impact for Muhammad was to comfort, assure, and strengthen him to carry forward his mission to its God-appointed fulfillment. The Meccan-Medinan Muslims were comparable to the few who believed Noah's message and who endured ridicule and danger in order to be faithful to the one God. Through the eyes of faith, they could see the signs of God's One-Only-ness, justice, and mercy in the world around them. Prayer, adherence to the emerging standards of conduct, loyalty to Muhammad, and Quranic revelations sustained their faith and testimony.

The Quranic Noah's Potential Relevance Today

Two areas seem relevant today. The first is Noah's immediate context. He addressed the leaders of his own people, calling them to repentance, faith in the true God, and obedience to God's will. He urged them to give up idolatry and become righteous or face God's wrath through catastrophe. Noah-based warnings are intensified with and after the ultimate Revelation in the Qur'an and the witness-model, Muhammad. There can be no excuses by leaders in nations and communities that have heard and had the God-blessed opportunity of Islam. How have the leaders of these countries and societies responded the Message? Have they taken the Qur'an as their guide in political, legal, economic, societal, educational and familial spheres? The Noah model may encourage some devout and frustrated Muslims to oppose governmental and religious leaders whom they perceive to be opposed to or careless in observing Islam. In other words, the Noah paradigm has potential political overtones, especially for the Muslim world.

Second, Noah was a messenger for all persons. There is a missionary dimension to the proclamation that reaches beyond the Muslim world. Muslims have a responsibility to take Islam to those who do not yet know or have not been made aware of the truth of Islam. As was true for Noah and Muhammad, time is running out. Now, after the full disclosure of the Qur'an and the spread of Islam through a substantial part of the world, Muslims are entering western Europe and the Americas, sub-Saharan Africa, and regions of Asia that have been relatively out of the orbit of Islamic presence. Since Noah is also a covenanted biblical figure, the Quranic delineation of his mission now comprehended in the fullness of the Revelation may serve as a fruitful point of contact with Jews and certainly Christian-influenced persons who are searching for God's truth. The "point of contact" might be in terms of interfaith dialogue or conversion. The example of Noah's 950 years of patience and persistence could imbue Muslims with the willingness to engage in long-term activities and commitments of resources to spread the Message and its way of life.

ABRAHAM (IBRAHIM)

> Who can be better in religion than one who submits his
> whole self to Allah, does good and follows the way of
> Abraham the true in faith? For Allah did take Abraham
> for a friend. But to Allah belong all things in the heavens
> and on earth: and He it is that encompasseth all things.
>
> *Surah 4:125–26*

Abraham, the friend of God, is the essential pre-Muhammad messenger.[13] He is the first Muslim, builder of the Ka'bah, founder of the city of Mecca, initiator of regular prayer, bearer of a revelatory book, the one through whom God made covenants with Jews, Christians, and the inhabitants of Arabia and who became the ancestral father of Isaac, Ishmael, Jacob and his sons, Moses, Mary, and Jesus. Muhammad, Abraham's progeny, completes the series of revealers. Abraham passed through fire in testifying to God's One-Only-ness. He was specially chosen, purified, and tested by God. Except for his even greater counterpart-descendant, Muhammad, God said of no one else:

> And who turns from the religion of Abraham but such as debase their souls with folly? Him [Abraham] We chose and rendered pure in this world, and he will be in the Hereafter in the ranks of the righteous. Behold! His Lord said to him: "Bow (thy will to Me)." He said: "I bow (my will) to the Lord and Cherisher of the universe." (Surah 2:130–31)

Abraham did on earth what Iblis refused to do in heaven; he bowed to and obeyed God's command. He rendered full obedience to God, was never deceived by the Evil One, and is the paradigm for subsequent messengers and especially Muhammad. His growth in faith and wisdom, along with his success in meeting the challenges and tests presented to him by God, earned him the designation "Imam to the nations" (Surah 2:124). He is regarded as the messenger through whom God made possible the restoration of the primal order God willed for this world.[14] Disorder and deception are the harsh results of Iblis's rebellion and humanity's sinful gullibility. Abraham sought to recover the original *fitra* (underlying order) and institute right worship around the location of the earthly home of Adam and his spouse and to build the Ka'bah as the center for prayer, pilgrimage, and obedient devotion to God. So when Muslims face Mecca and the Ka'bah for prayer and when they undertake the Hajj, they join in the way of Abraham, one of the greatest and most gracious guides on the Straight Path. Naming himself a Muslim, he prayed that his descendants would remain in the Faith and that they would have their own revelatory messenger (Surah 2:127–29).

Abraham in the Qur'an

The Genesis accounts are part of the Quranic backdrop, other points are amplified, and significant sections are added. According to Islam, the whole is given its true understandings in the Qur'an. We consider Abraham in three Quranic settings: his family of origin, in the land to which God first directed him, and in Arabia. I offer here a composite narrative of the Khalilullah, the Friend of God, among his people.

Abraham and His Family of Origin

Abraham, disdaining the polytheistic religion of his father, Azar, and his neighbors, sought the God who has created all. He was not satisfied with the skies, stars, moon, and sun. God revealed to him that He is the one and only God, is worthy of worship, and that all the heavenly bodies as well as all existence are signs pointing to Him. Sometime after Abraham came to believe in the One-Only God, God bestowed the first book to a messenger on Abraham.[15] He was now the first Muslim, and as such confronted his father and the local leaders, proclaiming the futility and irrationality of their idolatry, God's One-Only-ness, and God's summons that they follow Him.[16] The initial encounter was acrimonious, and his life was threatened.[17] But Abraham persisted in testifying to God and to the errors of his neighbors' religion. His angry father threatened to kill him because he chose to obey God and hated the ancestral deities. Yet Abraham continued to pray for the well-being of his father and community members (Surah 19:42–48). He attracted a few persons, notably Lot, to the Faith. The first Muslim and the small number who followed him threatened the political and religious order. In another encounter the leaders mocked Abraham for claiming that any divinity would reveal anything to the likes of him, then accused him of sorcery (Surah 43:26–32). Abraham increased tensions by smashing their idols, then infuriated them by scorning the gods when they did not retaliate against him. The leaders threw him into a fire, but God commanded the flames to be cool, and Abraham emerged safely.[18] God then commanded Abraham to leave his father and city to go to the land He had blessed for all nations.

Abraham in the New Land

Abraham and his small group left to settle where directed. In that new land Abraham established a righteous family-community that did what Allah commanded, engaged in regular prayers, and practiced charity. The Qur'an reports interesting incidents that are not in the Bible.

In one, a skeptic attempted to debunk the message proclaimed by Abraham. God had given the person some power, but he lacked understanding. Abraham confounded him by pointing out God's superior authority and power. The next event features a man who rejected the idea of resurrection from the dead. God caused him to die and then awakened him after a century, thereby showing him that God can do all things. The third account returned to Abraham. He asked God to prove to him the resurrection of the dead not because he did not believe that God will do it but because he wants to satisfy his understanding. God responded with instructions that involved the probable dismembering of birds and their reassembly when called to come to Abraham.[19]

Abraham in Arabia

Although the Qur'an does not share the details of Abraham's journeys to and in Arabia, it reports that he, Ishmael, and Ishmael's mother settled in what became Mecca.[20] There father and son built the Ka'bah and started the city of Mecca. Abraham's eloquent prayers petition God to make Mecca the center for Islam and a place of peace for all (Surahs 2:125–29 and 14:35–41). God's responses included the command for the Hajj:

> Behold! We gave the site to Abraham of the (Sacred) House (saying): "Associate not any thing (in worship) with Me; and sanctify My House for those who compass it round or stand up or bow or prostrate themselves (therein in prayer). And proclaim the Pilgrimage among men: they will come to thee on foot and (mounted) on every kind of camel lean on account of journeys through deep and distant mountain highways; that they may witness the benefits (provided) for them and celebrate the name of Allah through the days appointed over the cattle which He has provided for them (for sacrifice): then eat ye thereof and feed the distressed ones in want. Then let them complete the rites prescribed for them perform their vows and (again) circumambulate the Ancient House." (Surah 22:26–29)

The Qur'an mentions that Abraham was commanded to sacrifice his son.[21] More than willing, the son says: "'O my father! Do as thou art commanded: thou will find me, if Allah so wills, one practicing patience and constancy!' So when they had both submitted their wills (to Allah) and he had laid him prostrate on his forehead (for sacrifice), We called out to him 'O Abraham! Thou hast already fulfilled the vision!' Thus indeed do We reward those who do right" (Surah 37:102–105).

Abraham's Relevance for Muhammad and the First Umma

Muhammad, too, was a traveler. He traveled as a caravaneer and as a leader seeking refuge for his abused umma. He traveled to and was humiliated at Taif. Through God's benevolent and wise plan, he provided a safe haven for the nascent umma in Yathrib-Medina, thereby beginning the Muslim era. His final treks involved numerous military campaigns in Arabia before and after the capitulation of his opponents, the final Hajj, and the return to Medina. Muhammad also was a spiritual traveler. His dismay over polytheism led the hanif to climb Mount Hira. He returned the humble and empowered Messenger of Islam. He engaged in the struggle his predecessor prophets and messengers knew well. He undertook the Night Journey and, according to the Hadiths, ascended through the heavens where, he was greeted by Abraham and went where no human had ever gone before: into the closest possible presence of the Lord of the Worlds. Just as Abraham sought wisdom from God, the whole of Muhammad's subsequent life was one of spiritual awareness and growth, tempered with struggles and successes, loyalties and betrayals, and concerns vital to establishing a new community. He bore the burden of being God's ultimate revealer so as to guide all humans after him to the Straight Way. In all these travels Abraham, the first Muslim, was his most important human guide. As God revealed to Muhammad: "So We have taught thee the inspired (Message): Follow the ways of Abraham, the true in faith, and he joined not gods with Allah" (Surah 16:123).

Point by point, with the exception of the sacrifice of a son, Muhammad and the Quranic Abraham match each other. Muhammad was a direct descendant of the messenger-patriarch, was a Meccan, was involved in the rebuilding of the Ka'bah, was married and had children, lived in the midst of polytheists, rejected the idolatry of his family of origin and community leaders, was mocked and slandered by the leaders of the community, was the target of economic and physical dangers, and was protected by God when he left his birth city. As Abraham could be called the first Muslim, Muhammad was the first Muslim among the Arabs of his time and for all humanity to the Day of Judgment. Abraham was the Friend of

God; Muhammad was closer to God than any other human. He founded the community that God determined would be the greatest blessing to all nations. In that umma he established the religious practices, determined what the prayers would be and how they would be offered and usually led them. He was inspired by God to decide the proper interpretations of the revelations and relationships the umma had with God and one another. He was the city's ruler, judge, and sage. He determined how the fiscal and other material resources of the city were to be gathered and allocated. Moreover, he was the community's ruler who planned, as God willed, when and where to make war and was strategist, field general, and commander of the military forces. After battles he decided about prisoners of war and traitors and the division of plunder. In addition to being the key authority in dealing with the other inhabitants of the land, Muhammad determined and pursued foreign policies with the Persians and Byzantines. Throughout, he was guided by the revelations given him through and apart from the Qur'an. Abraham was the salient figure on whom he could draw for inspiration and example. Speaking of Muhammad, God said: "Without doubt among men the nearest of kin to Abraham are those who follow him as are also this Messenger and those who believe; and Allah is the Protector of those who have faith" (Surah 3:68).

The spiritual resonances are deeper yet between the two. Abraham was steadfast in trusting in, living by, and witnessing to God in spite of the dangers he faced initially, even to breaking the blood ties that bound him to his ancestors. He cared deeply for his father and family, but, as God commanded, he left them to the justice and mercy of God. Muhammad was a compassionate and loyal person who struggled with the same dilemma perhaps with greater anguish because he was convinced that on the Day of Judgment his unbelieving loved ones would be condemned. Muhammad could rely on the example of Abraham as a key figure for whom God cared and protected, gave victory and vindication, and through whom many were brought on the path to everlasting life.

Abraham also provided Muhammad with the style and means to face his detractors and the Hypocrites with words and actions. Abraham was unswerving in his insistence on the One-Only-ness of God. Muhammad was strengthened by that example, not only when he engaged with the polytheists, but also when he engaged with the Jews and Christians who debated with him and with whom he had to deal. In those latter encounters, Muhammad often cited Abraham as God's messenger for Islam.

The Quranic Abraham's Potential Relevance Today

Abraham and Muhammad have traveled well through the centuries; they belong together. Their determined efforts to proclaim the One-Only God in the face of opposition, especially the opposition of the leaders of their home city, gave members of the umma encouragement and a model to resist the secularization of their societies. In this regard Abraham is a Quranic support for a return to the ways of the Messenger. That Abraham established Mecca and erected the Ka'bah to be centers of peace, safety, and justice is a message to the political rulers and religious leaders of the Kingdom of Saudi Arabia. How that message is interpreted or attempted to be implemented may spur tensions and expressions aimed at achieving greater observances of Islamic law. Abraham's survival of fiery punishment through God's intervention may serve as an inspiration for those who are willing to go to the maximum lengths to defeat the forces, domestic and foreign, that threaten the Faith and the Faithful. While they may know that the flames, explosions, or time spent in prison will be real in this world, they may be convinced that they and their causes will be vindicated in the Hereafter.

MOSES (MUSSA)

Has the story of Moses reached thee? Behold he saw a fire.
So he said to his family, "Tarry ye; I perceive a fire; perhaps
I can bring you some burning brand therefrom or find some
guidance at the fire." But when he came to the fire, a voice
was heard: "O Moses! Verily, I am thy Lord! Therefore (in
My presence) put off thy shoes: thou art in the sacred valley
Tuwa. I have chosen thee. Listen then to the inspiration

(sent to thee). Verily, I am Allah: there is no god but I.
So serve thou Me (only) and establish regular prayer for
celebrating My praise.

Surah 20:9–14

Moses is a liberator-messenger for Jews and a forerunner of Jesus for Christians. The Qur'an's Revealer recalls events and persons mentioned in Exodus, Leviticus, Numbers, and Deuteronomy. The Quranic versions often include corrections, explanations, details, and supplements to the biblical accounts, along with episodes that are totally different from the Pentateuch.

Moses in the Qur'an

The Quranic accounts about Moses aim at strengthening Muhammad and the umma, gaining converts, refuting critics, and helping women and men on the Straight Way. God seeds Moses' story throughout the Qur'an without regard to temporal order. For our purposes I offer a connected sketch of the Qur'an's version of Moses' life.

Moses' Birth and Rescue

The Quranic account (Surah 28:7–13) confirms the basic outlines of the Exodus story but with differences.[22] Chapter 10 sketched the account about Moses as it related to his mother, sister, wife, and Pharaoh's queen. The child who grew to adulthood would make his own decisions about obeying or disobeying God. The Lord arranged for Moses to meet persons and engage in events that tested him, brought him closer to the Master, and empowered the revelation that God will disclose through him. The passage also notes the roles of two other women instrumental in moving God's plan forward by saving Moses. The "people of Pharaoh" take up the child, then present their bundle to the queen, whose response foreshadowed her later faith.[23] The last member of the female trio responsible for

Moses' rescue is his sister. While the Quranic and biblical accounts agree, the Revelation's detail about Moses needing a lactating nurse is reminiscent of the Qurayshi practice of giving their newborns to bedouin wetnurses, as Muhammad was nourished by Halima. The closing line, "but most of them do not understand," marks a transition to the next stage in the Qur'an's story of Moses.

Moses as Murderer and Fugitive

> When he reached full age and was firmly established (in life),
> We bestowed on him wisdom and knowledge, for thus do We
> reward those who do good. And he entered the City at a time
> when its people were not watching: and he found there two
> men fighting one of his own religion and the other of his
> foes. Now the man of his own religion appealed to him
> against his foe, and Moses struck him with his fist and made
> an end of him. He said: "This is a work of Evil (Satan):
> for he is an enemy that manifestly misleads!" He prayed:
> "O my Lord! I have indeed wronged my soul! Do Thou
> then forgive me!" So (Allah) forgave him: for He is the
> Oft-Forgiving Most Merciful. He said: "O my Lord! For
> that Thou hast bestowed Thy Grace on me never shall
> I be a help to those who sin!"
>
> *Surah 28:14–17*

God endowed Moses with wisdom and knowledge through practical experience and tests of his obedience. Before being called as a messenger, he made errors, repented, was forgiven, and moved forward in witnessing to God. The Qur'an shows him to be a person developing in obedience and faith.[24] The scene in Surah 28:14–17, probably set in the capital, pictures Moses being asked by a coreligionist for assistance in a fight with an idolater. Moses acted without seeking to end the fight by other means; his

punch killed the idolater. Immediately Moses realized such an act of unthinking violence was sinful, and he recognized that it was evil to kill a
God-created human without warning and without giving him the opportunity to change. Moses, a man with a hot temper and a man of prayer,
sought forgiveness from the God he already knew was just and forgiving.
In that prayer Moses indicated awareness that with God's pardon he would
be able to help other sinners. The Ever-Merciful forgave him. The next
day, another fight involved the same coreligionist:

> So he saw the morning in the City, looking about in a state of fear,
> when, behold, the man who had the day before sought his help called
> aloud for his help (again). Moses said to him: "Thou art truly, it is clear,
> a quarrelsome fellow!" Then when he decided to lay hold of the man
> who was an enemy to both of them that man said: "O Moses! Is it thy
> intention to slay me as thou slewest a man yesterday? Thy intention is
> none other than to become a powerful, violent man in the land and
> not to be one who sets things right!" (Surah 28:18–19)

Instead of striking first, Moses attempted to separate the men. Shaken
by the polytheist's accusation that his use of force would never restore
harmony, Moses realized that he could not hide from either the authorities or his own conscience. Suddenly an unnamed man came running from
the city to warn Moses that the Egyptian leaders were plotting to kill him
and that he must flee (Surah 28:20–21). Moses escaped and prayed to be
saved from wrongdoers, asking God, "Show me the smooth and straight
Path." Moses took his way through the wilderness to the land of Madyan.
Now a fugitive and an alien, Moses depended solely on God to be brought
to the Straight Path and to begin his mission in God's plan.

Moses as Servant, Householder, and Messenger

> And when he arrived at the watering (place) in Madyan
> he found there a group of men watering (their flocks), and
> besides them he found two women who were keeping back
> (their flocks). He said: "What is the matter with you?" They

said: "We cannot water (our flocks) until the shepherds take back (their flocks); and our father is a very old man." So he watered (their flocks) for them; then he turned back to the shade and said: "O my Lord! Truly am I in (desperate) need of any good that thou dost send me!" Afterwards one of the (damsels) came (back) to him, walking bashfully. She said: "My father invites thee that he may reward thee for having watered (our flocks) for us." So when he came to him and narrated the story he [the father] said: "Fear thou not. (Well) hast thou escaped from unjust people." Said one of the (damsels): "O my (dear) father! Engage him on wages. Truly the best of men for thee to employ is the (man) who is strong and trusty.

Surah 28:23–26

Moses learned to control his temper somewhat and channel his energies by doing the work of a servant without thought of a reward. Through prayer he put himself under the protection of God. Surah 28:23–26 omits any hint of violence in word or deed between Moses and the shepherds and adds that the women said their father was very old. The father's age, the unmarried state of the women, and the manner in which they were treated may indicate the barrenness of the land and the marginal social status of the family. Moses had exhausted himself physically and psychologically. Raised in Pharaoh's household and accustomed to luxury, the exile is now humbled and faithful. His prayer is that of an obedient believer who is ready to accept God's help. He seeks the Straight Way and is a recipient and future proclaimer of the Message. God responds through a woman. Within the passage is the germ of a tender love story. The old father believed Moses' account of what happened in Egypt and extended hospitality. Within the bounds of modesty, a daughter's reasonable proposal about employing this strong and trustworthy man resulted eventually in a marriage agreement. God set the stage for calling Moses to be His messenger to the Children of Israel.

The Qur'an shows Moses in the midst of his basic umma, the family, when the call came. He left them to get some free fire or "information" that could come only from God. The dialogue between God (via an angel?) and Moses resulted in God telling him that he had been prepared for decades for that moment and that he was to confront Pharaoh because "he has transgressed all bounds" (Surah 20:43). From that point on Moses was to lead his people out of Egypt and to be the first messenger to warn the Egyptians of the coming wrath if they did not serve and worship the one true God (Surah 28:46). Moses received nine signs, including the power to turn his staff into a serpent.[25] Realizing that he needed a human partner in his mission as well as divine help, Moses received permission to include Aaron in the work God gave him.

The Messenger Returns

[Allah commanded] "Go both of you to Pharaoh for he
has indeed transgressed all bounds; but speak to him mildly.
Perchance he may take warning or fear (Allah)." They
(Moses and Aaron) said: "Our Lord! We fear lest he hasten
with insolence against us or lest he transgress all bounds."
[Allah] said: "Fear not, for I am with you. I hear and see
(everything). So go ye both to him and say 'Verily we are
messengers sent by thy Lord. Send forth therefore the
Children of Israel with us and afflict them not. With a sign
indeed have we come from thy Lord! And peace to all who
follow guidance! Verily it has been revealed to us that the
penalty (awaits) those who reject and turn away.'"

Surah 20:43–48

Although Moses and Aaron probably contacted their people before the audience with Pharaoh, the Qur'an reserves the people's reactions to the brothers for a later point. Moses and Aaron are heralds who speak what their Lord told them. As God sent his heralds out, He noted the remote possibility that Pharaoh might take the warnings to heart and mend his cruel ways (Surahs 20:49 and 79:17–19). Pharaoh sneered as Moses extolled the God who created all and to Whom everything points and reported that there would be a resurrection of the dead and judgment (Surah 20:49–55). During the heated exchange, Pharaoh recalled to Moses his lowly origins and ingratitude. Moses responded that he had grown wiser through God's guidance and was now His messenger. He criticized the Egyptian ruler for enslaving the Israelites (Surah 26:18–22, al-Shu'ara', the Poets). Pharaoh jumped to the conclusion that the messenger was a sorcerer who wanted to replace him on the throne.[26] Convinced that his magicians and he could produce greater magic and wonders than Moses (and the God who sent Moses), he proposed a rod-throwing contest. The public contest of rods-becoming-serpents pitted Pharaoh's two magicians against Moses and Aaron (Surah 20:70–76). When Moses' rod-serpent devoured the magicians' rods, the men embraced Islam. Enraged, Pharaoh claimed that he was the almighty god and chief magician. He then had the magicians martyred in a grisly fashion,[27] showing that he did indeed exceed all bounds of justice and decency.

Another Quranic event featured Pharaoh commanding his vizier, Haman, to build a brick tower so that he could reach to the God of Moses (Surah 28:37–39).[28] He then revived the order to kill the "sons of those who believe with [Moses], and keep alive their females" (Surah 40:25). The next step was formulating a plot to kill Moses, prompting the messenger to pray to the All-Seeing, All-Knowing One (Surah 40:23–27).

God answered Moses' prayer with another stranger who stepped forward to state his previously concealed Islamic faith. His lengthy address rehearsed God's signs in creation and judgments on the Ad, Thamud, and people in Noah's time, then set forth warnings about the coming Judgment, the necessity for good works, and the mandate to walk the Straight Way. Apparently there was an attempt to burn the man alive (echoing Abraham's experience), but God rescued him (Surah 40:28–45). In addition to this unnamed believer, the Qur'an tells of another surprise Muslim, Pharaoh's wife, who prayed, "O my Lord! Build for me in nearness to Thee a mansion in the Garden and save me from Pharaoh and his doings and save me from those that do wrong" (Surah 66:11). The Qur'an lists several plagues and Pharaoh's broken promises (Surah 7:132–35). In the course of the calamities, Pharaoh's arrogance and murderous intentions multiplied. His blasphemies exceeded all bounds, even declaring himself "Lord Most High," thereby making his punishment inevitable and terrible (Surah 79:22–26). It was time for Moses and the Children of Israel to go.

Yet who were these people? Clearly but not always, they are termed the "Children of Israel." Not all accepted Moses' leadership prior to the departure. Given the reinstatement of the order to kill the male children and perhaps added pressures, the people to whom Moses was sent were understandably resistant. They complained that they had had nothing but trouble since Moses and Aaron came to them (Surah 7:128–29). The lure of Egyptian wealth and Pharaoh's claims for divinity were powerful. So Moses prayed that the Egyptian wealth not seduce his people, and God assured him that He would be with them on the way out of Egypt (Surah 10:88–89). The responses of a number of the people foreshadowed troubles in the wilderness.

The departure from Egypt is described graphically, yet not in Exodus-like detail. Pharaoh roused his people against the Children of Israel.[29] As in the biblical account, the massacre-minded Egyptians were caught in the sea (Surah 26:60–66). Pharaoh, as he was drowning, finally understood the error of his blasphemies and confessed God to be the only God, but it was too late. His corpse was returned to Egypt as a sign of God's power (Surah 10:90–92).

Moses in the Wilderness: Biblical Resemblances

The Quranic Voice did not repeat the wilderness rebellions, battles, problems, juridical decisions, feeding miracles, and ritual directions that occupied the authors of the Pentateuchal. Korah's rebellion is mentioned briefly. A key incident, the idolatry of the calf, stands out and is referred to several times in the Qur'an. Prior to the event an idolatrous desert people advised the Children of Israel to ask Moses to make an idol for them. He refused, recalled God's power, and warned about committing the sin of idol worship (Surah 7:138–41). Thinking the matter settled and eager to present himself to God, Moses put Aaron in charge of the last stage of the march to the sacred mountain and traveled ahead of the company. He was on the mountain for forty days and nights. In his absence (the?) Samiri led the "people astray" as part of a God-originated test.[30] Aaron and the Israelites failed the test (Surah 20:83–91).

Warned by God, Moses returned to the camp, and so did his old fury. He grabbed Aaron by his hair and beard, probably pummeling him just short of serious injury. On his (their?) part, Samiri lied about the idol, implying that Moses was the source of the calf idol; he (they?) claimed it was formed when dust from Moses' footprint was tossed into the fire. Moses cursed Samiri with the fate of all idolaters: hellfire in the Hereafter (Surah 20:96). God forgave repentant Israelites but the unrepentant were "overwhelmed with [God's] wrath" (Surah 7:152–53).[31] The incident was an act of shirk, a rebellion against God's messenger, and defiant disobedience to God. God will refer to the calf incident often when admonishing the People of the Book, especially the Jews.

While Moses was on the mountain he sought a vision of God. God told him to look at the mountain, and if it stood while God manifested His glory, then Moses would be granted his request. The mountain crumbled to dust, then apparently was reconstituted. Moses realized the greatness and transcendence of God's glory as well as the folly of his request. God then gave Moses the tablets that covered "all matters both commanding and explaining all things." He was commanded to promulgate the commandments—apparently the Tawrah—among his people and became a full-fledged messenger with a Book (Surah 7:143–47). God concluded both incidents with a version of the seventy elders that differs from Exodus 24:9–18 and with a prediction about the coming of an unlettered Messenger, a prophet who would come in the future to the people who were given the Tawrah and Ingil. God said: "For he commands them what is just and forbids them what is evil: he allows them as lawful what is good (and pure) and prohibits them from what is bad (and impure); he releases them from their heavy burdens and from the yokes that are upon them. So it is those who believe in him honor him help him and follow the light which is sent down with him it is they who will prosper" (Surah 7:156b–57).

Moses in the Wilderness: Three Distinctive Quranic Incidents

A trio of incidents unrelated to the biblical accounts heightens God's power manifested through his messenger. The first (Surah 2:67–74) may be related to Deuteronomy 21:1–9, the discovery of the corpse of a murdered Israelite between two settlements and the sacrifice of a heifer. In the course of the event Allah raises the murdered man from the dead. The second distinctive incident may report two events or different versions of the same occurrence (Surahs 7:163–66 and 2:65–67). In one the residents of a city fished on a Sabbath; in the other people despised God's messengers and His revelation. The punishment was the same: "We said to them, 'Be ye apes, despised and rejected.' " And it was so.

The third incident is long and complex (Surah 18:60–82). Traveling for the purpose of gaining further knowledge, Moses and his servant were guided by a special fish. The fish, undetected by the men, escaped and went as if in a tunnel straight to the sea. Moses and the servant returned to the spot where the fish disappeared and met a servant of God. He first rebuffed and then accepted Moses as a temporary traveling companion but under the condition that Moses was not to ask any questions about why the man acted as he did.[32] Moses, however, could not keep silent and protested when the man scuttled a ship, killed a youth, and rebuilt a crumbling wall without asking for payment. As he dismissed Moses for breaking his promise of watchful silence, the man explained that in each instance the appearances might have seemed senseless and even cruel, but God knew best. In each instance God was saving lives and dealing justly, although humans did not understand God's will without patience and guidance: "How canst thou have patience about things about which thy understanding is not complete?" (Surah 18:68).

Moses' Relevance for Muhammad and the First Umma

Say: "O men! I am sent unto you all as the Messenger of
Allah to Whom belongeth the dominion of the heavens
and the earth: there is no god but He: it is He that giveth

both life and death. So believe in Allah and His Messenger,
the unlettered Prophet, who believed in Allah and His
words: follow him that (so) ye may be guided."

Surah 7:158

Moses' relevance for Muhammad and the earliest umma was direct and
powerful. In the immediate situation he faced in Medina, Muhammad
expected the Jewish communities in the area and throughout Arabia to
acknowledge him as the Messenger promised by Moses and other biblical prophets. It is probable that he knew Jews personally in Mecca. In
Medina he encountered Jewish communities that had social and political
influence. During the Ascent into Heaven, he experienced Moses' presence
and received encouragement and advice from the earlier messenger. Soon
after arriving in Medina, Muhammad, obeying God, made the first qiblah
toward Jerusalem. One purpose of the Jerusalem qiblah appears to have
been literally to turn the Muslims from venerating the idol-filled Ka'bah
with all the traditional respect accorded the Qurayshi. The umma needed
to develop independence from the past before they were able to reclaim
the Ancient House and Abraham's city.

Following the Battle of Badr and under God's revelation, Muhammad changed the qiblah to the Ka'bah. He endured severe criticism from
his opponents, but the action signaled that the Muslims were now ready
to assert their independence of the Qurayshi-dominated religion and re-
take Mecca (Surah 2:142–50). The destruction of those Jewish communities was both a defensive and a retaliatory act. Why didn't the Jews embrace Islam, follow its Messenger, and see the truth of the Qur'an? From
the Muslim perspective, one answer lay in the relationship of the Children of Israel to God and to Moses. Significant numbers of Israelites and
key leaders resisted Moses from the time of his return to confront Pharaoh and throughout the wilderness period. Complaints, excuses, insults,
and revolts were topped by the calf idolatry. The Israelites of the past dis-
dained true worship and God's Straight Path. The Jews in Arabia carried on

in the same way with Muhammad the Messenger. What made the seventh-century Jews more liable for punishment was their consorting with the Meccans to defeat the Muslims. Another, related answer concerned the Jewish rejection of the Qur'an's divine origin and authority. In this instance contemporary teachers and leaders perpetuated the corruptions of the Tawrah and the distorted interpretations given by past leaders, and most Jews acquiesced in these errors.

Moses also provided a positive example for Muhammad in that the ancient messenger was an aya pointing the way to the final Messenger. Moses' experience from birth onward gave Muhammad encouragement and precedents and the umma's genuinely faithful believers. Muhammad stands at the end of the line of prophets and messengers in more than a historical sense. The exile, danger, accusations, anxieties, itinerations, and ridicule experienced by Moses and the other forerunners culminated and are transcended in Muhammad. So, too, are the prayers, submission, zeal, and growth of the Messenger as he carried out his mission. More than all the others, Muhammad took his umma to higher levels.

The Quranic Moses' Potential Relevance Today

Quranic presentations of Moses may have both negative and positive applications in and outside the Muslim contexts. On the negative side are representations of Jews as the rebellious and ungrateful descendants of the Children of Israel who continue to pervert the Tawrah and undermine Islam. Moses' predictions that God would punish treacherous and perfidious Jews in this world as well as in the Hereafter can be used to justify suspicions and violence against Jews and their supporters.

I see five positive opportunities related to the Quranic figure of Moses. First and probably the most obvious is that he is a leader who persevered in the face of powerful opponents, troublesome compatriots, and puzzling circumstances. His perseverance was animated by his obedience to the God Whose guidance and mercy was present throughout his life. Moses was willing to break with his past and the traditions in which he was raised. That break also meant listening to and taking advice from others. Moses is a messenger of heroic stature because he surrendered his life and will to

God. Second, Moses depended on women for his survival. His mother, sister, the Egyptian queen, and his wife were instrumental in safeguarding him when his life was at risk. His mother received Allah's revelations independent from her son. The queen awakened to Islam gradually in that she felt the need for a child and then grew in revulsion at her royal husband's arrogance and brutality. Muslims may be able to examine the roles of women through those linked to Moses in order to address concerns raised by non-Muslims.

Third, Moses led and stood in the midst of a community. He went beyond his own family to proclaim and do Allah's will to a diverse people so as to gather them into a coherent fellowship. He was instrumental in developing that community's faith, social structures, and relations with outsiders. As the Muslim umma grapples today with issues of claims made by persons seeking to be recognized as leaders and the nature of the umma, Moses' insistence on tawhid, justice, and mercy may be exemplary and helpful.

Fourth, Moses was a searcher. The Qur'an describes him as a person who intuited the importance of events and experiences, then sought to find their meaning and purpose. So he was attracted to the bush on the mountain, and he undertook the journey with the fish. He realized that there might be some knowledge or revelation from God for him. And he was correct. Here Moses' relevance may fit not only rulers and leaders but believers as well. The messenger went into obscure places, inquired, waited, and was rewarded. Islam has always been a religion that cherishes investigation for the sake of knowing more about God in order to enhance and expand obedience to Allah.

Fifth, Moses changed. The account of his coming to the defense of the first coreligionist introduced him as having a principle but enacting it in an unthinking and lethal way. He realized his error, repented, and was forgiven. Gradually, perhaps fitfully, his obedience to Allah and growth in responsibility led to increased self-control. At the same time his frequent prayers put him under Allah's protection, and from that position he asked God to forgive others. The need for a believer to mature from dedicated intentions but destructive action to obedience and mercy is clear at any time and especially now.

We sent Moses with Our Signs (and the command) "Bring out thy people from the depths of darkness into light and teach them to remember the Days of Allah." Verily in this there are Signs for such as are firmly patient and constant grateful and appreciative. (Surah 14:5)

JESUS (ISA)

One day will Allah gather the messengers together and ask: "What was the response ye received (from men to your teaching)?" They will say: "We have no knowledge: it is Thou who knowest in full all that is hidden." Then will Allah say: "O Jesus the son of Mary! Recount My favor to thee and to thy mother. Behold! I strengthened thee with the holy spirit so that thou didst speak to the people in childhood and in maturity. Behold! I taught thee the Book, and Wisdom, the Law, and the Gospel. And behold! Thou makest out of clay as it were the figure of a bird by My leave and thou breathest into it and it becometh a bird by My leave, and thou healest those born blind and the lepers by My leave. And behold! Thou bringest forth the dead by My leave. And behold! I did restrain the Children of Israel from (violence to) thee when thou didst show them the Clear Signs and the unbelievers among them said: 'This is nothing but evident magic.' And behold! I inspired the Disciples to have faith in Me and Mine messenger: they said 'We have faith and do thou bear witness that we bow to Allah as Muslims.'"

Surah 5:109–11

Jesus lives. He did not die—yet. Compared to the Qur'an's other covenant-messengers, accounts about Jesus are slim. While the Revelation gives us little narrative about Jesus and almost nothing about his disciples, nevertheless Jesus is a bridge between Moses and Muhammad, between Christians and Muslims, and between the earthly and spiritual realms.[33]

Jesus in the Qur'an

> He said: "I am indeed a servant of Allah: He hath given me
> revelation and made me a prophet; And He hath made me
> blessed wheresoever I be and hath enjoined on me prayer
> and charity as long as I live; (He) hath made me kind to my
> mother and not overbearing or miserable; so peace is on me
> the day I was born, the day that I die, and the Day that I shall
> be raised up to life (again)!"
>
> *Surah 19:30–33*

Six Basic Factors Characterizing Jesus' Messengership

Even before his virginal conception, Jesus was designated to be a special messenger who, like Moses, would be graced by God's signs as he testified to the One-Only God. The angels told Mary Jesus would be a messenger who would heal, animate clay birds, and restore the dead to life (Surah 3:45–51). As noted above, with the first words the baby Jesus uttered, he cleared her of any question about her morality. The Qur'an reports that he continued to witness to the One-Only God throughout his time on earth. Not quite parenthetically, the Quranic Jesus shows far more respect for and deference to his mother than did the Jesus of the canonical Gospels:[34]

> He said: "I am indeed a servant of Allah: He hath given me revelation
> and made me a prophet; And He hath made me Blessed wheresoever
> I be, and hath enjoined on me Prayer and Charity as long as I live;
> (He) hath made me kind to my mother and not overbearing or mis-

erable; So Peace is on me the day I was born, the day that I die, and the Day that I shall be raised up to life (again)!" (Surah 19:30–33)

The above passage indicates that Jesus' messengership was to be characterized by six factors First, he testified to the One-Only God from his infancy forward. Jesus will be especially instructed by God about the previous revelations and books revealed to and proclaimed by the prophets and messengers. As did Adam, Jesus received special guidance from God. Jesus stands in the line of prophets and messengers and was sent to confirm the Tawrah and to announce the coming of the greater and final messenger:

And remember Jesus the son of Mary said: "O Children of Israel! I am the messenger of Allah (sent) to you confirming the Law (which came) before me and giving glad Tidings of a Messenger to come after me whose name shall be Ahmad." But when he came to them with Clear Signs, they said "This is evident sorcery!" (Surah 61:6)

Jesus will be enabled to cancel or alter some of the regulations that were imposed on the Jews through the Tawrah given through Moses, such as dietary restrictions and probably ritual regulations. God, through Gabriel and Muhammad, recalls Jesus saying:

"(I have come to you) to attest the Law which was before me and to make lawful to you part of what was (before) forbidden to you; I have come to you with a Sign from your Lord. So fear Allah and obey me. It is Allah who is my Lord and your Lord; then worship Him. This is a way that is straight." (Surah 3:50–51)

Second, Jesus has a place in the line of prophets and messengers that God has sent to reveal His will and ways to humanity. God has proclaimed that "company" to be a united brotherhood serving the "Lord and Cherisher" of all: "Therefore serve Me (and no other) and he shall be (of the company) of the righteous" (Surah 21:92). Jesus stands with Moses, Salih, Hud, Noah, Abraham, and all the others. Indeed, on the Last Day the prophets and messengers will assemble and will be asked about their faithfulness to God (Surah 5:116–18). As were Moses and other biblical figures, Jesus was a prophet-messenger to the Jews. According to the Qur'an, the People of the Book were composed of two groups, the Children of Israel (Banu Isra'il) and the Christians (Nasara, i.e., Nazarenes). The existence of a brotherhood of human revealers points to God's plan to consummate the whole cosmos through the Day of Judgment and into the Hereafter.

Third, Jesus' being divinely instructed echoes God's teaching of the other human who was specially originated (Adam) and the messengers who were extraordinarily wise, gifted, and questing for deeper understanding (Abraham, Moses, and Solomon). To continue the educational figure of speech, God's curriculum will be based on the Book (perhaps the Umm Kitab that stands behind all revelatory books?), the Creator's wisdom that suffuses the earlier Tawrah disclosed to Moses and the gospel that was given to Jesus. The result is the eternal Message proclaimed since Adam and his wife entered this world and which continues into the present up to the Final Day. So far Jesus fulfills the Quranically expected roles of a prophet-messenger.

Fourth, Jesus transforms clay figures into live birds. The Christian Infancy Gospel of Thomas contains an account in which the five-year-old Jesus formed twelve sparrows on a Sabbath. When criticized for working on the Sabbath, he clapped his hands so that the birds came to life and flew away. Then Jesus is said to have cursed the boy critic, who withered immediately.[35] The Quranic "correction" of the Christian noncanonical story emphasizes that Jesus has been given power from God to breathe life into clay figures. This is not a manifestation of Jesus being more than a human but of being given such power by the God who can breathe life into clay to create Adam.

Fifth, although the Qur'an does not recount any healing or resuscitation miracles by Jesus, it seems to indicate that such actions took place. Probably the Revelation assumes that reader-listeners are aware of the basic events recounted in the canonical and noncanonical Gospels. Later reports about healings and resurrections circulated in Muslim and, in all likelihood, Christian circles.[36]

Sixth, Jesus is credited with being clairvoyant. He will know and be able to tell people what they have eaten and what possessions they have in their homes. The point of such knowledge may be that a person cannot dissemble before God or this messenger. A householder cannot claim not to have food to be shared with the hungry or wealth to relieve poverty.

Jesus as Warner and Promiser

Jesus' mission involved warnings and promises about an individual's destination in the Hereafter. If Moses' roles focused on establishing the community of the Children of Israel, then Jesus pointed Jews toward their spiritual condition and destiny. His Ingil was a clear revelation of God's compassion and mercy (Surah 57:27), yet Jesus was a sign of the coming Judgment (Surah 43:61). He proclaimed the One-Only-ness of God, and God added a dire warning to those who believed and taught otherwise: "But said Christ: "O Children of Israel! Worship Allah my Lord and your Lord.' Whoever joins other gods with Allah, Allah will forbid him the Garden, and the fire will be his abode. There will for the wrongdoers be no one to help" (Surah 5:72b). Nevertheless, as with all other prophets and messengers, Jesus was denounced as a sorcerer by most of the Jews. Rejected by many of his own people, Jesus turned to his disciples:

> O ye who believe! Be ye helpers of Allah. As said Jesus the son of Mary to the disciples: "Who will be my helpers to (the work of) Allah?" Said the disciples: "We are Allah's helpers!" Then a portion of the Children of Israel believed and a portion disbelieved: but We gave power to those who believed against their enemies and they became the ones that prevailed. (Surah 61:14)

God strengthened Jesus by means of the holy spirit (i.e., Gabriel) so that Jesus could withstand his opponents. At one point his disciples asked that he confirm their faith with a miracle that apparently the gospel writers misinterpreted or perverted as the ritual in which Jesus supposedly gave them wine and bread. God responded to the disciples' request with "the table spread" with food and issued a serious warning to all who follow Jesus' message and then fall away: "Allah said: 'I will send it down unto you: but if any of you after that resisteth faith I will punish him with

a penalty such as I have not inflicted on anyone among all the peoples'"
(Surah 5:112–15). The disciples' request may be an echo of Abraham's request about an intellectual proof of the resurrection and Moses asking to
see God.

Beyond the few passages that deal with Jesus' sayings and deeds, the
Qur'an addresses emphatically who Jesus is and is not. Plainly, Jesus is a
rasul, and his book is the Ingil. More specifically, Jesus and his mother are
not like the angels who conferred with Abraham, for as celestial beings
the latter did not eat. God stated bluntly that any who claim that Jesus is
divine or a form of the One-Only God is an idolater, that the concept of
God being a Trinity is blasphemy. Jesus testifies:

> They do blaspheme who say: "Allah is Christ the son of Mary." But
> said Christ: "O children of Israel! Worship Allah my Lord and your
> Lord." Whoever joins other gods with Allah, Allah will forbid him the
> garden and the Fire will be his abode. There will for the wrong-doers
> be no one to help. They do blaspheme who say: Allah is one of three in
> a Trinity: for there is no god except One Allah. If they desist not from
> their word (of blasphemy), verily a grievous penalty will befall the
> blasphemers among them. Why turn they not to Allah and seek His
> forgiveness? For Allah is Oft-Forgiving Most Merciful. Christ the son
> of Mary was no more than an Apostle; many were the Apostles that
> passed away before him. His mother was a woman of truth. They had
> both to eat their (daily) food. See how Allah doth makes His Signs clear
> to them; yet see in what ways they are deluded away from the truth!
> Say: Will ye worship besides Allah, something which hath no power
> either to harm or benefit you? But Allah He it is that heareth and
> knoweth all things." Say: "O people of the Book! Exceed not in your
> religion the bounds (of what is proper) trespassing beyond the truth
> nor follow the vain desires of people who went wrong in times gone by
> who misled many and strayed (themselves) from the even way. Curses
> were pronounced on those among the Children of Israel who rejected
> faith by the tongue of David and of Jesus the son of Mary: because
> they disobeyed and persisted in excesses." (Surah 5:72–78)[37]

I have aleady noted that on the Day of Judgment Jesus will reject any implication that he distorted the Message. Surah 5:116–18 takes the statement further:

And behold! Allah will say: "O Jesus the son of Mary! Didst thou say unto men 'Worship me and my mother as gods in derogation of Allah'? He will say: 'Glory to Thee! Never could I say what I had no right (to say). Had I said such a thing, Thou wouldst indeed have known it. Thou knowest what is in my heart though I know not what is in Thine. For Thou knowest in full all that is hidden. Never said I to them aught except what Thou didst command me to say to wit 'Worship Allah my Lord and your Lord'; and I was a witness over them whilst I dwelt amongst them; when Thou didst take me up, thou wast the Watcher over them and Thou art a Witness to all things. If Thou dost punish them they are Thy servants: if Thou dost forgive them Thou art the Exalted, the Wise.'" (Surah 5:116–18)

Jesus Raised to God's Presence

What happened to Jesus? Was he crucified? Did he die? Where is he now? Several Quranic passages and numerous Muslim interpretations of those ayas lean in the direction of rejecting an actual crucifixion and death of Jesus and therefore of his resurrection three days later. As indicated in the discussion in chapter 2 of the basic Christian narrative and creedal statements, Jesus' crucifixion, death, and resurrection are essential in normative Christianity. But that was not always the case. Gnostic Christians, deemed heretics by church authorities in the second and subsequent centuries, denied the actuality of Jesus' physical crucifixion, death, and resurrection because they denied that he was a human being; he only appeared to be human. Usually these positions held that the divine-angelic Christ-reality that dwelled in Jesus' physical body did not suffer but it was a shell body that died. Others held that someone else was substituted for Jesus either by divine design or by human error.[38]

Two passages in the Qur'an seem to agree with unorthodox accounts about a substitution for Jesus or an illusion that Jesus was crucified but with the crucial subtraction that Jesus was in any manner divine:

> And (then unbelievers) plotted and planned, and Allah too planned, and the best of planners is Allah. Behold! Allah said: "O Jesus! I will take thee and raise thee to Myself and clear thee (of the falsehoods) of those who blaspheme. I will make those who follow thee superior to those who reject Faith to the Day of Resurrection; then shall ye all return unto Me and I will judge between you of the matters wherein ye dispute." (Surah 3:54–55.)

> That they said (in boast) "We killed Christ Jesus the son of Mary the messenger of Allah." But they killed him not nor crucified him, but so it was made to appear to them, and those who differ therein are full of doubts with no (certain) knowledge but only conjecture to follow, for of a surety they killed him not. Nay, Allah raised him up unto Himself; and Allah is Exalted in Power Wise." (Surah 4:157–58)

The disbelieving People of the Book plotted against Jesus and thought they killed him. Whether someone else was substituted on the cross or whether the execution involved an optical illusion or whether by some other means not stated by the Qur'an, Jesus did not die but was taken by God into a heavenly place.[39] He will return from that heavenly place to participate in the Day of Judgment (Qur'an), although he is expected to defeat the Dajaal prior to a period of peace and prosperity at the conclusion of which he will die (Hadiths).

JESUS IS THE LATEST messenger to the Jews. His Ingil proclaims God's One-Only-ness with a particular emphasis on spiritual matters such as divine mercy and compassion. In unambiguously clear statements, Jesus is totally and only human. He is, however, alive in God's heavens, and is a sign of the imminent Day of Judgment.

Jesus' Relevance for Muhammad and the First Umma

Muhammad is the complete and the final Messenger. He fulfills the roles of Noah, Abraham, and Moses. Muhammad also fulfills the role of Jesus the messenger of spiritual depth, mercy, and compassion who is the aya to the end of this world and the beginning of the Hereafter. Jesus may serve as an interpretive exemplar for the Meccan period of Muhammad's activity. Certainly there are parallels between both servants of God, such as special conditions at their birth, enduring opposition, resisting the religious and political authorities, gathering followers, being accused of sorcery, and being targets for murderous plots. Beneath such resemblances is the development of Islam's spiritual and devotional foundations in those formative years. God determined that the Quranic method of establishing Islam through His final Messenger and revelatory Book required a firm grounding in tawhid through testimony, regular prayer, and Zakat.[40] All previous prophets and messengers included the dimension of full submission to God in heart and hand, but Jesus was the messenger who was the clearest sign pointing to the Judgment and the Hereafter without the admixture of this world's social issues. Perhaps Jesus' unique origin as the messenger born of a virgin predisposed him to his heavenly orientation. Muhammad's origins, described in the Hadith, showed him to be purified for his mission from early childhood. Finally, the Revelation quotes Jesus as it did Moses, saying that there will be a figure coming in the future who would advance God's revelatory action. Ahmad is one of the earliest appellations given Muhammad. The Meccan-born Messenger could gain strength and encouragement knowing that God had been preparing for his coming and the challenges of his mission.

The Quranic Jesus' Potential Relevance Today

The Qur'an's presentation of Jesus makes clear that there is an unbridgeable theological chasm between Islam and Christianity. Neither religion can be elided into the other. Given Muslim teachings about the Qur'an's origins and authority, the Revelation's position on Jesus' relationship to

God and humans, denial of his death and resurrection, and rejection of the Trinity, Christians must realize that any interfaith relationships with Muslims will be limited. Christianity and Islam are and will remain two separate religions. Nevertheless, any interfaith discussions and cooperation are bound to engage the disparate views of Jesus held by Muslims and Christians.

One area that Muslims and Christians may explore together is the spirituality attributed to Jesus in the Gospels and the Qur'an. The Muslim view of Jesus' focus on mercy and compassion as well as the Hereafter may aid Christians to review the Gospels and then reexamine the programs, structures, and liturgies of their churches. Another area pressing Christians that an examination of the Quranic Jesus may illumine is the nature of the New Testament canon and its relationship to noncanonical works that were used through the seventh century and beyond. Some Quranic accounts about Mary and Jesus are present in those works that orthodox Christians rejected or relegated to the status of semiforgotten legends. Periodically Christians and non-Christians, scholars and popularizers of religion turn to these materials to "find the real Jesus." The Qur'an offers a Jesus who needs to be studied in conjunction with the standard Christian account of Jesus. A third potential relevance relates directly to Muslims. If Jesus is the rasul who points to the Judgment and Hereafter and is an appropriate model for the pre-Medina stage of Islam, how does Jesus today summon Muslims to regard the devotional depth of the umma? Certainly Muslims will look to Muhammad as the complete rasul who conjoined spirit and politics. Yet in attempts to establish Islamic societies based on Shari'ah and Quranic-Hadith texts, there may be a need for Muslims to return spiritually to Mecca in order to arrive again in Medina so as to constitute or reconstitute the umma on a purified basis of Islamic law.

To Him belong the keys of the heavens and the earth: He enlarges and restricts the sustenance to whom He will: for He knows full well all things. The same religion has He established for you as that which He enjoined on Noah—the which We have sent by inspiration to thee—and that which We enjoined on Abraham, Moses and Jesus: Namely that ye should remain steadfast in Religion and make no divisions therein: to those who worship other things than Allah hard is the (way) to which thou callest them. Allah chooses to Himself those whom He pleases and guides to Himself those who turn (to Him). (Surah 42:12–13)

PEOPLE OF THE BOOK

> If only the People of the Book had believed and been
> righteous, We should indeed have blotted out their iniquities
> and admitted them to gardens of Bliss. If only they had stood
> fast by the Law the Gospel and all the revelation that was sent
> to them from their Lord, they would have enjoyed happiness
> from every side. There is from among them a party on the
> right course; but many of them follow a course that is evil.
>
> *Surah 5:65–66*

The Qur'an's message to Muhammad and the umma is plain: Be open to, beware of, and confront the People of the Book. Although the People of the Book are specifically identified separately as Jews and Christians in Quranic times, some passages regard Christians and Jews as a single group that refuses to acknowledge the divine origin of the Qur'an and the Messenger. Their refusal escalated into arguments, insults, conspiracies with polytheists and Hypocrites, and deceptions—all aimed at defeating the Muslim cause, the destruction of the umma, and the removal of Muhammad:

> Quite a number of the People of the Book wish they could turn you
> (people) back to infidelity after ye have believed, from selfish envy after
> the truth hath become manifest unto them; but forgive and overlook
> till Allah accomplish His purpose; for Allah hath power over all things.
> And be steadfast in prayer and regular in charity: and whatever good
> ye send forth for your souls before you ye shall find it with Allah; for

Allah sees well all that ye do. And they say: "None shall enter paradise unless he be a Jew or a Christian." Those are their (vain) desires. Say: "Produce your proof if ye are truthful." Such shall be no fear nor shall they grieve. (Surah 2:109–12)

Still, the People of the Book were in a special relationship to God. He had covenanted with them to give them prophets, messengers, revelatory books, care, and guidance to the Straight Way. By their rejection and opposition to the Qur'an and Muhammad, they disobeyed and defied the One True God. Their rebellion, if continued, will result in everlasting condemnation. In this world Muslim relationships with them are anticipated to be close, cautious and constrained. Muslims are warned not to make any of the People friends and confidants, at least at the expense of finding their primary fellowship with other Muslims: "O ye who believe! Take not the Jews and the Christians for your friends and protectors. They are but friends and protectors to each other. And he amongst you that turns to them (for friendship) is of them. Verily, Allah guideth not a people unjust" (Surah 5:51). The People of the Book knowingly distort and corrupt the earlier revelatory books and commit the shirk of giving Allah partners and set up intermediaries between God and the believer. A statement that may say something about Jews in Arabia and not Judaism as a whole is, "The Jews call Uzair [Ezra] a son of Allah" (Surah 9:30).[41] The Message accuses some or most of the People of the Book of hypocrisy, dishonesty, miserliness, and sin:

A section of the People of the Book say: "Believe in the morning what is revealed to the believers but reject it at the end of the day; perchance they may (themselves) turn back. And believe no one unless he follows your religion." Say {Muhammad]: "True guidance is the guidance of Allah; (fear ye) lest a revelation be sent to someone (else) like unto that which was sent unto you. Or that those (receiving such revelation) should engage you in argument before your Lord." Say: "All bounties are in the hand of Allah: He granteth them to whom He pleaseth; and Allah careth for all and He knoweth all things." For His Mercy He specially chooseth whom He pleaseth: for Allah is the Lord of bounties unbounded. Among the People of the Book are some who if entrusted with a hoard of gold will (readily) pay it back. Others who if entrusted with a single silver coin will not repay it unless thou constantly stoodest demanding because they say "There is no call on us (to keep faith) with these ignorant (pagans)." But they tell a lie against Allah and (well) they know it. Nay. Those that keep their plighted faith and act aright verily Allah loves those who act aright. (Surah 3:72–76)

The Qur'an recognizes that the umma will triumph over its enemies and that Muslims will govern the People of the Book. Since there was to be no compulsion in matters of religion (Surah 2:256), God commanded: "Fight those who believe not in Allah nor the Last Day nor hold that forbidden which hath been forbidden by Allah and His Messenger nor acknowledge the religion of truth (even if they are) of the People of the Book until they pay the Jizya with willing submission and feel themselves subdued" (Surah 9:29). The People of the Book and the pagans are to be met with the same Islamic witness:

The Religion before Allah is Islam (submission to His will): nor did the people of the Book dissent therefrom except through envy of each other after knowledge had come to them. But if any deny the signs of Allah, Allah is swift in calling to account. So if they dispute with thee say: "I have submitted my whole self to Allah and so have those who follow me." And say to the people of the Book and to those who are unlearned: "Do ye (also) submit yourselves?" If they do they are in right guidance but if they turn back thy duty is to convey the Message; and in Allah's sight are (all) His servants. (Surah 3:19–20)

THE QUR'AN ON JEWS

O children of Israel! Call to mind the (special) favor which
I bestowed upon you and fulfill your covenant with Me
as I fulfill My covenant with you and fear none but Me.
And believe what I reveal, confirming the revelation which

is with you, and be not the first to reject faith therein nor
sell My Signs for a small price: and fear Me and Me alone.
And cover not Truth with falsehood nor conceal the Truth
when ye know (what it is). And be steadfast in prayer;
practice regular charity; and bow down your heads with
those who bow down (in worship).

Surah 2:40–43

Jews and danger belong together. The Quranic theology of history with
progressive revelations and revealers and denunciations of shirk and injustice with admonitions and promises about the Hereafter have been high-
lighted previously, as have the circumstances that led to the massacres, expulsion, and destruction of Jewish settlements connected to Medina and
the life-and-death struggles of the umma with their Meccan foes.

Jews in the Qur'an

According to the Qur'an, Jews are in danger because of their greed,
treachery, and obstinate opposition to God, the Revelation, and Muhammad. According to the Hadith, those who fight against Islam in the last
days are in danger of slaughter in the End Time and of everlasting punishment in the Hereafter. The Qur'an maintains that the dangers are not
due to their ethnicity or Muslim malice: the Jews have brought the perils
on themselves by their unbelief and actions derived from that unbelief.
But, according to the Qur'an, such behavior and the hazards that accompany it are nothing new. The Pentateuch and Prophets contain a dismal
litany of Israelite-Jewish rejections of and rebellions against God. The
Qur'an agrees with the shape of the biblical accounts about revolts in the
wilderness over food and leadership (Surah 2:60–61). The Qur'an presents the Jews as being consistently arrogant, cruel, and treacherous. They
have earned the wrath of the All-Patient, Oft-Forgiving God by the calf
idolatry, breaking the Sinai covenant, and mocking, humiliating, and kill-

ing His spokespersons and revealers (Surah 2:90–96). The Jews who argued with Muhammad made themselves enemies of the mighty angels, Michael and Gabriel, cast away their holy God-given Book, and followed in the ways of Satan. They practiced magic and distorted basic human relationships. They will reap a terrible reward in Hell:

> Say: "Whoever is an enemy to Gabriel for he brings down the (revelation) to thy heart by Allah's will a confirmation of what went before and guidance and glad tidings for those who believe. Whoever is an enemy to Allah and His angels and apostles to Gabriel and Michael Lo! Allah is an enemy to those who reject faith." We have sent down to thee manifest signs (ayas); and none reject them but those who are perverse. Is it not (the case) that every time they make a Covenant some party among them throw it aside? Nay most of them are faithless. And when came to them a messenger from Allah confirming what was with them a party of the people of the Book threw away the Book of Allah behind their backs as if (it had been something) they did not know!" (Surah 2:97–101)

The Quranic indictment of the Jews included the conscious corruption of the Tawrah. They twist their tongues to give mispronunciations that are insulting and slanderous to Islam. They will be cursed for their distortions and rejection of belief (Surah 4:44–50).[42] One result of the "iniquity of the Jews" was God imposing dietary rules on them (Surah 2:160), while the rabbis and "doctors of the law" blasphemously interpreted God's stipulations about "sinful words and eating things forbidden" (Surahs 5:61–64 and 6:145–48).

The Quranic Jews' Relevance for Muhammad and the First Umma

The Qur'an rehearses some biblically grounded accounts and makes references to the various Israelite-Jewish rebellions and acts of disobedience against God and the disasters they experienced by the just and warning Lord. The Muslim case against the Jews stretched from the Bible to Medina. The Qur'an's rhetoric and passion fit the umma's situation. The

Muslim community faced dire threats from the Medinan Hypocrites and from the more powerful Confederates led by hostile Meccans. In such circumstances, the various Arab factions were a formidable threat. The Jewish clans in and around Medina not only complicated the situation; they threatened to sway the struggle significantly against Muhammad, the Companions, and the tentative cluster of Helpers.

On his part, Muhammad was prone to favor the Jews over the polytheists on account of their monotheism, having books from Moses and Jesus, and the mention of the Children of Israel in the Revelation. Given that the Ka'bah was in the hands of polytheists and jammed with idols, it was theological, logically, and tactically prudent for the Messenger to make Jerusalem's Temple Mount the umma's qiblah. After all, he had been there on the Night Journey for the Ascent through the heavens. Muhammad had every reason to expect the Jews to welcome him as their prophet and the Qur'an as the fulfillment of their scriptural promises—at least from his perspective. That the Jews did not become Muslims was a shock, but that they conspired with his Meccan enemies was a serious blow. The change in qiblah from Jerusalem to Mecca is symbolic and practical. From that point on, Muhammad knew he could not rely on the Jewish communities religiously, politically, or militarily. Nevertheless, God revealed to him that there were Jews who were quietly and secretly beginning to pray in the Islamic way and to practice the Faith. As long as he lived, Muhammad had wary hopes that the Jews would take the opportunity to enter the Straight Path. But the coming triumph of Islam in Arabia signaled another change was forthcoming: the expulsion of the People of the Book from Arabia.

The Quranic Jews' Potential Relevance Today

Jews, Muslims, and the Qur'an can be a dangerous combination. Generally and for centuries Jews were able to live and thrive in the Muslim world far better than they could in Christian-dominated areas. Granted there were political and social restrictions, as well as special taxes. And there were sporadic anti-Jewish acts and measures, but governmental authorities and the common sense of leaders usually contained these. Given the often-harsh tone of the Revelation and the tradition of reading the Qur'an through each month, the high degree of tolerance and security shown Jews in the Diaspora is surprising. The picture changed dramatically in the nineteenth and twentieth centuries with the rise of Pan-Arabism, Islamic consciousness, Western imperialism, the spread of European-style anti-Judaism, Zionism, the Holocaust, and the establishment of the state of Israel. The collapse and dismemberment of the Ottoman Empire after World War I together with the creation and subsequent demise of the League of Nations and its system of mandates—all culminating in and spreading out from the World War II—have uncovered smoldering and ancient animosities and created flaming new ones. Yet I see two potentially relevant prospects derived from Quranic views of Jews.

The first is a present tragic actuality that threatens to become even worse: deepening estrangement, animosity, and violence between Muslims and Jews based on religious grounds. Both sides have well-stocked supplies of rhetorical and scriptural ammunition that can be readily transformed into literal weapons against each other. The Shema and scores of passages in the Hebrew Bible specify a particular territory as God-given to the Jewish people from which they can never be uprooted. Within that divine mandate Jerusalem and the Temple Mount are held by many Jews as absolutely and forever Jewish. From the Muslim perspective, many persons and numerous organizations are willing to take the Quranic and Hadith texts literally in a countermandate to unite Arabs and Muslims either loosely or more formally in an international umma of Muslim Arabs and even of all Muslims that will be organized on the basis of Islamic law. And the territory, city, and hill are vitally important to such a vision. One result of such diametrically opposed expectations is that dedicated and impassioned persons on both sides justify acts of violence on the basis of God's will.

The second potential relevance of the Qur'an's views of the Jews takes a positive turn. Perhaps Jews and Muslims can focus on areas that they share religiously and historically so as to recover the Quranic and biblical contexts that deal with the one God and people seeking to obey that God through acts and structures of justice and compassion. The God they worship is the God they claim to be the Source of life, Guide, and Fulfiller for all people. Care of the creation, attitudes and deeds regarding the poor and needy, strengthening families, promoting just economic procedures, and construing charity and personal discipline are components of worship as vital as are prayer and pious learning. Islam and Judaism may be seen as sharing key portions of a common moral framework.

In spite of the conflicts and contradictions between them, Muslims and Jews have lived together and flourished in the past, despite differences in institutional structures and customs. Jews and Muslims also have lived side by side as minorities in Euro-American, Asian, and sub-Saharan diasporas. Perhaps those experiences may be helpful for sorting through the hostile and reconciliatory dynamics of their scriptures and their current situations, especially if they see an essential basis in the oneness of the God whom they seek to serve.

THE QUR'AN ON CHRISTIANS

They do blaspheme who say: "Allah is Christ the son of Mary." But said Christ: "O children of Israel! Worship Allah my Lord and your Lord." Whoever joins other gods with Allah, Allah will forbid him the garden and the Fire will be his abode. There will for the wrong-doers be no one to help. They do blaspheme who say: Allah is one of three in a Trinity: for there is no god except One Allah. If they desist not from their word (of blasphemy) verily a grievous penalty will befall the blasphemers among them. Why turn they not to Allah and seek His forgiveness? For Allah is Oft-forgiving Most Merciful.

Surah 5:72–74

Christians in the Qur'an

Paradoxically, the Qur'an absolutely rejects the central claims Christians make about Jesus, yet is gentler toward Christians than toward polytheists and Jews. The entire body of the church's Christology is diametrically opposed to Islam. For Islam, Christian understandings of Jesus verge on idolatry. But there were no attacks against Christian individuals or groups during the time of the Messenger. Perhaps the relatively positive relationships between Muhammad and Christians and the umma and Christians was a matter of power and precedent. In terms of power, the Christians had none to speak of. They were not organized into clans or tribes, so they did not pose a military, political, or social threat to the umma. Like the other hanifs in Arabia, the Christians did not seem to have been organized into blocs or coalitions that might have rivaled the Muslims. At the same time, there is the precedent of Muslims and Christians having had good relationships.[43]

Nevertheless, the Qur'an is only relatively well disposed toward Christians. They are regarded as blasphemers because of their beliefs that Jesus is God's son, the mediator between the Creator and the believer, the one through whom sins are forgiven and salvation achieved, and savior without works of the Law. This blasphemy is compounded by teachings about the Trinity and the distortions and corruptions introduced by Christians in their Scriptures (Surah 5:13). Topping all is the Christian rejection of the Qur'an and Muhammad. A related Quranic complaint is the polemics between Jews and Christians. Together they are the People of the Book, and both misinterpret and corrupt the Scriptures. They then accuse one another of such willful forgeries and errors. Such word wars signal that they are both in error and defy the divinely given truth in the Qur'an. The Qur'an suggests that enmity and jealousy, not legitimate faith issues, underlie their reciprocal heated denunciations.

At several points the Qur'an indicates that Christians in Arabia had numerous "intermediaries" between Christ and the believer as well as between God and the believer. These intermediaries appear to have been angels and saints (e.g., Surah 3:64). Christian popular piety may have given intercessory status to humans, sometimes of dubious honesty:

They take their priests and their anchorites to be their lords in derogation of Allah and (they take as their Lord) Christ the son of Mary; Yet they were commanded to worship but one Allah: there is no god but He. Praise and glory to him: (far is He) from having the parents they associate (with him). . . . O ye who believe! There are indeed many among the priests and anchorites who in falsehood devour the substance of men and hinder (them) from the way of Allah. And there are those who bury gold and silver and spend it not in the way of Allah: announce unto them a most grievous penalty. (Surah 9:31, 34)

Surah 5:82 indicates that humble monks are the closest in love to Muslims among the nonbelievers. But monastic asceticism is severely criticized: "But the monasticism which they invented for themselves We did not prescribe for them: (We commanded) only the seeking for the good pleasure of Allah; but that they did not foster as they should have done" (Surah 57:27).

The Quranic Christians' Relevance for Muhammad and the First Umma

Even before turning to Christians in Arabia, the Revealer took note of the Christian Roman Empire: "The Roman Empire has been defeated in a land close by; but they (even) after (this) defeat of theirs will soon be victorious within a few years" (Surah 30:2). The Persian incursion into Palestine and Syria (615–22) heartened both the Quraysh and the Jews. Any weakening of the Byzantine forces seemed advantageous for Arabs. The Jews thought the Temple might be rebuilt under Persian auspices. The Quranic passage, revealed before the Hijra, predicted correctly that the Persian victory would be short-lived. By 624 Emperor Heraclius's troops routed the Persians from Palestine and Syria, then counterattacked by invading Persia. Roman victories coincided with the Qurayshi defeat at Badr. Put in religious terms, the political-military struggles of the time were between Christians and Zoroastrians. As the polytheistic Quraysh supported the latter, it seems that the fragile Muslim umma risked offending the majority in Mecca by favoring the Byzantine Christians. Later, when Muhammad sent his emissaries to Ethiopia, Egypt, Yemen, Constantinople, and Susa, the Christians seemed bemused but not hostile.

But who were the Christians in Arabia? Perhaps most held to the official Christianity of the empire. Others may well have run afoul of the church by belonging to one or another of the several groups that rejected the standard views of Jesus and the Holy Spirit. They would have been marginalized as schismatics or denounced as heretics. In either case, while in Arabia they were beyond the reach of imperial enforcers of orthodoxy. Christian schismatics and heretics in Arabia may have been the chief sources for publicizing some aspects of noncanonical and rejected Gospels that dealt with Mary and Jesus.

The Quranic Christians' Potential Relevance Today

Islam and Christianity have had intertwined histories and have current intertwined relationships. The future will reflect that past and present. Expansions, wars, crusades, cultural cross-fertilization, the rise and fall of empires, and surges of intellectual and artistic activity are abetted and countered by reactionary movements both religious and secular, colonialism-imperialism, and the West's secularizing globalization. Muslim-Christian involvements are complicated tangles that sometimes explode. Today Christianity and Islam are two of the world's fastest-growing religions, and that growth is centered in sub-Saharan Africa. The collapse of the Soviet Union (1991) has led to a phenomenal rise of conservative Islam throughout central Asia, especially in the former republics. Islamic communities are growing rapidly and visibly throughout Western Europe. In the western hemisphere African Americans and Caribbean Americans are potential converts to Islam. Christians in the West who previously considered themselves among the leading shapers of their societies now recognize and respond to the growing Muslim presence among them. Western and worldwide attention is spurred by the actions of governments, paramilitary organizations, petroleum politics, international organizations, and outright war. In the present and foreseeable future, how and by whom and to what end the Qur'an and the Bible will be interpreted and applied are matters of life and death, war and peace. I see two potential areas for development.

First, interpretations of Quranic passages about Christians would move from Christians being closest to love than any other non-Muslims across a spectrum the opposite pole of which is that Christians are blasphemers and will be plunged into Hell with other idolaters. Passages of a similar nature could be cited from the Bible about non-Christians. Since, however, the Qur'an is held to be God's authoritative Word, is it possible for Muslims to venture to understand the Quranic denunciations of Christian doctrines in historical as well as theological contexts? Could such a view, even if taken, relieve some of the heat and passion in numerous passages without compromising Islam's total rejection of Christian Christological and Trinitarian teachings? Can Christians enter into a dialogue among themselves about those issues and also consider the exclusivistic claims about salvation through Jesus made in the Christian Scriptures and traditions?

Second, the Qur'an calls Christians and Jews "People of the Book." Throughout the twentieth and into the twenty-first century the People of the Book and Muslims have been in both amicable and hostile relationships. A positive step may be to return to the Books to search with one another not so much for what separates the believers but to discern the resemblances. Perhaps that may move Muslims, Jews, and Christians toward developing pragmatic moral visions that can be viable alternatives to mutual mistrust and antagonism. Obviously, such an undertaking could be pursued on scholarly and academic levels. Just as obviously, it also needs to be undertaken with respect and care in local communities of faith.

CONCLUSION

The Qur'an cites the Tawrah and the Ingil used by the People of the Book. Dozens of women and men, prophets and messengers, and the four special covenantal messengers attest to the plan and the Straight Path to life in this world. All point to the ultimate revealed Book and the Messenger to whom it was disclosed. Throughout the Qur'an God gives that Messenger the words he is to say, assurances to strengthen him, advice for the umma, and warnings to the People of the Book who reject the final Book. Biblical accounts and persons plus those accounts that are not in the Bible are intended to clarify, amplify, and deepen the basic message of the Qur'an stated in the al-Fatihah and epitomized in the Shahadah. In essence: the Bible and the Qur'an belong together. And Muslims, Jews, and Christians are called to make decisions about the sources, authority, uses, and meanings of the books in the present and for the future.

Say: "O People of the Book! Ye have no ground to stand upon unless ye stand fast by the Law the Gospel and all the revelation that has come to you from your Lord." It is the revelation that cometh to thee from thy Lord that increaseth in most of them their obstinate rebellion and blasphemy. But sorrow thou not over (these) people without Faith. Those who believe (in the Qur'an) those who follow the Jewish (Scriptures) and the Sabians and the Christians any who believe in Allah and the Last Day and work righteousness on them shall be no fear nor shall they grieve. (Surah 5:68–69)

TWELVE

THE QUR'AN ON JUSTICE AND JIHAD

Glorify the name of thy Guardian-Lord Most High Who
hath created and further given order and proportion,
Who hath ordained laws, and [Who] granted guidance.

Surah 87:1–3

In the Muslim world justice and jihad are watchwords for revolution, societal development, and spiritual renewal. The same words evoke anxiety
and repression by some Muslim-dominated governments and visions of
cruel punishments and fanatics in the Western world. We are indeed on
controversial territory, and the Qur'an may serve as a guide to understanding. This chapter has two major, related sections: justice and jihad.
The section on justice opens with considerations of three principles of
Quranic justice and then moves to directions in which Quranic justice
leads families and the umma's basic societal relationships, economic and
class relationships, civil and criminal prescriptions, and the question of
apostates. The second major section begins the subject of jihad as a spectrum of terms, concepts, and commitments. The discussion features key
passages, especially as they reflect the underlying unity of the Qur'an,
their contexts in Muhammad's efforts to proclaim the Message and organize the umma, and their potential present relevance. Contemporary

claims and counterclaims related to terrorism/wars of liberation or Islamic spirituality/psychology may be extrapolated from interpretations of the Revelation but often are independent of the Qur'an itself. Consequently, these derived positions are generally beyond the scope of the present study.

I do not use the terms *Fundamentalism* and *Fundamentalists* with regard to Islam. Although some generic characteristics are valid across religious lines, these are readily misunderstood in the North American context.[1] I also avoid the term *Radical Islam,* because *radical* actually means basic or from the roots, not at the edge or extreme. "Islamic extremists" and "militant Islamists" are used here and by Muslims interchangeably, yet cautiously; they connote "Islamic trends or movements that use violence to achieve their goals."[2] Islamic justice is a complex science. The post-Quranic development of jurisprudence (fiqh), several "schools" of interpretation, and the types of argumentation and exegesis of those schools are traced in other works.[3] Much of the following reflects the thoughts of influential Muslim scholars such as Fazlur Rahman and Sayyid Qutb.[4] Although they disagreed profoundly on many points, both emphasized that the proper response by Muslims to each other and all other persons is what may be called "just mercy" and that God's justice is mercy.

JUSTICE

Say: "My Lord hath commanded justice and that ye set
your whole selves (to Him) at every time and place of
prayer, and call upon Him making your devotion sincere
as in His sight. Such as He created you in the beginning
so shall ye return." Some He hath guided. Others have
(by their choice) deserved the loss of their way in that they
took the evil ones in preference to Allah for their friends
and protectors and think that they receive guidance.

Surah 7:29–30

THREE PRINCIPLES

Islamic justice is not Western justice. Post-Enlightenment Western views of justice are based in human actions, compromises, abilities, and resources. Islamic justice is given by God. Al Adl, the Just, is one of God's Beautiful Names, and justice reveals His will. The created world points to divine justice's principles, but the Qur'an and Muhammad's Sunna surpass all other testimonies. Keeping and obeying God's laws is a confession and an act of faith. Nations such as Iran, Afghanistan, Pakistan, and Saudi Arabia include in their constitutions and basic documents statements and provisions to the effect that their laws are based on the Qur'an and Muhammad's Sunna. Quranic-Islamic justice-mercy is based on three factors: tawhid, the unity-harmony of the universe, and the roles of humans in God's Plan.

The First Principle: Tawhid, God's One-Only-ness

> Behold! Verily to Allah belong all creatures in the heavens and on earth. What do they follow who worship as His "partners" other than Allah? They follow nothing but fancy, and they do nothing but lie. He it is that hath made you, the night that ye may rest therein, and the Day to make things visible (to you). Verily, in this are Signs for those who listen (to His Message).
>
> *Surah 10:66–67*

Whatever the sovereign One-Only God wills and does is just and merciful because God is sovereignly just and merciful. God, not humans, determines what justice is. Al-Fatihah states that God is Most Gracious, Most Merciful, the Cherisher and Sustainer of the Worlds, and can be reckoned thankfully to be the Master of the Day of Judgment Who aids humans on the Straight Path. No infernal or earthly power can rip believers or the umma out of His protective care. Women and men may reject the One because God permits such disobedience. As the Throne Aya led to the Light Aya, God's tawhid moves from transcendent authority and power to God's self-revelations in the world. He commanded Muhammad:

> Say: "To whom belongeth all that is in the heavens and on earth?" Say: "To Allah. He hath inscribed for Himself (the rule of) Mercy that He will gather you together for the Day of Judgment there is no doubt whatever. It is they who have lost their own souls that will not believe. To Him belongeth all that dwelleth (or lurketh) in the night and the day. For He is the One Who heareth and knoweth all things." (Surah 6:12–13)

Mercy, however, is not indulgence. Justice and awareness of human frailty are involved in the exercise of divine mercy. Because of mercy, persons who turn to God in sincere repentance and who then journey on the Straight Path will be forgiven by the gracious Master. Humans are enjoined by signs in creation and events as well as through prophets, messengers, and books to reject shirk and to establish prayer. Revelations of God's tawhid and will are evidence that He commands justice, and justice is concretized in good deeds and generosity as well as in obeying God's prohibitions regarding shameful acts, iniquity, rebellion, and breaking oaths (Surah 16:90–91). The Merciful-Just God sends down the Criterion (Furqan), that is, the Qur'an, that will never be surpassed and will stand forever (Surah 25:1, 6).

The Second Principle: The Unity-Harmony of God's World

> The revelation of the Book is from Allah, the Exalted in Power, Full of Wisdom. Verily, in the heavens and the earth are Signs for those who believe. And in the creation of yourselves and the fact that animals are scattered (through the earth) are Signs for those of assured Faith. And in the alternation of Night and Day and the fact that Allah sends down Sustenance from the sky and revives therewith the

earth after its death and the change of the winds are Signs
for those that are wise. Such are the Signs of Allah which
We rehearse to thee in truth: then in what exposition will
they believe after (rejecting) Allah and His Signs? Woe to
each sinful Dealer in Falsehoods.

Surah 45:2–7

The second basis for justice is the unity-harmony of God's world. The
world testifies that it has been made by the supremely transcendent Power.
Whatever God creates is not only in proper order and part of His plan; it is
suffused with God's justice-mercy. God has set a "balance" among the stars
as a sign that celestial bodies, weather conditions, geologic features, and
plants and animals are subject to, animated by, and responsible for expressing
God's justice.[5] Morality, then, is built into existence so that it is a matter of
relationship between God and all that was, is, and will be. Concomitantly,
morality that is grounded in God's will is a basic relationship among all the
entities that exist. All-pervasive morality-justice cancels every claim by any
human or jinni that a person or fire spirit was ignorant about the One
God and God's will for that being. The Islamically obedient world is an
oath-witness to God's goodness, will, and power.[6] The world is a moral
unity that moves toward the goal of justice: the Day of Judgment (Surah
77:1–13).

The Third Principle: Human Freedom and Responsibility

O man! What has seduced thee from thy Lord, Most
Beneficent? Him Who created thee, fashioned thee in
due proportion and gave thee a just bias. In whatever form
He wills, does He put thee together. Nay! But ye do reject
Right and Judgment! But verily over you (are appointed
angels) to protect you, kind and honorable, writing down
(your deeds). They know (and understand) all that ye do.

As for the Righteous they will be in Bliss; And the Wicked they will be in the Fire.

Surah 82:6–14, al-Infitar, The Cleaving Asunder

The third principle is the role of humans in God's plan. Humans take their place within the morally unified world. If they listen to and look at what is happening around them, they will hear, see, and join the responses that resound throughout the universe as all creation praises God with obedience and devotion.[7] The place and rank humans occupy is unique, for God designated humankind to be His caliphs, and humans freely accept that role (Surah 33:72–73). The covenant of trust was made not only with Adam but also is remade and reaccepted by everyone who enters the moral universe (Surahs 7:172–74; 76:1–3). The Creator has paid special attention to the souls of His caliphs: "By the soul and the proportion and order given to it; and its enlightenment [*taqwah*] as to its wrong and its right; truly, he succeeds that purifies it. And he fails that corrupts it!" (Surah 91:7–10, al-Shams, the Sun). Taqwah means awesome awareness of God's existence and will. By extension, it is religious devotion that protects the person from evil and is to be guarded by the individual so as not to be corrupted. Taqwah is the inner light or torch ingrained in the human soul through which men and women are able to discern right from wrong and good from evil (Surah 91:7–10). So the Qur'an is the external Furqan and the human soul matches it with its inner light—unless one rejects the moral world, the inner light, and the revealed messages.

Still, God knows that humans are frail. The chief human problem is ungrateful disdain for the taqwah within the soul and the revelations that the prophets and messengers have given to humanity. The fault is narrow-minded pettiness, which is a grave self-injury.[8] This leads to pride, greed, selfishness, miserliness, anger, envy, despair, and making oneself the standard for conduct.[9] The All-Knowing One knows what humanity needs and provides it through natural resources, yet people are ungrateful for the blessings they receive and behave badly toward God and each other when they do not get what they think they deserve. Tragically, humans tend to turn from God and toward shirk by resorting to other supposed gods, thinking these will satisfy them.[10] Nevertheless, God is patient. He does not turn against a person unless that person turns first against God.[11] The Quranic antidote for human ingratitude is taqwah and the Revelation. In this context taqwah is the awareness of God's justice so that women and men find the middle way between avarice and asceticism, overweening pride and craven abasement. The Oft-Forgiving and Merciful God gives guidance along the Straight Path to the Day (Surah 3:14–15).

Islam affirms the absolute freedom of the human conscience, equality before God, and responsibilities in relationships with others. The freedom of the human conscience is held in tension with the controversial teaching about the Divine Decree and Predestination as well as with Islamic views of freedom. Opinions within Islam may differ; I offer positions taken by Muslim scholars and leaders, including Qutb, Rahman, Glassé, al-Ghazali, and Mutahhari. A key passage is Surah 7:29–30:

> Say: "My Lord hath commanded justice, and that ye set your whole selves (to Him) at every time and place of prayer, and call upon Him, making your devotion sincere as in His sight. Such as He created you in the beginning, so shall ye return." Some He hath guided. Others have (by their choice) deserved the loss of their way in that they took the Evil Ones in preference to Allah for their friends and protectors, and think they receive guidance.

Since at birth every human enters a covenant with God, those who willfully reject God and His Straight Path earn their fates. While repentance is possible and God offers forgiveness, the person is to initiate the return to obedience through repentance and submission to God's ways. He foreknows the path that a person chooses to travel but does not determine or force that person to go in one way or the other (Surah 13:11b–12).[12] God acts subsequent to a people's action of faithfulness or rejection of the obligation to be faithful. Neither individuals nor communities are forced or fated into damnable disobedience; they bring it upon themselves. To gain forgiveness one must turn to God in sincerity and then practice the

Islamic way of worship and actions. Humans, then, are capable of exercising free will in acting justly.

The Muslim position on the "absolute freedom of the human conscience" is nuanced with divine tawhid and the essential meaning of "Islam."[13] The basis of the freedom of human consciences is the devout realization and acceptance of the facts that all creation is utterly contingent on God's will and "Islam" is obedience to God. Genuine freedom for any person and human community is total obedience to God's will. And that will is known most fully in the Qur'an and the Messenger's Sunna. God created humans, gave them bodies and souls, and gifted them with capacities to see His signs in nature and events. They are able and responsible to turn toward and obey Him. True freedom is being free from adherence to any thing or any one other than the One-Only God. Absolute freedom is absolute dependence on God, His Revelation, and His Messenger. Because Islam engages the whole person and entire communities in confessing, worshiping, and serving God, the individual and the community are to be structured according to God's will. God-obeying Muslims, then, are the only truly and absolutely free persons.

Justice, therefore, is both a goal and a process given by God and carried out through the absolute freedom of Muslims. The goal is to establish in this world God's intended just and equitable society. That society can be achieved by fulfilling the Pillars and Teachings as fully as humanly possible. That society is composed of persons who establish and keep with taqwah regular prayer, Zakat that ensures the welfare of the poor, the care and property of orphans, fasting, and Hajj, all under the aegis of the Shahadah—Confession of Faith. The umma's members will arrange their institutions so that God's tawhid will be taught and celebrated, angels affirmed as guardians, scriptures and messenger-prophets honored, and God's Day of Judgment anticipated with faithful confidence—all as part of the Sovereign One's decreed plan.

The process of justice engages the freedom of dedicated Muslims deliberately and carefully to present the Faith to their fellows in society, showing them the Straight Path so that they will accept the Qur'an's teachings and the Messenger's Sunna. Steadily and determinedly, Muslims are to take those steps to establish a genuinely free society, a society in which women

and men are not subjugated to any thing or any one but are fulfillingly obedient to the God who declares them to be His caliphs in the world. That
society will have Islam as the basis for its political institutions, legal interpretations, educational and cultural expressions, social and familial relationships, and economic arrangements. Its leaders will exemplify in their
public and personal life the Islamic Way under the guidance of God's will
grounded in the Qur'an and Muhammad's Sunna. Is such an umma possible? The devout answer is a resounding "Yes!" because it had been realized in the Messenger's Medina. The Muslim challenge is to achieve that
umma again in the modern world.

Obviously individuals differ from one another, as do their communities. Those differences are divinely willed and are part of His plan. God has
made them opportunities for people to demonstrate their obedience and
service to Him. The ultimate goal is to live toward God and His blessings
(Surah 6:164–65).

Within societies all persons share the equal responsibility for making
their communities just according to God's plan. Differences of social position, possessions, mental and physical capacities, and the like are also God-
willed tests for humans to use and share God's spiritual and material gifts
with others. In light of this, the Qur'an specifically condemns and requires
punishments for dishonesty, theft, greed, fornication, adultery, murder,
idolatry, and apostasy. Each is a form of ingratitude and disobedience to
God and violates other persons and their communities. Those whom God
blesses with authority, wealth, superior intellectual abilities, and strength
are to use those blessings to care for the creation and their fellow men and
women. Islam does not deny the right to own and use private property or
make a profit. Nations with substantial Muslim populations that have attempted forms of socialism or capitalism have been subject to resistance
from those who seek an Islamic sociopolitical umma.[14]

Wealth and authority are gifts from God, and portions of wealth are
to be used as "beautiful loans" to God in aiding others in the community
(Surah 2:245). Both success and failure are tests presented to persons and
groups to rely totally on God and to care for one another. God has provided for the needs of every person. Those who prosper are obligated to

share portions of their God-given bounty with others. Zakat is one but not the only form of such sharing. Ostentation, luxury, and vanity, naturally, are traps to be avoided through modesty, generosity, and humility before God and fellow humans:

> O ye who believe! Give of the good things which ye have (honorably) earned and of the fruits of the earth which We have produced for you, and do not even aim at getting anything which is bad in order that out of it ye may give away something when ye yourselves would not receive it except with closed eyes. And know that Allah is free of all wants and worthy of all praise. The Evil One threatens you with poverty and bids you to conduct unseemly. Allah promiseth you His forgiveness and bounties and Allah careth for all and He knoweth all things. He granteth wisdom to whom He pleaseth; and he to whom wisdom is granted receiveth indeed a benefit overflowing; but none will grasp the Message but men of understanding. And whatever ye spend in charity or devotion be sure Allah knows it all. But the wrongdoers have no helpers. (Surah 2:267–71)

DIRECTIONS

"Law is the divinely ordained system of God's commands."[15] God's justice involves directions both in terms of directives and the ongoing guidance needed to follow the Straight Path. Muslims attempt to discern God's will, then transpose what they have discerned into rules and patterns by which individuals and groups are to live. The divine component of those rules and patterns has come to be called Shari'ah, which originally meant "the way to the watering hole," that is, the way or method of living.[16] In terms of justice and law, Shari'ah is what God wills in personal and public behavior. The Qur'an and the Sunna do not themselves provide a uniform Shari'ah system recognized broadly by Muslims. A decision by a Shari'ah judge in Tunis may be different from that of his counterpart in Jakarta. Shari'ah is one of the most pressing and contentious issues among

Muslims today. In brief, the basic principles of justice indicated above are actualized in rules and patterns of conduct that can be characterized as a spectrum of directions.

One pole of justice's directions has the sense of commands and instructions. In this view, the Qur'an is essentially a compendium of God-given regulations that form a law code. So regarded, the Qur'an (and with somewhat less authority, the Hadith) decrees binding stipulations for individuals and society. Legal schools developed sets of interpretive procedures aimed at applying the Revelation and the Sunna to circumstances after the seventh century. Those schools leave room for shades of difference between what is *fard* (required) and what is *haram* (prohibited). Groups and movements such as the Afghani Taliban and Saudi Wahhabi have decidedly stringent understandings of Shari'ah.[17]

The other pole of the spectrum understands "directions" in the sense of pointing, guiding and moving toward the goal of an Islamic life and community. This position considers the Qur'an as the source for human conduct, relationships, and institutions. Muslims, then, are to use the Qur'an and the Sunna as the basis for adapting to, or abstaining from, or rejecting, or even rebelling against shifting developments and values in the cultures and societies in which the Faithful live.[18] Respected teachers-interpreters, past and present, are important for providing Muslims with decisions and guidance for their actions. With varying degrees of intensity and intention, Muslims share the conviction that when and if Islamic justice is established, every human being and the whole human community will be more just, merciful, prosperous, and fulfilled. Nevertheless, all injustice is derived from wronging oneself by making one's own interests, desires, and loyalties higher than the will of God. The devout Muslim is the human starting point and source for implementing God's justice in the world. From that individual starting point, Islam spreads to other spheres of life (e.g., Surah 4:105–10). We turn next to several spheres in which justice-directions are applied.

Justice for and in Families

The immediate community is the family, with the Messenger's family as the paradigm for all Muslim families. The Quranic "family" sets the individual

in home, clan, and tribe. Consequently, the Muslim family is the corner-
stone of the Muslim umma. Sexual promiscuity is a source of personal and
social disorder.[19] The father whispering the Shahadah and call to prayer
into the ear of his newborn child, the morning and evening settings of two
Salat prayers within family time and often before the family mihrab, the
Zakat paid from family resources, the evening meal during Sawm, and the
daily reading of the Qur'an, together with the nurturing care and observance of dietary regulations and modest dress by the mother, provide powerful witness, and genuine content within the family. Islamic worship and
taqwah are inseparable from Muslim justice as expressed in obedience to
God through morality, discipline, and law. These factors call on family leaders to embody and inculcate Quranic precepts extended into daily relationships and actions among elders and offspring. The head of the household
is called on to be just, merciful, and scrupulously honest.

In addition, heads of households are to care for and honor aged parents
(Surah 17:23–25), and they are obligated to share the bounty of what God
gave them as a sign of faithfulness to the God who renders justice to the
needy whether or not they are related to the family:

Thy Lord hath decreed that ye worship none but Him and that ye be
kind to parents. Whether one or both of them attain old age in thy life
say not to them a word of contempt nor repel them but address them
in terms of honor. And out of kindness lower to them the wing of
humility and say: "My Lord! Bestow on them Thy Mercy even as they
cherished me in childhood." Your Lord knoweth best what is in your
hearts: if ye do deeds of righteousness verily He is Most Forgiving to
those who turn to Him again and again (in true penitence). And render to the kindred their due rights as (also) to those in want and to the
wayfarer: but squander not (your wealth) in the manner of a spend-
thrift. Verily, spendthrifts are brothers of the Evil Ones; and the Evil
One is to his Lord (Himself) ungrateful. And even if thou hast to turn
away from them in pursuit of the Mercy from thy Lord which thou
dost expect yet speak to them a word of easy kindness. Make not thy
hand tied (like a niggard's) to thy neck nor stretch it forth to its utmost
reach so that thou become blameworthy and destitute. Verily, thy Lord

doth provide sustenance in abundance for whom He pleaseth, and He provideth in a just measure: for He doth know and regard all His servants. (Surah 17:23–30)

When rejected by unbelieving members of the kinship group because of their faith, Muslims are to recall that they are closer to Abraham than to their nearest relative. The Qur'an cancels kith and kin loyalties when the relatives reject the Revelation, a fact known only too frequently and painfully by Muhammad and his followers. The Muslim community, therefore, takes priority over family, clan, and tribe (Surah 9:23–24).[20] Family life and the witness to Allah's justice within and for extended families point toward justice-directions in the umma.

Justice for and in the Umma

God wills humans to take the leading role in maintaining and caring for all existence. To carry out their responsibilities women and men are to establish God-sanctioned justice and order among themselves. God has revealed the directions people are to follow and called into existence the Qur'an-based community led by Muhammad. From it the world would learn of the grace, mercy, and justice of God. Those on the Straight Path are drawn into the growing Islamic umma. They form a community called to be Islamically just and are summoned to extend God's justice so as to reduce unbelief, idolatry, and immorality as much as possible before the Judgment.[21] The Qur'an and Islamic practice indicate at least three sets of societal relationships among Muslims.

Basic Societal Relations among Muslims

The Meccan-Medinan umma is the framework for all expressions of the future Islamic umma. When quarrels arose in the umma, the preferred method was consultation on the basis of God's revealed will. The One-Only God wants His umma to be one in faith, worship, and actions. Disunity is a grave menace to the umma. God knows that rumors, gossip, and ethnic biases are corrosive. Surah 49 forbids rudeness, arrogance, sarcasm, gossip, slander, and mockery.[22] If fighting was necessary because one party persisted in opposing God's justice, then fighting was permitted by the umma against the defiant party until a fair and just peace could be arranged in compliance with God's commands. The sharing of Zakat by all members of the Islamic community strengthens the Muslim sense that the umma is indeed a commonwealth.

Economic and Class Relations among Muslims

Economic and class disparities may cause injustices and disunity. The umma is constituted not by ethnicity or social rank but by the unity of believers confessing-worshiping-serving the one God. Ideally, there is to be no hunger or destitution among Muslims or ostentatious displays of wealth and vanity:

> O ye who believe! Eat not up your property among yourselves in vanities: but let there be amongst you traffic and trade by mutual goodwill. Nor kill (or destroy) yourselves: for verily Allah hath been to you Most Merciful. If any do that in rancor and injustice, soon shall We cast them into the fire: and easy it is for Allah. If ye (but) eschew the most heinous of the things which ye are forbidden to do, We shall expel out of you all the evil in you and admit you to a Gate of great honor. And in no wise covet those things in which Allah hath bestowed his gifts more freely on some of you than on others: to men is allotted what they earn and to women what they earn: but ask Allah of His bounty: for Allah hath full knowledge of all things. To (benefit) everyone We have appointed sharers and heirs to property left by parents and relatives. To those also to whom your right hand was pledged give their due portion: for truly Allah is Witness to all things. (Surah 4:29–33)

A distinctive characteristic of Islam is its encouragement of commerce through which honestly gained reasonable profits are encouraged but in which usury (*riba*) is prohibited.[23] Riba is difficult to define, and its repeated stern condemnation is clearly a challenge to modern Muslim fiscal policies. The Quranic logic draws on the conviction that God has created all that exists and is the Owner of all. Commerce is a gift from God, but usury is from Iblis (Surah 2:275–81).

Contemporary anti-riba movements are usually linked to hostility to governments that claim to be Islamically based but adapt to or are seemingly in league with Western fiscal policies and practices. The intra-Muslim debate and conflict over riba is part of the struggle between militant Muslims, who insist on their understandings of a thoroughly Islamic political-economic-social state, and those Muslims who accommodate to non-Muslim monetary risks and rewards. From Quranic times to the present riba and the speculative nature of riba-based commerce has been seen as a form of gambling, a practice forbidden in Islam. Riba, opponents claim, is a source of humiliation and degradation, a satanic weapon that weakens the umma and extends the reach of Islam's demonic and human foes.

Civil and Criminal Directions among Muslims

The Qur'an provides both rules and guidance for dealing with what we may regard as legal situations. We have seen the earlier concern for orphans and heirs. Truthfulness is expected, and the umma's unity is damaged by deception and perjury. These violate obedience to God and dishonor the umma collectively and individually. Quranic judgments in criminal situations call for swift responses. The guilty person has harmed himself or herself, the people involved in the crime, and the umma's integrity. Worst of all, the criminal has defied God. The sanctions against fornicators and adulterers as well as those who deliberately bring false accusations have been considered earlier. Thieves are to be punished severely and are to bear the stigma of their crime for the rest of their lives, although God may extend forgiveness in the Hereafter:

> As to the thief male or female, cut off his or her hands: a punishment by way of example from Allah for their crime: and Allah is Exalted in Power. But if the thief repent after his crime and amend his conduct, Allah turneth to him in forgiveness; for Allah is Oft-Forgiving, Most Merciful. (Surah 5:38–40)[24]

Crimes of violence were reciprocated in kind. Although Surah
5:44–45 refers to God's instructions for the Jews, Islamic practice has followed suit:

> Life for life, eye for eye, nose for nose, ear for ear, tooth for tooth, and
> wounds equal for equal. But if anyone remits the retaliation by way of
> charity it is an act of atonement for himself. And if any fail to judge
> by (the light of) what Allah hath revealed they are (no better than)
> wrong-doers.[25]

A Quranic direction effectively provided grounds for ending blood
feuds through compensating the families of victims, assuaging their honor,
and restoring peace to the umma:

> Never should a believer kill a believer; but (if it so happens) by mis-
> take (compensation is due). If one (so) kills a believer, it is ordained
> that he should free a believing slave and pay compensation to the de-
> ceased's family unless they remit it freely. If the deceased belonged to
> a people at war with you and he was a believer, the freeing of a be-
> lieving slave (is enough). If he belonged to a people with whom ye
> have a treaty of mutual alliance, compensation should be paid to his
> family and a believing slave be freed. For those who find this beyond
> their means (is prescribed) a fast for two months running: by way of
> repentance to Allah: for Allah hath all knowledge and all wisdom. If
> a man kills a believer intentionally, his recompense is Hell to abide
> therein (for ever): and the wrath and the curse of Allah are upon him
> and a dreadful penalty is prepared for him. (Surah 4:92–93)[26]

The Question of Apostates

> Those who turn back as apostates after Guidance was clearly
> shown to them, the Evil One has instigated them and buoyed
> them up with false hopes. This because they said to those
> who hate what Allah has revealed "We will obey you in part
> of (this) matter"; but Allah knows their (inner) secrets. But

how (will it be) when the angels take their souls at death and
smite their faces and their backs? This because they followed
that which called forth the Wrath of Allah and they hated
Allah's good pleasure; so He made their deeds of no effect.

Surah 47:25—28, Muhammad

What is apostasy? A Western dictionary defines an apostate as a person who
once was within the believing community but who has repudiated that faith
and has become a renegade or a rebel against it.[27] The Western view im-
plies that persons who convert to another religious community but do not
actively oppose the first faith are not apostates; at worst, they are defectors.
Surah 47:25—28 appears to support that understanding. The term *apostate* in
the passage means literally "those who turn their backs" and go on to con-
sort with God's and Islam's enemies. The ayas spell out their eternal fate in
the Hereafter but do not prescribe any penalties in this world. Punishments
for apostates and opponents in this world are not specified in the Qur'an,
but a hadith describes Muhammad sentencing to a gruesome death several
apostates who were also guilty of deception, murder, and theft.[28]

The Qur'an is concerned with *kafirs,* unbelievers. The Arabic root
K-F-R means "cover, conceal, ignore, reject." It can be used for unbelief,
hypocrisy, and ingratitude toward and opposing God and the Messenger.[29] The "Hypocrites" seem to be persons who dissembled support for
Muhammad and the umma while in league with his opponents (Surah
2:8—16). Since some Medinan kafirs, both unbelievers and Hypocrites,
were involved in opposing and plotting against the umma and the Messenger even to the point of deserting before key battles, they were punished in
the aftermath of those conflicts.

Today, some Muslims, especially in Pakistan, Bangladesh, Egypt, Saudi
Arabia, Iran, and Afghanistan, regard as apostates those who were Muslims but have converted to another religion or simply stopped considering
themselves Muslims whether or not they are critical of or rebel against
Islam. Such persons may be subject to legal penalties, including death. De-

pending on local conditions, their neighbors may also take severe extra-legal actions against them. In chapter 14 we will encounter two persons, Salman Rushdie and Taslima Nasrin, who have repudiated the Faith and who denounce Islam, the Qur'an, and the Messenger. Both have been threatened with death. A serious issue facing Muslims in predominantly Muslim societies and in the Muslim diaspora concerns the freedom of persons to convert to other religions, the sociopolitical freedom and safety of non-Muslim missionaries to propagate their faiths in Islamic lands, and the futures of those who renounce Islam.

> Allah created the heavens and the earth for just ends and in order that each soul may find the recompense of what it has earned and none of them be wronged. (Surah 45:22)

JIHAD

> O, ye who believe! Bow down and prostrate yourselves, and
> worship your Lord, and do good, that haply ye may prosper.
> And strive [j-h-d] for Allah with the endeavor [j-h-d] which
> is His right. He hath chosen you and hath not laid upon you
> in religion any hardship; the faith of your father Abraham
> (is yours). He hath named you Muslims of old time and in this
> (Scripture), that the Messenger may be a witness against you,
> and that ye may be witnesses against mankind. So establish
> worship, pay the poor due, and hold fast to Allah. He is your
> Protecting Friend. A blessed Patron and a blessed Helper![30]
>
> *Surah 22:77–78*

"Jihad" is a cluster of terms, concepts, and commitments covering the spectrum from physical war to individual spiritual struggle. For some Muslims, it is "an absolute necessity," "a neglected duty," "the peak of this religion."[31]

For numerous non-Muslims, jihad is evidence that a sinister power lurks behind the word *Allah;* Islam is a satanic and fanatical religion; jihad is a tactic used by Muslims in their plot to dominate the world; and jihad reveals the Qur'an to be steeped in violence, bloodshed, and institutionalized hate from Muhammad to the present.[32] What has been termed "classical jihad theory" among medieval and later Muslim legal scholars considers jihad an unconditional duty for Muslim individuals and countries to fight nonbelievers until they submit to Muslim rule or are converted to Islam.[33] Non-Muslims who are well disposed to Islam and many devout Muslims quote a tradition that appears to minimize warlike interpretations of jihad. The sense of that tradition is that Muhammad called physical warfare the "Lesser Jihad" and the spiritual jihad within individuals the "Greater Jihad."[34] Other scholars take a more neutral or descriptive stand.[35] The Qur'an is sparing in its use of jihad. The hadith collections are more ample and give rise to understanding jihad as conflicts undertaken for religious goals. So to enter into a discussion of jihad is to step onto highly controversial ground. As we venture into that territory I focus chiefly on the Qur'an and the contexts in which pertinent references are made. The first concern is with three closely connected terms, *jihad, qitaal,* and *fi sabil-Allah.* The second concern is twofold: abrogation/canceling of earlier ayas in favor of later ayas and the possibility that the concept of jihad "evolved" in the Qur'an. I return to the familiar pattern of the underlying unity of the Qur'an, the contexts for Muhammad, and the potential ongoing relevance for Muslims and non-Muslims.

JIHAD, QITAAL, AND FI SABIL-ALLAH

Jihad, qitaal, and fi sabil-Allah are usually closely connected in the Qur'an. Sometimes jihad and qitaal are virtually interchangeable; Fi sabil-Allah puts both under God's jurisdiction and in His purpose.

Jihad

J-H-D, the triconsonantal root for jihad-related words, occurs forty-one times in the Qur'an.[36] The root connotes striving, endeavoring, being in earnest, power, ability, struggle, and fighting. Most of the references in the Qur'an do not deal with an obvious call to Muslims to wage war or to fight. For example, one passage urges believers to remain faithful to Islam even though their nonbelieving parents struggle (jihad) to have them return to the religion of their ancestors, and five passages are related to taking oaths in earnest.[37] The Yusuf Ali translation tends to tame jihad expressions by adding parentheses or selecting alternate wordings that are gentler than the context indicates. Two uses that Marmaduke Pickthall properly rendered as "endeavor" might reflect a military context.[38] A set of ayas relates the Hijra to jihad by indicating that those who emigrated to Yathrib-Medina had striven with their wealth and risked their lives while in Mecca and by leaving their property and relatives in Mecca.[39] Surah 22:77–78, the passage that opened the jihad section of this chapter, is a general exhortation to put faith into action without a direct reference to war. Several ayas that use the word *jihad* and to which we will return are critical of or refer to men who were either unwilling or unable to participate in a military conflict ordered by God through Muhammad.[40] Of the forty-one references, ten clearly are military in nature and significance.[41] All ten are in Surahs 2, 8, and 9. Nevertheless, the military roles of jihad and its related terms are not thereby minimized.

Qitaal

Q-T-L, the root that means "to kill, slay, fight, and assail" is the most important of several terms translated as "war" or "conflict."[42] It and its derivatives appear one hundred sixty times in the Qur'an, forty-four of them clearly in terms of warfare. *Qitaal* is often used in conjunction with *jihad* or by itself in the sense of a conflict sanctioned by God. Sometimes *qitaal* is used to cite killings, attempts to murder, or conflicts that occurred to earlier figures such as Joseph's brothers plotting to slay him or Moses killing the Egyptian polytheist or attempts to kill God's messengers and prophets. The word also is used to refer to battles and wars against Muslims or as advice to believers to defend themselves or to make promises to those who might die defending the Faith. A lexicographic examination of where the term appears shows that there are "qitaal clusters" in the Qur'an and that these fall almost exclusively in Medinan surahs, especially Surahs 2, 3, 4, 5, 8, and 9.[43] Frequently there are multiple uses in an aya or closely connected ayas. The qitaal clusters, logically, usually deal with conflict situations faced by the umma. It is more helpful to recognize the varied uses of the term and to see its contexts than to make the generalization that the Qur'an inculcates violence.[44]

Fi sabil-Allah

Fi sabil-Allah means "In the way of God/In the cause of God." It is the key factor in determining whether or not a jihad and/or qitaal is divinely sanctioned. The term appears seventy times in the Qur'an. A root expressing the God-given result of fighting-striving in the way of God is *F-T-H*, opening (as in al-Fatihah), and victory. Used thirty-eight times in the Qur'an, *Fath, Victory,* is the traditional name given Surah 48. The only proper cause for war is that it be undertaken for the way of God and that it be conducted in the way of God. In the Jahiliyyah Arabs conducted raids (*ghazwah*) on the caravans of rival powers for the purpose of gaining plunder, slaves, women, and animals. Raids or expeditions involved cleverly laid ambushes, and the raiders took care not to inflict fatalities or wound the defenders. Killing a person in a raid provoked a feud between the tribes or clans involved that could be assuaged only by blood-for-blood vengeance or the acceptance by the aggrieved family of an indemnity in terms of animals, slaves, or money. As noted earlier, during the Jahiliyyah, Arabs honored the months of Dhu l-Hijjah, Qa'dah, Muharram, and Rajab as times when raids and fighting were forbidden. But after the Revelation began, could one fight for God during one of those times? That question pressed on Muhammad soon after the Hijra.

Herem and Jihad-Qitaal

Not all wars said to be commanded or encouraged by God are the same. The biblical herem enjoined on the Israelites as they invaded or infiltrated Canaan and later fought against the peoples who lived there that these were to be wars of annihilation. Indigenous persons—regardless of combat status—their property, livestock, and especially shrines were to be destroyed and no prisoners allowed to live.[45] The ostensible reason was to eliminate to the extent possible any residue of native customs, gods, and influences that might be absorbed into and corrupt the Israelites' worship and morals. Given repeated condemnations of syncretism and blatant Baalism by the prophets, the policy failed to achieve its goal.

Islam regarded polytheism as the result of reprehensible demonic rebellion against God and as a Satan-originated deception through which humans disobeyed the One-Only God. Accordingly, when Islam triumphed, the Ka'bah was cleansed and idolatry banned. But, in principle, polytheists as well as the People of the Book who did not fight against Islam were not to be slaughtered.[46] Further, during a jihad-qitaal, God ordered that property and natural resources such as trees and wells were not to be destroyed. Captured soldiers and enemy civilians rarely were killed, except for causes such as harming the Messenger. Prisoners often were ransomed or enslaved. The Quranic approach to the jihad-qitaal-fi sabil-Allah shifted as a result of the rapid expansion of Muslim-controlled territory beginning in the late eighth century and with the western European–Christian crusades that started in the late eleventh century. During the crusades, both sides routinely butchered prisoners who were not held for ransom. The Euro-Christians were known for massacring civilians when sacking cities. Uncomfortable with the ready conflation of the biblical holy war and medieval crusade with jihad for the cause of God, Muslim scholars suggest not calling a jihad a "holy war" but a "just war." This, however, may compound confusion because the expression "just war" has significantly different meanings and history in Western legal, philosophical, and theological theory.[47]

JIHAD INVOLVES MORE than a particular word. Its basic meaning of struggle may be used in several ways and is to be understood in its Quranic contexts. Qitaal is unambiguously used in military and physical senses, frequently in connection with jihad. Again, the contexts of qitaal, like those of jihad, vary. To fight in/for the cause/way of God is crucial for understanding the roles of jihad and qitaal in the Qur'an and in subsequent

Islamic developments. Using the expressions "holy war" and "just war" with reference to jihad raises problems and is unhelpful. Perhaps one may regard "In the way of God/For the cause of God" as the Islamic umbrella under which jihad and qitaal should be seen. Finally, Muslim theories about and practices of jihad–qitaal–fi sabil-Allah developed over centuries through interpretations of the Qur'an, the Hadith, and situations faced by Muslims. The entire subject embraced under "jihad" is and will remain controversial within Islam and between Muslims and non-Muslims.

> O ye who believe! What is the matter with you then when ye are asked to go forth in the cause of Allah, ye cling heavily to the earth? Do ye prefer the life of this world to the Hereafter? But little is the comfort of this life as compared with the Hereafter. Unless ye go forth, He will punish you with a grievous penalty and put others in your place; but Him ye would not harm in the least. For Allah hath power over all things. (Surah 9:38–39)

JIHAD AND THE QUR'AN'S UNDERLYING UNITY

> O ye who believe! If any from among you turn back from
> his faith, soon will Allah produce a people whom He will love
> as they will love Him, lowly with the believers mighty against
> the rejecters fighting [*jihad*] in the way of Allah and never
> afraid of the reproaches of such as find fault. That is the
> Grace of Allah which He will bestow on whom He pleaseth:
> and Allah encompasseth all and He knoweth all things. Your
> (real) friends are (no less than) Allah, His Messenger, and
> the (fellowship of) believers, those who establish regular
> prayers and regular charity, and they bow down humbly
> (in worship). As to those who turn (for friendship) to Allah,
> His Messenger, and the (fellowship of) believers, it is the
> fellowship of Allah that must certainly triumph.[48] O ye who
> believe! Take not for friends and protectors those who take
> your religion for a mockery or sport whether among those

who received the Scripture before you or among those who reject faith; but fear ye Allah if ye have Faith (indeed).

Surah 5:54–57

God's plan for this world requires jihad, but not all jihads involve violence, killing, and war. The underlying unity of the Qur'an may be seen through the lens of jihad. That unity is posited on the singularity and transcendent power-authority of the One-Only God. The Creator's covenant with all that exists is based on God's most gracious, merciful, and just will and the creation's joyful, free obedience-testimony to God. Al-Ahad (the One) could have made all to be obedient and united, yet He elected to give His creatures the ability to obey or disobey Him. Except for some jinn and the humans who joined them, the heavens and earth and all in them submit gladly and worshipfully to God. Iblis and his doomed ilk rebelled and set themselves in enmity against God and set about the task of deceiving and dragging into damnation as many humans as possible. The expulsion of Iblis and the primal human couple from the heavenly Garden to this world of space and time began the jihad-struggle between truth and deception, obedience and rebellion, right worship and idolatry, and the Way of God and the Way of Satan. That jihad will continue until the end of this world and the beginning of the Hereafter.

In addition to providing humanity with signs, successes, and supports through nature to direct humans to the Straight Path, God sent prophets and messengers in words and with books to proclaim His One-Only-ness and will. That Message, if heard and obeyed, undercuts and exposes Iblis's idolatrous deceptions. Hearing and obeying God will lead to the establishment of the God-united and blessed umma in which there will be proper worship, justice, and peace. Living according to God's will is a matter of jihad. Prophets and messengers as well as women and men who seek to worship-obey-serve the One-Only God have had to struggle against Iblis's formidable deceptions, the unbelief and ingratitude of their families and neighbors, and the murderous hostility of governments. In spite of the opposition and machinations of evil powers and human foes, God promises His faithful, obedient struggler-fighters the glorious rewards of the Hereafter. In that Hereafter there will be no more jihads but eternal Salaam, peace.

The Qur'an recognizes the struggles necessary for believers in order for them to be faithful Muslims and to establish the God-willed umma. Those struggles involve fighting the rebellious demons and deceived humans. Because the struggles are carried out in different ways and under different circumstances, we turn to two key issues and then Muhammad's contexts to consider how he conducted himself and led the umma in the jihad for the cause and way of God.

> Those who believed and those who suffered exile and fought [*jihad*] (and strove and struggled) in the path of Allah, they have the hope of the Mercy of Allah; and Allah is Oft-Forgiving Most Merciful. (Surah 2:218)

TWO KEY ISSUES

> Lo! The number of the months with Allah is twelve months by Allah's ordinance in the day that He created the heavens and the earth. Four of them are sacred: that is the right religion. So wrong not yourselves in them. And wage war [*qitaal*] on all the idolaters as they are waging war [*qitaal*] on all of you. And know that Allah is with those who keep their duty (unto Him).
>
> *Surah 9:36*

The issues that need to be addressed before examining Muhammad's contexts are whether or not passages revealed toward the close of the revelatory period abrogated earlier passages and whether or not the concept of jihad evolved in the Qur'an.

Abrogation

Here we return to the possibility that some Quranic passages were abrogated or modified by later passages in the Qur'an or by the Hadith. Precisely, are passages such as Surah 2:62—"Those who believe (in the Qur'an) and those who follow the Jewish (Scriptures) and the Christians and the Sabians and who believe in Allah and the last day and work righteousness shall have their reward with their Lord; on them shall be no fear nor shall they grieve"—and Surah 2:256—"Let there be no compulsion in religion. Truth stands out clear from error; whoever rejects evil and believes in Allah hath grasped the most trustworthy hand-hold that never breaks. And Allah heareth and knoweth all things."—abrogated by passages such as the Sword Aya? The following excerpts are from Pickthall's translation:

> Those who believed and adopted exile and fought [*jihad*] for the faith with their property and their persons in the cause of Allah as well as those who gave (them) asylum and aid, these are (all) friends and protectors one of another. As to those who believed but came not into exile, ye owe no duty of protection to them until they seek your aid in religion. It is your duty to help them, except against a people with whom ye have a treaty of mutual alliance: and (remember) Allah seeth all that ye do. The unbelievers are protectors one of another: unless ye do this (protect each other) there would be tumult and oppression on earth and great mischief. Those who believe and adopt exile and fight [*jihad*] for the faith in the cause of Allah as well as those who give (them) asylum and aid, these are (all) in very truth the believers: for them is the forgiveness of sins and a provision most generous. And those who accept faith subsequently and adopt exile and fight [*jihad*] for the faith in your company, they are of you. But kindred by blood have prior rights against each other in the

Book of Allah. Verily, Allah is well acquainted with all things. (Surah 8:72–75)

Then, when the sacred months have passed, slay [*qitaal*] the idolaters wherever ye find them, and take them (captive), and besiege them, and prepare for them each ambush. But if they repent and establish worship and pay the poor due [*Zakat*], then leave their way free. Lo! Allah is Forgiving, Merciful.[49] (Surah 9:5, Ayat al-Sayf, the Sword Aya)

Other important passages with a similar thrust are:

Fight [*qitaal*] in the way of Allah against those who fight [*qitaal*] against you, but begin not hostilities. Lo! Allah loveth not aggressors. And slay [*qitaal*] them wherever ye find them, and drive them out of the places whence they drove you out, for persecution [*fitna*] is worse than slaughter [*qitaal*]. And fight [*qitaal*] not with them at the Inviolable Place of Worship until they first attack [*qitaal*] you there, but if they attack [*qitaal*] you (there) then slay [*qitaal*] them. Such is the reward of disbelievers. But if they desist, then lo! Allah is Forgiving, Merciful. And fight [*qitaal*] them until persecution [*fitna*] is no more, and religion is for Allah. But if they desist, then let there be no hostility except against wrongdoers. The forbidden month for the forbidden month, and forbidden things in retaliation. And one who attacketh you, attack him [in] like manner as he attacked you. Observe your duty to Allah, and know that Allah is with those who ward off (evil). (Surah 2:190–94)

Fight against such of those who have been given the Scripture as believe not in Allah nor the Last Day, and forbid not that which Allah hath forbidden by His Messenger, and follow not the religion of truth, until they pay the tribute [*jizya*] readily, being brought low. (Surah 9:29, The Jizya Aya)

Three conclusions may be drawn if the later passages such as the Sword and Jizya Ayas and Surahs 2:190–94 and 9:36 abrogate passages such as Surah 2:62 and 2:256. One is that Islam is in unremitting warfare with all other religions and with the societies that permit those religions until the other peoples either submit to Islam or are killed. The second conclusion based on the Jizya Aya is that the People of the Book are to be protected in Muslim-controlled territories only if they submit to be ruled by Muslims and pay the jizya tax. A third, more moderate conclusion is that nonbelievers are to be fought until they are driven from the land under contention or until their fitna against Muslims ceases and they consent to live unresistingly under the just rule of Muslims.

Medieval Muslim jurists cited by modern militant Islamists who argue in favor of abrogation may be in the minority, but their positions often fuel adherents to direct action, calling such action jihad in the way and for the cause of God.[50] Obviously, those non-Muslims who regard the Qur'an and Islam as violent and demonic would find support for their positions on the basis of the interpretations that would abrogate the "tolerant" and peaceful passages of the Qur'an.

Muslim scholars who argue against abrogation are no less firm in holding that Islam has a mission to bring as many persons as possible to the Truth (Islamically understood) and to seek to establish just and equitable societies on Islamic principles. For example, although his writings have been adapted by revolutionary militant Muslims, Qutb moved from regarding jihad as essentially the struggle to defend Islam from aggression to combating all forms of injustice no matter where they might occur. In his view, the justice to be established was Islamic justice, not simply authority exercised by those who claimed to be Muslims.[51] Rahman, scarcely a militant Islamist, also rejected the abrogation justification advanced by militant Islamists. He argued that jihad is an absolute necessity and instrument willed by God in order to eliminate by the nonviolent means of witness, work, education, and reform "corruption on earth" in cooperation with like-minded non-Muslims.[52] Mahmud Shaltut (1893–1963), the Shaykh al-Azhar, countered the abrogationists by insisting that all the Quranic ayas are to stand as they are, making distinctions among seemingly contradictory passages on the basis of context.[53] I open the Qur'an and continue our study in agreement with Shaykh Shaltut, Qutb, and Rahman with regard to the abrogation issue.

The Evolution of Jihad

Did the concept of jihad in the Qur'an evolve from relatively benign and tolerant strivings to aggression, killing, and war? In fact, to maintain that such an evolution took place is a milder version of the abrogation issue for it allows the early passages to stand but to lose practical relevance as the umma became a powerful community under the leadership of the Messenger-General. Clearly, the concept of jihad underwent significant development after the cessation of the Revelation on Muhammad's death. And the concept of jihad is still being studied and elaborated.[54] The evolutionary view was described by the medieval jurist and commentator Shamseddin al-Sarakhsi (1010–90). He held that Muhammad was commanded to engage in jihad in four developing stages:

1. to spread the Islamic Message and Faith peacefully (early Meccan period);
2. to confront and argue with unbelievers in a wise and fair manner (mainly pre-Hijra and early Medinan period);
3. to fight the umma's enemies if Muslims were unjustly wronged, and such fighting was not to be undertaken in the sacred months; and
4. to wage war against unbelievers unconditionally and constantly to bring about the victory of Islam.[55]

The evolutionary view, as does the abrogationist position, concludes with Islam as a religion hostile to the point of war with other religious, social, and political systems. I find the "new reading" proposed by Reuven Firestone to fit the Qur'an more adequately and in accord with Muhammad's contexts.[56] Firestone grouped jihad-qitaal passages into four types. Instead of being in stages, the passages range through the Qur'an and need to be understood in their own contexts:

1. passages expressing nonmilitant means for propagating or defending the Faith;
2. passages expressing restrictions on fighting;

3. passages expressing conflict between God's command to fight and
    the reactions of Muhammad's followers; and
4. passages strongly advocating war for God's religion.

JIHAD-QITAAL IN MUHAMMAD'S CONTEXTS

Let those fight [*qitaal*] in the cause of Allah who sell the
life of this world for the Hereafter. To him who fighteth
[*qitaal*] in the cause of Allah, whether he is slain or gets
victory, soon shall We give him a reward of great (value).
And why should ye not fight [*qitaal*] in the cause of
Allah and of those who being weak are ill-treated (and
oppressed)? Men, women and children whose cry is:
"Our Lord! Rescue us from this town whose people
are oppressors; and raise for us from Thee one who will
protect; and raise for us from Thee one who will help!"
Those who believe fight [*qitaal*] in the cause of Allah,
and those who reject faith fight [*qitaal*] in the cause of
evil. So fight [*qitaal*] ye against the friends of Satan: feeble
indeed is the cunning of Satan.

Surah 4:74–76

The Hijra to Yathrib-Medina marks the chief decisive historical before-
and-after point in the Qur'an. Following that basic distinction, a series
of battles and expeditions put Muhammad's and the umma's situations in
different lights. The following, focused on jihad-qitaal for the cause/way of
God, traces Muhammad's contexts first in Mecca, then in Yathrib-Medina.
The umma and Muhammad were engaged in numerous expeditions, skirmishes, and battles. In the Medinan setting, I comment mostly on the key
Battles of Destiny: Badr, Uhud, the Trench, and the War of the Confederates. Finally, we turn to the expedition to Tabuk.

Muhammad's Context in Mecca, 610–622

As noted in earlier chapters, the Meccan responses to Muhammad's proclamation, exhortations, warnings, and influences moved from initial mockery to malicious hostility and finally to murder. The Revealer advised Muhammad to bear patiently with the negative responses of the unbelievers.
He was to pray and persevere and be confident that the Day of Judgment
was coming. His gentle demeanor was due in part to his lack of personal
authority and perhaps eloquence at this early stage:

> Verily, in this is a Message for any that has a heart and understanding
> or who gives ear and earnestly witnesses (the truth). We created the
> heavens and the earth and all between them in six days nor did any
> sense of weariness touch Us. Bear then with patience all that they say,
> and celebrate the praises of thy Lord before the rising of the sun and
> before (its) setting. And during part of the night (also) celebrate His
> praises and (so likewise) after the postures of adoration. And listen for
> the Day when the Caller will call out from a place quite near. (Surah
> 50:37–41)

Apparently he developed debating and rhetorical skills that enhanced
his efforts to gain converts. Success, however, bred increased opposition
from the Qurayshi oligarchy. Plots began to be hatched against him and the
growing Muslim community. Some followers may have desired to strike
back at those who opposed the Way of God. Still, God advised Muhammad
to continue with patience and perseverance: "Allah is with those who restrain themselves, and those who do good" (Surah 18:125–28).[57] In 615 a
group of beleaguered believers, including one of his married daughters,
fled Mecca and took refuge among the Christians in Abyssinia. Muhammad was commanded to be more forceful and determined in proclaiming
the Message even to the point of breaking family ties:

> Therefore expound openly what thou art commanded and turn away
> from those who join false gods with Allah. For sufficient are We unto

thee against those who scoff, those who adopt with Allah another god. But soon will they come to know. We do indeed know how thy heart is distressed at what they say. But celebrate the praises of thy Lord and be of those who prostrate themselves in adoration. And serve thy Lord until there come unto thee the Hour that is Certain. (Surah 15:94–99)

Muhammad had grown to be a persuasive and powerful preacher-teacher who challenged the established authorities. He and his followers broke with their natural tribal, clan, and family communities to begin a new community based on worship-obedience to the One-Only God. The Qurayshi attacks on Muhammad and the Meccan Muslims foreshadowed further assaults and, once he had the resources and divine mandates, qitaal responses.

Traditionally two Quranic references to jihad are associated with the Meccan situation, although they could be applied to subsequent times as well. One, Surah 29:8, concerning the jihad efforts of parents to sway their offspring to cease being Muslims, was mentioned earlier. The second passage proclaims that individual Believers will not be exempt from God's tests. The tests will disclose who is a sincere Believer and who is a Hypocrite:

Do men imagine that they will be left (at ease) because they say, "We believe," and will not be tested with affliction [fitna]? Lo! We tested those who were before you. Thus Allah knoweth those who are sincere, and knoweth those who feign. Or do those who do ill deeds imagine that they can outstrip Us: Evil (for them) is that which they decide. Whoso looketh forward to the meeting with Allah (let him know that) Allah's reckoning is surely nigh, and He is the Hearer, the Knower. And whosoever striveth [jihad], striveth [jihad] only for himself, for lo! Allah is altogether independent of (His) creatures. And as for those who believe and do good works, We shall remit from them their evil deeds and shall repay them the best that they did. (Surah 29:2–7)[58]

Muhammad's Medinan Contexts

The Messenger's and the emigrants' situation changed dramatically with their arrival in Yathrib-Medina. Once in the oasis city the Messenger of God, head of the community of Believers and father–father-in-law, also became the judge, civic leader, general, soldier, husband, and diplomat. The Medinans wanted him to restore order and to end their hostile attitudes toward one another. Muhammad had to deal with a number of constituencies, trying to compose them into a God-worshiping-serving umma. Among those who anticipated his leadership were Meccan emigrants and the refugees who returned from Abyssinia. They had lost property and wealth because of their adherence to Islam and the Messenger. They wanted restitution as soon as possible. Apparently, some among the emigrants and new believers from Medina chafed under Muhammad's leadership, much as the Israelites did with Moses in the wilderness. The critical areas seem to have been his political-moral policies on alcohol consumption and military strategy. These critics appear to have been included in the category "Hypocrites," also known as "dissenters." Added to these interest groups were Medinan polytheists, the People of the Book, and, on the margins, nomadic bedouin. The emigrants also faced an immediate problem: they had no property or wherewithal to sustain themselves. They were dependent on the few resources they could take from Mecca and on the temporary generosity of the Yathribans.

If the situation inside Yathrib-Medina was complicated, the predicament looming outside was simpler and more dangerous. According to Muslim traditions, the polytheists of Mecca, Taif, and other settlements realized that their caravan routes to and from Syria were in reach of raiding parties from Yathrib-Medina. As long as Muhammad and the Muslims were abroad and determined to bring Arabia into the umma of Islam, their economies, political stability, and religious traditions were endangered. Further, as long as Muhammad was alive, the honor of Mecca's leaders was compromised. Another menace loomed on the geographic and religious horizons: the Byzantine Empire. Under these circumstances jihad often, but not always, was expressed in terms of qitaal Fi sabil-Allah, war in the way of God.

From Hijra through the Battle of Badr

Although once in Medina the Muslims fought a number of engagements with the Meccans before the Battle of Badr (March 17, 624), the so-called Raid at Nakhlah confronted Muhammad with a double dilemma.[59] First, the death of the Meccan leader was bound to set in motion a blood feud. Should Muhammad fight the more powerful Meccans, or should he negotiate an indemnity? To do the latter would be to recognize the legitimacy of the polytheists and dishonor his own soldiers. Second, they were concerned with the violation of the holy month. What ought the Muslims do with the plunder and prisoners? Should they recognize the religious customs of the idolaters? Could they legitimize the violation of ancient custom? At this juncture, Muhammad received a revelation, Surah 2:217:

> They ask thee concerning fighting [*qitaal*] in the Prohibited Month. Say: "Fighting [*qitaal*] therein is a grave (offence); but graver is it in the sight of Allah to prevent access to the path of Allah to deny Him to prevent access to the Sacred Mosque and drive out its members. Tumult and oppression are worse than slaughter [*qitaal*]." Nor will they cease fighting [*qitaal*] you until they turn you back from your faith if they can. And if any of you turn back from their faith and die in unbelief their works will bear no fruit in this life and in the Hereafter; they will be Companions of the Fire and will abide therein.

In other words, the Raid at Nakhlah was the presenting cause for authorizing Muslims to break with the prevailing non-Muslim traditions if and when keeping those traditions hindered significantly the practice of Islam or threatened the Muslim community or any of its members. Violations were not made for the sake of convenience or opportunistic reasons. But if the Muslims felt vindicated by the revelation, the Meccans were incensed, and the other tribes recognized that a new force that could operate outside the boundaries of accepted custom had to be dealt with. And the Meccans still sought revenge for the death of one of their own.

The story behind the Battle of Badr is instructive. In March 624 the Medinans learned that a rich Qurayshi caravan was on its way from Syria to

Mecca. The Medinans, believers and unbelievers, agreed to Muhammad's initial plan to attack the caravan. The Meccans, learning of the planned assault, sent a thousand-man force to beat off any Muslim-Medinan foray. Inspired by a God-given dream, Muhammad announced that his forces were to engage the larger Meccan contingent. As this made no military sense, many Medinans and Muslims refused to go into battle with him. According to some Muslim traditions, Muhammad sent messages to the Qurayshi leaders indicating that while he was prepared to do battle, he would prefer that the armies disengage. The Qurayshi, however, seeking revenge for the death of their tribesman and convinced that they could annihilate the Muslims, refused.[60] Some able-bodied and willing men were delegated to remain in Medina to keep order and maintain proper worship. The Muslim army consisted of some 70 emigrants and approximately two 230 Medinan converts against a thousand. God commanded him: "O Messenger! Rouse the Believers to fight [qitaal]. If there are twenty amongst you patient and persevering, they will vanquish two hundred; if a hundred, they will vanquish a thousand of the unbelievers, for these are people without understanding" (Surah 8:5–6). The Messenger demanded strict obedience to his orders, especially the order that the troops not be distracted by taking plunder during the engagement. He assured them that God would provide a thousand angels to fight with them. The result was the stunning victory at the Battle of Badr Springs. Several of the Quranic passages related to the battle for the cause and in the way of God are in Surah 8.[61]

Humans did not gain the victory at Badr. God won the battle and thereby validated Muhammad's leadership and the Truth of the Message. Surah 8:72–75 declares the battle a jihad:

Those who believed and adopted exile and fought [jihad] for the faith with their property and their persons in the cause of Allah as well as those who gave (them) asylum and aid these are (all) friends and protectors one of another. As to those who believed but came not into exile, ye owe no duty of protection to them until they seek your aid in religion it is your duty to help them except against a people with whom ye have a treaty of mutual alliance: and (remember) Allah seeth all that ye do. The unbelievers are protectors one of another: unless ye do this (protect each other) there would be tumult and oppression on earth and great mischief. Those who believe and adopt exile and fight [*jihad*] for the faith in the cause of Allah as well as those who give (them) asylum and aid these are (all) in very truth the believers: for them is the forgiveness of sins and a provision most generous. And those who accept faith subsequently and adopt exile and fight [*jihad*] for the faith in your company they are of you. But kindred by blood have prior rights against each other in the Book of Allah. Verily, Allah is well acquainted with all things.

The "way of fighting" was also a matter of revelation:

Say to the unbelievers if (now) they desist (from unbelief) their past would be forgiven them; but if they persist the punishment of those before them is already (a matter of warning for them). And fight [*qitaal*] them on until there is no more tumult or oppression and there prevail justice and faith in Allah altogether and everywhere; but if they cease, verily Allah doth see all that they do. If they refuse be sure that Allah is your protector the best to protect and the best to help. (Surah 8:38–41)

Jihad is limited on several counts. One is that the enemy is given the opportunity to become a believer, according to Yusuf Ali's parenthetical insertion. The passage could be interpreted differently. The Qurayshi moved to attack the Muslims as part of their campaign to destroy Islam. The ayas indicate that if and when the opponents desist from their plans and actions to defeat the faithful and the faith, the jihad will be ended. In that sense jihad is defensive, not aggressive. The expectation seems to be that the enemies will become monotheists and establish a just society. The implication may be that the foe will gradually adopt Islam. A second and related limitation comes at Surah 8:61: "But if the enemy inclines toward peace [*salaam*], do thou also incline towards peace [*salaam*] and trust is Allah, for He is the One who heareth and knoweth (all things)."

As noted earlier, the Battle of Badr raised another issue: the disposition of the plunder taken in a jihad. A war or conflict for the cause and in the way of God was not undertaken to enrich the fighters. Surah 8's traditional title, "The Spoils of War" (al-Anfal), indicates that the umma comes first. All booty was put into a common pool. From it various shares were distributed so there was to be no greedy taking on the battlefield or squabbling in the battle's aftermath. The share given to the Messenger was quickly given to those widowed and orphaned in the battle, then to the needy in the umma. Those who engaged directly in the battle shared equally in another portion. The individuals who were willing but unable physically to fight or did not have the proper equipment or were assigned to stay in Medina received their due shares as well.

The Battle of Badr established several important precedents for jihads. First, a jihad is undertaken by God's command and under a person who is authorized to be the leader of the struggle. Second, it is God who gives victory, no matter how daunting the odds may be for the Muslims. Third, jihad is limited and may be ended when the enemy "inclines toward peace" or seeks conversion or agrees to stop hostile actions against Islam and Muslims. Fourth, prisoners taken at the battle was not slaughtered or abused. The practice of ransoming captives or enslaving them was common. Prisoners were also given the option of converting to Islam and then being treated as fellow Believers. But Badr was not the last battle.

From Badr to Uhud

Several weeks after the victory at Badr, Muhammad began to consolidate Muslim-Medinan influence among the surrounding bedouin tribes and to reduce or eliminate those who resisted the state that was emerging under his leadership. His efforts brought him into conflict with some Arab chiefs and Jewish settlements.[62] Some of Ibn Ishaq's lengthy recounting of events in Medina involving the deteriorating relationships between Jews and Muhammad may come from this interim period or shortly after the Battle of Uhud.[63] At the same time the Medinans prevented Meccan caravans from making the round-trip journey between Syria and the Holy City unscathed. The Meccan leader, Abu Sufyan, gathered his forces and allies to attack Medina. A number of Medinans who opposed Muhammad directly and covertly, as well as some Jewish leaders, conspired against Muhammad and the Muslims. In March 625 more than 3,000 Meccan warriors on foot and mounted on camels joined battle with some 700 Muslims in the valley at the foot of Mount Uhud fewer than twenty miles from Medina. Muhammad expected to field a larger army, but at the last hour several valued contingents went over to the enemy or deserted him.

Muhammad had a sound battle plan as well as divine assurance that if his soldiers conducted themselves in the way of God and took no plunder during the fighting, he would win. A number of his archers disobeyed his clear instructions, broke ranks, and started to loot the enemy camp and bodies. The Meccan counterattack almost overwhelmed the Muslims, and Muhammad himself was wounded. The Muslims were able to disengage and return to their city. The Meccans, however, did not win a clear victory. They were unable to rout the Muslims and follow their advantage at Uhud so as to assault Medina. If anything, the Battle of Uhud was indecisive. If any of the Faithful took the result of the battle as a sign that God deserted them or that the Messenger was a poor leader, such thoughts were corrected by revelations now in Surah 3.[64]

It was not the jihad that failed at the Battle of Uhud but the Muslims who failed to obey God through the Messenger. Instead, they were led by Satan to satisfy greed and then to lost confidence in their dependence on God. In the latter sense, they failed God's test of their obedience. What happened at Uhud was symptomatic of events and conspiracies in Medina. Soon after (some think soon before) the battle, Muhammad followed God's directions to change the direction of the qiblah. Also after the battle, Muhammad took bold steps to organize the umma on the basis of the Revelation concerning morals, family life, and law. Uhud stands as a warning to Muslims that if they follow their own interests, departing thereby from the way and cause of God, they risk defeat and humiliation.

From Uhud to the Trench and Early Aftermath

On March 31, 627, the huge army of confederated opponents to Muhammad, Medina, and Islam began to lay siege to Medina. The Battle of the Trench, actually a lengthy struggle at the end of which the Confederates withdrew, resulted in the treaty of Hudaybiyyah in 628. The termination of the treaty led to the surrender and conversion of Meccans and others to Islam, the crushing of the Jewish communities whose leaders collaborated with the Confederates, and the adherence of bedouin tribes to Muhammad.

Surah 2:190–93 and Surah 9, often cited as portions that abrogate earlier ayas concerning jihad, was revealed in the context of the Battle of the Trench and its aftermath. Surah 33 (al-Ahzab, the Confederates,) may be read as a dramatic account of the situation during the siege. Surah 33:9–27 depicts the panic, dissension, and testing of the Hypocrites and believers as the struggle wore on. Some of the Medinan Hypocrites moaned that all Muhammad revealed to them was delusions (33:12), and others were plainly cowards who wanted to guard their own possessions in spite of the agreement they made with Muhammad to be loyal to God and the Messenger (33:13). Defeatists predicted that the enemy was certain to cross the ditch and put the defenders to the sword (33:13), so it would be better to revolt against Muhammad and surrender the city on the best possible terms (33:14). True believers, however, were convinced that Muhammad was God-inspired and that they would be obedient to God and loyal to Muhammad (33:22–23). God sustained and vindicated Muhammad through a devastating windstorm and invisible celestial forces that scattered the enemy (33:9). Even after the Confederates withdrew, the doubters and complainers predicted that the enemy would return in greater force to slaughter whom they could (33:20). The section also makes clear that a number of People of the Book showed themselves disloyal and even treasonous during the struggle (33:24–26). God then granted that the property of those who were expelled the city and the surrounding area was to be given to the believers (33:27).

Surah 9 and Surah 2:190–93, read in context, do not abrogate previous passages or propose that they are now the only ways to construe jihad-qitaal in the way of and for the cause of God. "Read in context" does not mean, however, that these passages can be domesticated. They do inculcate fighting, yet not as a universal Islamic policy. A brief summary of the events from 628 to 630 puts them in historical perspective. Recalling the historical survey of chapter 5, both the Byzantine and Persian Empires were in states of disarray and weakness, leaving the Arabian Peninsula relatively free of foreign domination and open to incursions from Arabia. By the Treaty of Hudaybiyyah Muhammad gained significant stature as the leader of what was becoming the most powerful and wealthiest state in Arabia. The Muslims also gained the agreement of the Meccans that they would be able to undertake the Hajj in 629. The Meccans withdrew from the city during the time the Muslims (without Muhammad) performed their rites in and around the Ka'bah. From 628 to 630 the Muslims under Muhammad's leadership consolidated their control over Arabia by bringing the bedouin into their orbit, sometimes forcefully, sometimes by conflict, and by gaining authority over Taif and other towns as well as bringing Yemen into the Islamic orbit. In late summer 630, or perhaps in October, the Messenger led a 3,000-man expedition to Tabuk on the border between Arabia and Syria in order to do battle with a reported Byzantine force. The Byzantine contingents were not where he expected, but on the march he gained the grudging loyalty of various nomadic tribes. Between the 629 Hajj and early 630 relations deteriorated between the Meccans and their allies on the one hand and the Muslims on the other. After a series of incidents Muhammad received the revelation to scrap the Treaty of Hudaybiyyah. Surah 9 opens with that repudiation and the forecast of what would happen if the Meccans decided to defend the city. In that context the sternest words about jihad-qitaal were revealed.

Surah 9 opens with the announcement that the treaty would be terminated at the end of four months. Surah 9:4 provides a condition that those unbelievers who have not violated the treaty or given aid to those who oppose the Muslims will be exempt from the treaty's repudiation. They will be secure until the stated end of the agreement in 638 (9:4, 7). A possible underlying reason may be that the treaty was a temporary arrangement that allowed time for a more permanent settlement to be reached, a settlement that by implication involves the cleansing of the Ka'bah and the establishment of Islam as the religion of Mecca. Muslims would not engage in any surprise ambushes or battles during the four-month period that probably included sacred months. If, however, polytheist partners to the treaty would convert to the Faith, there would be no hostilities.

A closer reading of Surah 9 indicates that any permanent treaty with the idolaters of Mecca was bound to disadvantage the Islamic cause and the Muslim umma:

> How can there be a league before Allah and His Messenger with the pagans except those with whom ye made a treaty near the sacred mosque? As long as these stand true to you stand ye true to them: For Allah doth love the righteous. How (can there be such a league) seeing that if they get an advantage over you, they respect not in you the ties either of kinship or of covenant? With (fair words from) their mouths they entice you, but their hearts are averse from you; and most of them are rebellious and wicked. The signs of Allah have they sold for a miserable price and (many) have they hindered from His way: evil indeed are the deeds they have done. In a Believer they respect not the ties either of kinship or of covenant! It is they who have transgressed all bounds. But (even so) if they repent establish regular prayers and practice regular charity, they are your brethren in faith: (thus) do We explain signs in detail for those who understand. But if they violate their oaths after their covenant and taunt you for your faith, fight ye the chiefs of unfaith: for their oaths are nothing to them: that thus they may be restrained. Will ye not fight people who violated their oaths plotted to expel the apostle and took the aggressive by being the first (to assault) you? Do ye fear them? Nay it is Allah whom ye should more justly fear, if ye believe! Fight them and Allah will punish them by your hands cover them with shame help you (to victory) over them heal the breasts of believers. (Surah 9:7–14)

Surah 2:190–93 addresses the same situation as Surah 9:

> Fight in the cause [*jihad*] of Allah those who fight you but do not transgress limits; for Allah loveth not transgressors. And slay them wherever ye catch them and turn them out from where they have

turned you out; for tumult and oppression are worse than slaughter; but fight them not at the Sacred Mosque unless they (first) fight [*jihad*] you there; but if they fight you slay them. Such is the reward of those who suppress faith. But if they cease Allah is Oft-Forgiving, Most Merciful. And fight them [*jihad*] on until there is no more tumult or oppression and there prevail justice and faith in Allah; but if they cease let there be no hostility except to those who practice oppression. (Surah 2:190–93)

Except for 9:38, a reference to the malingerers on the Tabuk expedition, Surah 9 and Surah 2:190–93 in their original settings are directed to the specific situation that resulted in the surrender of Mecca with very little bloodshed. To cite the Surah's view of jihad to justify continual conflict against non-Muslims is an expansion that is arguable at best.

TO THIS POINT we have traced the meanings of important terms used in the Qur'an with jihad, found interpretations of jihad that argued for and against expanding the term to continual warfare, and considered how jihad language was used in Muhammad's contexts. I hold that later passages did not abrogate earlier passages and that the concepts covered by jihad are best considered in their Quranic contexts. Nevertheless, jihad's original root meaning of struggle, earnestness, power, ability, and fighting express purposeful, determined, faithful action—including war—in and for the cause and way of God.

JIHAD'S MOMENTUM FOR CONTINUAL RELEVANCE

Fighting is prescribed upon you, and ye dislike it. But it
is possible that ye dislike a thing which is good for you.
And ye love a thing which is bad for you . . .

Surah 2:216

Of all the aspects of Islam, two emerge as the most problematic for many Muslims and almost all non-Muslims: women and jihad. Numerous Muslim societies are seeking to deal forthrightly with the former.[65] Jihad, however, is a complex and demonstratively dangerous topic.[66] Struggle, conflict, effort, and war have momentums that take them across centuries and continents.

On the basis of the Qur'an, I discern six "momentums" acting on jihad's energy in the twenty-first century:

1. Witnessing at all times to the Faith, especially when Islam is in a minority position in society;
2. Opposing treacherous hypocrites and dhimmi in predominantly Islamic societies;
3. Defending Islam from external enemies;
4. Recovering territory that once was Muslim;
5. Extending the territory ruled by Islamic justice; and
6. Stopping the spread of apostasy and heresy and punishing apostates and heretics.

Each of these has serious applications to the twenty-first century. Momentums 2 and 6 are applicable especially by those who seek to overturn governments that regard themselves as Muslim, that is, based on the Qur'an and Sunna, but that are not deemed genuinely Islamic by their detractors. Momentums 1 and 5 are applicable in terms of dedicated witnesses to Islam, the Qur'an, and the Messenger. In some sub-Saharan areas such as Nigeria this is taking the form of imposing versions of Islamic law in regions that are not yet officially Muslim. Momentum 4 is especially critical to the conflict involving the state of Israel, the Palestinians, and the Muslim nations opposed to Israel. Some militant Islamists seek to add Spain to the Islamic world. In addition, there are large organizations that engage in social service projects and charity while carrying on military-style operations under the banner of jihad.[67] Momentum 3, defending Islam from external enemies, can take the form of preemptive strikes against nations, institutions, and systems by those who have the motivation and means. Those individuals and groups are convinced that the "enemy" is attacking

Islam directly or indirectly through anti-Islamic economic policies, assaults on Islamic morality via mass media, defamatory publications, and suborning officials and leaders. The West, especially the United States, has been the enemy of such persons and groups.

A critical issue among Muslims is who has the authority to proclaim a jihad. Modern Twelver Shiʻites have declined numerous opportunities to declare a jihad because of their conviction that only the Hidden Imam bears such authority. Among Sunni Muslims the situation is mixed. Various teachers and others who claim authority have and probably will declare jihads. Their authority rests with those men and women who accept such authority and act accordingly. So the charismatic Osama bin Laden (al-Qaeda, "the Foundation") and supporting shaykhs declared jihad against the government of Saudi Arabia and the United States. The blind Egyptian shaykh Umar Abdel Rahman (Jamaʻat al-Islamiyyah) allegedly inspired the assassins of Egypt's president, Anwar Sadat (1980), was accused of complicity in the 1993 attack on New York's World Trade Center, and was convicted of plotting to blow up several New York facilities and monuments. Mullah Muhammad Omar provided the spiritual energy and apparently some of the strategy of the Taliban. Other Muslim leaders condemn such militants and consider those who attack civilians and often destroy themselves damned rather than martyrs. Given the Shiʻite avoidance of the term *jihad* and the absence of a centralized authority among Sunni Muslims, jihad is used by militant groups that recruit and deploy what John Kelsay calls "soldiers without portfolio."[68]

Nevertheless, jihad has definite positive and constructive momentum. The first momentum cited, "Witnessing at all times to the Faith, especially when Islam is in a minority position in society," is a vital concern among Muslims and, for sometimes conflicting reasons, among non–Muslims. Within predominantly Muslim lands religious teachers and government officials are being challenged to examine and change, where necessary, their educational patterns so that believers of all ages are able to meet and express the Faith in a globalized economy with shifting societal patterns. Muslims in minority contexts struggle with expressing the Faith and their devotion to it when there are legal and social constraints on wearing distinctive religious garb such as veils and head coverings, setting aside places and times at work or school for prayer, and handling the pervasive influence of Western secularizing media. In light or under the shadow of violence in word and deed by militant Islamists, how can Muslims explain who they are, what they believe, and how they relate to their surroundings? What are the roles of and needed levels of support for mosques and religious schools? Jihad will mean thoughtful, creative, and earnest struggle for many Muslims living in the West. And that will include attracting and bringing into the umma converts to Islam.

The same momentum has possibilities for Muslims to engage persons of goodwill from the so-called majority culture. The dimensions of jihad include positive as well as negative relationships with the People of the Book. Areas of common endeavor without compromising one's broader faith commitments need exploration. Perhaps opening the Qur'an together may be an initial step.

Fazlur Rahman and, in his own situation, Sayyid Qutb understood jihad in terms of the struggle for justice. They claimed, with considerable justification, that Islam is an intensely practical religion grounded in God as the Creator and the world as made to respond to Him. Hunger, poverty, and oppression, as well as immense wealth, power, and pride, may be simultaneously demonic deceptions and tests from God. The Qur'an, as the final revelation, included all the previous revelations about justice and human responsibility. Jihad, then, is the determined and varied striving and effort to care for the creation and to care for all humans.

> Let those fight in the cause of Allah who sell the life of this world for the Hereafter. To him who fighteth in the cause of Allah, whether he is slain or gets victory, soon shall We give him a reward of great (value). And why should ye not fight in the cause of Allah and of those who being weak are ill-treated (and oppressed)? Men women and children whose cry is: "Our Lord! Rescue us from this town whose people are oppressors; and raise for us from Thee one who will protect; and raise for us from Thee one who will help!" Those who believe fight in the cause of Allah and those who reject faith fight in the cause of evil. So fight ye against the friends of Satan: feeble indeed is the cunning of Satan. (Surah 4:74–76)

JUSTICE AND JIHAD belong together. They are woven throughout the Qur'an and Islamic history. Justice without jihad might become a series of principles and rules without energy. Jihad without justice is a denial of the very nature of Islam: earnest strivings, struggles, and even fighting for the cause of God and in the way of the God who is all-gracious, merciful, and just. How justice-jihad expresses and implements the will of the One-Only God for and in this world is an ongoing challenge for Muslims and non-Muslims.

> Allah chooses Messengers from angels and from men: for Allah is He Who hears and sees (all things). He knows what is before them and what is behind them: and to Allah go back all questions (for decision). O ye who believe! bow down prostrate yourselves and adore your Lord; and do good, that ye may prosper. And strive in His cause as ye ought to strive (with sincerity and under discipline). He has chosen you and has imposed no difficulties on you in religion; it is the cult of your father Abraham. It is He Who has named you Muslims both before and in this (Revelation); that the Messenger may be a witness for you and ye be witnesses for mankind! So establish regular Prayer, give regular Charity, and hold fast to Allah! He is your Protector, the Best to protect, and the Best to help! (Surah 22:75–78)

CONCLUSION

Thus far we have opened the Qur'an through a series of increasingly intense studies that culminated in what are probably the most difficult issues raised by and to Muslims and non-Muslims. Ever-present have been pressing concerns such as the relationships between the People of the Book and Muslims, the roles of women, and interpretations of jihad. The two essential factors in engaging the Qur'an have been the relationship of passages and themes to the Qur'an's underlying unity and the contexts in which Muhammad received and transmitted the Revelation to those around him. Those factors have kept us anchored in the text so that we could follow and be open to the momentum the Qur'an generates into the present.

Islam is a religion that claims the total loyalty of individuals and societies that venture to call themselves Islamic. The forms of worship set the agendas of daily life; the Pillars and Teachings integrate individuals into local communities, then step by step to the worldwide umma. The Qur'an provides directions as rules and guidance at every major step along the Straight Path. At the same time serious and searching questions about the challenges posed by modernization, Westernization, and tensions in the Muslim world are being raised by Muslims and non-Muslims alike.

The Word of thy Lord doth find its fulfillment in truth and in justice. None can change His Words, for He is the one Who heareth and knoweth all. (Surah 6:115)

PART III

THE EVER-OPEN QUR'AN

Whoever submits his whole self to Allah and is a doer of
good has grasped indeed the most trustworthy hand-hold:
and with Allah rests the End and Decision of (all) affairs. But
if any reject Faith, let not his rejection grieve thee. To Us is
their return, and We shall tell them the truth of their deeds:
for Allah knows well all that is in (men's) hearts. We grant
them their pleasure for a little while: in the end shall We
drive them to a chastisement unrelenting. If thou ask them
who it is that created the heavens and the earth they will
certainly say "Allah." Say: "Praise be to Allah!" But most of
them understand not. To Allah belong all things in heaven
and earth: verily Allah is He (that is) free of all wants, worthy
of all praise. And if all the trees on earth were pens and the
Ocean (were ink) with seven Oceans behind it to add to its
(supply), yet would not the Words of Allah be exhausted (in
the writing): for Allah is Exalted in Power, Full of Wisdom.

Surah 31:22–27

The Qur'an is an open book. From the beginning of the revelation the
Message was shared, then gradually became more public. Today and into
the foreseeable future millions of women and men will open it in Arabic
and in interpretation-translations. It will continue to inspire, confuse, and
offend those who seek to understand it. The Qur'an is "open" in that it
is available to believers and nonbelievers, interpreters within Islam, those
curious about Islam and the Book, and those who will criticize the Book
and Islam. Once the Book has been opened and made public, the umma
cannot fully control what others make of it. During our journey, I sought
to have the Qur'an speak for itself in its context as the basis for the Faith of
Islam and in its context in the time of Muhammad and the first umma.
Along the way I have indicated areas of potential momentum for the
present.

Part III brings us into the "nearly present" and points toward the future. Chapter 13 introduces three of a number of approaches current among Muslims as they use the Qur'an to confront the umma and the West. Chapter 14 cites two major types of criticism brought against the Qur'an and, thereby, against Islam. The closing chapter reflects on where we have been, how to read the Qur'an now, and how we might respond to the questions raised in chapter 1. A brief coda concludes—and begins— our journey.

> To Allah belongeth the dominion of the heavens and the earth; and Allah hath power over all things. (Surah 3:200)

THIRTEEN

CHALLENGES FROM THE QUR'AN

To every People have we appointed rites and ceremonies
which they must follow. Let them not then dispute with
thee on the matter, but do thou invite (them) to thy Lord:
for thou art assuredly on the Right Way. If they do wrangle
with thee say, "Allah knows best what it is ye are doing."

Surah 22:67–68

Iqra! Read! Recite! Proclaim! The words Muhammad began to hear on
the Night of Power still challenge men and women to obey the One-Only
God. Political to its core, social in its structures, missionary in its purpose,
and confident in its ultimate success, Islam always challenges its believers
and others to respond to God, the Message, and the Messenger. Quranically energized Islam has endured sweeping dynastic changes, the Western
Enlightenment and its several cultural aftermaths, the rise and fall of indigenous and invading empires, colonialism and imperialism, nationalist
and ethnic emphases, and grave internal strife. *Iqra!* is still the living voice
that moves Muslims to proclaim the God who is revealed in all times, all
cultures, and finally in the Qur'an, which summons every person to obey
His will in every aspect of life.

This chapter presents some key challenges posed by the Qur'an
and by those who use the Qur'an. First, we return to a discussion of the

Transcendent Time of the Revelation. Second, we set, although briefly, the context for the current Islamic resurgence. Third, we turn to three uses of the Qur'an in the current Islamic resurgence that I refer to as Revolution, Reformation, and Neo-Awakening.

THE REVELATORY TIME

By (the Token of) time (through the Ages), verily Man is in loss,
Except such as have Faith and do righteous deeds, and (join together)
in the mutual teaching of Truth and of Patience and Constancy.
Surah 103, al 'Asr, Time through the Ages

The Time that transcends all times encompassed twenty-two to twenty-three years, from the Night of Power to Muhammad's death. God's action in that brief period provides the basis for human society and sets the course for the consummation of all times.

God's revelations in the Qur'an to the Messenger, the Messenger's obedience to his Lord, and the establishment of the umma are the core of the Revelatory Time. One human lived so Islamically that he and the community he shaped are the model for all times and persons to emulate in obedience to God. Three consequences of the Revelatory Time call for comment.

First, the Qur'an and Muhammad's Sunna are unchangeable, yet interpretations may be offered and understandings deepened. Muslims are wary, however, of un-Islamic innovations (*bid 'ah*) that will corrupt the Faith and the Faithful. The Qur'an does not need to be updated, adapted, or adjusted to subsequent cultures and conditions. Later times and people are challenged to measure up to the Qur'an's revelations of God's will and the best ways for humans to live. God's tawhid, the Qur'an, Muhammad, and the first umma are the basis on which Muslims and non-Muslims engage, adjust, accept, or reject the changes and values of their times. Because Islam claims that all wisdom and creative abilities come from God and are intended for the establishment of justice in the world prior to the Day of Judgment, Islam is the most modern religion and the best way of life.

The second consequence of the Revelatory Time is its challenge to current societies. God demands that all societies structure themselves in Islamic-style justice and equity. Are the Quranic passages dealing with issues such as social and legal matters, usury and economics, family relations and spousal duties, rules about inheritance and bequests, treatment of criminals and nonbelievers, conflict and war to be enacted and institutionalized in times that are far different from those of seventh-century Arabia? Is Islam limited to individual piety and customs? Is the Qur'an being manipulated by teachers controlled by governments claiming to be Islamic? A growing number of Believers insist that God wills the implementation of Qur'an's societal directives so that Muslims will establish an Islamic society or "nation," that is, an umma unrestricted by borders, ethnicities, cultural traditions, economic systems, or political compromises. Militant Islamists hold that God commands Muslims to create an umma that uses the Qur'an and Muhammad's Sunna as its core and the Mecca-Medina umma as its operational model. That will mean changing, even ousting, regimes that are hypocritical and corrupt in their alleged adherence to the Faith. And that includes confronting foreign unbelievers who support such regimes.

The two consequences raise the third: leadership. Muhammad's death initiated a crisis in the umma's leadership that persists into the present. For several decades Muslims used the word *caliph* for the person who exercised spiritual and political leadership in the umma. The rapid spread of Islam together with the divisions over leadership chiefly along the lines of Sunni and Shi'ia led to the development of over leadership offices, caliph and sultan.[1] Roughly, *sultan* has the sense of God-given political authority, and the caliph was the chief religious leader-interpreter. Sultan and caliph were to work in harmony, with the sultan being advised by the caliph and his circle of jurists and scholars. The Ottomans reasoned that a true Islamic nation-umma could be established only if there was a devout and competent sultanate along with a vibrant, faithful caliphate.[2] The obverse is that if the sultanate and caliphate were abolished, Islam would be seriously endangered, corrupt leaders would pervert the Faithful, and damnable bid'ah would open the realm of Islam to infiltration from the realm of unbelief and deception.

Shi'ia leadership differed. Eventually the Persian shahs recognized a cadre of Twelver imam-leaders, the *ulama,* and gave them authority to decide matters of religious law regarding the health and welfare of believers and to distribute funds to the poor. The imams developed a system of educating and certifying other imams so that the imamate came to resemble a guild of learned, devout, and skilled men connected to the people rather than to imperial authority. Until the 1960s Shi'ia imams tended to be overtly apolitical but had definite influence among most levels of society, except for an aristocratic, Westernized elite close to and including the last Iranian shah, Reza Pahlevi (1919–80). Since the triumph of the Islamic revolution in Iran (1979), Shi'ia leaders in Iran and Iraq has been intensely involved in politics and governance.

Sunni and Shi'ia Muslims trace their forms of leadership in the Qur'an and Sunna of the Revelatory Time. The restoration and implementation of authoritative leadership in the umma is a challenge being pressed by militant Islamists.

A Brief Examination of Times after the Revelatory Time

Muslim political-social structures and authority in areas where Islam is the dominant religion underwent far-reaching and generally negative developments. A full recounting of events and personalities is outside the scope of this study.[3] I offer here a description of what has become a crisis of confidence and leadership and the resurgence of Islamic-Quranic fervor relevant to understanding and using the Qur'an.[4]

From the late 1600s to the end of World War II, Muslim political stability, economic drive, and confidence diminished significantly.[5] Muslim rulers and elites borrowed increasingly and superficially from secularizing Euro-Christians. The result was a broad cultural-political-economic vulnerability to Western influence and expansion. During the seventeenth through nineteenth century Britain, France, Holland, the Austro-Hungarian

Empire, Spain, and Russia acquired colonies and spheres of influence from China through Morocco, from the Nile Delta to the Cape of Good Hope, from the Indian subcontinent and the Malaysian-Burmese peninsulas to the Pacific islands. Much of the European expansion was at the expense of the Muslim Ottoman Empire. At its territorial zenith in the 1690s the Ottomans ruled much of Hungary, the Balkans, the Middle East including Arabia, and most of North Africa. As the Ottoman bureaucracy faltered and the empire lost territory, respect, and authority as a result of wars and ineptness, two nineteenth-century sultans embarked on a reform plan called the Reorganization, or Tanzimat. Tanzimat welcomed Westerners and Western values into the empire, making the Ottomans increasingly dependent on the western Europeans.[6] In the remainder of the nineteenth century the decline of the Ottoman Empire continued. Almost incidentally for the Ottomans but of future consequence for the region, European Jews began to immigrate to Palestine.[7] When oil was discovered in Iran in 1908, the Muslim world took on new significance for Russia and the West.

World War I prompted major changes for Muslims as well as for the rest of the world. The Ottoman Empire was one of the Central Powers.[8] Some Arab theorists hoped that the postwar settlement would result in an "Arab nation" that would unite the Arab peoples in a coherent confederation. From the perspective of the Muslim world and Arab nationalists, the treaties and actions of the white Euro-Christian imperialist nations in the 1920s betrayed the Arab people.[9] Stunned by the corruption and collapse of the Ottoman state and convinced that the "backwardness" of their fellow Turks was largely due to reactionary Muslim religious authorities, a group of Turkish army officers led by Mustafa Kemal (later Ataturk, 1881–1938) staged a successful coup (1920). The new and determinedly pro-Western secular government abolished the sultanate (1922), proclaimed Turkey a republic (1923), and dissolved the caliphate (March 23, 1924). The rapid steps that followed superficially secularized Turkey, marginalized Islam, and pleased the elite that sought a future tying Turkey to Europe.[10] Conservative Muslims were appalled. Many thought that a restoration of the caliphate and a return to Islamic faith and values was God's will—and the duty of all right-thinking Muslims to pursue. Considering the termination of the caliphate the biggest calamity for Islam and revolted by the corruption of Egypt's government, a number of Egyptian intellectual-activists formed the Muslim Brotherhood in 1928.[11] Throughout the 1920s and 1930s Western petroleum companies developed and exploited oil fields in the Arabian Peninsula, the Persian Gulf, Iraq, and Iran.[12] The West's economic, political, and cultural penetration in the Islamic world included Christian missionaries, often from the United States. They established schools, hospitals, and orphanages. The flow of Jewish immigrants into Palestine increased after the 1933 Nazi accession to power in Germany. Nationalist anticolonialist movements spread from North Africa through the Indian subcontinent and Malaysia and into the Dutch East Indies. At times they appealed to Islam and the Qur'an but were motivated largely by anti-imperialism. Sometimes cooperatively, yet often in tension with the nationalists, Islamists also began to see Islam as the way to liberation, morality, and justice.

World War II set the stage for the resurgence within Islam and widespread struggles for independence from foreign powers. The war revealed that the secularized Euro–North American–Christian nations fought ferociously among themselves and used weapons of mass destruction against one another. The once-subjugated peoples of Africa, the Middle East, and Asia realized they could successfully fight their former colonial masters. They also were caught up in the cold war in which a pro-American bloc was pitted against a Soviet bloc. Both Superpowers attempted to bring predominantly Muslim nations into their spheres of influence. The struggle for mastery between the two camps involved geopolitical strategies and access to petroleum. One result was the enriching of some oil-producing governments and the concomitant penetration of secularizing Western and Marxist cultural influences in traditionally Islamic societies.

Before World War II some Arab leaders' visions of a secular Pan-Arab nation or a Pan-Islamic nation sometimes overlapped, with advocates of both recognizing that one could be used as a temporary stepping-stone to the other, but each realized the long-term incompatibility of their ideals. In 1945 the League of Arab States (usually known as the Arab League) was established.[13] After a deranged Australian Christian attempted to set fire to the al-Aqsa Mosque (August, 21, 1969), considered the third holiest site in Islam, a number of Muslim representatives met in Rabat, Morocco, to establish the Organization of the Islamic Conference (OIC). This international body of fifty-six nations parallels the intentions of the League of Arab Nations but with decided international Islamic aims such as strengthening Islamic solidarity among members, fighting colonialism, and assisting the Palestinian people to recover their rights and liberate their occupied territories.[14] The OIC, as does the Arab League, seeks to avert conflicts and violence among member states through negotiation and discussion.

Two other factors have had an impact on Islam and the world after 1945. On the Indian subcontinent Mohammad Iqbal (1877–1938) and Abul A'la Maududi (1903–79) agitated for a Muslim state within India while Mohammad Ali Jinnah (1876–1948) worked for a "moderate" Muslim nation separate from a Hindu-dominated India. The result was the partition of the subcontinent into theoretically secular India and Muslim Pakistan. Maududi worked tirelessly for what he considered a genuinely Muslim nation. The second instance is the formation of the state of Israel in May 1948. From Arab and many Muslim perspectives, the establishment and maintenance of what some prefer to call "the Zionist entity" was a Western political-cultural invasion and an illegitimate occupation of Arab territory and of land that is holy to Islam. The Arab-Israeli conflicts enmeshed the Arab world, the Muslim world, and the Soviet and American antagonists of the cold war.[15] The region has been embroiled in violence both physical and verbal. Among the Muslim organizations that emerged are the Jama'at al-Jihad (the organization that assassinated President Sadat in 1981 and whose views are presented in *The Neglected Duty*); the Palestinian Liberation Organization (PLO, a fragile coalition of religious and secular groups organized in 1970); and the Lebanese Harakat al-Mahrumin (Movement of the Deprived), Amal (1975), and Hizbullah.[16] Hamas (Harakat al-Muqawamah al-Islamyyia, Islamic Resistance Movement) formed in the 1980s among Palestinians.[17]

The last three decades of the twentieth century saw the overthrow of the Pahlevi regime in Iran, the establishment of the Islamic Republic of Iran (1979) and subsequent rupture of relations between Iran and the United States, and the Iran-Iraq War (1980–88). The 1979 seizure of the Grand Mosque in Mecca by a madhi-expecting group was a symptom of increasing hostility to the government of Saudi Arabia, the Soviet incursions into Afghanistan (1973, 1978), and the U.S. support of anti-Soviet resistance groups, including those associated with Osama bin Laden. Bin Ladin established al-Qaeda, the Foundation, in 1986. Among the plethora of events that continued throughout the 1990s and into the twenty-first century were the intifadas, or uprisings, in Israeli-occupied Palestinian territories, the Iraqi invasion of Kuwait (1990), and the resulting U.N. and U.S.-led military action to drive the Iraqis from Kuwait. The latter campaign moved bin Laden to commit like-minded Muslims to driving Western powers and influences from Muslim lands, reestablishing the caliphate, restoring Islam to its past glory, and overthrowing what they consider Muslim apostate governments. Subsequently, various groups from Indonesia through Spain, from India to Jersey City, New Jersey, from Kabul to Chechnya were inspired by al-Qaeda and similar groups to read the Qur'an as God's summons to qitaal-jihad as they understood it. The motivations and actions of such persons, although few in number, are beyond the scope of this study.[18]

As the twentieth century ended and the twenty-first began the United States sustained attacks on embassies, the World Trade Center, the Pentagon, and military installations—all with the perpetrators using the Qur'an and Hadith for justification.[19] The October 2001 U.N.-sanctioned invasion of Afghanistan to capture bin Laden and his associates and the 2003 U.S.-led invasion of Iraq were seen by many Muslims as anti-Islamic actions that recalled the language and intentions of medieval crusaders. Shortly before the attack on Iraq began, Shaykh al-Azhar issued "An Appeal to the Civilized World and to All Peace-Loving Powers." He stopped just short of considering Muslim defensive response as a jihad.[20]

Yet Muslim reactions to secularizing Western influences and power, especially in a globalized economy, are part of a larger and more explosive issue in the resurgence of Islamic consciousness. The postcolonial Muslim world is crowded with poor, striving persons who understand themselves as betrayed by their leaders. Many, especially the youthful, turn to Islam's Holy Book to provide answers, incentives, and power. Their often-repressive regimes promise reforms and an equitable sharing of fiscal resources, improved health care, and sound educational advances, but dire conditions remain entrenched. A few nations, such as Sudan and Ethiopia and the central Asian republics of the former Soviet Union, tried Marxism; it did not work. Others have tried Euro-American capitalism; it has not improved their lives either. Increasingly, the call, as put by the Muslim Brotherhood, is "Islam is the answer!" And that means turning to the Qur'an and its message for social justice and change through obedience to the One-Only God.

THE QUR'AN'S CHALLENGES FOCUSED

Whatever is in the heavens and on earth doth declare the
Praises and Glory of Allah: to Him belongs Dominion and
to Him belongs Praise: and He has power over all things.
It is He Who has created you; and of you are some that are
Unbelievers and some that are Believers: and Allah sees well
all that ye do. He has created the heavens and the earth in just
proportions and has given you shape and made your shapes
beautiful: and to Him is the final Goal. He knows what is in
the heavens and on earth: and He knows what ye conceal and
what ye reveal. Yes Allah knows well the (secrets) of (all) hearts.

Surah 64:1–4

The resurgence of Islamic consciousness is energized by activist appeals to and interpretations of the Qur'an, the Messenger, and the umma. The Qur'an is living speech through which God addresses all times and all peoples. Humanity, not the Qur'an, develops. Below I discuss three ways in which individuals or groups use the Qur'an to challenge fellow Muslims and non-Muslims.[21] I term them the revolutionary challengers, a reformation challenger, and neo-awakening challengers.

REVOLUTIONARY CHALLENGERS

Sayyid Qutb, Abdul A'la Maududi, and the *Neglected Duty* clearly expressed the Qur'an's challenges. Each is used by advocates of violent actions and makes use of Quranic references and insights.

Sayyid Qutb

Even after his death in 1966 Qutb has remained the leading intellectual voice for the Brotherhood and radical Islamists.[22] Following the failure of the Nasserites to implement the reforms Qutb and the Brotherhood advocated, the Brotherhood moved in two directions, both claiming Qutb as its guide. One adopted aggressive tactics against what they consider pseudo-Muslim governments and their Western allies; the other opts for a gradual process of change. Both retained the goal of establishing an Islamic state that would restore the caliphate and establish an international Islamic nation.

Most of Qutb's thirty-volume tafsir was written while he was imprisoned. *In the Shade of the Qur'an* differs from most earlier tafsirs on several counts. One is the obvious skipping of the technical philological considerations of words and passages and the addition of pages of citations from earlier commentators and Hadith collections. Second, it is clearly hortatory and does not shun sharp polemics, especially against Zionism and Western secularism. Third, as his brother, Mohammad Qutb, observed, the *Shade* "is a campaign of struggle, because it is much more than a 'commentary' on the Qur'an."[23] Since, Qutb held, the Qur'an is the God-given constitution for all life, it has a twofold function. The first is to educate the Faithful and all humanity intellectually, communally, and spiritually as to the principles and guides to lift human beings to the high status that God intends for his human creatures. The second function is practical. The Qur'an deals with the realities of human conduct, providing a life-giving code that, if followed, leads to peace among the Believers and then among all peoples. To understand the Qur'an fully, one must read it faithfully and in faith. Qutb tends to deal with clusters of ayas and whole sections rather than with passages in isolation. The result is a tafsir that is inspiringly sermonic and immediate in impact, while it sheds critical light on cultural and political situations. His *Milestones* epitomizes most of his Quranic thinking. His opening the Qur'an and expressing what he discerned as Milestones helps us to understand the Qur'an's challenges.

Qutb wrote largely for the vanguard that will take responsibility for doing God's will. He considered the Revelatory Time the generation of the Messenger and his Companions and Helpers. The preceding period, that of the first Jahiliyyah, is the paradigm for unbelief and the degradation of humanity. The Meccan-Medinan years established the best of all societies, and it is to those principles and values that the world must return. Qutb argued that after the generation of the Messenger corruption and deception infiltrated Islam, beginning a second Jahiliyyah, which is worse than the first. The present umma's mission is to take all positive, constructive, and practicable steps to achieve the Quranic goal for the sake of humanity once more becoming God's caliphs in creation.

Qutb's analysis of the human condition in the second Jahiliyyah affirmed the positive aspects of Western culture in the sciences and humanities as the actions of the God Who is the Source of wisdom. During the Renaissance, the West was animated by creative genius and life-giving values, but lust for power, imperialism, and depraved morality has made the West the leader of the second Jahiliyyah. Clearly, the United States is the present head of the West. Humanity needs a totally different system of life, values, social arrangements, justice, and ideals than it has now. It needs Islam to be the new leader. Islam is the only system that has the values and the structure for that way of life.[24]

If Qutb's strictures on the West are stern and cutting, his attacks on so-called Islamic governments are more so. Islam itself needs to be revived through being restored to its original form. That entails removing the accretions of pagan and other human traditions that have weighed Islam down for centuries. He insisted that Islam is positive and liberating, not regressive or repressive. Tawhid means that obedience to the One God frees humans for faithful action in all areas of their lives. People are to be educated, shown the wisdom of the Islamic way, and encouraged to give their hearts to the God who has created them. There is to be no compulsion in matters of religion; God's truth will be self-evident. Yet Muslims must be persistent. Islam can only be real if it is expressed in the living people and institutions of a society. He projected milestones or guideposts for the vanguard in achieving the goal of a new society that used Muhammad's Mecca and Medina as the ideal patterns. Three milestones are noted.

The first milestone is making the Qur'an the only source for belief, organization, and action. That step entails having the Book-Message become part of the believer's personality through worship, education, home life, public discourse, and social institutions. Qutb advocated a spirituality imbued with the Qur'an, an awareness of the greatness of humanity willed by God, consciousness of the coming Day of Judgment, and the need for justice in all human endeavors. Second, the vanguard is to turn the Quranic instructions into actions. Study leads to actualization. Islam's mission is to establish that humanity-embracing community in which human values and ideals will be harmonized with the external structures of society, all for the praise-obedience of God. That is the true consummation of women and men as God's righteous caliphs. The third milestone is the elimination of all traces of Jahiliyyah ways of thinking and acting. There can be no compromises with the forces of greed, immorality, and injustice. The fruits of Western culture are valuable, but the selfish principles of capitalism, imperialism, and idolatry are to be totally and, if necessary, forcibly rejected. He denounced the sexual permissiveness, materialism, and racism of the United States as evidence that is the center of the Jahiliyyah. As social justice is an imperative for Muslims, Qutb turned toward the Zakat as a major means to alleviate poverty and to meet human need. On the basis of the Qur'an, he offered a vision of what Islam ought do and why—and criticized the existing Muslim states that are covertly and sometimes openly in league with the Western Jahiliyyah powers.

The Neglected Duty

The Neglected Duty (al-Faridah al-Gha'ibah) contains scores of quotations from the Qur'an and Hadith collections and interpretations of medieval and modern commentator-scholars. The Jama'at al-Jihad conspirators denounced Muslim apostates, Western crusaders, Zionist enemies, go-slow reformers, spiritualizing mystics, and manipulated government-appointed imams. Jihad is the duty that has been neglected, delayed, betrayed, domesticated, co-opted, and etherealized. But the jihad of the Qur'an and Sunna is the actual fight against Islam's internal and external enemies. The document's basis is Qutb's two Jahiliyyahs, restoration of the caliphate and establishment of a just society on the basis of the Qur'an and Sunna. As the first Jahiliyyah was characterized by idolatry, corruption, injustice, and Meccan authorities' abuse of religion and power, so the present state of Egypt is worse because the leaders claim to be Muslim. God struck Islam's Meccan opponents not through reforms but, after warnings and revelation, through war. So, too, God now demands genuine Muslims not to compromise or delay. The duty of jihad can no longer be neglected. Muslims must fight to establish the faith and patterns of the first umma. Both the Qur'an and Muhammad sanctioned the use of covert action and dissembling as jihad strategies, so the members of Jama'at al-Jihad assassinated the nation's leader. Loyalty to Islam and obedience to God come before any pledges to the nation or its flawed constitution. And jihad begins not in Palestine, as some advocated. Jihad begins now, in Egypt.

The justification for killing the leaders and those so-called Muslims who supported them derives from the Quranic and Sunna punishments for apostates. Death is the only punishment in al-Dunya and damnation in al-Akhira. Sadat and those who stood with him, reasoned the Jama'at al-Jihad, are apostates. The types of jihad presented in the pamphlet justify holy struggle against all who encourage and aid the apostates and those who fight against Islam. The "crusaders" (Westerners) and Zionists (Israelis and Jews who support Zionism) and their property and institutions are, therefore, legitimate targets. The men behind the *Neglected Duty* did not attempt a coup d'état. They commended themselves to God, expecting God to act once they destroyed the new pharaoh. *The Neglected Duty* influences jihadist groups throughout the Muslim world.

Abul A'la Maududi

Abdul A'la Maududi, an Indian-Pakistani, influences the Islamic resurgence from North Africa through Indonesia.[25] Originally opposed to political nationalism as an obstacle to the establishment of an Islamic nation, he kept aloof from the process that resulted in the formation of India and Pakistan. Eventually, however, he saw Pakistan, Islamically rightly organized, as the model for the rest of the Islamic world. Maududi spent years in jail both in prepartition India and in postindependence Pakistan. One Pakistani government found him so subversive that he was sentenced to death. He was a severe critic of the several military governments and what he took to be Islamically diluted constitutions promulgated by those governments. Maududi recognized that education was crucial to the formation of such a pure state and that dedicated Muslims needed to be persistently active in preventing the secularization of Pakistan's educational-cultural institutions. From his perspective, the Muslim world in his region was beset by Western secularism, atheistic Marxism, and aggressive Hindu polytheism.

Tafhim al-Qur'an (Towards Understanding the Qur'an), his tafsir on the Qur'an, written largely while he was jailed, is widely used. His enthusiastic translator, Zafar Ishaq Ansari, said that it was "revivalist and revolutionary. Its emphasis is on movement, activism and dynamism. . . . It is a plea for purposive change and tries to develop the faculty to discriminate between the essential and the coincidental, between the divine, and as such permanent, and the human, and as such changeable."[26] The tafsir also offers the author's own translation of the Arabic in what he called a personal voice intended not for scholars but for the general reader.[27] Unlike Qutb, Maududi proceeds on an aya-by-aya exposition, providing insights into the history and context of the passages. This method accords with his didactic purpose for the lay reader and to some extent in contrast to Qutb's writing for the vanguard. For example, Maududi's handling of passages in Surah 2 concerning Zakat and generosity engages readers in considering their personal and communal opportunities and responsibilities to aid the poor from the riches given by God.[28]

He also raised political concerns in the tafsir and disclosed his opposition to most Pakistani governments. He suspected that the authorities were not sincere or dedicated enough to move with reasonable speed to install what he called a "theo-democracy," or democratic caliphate, that is, a theocracy that took into account the Quranically revealed rule of God implemented by persons who were competent and devout Muslims:

The belief in the Unity and the Sovereignty of Allah is the foundation of the social and moral system propounded by the Prophets. . . . The basic principle of Islam is that human beings must, individually and collectively, surrender all rights on overlordship, legislation and exercising authority over others. . . . None is entitled to make laws on his own authority and none is obliged to abide by them. This right vests in Allah alone. . . . Islam from the viewpoint of political philosophy is the very antithesis of secular Western democracy [which is based on] the sovereignty of the people. Islam . . . altogether repudiates the philosophy of popular sovereignty and rears its polity on the foundations of the sovereignty of God and the vice-gerency (Khilafat) of man. . . . The theocracy built up by Islam is not ruled by any particular religious class but by the whole community of Muslims including the rank and file. The entire Muslim population runs the state in accordance with the Book of God and practice of His Prophet. . . . [T]he distinguishing mark of the Islamic state is its complete freedom from all traces of nationalism and its influences . . . having its foundations in certain recognized moral principles. God has retained the right of legislation in His own hand not in order to deprive man of his natural freedom but to safeguard that very freedom. His purpose is to save man from going astray and inviting his own ruin.[29]

His interpretation of the Qur'an and the Sunna emphasized social justice, the honesty of leaders, and the banning of alcohol, usury, and innovations contrary to the spirit of Islam. While in power, General Zia al-Haqq (1977–88) affirmed Maududi's insistence on a morally clean government and attempted to enact Maududi's reforms. In 1978 the "Renewal of Covenant" brought the Qur'an and the Sunna forward as the basis for political and social life, and in 1979 then-President al-Haqq announced the imposition of Zakat and Islamic punishments for crimes mentioned in the Qur'an, prohibition of usury and the drinking of wine (allowances were made for Christians to have communion wine), and the abrogation of laws that were counter to the Qur'an and the Sunna. Through Maududi's regular appearances on Pakistani radio and television, he became a national moral conscience. Members of his Jamaat I-Islamyya were ministers in the al–Haqq government. In early 1979 Maududi made ten proposals to put the nation on the Straight Path: the steady Islamization of the educational curriculum and teachers; special police supervision of governmental officials to monitor their continued honesty; the speedy dismissal of corrupt officials; the banning of all anti-Islamic literature, pornography, and crime news; the requirement that communications media "teach Islamic beliefs and commandments . . . to create fear of God and the fear of the Day of Judgment"; the distribution of wealth so that the poor and needy would be cared for; and the confiscation of illegally gotten wealth.[30] He died in September 1979. His relative success and certainly the steps he advocated are used especially by those who challenge Islamic societies on the basis of the proper interpretation of the Qur'an.

A REFORMATION CHALLENGER

Fazlur Rahman accepted fully the verbal inspiration of the Qur'an.[31] He concluded that Islamic intellectual, mystical, and legal traditions, whether medieval or modern, misrepresented and misunderstood the Qur'an. He held that Sunni teachers and scholars often developed laws and legal pronouncements from passages torn from contexts that did not relate to the issues these passages were called on to resolve. He said that the Qur'an was not a law book in a legalistic sense but was the *religious source* of all law.[32] He wrote, "The Qur'an is the divine response, through the Prophet's mind, to the moral and social situation of the Prophet's Arabia, particularly to the problems of the commercial Meccan society."[33] He criticized those Muslims who, eager to adapt or counter Western techniques, claimed for the Qur'an a specious clairvoyance in anticipating technology, astronomical discoveries, and scientific developments.[34] He felt that past and present struggles within Islam concerning the relationship of philosophical reasoning and reliance on revelation led to artificial arguments and assertions about Islam's character. These factors, in turn, gave the non-Muslim world a false understanding of the Faith and its role in the modern world. Rahman called for a transformation of Islamic intellectual and theological thinking and practices through understanding the Qur'an's deeper unity and

Muhammad's mission of the moral improvement of humanity in a concrete and communal sense.[35] Islam and the Qur'an are practical and social and aimed toward justice. His hermeneutical approach, therefore, emphasized Muhammad's sociopolitical context as the key to understanding the Revelation and how humans were to respond. While in Pakistan, Rahman headed the nation's Institute for Islamic Research (1962–68). In the aftermath of the civil war that led to the independence of Bangladesh and several governmental changes, Rahman, denounced by Maududi's followers, left Pakistan for the United States.[36]

Rahman sought to find the Qur'an's underlying unity and principles. He understood humanity to be the subject of the Qur'an and took that as a starting point for his interpretation: "The Qur'an is a document that is squarely aimed at man; indeed it calls itself "guidance for mankind . . . [2:185]. . . . Still, the Qur'an is no treatise about God and His nature: His existence, for the Qur'an, is strictly functional—He is Creator and Sustainer of the universe and of man, and particularly the giver of guidance for man and He who judges man, individually and collectively, and metes out to him merciful justice."[37]

God intends the Qur'an to shake humans into believing and serving the God whose goodness and will are present throughout creation and events. It testifies to God's greatness and power chiefly through acts of mercy, and mercy guides humans on the Straight Path, and the Straight Path is the way of the return to God on the Day of Judgment. The Qur'an, then, discloses a chain of divine mercy that begins and ends with God: creation-preservation-guidance-judgment.[38] His challenge to Muslim scholars rested on his understanding of *itjihad*.

Originally a form of legal reasoning, itjihad comes from the same root as jihad, that is, struggle.[39] In legal thought, it means to exert effort, to struggle to find the underlying causes and principles, to search beyond analogy, precedent, and consensus so as to use reason. Itjihad is the use of reason, one of God's gifts, as a culminating step to discern God's will in a particular situation. When Rahman employed the term for interpreting the Qur'an, therefore, he dealt not only with texts but also with opening the intellectual doors and windows of conservative Islam and set limits on the speculations of mystics and those who seemed too quick to justify their adaptations and/or rejections of Western ways. Rahman understood the Qur'an as the final document that is ever-speaking to believers and non-believers. Understanding the Qur'an leads to an understanding of the full range of human activity in light of the merciful will and merciful justice of God. The everlasting Book cannot be divorced from the actual, changing situations of women and men, God's will for worship-obedience, and the establishment of a just society.

NEO-AWAKENING CHALLENGERS

Two loosely related groups have emerged and promise to be significant in the future. Both employ the Qur'an, and both advocate a nonviolent, steady approach to revive and reassert Islam as the basis for just, humane, and modern societies.

The New Islamists

First, a growing number of Egyptian scholars, journalists, and jurists call themselves the "New Islamists." They feel that genuine Islam was caught between the extremism of the revolutionary jihadists and the rejection-ism of secularists.[40] Claiming roots in the nonconfrontational wing of the Egyptian Ikhwan, they regard Islam as having a centrist midstream and claim that they are the intellectual leaders and spokespersons of that middle ground, Wassettiyya. Among their recognized writers and authorities are Shaykh Muhammad al-Ghazali (d. 1996), Kamal Ahmad Abu al-Magd (or Majd, b. 1930), and Yusuf al-Qaradawy (or Qaradawi).[41] Although they formulated a set of principles in the early 1980s, the tense political climate in Egypt before and after Sadat's assassination delayed their presenting it to the public.[42] The Egyptian government has often shifted attitudes and policies toward groups and movements that it deems suspicious and potentially subversive. Some leaders, such as al-Ghazali and Magd, were officials in the administration but were dismissed or resigned. They have learned to be adroit, offering accommodations but persisting in their overall vision. And the Qur'an is integral to that vision.

In *Islamic Awakening between Rejection and Extremism,* Yusuf al-Qaradawy
(b. 1926) addressed the need for Islamic leaders to engage youth.[43] He
called Muslim extremism a genuine menace to the Faith, attributing it to
a failure of intellect and communication by religious and political leaders.
He described extremism as promoting bigotry, intolerance, and obstinate
devotion to one's own views as infallible, all of which grow out of ignorance of the Qur'an and the Sunna, vanity and pride. It is not only that
youth are tainted with such errors but also the shallowness and conceit of
teachers who know neither the fullness of the Qur'an nor the history of
Islam. He was unsparing in his criticism of those Muslims who wanted
a secular state and to reject the political-social role of Islam: "The problem [of Muslim governments and societies] can basically be attributed to
the imposition on Muslim societies of secularism—an alien trend which
is at odds with all that is Islamic. . . . Secularism may be accepted in a Christian society, but it can never enjoy a general acceptance in an Islamic society. . . . For Muslim societies, the acceptance of secularism means . . .
abandonment of Shariah, a denial of the divine guidance and a rejection of Allah's injunctions. . . . For this reason, the call for secularism
among Muslims is atheism and a rejection of Islam."[44] Muslim youth, he
argued, are caught between the secularist rejection of the wholeness of
Islam and the extremism of those who are fixed on an illusionary, violence-
prone view of Islam. He argued that real freedom is not doing whatever one wants to do but engaging in meaningful, informed discussions
in the context of realizing that Islam is both din (devotion-faith) and
Shari'ah (ways to live). That will take constructive dialogue, mutual respect, and time.

The New Islamists recognize that there are numerous passages in the
Qur'an that may be taken in jihadist and Wahhabist ways, but they argue
that the revolutionaries misunderstand and abuse the Qur'an. In terms that
echo Rahman, they seek to apply a form of itjihad that grows out of their
understanding of the wholeness and unified Message of the Qur'an and
the Sunna. What is sorely needed in Islamic circles is a renewal of serious
theological discourse, and that will lead to a renewal of Islamic society.
Their method of interpreting the Qur'an, as summarized by al-Ghazali,
includes four basic principles:[45]

1. "All matters pertaining to Islam have their ultimate and most reliable source in the Qur'an. In some areas the Qur'an provides explicit provisions, in others, guidelines for believing, thinking, and acting. In all cases the Qur'an provides the rightful starting point."

2. "Since *Sunnah* came later, to elaborate and facilitate the understanding of the Qur'an, *Sunnah* cannot contradict what it explains. Qur'an and *Sunnah* must be taken together, but in the end, Qur'an has precedence."

3. "Since both Qur'an and *Sunnah* are texts that may have unspoken meanings that are not accessible to literary readings alone, both the necessity of interpretation and the acceptance of differences that interpretation will unavoidably generate are an inherent element of Islam and one that is to be cherished."

4. "The flexibility that *itjihad* affords and the differences within *fiqh* [i.e., their term for understanding the Qur'an and the Sunna] that it yields explain the capacity of Islam to meet human needs in all times and places. What remains constant are the general purposes and higher values of Islam, expressed in the Qur'an and *Sunnah*."

The New Islamist approach addresses three Quranic challenges. The first is the challenge of interpreting the Qur'an so as to address social and religious distortions or misreadings that lead to the suppression of justice and human dignity regardless of national location. The New Islamists are dedicated to the equality of all persons, especially women, in Islamic society. For example, in a study of Surah 4, al-Ghazali argued that, taken as a whole and placed in the context of the Qur'an, God clearly advocates the equality of men and women. In spite of physical differences and complementary social roles, the Qur'an infers that because women are equal, they are to be granted equal access to education and the professions. Husbands and wives are to share care of the home and children. Such opinions and their use of the Qur'an to challenge existing as well as extremist thinking among Muslims have led to threats against the New Islamists, yet they persist and appear to be making headway, at least among those who are disaffected from the option of revolution and violence.

Second, the New Islamists challenge the Egyptian government, society, and the religious establishment. They do not regard as evil Jahiliyyah Egypt's glorious millennia-long history; the genius of its forebears in matters of art, engineering, philosophy, science, and literature; and rich religious heritage that includes Christianity. Egypt must again have a leading role in world events and culture. The Qur'an reveals that Islam does not seek to obliterate previous faiths but fulfills them. Islam today must build contacts between Muslims and non-Muslims. The centuries during which Christians and Muslims lived together are models for how Christians and Muslims can think, work, serve, and join together to build a moral, just, and peaceful society. Advocating the Quranic concept of the People of the Book, the New Islamists build on the concept of a covenant of God-dedicated servant-peoples of the Book. Christians and Muslims are tied together in common bonds of devotion to one God and serving humanity. So Christians are to have the same civil rights and legal equality before the law, not on secular grounds, but on Quranic grounds.[46]

The third challenge is directed to the revolutionary jihadists and to the secularists. Secularism is morally, politically, and economically bankrupt. The current misery of the poor, the failing educational system, and the repressive government are misguided forms of secularism. If the West is the model, then an examination of Western tactics and their results ought be sobering antidotes to the unreal expectations of Egyptian secularists. The New Islamists claim that the revolutionary jihadists are ignorant of the Qur'an's unity and use, and their tactics are opposed to the Qur'an's message. Instead of violence and plans to overthrow governmental institutions, the Qur'an and Islam encourage a graduated and gradual accommodation with the Egyptian government. They push for developing and spreading an Islamic consciousness throughout the state not for creating another Iran or Taliban or for restoring a defunct caliphate. That Islamic consciousness is broad enough to include Christians and minority groups of Muslims on the basis of a God-centered morality and commitment to justice.

Progressive Muslims

The second group designates itself "Progressive Muslims."[47] Generally its members are female and male scholars drawn from a wide variety of nations, including the United States and Canada. Some have been born into Muslim cultures, and others are converts. Among them are Arabs, African Americans, Caucasians, Malaysians, and Pakistanis. All have studied in Western Europe and North America. Most are faculty members in U.S. colleges and universities, often in Islamic studies programs. They have repudiated violence and jihadist actions but are vigorous and articulate in exposing, criticizing, and applying Quranic insights to what they see as abuses, injustices, and corruption in Muslim and non-Muslim societies.

Their choice of the term "Progressive Muslims" is carefully described by Omid Safi. The progressive Muslim agenda and person are described as developing from the axiom that

> "every human life, female and male, Muslim and non-Muslim, rich or poor, 'Northern' or 'Southern,' has exactly the same intrinsic worth. The essential value of human life is God-given and is in no way connected to culture, geography, or privilege. A progressive Muslim is one who is committed to the . . . idea that the worth of a human being is measured by a person's character, not the oil under their soil, and not their flag. A progressive Muslim agenda is concerned with the ramifications of the premise that all members of humanity have this same intrinsic worth because, as the Qur'an reminds us, each of us has the breath of God breathed into our being. . . . 'Progressive' in this usage refers to a relentless striving towards a universal notion of justice in which no single community's prosperity, righteousness, and dignity comes at the expense of another. Central to this notion of a progressive Muslim identity are the fundamental values that we hold to be essential to a vital, fresh, and urgently needed interpretation of Islam for the twenty-first century. These themes include social justice, gender justice, and pluralism. . . . To put it slightly differently, being a progressive Muslim means not simply thinking more about the Qur'an and the life of the Prophet, but also thinking about the life we share

on this planet with all human beings and all living creatures.... [O]ur relationship to the rest of humanity changes the way we think about God, and vice versa."[48]

Progressive Muslims are well within the themes of the Qur'an and use those themes to address and challenge the "arrogance" of Western modernity and postmodernism, particularly with a focus on the United States. They are similarly critical of the hidebound traditionalism of Muslim literalist-exclusivists, the extremist jihadists, the "liberal" Muslims who actually make their Islamic heritage a veneer for capitulating to Western secularism, the reformers who seek to abolish any dependence on Islamic legal and theological traditions in order to create a thoroughly "modern" Islam, and, of course, secularists who would abandon all vestiges of supernatural religion. The Progressives are willing to quote popular American singers, as well as Martin Luther King Jr., and Mohandas Gandhi.

They understand Islam as the truly natural religion that serves as the basis and also the goal of all religions. On that basis they advocate the Quranic understanding of the caliphate of all humans in caring for God's world and for the equality of all persons before God. On those grounds, Progressives move to analyze and criticize, then propose principles of cooperation and action for ecological and social justice. On the same grounds, they lift up the condition of women and men through their lens of "gender justice." Recognizing the God-given equality and God-given abilities of women will work to the fulfillment of men in a God-willed empowerment of humans to care for the world, one another, and future generations. In the course of arguing for gender justice, the progressive Muslims push for changes in attitudes and practices in marriage and divorce.[49]

The third item on the agenda is "pluralism." The issues in this area are not so much racial and ethnic pluralism but the pluralism of points of view within religious traditions (obviously including Islam) and the pluralism of interreligious relations. Given the perspective of God as Creator of all persons and their value before God, progressive Muslims encourage interreligious dialogues and urge Muslims to be patient, probing, and appreciative of the different positions taken by other Muslims. This is not a plea for tolerance but for seeking and finding the will and revelation of God in the faith and expressions of others.[50] As is the case with the New Islamists, the progressive Muslims do not advocate the restoration of the caliphate.

Progressive Muslims use the history and culture of Islam along with the Qur'an to express their critiques of Islam and the non-Muslim world. Their threefold challenges of social justice, gender justice, and pluralism certainly are trenchant. Nevertheless, the progressive Muslims are looking to a future in which the universal message of the Qur'an and Muhammad, the wisdom and strength of Islam will be brought together with people who have responded to God's other revelations so as to fulfill Surah 16:90 as Safi rendered it: "Indeed God commands justice, and the actualization of goodness, [and] the realization of beauty."

CONCLUSION

Iqra! Read! Recite! Proclaim! The words still challenge men and women to obey the One God. As we have seen, who holds, hears, and proclaims those challenges is critically important. To pose those challenges involves interpreting the Message and the several contexts that are to be addressed. The human condition, the exploitation of persons by persons, the entrenched structures of society, the roles of past successes and failures, the political realities of the present, and the anxieties about and hopes for the future are all subject to Quranic analysis. Yet the Qur'an does more than expose; it also proposes. Here, particularly in the darkness generated by wars, Muslims and non-Muslims may turn to the Qur'an, as well as other sources, for enlightenment, for understanding, and even for cooperation.

> These are Verses of the Wise Book, a Guide and a Mercy to the Doers of Good, those who establish regular prayer and give regular charity and have (in their hearts) the assurance of the Hereafter. These are on (true) guidance from their Lord; and these are the ones who will prosper. (Surah 31:2–5)

FOURTEEN

CHALLENGES TO THE QUR'AN

But the misbelievers say: "Naught is this but a lie which he
[Muhammad] has forged, and others have helped him at it."
In truth it is they who have put forward an iniquity and a
falsehood. And they say: "Tales of the ancients which he
has caused to be written, and they are dictated before him
morning and evening."

Surah 25:4—5

In the beginning there was ridicule and rejection. Meccans scoffed at Muhammad's claims to have received revelations through an angel, dismissed his calls for them to forsake their ancestral gods, and opposed the Message that threatened to change their lives and livelihoods. Some medieval Christians theorized that the Qur'an was written by a devil named Mahound and branded the religion grossly immoral. Until the mid-nineteenth century Western scholars generally approached the Qur'an as defenders of their own faith positions in Judaism and Christianity. They mounted polemical theological arguments against the Qur'an rather than engage in textual and historical analysis. But it was only a matter of time before some would approach the Qur'an grammatically, historically, and critically.[1] Polemical defenders of Christianity, usually conservative Protestants, have already been discussed. More recently the challenges have expanded to textual and historical skeptics, advocates of free expression, and social analysts. This chapter presents two contemporary types of challengers that I term rejecters and disparagers.

REJECTERS

In essence, the rejecters deny the historicity of what may be called the traditional Muslim account of Islam's origins. They reject what Muslims hold concerning pre-Islamic Arabia, the Qur'an, Muhammad, Hijra, the first four caliphates, and the authenticity of the Hadith collections; the existence of Muhammad's Meccan and Medinan families and Companions and Helpers; the Battle of Badr, Uhud, and the Trench; the centrality of Mecca; and the paradigmatic role of the Medinan umma. In place of the traditional account, the rejecters propose radically different scenarios that they claim are based on hitherto ignored and misinterpreted archaeological evidence (or the lack thereof), datings, variant and reinterpreted Quranic texts, non-Muslim references, arguments from silence, and, in one instance, admitted speculation. They argue that there are no clear, surviving passages from the Qur'an prior to the 690s, that archaeological remains of pre-Islamic Arabia do not confirm the Muslim version of active trade routes or the social conditions of what Muslims term the Jahiliyyah, or that a Meccan merchant named Muhammad ever existed, or that a series of Muslim victories united the Arabs during or immediately after the traditional dating of Muhammad's life. Instead, they maintain that contemporary and near-contemporary evidence cuts the ground from under the historical basis for Islam. The key rejectionist arguments may be summarized as follows:[2]

1. Polytheistic Arabs from Arabia began to assert themselves in southern Palestine in the late 630s and through the 640s, slowly taking control of Palestine, Syria, and Egypt by 643.
2. During the period 643–680, under Damascus-based Mu'awiyah, coins were struck that reflect an indeterminate monotheism that could fit Jews, Christians, and other monotheists.

3. The first coins mentioning Muhammad appear in 691. Quranic (with variants to traditional text) ayas first appear inscribed inside the Jerusalem's Dome of the Rock, and these aim to refute Christian claims. The religion the inscriptions support appears to be a melding of Judaism with Christianity plus Muhammad but lacks Islamic specificity.

4. By 720–50 biographies of the "traditional" Muhammad appear. The first official mention of the "Book of Allah" appears in 752, and by 780 there are inscriptions indicating beliefs and practices that may be defined as Muslim.

5. Therefore, "Muhammad is not a historical figure, and his biography is the product of the . . . 2nd century A. H." He "entered the official religion only ca. 71/690. . . . The Qur'an is a late compilation; it was not canonized until the end of the 2nd century A. H. or perhaps early in the 3rd"; and

6. Islam grew out of the need for Arab rulers to stabilize their new state. Later storytellers developed the traditions about Muhammad the merchant from Mecca, using the name of a desert prophet named Mahmet who was linked to a Jewish-based Abrahamic messianic-apocalyptic monotheism.

The rejectionist version has the caliph Abd al-Malik (r. 685–705) introduce the "traditional" Muhammad as the Messenger of God. The Qur'an, then, was composed from various sayings derived from various sects and groups in the Arab empire and evolved over time. One could read the Qur'an as featuring an unnamed prophet or prophets who proclaimed a basic monotheism, justice, judgment, and rewards/punishments without identifying that prophet as the traditional account's Muhammad. Specific references to Muhammad would then be explained as interpolations by pious (or deliberately fraudulent) scribes. Islam is, therefore, a fabricated religion, Muhammad a fictitious character, and the Qur'an "strikingly lacking in overall structure, frequently obscure and inconsequential in both language and content, perfunctory in its linking of disparate materials, and given to the repetition of whole passages in variant versions." The appraisal continues: "On this basis it can be argued that the book is the product of the belated and imperfect editing of materials from a plurality of traditions. At the same time the imperfection of the editing suggests that the emergence of the Koran must have been a sudden, not to say, hurried event."[3]

The rejectionist conclusion is that the Qur'an evolved over time among Western scholars since the late nineteenth century. Some terms related to legal prescriptions appear to have been generated after the traditional dating of Muhammad's death. Other Westerners posited that the Qur'an "developed" or "evolved" into its present form but that Muhammad's religious experience was still its source.[4] The more negative approach began to emerge in the 1970s with views that the Qur'an as a whole was a late document and that Muhammad may never have existed. The modern scholarly repudiation of the traditional account was mounted in the 1970s by Western academics. The significant leader in the investigation of the Qur'an that is the basis for the above summary was John Wansbrough. He and two colleagues, Michael Cook and Patricia Crone, concluded that the Muslim version did not match the available archaeological and other manuscript materials and that the contradictions in some of the Muslim materials could not be reconciled with the Muslim version.[5] Wansbrough himself was not interested in proving or disproving the validity of Islam. His focus was on the process by which the scripture called the Qur'an emerged. He concluded that the Qur'an as a written document came into being long after the traditional account says it was revealed. He sought to make an extended and complex case about oral proclamation, existing oral-literary materials common to Judaism and Christianity, and the process of developing written texts using words from later times. Yet if Wansbrough did not intend to disprove the authenticity of Islam as a religion and the Qur'an as the proclamation to Muhammad, he can be read as giving grounds for those who want to take the position further.

Crone and Cook went further.[6] They mounted an assault on the nature of Islam, admitting that their *Hagarism: The Making of the Islamic World* is "a book written by infidels for infidels."[7] As did Wansbrough, they employ arguments from the silence of archaeological texts and surmises from admittedly murky archaeological tribal remains in Arabia. They concluded, as did Wansbrough, that there are no surviving references to the Qur'an prior to the end of the seventh century. They then posit the existence of a heterodox Jewish sect living in Arabia that featured Hagar and Abraham. Citing post-632 Jewish sources about a prophet-warrior among the Arabs who proclaimed a messianic message about the end of the age, Cook and Crone referred to other Jewish sources about a group of Jews who left Edessa and settled among the Arabs ("children of Ishmael") around 628. Combined with an Armenian chronicle dated in the 660s that mentioned a monotheistic Ishmaelite prophet named Mahmet who knew much concerning Moses and Abraham and summoned his followers to live under his law that prohibited idolatry, alcohol, and fornication, the two modern scholars speculate that there was an Abrahamic-Ishmaelite-Hagar-centered sect in Arabia that they call the "Hagarenes." The sect was also heavily influenced by the Samaritans and Zoroastrians. From the former they derived an attachment to the Pentateuch and from the latter the dualism that developed into Dar al-Harb and Dar al-Islam.

While the details of Crone and Cook's construction are not germane to our focus, they maintain that the Hagarenes were disappointed by being rebuffed by Jews and, after a period of positive relations with Christians, decided to combine their religion of Abraham and Moses' Pentateuch with a version of Christian messianism-apocalypticism (minus Christology) to "elaborate a full scale religion of Abraham."[8] By a theological transposition of biblical geography to Arabia, Mecca replaced Jerusalem, the Ka'bah became the Ishmaelized Mount Moriah–Temple, Mount Hira was the new Sinai, the Jahiliyyah was the period of Egyptian bondage, the Hijra is the Exodus, the Medinan period was the shaping of the community in the wilderness, and the return to Mecca was the entry into the Promised Land. Muhammad, a construction of Hagarenes plus Abd al-Malik's advisers, was the prophet greater than Moses, and the Qur'an was the new and superior Pentateuch-Gospel that gave theological credibility to the new Arab state. Whatever one may think of Cook and Crone's scenario, they were right in stating that no believing Muslim would accept their version of Islam's origins. Nevertheless, Wansbrough's and Cook and Crone's points about the archaeological evidence and silences, as well as variant texts, raise significant questions about the traditional account.[9]

Another rejectionist approach began in the 1920s among those who, like Wansbrough, built on a linguistic basis. Alphonse Mingana wrote in 1927 that it was time to subject the Qur'an to the same kind of analysis used in biblical studies.[10] He posited that the Qur'an is a pastiche of texts drawn from Jewish, Christian, and Zoroastrian sources. He believed that Syriac was the most important language that influenced the growth and development of the Qur'an. Simply by positing that there was growth and development in Quranic texts runs counter to the traditional account and the role of the Messenger. Others also have noted the appearance of loanwords from other languages and the possible use of terms from times subsequent to Muhammad's life.[11]

The most recent attempt to show that the Qur'an is not from Muhammad and is greatly misinterpreted is that of the pseudonymous Christof Luxenberg (sometimes given as Luxenburg), rumored to be a Lebanese Christian.[12] He claims that he is working on a "critical edition" of the Qur'an. Logically, that means he is working through variant texts in order to produce a composite text. Also logically, that means the person(s) working on the project assume that there was not one definitive, inspired, and uncorrupted Qur'an revealed to Muhammad that was transmitted and copied without error by his secretaries. Luxenberg has also published in German a work that seeks to prove that the Qur'an is heavily indebted to Syriac and Aramaic, which is later than the traditional account posits.[13] Luxenberg noted that he is translating *houri* not as the virginal beings in the Gardens but as white raisins or white grapes. This would certainly be interesting news to future jihadists. Luxenberg is reluctant to emerge publicly because of the fatwa issued against Salman Rushdie. Cook, Crone, and Wansbrough, as well as other Westerns scholars, seem not to fear such condemnations for their conclusions about the Faith, the Messenger, or the Book.

DISPARAGERS

Salman Rushdie and Taslima Nasrin represent different, yet related challengers to the Qur'an. They were born into Sunni Muslim families, know

Muslim practices, and are acquainted with the Qur'an. Both are writers who state openly their personal rejections of Islam and the Qur'an, are atheists, and are living under condemnations and death threats for their published work concerning the Qur'an, Muhammad, and Islam. Neither is an Islamic or Quranic scholar, nor has either engaged in deep study of the Qur'an and Hadith. Yet both have gained worldwide attention, sympathy, and enmity. Their disparagements of the Qur'an, however, have been different.

SALMAN RUSHDIE

Salman Rushdie is an Islamic "outsider" who is perceived as an "insider" or as someone who could be regarded as a "cultural Muslim," but most Muslims consider him an apostate.[14] He claims that he never intended to insult or blaspheme Islam, Muhammad, or believers but writes only about the immigrant experience.[15] The publication of his *Satanic Verses* (1988) provoked widespread, violent, and deadly responses. A complex book, it raises numerous issues ranging from its literary merits and authorial intentions and responsibilities, an author's freedom of and accountability for expression, racial and religious antagonisms, political and communal authority, and life and death.[16] Hewing to our Quranically focused purpose, I forgo any attempt to discuss the novel per se or the dynamics of British and American responses to the storm it and Rushdie generated.

The novel's title signals that it involves the highly controversial account of the Satanic Verses concerning allegations that Shaytan deceived Muhammad into making a positive statement about the three daughter-wives of Allah. The so-called Satanic Verses have been deemed blasphemous, and blasphemy against God, Muhammad, and the Faith is punished by God with eternal death. The novel has convoluted plot lines and important dream sequences. A major character named Gibreel recalls in a dream that his mother sometimes referred to him as Shaytan. Another major character, Saladin, grows horns and hooves. Two related dream sections of the novel especially provoke Muslims. Briefly, a prophet named Mahound establishes a new religion in the city of Jahili. His scribe is Salman, a Persian. Mahound begins with stirring revelations that he claims come from God. A new character, Salman, becomes Mahound's secretary and begins by recording Mahound's "revelations." Salman alters, then fabricates revelations into the text, sometimes making one contradict another and then making some outrageous statements. Neither Mahound nor anyone else notices the false revelations. Mahound engages in sexual excesses with a dozen prostitutes who become his wives. Their brothel, the Covering or Veil, is circumambulated by those who believe Mahound. There also are references to a deranged prophetess named Ayesha who leads her followers in a suicidal mission to make a pilgrimage from India to Arabia by walking into the sea. The revelations and religion promulgated seem to make God a petty businessman. Throughout the novel characters confuse good and evil, morality and immorality, God and Satan, revelation and delusion.

Rushdie's claims about his purposes and artistic freedom notwithstanding, I think the novel disparages Islam, the Messenger, and the Qur'an. Neither Rushdie nor his publisher responded to requests by British Muslims to insert a clear and prominent disclaimer in the book's opening pages that it is totally fictional or to withdraw it from publication. Some Shi'ia Muslims brought the book to the attention of the Ayatollah Khomeini. In February 1989 he issued the fatwa: "I inform the proud Muslim people of the world that the author of the *Satanic Verses* book which is against Islam, the Prophet and the Koran, and all involved in its publication who were aware of its content, are sentenced to death." An Iranian-based foundation established a $2.5 million fund to reward the assassin or assassins who carried out the fatwa. Because the issuer of the fatwa died, it cannot be rescinded. Still Ayatollah Khomeini spoke only for Twelver Shi'ites. The general response of Sunni Muslim leaders was that the author should be brought to trial. Both Sunni and Shi'ia spokespersons demanded the withdrawal of the book from circulation and the destruction of all copies. In the West the Muslim response to Rushdie made Islam appear intolerant, repressive, and menacing. From the Muslim side, the Western press, publishers, and public disclosed how secularized, Godless and irreverent the West really is in the name of "freedom" and is intent on mocking Islam.

TASLIMA NASRIN

Born in 1962 in what is now Bangladesh, Nasrin was raised in an upper-middle-class family. Her autobiographical reflections tell of her moving from childhood acceptance of religious practices to blunt denunciation of Islam and outright atheism. According to Nasrin, her mother was an unquestioningly devout, repressed, even superstitious person who frequented spiritual advisers whom Nasrin describes as domineering and abusive to females. On the one hand, her physician father encouraged her to study science and become a physician. On the other hand, he beat his wife and children, apparently using religion as justification, and restricted his daughters' freedom to be out of the house or to read books not connected to their studies. Nasrin recited and memorized portions of the Qur'an in Arabic, but only when an early teenager did she obtain a Bengali translation of the Book. Her reaction was entirely negative, especially concerning what she perceived as the Qur'an's and Islam's views and teachings on women:

> Islam does not consider woman a separate human being. Man was the original creation and womankind was created secondarily for the pleasure of man. Islam considers a woman as a slave or sexual object, nothing more. Women's role is to stay at home and to obey her husband, for this is her religious duty. Women are considered weak, so they should be taken care of, their body and mind, their desire and wishes, their rights and freedom must be controlled by men. Islam treats women intellectually, morally and physically inferior. . . . Islam considers women psychologically inferior.
>
> And after all the rights and freedom, after getting all the sexual pleasure and pleasure of being the master, Allah will reward the men with wine, food, and seventy-two virgins in Paradise, including their wives of the earth. Allah said, *Eat and drink happily, in return for your works. They relax on luxurious furnishings, and we match them with beautiful virgins (52.19–20). Near them, shall be blushing virgins with large beautiful eyes who will be like hidden pearls (37.48–49).*

And what is the reward for the pious woman? Nothing. Nothing but the same old husband, the same man who caused her suffering while they were on earth.[17]

Told to be silent or risk hellfire, Nasrin's doubts grew about the Qur'an's cosmology and versions of creation. Yet it was the issue of the treatment of women that ignited her psychological and literary ire. She began to write for newspapers, and had poetry and novels published. All the while she concluded:

I came to suspect that the Qur'an was not written by Allah but, rather, by some selfish greedy man who wanted only his own comfort. Then I read the Hadith, the words of Muhammad. I found different events of Prophet Muhammad's life in which, when he had problems, Allah solved them right away. For example, he was sexually aroused by seeing his daughter-in-law, so Allah sent him a message saying he could marry her because his son was adopted and not a real son, so the marriage was therefore justified. Further, he created a new rule, that Muslims would not be allowed to adopt any child. Muhammad married thirteen times, one of his brides being six-year-old Ayesha. Allah, he said, told him that he was allowed to enjoy his wives, his female slaves and all the captive women he had. He put Ayesha in a veil because he was jealous and did not want his friends looking admiringly at her. Allah, he said, told his friends that they should not go to the Prophet's house any time they want but if they go, they should not look at any of his wives or ask any of them for something. He was so jealous that he introduced the veil for his wives and, ultimately, for all Muslim women. . . . It became clear to me that Muhammad had written the Koran for his own interest, for his own comfort, for his own fun. So I stopped believing in Islam. When I studied other religions, I found they, too, oppressed women. When I stopped practicing religion and made some offensive comments about religion to my mother, she became both nervous and furious, sure that I would go to Hell, and she started praying for me.[18]

Her antipathy to Islam and all religions appeared in her writings. Although given awards for Bengali literature by Indian literary societies, she was criticized, then vilified in Bangladesh. She claimed she proposed changing the Shari'ah with regard to women but was understood as seeking to change and possibly undermine the Qur'an. In 1993 a shaykh in the militant Bangladeshi organization Soldiers of Islam issued a fatwa condemning her and called for her arrest, trial, and execution by hanging. Whatever she may have said, it is clear that she had rejected all religions and had harsh words for Islam:

> Then I studied the Koran. . . . I found it total bullshit. The Koran, believed by millions, supported slavery and inequalities among people—in other countries the equality of women had been established as a human right. . . . Men had the right to marry four times, divorce, have sex with female slaves, and beat their wives. Women were to hide their bodies because the female body is simply a sexual object. Women were not allowed to divorce their husbands, enjoy inheritance, or have their testimony in court considered as seriously as men's. I found that Allah prescribed Muslims to hate non-Muslims and kill apostates. . . . With my own conscience I found religion ridiculous because it stops free thought, reason, and rationality. . . . So I don't accept Allah, His cruel unholiness. I have my own conscience, which inspired me to support a society based on equality and rationality. Religion is the cause of fanaticism, bloodshed, hatred, racism, conflict. Humanism can only make people humane and make the world livable.[19]

Encouraged by friends, family, and the Bangladeshi government, Nasrin has gone into exile, living usually in Sweden or France. A number of her novels and poems have been published. In addition, she lectures widely on the plight of women, what she understands is the wicked conjunction of religion and politics, and on the need for a humanism gives opportunities for persons to fulfill themselves in freedom and peace. The prospects of returning to Bangladesh or of having the bans on her writings dropped seem remote under present conditions.

CONCLUSION

The rejecters and disparagers share an aggressive defensiveness and a defensive aggressiveness. The rejecters take the Qur'an and Islam seriously, then undercut its foundations so that it is either a fraud or a mistake based on wrong readings. The disparagers denounce the Qur'an and Islam as repressive, ludicrous, and, in Nasrin's inelegant expression, bullshit. Do the Islamicist militants and these critics have the last words? Or can we go further? That leads us to the final chapter.

> Praise be to Allah to Whom belong all things in the heavens and on earth: to Him be Praise in the Hereafter: and He is Full of Wisdom acquainted with all things. . . . The Unbelievers say "Never to us will come the hour": say "Nay! But most surely by my Lord it will come upon you by Him Who knows the unseen from Whom is not hidden the least little atom in the Heavens or on earth: nor is there anything less than that or greater but is in the Record Perspicuous: That He may reward those who believe and work deeds of righteousness: for such is Forgiveness and a Sustenance Most Generous." (Surah 34:1–4)

FIFTEEN

THE QUR'AN OPENED AND OPEN

In the name of Allah, Most Gracious, Most Merciful.
Say: I seek refuge with the Lord and Cherisher of Mankind,
The King (or Ruler) of Mankind,
The Allah (or Judge) of Mankind,
From the mischief of the Whisperer (of Evil) who
withdraws (after his whisper),
(The same) who whispers into the hearts of mankind
Among Jinn and among Men.

Surah 114

The Qur'an's last words open this book's final chapter. We have traveled not only from an Arabia distant in geography and time but also into the present with some intimations of the future. As is the case with any serious study of religion, we have also seen and heard how other persons think about God and themselves, how they worship and seek to live their lives. And we have taken some steps to understand ourselves and how we relate to others. This opening of the Qur'an is only an introduction. Once we have been introduced to someone, we grow into conversations and relationships, work through mishearings and misunderstandings, and then make choices about deepening or terminating the relationship. The same image fits our introduction to the Qur'an. Given the conditions of our

437

world and the changing nature of society, opening and being introduced to the Qur'an is a necessity, a challenge, even a privilege.

The religious confrontations that mark the twenty-first century are abetted and heightened by the globalization of technology, integrated world markets, and cultural challenges. The Islamic resurgence competes with the rapid growth of indigenous Christian movements in sub-Saharan Africa and Asia while traditional Euro-American Christianity is static. Tensions over Kashmir, Israel-Palestine, wealth and poverty, policies and power exercised by the United States, and the escalating expectations of youth throughout the non-Western world are inseparable from religious claims and commitments. Surah 114 warns that evil forces insinuate themselves into the minds and actions of jinn and humans. Those who still seek versions of the Straight Path and those who have yet to recognize their responsibilities to their fellow humans know too well that whispers can be amplified into explosions and sobs. The Qur'an holds that it contains the core principles and practices to resist the whisperer and to form the truly free human community. This chapter projects some opportunities and questions for the future.

THE QUR'AN AS BOOK AND MORE THAN A BOOK

In chapter 1 I began to raise the question of the Qur'an as a book and more than a book. I return to that point now. We have traced the Qur'an from being a bundle of sheaves, sayings memorized by believers, revelations passed through Gabriel from God to a man, and a Message linked to the Mother of the Book. Before that and always, the Qur'an belongs to, originates with, and is consummated over time by God for every person and community. Moreover, the Qur'an is a library housing the matching Meccan and Medinan revelations. The former discloses God's will by informing nonbelievers and opponents about the merciful and just One God, exhorting and warning its listeners and readers to obey the Master of the Worlds. The Medinan ayas disclose God's will for shaping the Islamic umma's individual piety, family relations, public policies, military strategies, interfaith contacts, and international relations. Interwoven through both portions are assurances of God's care for His umma, the certainty that His will for this world shall be fulfilled, and the welcome that believers will receive into eternal blessedness.

Yet beyond all that the Qur'an is more than a book. It is a proclamation. It is meant to be heard, with ears tuned to its Message about the One-Only God Who has created the world for human beings and then gives them—us—guidance on the Straight Way. After more than initial confusion and frustration, I have found it helpful to read the Qur'an as if it were a person.[1] Sometimes the person is in a pulpit preaching or in a classroom teaching or in a courtroom interpreting the law or arguing a case, or sitting quietly, listening and speaking. In those and whatever circumstances one may be open to the Qur'an. Listening and seeing beneath and behind the words are vital to carrying on a conversation with the Qur'an. Since we are still reading with our ears, I suggest looking at the ruku's in those surahs that have such designations. I view the first ruku' as setting out the surah's theme and the last ruku' as providing a summary of or further insight into the whole surah. Where there are no ruku' designations, the reader-listener may want to go several ayas into the text until a shift of subject is determined and so make one's own ruku', then do the same at the end of the surah. In spite of some critics who find no unity within surahs or the Qur'an as a whole, I think Muslims are correct when they contend that the unity is in the dialogue between the reader and the Qur'an. The Qur'an is more than a book; it is a partner in conversation as well as a proclamation.

Nevertheless, the Qur'an is a book, As such, it contains different literary forms and themes to instruct humans about God, warn against the deceitful whisperer, and strengthen as well as inspire believers. The Book's texts separately and as a whole encourage scrutiny and examination. Discerning the literary form of a text or portion of a text is basic to a reasonably accurate interpretation. But such efforts can be controversial when an interpreter is perceived as questioning the validity of the Qur'an and the authority of traditional interpreters.[2] In chapter 7 I broached the subject of interpretation, Western and Islamic forms of interpretation, and the freedom as well as the responsibility of interpreters to their reference communities. The discipline of interpretation, usul tafsir, links hadiths and past commentators in a wide-ranging, yet deep continuum of analysis and application across the span of Islamic history into the present. Most Muslim interpreters seek to harmonize their understandings and conclusions with traditional sources even when those sources were innovative and controversial in their time. There is no guarantee that Muslims will regularly interpret the Qur'an correctly or be unchallenged by other believers. In line with Surah 114's warnings about the whisperer, when a Muslim opens the Qur'an, he or she prays, "I seek refuge with God from the accursed Satan. In the name of God, the Merciful and the Compassionate." Reading and interpreting the Book is a form of worship, yet with awareness that one might be misled if one strays from the Straight Path.

Still, what a person or group draws from the Revelation may have lethal consequences, as in the instance of the activists whose thinking is expressed in *The Neglected Duty.* Both Shi'ia and Sunni Muslims, in their distinct ways, have different means of weighing and expressing interpretations. Yet how binding is an interpretation based on the Qur'an made by a shaykh or imam, even when expressed as a fatwa by the council of al-Azhar or the Noble Scholars of Saudi Arabia? The Book seems to have wide margins and ample spaces between lines to accommodate many interpretations within the framework of the Pillars and Teachings.

A further question about the Book: Who "owns" the Qur'an? To "own" can mean both to possess and to profess. Certainly, the umma "owns" the Qur'an in the sense of professing it as God's revealed, final word that guides Muslims on the Straight Path. "Owning" the Qur'an in the sense of professing it has engaged Muslims for fourteen centuries. To profess the Qur'an is to join one's heart and mind in fathoming its meanings, rejoicing in its Message, and then applying those meanings to life amid the changes wrought by time and location in this world.

Theologically, only God owns the Qur'an in the double senses of professing and possessing it. God revealed the Qur'an with a twofold purpose. The first was to reveal to the Arabs the Message of God's tawhid and the proper human response to that disclosure. All other peoples had received preliminary versions of the total Message through prophets and messengers sent to them previously. Those Arabs who accepted the Message and the Messenger and later believers are the custodians and first-line interpreters-proclaimers of the Revelation. Second, the Qur'an is a Message for human-kind and the jinn. God made it a Book for all to hear, consider, and re-spond. The Qur'an, then, is a book open for not-yet and never-ever believ-ers to examine, question, be answered by, and answer in turn.

When non-Muslims open the Qur'an they have the opportunity to enter into and understand it and, through it, Islam. One opportunity is for Muslims and non-Muslims to engage in joint study of the Book. The Mus-lim co-reader may be an author such as Rahman, Esack, Qutb, or Ayub. If circumstances permit, the Muslim co-reader may be an individual who is willing to work through the text with the non-Muslim. A pair of cau-tionary observations. You may recall the Pakistani and New Jersey students mentioned in the introduction. One was convinced that the Qur'an would convince me to become a Muslim, the other thought it incredible that I did not denounce Islam. As in any genuine interfaith engagement, each party needs to set aside overt pressure to convert or controvert the other party if their agreed upon purpose is to understand the book considered sacred by one of them. The other caution is that non-Muslims need to recognize that many Muslims in North American societies are wary of being misunder-stood or of being drawn into heated political discussions.

Another opportunity for understanding the openness of the Qur'an in the hands of a non-Muslim is for the inquiring non-Muslim to link herself or himself with someone I termed previously a resident alien. Such per-sons are grounded in their own positions, yet are aware and knowledgeable enough to present the Qur'an honestly and understandably to another non-Muslim. For Esack my "resident alien" is his "friend of the [Muslim] lover" of the Qur'an.[3] Such resident aliens or friends may accompany the inquirers through books about the Book.[4] Increasingly such persons are present in local communities and willing able to engage fellow non-Muslims in fruitful study and explication of the Qur'an.[5]

The question of owning the Qur'an leads to the issue of the respon-sibilities of the umma and interpreters in their study and exposition of the Qur'an. The umma is responsible for the proper preservation and publica-tion of the text. It also reserves to itself the authority to respond to Mus-lims and those who regard themselves as no longer Muslims. There may be degrees of response ranging from praise (e.g., Esack and Sulayman Nyang) to outright condemnation (e.g., Rushdie and Nasrin). Muslim interpreters are responsible to the umma for reverential handling of Quranic texts and for relating their positions to the basic theological-social positions of Islam. This does not preclude working toward reforming a religious community. At the same time, the circle of believers has the authority to probe, argue with, accept, or reject the interpreter's positions. How various subcommunities within the Islamic umma exercise their responses to interpreters is not only a controversial issue within Islam but also in the wider society. Yet to whom or what is the non-Muslim accountable for his or her exegesis of and presentation of the Qur'an? Are non-Muslim commentators free agents? This is a significant issue in regard not only to the Qur'an but also to the Bible. Even among Christians, the Western idea of freedom of expression clashes with the traditions and theologies of the churches. Indeed, it appears that the marketplace and popular opinion determine appeal and acceptance of interpretation. Such a situation of virtually untrammeled freedom of expression about sacred texts is incomprehensible to most Muslims. Nevertheless, a number of sound "nonaffiliated" scholars are highly respected among Muslims.

I think any commentator-interpreter has three basic responsibilities to the texts and the communities that consider those texts sacred whether or not the commentator-interpreter is a member of the community. First, one is to regard the text and the community with respect no matter what one's experience has been with the community or its members' interpretations of its passages. Due care is to be given to the reality that thousands or millions of persons living over the course of centuries have found meaning and purpose in and through these materials. To honor the faith of believers does not impinge on the analysis of the materials but imposes discipline on the rhetoric employed. Second, one is to give sufficient regard to the range of interpretations that the community has adopted and even rejected. The community's ongoing involvement with its own scriptures will inform all present and future commentator-interpreters of manners and angles of meanings attempted and presented by believers. The benefits to the commentator-interpreter are that he or she may be saved from errors in judgment about the community's ability to understand its own writings and to learn the permutations of the community's hermeneutics. Third, especially for those in academic settings, commentator-interpreters are accountable to the scholarly community so that their methods, style, analysis, and conclusions are open to critique, discussion, and revision. To be sure, institutional commitments may circumscribe a scholar's presentations, for example, arguing for abortion in a Roman Catholic or conservative Protestant university or explaining Islamic origins based on Hagarism in a Muslim university.

So the Qur'an is a book and more than a book, "a Book with verses basic or fundamental (of established meaning)—further explained in detail—from One Who is wise and Well-Acquainted with all things" (Surah 11:1).

QURANIC AFFIRMATIONS FOR THE FUTURE

What will be the roles of Islam, other religions, and secularizing societies as future risks and opportunities open to us? Can we hear and engage the Qur'an whether or not we are Muslim or have a religious commitment?

The Quranic answers are all fully and clearly affirmative. Through that affirmation the Qur'an's responses to the world's religions and secularizing societies are consistent with, although nuanced differently than, those made to the People of the Book and the Muslim umma. The center is still the God Who commands His community to proclaim, do, and be the living witnesses of the Message of justice and mercy so that all persons will join Muslims on the Straight Path. The world's religions are still part of God's gracious action even though their adherents do not accept the full Islamic understanding of God's revelation. These religions, together with the People of the Book, form a God-centered cadre to address the often Jahiliyyah-like leaders, institutions, and forces of the twenty-first century. Working in concord with each other and Islam, these religions may serve to expose the whisperer who deludes and degrades God's human caliphs.

The Qur'an's questions to secularizing societies are based on the conviction that the human community is not split into one sphere for religion and another for political-social affairs. We live in a world that is not self-generating, self-sufficient, or self-sustaining. Secularizing tendencies to lift up human abilities and techniques can be met positively and critically by

Muslim assertions of the Divine Source of human knowledge and the roles of humans as God's caliphs. The Qur'an provides personal and communal ethical counterpoints and contents to the shaping of human accomplishment and prospects for the future.

Quranic-Islamic questions invite positive responses that may recall to the members of secularizing societies that humans depend for their existence on that which is beyond them, are in continuity with the generations that have preceded and will follow them, and are connected to one another in the present through physical, moral, and spiritual networks. Human beings have an intrinsic worth that gives them mighty claims on the leaders of societies for sustenance, shelter, and justice. Since those who have authority as well as those whose abilities lead to technological advances also are human, they are caliphs with power to work toward the welfare of the members of their communities. Although not all such leaders will confess the Shahadah, they can fulfill the intentions of Zakat and strengthen the general human umma.

We opened this study with a consideration of religious attitudes ranging through exclusivism, inclusivism, and pluralism. Now some questions return for response. The answers are not simple, and they are far-reaching.

1. Do Jews, Christians, Muslims, and people of other religions worship and seek to serve the same God?
2. Is the Qur'an a book and message inspired by God?
3. Is Muhammad a person inspired by God?

CODA

When we began our journey with the Qur'an, I shared three accounts. The students from Pakistan and New Jersey lambasted me, one for not becoming a Muslim and the other for not condemning Islam, the Qur'an, and Muhammad. In symbolic retrospect, this book grows out of their criticisms and from the other encounters. The wife-mother-veterinarian and the husband-father-businessman witnessed to the centrality of the Qur'an in shaping their personal devotion, family relations, professions, community involvement, and participation in their mosque umma. The initially testy parishioner began to revise his presuppositions about Islam and Muslims and started to deal with his anxieties and hostilities. He wanted to know more about Islam, but more important, he wanted to know more about and deepen his commitments to his own faith and self-understanding. To do that means to open the Qur'an in its own context, to listen to its message, to begin to make connections to the Bible and the People of the Book, and to be challenged as well as to challenge it. The seminary student who was considered a security risk by her coworkers is a sign that misunderstandings and hostilities darken lives and relationships. Our journey is an attempt to continue the process of introducing Islam by opening its sacred Book. And in that venture we may even start to understand ourselves.

This chapter began with the final surah, a warning against distortions, and a prayer of confidence in the Lord and Cherisher Who is Most Gracious and Merciful. In Quranic style, the end leads us again to the Opening:

In the name of Allah Most Gracious, Most Merciful.
Praise be to Allah the Cherisher and Sustainer of the Worlds.
Most Gracious Most Merciful.
Master of the Day of Judgment.
Thee do we worship and Thine aid we seek.
Show us the straight way.
The way of those on whom Thou hast bestowed Thy Grace
Those whose (portion) is not wrath and who go not astray.

APPENDIX A

Traditional Names and Order of Surahs

Number	Arabic Name	English Name	Associated with
1	Fatihah	Opener	Mecca
2	Baqara	Cow or Heifer	Medina
3	'Imran	Family of Imran	Medina
4	Nisa'	Women	Medina
5	Ma'ida	Repast or Table Laid	Medina
6	An'am	Cattle	Mecca
7	A'raf	Heights	Mecca
8	Anfal	Spoils of War	Medina
9	Tauba/Bara'ah	Repentance/Disavowal	Medina
10	Yunus	Jonah	Mecca
11	Hud	Hud	Mecca
12	Yusuf	Joseph	Mecca
13	Ra'd	Thunder	Medina
14	Ibrahim	Abraham	Mecca
15	Hijr	Rocky Tract	Mecca
16	Nahl	Bees	Mecca
17	Isra'/Bani Isra'il	Night Journey/ Children of Israel	Mecca
18	Kahf	Cave	Mecca
19	Maryam	Mary	Mecca
20	Ta-ha	Ta Ha	Mecca

Number	Arabic Name	English Name	Associated with
21	Anbiya'	Prophets	Mecca
22	Hajj	The Pilgrimage	Medina
23	Mu'minun	Believers	Mecca
24	Nur	Light	Medina
25	Furqan	Criterion	Mecca
26	Shu'ara'	Poets	Mecca
27	Naml	Ants	Mecca
28	Qasas	Narrations	Mecca
29	'Ankabut	Spider	Mecca
30	Rum	Romans	Mecca
31	Luqman	Luqman	Mecca
32	Sajda	Prostration	Mecca
33	Ahzab	Confederates	Medina
34	Saba'	Sheba	Mecca
35	Fatir	Originator of Creation/Angels	Mecca
36	Ya Sin	Ya Sin	Mecca
37	Saffat	Those Ranged in Ranks	Mecca
38	Sad	Sad	Mecca
39	Zumar	Crowds	Mecca
40	Mu'min/Ghafir	Believer/Forgiver	Mecca
41	Ha-Mim/Fussilat	Ha Mim/Expounded	Mecca
42	Shura	Consultation	Mecca
43	Zukhruf	Gold Adornments	Mecca
44	Dukhan	Smoke	Mecca
45	Jathiyah	Kneeling Down/ Crouching	Mecca
46	Ahqaf	Winding Sand Tracts	Mecca
47	Muhammad	Muhammad	Medina
48	Fath	Victory	Medina
49	Hujurat	Chambers	Medina
50	Qaf	Qaf	Mecca
51	Dhariyat	Winds That Scatter	Mecca

Number	Arabic Name	English Name	Associated with
52	Tur	Mount	Mecca
53	Najm	Star	Mecca
54	Qamar	Moon	Mecca
55	Rahman	Most Gracious	Medina
56	Waqi'a	Inevitable	Mecca
57	Hadid	Iron	Medina
58	Mujadila	Woman Who Pleads	Medina
59	Hashr	Mustering	Medina
60	Mumtahinah	That Which Examines	Medina
61	Saff	Battle Array	Medina
62	Jumu'ah	Friday	Medina
63	Munafiqun	Hypocrites	Medina
64	Tagabun	Mutual Loss and Gain	Medina
65	Talaq	Divorce	Medina
66	Tahrim	Prohibition	Medina
67	Mulk	Dominion	Mecca
68	Qalam/Nun	Pen/Nun	Mecca
69	Haqqa	Sure Reality	Mecca
70	Ma'arij	Ways of Ascent	Mecca
71	Nuh	Noah	Mecca
72	Jinn	Jinn/Spirits	Mecca
73	Muzzammil	Enfolded One	Mecca
74	Muddaththir	One Wrapped Up	Mecca
75	Qiyamah	Resurrection	Mecca
76	Dahr/Insan	Time/Man	Medina
77	Mursalat	Those Sent Forth	Mecca
78	Naba'	Great News	Mecca
79	Nazi'at	Those Who Tear Out	Mecca
80	'Abasa	He Frowned	Mecca
81	Takwir	Folding Up	Mecca
82	Infitar	Cleaving Asunder	Mecca
83	Mutaffifin	Dealers in Fraud	Mecca

Number	Arabic Name	English Name	Associated with
84	Inshiqaq	Rending Asunder	Mecca
85	Buruj	Constellations	Mecca
86	Tariq	Night Star	Mecca
87	A'la	Most High	Mecca
88	Ghashiya	Overwhelming Event	Mecca
89	Fajr	Dawn	Mecca
90	Balad	City	Mecca
91	Shams	Sun	Mecca
92	Lail	Night	Mecca
93	Dhuha	Glorious Morning Light	Mecca
94	Sharh/Inshirah	Expansion of the Breast	Mecca
95	Tin	Fig	Mecca
96	'Alaq/Iqra'	Clinging Clot/Read	Mecca
97	Qadr	Night of Power/ Night of Honor	Mecca
98	Baiyina	Clear Evidence	Medina
99	Zalzalah	Earthquake	Medina
100	'Adiyat	Those That Run	Mecca
101	Qari'a	Great Calamity	Mecca
102	Takathur	Piling Up	Mecca
103	'Asr	Time through the Ages	Mecca
104	Humaza	Scandalmonger	Mecca
105	Fil	Elephant	Mecca
106	Quraish	Quraysh	Mecca
107	Ma'un	Neighborly Assistance	Mecca
108	Kauthar	Abundance	Mecca
109	Kafirun	Those Who Reject Faith	Mecca
110	Nasr	Help	Medina
111	Lahab/Masad	Flame/Plaited Rope	Mecca
112	Ikhlaas	Purity of Faith	Mecca
113	Falaq	Daybreak	Mecca
114	Nas	Mankind	Mecca

APPENDIX B

Biblical Figures Mentioned in the Qur'an

Biblical Name	Quranic Name	Biblical Name	Quranic Name
Aaron	Harun	Jonah	Yunus
Abel	Habeel	Joseph	Yusuf
Abraham	Ibrahim	Korah	Qarun
Adam	Adam	Lot	Lut
Amran	Imran	Mary	Maryam
Cain	Qabeel	Noah	Nuh
David	Dawood	Pharaoh	Firon
Elijah	Ilyas	Saul	Talut
Elisha	al–Yasha	Solomon	Suleiman
Enoch	Idris	Terah	Azar
Ezra	Uzair	Zechariah	Zakariya
Gog and Magog	Yajuj and Majuj		
Goliath	Jalut		
Isaac	Ishaq		
Ishmael	Isma'il		
Jacob	Yaqoub		
Jesus	Isa		
Job	Ayub		
John the Baptist	Yahya		

APPENDIX C

Glossary of Key Terms

adhan	Call to Salat prayers.
al-Akhira	The Hereafter, existence following the end of this created world.
Allah	Arabic word for the Supreme Deity, God.
ansari	Helpers. Persons in Medina who aided and allied themselves with Muhammad.
aya, ayah (pl. ayat)	Sign, pointer. Used to refer to a "verse" in the Qur'an.
Basmillah	Opening words of 113 of the surahs: "In the Name of Allah, Most Gracious, Most Merciful."
bid'ah	Innovation. Practice or belief not from the Qur'an, Sunna, or earliest traditions. Denounced by conservatives.
Dajjal, Dajaal	Deceiver; "Antichrist."
dawah	Literally, "call." God calling persons to become Muslims, to provide information about Islam to non-Muslims, and to recall to the Faith those who have lapsed.
dhanb	Sin that is an infraction or trespass.
din, deen	Divine sovereignty; obedience to God, religion, meting out rewards and punishment, judgment.
al-Dunya	This created world.

fi sabil-Allah	For the cause of God; in the way of God.
fitna	Ordeal, serious testing.
hadith	Collection or parts of a collection of Muhammad's sunna.
hafiz (pl. huffaz) al-Qur'an	Person who has memorized the Qur'an.
Hajj	One of Islam's Five Pillars. Obligatory pilgrimage to Mecca, undertaken in the month Dhul l-Hijjah.
hanif (pl. hanáfa)	Monotheist.
Hashem	Clan within the Quraysh tribe. Muhammad was a member of this clan.
Hijra, Hijrah	Departure from Mecca for Medina, beginning of the Muslim era, 622.
hizb (pl. ahzab)	Literally, "one-fourth." One of four portions into which Muslim scholars divided the Qur'an so that it may be read in four days or four sessions.
Houri(s)	Beautiful Companion(s) in the Gardens of Bliss.
Iblis	The Evil One, Satan; also called Shaytan.
ilaha	Something worthy of worship, a god.
imam	Basic meaning: Leader in prayer. Extended meaning: Leader of a mosque; interpreter-commentator who has followers.
iman	Faith.
Ingil	Gospel. Allah's message and book brought by Jesus.
Islamists	Muslims who hold that Allah commands faithful Muslims to create an Islamic umma if that means the use of coercion.
ithum, ithm	Sin that is a major offense and disobedience of God's will.
itjihad	Use of reason in interpretation and legal decisions.
Jahannam	A term for Hell.
al-Janna	The Garden(s) of Bliss in Al-Akhira.

jihad	Effort, endeavor, struggle, fight.
jinn (sing. jinni)	Spiritual beings made from fire and smoke. Some are obedient to Allah; most seem allied with Iblis.
jizya	"Poll tax," or payment made by the People of the Book to Muslim authorities.
juz (pl. ajza)	Literally, "one-thirtieth." One of thirty equal portions into which Muslim scholars divided the Qur'an. Devout Muslims read one juz each day. It is customary to read a juz each day of Ramadan.
kafir	Unbeliever.
khalifah	Caliph. Leader of the umma after Muhammad.
al-Kitab	The Book. Often used of the Qur'an or earlier books given by prophets and messengers.
madrassa	Religious school, often affiliated with a mosque.
manzil (pl. manazil)	Literally, "one-seventh." One of seven portions into which Muslim scholars divided the Qur'an so that it may be read in seven days or seven sessions.
masjid	Mosque.
mihrab	Position of the qiblah, often indicated by an indentation in the wall.
Muhajirun	Emigrants. Persons who left Mecca for Yathrib/Medina on the Hijra.
mushrik	Idolater.
People of the Book	Jews and Christians. Later expanded to include Hindus and Zoroastrians.
qari	Qur'an chanter.
qiblah, qibla	Direction of prayer toward the Ka'bah in Mecca.
qitaal	Kill, slay, slaughter, conflict, war.
Qur'an	Scripture-Proclamation-Message directly from God, first revealed to Muhammad by the angel Gabriel on Mount Hira during the Night of Power, 610 CE.
Quraysh	Tribe in control of Mecca. Muhammad's tribe.

Ramadan	Month during the Muslim year during which most persons fast totally during the day. A month for prayer and reflection.
rasul	Messenger.
rasuliyyah	"Messengerhood"; the position of one called to be a Messenger.
riba	Usury; prohibited rate of interest on loans and investments.
rihal	Wooden stand or holder for a Qur'an.
sahabah (sing. sahib)	Companions. Several classes: those who were closest associates of the Messenger, those who memorized the Qur'an and hadiths before they were written, and those Muslims who saw Muhammad.
Salat	One of Islam's Five Pillars: obligatory five prayers each day.
Sawm Ramadan	One of Islam's Five Pillars: fasting during the month of Ramadan.
Shahadah	First of Islam's five pillars: Muslim confession of faith, "I testify that there is no allah but Allah, and I testify that Muhammad is the Messenger of Allah."
Shari'ah	God's law in its quality as divine and presented in the Qur'an and Sunna.
Shaytan	Evil One, Satan; also called Iblis. Sometimes used to refer to a devil.
Shi'ia	"Party of Ali." Muslims who believe Ali was the rightful first caliph. About 10 to 12 percent of Muslims are Shi'ites.
shirk	Idolatry; worship of something or someone other than the One God.
Sirataal mustiqiim	Straight Path or Way.
Sunna, Sunnah	Traditions of the customs and sayings of Muhammad.
Sunni	Largest group of Muslims.

Surah, Sura	A "chapter" of the Qur'an.
Tanzil	Revelation sent down from God. Linked to wahy.
taqwa	Piety that comes from the awe of God.
Tawrah	Torah. God's message and book brought by Moses.
ulama, uelema	Recognized and authoritative Muslim teachers.
Umm al-Kitab	Mother of the Book. Heavenly source of Qur'an.
umma	Muslim community extended in time and space.
wahy	Inspiration, revelation from God. Linked to Tanzil.
Yawm Din	Day of Judgment.
Zakat	One of the Five Pillars: the obligatory "tax" that is given to the poor.

NOTES

Introduction

1. The comment was made during a 1992 seminar held at De Sales University, Center Valley, Pa.
2. From Surah 25:1, 6 al-Furqan, The Criterion.
3. The Dawood and Arberry translations are smoother than Yusuf Ali's but lack notes and appendixes. The Pickthall translation is quite literal and contains little explanatory material, while Ahmed Ali makes some decisions that are not literal enough. Ahmad von Denffer concludes that all translations by non-Muslims "should be rejected" because a proper translation can be rendered only by a devout Muslim who is skilled in the classical Arabic language and Islamic literature. He is moderately critical of Yusuf Ali's translation (see pp. 144–45). Bilal Philips likewise rejects translations by non-Muslims because he feels that there are now sufficient translations by competent Muslim scholars (see his *Usool at-Tafseer,* pp. 73–83). Note that the readily available translation and other works by Maulana Muhammad Ali (d. 1951) are problematic. He was a member of the Ahmadiyya community, and the translation as well as notes reflect that community's teachings. The Ahmadiyya are considered heretics by Sunni and Shi'ia Muslims.
4. Glassé, pp. 159–62.
5. Bukhari, in the Khan translation, vol. 1, p. 8.
6. See Glassé, p. 416.

One. *Risks, Perspectives, and Understandings*

1. See Said, pp. 62–63, 72–75, 235–38, 300–321. Throughout the work Said (1935–2003), a secularized Palestinian whose religious background was Christian, argued that the Western construction of the "Oriental" and the "Orient" depicts Oriental men as effeminate, weak, inscrutable, sneaky, dangerous, and

a threat to white Western women and Oriental women as exotic and eager to be dominated. He argues that the general Western "Orientalist" view is that especially Arabs and Islam are backward, foreign, sensual, passive, despotic, antiprogress, and inferior to the West. See also von Denffer, pp. 156–62.

2. Dalai Lama, p. 226.

3. Maimonides, vol. 3, bk. 14, treatise 5, chap. 11, p. xxiii. In 1743 the Venetian censors deleted a lengthy passage concerning Jesus and the Messiah in which the quotation occurs.

4. See, for example, Hick, *A Christian Theology of Religions* and *God Has Many Names*; Hick and Knitter; Race; W. C. Smith; and Swidler.

5. See Dupuis. The book is a study in the history, present state, and future of what he terms "religious pluralism." While the Jesuit former missionary active in India does not deal explicitly with Islam, his theological analysis of Christian views is valuable; see pp. 6–23, 330–58. Note also Braaten's essay, "Lutheran Theology and Religious Pluralism" (p. 107), in Rajashekar, *Religious Pluralism,* pp. 105–28.

6. See Race. He deals extensively with the three modes of response. The threefold paradigm has limitations but is generally useful. Note also McGrath, pp. 520–38. McGrath argues for the use of the term *particularism* because "exclusivism sounds polemical" (p. 534). I prefer *exclusivism* for the sake of clarity.

7. See especially Kraemer. While respecting the intentions of other faiths, Kraemer maintained that it is only God's revelation in Jesus that gives the power and truth that lead to salvation. Note also the discussion in McGrath, pp. 532–34.

8. Some outspoken contemporary American "exclusivists" who have addressed directly the question of whether Jews, Christians, and Muslims worship the same God are considered in chapter 14. Among the New Testament passages often cited by exclusivist Christians to support the view that salvation is only through Jesus are John 3:16 f; John 6:28–65; Acts 2:37–39; Romans 1:16–3:26; 1 Tim. 2:1–7; 1 Pet. 3:18–22; 2 John 8:11; Jude 3–23; and Rev. 22:6–21. Second-century "fathers" who held that there was no salvation apart from confessing Jesus as Lord and Savior are, e.g., Ignatius of Antioch (*Magnesians* 5–9; *Smyrnaens* 6 in *Ante-Nicene Fathers,* vol. 1); Tertullian (*Apology* 21; *On Prescription against Heretics*) in *Ante-Nicene Fathers,* volume 3; and Hippolytus (*Refutation of All Heresies,* chaps. 29–30, in *Ante-Nicene Fathers,* vol. 5). A third-century bishop-theologian carried the logic of no salvation apart from Jesus to no salvation apart from the Christian Church; see Cyprian, "On the Unity of the Church" (Treatise 1, in *Ante-Nicene Fathers,* vol. 5, pp. 421–29), "Whoever is separated from the Church and is joined to an adulteress, is separated from the promises of the Church; nor can he who forsakes the Church of Christ attain to the rewards of Christ. He is a stranger; he is an enemy. He can no longer have God as his Father, who has not the Church as his mother" (p. 423).

9. The demonic option is rooted in early Christian polemics against pagans and those accused of heresy, e.g., Tertullian, *On Idolatry, Prescription against Heretics* 40; and Cyprian (*Treatise on the Unity,* p. 422). See also W. H. Wagner, "Interpretations of Genesis 6:1–4." Athenagoras, *Plea for Christians,* in *Ante-Nicene Fathers,* vol. 2, claims the demons related to interpretations of Gen. 6:1–4 deluded polytheists into worshiping those demons as gods. Martin Luther (1483–1546) linked Jews, the papacy, and Muslims to the devil and denounced non-Christian religions as Satan-stimulated error ("Lectures on Genesis," in *Luther's Works,* vol. 6, p. 127; and Sermon on John 3:20, in *Luther's Works,* vol. 22, p. 365). He called Muhammad the devil's panderer, whoremaster, uncouth blockhead, and ass, and depicted him studying the Qur'an "in his bed of harlotry . . . [boasting that the devil] had endowed him with so much physical strength that he could bed as many as 40 women and yet remain unsatisfied" ("Last Words of David," in *Luther's Works,* vol. 15, comments on 2 Sam. 23, pp. 339–44).

The false god–idolatry extension was clearly articulated by John Calvin. *Institutes* 1.4 states that God has "sown a seed of religion in all men," but humans "measure [God] by the yardstick of their own carnal stupidity, and neglect sound investigation, thus out of curiosity they fly off into empty speculations." One result is that humans plunge into ruin through idolatry and attendant immorality. Worship apart from the God revealed in Jesus through the Spirit, therefore, is directed to a false god: "Now we must also hold that all who corrupt pure religion—and this is sure to happen when each is given to his own opinion—separate themselves from the one and only God. Indeed, they will boast that they have something else in mind; but what they intend, or what they have persuaded themselves of, has not so much bearing on the matter, seeing that the Holy Spirit pronounces them all to be apostates who in the blindness of their own minds substitute demons in place of God" (*Institutes* 1.5, 13). The influential twentieth-century Reformed theologian Karl Barth (1886–1968) carried through the same views in his *Church Dogmatics.* He remarked that Islam makes a "noisy fanaticism" out of its version of monotheism and that Muhammad is a "baroque figure" to be regarded with humor, but that Islam's "artifice . . . consists in developing to a supreme degree what is at the heart of all paganism, revealing and setting at the very center its esoteric essence, i.e., so-called 'monotheism.' In this way it was able to become a deadly danger to all other forms of paganism and to a Christianity with a pagan conception of the oneness of God" (Barth, *Church Dogmatics,* vol. 2, pt. 1, p. 448).

10. See, e.g., Feiler.

11. The New Testament and traditional theologians lend less support for the inclusivist and pluralist positions than for the exclusivist perspective. Among passages that may be adduced are the creation accounts of Gen. 1–2 and Psalms, the Wisdom portions of the Wisdom of Solomon and Sirach, in that these present God's gracious involvement with all persons, especially through wisdom. Deut.

4:15–20 has YHWH through Moses say that he gave celestial powers (made by and subject to YHWH) to the other nations for worship but that Israel is to worship only YHWH. Among the New Testament passages are Matt. 25:31–46; John 1:1–18; and Acts 10:34 and 17:16–31. The cosmic theological passages in Ephesians and Colossians indicate a restoration of all creation through the ultimate glorification of Jesus according to the hidden plan-mystery of God. Among second- and third-century theologians who occasionally wrote of the Creator and the incarnate Word-Jesus moving all humans and spiritual beings to eternal fulfillment are Clement of Alexandria, Athenagoras, and Origen (See *Ante-Nicene Fathers,* vol. 2 and 4). Justin Martyr's suggestive but undeveloped concept of the "spermatic word" resonates with the wisdom tradition (*Ante-Nicene Fathers, Second Apology*). Clement of Alexandria may be quoted as indicative of the other early theological writers: "The Father, then, and Maker of all things is apprehended by all things, agreeably to all, by innate power and without teaching. . . . But no race anywhere of tillers of the soil, or nomads, not even of dwellers in cities, can live without being imbued with the faith of a superior being. . . . [A]ll have one and the same preconception respecting Him who hath appointed government, since the most universal of His operations equally pervade all" (*Miscellanies* 5.14, 133). "Men must then be saved by learning truth through Christ, even if they attain philosophy. For now that is clearly shown 'which was not made known to other ages, which is now revealed to the sons of men' [Eph. 3:5]. For there was always a natural manifestation of the one Almighty God among all right thinking men, and the most, who had not quite divested themselves of shame with respect to the truth apprehended the eternal beneficence in divine providence" (*Miscellanies* 5.14, 87).

12. See Flannery, Declaration on the Relation of the Church to Non-Christian Religions, *Nostra Aetate* 3, pp. 739–40.

> The Church also has a high regard for the Muslims. They worship God, who is one, living and subsistent, merciful and almighty, the Creator of heaven and earth, who has also spoken to men. They strive to submit themselves without reserve to the hidden decrees of God, just as Abraham submitted himself to God's plan, to whose faith Muslims eagerly link their own. Although not acknowledging him as God, they venerate Jesus as a prophet, his virgin Mother they also honor, and even at times devoutly invoke. Further, they await the day of judgment and the reward of God following the resurrection of the dead. For this reason they highly esteem an upright life and worship God, especially by way of prayer, alms-deeds and fasting. Over the centuries many quarrels and dissensions have arisen between Christians and Muslims. The sacred Council now pleads with all to forget the past, and urges that a sincere effort be made to achieve mutual understanding; for the benefit of all men, let them together preserve and promote peace, liberty, social justice and moral values.

See also Flannery, *Lumen Gentium's* statement: "The plan of salvation also includes those who acknowledge the Creator, in the first place amongst whom are the Moslems: these profess to hold the faith of Abraham, and together with us they adore the one, merciful God, mankind's judge on the last day" (chap. 2, para. 16). The quotation is repeated in the *Catechism of the Catholic Church,* pt. 1, sect. 841, p. 223. Dardess recognizes that the Vatican Council left issues unresolved. He addresses the relationship of the Bible and the Qur'an in a positive manner, aiming his work at Roman Catholics in interfaith dialogue with Muslims.

Nicholas of Cusa (1401–64) held in *De Pace Fidei* that there was one true religion common to all faith-expressions but that believers worship through different rites. He considered Christianity the common unity that the other religions, through discussion and study, would come to acknowledge and accept. In his *Cribratio Alkoran,* dedicated to Pope Pius II, however, the cardinal took an entirely negative view of the Qur'an. Cusanus reports a tradition that Muhammad was instructed about Christianity by a Nestorian monk and became a Christian while in Mecca. Some Jews perverted Muhammad, and the religion therefore is an amalgam of Nestorian heresy and Judaism (p. 79). Cusanus also reports that some Arabs say that seven men wrote the Qur'an and others say that four men who opposed each other wrote their own Qur'ans. There are accounts told to Cusanus that someone named Elag deleted eighty-five passages and added others (pp. 84–85). In the course of his examination of the Qur'an, Cusanus concludes that Muhammad has blasphemed God (p. 148). His versions of the Qur'an's origins and Muhammad became part of the opposition to Islam, the Book, and the Messenger that appears in modern exclusivist criticisms. See Nicholas of Cusa.

13. McBrien, p. 275. Among Roman Catholic theologians with distinctive views, note especially Rahner, pp. 311–21. Note Hans Küng's essays and Knitter's response in Swidler, pages 192–209, 231–50, and Knitter, pp. 224–30.

14. John of Damascus (d. before 753), an official of the Ummayid caliph before he entered the monastic life, termed Islam a "heresy" and wrote disparagingly of the "superstition of the Ishmaelites," in his Fount of Knowledge. While he referred to the Qur'an and some Muslim practices, he may report some legends; see John of Damascus, pp. 153–60.

15. For succinct surveys of Orthodox positions see Papademetriou's two articles cited in the bibliography and Yannoulatos.

16. Quoted by *Papademetriou,* "Recent Patriarchal Encyclicals."

17. Papademetriou, "An Orthodox Christian View," closing paragraph.

18. See, e.g., T. Peters and his view of *ecumenē,* pp. i, vii–xvii, 352–54; and W. H. Wagner, "Toward a Christian-Islamic Ecumenic Encounter."

19. See, e.g., Paul Sponheim and Philip Hefner, in Braaten and Jenson, vol. 1, pp. 197–321.

20. See Macquarrie, pp. 163–64. He sees a resemblance between austere Calvinism and Islam.

21. The first quotation is from Watt, *Islam,* introd.; and the second is from Watt, *Muhammad,* p. 240.

22. See, e.g., Cragg, *Muhammad and the Christian:* "There are to be sure acute problems for the theologian in the Islamic doctrine of God and in its characteristic 'distancing' of the divine/human relationship. But these, critical as they are, do not detract from the relevance of this most resolute of theisms. It is within, rather than against, this witness to the divine Lordship that the Christian can find community with Muslims and ground his estimation of Muhammad. . . . [F]rom this angle and with this dimension, the Qur'an can become the Christian's territory in a positive sense" (pp. 7–8). Cragg recognizes that the idea of a "suffering God" is rejected by Muslims, whereas it is essential for Christians. He claims that Islam exempts God from the turmoil and tragedy of humans because of Islam's emphasis on divine transcendence. See Cragg, *Muhammad and the Christian,* pp. 137–39. See David Kerr's essay, "The Prophethood of Muhammad," in Haddad and Haddad, pp. 426–46, for criticisms of Cragg and others with a milder view of Watt.

23. See McGrath, pp. 537–38.

24. Note especially Armstrong (a former Roman Catholic religious).

25. See Hick, *A Christian Theology of Religions,* esp. pp. 124–39. He sees two types of Christianity by the mid-twenty-first century, one traditional with the creeds and doctrines about Jesus and his atonement and another motivated by a pluralistic vision that takes Jesus as one outstanding incarnation of God's presence among humans and that considers the other religions as valid paths to God.

26. See Ford, pp. 268–72, on Hick; and Hick, *A Christian Theology of Religions.*

27. Muslims traditionally consider the Night to have been between Ramadan 23 and 27.

28. See Glassé, p. 381.

29. See Hind and Saeed. A saying or action by Muhammad is termed *hadith sharif* (noble hadith). See Glassé, pp. 159–62.

30. See also Surah 73:4, in which Muhammad is told to recite the passages in "slow, measured, rhythmic tones."

31. Surah 12 fits the context of a controversy.

32. For the revelations concerning his being authorized to take more than four wives and the resolution of the rumors concerning Aisha's morality (which led to wider instructions on gossip and accusations against women), see Surahs 33:50–52 and 24:1–26 respectively.

33. The number of ayas differ from edition to edition because some include the Basmillah ("In the Name of God, Most Gracious, Most Merciful"), which appears at the start of every surah (except Surah 9), as a verse while others do not.

Also, there are passages that are linked and some that are separated. The Qur'an is somewhat shorter than the New Testament.

34. *Tajwid* (adornment, beautification) is the term for the science of reciting the Qur'an. There are different tempi, styles, and pronunciations. See Glassé, pp. 268–69.

35. The constitutions of nations such as Saudi Arabia, Iran, and Pakistan declare the Qur'an and Sunna the basis of national law. The Pakistani Penal Code, 295-B, reads, "Whoever willfully defiles, damages or desecrates a copy of the Holy Qur'an or an extract therefrom or uses it in any derogatory manner or for any unlawful purpose shall be punishable for imprisonment for life." Pakistan Penal Code 295-C reads, "Use of derogatory remarks, etc.; in respect to the Holy Prophet. Whoever by words, either spoken or written or by visible representation, or by any imputation, innuendo, or insinuation, directly or indirectly, defiles the sacred name of the Holy Prophet Mohammad (PBUH) shall be punished with death, or imprisonment for life, and shall also be liable to fine." Penal Code 298-A covers the Messenger's wives, family, four "righteous caliphs," and Companions (up to three years' imprisonment and possible fine). The "anti-blasphemy" laws were enacted in 1985–86.

36. Surah 56:77–79: "[T]his is indeed a Qur'an most honorable, in a Book well guarded which none shall touch but those who are clean."

37. See Surah 16:98–99: "When thou dost read the Qur'an seek Allah's protection from Satan the rejected [or "stoned"] one. No authority has he over those who believe and put their trust in their Lord."

38. See von Denffer, pp. 163–65; and the conservative Ahmad Khan. The latter would prevent non-Muslims from touching the Qur'an. Muslims are also advised by Khan to be careful when writing passages of the Qur'an so that good penmanship is used, papers with Quranic passages are treated with respect, and, when written on blackboards, are removed with water rather than a common eraser.

39. See von Denffer, p. 166. Fourteen or fifteen ayas promote the response called *Sajda al-Tilawa*: 7:206; 13:15; 16:49/50; 17:109; 91:58; 22:18 (22:77); 25:60; 27:25/26; 32:15; 38:24/25; 41:38; 53:62; 84:20/21; and 96:19.

Two.   *Basic Narratives for Judaism and Christianity*

1. The Jewish references are from Josephus's *Antiquities of the Jews,* pseudepigraphal writings (Jubilees, Sibylline Oracles, and Enoch as translated in Charlesworth), the so-called Old Testament Apocrypha and Deuterocanonicals (as in the *New Revised Standard Bible*), and the Babylonian Talmud as reported in Ginzberg. In the case of Christian materials I used Hennecke and Schneemelcher; Ehrman; and M. A. Yusseff's edition of the Gospel of Barnabas.

2. While there is continuity between the biblical Hebrews-Israelites and Jews, there are also differences. See Jer. 34:9; Zech. 8:23; and Esther. "Covenant" is used in numerous ways, some of which are not relevant to our study. See *Anchor Bible Dictionary,* vol. 1, pp. 1179–1202.

3. See Neusner, *The Way of the Torah,* p. xiv.

4. The first "age" includes what is often termed the apostolic period (30–100 CE and the patristic period up to the First Council of Nicea) and the second is from the First Council of Nicea to the Second Council of Nicea. The latter concludes a series of seven ecumenical councils accepted both by Latin (Western) and Greek (Orthodox) Christianity.

5. Gen. 2:3: "So God blessed the seventh day and hallowed it, because on it God rested from all the work that he had done in creation." See Exod. 20:8–11; Deut. 5:12–15.

6. W. H. Wagner, "Interpretations of Genesis 6:1–4."

7. But see the fragmentary *Life of Adam and Eve* in Charlesworth, vol. 1, pp. 258–61.

8. See, e.g., 2 Esd. 3:20–26; 4:30; 7:48, 166–18. Some persons are able to keep God's commandments without sinning (3:36).

9. Books attributed to Enoch form an important backdrop for Jewish and Christian demonology and apocalypticism; see Charlesworth, vol. 1, pp. 14–89.

10. See, e.g., Josephus, *Antiquities* 1.3, 73; and *Sibylline Oracles* 1.146–98, in Charlesworth, vol. 1, pp. 338–39. Josephus wrote ca. 90–100.

11. Gen. 9:9–17.

12. Josephus, *Antiquities* 1.6, 3.

13. See Gen. 9:20–28.

14. See Goldberg and Raynor, p. 274.

15. See Josephus, *Antiquities* 1.7, 154–57; and Ginzberg, vol. 1, pp. 174–75, 184–86.

16. Gen. 17:1–21.

17. Gen. 16:1–16; 21:8–21.

18. See Gen. 22:1–19.

19. See Jubilees 17:15–18 (Charlesworth, vol. 2, p. 174); and Josephus, *Antiquities* 1.13, 222–36. The latter specifies Isaac's age.

20. Exod. 19:1–6. For another formulation of the election of Israel, see Deut. 7:7–16; 12:12–22.

21. Exod. 19:7–9; 34:1–28.

22. See esp. Deut. 30:1–20.

23. See, e.g., Deut. 4:19.

24. See Isa. 44:1–28.

25. See Exod. 24:1–8; 19–40. Leviticus continues exhortations and rules often with the theme of the holiness God expects from God's people since God

is also holy. Numbers contains narrative materials of Israel's time in the wilderness, and Deuteronomy is Moses' farewell testament.

26. Exod. 33:11. In the pseudepigraphal Book of Jubilees, God gives Moses Enochlike revelations about the past stretching to the hierarchies of angels and the future of Israel; see Charlesworth, vol. 2, pp. 52–142.

27. For Moses' ascension after his death, see Josephus, *Antiquities* 4. 8, 48; the New Testament's Jude 8; Ginzberg, vol. 2, pp. 831–39. For some traditions and legends about Moses in Jewish apocalyptic writings, see Charlesworth; Ginzberg.

28. See also 1 Chron. 17:7–14. 2 Sam. 7:18–29 and 1 Chron. 17:16–27 recount David's prayer in which he accepted the Lord's promise.

29. See, e.g., 2 Esdras 6:11–7:45 for a description of the end and a heavenly messiah called the son of God who will reign four hundred years and die before the general resurrection. 1 Enoch 37–69 has the supreme angel, Son of Man, defeat the power of evil and be involved in the judgment (Charlesworth, vol. 1, pp. 29–48). 3 Enoch refers to the Messiah of Joseph, the Messiah the son of David, and battles involving Gog and Magog in the days of the Messiah (3 Enoch 45:5, in Charlesworth, vol. 1, p. 298).

30. The parallel passage is Micah 4:1–4.

31. E.g., the destructions of the northern kingdom of Israel (722 BCE) and the southern kingdom of Judah (590s–586 BCE); the surrender to the Macedonian Greeks (330 BCE); the Maccabean revolt and later civil war (160s–63 BCE); the reality of Roman domination beginning in 63 BCE; and the ill-fated rebellions against the Romans (67–72 and 132–35 CE).

32. See both volumes of Charlesworth for the numerous pseudepigraphal works. Among the so-called intertestamental apocalyptic works are three books of Enoch, Jubilees, Testament of the Twelve Patriarchs, 2 Esd., 2 Bar., Dan., and Zech. 9–14.

33. Among the fringe groups were the Qum Ran Covenanters. Pharisees and Zealots also used some of the widely circulated works.

34. See 2 Maccabees as a whole, esp. 2 Macc. 7.

35. See, e.g., Neusner, *Torah: From Scroll to Symbol*; Ruderman, pt. 1, pp. 21–37.

36. See 2 Esd. 14:37–48.

37. In addition to G. Robinson, see Neusner, *From Testament to Torah*; *Midrash in Context*; and *Torah: From Scroll to Symbol*; Cohen; Goldberg and Raynor.

38. G. Robinson, pp. 201–19.

39. Neusner, *Introduction to Rabbinic Literature,* pp. 223–45.

40. Reven Kimelman, "Birkat Ha-Minim and the Lack of Evidence for an Anti-Christian Jewish Prayer in Late Antiquity," pp. 226–44; and Lawrence Shiffman, "At the Crossroads: Tannaitic Perspectives on the Jewish-Christian Schism," pp. 115–56, both in Sanders, Baumgartner, and Mendelson.

41. See John Chrysostom; Wilken; and Charlesworth, "Christians and Jews in the First 6 Centuries," pp. 305–25 in Shanks.

42. The Septuagintal texts of Esther and Daniel are longer than the Hebrew, the Psalms are divided differently, and Jeremiah has a different arrangement. The following are in the Septuagint and not in the Hebrew Bible: 1–4 Macc., Wisdom of Solomon, Sirach (Ecclesiasticus), Judith, Tobit, and Baruch.

43. 1 Cor. 15:3–11.

44. E.g., see 1 John 4:1–6.

45. E.g., see 1–3 John, Galatians, Philippians, and Revelation.

46. For the earliest such reference to Enoch, see Jude 14–15.

47. The Infancy Gospel of Jesus, the Infancy Gospel of Mary, several Gospels, and Acts of Thomas. In addition there were Acts of Thomas, John, Pontius Pilate, Paul and Thecla, and Nicodemus along with treatises and apocalyptics such as the Didache and the Apocryphon of John. For reasons still unknown, a group of Christians deposited numerous manuscripts in Nag Hammadi, Egypt. See J. Robinson; Hennecke and Schneemelcher, both volumes; and Ehrman.

48. The Infancy Gospel of Thomas, 2:2–5; 4:1–2; 9:1–3; in Ehrman, pp. 127–29. The work probably dates from the second or third century.

49. Proto-Evangelium of James, 7:1–3, in Hennecke and Schneemelcher, vol. 1, p. 378.

50. See among many New Testament passages, Luke 24:44–47; 1 Cor. 15:3–4; and W. H. Wagner, *After the Apostles,* pp. 13–23.

51. Psalm 22 also functions as a significant early Christian prediction-interpretation of Jesus' death and exaltation.

52. See Exod. 12:21–32; 24:3–8; and Lev. 16:7–34.

53. See Rom. 1:16.

54. See esp. Gal. 4:21–5:12.

55. See 1 Pet. 3:13–22.

56. See esp. 1 Cor. 15:20–58; Rom. 5:12–21; John 20:1–31.

57. See W. H. Wagner, *After the Apostles,* pp. 79–94, for a fuller discussion.

58. See especially a chain of passages quoted by Paul in Romans 3:9–18. The Old Testament quotations are drawn from Ecclesiastes, several Psalms, and Isaiah.

59. See, e.g., 1 Tim. 2:8–18, 1 Cor. 15:45–49. An important second-century source is Tertullian's treatises "On the Veiling of Virgins" and "On The Apparel of Women," in *Ante-Nicene Fathers,* vol. 4. Note also W. H. Wagner, "Interpretations of Genesis 6:1–4."

60. See, e.g., Justin Martyr, *Dialogue with Trypho, a Jew,* in *Ante-Nicene Fathers,* vol. 1; and Clement of Alexandria's *Exhortation, Instructor, and Stromateis,* in *Ante-Nicene Fathers,* vol. 2; and W. H. Wagner, *After the Apostles,* pp. 95–115, 157–86.

61. The following version of the creed developed at the First Councils of Nicea (325) and Constantinople (381) was approved by the Council of Chalcedon (450).

We believe in one God the Father All-sovereign, maker of heaven and earth, and of all things visible and invisible.

And in one Lord Jesus Christ, the only-begotten Son of God. Begotten of the Father before all the ages, Light of Light, true God of true God, begotten not made, of one substance with the Father, through whom all things were made; who for us men and for our salvation came down from the heavens, and was made flesh of the Holy Spirit and the Virgin Mary, and became man, and was crucified for us under Pontius Pilate, and suffered and was buried, and rose again on the third day, according to the Scriptures, and ascendeth into the heavens, and sitteth on the right hand of the Father, and cometh again with glory to judge living and dead, of whose kingdom there shall be no end:

And in the Holy Spirit, the Lord and the Life-giver, that proceedeth from the Father, who with the Father and Son is worshipped together and glorified together, who spake through the prophets:

In one Holy, Catholic and Apostolic Church:

We acknowledge one Baptism unto remission of sins. We look for a resurrection of the dead, and the life of the age to come. (Bettenson and Maunder, pp. 28–29)

62. One often-cited list is the seventh- or eighth-century Latin Muratorian Canon. It probably reflects a second- or third-century list. It omits 1 and 2 Peter and Hebrews and puts the Wisdom of Solomon in the New Testament.

63. Eusebius, *Ecclesiastical History,* in *Nicene and Post-Nicene Fathers,* ser. 2, vol. 1, bk. 2, chap. 25, pp. 1–7.

64. See Athanasius, Letter 39, in *Nicene and Post-Nicene Fathers,* ser. 2, vol. 4, pp. 551–52. He noted that heretics have used other works that are to be rejected.

65. The names of the twelve vary in the Gospels (see Matt. 10:2–4; Mark 3:16–19; and Luke 6:12–16). The Gospel of John does not list the disciples and mentions several not named in the other three Gospels. A number of women followed Jesus. Other followers were Lazarus, Mary and Martha of Bethany, Joseph of Arimathea, the owners of the Jerusalem house in which Jesus met the night of his arrest, and the five hundred referred to in 1 Cor. 15.

66. Note, e.g., 1 Cor. 12:1–11; Eph. 4:11; Acts 6:1–6; and 1 Tim. 3:13.

67. Byzantine rule extended into North Africa and at times into Sicily, Italy, and the Balkans. See Treadgold for a compact, yet complete history.

68. See Ferguson, vol. 1, p. 266. Bishops who were already married were required to put their wives into distant convents.

Three.   *Islam's Basic Narrative and Core Positions*

1. See the entry "Divine Names" in Glassé, pp. 99–100. The first four titles cited are in the passage quoted. Note the brackets in the quotation. Yusuf Ali translated Az-Zahir as "The Evident" and Al Batin as "The Immanent." I follow Glassé's version. The other titles are in Surahs 112:3; 13:9; and 112:1 respectively.

2. Surah 50:16. See also Surah 7:180: "The most beautiful Names belong to Allah, so call on Him by them; but shun men as use profanity in His Names. For what they do, they will soon be requited."

3. See Glassé, p. 334.

4. See Maududi, *Four Basic Qur'anic Terms,* p. 94.

5. Other words include *'uqud* (probably treaty, in Surah 5:1) and *aqd* (legal act, contract, and will).

6. See McAuliffe, *Encyclopedia of the Qur'an,* vol. 1, pp. 464–67.

7. *'Ahd* is used in civil and political senses at Surahs 17:34; 23:8; and 70:32. *Mithaq* is at Surahs 4:90, 92; 8:72. The words are used interchangeably at Surahs 2:27 and 13:20, 25.

8. God as guarantor is at Surah 12:66, 80. The Qur'an as covenant of the Book is at Surah 7:169. God voiding the covenant with violators is at Surah 2:123–24.

9. Each of God's days might be thousands of human years (Surah 22:47). Although the Qur'an does not mention Gen. 1–3, the general structure of those accounts is reflected in the Quranic passages.

10. See also Surah 7:54.

11. See, e.g., Surahs 2:30–39; 7:11–26; and 15:26–50.

12. See also Surah 55:15.

13. See Surah 2:29. Often translated as "vicegerent," *khalifah* (caliph) is a deputy or representative authorized and empowered to act on behalf of and carry out the will of a superior authority.

14. Surah 15:28–29.

15. Among other passages, see Surahs 15:32–43 and 2:34.

16. In his translation of the Qur'an Maududi renders the term as the "Tree of Eternal Life" and Dawood as the "Tree of Immortality." Note that in Gen. 2:17 the specifically forbidden tree is that of good and evil. The tree of life is not mentioned until the couple are expelled from the Garden (Gen. 3:24). In addition, the Genesis Garden is on earth and not in one of the heavens. See also Surah 24:50 and Surah 7:19–23.

17. See Surahs 20:115; 33:72.

18. Surah 20:121 included a reference to Adam and the woman sewing together leaves from the Garden to cover themselves.

19. See Glassé, p. 372, on sin.

20. See also Surah 20:123–24.

21. See Maududi, *Birth Control,* pp. 73–74: "Islam is the natural way of life: it is the natural religion for man. All the rules laid down by it, individual as well as collective, are based on a fundamental principle: that man should behave and act in consonance with natural laws that he finds working in the universe; and that he should refrain from a course of life that might force him to deviate from the purposes for which nature is operating. The Holy Qur'an informs us that God Almighty has not only created everything that we find in the universe but has also endowed it with an instinctive knowledge of the ways by which it can most suitably perform the tasks assigned to it in the general scheme of things."

22. See Glassé, p. 372.

23. See, e.g., Surahs 17:11; 21:37; 70:19–21; 4:278; 30:54; 16:4; 18:54; 21:1–3; 2:243; and 7:10–17.

24. See, e.g., Surahs 2:10; 5:52; 8:49; 9:125; and 74:31.

25. See, e.g., Surah 2:40–46.

26. Bakkah seems to have been an ancient name for Mecca. See Yusuf Ali, p. 152 n. 422.

27. Glassé, p. 318.

28. See also Surah 14:4, 9–14.

29. See, e.g., Surahs 33:7; 17:54; 6:10; and 2:87.

30. According to Yusuf Ali, the root of the word *dhari* connotes humiliation and is a plant that is "bitter and thorny, loathsome in smell and appearance[,] . . . a fit plant for Hell" (p. 1640 n. 6099).

31. See the introduction for the written and vocalized Arabic form of the Shahadah.

32. The names and times of the prayers are (a) Early Morning Prayer, Salatu-l-Fajr, from dawn to sunrise; (b) Noon Prayer, Salatu-l-Zuhr, from the time the sun is directly overhead until an object's shadow is as long as the object itself; (c) Afternoon Prayer, Salatu-l-Asr, between the noon prayer to the end of sunset; (d) Sunset Prayer, Salatu-i-Maghrib, between the end of sunset and the disappearance of evening twilight; and (e) Night Prayer, Salatu-l-'Isha, from the end of evening twilight to just before dawn.

33. Many Muslims contribute to various benevolent societies and charities that transmit the funds to believers in poor countries or to Muslim hospitals, schools, development projects, and so on.

34. The Ka'bah is 42.65 feet high. The northeast wall is 41.44 feet long, the east wall is 36.81 feet long, the west wall is 42.98 feet long, and the south-

west wall is 36.19 feet long. The door in the northeast wall is 6.5 feet from the ground and 5.58 feet wide. See Glassé, p. 179; and Muhammad Ali, *Religion of Islam,* pp. 378–83.

35. See Glassé, p. 400, on the Wahhabi position that nothing is "real" but God. The Sufi position attempts to balance union with God and the distinction between the Lord and the servant. Thirteen qualities or holy attributes that apply to God are existence, eternity, perpetuity, dissimilarity (from all else), self-sufficiency, unity, might, will, knowledge, life, hearing, sight, and speech. The thirteen that must not be applied to God are nonexistence, beginning, ending, similarity, need, plurality, weakness, coercion, ignorance, death, deafness, blindness, and muteness.

36. See Surah 17:1 for the reference to the "Farthest Mosque." Muhammad and Gabriel's journey began from and ended at the Ka'bah. They used the rock now within the Dome of the Rock in Jerusalem as the point of departure through the heavens. In the order of the heavens from the closest to earth to the highest the gatekeepers are Adam, Jesus and John the Baptist, Joseph the Patriarch, Enoch, Aaron, Moses, and Abraham. Some hadiths transpose Moses and Abraham. Through the Night Journey and the Ascent, Jerusalem has become the third holiest site in Islam. Note Muslim, vol. 1, bk. 1, chap. 75, item 309, pp. 101–2. Also, see W. H. Wagner, "Journeying to God."

37. The hadith and a cherished traditional account in the most widely read traditional biography (*Sira or Life of Muhammad,* by Muhammad ibn Ishaq) of Muhammad tells of his being opened by angel-presences, having the dark spot of resistance to God present in every human heart removed, and his interior being cleansed by the angels; see Muhammad ibn Ishaq, pp. 71–72. The cleansing account is repeated in the hadith before the Prophet went on the Night Journey, see Muslim, vol. 1, bk. 1, chap. 75, item 309, pp. 102–4.

38. The first reference is from Muslim, vol. 1, bk. 1, chap. 1, sect. 1, pp. 1–2. The second reference is from *Mishkat-Ul-Masabih,* bk. 2, the Book of Destiny (Qadr), chap. 4, sect. 1, hadith 79 and 80. *Mishkat* agrees with Muslim but makes the event the second reported in Book 1.

39. See Muhammad Ali, *Religion of Islam,* pp. 235–260, for a full discussion, including mistranslations and confusions among scholars. The debate can be traced in the later Umayyid dynasty in Damascus, exemplified in the struggle between the Qadarites (free will) and the Jabarites (absolute predestination).

40. Quoted in Denny, p. 112.

Four.   *The Setting: Reflections on Arabia*

1. For a view of pre-Islamic conditions in Arabia with special emphasis on culture, see Hoyland.

2. See, among various passages, Surahs 7:65–93; 11:50–68; and 27:45–53.

3. See Surahs 2:62 and 27:22–44.

4. See Ben-Sasson, pp. 358–59; and Biale, pp. 207–9.

5. See the florid account of how Christianity came to Arabia and the defeat of Abrahah in ibn Ishaq, pp. 12–30.

6. See Hennecke and Schneemelcher, vol. 1, on Gospels; Cameron, for the Proto-Evangelium of James (pp. 107–22) and the Infancy Gospel of Thomas (pp. 124–30); and J. Robinson, pp. 244–55, for the Dialogue with the Savior.

7. See Ferguson, vol. 1, p. 98, for a helpful survey.

8. Zoroastrianism and Manichaeanism saw the cosmos as divided between the powers of light and dark. This world was a temporary mixture of both until the time when the two powers would be separated from each other. Mani, a Persian prophet active in the third century CE, was executed by the Persian authorities. He claimed to be the last of the divine prophets sent by the god of light-goodness into the cosmos to proclaim salvation.

9. See also Surah 48:11–12.

10. See Glassé, p. 206, for other deities and their functions.

Five.   *Times and the Messenger*

1. Among those who heeded when most around them rejected the Message and its proclaimers were some aristocratic Egyptian women (Surah 12:51–53), two Egyptian sorcerers (Surah 7:109–26), Pharaoh's wife (Surah 66:11), some anonymous persons (Surah 27:53), and the queen of Sheba (Surah 27:44).

2. See Treadgold, pp. 149–309, for a detailed description.

3. The successors were Tiberius II Constantine (r. 578–82), Maurice Tiberius (r. 582–602), and Phocas (r. 602–10).

4. Bukhari 1.7. See also Ibn Ishaq, pp. 653–59.

5. See Salahi, pp. 6–16. Generally he repeats Ibn Ishaq's versions.

6. Ibn Ishaq pp. 35–52.

7. Ibn Ishaq, p. 36.

8. Ibn Ishaq, p. 97.

9. Ibn Ishaq, p. 55.

10. Among relevant passages are those also from surahs that contain Medinan as well as Meccan ayas, e.g., 2:177, 215–20; 4:2–8; 3:32, 132; 4:59–66, 80–81.

11. See Watt and Bell, pp. 3–9; Salahi, pp. 47–55.

12. See especially Qutb, *Milestones*; *Social Justice In Islam*; and *In the Shade of the Qur'an*. Also see Maududi, *Four Basic Qur'anic Terms* and *Islamic Law and Constitution*; Mutahhari; Saulat; Hussain; Khomeini; and Safi.

13. See Ibn Ishaq, pp. 68–82, for some of the accounts about Muhammad's birth and family, the near-sacrifice of his father when a youth, his father's probity in sexual matters, and the signs and wonders that accompanied Muhammad's birth. Included are accounts of various persons, such as Ethiopian Christians, who recognized that he would be a great person in God's plan.

14. Ibn Ishaq, pp. 71–72. See also Muslim, vol. 1, bk. 1, chap. 75, items 310–11, pp. 100–103.

15. Ibn Ishaq, pp. 79–81. He gave the monk's name as "Bahira." See also Muslim, vol. 4, bk. 29, chaps. 972–79, items 5758–98, pp. 1247–52, for a description of the Messenger including the report that the "seal" was about the size of a pigeon's egg toward his left shoulder and had molelike spots. Muslim's description holds that Muhammad was handsome and plain, kindly and firm, smiling and serious, brave and judicious.

16. Glassé, p. 214; and Salahi, pp. 43–46.

17. While the exact night is not known, Muslims hold that it was within ten nights before the end of Ramadan. Some identify Ramadan 27 as the Night. See Glassé, p. 276.

18. Bukhari 1.3. See also Muslim, vol. 1, bk. 1, chap. 74, item 301, p. 96.

19. See, e.g., Surah 7:157.

20. Bukhari 1.3.

21. Bukhari 1.4.

22. See Surahs 81:19–25 and 53:2–18.

23. Ibn Ishaq, pp. 165–66.

24. See W. H. Wagner, "Journeying to God"; and Muslim, vol. 1, bk. 1, chap. 75, item 309, p. 100. Sometimes the order of Moses and Abraham is reversed. Muslim, 1.75.312–13, quotes Abu Malik's description of angels cleansing Muhammad's internal organs as a prelude to the Night Journey with water drawn from Zamzam. The same source saying that Gabriel opened the roof of Muhammad's home, cleansed him, and then took him on the journey.

25. Surah 61:4 also refers to the battle.

26. Muhammad used his portion to aid the widowed, orphaned, and needy.

27. Muhammad's Last Sermon was delivered on the Ninth Day of Dhu l-Hijjah 10 AH in the Uranah Valley of Mount Arafat. The text is taken from the Alim, The Messenger's Last Sermon.

28. *Sahabah* may be defined in two ways. Strictly speaking, they were Muhammad's closest associates and attempted to absorb his teachings. They memorized the Qur'an and hadith before these were committed to writing. The term is also used to refer to anyone who saw the Messenger and converted to Islam during his lifetime.

29. There were numerous other prophetic claimants, including a woman. See Glassé, p. 331.

Six.   *The Origin, Transmission, and Structures of the Qur'an*

1. Yusuf Ali, p. 13, n. 15. Glassé, pp. 441–42, connected *surah* to "a row."

2. Muslim tradition explains that Muhammad, in a revelatory mode, opened the start of each surah, with the exception of Surah 9, with the Basmillah. Most of Surah 8 was revealed seven years before Surah 9. When the Qur'an was collated, it was decided that Surah 9 would be taken as distinct from Surah 8. See Yusuf Ali, p. 435; and Usmani, vol. 1, p. 813.

3. See Muhammad Ali, *The Religion of Islam,* p. 37 and n. 42. He added that the Kufan tradition counts 6,239; the Basran, 6,204; the Syrian, 6,225; the Meccan, 6,219; and the Medinan, 6,211. It is important, therefore, for readers to find out which version they are using when citing Quranic passages. See also Watt and Bell, pp. 57–64; and *Gätje,* p. 42.

4. See Muhammad Ali, *Holy Qur'an,* pp. 1–25. Earlier scholars have put the Arabic diacritic hamza in the margin to indicate a ruku'. The word *ruku'* also means "to bow." As noted in chapter 1, when one of these fourteen or fifteen ayas (called Sajda al-Tilawa) are recited, the persons present often bow toward Mecca. See Glassé, p. 388; and von Denffer, pp. 163–65.

5. For further explanation, see *Esack, The Qur'an, A Short Introduction,* pp. 63–64.

6. See Esack, *The Qur'an: A Short Introduction,* pp. 64–66.

7. See Bukhari 9.71/Khan 7374. The Messenger, ever understanding of human limitations, advised a follower who had a poor memory to recite Al Ikhlas three times for in doing so it was equal to saying the entire Qur'an.

8. See Yusuf Ali, pp. 122–24, for his explanation and a chart of the way in which the letters are combined letters. See also Esack, *The Qur'an, A Short Introduction,* pp. 62–63, who calls them "Disjointed Letters" (*al-huruf al-Muqatta'at*), and Sherif, pp. 45–47.

9. Yusuf Ali, p. 122.

10. See Sherif, pp. 61–62; and Uri Rubin's essay, "Exegesis and Hadith: The Case of the Seven Mathani," in Hawting and Abdul, pp. 141–72.

11. See Watt and Bell, pp. 127–35, for the punishment thesis.

12. See Esposito, *Oxford Encyclopedia,* vol. 3, p. 386.

13. Surah 24:11–19.

14. See, e.g., Platonic speculations on the eternal forms, or *ideai.* Jewish intertestamental apocalyptic writings such as Enoch, Testament of the Twelve Patriarchs, Jubilees, and 2 Esdras refer to heavenly revelatory scribes, scrolls, and books.

15. See Surahs 13:39; 43:2–4; and 85:22.

16. See Ibn Kathir, vol. 1, p. 43. He explains the reasoning behind some calling al-Fatihah the Umm Kitab.

17. E.g., see the relevant comments on the cited passages in Daryabadi; and Maududi, *Towards Understanding.*

18. In the eighth and ninth centuries CE the Mu'tazilite school of law and theology, heavily influenced by Neoplatonism and Persian thought, held that the Umm al-Kitab was created. The theological point appears to have been an attempt to preserve the singular unity of God. Backed by the Abbasid caliph al-Mamun (783–833), the Mu'tazilite position became part of a litmus test for teachers and their disciples. Those who held the view that the Umm al-Kitab was uncreated were suppressed and punished. This period of inquisition and suppression, called the *mihnah,* lasted from 833 to 847. Among those who were flogged for their rejection of the Mu'tazilite view was Ahmad ibn Hanbal (780–855), founder of the rival legal-theological school named after him (Hanbali or Hanbalite). Ibn Hanbal insisted that the Umm al-Kitab was uncreated. Sunnis adopted that position, whereas Shi'ia hold the Mu'tazilite view.

19. Philips, *Usool al-Tafseer,* p. 131 and the explanation continuing to p. 137 with footnotes.

20. See Esack, *The Qur'an: A Short Introduction,* pp. 105–11.

21. In biblical literature see Saul and his messengers (1 Sam. 10:9–13; 19:18–24) and Amos 7:10–16. See also Cragg, *Weight in the Word.*

22. See 2 Esdras 14:37–15:4.

23. Muslim, vol. 4, chap. 973, items 5764–67, p. 1248.

24. See especially Bukhari 6.501–82/Khan 5001–62.

25. Bukhari 4.819/Khan 3623. The same is reported several times without Aisha being mentioned at Bukhari 6.520/Khan 4998.

26. Bukhari 6.514/Khan 4992.

27. Al-Khu'i, a Shi'ia scholar, esp. chap. 4. Al-Khu'i attacked ten Sunni positions, arguing that the best and authentic custodians and interpreters of the Qur'an were Ali and those related to him. Both Bukhari and Muslim cite the incident reported by Hisham b. Hizam. Muslim included in the account that the Messenger said Gabriel said the Qur'an could be recited in one of the then-existing dialects in Arabia. See Muslim, vol. 2, bk. 4, chap. 289, items 1782–89, p. 389. Some Sufi brotherhoods regard the seven ahruf as seven styles or levels of spiritual-mystical interpretation.

28. Bukhari 6.581/Khan 5061.

29. See von Denffer, pp. 44–56, for a discussion of the sheaves and the various collections that were brought together in the final collation. Note also Philips, *Usool at-Tafseer,* pp. 155–60.

30. Tirmidhi 5823.

31. Bukhari 4.84. The traditional text is in the Alim. The passage does not appear at that point in Khan.

32. Bukhari 9.487/Khan 7390.

33. See Esack, *The Qur'an: A Short Introduction,* pp. 85–90.

34. The Medinan-Meccan tradition was claimed by those who held they were the closest to Muhammad, his family, and the many Companions in Arabia. Zaid b. Thabit, Umar, and Abu Bakr were identified with that position. The tradition of Basra centered on the Companion, Abu Musa al-Ashari (known originally as Abdullah ibn Qays, d. ca. 662). The Kufan position was led by Abdullah ibn Masud (d. ca. 653). He was one of four men whom, it was said, the Messenger singled out as sound teachers of the Qur'an. The others were Salim (an emancipated slave), Ubayy b. Ka'b, and Mu'adh b. Jabal (Bukhari 3758–60). The Syrian mushaf tradition centered in Damascus was associated with Ubayy bin Ka'b (d. ca. 639), also known as Abu Mundhir. For a time, according to tradition, he was one of Muhammad's several secretaries. In Muslim tradition the Messenger told him that the seven mathani were the seven ayas of al-Fatihah. Also associated with and credited with having a mushaf was Miqdad b. Amr (d. ca. 653). For fuller discussions of the collection and collation of the Qur'an, see Burton; Gätje; and Welch.

35. Bukhari 6.509/Khan 4986.

36. The editor's note 2760 to Muslim, vol. 4, bk. 29, chap. 1,014, p. 1313, states: "There were hundreds, if not thousands, of Companions who had recorded the verses of the Qur'an and committed them to their memories. What this means is that these four eminent Companions completely devoted themselves to this work."

37. Some Sunnis claim that the Shi'ia have unorthodox variant readings of and interpolations in the text, as well as another (and for Sunnis, false) surah. Modern Shi'ites deny the accusation. They do say, however, that the Sunnis have suppressed a number of Muhammad's hadith that favor Ali and his offspring.

38. Bukhari 6.510/Khan 4987.

39. Bukhari 6.556 and 6.558/Khan 5068–42, both narrated by Aisha.

40. Bukhari 6.550/Khan 5032.

41. Bukhari 3.263/Khan 2047.

42. See Gätje, pp. 57–59; Sherif, pp. 58–60; Burton, 27, 47–61, 93, 161–63; and Esack, *The Qur'an: A Short Introduction,* p. 126. Sherif cites three kinds of abrogation within the Qur'an: "(1) where both the written word and the content are eliminated (as reported cases where a recorded verse is said to have disappeared mysteriously and its substance to have faded from memory); (2) where the written word somehow vanished but the content remained in force (a once-existing verse that ordered the stoning of adulterers is believed to have disappeared, but the commandment has been maintained by tradition); (3) where a still-existing verse is in effect repealed or modified by the introduction of a new text (all references in the commentaries to the doctrine of abrogation fall into this category)" (p. 59). Burton entered into a complex and lengthy argument on whether there were two or three modes of abrogation and whether the Messenger's Sunna could

be taken as abrogating a Quranic passage or pointed to the abrogation of a Quranic ruling. He also moved in the direction of claiming that the mushafs that were used for the Uthmanic recension of the Qur'an were incomplete and/or that material was omitted. Muslims reject the view that the Qur'an is incomplete. See Burton, pp. 46–104.

43. Sherif, p. 58.

44. See also Esack, *The Qur'an: A Short Introduction,* pp. 118, 126–28. He notes that many Muslim jurists say that since Muhammad's life was an interpretation of the Qur'an, a tradition in the Hadith "reinterprets" and/or abrogates the Quranic text.

45. Numerous hadith speak disparagingly of individual Jews and Christians. For example, Bukhari 9.77/Khan 6944 reports that Muhammad said that if Jews fought against Muslims in the Last Hour, Muslims would kill them, and even trees and stones would call on the Muslims to slay the Jews (Bukhari 4.177/Khan 2925). This is virtually duplicated at several other points. Supposedly when Muhammad was dying he also cursed Jews (Bukhari 4.660/Kahn 3453 and 3454). According to Bukhari 4.394/Khan 3169, some Jewish leaders lied to him about the punishment required in the Torah concerning adultery. Muhammad then ordered that the accused Jew brought before him be stoned in accord with Jewish law (see Muslim, vol. 3, bk. 16, chap. 683, item 4214, p. 919, for one version, which is repeated with a man and a woman at other points in Bukhari 4.829/Khan 3635). On another occasion the Jewish survivors of the defeat of Khayber attempted to kill Muhammad by serving him poisoned mutton.

46. The Muslims and Meccan attackers thought it was still the holy month of Jumada l-Akhira, but according to some sources it was already the month of Rajab.

47. Bukhari 5.462/Khan 4141. Aisha said that she was inadvertently left behind when the company she was with broke camp. Safwan bin Al-Muattal, a young man, found her. Without speaking or looking at her (she was veiled), he brought her back to Medina. Some Medinan Hypocrites, attempting to sow discord in the umma, spread rumors about her. The Quranic revelation vindicated her and Safwan and led to the severe beating of the slanderers.

48. See Bukhari 8.815 for the first quotation and Bukhari 8.817. The Khan references are 6829–30.

49. See, e.g., Dawood, p. 5; Cragg, *Readings in the Qur'an,* p. 16; and Cragg, *The Qur'an and the West,* p. 12. In the last reference, Cragg suggests that by beginning at Surah 114 one reads the Qur'an "inward."

50. Rumi, Discourse 44, p. 173.

51. Cragg, *Readings in the Qur'an,* p. 14.

52. Yusuf Ali, p. 1419.

53. Yusuf Ali, p. 1.

Seven.   *Interpreting the Qur'an*

1. See esp. Ackroyd and Evans, the *Anchor Bible Dictionary,* vol. 3, pp. 425–43; Epp and MacRae.

2. Geographically, culturally, and religiously the "West" includes western and northern Europe, the continental United States, and Canada. Its traditions originated in Greece and Rome. The "Islamic world" embraces those nations and areas in which Islam is the dominant religious-cultural-intellectual perspective. Geographically, that includes North Africa, reaches into areas in sub-Saharan Africa, sweeps through the Syrio-Palestinian corridor (with the exception of Israel), from Turkey through the central Asian republics of the former Soviet Union, the Indian subcontinent, Malaysia, Indonesia, and numerous islands in the Indian Ocean. In Europe, the term could be used more gingerly of Albania, Bosnia, and some regions of Russia (such as Chechnya). I do not assume that either the West or the Islamic world are without great diversity and divisiveness.

3. See Smalley; Ackroyd and Evans; and *Interpreters Bible,* vol. 1, pp. 106–26.

4. The senses usually cited were the literal, the moral, and the spiritual. See Ackroyd and Evans, vol. 1, p. 467, for Origen of Alexandria's often-used view.

5. The first known such "harmony" was Tatian's *Diatessaron.* The tradition continues to the present; see Daniel.

6. For a comprehensive study of rabbinic literature and interpretation, see Neusner, *Introduction to Rabbinic Literature; From Testament to Torah*; and *Midrash in Context*. In addition, see *Anchor Bible Dictionary,* vol. 3, pp. 425 f.; and *New Interpreters Bible,* vol. 1, pp. 65–82.

7. See Neusner, Avery-Peck, and Green, pp. 217–41.

8. See esp. Thompson, pp. 205–28; Acton, vol. 1, pp. 532–73. Valla was ordained as a priest in 1431 and for part of his career was a member of the papal curia. In 1440 he proved that the Donations of Constantine was a forgery. His *Elegances of the Latin Language* (1444) demonstrated that the Vulgate Latin version of the New Testament used throughout Western Christendom contained grammatical errors and clumsy constructions.

9. See Spinoza, esp. chaps. 17–20.

10. See, e.g., Schweitzer; and Witherington.

11. See, e.g., Crossan, *Birth of Christianity,* and Pagels, *Beyond Belief.*

12. E.g., the American Roman Catholics Raymond Brown, Joseph Fitzmyer, and Luke Timothy Johnson; the Anglican Nicholas Thomas Wright; and the American Methodist Ben Witherington III.

13. Among the early leaders of the Reform movement were Abraham Geiger (1810–74), Hermann Cohen (1842–1918), and Leo Baeck (1873–1956). In the *Essence of Judaism,* Baeck wrote: "The distinctiveness of Judaism, which it has passed on to the rest of mankind, is its ethical affirmation of the world: Ju-

daism is the religion of ethical optimism. . . . Judaism never abandons the goal of the world since it has no doubt in the God who has bid men to march toward that goal. Its optimism is the strength of the mortal will; its call is 'Prepare the way!' (Isaiah 40:3)" (1974: 84–85, 86).

14. Among the early Conservative leaders were Zecharias Frankel (1801–75) and Solomon Schechter (1847–1915).

15. Kaplan, especially pp. 25–35, 330–59.

16. Sherif, p. 42. The citation from Surah 16 begins at aya 98: "When thou dost read the Qur'an, seek Allah's protection from Satan the rejected one. No authority has he over those who believe and put their trust in their Lord. His [Satan's] authority is over those only who take him as patron and who join partners with Allah."

17. Von Denffer, pp. 122–23, slightly altered. See also Philips, *Usool at-Tafseer*, pp. 48–50. His conditions for an interpreter are correct belief, correct methodology, and correct knowledge.

18. See Philips, *Usool at-Tafseer*, p. 50.

19. The Sunni schools are Hanafi, Hanbali, Maliki, and Shafi'i. The Shi'ia schools reflect divisions among Shi'ites. The Sadiqi is most prominent because it is followed by Twelver Shi'ia. Other Shi'ia groups follow one or the other Zayidis, Kharijis, and Ismailis. For general overviews, see Esposito, *Oxford Encyclopedia*, pp. 450–72; and Glassé, p. 419–20.

20. See Denny, pp. 195–206; Glassé, pp. 419–20; Esposito, *Oxford Encyclopedia*, pp. 178–81, 450–72;

21. Shi'ia emphasize the role of itjihad; very conservative Sunnis such as the Wahhabis insist that the "gates of itjihad" were closed in the ninth century.

22. Esposito, *Oxford Dictionary*, p. 134.

23. See, e.g., Baker; Safi; Wadud; and Rahman, *Islam and Modernity.*

24. Although I draw on a number of Muslim sources in the following discussion, I use mainly Philips, *Usool at-Tafseer*; von Denffer; Maududi, *Towards Understanding*; Glassé; Gätje; and Daryabadi.

25. Among the traditional forms of *ilm al-Qur'an* are tafsir (exegesis), recitations, Uthmanic script, miraculous aspects of the Qur'an, reasons for the Revelation, abrogated ayats, Quranic grammar, unusual Arabic terms, religious rulings, and Arabic language and literature. The branches of Quranic sciences number over one hundred. See *Philips, Usool at-Tafseer,* pp. 9–13.

26. The citation is from von Denffer, pp. 123–29. He used Ibn Taymiyah's *Muqaddima Fi Usul al-Tafsir* (Kuwait, 1971), pp. 93–102.

27. See von Denffer, pp. 134–35.

28. See von Denffer, pp. 136–37. Some hold that the tafsir by Umar al-Baidawi is the most authoritative among Sunni Muslims, but his tafsir was not completed before his death in 1286.

29. Philips, *Usool at-Tafseer,* pp. 245–64.

30. Philips, *Usool at-Tafseer.* Examples are stated at 2:17–20 and 13:17; and inferred at 25:67 and 17:110. Aphorisms at 2:116, 55:60, and 5:100.

31. Sherif, pp. 47–50.

32. See Yusuf Ali, pp. 1694–96, for details on oaths and their social importance.

33. See Safi, pp. 147–250, for several essays focused on gender justice; and chap. 13.

34. See Wadud, ix–xix, for the reactions to her work; and pp. 3–10, for her methodological statement.

35. Rahman, *Islam and Modernity,* from pp. 18, 19, 20. Original emphasis.

Eight.   *Four Cherished Passages*

1. The transliteration is from the Eliasi rendition in the Pickthall translation.

2. Other translations use "Lord" for *Rabb,* instead of "Cherisher and Sustainer," e.g., Pickthall; and Maududi, *Holy Qur'an.* Yusuf Ali supported his translation by stating, "The Arabic word *Rabb* usually translated Lord, has also the meaning of cherishing, sustaining, bringing to maturity" (p. 14, n. 20). Muhammad al-Ghazali called al-Fatihah the "Surah of Praise," "the Mother of the Book," and the Qur'an's greatest surah (p. 3).

3. See Ibn Kathir, vol. 1, p. 41–50. He indicated several hadiths that cited those titles.

4. Ibn Kathir, vol. 1, p. 43.

5. Qutb, *In the Shade,* vol. 1, p. 2.

6. See Glassé, p. 99–100, for the list.

7. The Qur'an's collators recognized that Surah 9 was an anomaly, and some thought it was a continuation of Surah 8. Because they recalled that the Messenger himself regarded it as a surah, they followed suit. See, however, Ibn Kathir, vol. 4, pp. 369–70. See Usmani, vol. 1, pp. 813–14.

8. Note, e.g., Martin Luther's sermon for St. Thomas Day in *Luther's Works,* vol. 51, pp. 17–23. The second-century Christian heretic, Marcion, posited two divine beings: the deity of wrath and judgment and the deity of love and grace.

9. The passages are Surahs 68:2–6; 73:1–5; and 74:1–7.

10. Spoken devoutly in Arabic, the aya is said to put the speaker under Allah's special protection. It is an *ayat al-hifz,* a verse of protection and refuge. See Bukhari 6.530/Khan 1510.

11. Tirmidhi 2169 and 2144.

12. Tirmidhi 2169.

13. See especially Qutb, *In the Shade,* vol. 1, p. 412–15, for the claim that Islam does not force conversions or religious conformity.

14. The surahs are 2, 7, 9, 10, 11, 13, 17, 20, 21, 23, 25, 32, 39, 40, 43, 57, 69, 81, 85. Note that 2:255 is in the third juz of the daily readings.

15. The complex tradition used by al-Ghazzali depicts the transcendent God as behind 70,000 veils. Various human souls can rise through the bottom layers of Pure Darkness through belief in and obedience to God until the rare soul stands naked before the full presence of God. See pp. 84–98.

16. Al-Ghazzali, *Mishkat,* p. 98.

17. See al-Ghazzali, *Mishkat.*

18. Yusuf Ali translates 24:1, "A Surah which We have sent down and which We have ordained. In it We have sent down clear signs in order that ye may receive admonition."

19. It is also a whole in its juz portion.

20. This can be precariously close to pantheism or to a Muslim gnosticism. Ibn Rashid accused al-Ghazzali of just such a lapse.

21. Ibn Kathir, vol. 7, p. 88, reports that Muhammad said that "houses" here meant "hearts," as related by Abu Said al-Khudri.

22. See, e.g., Surahs 7:54; 16:12, 16; 37:6–10; 67:5; 77:8–11; 81:2; and 82:2. Surah 7:54 relates Allah's Throne to the veils of night, then the sun, moon, and stars that are governed by the Rabb's commands.

23. See Yusuf Ali, notes 3000–3002, pp. 876–77.

24. See Surah 95.

25. For example, the Lote Tree, which has its roots in the fifth or sixth heaven and reaches into the seventh heaven (see Surahs 34:16; 56:28; and W. H. Wagner, "Journeying to God"). There is also a "cursed tree," (Zaqqum) that grows at the bottom of Hell. See Surah 17:60, with note 2250, in Yusuf Ali, p. 691; Surahs 37:62–65; 44:43–46; and 56:62.

26. Three men were beaten. See Surah 24:4–5 for the penalty for bringing false accusations.

27. See Surah 24:6–9.

28. Female slaves who consented, however, could be legitimate sexual partners for their male owners.

29. Bukhari 9.38B/Khan 6901.

30. Tirmidhi 2147: "Allah's Messenger (peace be upon him) said, 'Everything has a heart, and the heart of the Qur'an is Ya-Sin. Allah will record anyone who recites Ya-Sin as having recited the Qur'an ten times.'" 2148: "Allah's Messenger (peace be upon him) said, 'A thousand years before creating the heavens and the earth, Allah recited Ta-Ha and Ya-Sin, and when the angels heard the recitation they said, 'Happy are the people to whom this comes down, happy are the minds which carry this, and happy are the tongues which utter this.'"

31. See Ibn Kathir, vol. 8, pp. 178–79. On the basis of Ibn Ishaq and Hadith readings, he identified the city as Antioch and the three messengers as Sadiq, Shaduq, and Shalum. Another source cited by Ibn Kathir agreed that the city was Antioch, but the messengers were Shamun and Yuhannah, with Bulus as the runner.

Nine.   *The Qur'an on the End of This World and Life in the Hereafter*

1. The Qur'an uses several terms for the term translated as "Hell" and its attributes. These include *an-Nar* (the Fire), *Jahannam* (Gehenna), *al-jahim* (burning), *as-sa'ir* (raging flame), *as-saqar* (scorching fire), *al-hawiyah* (abyss), and *al-hutamah* (crushing pressure). See Glassé, pp. 175–76.

2. See Surahs 15:85—"We created not the heavens the earth and all between them but for just ends. And the Hour is surely coming (when this will be manifest)"—and 16:3—"He has created the heavens and the earth for just ends: far is He above having the partners they ascribe to Him!"

3. Muslim, vol. 4, bk. 39, chap. 1210, item 7023, p. 1520. See also, e.g., Surahs 7:158; 24:62; and 47:32.

4. See, e.g., Surah 29:2–5: "Do men think that they will be left alone on saying 'We believe' and that they will not be tested? We did test those before them and Allah will certainly know those who are true from those who are false. Do those who practice evil think that they will get the better of us? Evil is their judgment! For those whose hopes are in the meeting with Allah (in the Hereafter let them strive); for the Term (appointed) by Allah is surely coming: and He hears and knows (all things)." See also Surahs 18:7; 2:155–57 and 212–15.

5. See Surahs 39:42 and 6:60.

6. In Muslim tradition 'Izar'il is the Archangel of Death who has other angelic messengers to assist him. See Glassé, p. 42.

7. See Surah 32:5: "He rules (all) affairs from the heavens to the earth: in the end will (all affairs) go up to Him on a Day the space whereof will be (as) a thousand years of your reckoning." See also the biblical passages Ps. 90:4 and 2 Pet. 3:8.

8. Al-Awlaki, for example, cites fifty-two minor signs. Among these are wars between the Muslims and the Jews in which trees and rocks serve the Muslim cause and a war between the "Greeks" (the Byzantine Empire) and polytheists in the West. Most agree that Muhammad spoke of ten major signs. According to a hadith verified by Imam Muslim and derivable from the Qur'an, Muhammad mentioned ten signs: the smoke; Dajjal; the beast; the sun rising in the west; the descent of Jesus; Gog and Magog; landslides in the east, west, and in Arabia; and a fire from Yemen. See Muslim, vol. 4, bk. 39, chap. 1202, item 6931, p. 1502 f. Book 39 is devoted to the *fitnas* (drastic tests of faith, excruciating ordeals) that

will occur as al-Dunya is destroyed. Muslim, vol. 4, bk. 39, chap. 1212, item 7039, p. 1525, mentions six of the ten signs. See also Muslim, vol. 1, bk. 1, chap. 73, item 296, p. 94. There are few references to the beast, and it does not appear to have a significant role in the hadiths. There is a strange creature or beast who introduces some seafarers to Ad-Dajjal according to the cited hadiths. Clearly nine of the events must occur before the dissolution of the cosmic order (the rising of the sun from the west). Hadith references to Ad-Dajjal occur especially in Muslim's book 39. Khouj and Mabruk put the battle with Ad-Dajjal after the sun rising in the west.

9. See, e.g., D. Cook, *Contemporary Muslim Apocalyptic Literature.*

10. The name appears to mean "king with two horns" or "Lord of two epochs" (Yusuf Ali, n. 2428, p. 731). The barrier was built of molten iron and lead and was intended to protect a poor, oppressed people. Sometimes Alexander the Great is thought to have been Zul-qarnain. (Surah 18:94–101). Elements of the battle are at Surah 21:94–106. The polytheists will recognize and lament their heedless rejection of Islam.

11. See esp. Muslim, vol. 4, bk. 38, chap. 1183; and bk. 39, chap. 1215.

12. Sunni as well as Shi'a Muslims have traditions about the Mahdi. Twelver Shi'a have a distinctive position related to the occultation of the Twelfth Imam. Abu Dawood's collection of the sayings of Muhammad includes: "The Prophet (peace be upon him) said: The Mahdi will be of my stock, and will have a broad forehead a prominent nose. He will fill the earth will equity and justice as it was filled with oppression and tyranny, and he will rule for seven years" (Hadith 4272). Tradition says that he will be named Muhammad Mahdi. Some conservative Sunni scholars reject "mahdism" as a form of messianism perilously close to Christianity, and others see it as balancing Quranic references to Jesus. See Glassé, pp. 280–81.

13. Muslim, vol. 4, bk. 39, chap. 1210, item 7023, pp. 1520–21.

14. See Surah 56:7–14: "And ye shall be sorted out into three classes. Then (there will be) the Companions of the Right Hand. What will be the Companions of the Right Hand? And the Companions of the left hand what will be the Companions of the Left Hand? And those Foremost (in Faith) will be Foremost (in the Hereafter). These will be those nearest to Allah: In Gardens of Bliss: A number of people from those of old And a few from those of later times."

15. Some, including Khouj (pp. 79–80), hold that the bridge is the same for both believers and damned.

16. "And what will explain to thee what Hell-Fire is? Naught doth it permit to endure and naught doth it leave alone! Darkening and changing the color of man! Over it are Nineteen. And We have set none but angels as guardians of the Fire; and We have fixed their number only as a trial for Unbelievers in order that the people of the Book may arrive at certainty and the Believers may increase in Faith and that no doubts may be left for the People of the Book and the Believers

and that those in whose hearts is a disease, and the Unbelievers may say 'What symbol doth Allah intend by this?' Thus doth Allah leave to stray whom He pleaseth and guide whom He pleaseth; and none can know the forces of the Lord except He, and this is no other than a warning to mankind" (Surah 74:27–31).

17. See O'Shaghnessy, pp. 48–73. The layers and intensities of Hell-fire Hawiya (abyss, chasm), in 101:9; Jahim (kindled to intense heat, vehement fire), in 82:14; Sa'ir (place of punishment with hot fire and disease), in 76:4; Jahannam (place of bitter torment, bottomless pit), in 89:23; Laza (fiercely blazing sharp flame), in 74:42; and Hutama (crushing, vehement flame that devours as it burns), in 104:4. Jahannam is the most commonly used term.

18. See Surahs 37:62; 14:13–17; and 47:15. See also Surah 88:1–7. The damned will drink of a boiling hot spring and eat bitter Dhari, "a plant, bitter and thorny, loathsome in smell and appearance" (Yusuf Ali, p. 1640 n. 6099).

19. Some Muslims hold that Hell is not permanent but is meant for purification. Passages cited to indicate that teaching are Surahs 11:119; 51:56; 6:128; and 11:106–8. The Ahmadiyah believe that the soul makes progress toward fulfillment. See M. Ali, *The Holy Qur'an,* pp. I-49–51. The Ash'ari school of Islamic law and interpretation holds that if a person was not an idolater, God could forgive his sins so that he could enter the Garden after he had paid the penalties for noncompliance with God's will in his earthly life. Hell, in other words, may be a Purgatory-like place. Muslim theologians regard only God as "eternal" (*abad*), while Hell and the Gardens are "perpetual" (*khuld*). See Glassé, p. 176.

20. Muslim, vol. 4, bk. 38, chap. 1180, item 6807, p. 1481, includes the Sayhan, Jayhan, Euphrates, and Nile among the Garden's rivers.

21. Muhammad saw it on the Night Journey-Ascent. See W. H. Wagner, "Journeying to God."

22. The talh tree is probably a type of flowering acacia.

23. In addition to citations in Surahs 55 and 56, see Surahs 2:25; 3:15; 4:57; and 44:54.

24. Smith and Haddad, pp. 164–68.

25. Bukhari 4.53/Khan 2796.

26. Tirmidhi 3834.

27. Muslim, vol. 4, bk. 38, chaps. 1171–78, items 6784–97, pp. 1477–80.

Ten. *The Qur'an on Woman and Women*

1. See Charlesworth, vol. 1, for Enoch and the Testament of the Twelve Patriarchs. See Tertullian, treatises *On Modesty, On the Apparel of Women, On The Veiling of Virgins, On Exhortation to Chastity,* and *To His Wife.* Also see W. H. Wagner, "Interpretations of Genesis 6:1–4" and *After the Apostles,* pp. 190–92.

2. While there is no Quranic reference to clitoridectomy, a hadith attributed to Muhammad by Abu Dawood 5251, with Umm Atiyyah al-Ansariyyah as the narrator, states: "A woman used to perform circumcision in Medina. The Prophet (peace be upon him) said to her:'Do not cut severely as that is better for a woman and more desirable for a husband.'"

3. See especially Wadud; and Smith and Haddad.

4. See Surahs 4:1; 6:98; 7:89; and 39:6. Yusuf Ali translated *nafs* as "person."

5. See Gen. 1:26–28; 2:18–23. See also tafsirs on Surah 4:1 in Ibn Kathir, vol. 2, pp. 368–71; and Qutb, *In the Shade of the Qur'an,* vol. 3, pp. 22–25. The commentators are explicit about the passage referring to the Gen. 2:18 f. account.

6. Exceptions for women during the Ramadan fast are derived from later traditions, not the Qur'an.

7. See, e.g., Surahs 6:136, 141; 30:51; 42:20; and 68:22.

8. In addition to those listed, there are passing references to Zakariya's wife at Surah 3:40 (in the Gospel of Luke, Elizabeth) and Lot's daughters at Surah 11:78. The biblical names for the listed women are Eve, Sarah, Jochabed (Moses' mother), Miriam, and Zipporah (Moses' wife). Muslim non-Quranic traditions name Potiphar's wife who attempted to seduce Joseph as Zuleika, the wife of Pharaoh as Asiyah, and the queen of Saba as Bilquis.

9. See Muslim, vol. 4, bk. 19, chap. 1004, items 5965–66, pp. 1296–97.

10. One of Noah's sons also drowned. The deaths of Noah's wife and son are at Surah 11:40–43. Lot's wife preferred to stay in the doomed city rather than join her husband and daughters. She is also called derisively an "old woman" (Surah 11:81).

11. Ibn Ishaq, p. 310.

12. 1 Kings 10:1–13; 2 Chron. 9:1–12.

13. Surah 19:28: "The townspeople who knew her and then saw that she brought a baby with her after her sojourn in the east said, accusingly,'O sister of Aaron! Thy father was not a man of evil nor thy mother a woman unchaste!'"

14. See Cameron, pp. 107–21; and Hennecke and Schneemelcher, vol. 1, pp. 378 f.

15. Surah 3:38–41 and the nearly identical passage at Surah 19:2–15.

16. See Cameron, *Protoevangelium,* pp. 113–44, in *The Other Gospels.*

17. The noncanonical document called the Gospel of Pseudo-Matthew contains a story of a palm tree bending down to shelter Mary, Joseph, and Jesus from the heat. The tree was transported to heaven as a reward. In its place a spring bubbled up to refresh Mary. See Hennecke and Schneemelcher, vol. 1, p. 412.

18. With various spellings, the hadiths identify her as Khaula bint Tha'laba (or Khaulah or Khuwaillah), the wife of Aws ibn as-Samit. The context in Bukhari is that her husband seems to have taken a slave girl as his sexual partner and has rejected Khaula (Bukhari 7.24/Khan: no number given for the specific hadith and

a different hadith that follows; the passage is between 5292 and 5294). Abu Dawood 2212 reports that her husband, Aws ibn as-Samit, was addicted to sex and apparently considered her unable to satisfy him, so he wanted another wife. Allah answered Khaula's petition with the ayas relating to zihar. Abu Dawood 2208 gives a more ample account.

19. The sons born to Khadijah and Muhammad also died in infancy.

20. Briefly, Zayd was a captive slave bound to Khadijah, who gave him to Muhammad. When given the opportunity to return to his father, al-Harith, Zayd opted to stay with the Messenger. Muhammad then adopted him as a son and emancipated him, so the young man was known as Zayd ibn Muhammad. After Khadijah's death and the Hijra, Muhammad arranged a marriage between one of his aunt's daughters, Zaynab bint Jahsh, and Zayd. The marriage was not happy. During a visit to their home, Muhammad was attracted to Zaynab. Developing Muslim marriage practices prohibited a man from marrying the divorced wife of his son. In that context Surah 33:37 was handed down. Through it past and future adoptions in which the adoptee was considered a blood son were canceled. A person was to bear the name of his or her own family of origin. This meant that Zayd became Zayd ibn al-Harith. Zayd and Zaynab agreed to divorce, making her eligible to be married to the Messenger. But he already had the Quranic maximum of four wives. Another revelation (33:52) made the exception for Muhammad so that he could have more than four wives at one time. Zayd ibn al-Harith was killed in battle in 630.

21. Some Sunni Muslims consider Aisha foremost among the Mothers of the Faithful. Aisha resented his continuing to honor Khadijah instead of giving her what she felt she deserved. See Muslim, vol. 4, bk. 19, chap. 1004, items 5971–76, pp. 1297–98.

22. Muslim, vol. 4, bk. 19, chap. 1004, items 5971–76, pp. 1297–98.

23. Ordani, pp. 78–83. The circumstances are different. The Shi'ia hadith quoted has Muhammad come to Fatimah and Ali's home. When her father said that he did not feel well, she covered him with a Yemeni cloak. Eventually she, Ali, Hasan, Hussein, and the angel Gabriel were gathered there. Gabriel is reported to have said, "Allah sends His revelation to you people and says, 'Surely Allah has decided that He shall keep you and your Ahul-Bayt clean of all pollution with a thorough purification.'" The passage continued with assurances that the Shi'ites will be blessed, although they will suffer and be misunderstood. See also Lalljee, pp. 244–51.

24. Muslim, vol. 4, bk. 19, chap. 1007, items 5999–6002. Ali was negotiating a marriage with the daughter of one of Muhammad's Meccan foes, a man nicknamed "Father of Ignorance" (Abu Jahl). He was killed fighting for the Qurayshi at Badr.

25. See, e.g., Armstrong; Glassé; F. Peters; and Salahi. The term *Umm* means "mother." Hind and Ramlah are usually referred to by their "umm" title.

26. Muslim, vol. 4, bk. 19, chap. 1005, item 5984, pp. 1299–1301.

27. Al-Ghazali, *Muhammad,* pp. 298–306.

28. Bukhari gives contrasting versions for the revelation of the Veil Aya: Bukhari 8.255/Khan 6238 claimed to be the most authoritative. Anas bin Malik claimed to know more than others about the occasion of the revelation of the al-Hijab verse. He recounted that the male guests at the wedding to Zainab over-stayed the feast on the wedding night. Muhammad was too polite to ask them to leave. Allah then sent down the Veil Aya, and Muhammad set a screen between the outsiders and his family.

29. Yusuf Ali, p. 1077 n. 3765.

30. When Aisha was alone with Safwan, she and Safwan insisted she was covered and veiled.

31. Abu Dawood 4092, narrated by Aisha.

32. M. Ali, Qur'an, pp. 1106–7.

33. Bukhari 7.119/Khan 5191, narrated by Ibn Abbas, is a lengthy hadith. Aisha and Hafsa were identified as the two wives involved in the breach of confidence.

34. Al-Musnad, p. 128. As of this writing, some examples of governmental regulations enforced by the religious police prevent Saudi women from driving automobiles and appearing in public without male escorts, Saudi female physicians from examining male patients, and male physicians from examining female patients under nonemergency circumstances.

35. Yusuf Ali, p. 873 n. 2985: "Zinat means both natural beauty and artificial ornaments. I think both are implied here, but chiefly the former. The woman is asked not to make a display of her figure except to the following classes of people: (1) her husband, (2) her near relatives whom a certain amount of *neglige* is permissible; (3) her women, (4) slaves, male and female, as they would be in constant attendance; but this item would now be blank, with the abolition of slavery; (5) men who are free from sexual desire and who usually frequent the houses; and (6) infants or small children before they get a sense of sex."

36. Male and female homosexuality is condemned in the Qur'an (Surah 4:15–17). When proven against women, the penalty is confinement to their homes until they die or God directs some other action. Repentant men are to be punished in some unstated manner and then left alone. On the virtual necessity of marriage, see M. Ali, *Religion of Islam,* pp. 444–45.

37. Translations of this aya vary significantly. Pickthall, Shakir, Arberry, and M. Ali agree that men are "in charge of" or "manage" the affairs of their wives and that women therefore owe their husbands obedience. The process for "rebellious women" is the same as in Yusuf Ali's translation without his added parenthetical "lightly." Ahmed Ali renders the aya: "Men are the bread-earners of women as God has given some edge over the others, and because they spend of their wealth

(to provide for them). So women who are virtuous are obedient to God and guard the hidden as God has guarded it. As for women you feel are averse, talk to them suasively; then leave them alone in bed (without molesting them) and go to bed with them (when they are willing)."

38.　M. Ali, *Qur'an,* p. 206 nn. 34c and 34d.

39.　Tirmidhi 3294, narrated by Mu'adh ibn Jabal: "Allah's Messenger (peace be upon him) said to him, 'Mu'adh, Allah has created nothing on the face of the earth dearer to Him than emancipation, and Allah has created nothing on the face of the earth more hateful to Him than divorce.'"

40.　See Esposito, *Oxford Encyclopedia,* vol. 4, p. 337, for modern practices. *Talaq* is now one of several forms of divorce.

Eleven.　*The Qur'an on Biblical Figures, Jews and Christians*

1.　Five other figures who appear in the Bible and the Qur'an are Lot (Lut), Joseph (Yusuf), Jonah (Yunus), David (Dawood) and Saul (Talut). The Quranic Lot did not drink wine, commit incest with his daughters, dispute with Abraham over grazing rights, etc. See Surahs 15:62–77; 11:78; and 7:80–82. Surah 12 presents Joseph as protected by God and as one who endured adversity, betrayal, seduction, and deception. The Quranic story of Jonah (Surah 37:139–48) is well disposed toward the prophet. Saul (Surah 2:249) and David (Surah 2:250–51) are mentioned briefly. See Appendix B for the biblical figures mentioned in the Qur'an.

2.　The Tawrah is not identical with the biblical five books of the Torah (Pentateuch), and the Ingil is not the same as the four canonical Gospels of the Christians. Quranically, the Tawrah and the Ingil were books that contained the Islamic message of God's sovereign One-ness, the commands related to how to worship Him alone, and the Straight Way of living individually and communally in obedience to Him.

3.　The surahs are Imran (for Amran, the father of Moses, Aaron, and their sister; Surah 3), Jonah (Surah 10), Joseph (Surah 12), Abraham (Surah 14), Mary (Surah 19), and Noah (Surah 71).

4.　For Ezra, see 2 Esdras 14:9 and Surah 9:30; Mary in the Temple and the source of her food (Proto-Evangelium of James, in Hennecke and Schneemelcher, vol. 1, pp. 376–78; Jesus and the sparrows in the Infancy Gospel of Thomas, in Hennecke and Schneemelcher, vol. 1, pp. 392–93. Some versions of Christ not being crucified are the Nag Hammadi *Second Treatise of the Great Seth,* in which the victim is Simon of Cyrene (J. Robinson, pp. 365–66); and the so-called Gospel of Barnabas (Yusseff, pp. 220–26).

5.　Surah 7:61. See Glassé, p. 303, for further traditions about Noah and the ark.

6. But see Surah 11:49a: "Such are some of the stories of the Unseen which We have revealed unto thee: before this neither thou nor thy People knew them."

7. Surah 7:59–64.

8. Surah 11:25–27.

9. Surah 71:21–28.

10. Surahs 11:37–39; 23:26–30.

11. Surah 66:10.

12. See also Surah 10:73.

13. Exod. 33:11 calls Moses the friend of the Lord with whom God spoke face-to-face.

14. See Glassé, p. 18–19.

15. Surah 87:14–19.

16. See Surah 22:78. Abraham designated those who believe as he did "Muslims."

17. Surah 6:74–82.

18. Surahs 21:51–75; 37:83–99.

19. Surah 258–60. With regard to Abraham and the birds, see Yusuf Ali, p. 108 n. 303, and p. 109 n. 308; and Ibn Kathir, vol. 2, p. 43. See also Yusuf Ali.

20. The tradition is that of the near-death of Ishmael and his mother, the running between Marwa and Safa, and the uncovering of the spring of Zamzam. The Qur'an does not explicitly contain the account.

21. The son is not named in the Quranic account.

22. See also Surah 20:39 for a shorter version.

23. The passage also mentions an adviser to Pharaoh named Haman. Haman is also the name of the Persian king's vain anti-Jewish vizier in the biblical book, Esther.

24. Exod. 2:11–12.

25. See Surahs 28:31–32; 27:12.

26. See Surah 20:56–58.

27. He had their hands and feet cut off on opposite sides and crucified them on the trunks of palm trees.

28. See also Surah 40:36–37.

29. Somehow the Israelites garnered Egyptian treasures. There is a hint of an earthquake that leveled the Egyptian's great and conceited works and buildings at Surah 7:137.

30. The Qur'an does not identify "Samiri" as an individual or an Israelite group or another desert people.

31. See Exod. 32:25–35.

32. In Muslim tradition the unnamed servant of God is Khider, i.e., "Green."

33. For a general and helpful survey of Jesus in the Qur'an, the Hadith, and Muslim tafsir traditions, see N. Robinson, esp. pp. 3–7, 35–40, and 50–77. His

treatment of Surah 4:159 and other passages on the crucifixion and return of Jesus provide insight into interpretive flexibility among Muslim scholars; see pp. 78–105, 106–41. Robinson reserved for special treatment the incident of the clay birds that were given life and Jesus' virginal birth, pp. 142–66.

34. See Luke 2:41–51; Matt. 12:46–50; and John 2:1–5.

35. See Cameron, p. 125.

36. See Khalidi, p. 177–78, for the healing of a blind, leprous, crippled, and paralyzed man; and p. 211 for a comment by Jesus that he healed people. Accounts about Jesus raising persons from the grave appear to have been common after the mid–eighth century; see pp. 85, 115, 154–57, 163, 188–89, 191, and 206–08. In the resurrection stories the person often was raised from a grave and then returned to the grave after testifying to the power of God. Ibn Kathir, vol. 2, p. 164, explained that "Allah sent every Prophet with a miracle suitable to his time." Magic was the way miracles were accomplished in the time of Moses. In Jesus' time "medicine and physics were advancing. Isa brought them the types of miracles that could not be performed, except by one sent from Allah. How can any physician bring life to clay, cure blindness and leprosy and bring back to life those entrapped in the grave? Muhammad (PBUH) was sent during the time of eloquent people and proficient poets."

37. See also Surah 4:171.

38. In the Nag Hammadi Apocalypse of Peter, Peter reports: "I saw him seemingly being seized by them. And I said, 'What do I see, O Lord, that it is you yourself whom they take, and that you are grasping me? Or who is this one, glad and laughing on the tree? And is it another one whose feet and hands they are striking?' The Savior said to me, 'He whom you saw on the tree, glad and laughing, this is the living Jesus. But this one into whose hands and feet they drive the nails is his fleshly part, which is the substitute being put to shame, the one who came into being in his likeness'" (J. Robinson, p. 344). See also Cameron, pp. 89–96, for a similar "Jesus-out-of-body" account in *John's Preaching of the Gospel*. In the Nag Hammadi *Second Treatise of the Great Seth* (J. Robinson, pp. 332–33), "Christ" inhabits the body of a human and mockingly thwarts the plots of those who seek to kill him. Instead the victim is Simon (undoubtedly Simon of Cyrene, e.g., Luke 23:26 f.). In the Gospel of Barnabas (Yusseff), the features of Jesus are projected on to Judas, and Judas is crucified and killed.

39. Questions over the crucifixion of Jesus persist in several circles. Some take a grammatical view of Surah 3:55, Surah 4:157, and Surah 5:110 that Jesus was crucified, died, then was resurrected. The traditional Muslim interpretation holds that Jesus was not crucified and that he did not die. Ibn Kathir, vol. 3, pp. 26–27, accepts the view that before his impending arrest, Jesus asked for volunteers to take his place. When the officers came to seize Jesus in the house he occupied, they took the volunteer. Jesus then ascended to heaven from an upper room. See

N. Robinson, pp. 127–41, for a full discussion of Muslim interpretations and of Jesus being taken by God. Ibn Ishaq essentially repeats the Quranic passages (pp. 275–76). See Cragg, *Jesus and the Muslim,* pp. 172–73. See also Khalidi, p. 205.

40. See Qutb, *Milestones,* pp. 23–43.

41. See 2 Esdras 14:1–9.

42. Yusuf Ali, p. 200 n. 566, noted: "*Ra'ina,* if used respectfully, in the Arabic way, would have meant 'Please attend to us.' With a twist of the tongue, they suggest an insulting meaning, such as 'O thou that takest us to pasture!' or in Hebrew, 'Our Bad One.'"

43. See W. H. Wagner, "Toward a Christian-Islamic Ecumenic Encounter."

Twelve.   *The Qur'an on Justice and Jihad*

1. See Marty and Appleby, pp. vii–x, 817–42, for the characteristics, and chaps. 6–8 for reflections on "fundamentalisms" in Islam. See also Piscatori for a more concise version of Marty and Appleby.

2. Baker, p. 268.

3. For general information see Denny; Esposito, *Oxford Dictionary*; Esposito, *Oxford Encyclopedia*; Coulson; Goldziher; and Glassé. The four major Sunni schools are Hanafi, Hanbali, Maliki, and Shafi. Shi'ite groups have separate schools of interpretation.

4. An Egyptian, Qutb studied and taught in the United States (1948–51). His fervor to build an Islamic society led the Egyptian government to execute him for treason. See his *In the Shade of the Qur'an, Milestones,* and *Social Justice.* Esposito, *Oxford Encyclopedia,* contains biographical sketches of Qutb and Rahman and a description of the Muslim Brotherhood (al-Ikhwan al-Musilmun). *Return of the Pharaoh* by Zainab al-Ghazali (b. 1917) is an autobiographical account of a woman associated with the Brotherhood. See also Yvonne Haddad's essay on Qutb in Esposito, *Voices of Resurgent Islam,* pp. 67–98.

5. See Yusuf Ali, pp. 1397–98 n. 5177. He suggests that the "balance" is the constellation Libra.

6. See Surah 91:1–6; and Yusuf Ali, Appendix 11 on Oaths and Adjurations, pp. 1694–96.

7. Qutb, *In The Shade of the Qur'an,* vol. 30, pp. 184–90.

8. Rahman, *Major Themes,* pp. 25–36. *Qatr* is the term for narrow-mindedness; *da'f* is pettiness.

9. See, e.g., Surahs 4:128; 9:75–79; 89:15–20; and 64:15–18.

10. See, among many ayas, 2:164–67.

11. See Surahs 4:115; 8:53; and 13:11.

12. See Rahman, *Major Themes,* pp. 19–20; Surahs 2:59, 88; 4:115; and 6:49.

13. See Qutb, *Social Justice,* pp. 53–57; and *In the Shade of the Qur'an,* vol. 30, pp. 184–89.

14. Note past connections to "Arab nationalism" and "Arab socialism" in Syria, Iraq, Yemen, and Egypt and those countries that have tried or are trying Western-style capitalism, e.g., Malaysia, Turkey, Indonesia, Pakistan, Algeria, Saudi Arabia, and pre-1979 Iran.

15. Coulson, p. 1.

16. Denny, p. 394.

17. The Taliban and Wahhabi prohibit music, chess, cosmetics, pictures of women with faces exposed, and women being in public without a male escort and also prescribe the garments women are to wear in public. The Taliban specified the type of beards men may have and denied education to women. Qutb was close to but not in total agreement with the position that the Qur'an provides the laws and regulations that must govern a truly Islamic society. See, e.g., *Milestones,* pp. 38–43. The Muslim Brotherhood's brief collaboration with the Wahhabi and the Saudi government did not include Quranic interpretation.

18. Rahman is a spokesperson for this end of the spectrum. See, e.g., his *Major Themes,* p. 47, and his previously cited hermeneutic.

19. Surah 17:32: "Nor come nigh to adultery: for it is a shameful (deed) and an evil opening the road (to other evils)."

20. See also Surahs 4:135–36; 9:113–14; and 26:214–16.

21. Some later Muslim scholars and leaders posited two realms, the Dar al-Islam and the Dar al-Harb. The Dar al-Islam is the realm of submission-obedience-peace in which Shari'ah prevails and the governing authorities are Muslims. Its polar opposite, Dar al-Harb, is the realm of defiance-rebellion-conflict over which nonbelievers rule. Since the nineteenth century and into the present, Muslim views of the two realms have been especially important in developing dimensions of jihad both for individual spirituality and political action.

22. See esp. Surah 49:9–12.

23. For references to interest, usury, and banking, see Qutb, *In the Shade of the Qur'an,* vol. 1, pp. 449–69; Esposito, *Oxford Encyclopedia,* vol. 2, pp. 205–7; and Glassé, pp. 335, 192–93. For a fuller discussion of basic meanings, see Esposito, *Oxford Dictionary,* pp. 265–66. It appears that in the Jahiliyyah if a borrower defaulted on a payment the debt would be doubled and a second default resulted in doubling the new total.

24. Later Islamic jurisprudence specified some mitigating circumstances. Thieves who had one limb amputated and stole again were punished by the loss of the other hand.

25. See Exod. 21:12–26; Lev. 24:13–22; and Deut. 19:15–21. There is no evidence that the Israelites maimed or blinded offenders.

26. See also Surah 2:178–79 and Bukhari 6.27/Khan 4611.

27. See Webster, p. 66.

28. See Bukhari 9.37/Khan 6899. The hadith states that Muhammad imposed the death penalty only in the case of deliberate murder, a married person who "committed illegal sexual intercourse," and "a man who fought against Allah and His Messenger and deserted Islam and became an apostate." The narrator then told of the men who murdered one of Muhammad's supporters, stole from the Messenger, and were apostates. According to the hadith, Muhammad ordered that the men have their hands and feet cut off, their eyes branded with a hot iron, and then had them thrown out in the blazing sun to die.

29. See Esposito, *Oxford Encyclopedia,* vol. 2, pp. 439–42. The *Encyclopedia* includes apostates under the category *kafir.*

30. The text uses the Pickthall translation because it is more literal at key points than the Yusuf Ali rendering because of the latter's added "with sincerity and under discipline": "O ye who believe! Bow down prostrate yourselves and adore your Lord; and do good; that ye may prosper. And strive [*j-h-d*] in His cause as ye ought to strive [*j-h-d*] (with sincerity and under discipline): He has chosen you and has imposed no difficulties on you in religion; it is the cult of your father Abraham. It is He Who has named you Muslims both before and in this (Revelation); that the Messenger may be a witness for you and ye be witnesses for mankind! So establish regular Prayer give regular Charity and hold fast to Allah! He is your Protector the Best to protect and the Best to help!"

31. In the order quoted: Rahman, *Major Themes,* p. 63; Jansen; and bin Laden, p. 49. Note that both Bukhari (bk. 56) and Muslim (bk. 10) dedicate a book each in their Hadith collections to Muhammad's sayings and actions on jihad.

32. In the order reflected: Richardson, p. 229, and Safi, p. 10; W. Wagner, (throughout his book) and Miller, pp. 183–91; and Lindsey, preface and p. 92. Bostom shares ideas similar to those noted above. Pipes distinguishes between what he terms "militant Islamists" and most Muslims in the world, yet his concentration on militants dominates his writings so that the "Islamic threat" is in the foreground; see his *Militant Islam* and *In the Path of God.* In *After Jihad* Feldman argues, perhaps overoptimistically, that we are in a postjihad age, even though occasional terrorist outbursts will be perpetrated by desperate ideologues and groups.

33. See Esposito, *Oxford Encyclopedia,* vol. 2, pp. 370–73.

34. Feldman, p. 235, notes that the saying was quoted in two versions by the medieval scholar al-Ghazzali. The shorter version cites Muhammad telling his soldiers as they returned from a successful military campaign, "We have returned from the lesser jihad to the greater jihad." When the men questioned him further, he replied that the greater struggle was the "jihad of the heart." The longer version remembers him saying that the greater jihad was "man's struggles with his desires." Some Muslims understand jihad in two dimensions, the spiritual struggle with

oneself (*jihad al-nafs*) and the struggle with evil (*jihad al-Shaytan*); see McAuliffe, Encyclopedia, vol. 3, pp. 35–43.

35. See, e.g., Armstrong, pp. 164–210; Rahman, *Islam,* pp. 37, 86, 200–213; Denny, p. 136; Rashid, *Jihad,* pp. 1–4; Kelsay; bin Humaid; and Esposito, *Oxford Encyclopedia,* vol. 2, pp. 369–73. Armstrong and Rashid attribute the distinction to a saying in the Hadith, while Esposito regards it as a later development. Glassé (pp. 209–10) and bin Humaid do not mention the Greater Jihad.

36. See Kassis, pp. 587–88; and McAuliffe, *Encyclopedia,* vol. 3, pp. 35–43. Bonney counted 35 (p. 28, n. 44); he probably did not count several occurrences that are clearly not associated with war or conflict.

37. See respectively Surah 29:8 and Surahs 5:53; 6:109; 16:38; 24:53; and 35:42.

38. Surah 9:79's *yajiduuna* is obscured by Yusuf Ali's translation, "fruits of their labors." At Surah 25:52 Yusuf Ali added in parenthesis "Qur'an" where the text is "So obey not the unbelievers (*kafiriina*) but strive against them herewith with a great endeavor (*jaalidhum-bikii jihaadan-ka-biriinaa*)" according to Pickthall's translation and transliteration.

39. See Surahs 2:218; 8:72–75; 9:20, 24; and 16:110.

40. See Surahs 9:44, 86; and 4:95.

41. The passages are Surahs 2:190–93; 8:72–75; 9:41, 44–46, 87–92.

42. Kassis, pp. 928–33. Richardson, p. 28, commented, pejoratively, on the prevalence of warlike expressions in the Qur'an, calculating that one of every fifty-five ayas deals with war or conflict.

43. The statistics are Surah 2 (27 times), Surah 3 (21 times), Surah 4 (25 times), Surah 5 (11 times), Surah 8 (6 times), and Surah 9 (15 times).

44. See Gabriel, pp. 33–39, for such a generalization.

45. See Bonney, pp. 15–18; Deut. 7 and 20; Josh. 6; and 1 Sam. 15.

46. The execution of the 600 Jews of Qurayza was due to their attempt to betray the Muslims to the Qurayshi. The sentence was proposed by a Jewish leader.

47. See Bonney, p. 13. He argues that the Qur'an advocates only defensive wars and notes that the Qur'an never uses the term *holy war.*

48. In rendering the prediction at the end of Surah 5:56 that Islam will be triumphant, Yusuf Ali translated *hiz-ballaahi* as the "fellowship of Allah." Pickthall (p. 119) and Shakir (p. 71) translate it as "party of God." The Lebanese political and paramilitary organization, Hizbullah, takes its name from this aya.

49. Yusuf Ali renders the passage as "But when the forbidden months are past then fight and slay the pagans wherever ye find them and seize them beleaguer them and lie in wait for them in every stratagem (of war); but if they repent and establish regular prayers and practice regular charity then open the way for them: for Allah is Oft-Forgiving Most Merciful."

50. See bin Laden, pp. 4–19, 20–30. Bin Laden, Wahhabis, and others refer to Ahmad ibn Taymiyya (1263–28) for their militant understanding of jihad. Ibn Taymiyya wrote of jihad-qitaal-style resistance to the superficially Muslim Mongol invaders who destroyed Baghdad, devastated Muslim territories, and ruled Muslims harshly. His often-blunt language and courageous stance earned him death in prison. See Glassé, p. 202. Kelsay provides a helpful study relevant to post-1990 jihad considerations.

51. See Bonney, pp. 216–17, 356–69, and Qutb's arguments throughout his *Milestones* and *Social Justice*.

52. See Rahman, *Major Themes,* pp. 62–64. He argues that Islam was never spread by the sword, but the political domain of Islam was spread through conversion and conquest.

53. R. Peters, pp. 26–79.

54. See Esposito, *Oxford Encyclopedia,* vol. 3, pp. 370–73. See n. 21 above concerning the development of a theory of the Dar al-Harb and Dar al-Islam. See also Kelsay.

55. Bonney, pp. 25–27.

56. See Firestone generally and esp. p. 69.

57. For traditions about the pressures and persecutions as well as tortures inflicted on Meccan Muslims, see Salahi, pp. 92–134.

58. Pickthall, pp. 391–92.

59. See Salahi, pp. 225–33 for a description of some of the expeditions.

60. See Salahi, pp. 234–52.

61. Salahi, pp. 234–52, provides colorful and traditional background material.

62. See Salahi, pp. 253–98; and *Cambridge History of Islam,* vol. 1a, pp. 46–49.

63. See ibn Ishaq, pp. 236–70. The biographer reported that Surah 2:1–100 was revealed as a result of the Jews mocking Muhammad by asking insolent questions.

64. See also Surah 3:121–29, 149–55, 165–67.

65. Indonesia and Pakistan, two of the largest Muslim states, have had female presidents, and Turkey has had a female prime minister. Women have been elected to national positions in many countries such as Iran, Egypt, Jordan, and Bangladesh. Granted there are stark contrasts as well, e.g., Saudi Arabia, Kuwait, and Afghanistan. The Islamic legal systems of parts of Nigeria and other countries are deeply suspicious and punitive with regard to women.

66. Note the assassination of Anwar Sadat and *The Neglected Duty,* the writings and actions of Osama bin Laden, the rhetoric of militant Islamists such as Hamas, Hizbullah, and Islamic Jihad. See Esposito, *Oxford Encyclopedia,* vol. 3, pp. 373–76, for a listing and brief description of some groups.

67. Note the al-Aksa Martyrs' Brigade, Islamic Jihad, and Hamas in the Palestinian territories and Hizbollah based in Lebanon.

68. Kelsay, pp. 77–110.

Thirteen.   *Challenges from the Qur'an*

1. See Esposito, *Oxford Encyclopedia,* vol. 4, pp. 135–36, for further details.

2. In 1517 Sultan Selim I (r. 1512–20) conquered Egypt. He transported the remaining caliph to Istanbul-Constantinople, thereby making the caliphate an Ottoman-sponsored office. His successor, Suleyman I (the Magnificent, r. 1520–66) unsuccessfully besieged Vienna in 1529. For further treatment of Sunni sultanate and caliphate, see Denny, pp. 206–11.

3. For more information, see, for example, the works of Esposito; the works of Bernard Lewis (some scholars, e.g., Edward Said, criticize him); Eickelman and Piscatori; Rahman, esp. *Islam and Modernity*; Esack, *Qur'an: Liberation and Pluralism*; and the works of Sayyid Qutb.

4. See Esposito, *Voices of Resurgent Islam*; and Esposito and Voll.

5. See, e.g., Lewis, *What Went Wrong?*

6. The historical situation was complicated by intra-Western rivalries and Western European-Russian hostilities. The Russo-Turkish conflicts (1768–74, 1787–92) depleted Ottoman fiscal and military resources. Revolts in the Balkans (1829–30) and French incursions in Algeria (1830) exposed the weakness of the Ottoman government. Tanzimat was begun by Sultans Mahmud II (r. 1808–39) and Abdulmecid I (r. 1839–61). The *Hatt-I-Serif* (Noble Edict of the Rose Chamber, 1839) set up provincial assemblies, state courts that were largely independent of religious jurists, new codes of criminal and commercial law, a uniform taxation system, a Prussian-style military conscription system, rights for minorities in the empire, and a Western-style educational system in place of a largely Islamically oriented system. The Crimean War (1853/4–56) allied Britain, France, and Sardinia with Ottomans to thwart the Russian drive for access to the Mediterranean Sea. In the war's aftermath, Sultan Abdulaziz (r. 1861–76) led a backlash against Tanzimat. In 1875 the empire was bankrupt and by 1881 was forced to accept European involvement in its fiscal policies and, consequently, political authority. In 1878 Romania, Serbia, Montenegro, and part of Bulgaria became independent. In 1830 the French took most of Algeria and in 1881 took Tunisia. The next year Britain occupied Egypt. In 1912 Italy annexed Libya.

7. Late nineteenth- and early twentieth-century pogroms against European Jews and the Dreyfus case in France (1894–1906) convinced numerous Jews that they needed their own homeland. For many, the logical option was Palestine. The

type of Zionism guided by Theodor Herzl (1860–1904) led to Jewish emigration to Palestine. By the 1920s both Arab and Jewish leaders warned of impending intercommunal strife over land and political power. Among the seriously considered alternatives were various locations in Russian Asia, Australia, South Africa, Latin America, and especially Uganda. Bloody riots and massacres broke out in the 1920s and 1930s, with both sides attacking the other.

8. Sultan Mehmed V (1909–18) declared a jihad against Britain, France, and Russia in 1914. His call to arms was largely unheeded.

9. The secret protocols of the Anglo-French Sykes-Picot Agreement (1916) set out French and British spheres of influence, the internationalization of Jerusalem, and left desert areas for Arab rule. Prime Minister Henry McMahon had assured the Arabs that they would be given "self-determination" after the war. The Arabs thought that included Palestine, but the British rejected that interpretation. On November 2, 1917, the British government's Balfour Declaration stated that it looked with favor on the creation of a Jewish homeland in Palestine. But did that declaration mean a politically autonomous Jewish state? Jerusalem fell to the British in December 1917. See Tuchman as a whole and pp. 310–48.

Under the treaty and the League of Nations' mandate system the British were given a permanent mandate over Palestine and the French over Greater Syria. From this and other actions in the 1920s, the current boundaries within Arabia were developed and the al-Saba clan's rule over Kuwait was established, as well as the authority of the Saud family in what is now Saudi Arabia and the Hashem family in Jordan. Muslims and Hindus in India had their hopes for autonomy blunted too. The ultimate victory of the Bolsheviks in the old imperial Russian domain meant that the new Union of Soviet Socialist Republics replaced the czars with atheistic Soviet authority in central Asia until 1991. See esp. Eickelman and Piscatori; Esposito, *The Islamic Threat* and *Unholy War*; Kepel; Matinuddin; and Rashid, *Jihad* and *Taliban*.

10. All educational institutions were put under the authority of a governmental Ministry of Public Instructions; all cases relating to Islamic teaching and practice were to be considered by a Directorate for Religious Affairs. By 1925 various Islamic and traditional activities such as pilgrimages (permission to participate legally in the hajj was restored in 1948) were banned, and wearing the distinctive Turkish fez was prohibited. In the same period the Gregorian (Western) calendar replaced the Muslim calendar. The government attempted, unsuccessfully, to install churchlike pews in mosques and use music in the religious services. A law was passed ordering that the Turkish language replace Arabic in religious services and the reading of the Qur'an. In 1926 a modified version of the Swiss legal code replaced Shari'ah as the basis for law, and in 1928 the provision that Islam was the official religion of Turkey was deleted from the constitution.

11. See Esposito, *Oxford Encyclopedia,* vol. 3, pp. 183–201.

12. Petroleum was discovered in Arabia (1938). Standard Oil of California (Chevron) and the Saudi government formed the Arabian-American Company (Aramco).

13. In 1943 Iraqi leaders proposed a union of Arab nations and territories consisting of Iraq, Transjordan, Syria, and Lebanon. In 1944–45 Egypt responded with a plan that added Saudi Arabia, Egypt, and Yemen. Today it includes twenty-two nations. According to its founding Alexandria Protocol (October 1944) the League is to coordinate political plans, resolve problems and conflicts that arise between member states, protect the sovereignty and independence of the members against aggression by non-Arabs, "and . . . supervise in a general way the affairs and interests of the Arab countries." See League of Arab States, www.arableague.org/arableague/english/details.

14. According to its charter, adopted in 1972, the OIC seeks to strengthen Islamic solidarity among its members and to cooperate in fields such as science and political policies. It is dedicated to "the struggle of all Muslim people to safeguard their dignity, independence and national rights . . . [; to] [c]oordinate action to safeguard the Holy Places; support the struggle of the Palestinian people and assist them in recovering their rights and liberating their occupied territories; work to eliminate racial discrimination and all forms of colonialism; [and] create a favorable atmosphere for the promotion of cooperation and understanding between Member States and other countries." The OIC is pledged "to refrain, in relations among Member States, from resorting to force or threatening to resort to the use of force against the unity and territorial integrity or the political independence of any one of them." See Organization of the Islamic Conference, www.oic-oci.org/oicnew/home.asp.

15. Among other important events were the toppling of the Egyptian monarchy and the proclamation of the Republic of Egypt (1952); Gamal Abdel Nasser (1918–70) becoming prime minister and then president of Egypt (1954 and 1956 respectively); the Egyptian nationalization of the Suez Canal and subsequent attacks on Egypt by France, Britain, and Israel (1956); and the Baathist coup in Iraq and eventually accession to power of Saddam Hussein (1963).

16. *Amal* is the acronym for Afwaj al-Muqawamah al-Lubnaniyah, the Lebanese Resistance Movement. Imam al-Sadr disappeared in Libya and probably was killed by the Libyan regime. See Saad-Ghorayeb. Hizbullah's origins reach back to Lebanese Shi'ite protest groups, especially the Movement of the Deprived (Harakat al-Mahrumin). Hizbullah began as a militant organization whose only purpose was to end Israeli occupation of Lebanese territory. After the Israelis withdrew from Lebanon (May 2000), Hizbullah suspended most cross-border attacks on Israel and became an important political party in Lebanon. In 2006, however, a small-scale war was fought between Israel and Hizbullah in Lebanon.

17. Hamas presents itself as one of the wings of the Muslim Brotherhood in Palestine. Its 1988 Covenant is replete with Quranic quotations. Hamas' slogan is "Allah is its target, the Koran its constitution: Jihad is its path and death for the sake of Allah is the loftiest of its wishes." Hamas seeks to "raise the banner of Islam over every inch of Palestine, for under the wing of Islam followers of all religions can coexist in security and safety where their lives, possessions and rights are concerned. In the absence of Islam, strife will be rife, oppression spreads, evil prevails and schisms and wars will break out. . . . There is no solution for the Palestinian question except through Jihad. Initiatives, proposals and international conferences are all a waste of time and vain endeavors." The movement rejects all forms of secularism for "[s]ecularism completely contradicts religious ideology." See Hamas Charter, at www.mideastweb.org/hamas.htm.

18. See especially Matinuddin; and Kepel, esp. pp. 222–36. For the chronology of the crisis of the first Gulf War, see Piscatori, pp. 209–44. The stationing of Western (mostly U.S.), forces in Saudi Arabia and the launching of the attack to drive the Iraqis from Kuwait led bin Laden into serious opposition to the West and especially the United States. In 1998 bin Laden established a new organization, the International Islamic Front for Jihad against Jews and Crusaders. In 1998 the organization issued a Qur'an-quoting fatwa from several shaykhs including Osama bin Laden urging Muslims "to kill the Americans and their allies, civilians, and the military . . . in any country in which it is possible to do it, in order to liberate al-Aqsa Mosque and the Holy Mosque from their grip and in order for their armies to move out of all the lands of Islam, defeated, and unable to threaten any Muslim" (bin Laden, pp. 58–62). The December 1991 collapse of the U.S.S.R. led to the former fifteen republics of the old Soviet Union becoming independent nations. Confrontational Islamists began to spread their versions of Islam among the republics that bordered Afghanistan. In 1994 the particularly brutal murder of pilgrims by an Afghan warlord's adherents galvanized a strong-willed mullah, Muhammad Omar, to organize Qur'an students (*talibani*) to fight the warlords and their supporters. The Taliban was born. With literally smashing success the Taliban soon controlled most of Afghanistan. They imposed a stringent version of Islam that saw the Revelatory Time as the ideal.

19. Note the 1993 attack on the World Trade Center and the plot to destroy monuments and facilities in New York City. After a brief hiatus, in 1995 and 1996 more explosions killed and injured Americans in Saudi Arabia. The U.S. embassies in Kenya and Tanzania were destroyed on the same day in 1998, prompting the United States to attack suspected al-Qaeda installations in the Sudan and Afghanistan, and in October 2000 a U.S. naval vessel was heavily damaged in a port in Yemen. The September 11, 2001, attacks by nineteen al-Qaeda–connected men on the World Trade towers were met by an overriding response in Muslim areas of horror and foreboding. Most Muslim leaders condemned the action. Grand

Imam of Al-Azhar, Shaykh Mohamed Sayed Tantawi, said, "Al-Azhar is against terrorism, regardless of its source or target. The killing of innocent men, women, and children is a horrible and ugly act that is against all religions and against rational thinking." The Egyptian Ikhwan issued a statement that expressed its horror at the attack and "such activities that are against all humanist and Islamic morals.... [We] condemn and oppose all aggression on human life, freedom and dignity anywhere in the world." Hamas's spiritual leader, Shaykh Ahmad Yassin, and several Islamically oriented Palestinian resistance groups, as well as the PLO, expressed sympathy with the survivors and families of the dead. Nevertheless, most observed that successive U.S. governments had set the stage for the tragedy through economic policies, support of Israel, and refusal to lift embargos on Iraq.

20. See al-Azhar. Using terms such as the "insanity of powers that tread on all international values and tradition," the statement says that the Americans will target "the millions of children of our [Arab and Islamic] nation as well as our faith, our holy places, and all [our] sources of wealth and power. All this is clear in the occupation of Iraq and the acquisition of its petroleum wealth." The al-Azhar *Appeal* continued that the al-Azhar Council "learned with certainty that the insistence on striking Iraq is only an introduction to other strikes to the rest of the Arab countries. The anti-Arab and anti-Islamic powers announced that after their full control of Iraq, they are going to rearrange situations in the Arab areas in a way that guarantees the American and Israeli interests, and put an end to the Palestinian resistance." The *Appeal* signaled that Muslims from other countries were fully within their religious rights and duties to resist and to fight the U.S.-led invasion and subsequent occupation. Toward the conclusion of the *Appeal,* the Council stated: "Therefore, and in application of the Islamic law that stipulates that if an aggression against a Muslim country took place, al-Jihad becomes an obligation for every male and female Muslim. It is so because our [Islamic] nation faces a new crusade aiming at the land, honor, belief and territory. Accordingly, the Islamic Supreme Council of Al-Azhar calls the Arabs and the Muslims all over the world to be ready to defend themselves, their belief, and to adhere to Allah, and not to scatter, and to rise above their disagreements until Allah's will is enforced. The Council calls all Arabs and Muslims all over the world not to be weak or languish in front of this aggression because Allah (SWT) guarantees victory to His religion, and to keep it above all."

21. Another view, for example, is Libya's Mu'ammar al-Qadhdhafi's "Third Universal Theory" of family, nation (people), and world in which Islam is the "natural religion" and framework of history with the Qur'an as the referent point. See Esposito, *Oxford Encyclopedia,* vol. 4, pp. 373–74.

22. Paul Berman's March 23, 2003, *New York Times* article on Qutb was titled "The Philosopher of Islamic Terror." The article itself did not brand him a terrorist but maintained that he is used by those whom the United States considers "terrorists."

23. Qutb, *In the Shade of the Qur'an,* vol. 30, p. xi.

24. See esp. Qutb, *Milestones,* pp. 7–17.

25. *Mawlana,* rendered also as *mulla(h)* in Persian, is similar to the Arabic *shaykh.* Meaning companion, friend, helper, and patron, it is an honorific for a respected teacher's religious devotion, accomplishments in Quranic law and theology, and spiritual-intellectual leadership.

26. Maududi, *Towards Understanding,* vol. 1, p. xvii.

27. Maududi, *Towards Understanding,* vol. 1, p. 1.

28. Maududi, *Towards Understanding,* vol. 1, pp. 184–91.

29. Maududi, *Islamic Law,* pp. 136, 138, 140. See also *Saulat,* pp. 134 ff.

30. Saulat, pp. 110–11.

31. See Cragg, *Pen and the Faith,* pp. 91–108, for a helpful presentation on Rahman.

32. Rahman, *Major Themes,* p. 47. Emphasis is Rahman's.

33. Rahman, *Islam and Modernity,* p. 5.

34. See, e.g., Qush.

35. See especially Rahman, *Islam and Modernity,* pp. 1–11.

36. See Esposito, *Oxford Encyclopedia,* vol. 3, p. 408.

37. Rahman, *Major Themes,* p. 1.

38. Rahman, *Major Themes,* p. 9.

39. The legal forms in *usul al-fiqh* following the Qur'an and the Sunna are analogy (*qiyas*), consensus of the recognized teachers and umma (*ijma*), and effort (*itjihad*).

40. See Baker for a description of and references for the New Islamists. See also al-Qaradawy.

41. See Esposito, *Oxford Dictionary,* p. 94, for a brief entry about al-Ghazali; and p. 187 for Majd (Magd). See also Eickelman and Piscatori, pp. 71 and 132, for references to al-Ghazali.

42. Baker cites the document throughout his introduction and indicates that it was published under the authorship of Magd as *A Contemporary Islamic Vision: Declaration of Principles* (Cairo: Dar al-Shuruq, 1991). I have not been able to locate it. It apparently was published by al-Ahram.

43. al-Qaradawi, pp. 15, 21, 32–35.

44. al-Qaradawi, selected from pp. 85, 86 and 87.

45. Baker, p. 92. He refers to al-Ghazali's book *The Prophet's Sunnah.*

46. When considering Judaism, the religion, the New Islamists cite the Quranic passages that speak well of Jews. The case is different when regarding Jews who support Zionism and the occupation of Palestine, meaning political Israel as well as the Palestinian Authority. They hold that Palestinian-Israeli problems can be resolved by negotiations after Muslims renew their own societies first.

47. See Safi. The book is a series of fifteen essays prefixed by an excellent introduction. Amina Wadud is one of the contributors.

48. Safi, p. 3.

49. Safi, pp. 147–250.

50. Safi, pp. 251–332, is a series of five essays on Muslims and race relations in the United States.

Fourteen.   *Challenges to the Qur'an*

1. See, in Wansbrough, Andrew Rippin's introduction, pp. ix–xi, for his citations of Abraham Geiger and Theodor Nöldeke. Geiger and Ignaz Goldziher (see Goldziher, p. 28 n. 37) credited much of the Qur'an to Muhammad and felt that he had genuine religious experiences. They argued that the Qur'an, however, was collated and arranged by careless Companions, thereby accounting for its seeming disorder and illogical combinations of passages.

2. See Nevo and Koren. The first four items are taken from pp. 361–64 and the fifth from p. 11. The sixth point is from pp. 171 and 247–70, as well as the basic argument in Crone and Cook.

3. The quotations are from Crone and Cook, p. 18. Cook may have moderated his position in his *Koran: A Very Brief Introduction.*

4. See, e.g., Jeffreys, *The Qur'an as Scripture,* pp. 3, 8; and McAuliffe, *Qur'anic Christians,* pp. 12–17.

5. See Stille.

6. In 2004 Crone was a fellow at the Institute for Advanced Study in Princeton and Cook was a faculty member at Princeton University.

7. Crone and Cook, p. viii.

8. Crone and Cook, pp. 12–17.

9. I note that the same arguments from silence can be used to posit that the Hebrews were not enslaved in Egypt or that Jesus existed.

10. See "Syriac Influence on the Style of the Koran," in Ibn Warraq, pp. 171–92. Mingana was an Iraqi Christian.

11. See the article by Jeffreys and Bell in Ibn Warraq, an anthology of articles and essays by Western Orientalists from the early twentieth century to its close.

12. See Stille; and Kristof.

13. His work is *Die syro-aramäische Lesart des Koran: Ein Beitrag zur Entschlüssung der Koransprache.*

14. Rushdie was born in 1947 just prior to the partition of colonial India into Pakistan and India. His wealthy Muslim parents sent him to a Christian missionary school in India for his primary education. At the age of thirteen he went

to England to a public school and then to Cambridge University. After a stay in Pakistan (to which his family moved while he was in England), he returned to England and became a naturalized British citizen. His novel *Midnight's Children* (1981) won the Booker Prize and the enmity of Indira Gandhi. His *Shame* (1983) was set in an imaginary country that obviously was Pakistan, and it was soundly condemned by Maududi's followers. Later novels are eclectic in that they combine Muslim, Hindu, Christian, Jewish, Jain, Sikh, and pagan elements in an Indian matrix flavored variously by British, Spanish, American, and Mexican elements. "Salman" is the name of the first Persian convert to Islam, a man who became a Companion to Muhammad. Most recently, in an account of his marriage to a Hindu woman, he stated again that he was an atheist who had no need for a g/God (*New York Times,* April 25, 2004).

15. See Cohn-Sherbok, p. 132. In a letter to Rajiv Gandhi, he wrote: "The book isn't about Islam, but about migration, metamorphoses, divided selves, love, death, London and Bombay."

16. See Cohn-Sherbok; Maitland and Appignanesi; and Pipes, *The Rushdie Affair.*

17. Nasrin, Speech at the Free Thought Society Convention, San Diego, California, 2002.

18. Nasrin, Speech at the Free Thought Society Convention, San Diego, California, 2002.

19. Nasrin, www.mukto.mona.com/articles/taslima.

Fifteen.   *The Qur'an Opened and Open*

1. The idea of the Qur'an as a person is suggested, quite differently, by Esack, *The Qur'an: A Short Introduction,* pp. 1–3, 17.

2. See the case of Muhammad Ahmad Khalaf recounted by Haddad, *Contemporary Islam,* pp. 47–53.

3. Esack, *The Qur'an: A Short Introduction,* pp. 1–6.

4. E.g., Cragg, Esposito, Watt, Annemarie Schimmel, and W. H. Wagner. But see David Kerr's essay, "The Prophethood of Muhammad," in Haddad and Haddad, pp. 426–46, for criticisms of Cragg and Küng and a milder view of Watt. Cragg is an Anglican, Esposito and Küng are Roman Catholics, Schimmel was rooted in Lutheranism, and Watt is a priest of the Episcopal Church of Scotland.

5. Often such persons are on college, seminary, and university faculties, as well as among local clergy. Local Muslims also may know who their "friends" are in the community.

SELECTED BIBLIOGRAPHY

Primary Sources and Translations

Arabic Text

al-Qur'an al-Kareem. Abu Dhabi: n.p., 1977–79.

English Translations of the Qur'an

Ali, Ahmed. *Al-Qur'an: A Contemporary Translation*. Rev. ed. Princeton: Princeton University Press, 1988.

Ali, Muhammad. *The Holy Qur'an*. Arabic Text with English Translation and Commentary. Dublin, Ohio: Ahmadiyya Anjuman Isha'at Islam Lahore, 2002.

Ali, Yusuf Abdullah. *The Meaning of the Holy Qur'an*. 4th ed. Arabic and English texts. Brentwood, Md.: Amana Corporation, 1991.

Arberry, Arthur. J. *The Koran Interpreted*. New York: Macmillan, 1955.

Cragg, Kenneth. *Readings in the Qur'an: Selected*. San Francisco: Collins, 1988.

Dawood, Nessim Joseph. *The Koran*. 6th ed. New York: Penguin Books, 2003.

Malik, Abdul, Mujahid, supervisor. *The Noble Qur'an: Word for Word from Arabic to English*. 3 vols. Riyadh: Darussalam, 1999–2000.

Maududi [Mawdudi], Abul A'la. *The Holy Qur'an*. 12th ed. Lahore: Islamic Publications, 1995.

Pickthall, Muhammad Marmaduke. *The Holy Qur'aan*. Rev. ed. Transliteration in Roman Script by Muhammad Abdul Eliasi. New Delhi: Idara Ishaat-E-Diniyat, 1978.

Shakir, M. H. *The Qur'an*. 10th ed. Elmhurst, N.Y.: Tahrike Tarsile Qur'an, 1997.

English Translations of Hadith Collections

Abu Dawood. *Sunan*. Shahid Shah, The Alim, Windows Release 4.5. Alexandria, Va.: ISL Software Corp., 1986–96.

Alim, The. (A multimedia CD-ROM program with databases of primary resource materials of the Islamic tradition.) Developed by Shahid Shah. Windows Release 4.5. Alexandria, Va.: ISL Software Corp., 1986–96.

Bukhari, Muhammad ibn Ismail. *Al Hadith Sahih of al-Bukhari*. 5th ed. rev. 9 vols.
Translated by Muhammad Muhsin Khan. Riyadh: Darussalam, 1997.

———. *Al Hadith Sahih of al-Bukhari*. Shahid Shah, The Alim, Windows Release
4.5. Alexandria, Va.: ISL Software Corp., 1986–96.

Hind, Sahbanul, and Ahmad Saeed. *Hadees-E-Qudsi (Commands of Allah)*. Translated
by Mohammad Salman. New Delhi: Arshad Saeed, Dini Book Depot, 1988.

Muslim, Husayn Abu. *Al Hadith Sahih of Imam Muslim*. 4 vols. Translated by Abdul
Hamid Siddiqi. New Delhi: Kitab Bhavan, 1986.

Tabrizi, Wali-ud-Din Muhammad bin Abudullah. *Mishkat-Ul-Masabih*. English
and Arabic. 2 vols. Translated by Abdul Hameed Siddiqui. New Delhi: Kitab
Bhavan, [1980] 1987.

Tirmidhi, Abu Isa Muhammad. *Al Hadith Sahih of Tirimidhi*. Shahid Shah, The
Alim, Windows Release 4.5. Alexandria, Va.: ISL Software Corp., 1986–96.

Qur'an Interpretation (Tafsir)

Ali, Muhammad. *Introduction to the Study of the Holy Qur'an*. Columbus, Ohio:
Ahmadiyyah Anjuman Ish'at Islam Lahore, 1992.

Cook, Michael. *The Koran: A Very Short Introduction*. New York: Oxford University Press, 2000.

Daryabadi, Abdul Majid. *Tafsir-Ul-Qur'an: Translation and Commentary of the Holy
Qur'an*. 4 vols. Karachi: Darul Ishaat, 1991.

Doi, A. Rahman I. *Introduction to the Qur'an*. Ibadan: Nigerian Publishers Services, 1981.

Esack, Farid. *The Qur'an: A Short Introduction*. Oxford: Oneworld, 2002.

al-Ghazali, Muhammad. *Journey through the Qur'an: The Content and Context of the
Suras. Themes and Messages of the Holy Qur'an*. Translated by Aisha Bewley,
abridged by Abdalhaqq Bewley. London: Dar al-Taqwa, 1998.

Hawting, Gerald R., and Abdul-Kader Shareef, eds. *Approaches to the Qur'an*.
London: Routledge, 1993.

Ibn Kathir, Abu al-Fida'. *Tafsir al-Qur'an*. 10 vols. Abridged under supervision.
Riyadh: Darussalem, 2000.

al-Khu'i, Abu al-Qasim al-Masawi. *The Prolegomena to the Qur'an*. Translated by
Abdulaziz A. Sachedina. New York: Oxford University Press, 1998.

Maududi [Mawdudi], Abul A'la. *Towards Understanding the Qur'an*. 6 vols. Translated by Zafar Ishaq Ansari. Leicester: Islamic Foundation, 1999.

Philips, Abu Ameenah Bilal. *Usool at-Tafseer: The Methodology of Qur'aanic Explanation*. Sharjah, UAR: Dar al-Fatah, 1997.

Qutb, Sayyid. *In the Shade of the Qur'an*. 30 vols. New Delhi: Islamic Book Service, 1998–.

Usmani, Shabbir Ahmed. *The Noble Qur'an: Tafseer-E-Usmani*. 3 vols. New Delhi: Idara Isha'at-E-Diniyat, 2002.

von Denffer, Ahmad. *'Ulum al-Qur'an*. Leicester: Islamic Foundation, 1994.

Watt, Montgomery, and Richard Bell. *Introduction to the Qur'an*. Edinburgh: University of Edinburgh Press, 1991. [Watt's enlargement and revision of Bell's earlier work.]

Other Works and Works Cited

Ackroyd, P. R., and C. F. Evans, eds. *The Cambridge History of the Bible*. 2 vols. Cambridge: Cambridge University Press, 1975.

Acton, Lord [John Dahlberg]. *Cambridge Modern History*. Vol. 2. Edited by A. W. Ward, G. W. Prothero, and Stanley Leathes. Cambridge: Cambridge University Press, 1903.

Ajami, Fouad. "The Summoning." *Foreign Affairs* 72, no. 4 (1993): 2–9.

Ali, Muhammad. *Muhammad and Christ*. Columbus: Ahmadiyya Anjuman Isha'at Islam Lahore, 1993.

———. *The Religion of Islam*. 6th ed. Columbus: Ahmadiyya Anjuman Isha'at Islam Lahore, 1990.

Anchor Bible Dictionary. 4 vols. New York: Doubleday, 1992.

Ante-Nicene Fathers. Edited by Cleveland A. Cox. Grand Rapids, Mich.: Eerdmans, 1957.

Armstrong, Karen. *Muhammad: A Biography of the Prophet*. San Francisco: HarperSan Francisco, 1992.

al-Awlaki, Anwar. *The Hereafter*. Denver: Al-Basheer Company Audiotapes, 2002.

al-Azhar Supreme Council. "An Appeal to the Civilized World and to All Peace Loving Persons." alazahar@gam3a.com through webmaster@islamic-council.org, 2003. [Translated for Walter Wagner by Hanni Khouri, al-Azhar University, Cairo.]

Baeck, Leo. *The Essence of Judaism*. New York: Schocken Books, 1974.

Baker, Raymond William. *Islam without Fear: Egypt and the New Islamists*. Cambridge, Mass.: Harvard University Press, 1993.

Barth, Karl. *Church Dogmatics*. Vol. 2, pt. 1. Edinburgh: T. and T. Clark, 1957.

Ben-Sasson, H. H., ed. *A History of the Jewish People*. Cambridge, Mass.: Harvard University Press, 1976.

Bergen, Peter. *Holy War, Inc.: Inside the Secret World of Osama bin Laden*. New York: Touchstone, 2002.

Berman, Paul. "The Philosopher of Terror." *New York Times*, March 23, 2003.

Bettenson, Henry, and Chris Maunder, eds. *Documents of the Christian Church*. 3d ed. New York: Oxford University Press, 1999.

Biale, David. *Cultures of the Jews: A New History.* New York: Schocken Books, 2002.

Bill, James A. *The Eagle and the Lion: The Tragedy of American-Iranian Relations.* New Haven: Yale University Press, 1988.

bin Humaid, Abdullah bin Muhammad. *Jihad in the Qur'an and Sunna.* Riyadh: Maktaba Dar-Us-Salam, 1995.

bin Laden, Osama. *Messages to the World: The Statements of Osama bin Laden.* Edited by Bruce Lawrence. London: Verso, 2005.

Boase, Roger, ed. *Islam and Global Dialogue: Religious Pluralism and the Pursuit of Peace.* Burlington, Vt.: Ashgate, 2005.

Bonney, Richard. *Jihad: From Qur'an to bin Laden.* Houndsmills: Palgrave-Macmillan, 2004.

Bostom, Andrew. *The Legacy of Jihad. Islamic Holy War and the Fate of Non-Muslims.* Amherst, N.Y.: Prometheus Books, 2005.

Braaten, Carl, and Robert Jenson, eds. *Christian Dogmatics.* 2 vols. Philadelphia: Fortress Press, 1984.

Burton, John. *The Collection of the Qur'an.* Cambridge: Cambridge University Press, 1977.

Calvin, John. *The Institutes of the Christian Religion.* 2 vols. Translated by Floyd Lewis Battles. Philadelphia: Westminster Press, 1973.

Cameron, Ron. *The Other Gospels: Non-Canonical Gospel Texts.* Philadelphia: Westminster Press, 1982.

Charlesworth, James, ed. *The Old Testament Pseudepigrapha.* 2 vols. Garden City, N.Y.: Doubleday, 1983.

Cohen, Shaye, J. D. *From Maccabees to the Mishna.* Philadelphia: Westminster Press, 1987.

Cohn-Sherbok, Dan, ed. *The Salman Rushdie Controversy in Interreligious Perspective.* Lewiston, N.Y.: Edwin Mellin Press, 1990.

Cook, David. *Contemporary Muslim Apocalyptic Literature.* Syracuse: Syracuse University Press, 2005.

———. *Understanding Jihad.* Berkeley: University of California Press, 2005.

Coulson, Noel J. *Conflicts and Tensions in Islamic Jurisprudence.* Chicago: University of Chicago Press, 1969.

Cragg, Kenneth. *A Certain Sympathy of Scriptures: Biblical and Quranic.* Brighton: Sussex Academic Press, 2004.

———. *The Christ and the Faiths.* Philadelphia: Westminster Press, 1986.

———. *The Dome and the Rock.* London: SPCK, 1964.

———. *The Event of the Qur'an: Islam in Its Scripture.* London: George Allen and Unwin, 1971.

———. *Jesus and the Muslim: An Exploration.* Oxford: Oneworld, 1999.

————. *The Mind of the Qur'an: Chapters in Reflections.* London: George Allen and Unwin, 1973.

————. *Muhammad and the Christian: A Question of Response.* Oxford: Oneworld, [1984] 1999.

————. *The Pen and the Faith: Eight Modern Muslim Writers and the Qur'an.* London: George Allen and Unwin, 1985.

————. *The Qur'an and the West.* Washington, D.C.: Georgetown University Press, 2006.

————. *The Weight in the Word: Prophethood: Biblical and Quranic.* Portland, Ore.: Sussex Academic Press, 1999.

Crone, Patricia, and Michael Cook. *Hagarism: The Making of the Islamic World.* Cambridge: Cambridge University Press, 1977.

Crossan, John Dominic. *The Birth of Christianity: Discovering What Happened in the Years Immediately after the Execution of Jesus.* San Francisco: HarperSan Francisco, 1998.

————. *The Historical Jesus: The Life of a Mediterranean Jewish Peasant.* San Francisco: HarperCollins, 1991.

Cullison, Alan. "Inside al-Qaeda's Hard Drive: A Fortuitous Discovery Reveals Budget Squabbles, Baby Pictures and Office Rivalries—and the Path to 9/11." *Atlantic Monthly* 294, no. 2 (September 2004): 55–70.

Dalai Lama. *Ethics for the New Millennium.* New York: Riverhead Books, 1999.

Daniel, Orville. *Harmony of the Four Gospels.* Grand Rapids, Mich.: Baker Book House, 1996.

Dardess, George. *Do We Worship the Same God? Comparing the Bible and the Qur'an.* Cincinnati: St. Anthony Messenger Press, 2006.

Denny, Frederick. *An Introduction to Islam.* 2nd ed. New York: Macmillan, 1994.

Doi, A., and I. Rahman. *Hadith: An Introduction.* Chicago: Kazi Publications, 1980.

Dupuis, Jacques, S.J. *Toward a Christian Theology of Religious Pluralism.* Maryknoll, N.Y.: Orbis, 1997.

Ehrman, Bart D. *The New Testament and Other Early Writings: A Reader.* New York: Oxford University Press, 1998.

Eickelman, Dale, and James Piscatori. *Muslim Politics.* Princeton: Princeton University Press, 1996.

Epp, Eldon, and George MacRae, eds. *The New Testament and Its Modern Interpreters.* Atlanta: Scholars Press, 1989.

Esack, Farid. *Qur'an: Liberation and Pluralism. An Islamic Perspective on Interreligious Solidarity against Oppression.* Reprint. Oxford: Oneworld, 2002.

Esposito, John. *Islam: The Straight Path.* Expanded ed. New York: Oxford University Press, 1998.

————. *The Islamic Threat: Myth or Reality?* New York: Oxford University Press, 1995.

————. *Unholy War: Terror in the Name of Islam.* New York: Oxford University Press, 2002.

————, ed. *The Islamic World Past and Present.* 3 vols. New York: Oxford University Press, 2004.

————, ed. *The Oxford Dictionary of Islam.* New York: Oxford University Press, 2003.

————, ed. *The Oxford Encyclopedia of the Modern Islamic World.* 4 vols. New York: Oxford University Press, 1995.

————, ed. *Voices of Resurgent Islam.* New York: Oxford University Press, 1983.

Esposito, John, and John Voll. *Makers of Contemporary Islam.* New York: Oxford University Press, 2001.

Feiler, Bruce. *Abraham: A Journey to the Heart of Three Faiths.* San Francisco: Harper-Collins, 2002.

Feldman, Noah. *After Jihad: America and the Struggle for Islamic Democracy.* New York: Farrar, Straus and Giroux, 2004.

Ferguson, Everett, ed. *Encyclopedia of Early Christianity.* 2 vols. 2nd ed. New York: Garland, 1997.

Fiorenza, Francis Schüssler, and John P. Galvin, eds. *Systematic Theology: Roman Catholic Perspectives.* 2 vols. Minneapolis: Fortress Press, 1991.

Firestone, Reuven. *Jihad: The Origin of Holy War in Islam.* New York: Oxford University Press, 1999.

Flannery, Austin, gen. ed. *Vatican Council II: The Conciliar and Post-Conciliar Documents.* New rev. ed. Northport, N.Y.: Costello, 1996.

Fletcher, Richard. *The Cross and the Crescent: Christianity and Islam from Muhammad to the Reformation.* New York: Viking, 2003.

Ford, David F., ed. *The Modern Theologians: An Introduction to Christian Theology in the Twentieth Century.* 2nd ed. Oxford: Blackwell, 1997

Gabriel, Mark. *Islam and Terrorism: What the Qur'an Really Teaches about Christianity, Violence, and the Goals of Jihad.* Lake Mary, Fla.: Charisma House, 2002.

Gätje, Helmut. *The Qur'an and Its Exegesis.* Oxford: Oneworld, 1996.

al-Ghazali, Zainab. *The Return of the Pharaoh.* Leicester: Islamic Foundation, 1994.

al-Ghazzali, Abu Hamid. *Al-Ghazaali's Mishkat Al-Anwar: "The Niche for Lights."* Translated by W. H. T. Gairdner. New Delhi: Kitab Bahvan, 1994.

Ginzberg, Louis. *Legends of the Jews.* 2 vols. Classic Reissue. Philadelphia: Jewish Publication Society, 2003.

Glassé, Cyril. *The New Concise Encyclopedia of Islam.* Rev. ed. New York: Altamira Press, 2001.

Goldberg, David, and John Raynor. *The Jewish People: Their History and Their Religion.* New York: Penguin, 1989.

Goldziher, Ignaz. *Introduction to Islamic Theology and Law.* Princeton. Princeton University Press, 1981.

Graham, Franklin William. *The Name.* Nashville: Thomas Nelson, 2002.

Haddad, Yvonne, ed. *Contemporary Islam and the Challenge of History.* Albany: State University of New York Press, 1981.

Haddad, Yvonne, and John Esposito, eds. *Muslims on the Americanization Path?* Atlanta: Scholars Press, 1998.

Haddad, Yvonne, and Wadi Haddad, eds. *Christian-Muslim Encounters.* Gainesville: University of Florida Press, 1995.

Hawting, G. R., and Kader A. Shareef, eds. *Approaches to the Qur'an.* London: Routledge, 1993.

Hedrick, Charles, and Robert Hodgson, eds. *Nag Hammadi Gnosticism and Early Christianity.* Peabody, Mass.: Hendrickson Press, 1986.

Hennecke, Edgar, and Wilhelm Schneemelcher. *The New Testament Apocrypha.* 2 vols. Translated and edited by Robert McL. Wilson. Philadelphia: Westminster, 1963.

Hesiod. *Hesiod: Theogony and Works and Days, and Theogonis Elegies.* Translated and edited by Dorothea Wender. New York: Penguin, 1973.

Hick, John. *A Christian Theology of Religions: The Rainbow of Faiths.* Louisville: Westminster/John Knox Press, 1995.

———. *God Has Many Names.* Philadelphia: Westminster/John Knox Press, 1982.

Hick, John, and Paul Knitter, eds. *The Myth of Christian Uniqueness: Toward a Pluralistic Theology of Religions.* Maryknoll, N.Y.: Orbis, 1987.

Holt, P. M., Alice Lambton, and Bernard Lewis. *The Cambridge History of Islam.* 4 vols. New York: Cambridge University Press, 1970.

Hoyland, Robert G. *Arabia and the Arabs: From the Bronze Age to the Coming of Islam.* London: Routledge, 2001.

Huntington, Samuel P. "The Clash of Civilizations?" *Foreign Affairs* 72, no. 3 (1993): 22–49.

———. *The Clash of Civilizations and the Re-Making of World Order.* New York: Simon and Schuster, 1997.

———. Interview. PBS *NewsHour.* www.pbs.org/newshour/gergan/january97.

———. *Who Are We? The Challenges to America's National Identity.* New York: Simon and Schuster, 2004.

Huntington, Samuel P., and Anthony Giddens. "The Two Wests." *New Perspectives Quarterly* (Fall 2003). www.digitalnpq.org/archive/2003index.html.

Hussain, Shaukat. *Human Rights in Islam.* New Delhi: Kitab Bhavan, 1990.

Ibn Ishaq, Muhammad. *The Life of Muhammad.* Translated by A. Guillaume. Karachi: Oxford University Press, [1955] 1990.

Ibn Taymiyya, Ahmad. *A Muslim Theologian's Response to Christianity.* Edited and translated by Thomas Michel. Delmar, N.Y.: Caravan Books, 1984.

Ibn Warraq. *What the Koran Really Says: Language, Text and Commentary.* Amherst, N.Y.: Prometheus Books, 2002.

Interpreters Bible. Nashville: Abingdon, 1955.

Jansen, Johannes J. G. *The Neglected Duty: The Creed of Sadat's Assassins and the Islamic Resurgence in the Middle East.* New York: Macmillan, 1986.

Jeffreys, Arthur. *Materials for the History of the Text of the Qur'an.* Leiden: Brill, 1937.

———. *The Qur'an as Scripture.* New York: Russell Moore, 1952.

Jenkins, Peter. *The Next Christendom: The Coming of Global Christianity.* New York: Oxford University Press, 2002.

John Chrysostom. *Discourses against Judaizing Christians.* Translated by Paul W. Harkins. Washington, D.C.: Catholic University of America Press, 1979.

John of Damascus. *Writings.* Translated by Frederic H. Chase Jr. Washington, D.C.: Catholic University of America Press, 1958.

Josephus, Flavius. *The Works of Josephus.* Translated by William Whiston. Peabody, Mass.: Hendrickson, 1987.

Kaltner, John. *Ishmael Instructs Isaac: An Introduction to the Qur'an for Bible Readers.* Collegeville, Mich.: Liturgical Press, 1999.

Kaplan, Mordecai. *The Meaning of God in Modern Jewish Religion.* Detroit: Wayne State University Press, 1994.

Kassis, Hanna. *Concordance of the Qur'an.* Princeton: Princeton University Press, 1984.

Kathir, Abu al-Fida' Ismail ibn. *The Life of the Prophet Muhammad.* 4 vols. Translated into English by Trevor Le Gassick. Reading, U.K.: Garnet, 1998.

Kelsay, John. *Islam and War. The Gulf War and Beyond: Study in Comparative Ethics.* Louisville: Westminster/John Knox Press, 1993.

Kepel, Gilles. *Jihad: The Trail of Political Islam.* Cambridge, Mass.: Belknap, 2002.

Khalidi, Tarif, ed. *The Muslim Jesus: Sayings and Stories in Islamic Literature.* Cambridge, Mass.: Harvard University Press, 2003.

Khan, Ahmad. "Etiquettes of Reading and Handling the Qur'an al-Kareem." www.themodernreligion.com/basic/quran/etiquette.html.

Khomeini, Ruhullah. *Islam and Revolution: Writings and Declarations of Imam Khomeini.* Vol. 1. Berkeley: Mizan Press, 1981.

Khouj, Abdullah Muhammad. *The End of the Journey: An Islamic Perspective on Death and the Afterlife.* Washington, D.C.: Islamic Center, 1988.

Knitter, Paul. *Introducing Theologies of Religions.* Maryknoll, N.Y.: Orbis, 2005.

Kraemer, Hendrick. *The Christian Message in a Non-Christian World.* New York: Harper, 1938.

Kristof, Nicholas. "Martyrs, Virgins and Grapes." *New York Times,* August 4, 2004.

Küng, Hans. *On Being a Christian.* Garden City, N.Y.: Doubleday, 1976.

———. *Theology for the Third Millennium.* New York: Doubleday, 1988.

Lalljee, Yousuf. *Know Your Islam.* 2nd ed. Elmhurst, N.Y.: Tahrike Tarsile Qur'an, n.d.

Lewis, Bernard. *The Crisis of Islam: Holy War and Unholy Terror.* New York: Modern Library, 2003.

————. *Islam and the West.* New York: Oxford University Press, 1993.

————. *Islam in History: Ideas, People, and Events in the Middle East.* New and expanded ed. Chicago: Open Court, 1993.

————. *The Political Language of Islam.* Chicago: University of Chicago Press, 1991.

————. "The Roots of Muslim Rage." *Atlantic Monthly,* 266, no. 4 (September 1990): 49–61.

————. *The Shaping of the Modern Middle East.* New York: Oxford University Press, 1994.

————. *What Went Wrong? Western Impact and Middle Eastern Response.* New York: Oxford University Press, 2002.

Lindsey, Hal. *The Everlasting Hatred: The Roots of Jihad.* Murrieta, Calif.: Oracle House, 2002.

Luther, Martin. *Luther's Works.* Edited by Jaroslav Pelikan and Helmut Lehmann. St. Louis: Concordia; Philadelphia: Fortress Press, 1959.

Mabruk, Laila. *The Day of Rising.* London: Dar al-Taqwa, 1997.

Maimonides, Moses. *The Code of Maimonides (Mishneh Torah).* Vol. 3. Translated by Abraham M. Hershman. New Haven: Yale University Press, 1977.

Maitland, Sara, and Lisa Appignanesi. *The Rushdie File.* London: Fourth Estate, 1989.

Marcinkowski, Muhammad. "Some Reflections on Alleged Twelver Shi'ite Attitudes toward the Integrity of the Qur'an." *Muslim World* 91, nos. 1–2 (Spring 2001): 137–53.

Marty, Martin, and Scott Appleby, eds. *Fundamentalisms Observed.* Chicago: University of Chicago Press, 1994.

Matinuddin, Kamal. *The Taliban Phenomenon: Afghanistan, 1994–1997.* London: Oxford University Press, 1999.

Maududi [Mawdudi], Abul A'la. *Birth Control: Its Social, Political, Economic, Moral, and Religious Aspects.* Reprint. New Delhi: Isha'at-E-Islam Trust, 2000.

————. *Four Basic Qur'anic Terms.* 3rd ed. Lahore: Islamic Publications, 1993.

————. *Islamic Law and Constitution.* Lahore: Islamic Publications, 1992.

Macquarrie, John. *Principles of Christian Theology.* 2nd ed. New York: Scribners, 1977.

McAuliffe, Jane Dammen. *Qur'anic Christians: An Analysis of Classical and Modern Exegesis.* Cambridge: Cambridge University Press, 1991.

————, ed. *Encyclopedia of the Qur'an.* 3 vols. Leiden: Brill, 2001–4.

McBrien, Richard. *Catholicism.* Study ed. Minneapolis: Winston Press, 1981.

McGrath, Alister. *Christian Theology: An Introduction.* 2nd ed. Oxford: Blackwell Publishers, 1997.

Miller, David. *The Quran Unveiled: Islam and New Testament Christianity in Conflict.* Montgomery, Ala.: Apologetics Press, 2005.

Moin, Baquer. *Khomeini: The Life of the Ayatollah.* New York: St. Martin's Press, 1999.

Momen, Moojan. *An Introduction to Shi'ia Islam: The History and Doctrines of Twelver Shi'ism*. New Haven: Yale University Press, 1985.

al-Musnad, Muhammad bin Abdul, collector. *Fatawa Islamiyah: Islamic Verdicts*. Vol. 8. Riyadh: Darussalam, 2002.

Mutahhari Murtaza, Ayatollah. *Fundamentals of Islamic Thought: God, Man, and the Universe*. Berkeley: Mizan Press, 1985.

Nagel, Tilman. *The History of Islamic Theology: From Muhammad to the Present*. Princeton: Marcus Wiener Press, 2000.

Nasr, Hossein, ed. *Islamic Spirituality*. World Spirituality, vols. 19, 20. New York: Crossroad, 1987, 1991.

Neusner, Jacob. *From Testament to Torah: An Introduction to Judaism in Its Formative Age*. Englewood Cliffs, N.J.: Prentice Hall, 1988.

———. *Introduction to Rabbinic Literature*. New York: Doubleday, 1994.

———. *Midrash in Context: Exegesis in Formative Judaism*. Philadelphia: Fortress Press, 1983.

———. *Torah: From Scroll to Symbol in Formative Judaism*. Philadelphia: Fortress Press, 1985.

———. *The Way of the Torah: An Introduction to Judaism*. 4th ed. Belmont, Calif.: Wadsworth Press, 1988.

Neusner, Jacob, Alan Avery-Peck, and William Scott Green. *Encyclopedia of Judaism*. New York: Continuum, 2003.

Nevo, Yehuda, and Judith Koren. *Crossroads to Islam: The Origins of the Arab Religion and the Arab State*. Amherst, N.Y.: Prometheus Books, 2003.

New Interpreters Bible. Gen. ed. Leander Keck. Nashville: Abingdon Press, 1994.

Nicene and Post-Nicene Fathers of the Christian Church. Ser. 2. Edited by Philip Schaff and Henry Wace. Grand Rapids, Mich.: Eerdmans, 1961.

Nicholas of Cusa. *Nicholas of Cusa's De Pace Fidei and Cribratio al-Koran*. Translation and analysis by Jasper Hopkins. Minneapolis: Arthur Banning Press, 1990.

Ordani, Abu-Muhammad, comp. *Fatima the Gracious*. Qum, Iran: Anssarian Publications, 1987.

O'Shaghnessy, Thomas. *Muhammad's Thoughts on Death: A Thematic Study of Qur'anic Data*. Leiden: Brill, 1969.

Pagels, Elaine. *Beyond Belief: The Secret Gospel of Thomas*. New York: Vintage Books, 2004.

———. *Gnostic Gospels*. New York: Random House, 1979.

Papademetriou, George. "An Orthodox Christian View of Non-Christian Religions." Web page of the Greek Orthodox Diocese of America, Ecumenical Issues. www.//goarch.org/en/ourfaith/articles8072.asp.

———. "Recent Patriarchal Encyclicals on Religious Tolerance and Peaceful Coexistence." *Journal of Ecumenical Studies* 39, no. 4 (2002): 105–9.

Parrinder, Geoffrey. *Jesus in the Qur'an*. London: Faber and Faber, 1965.

Partner, Peter. *God of Battles: Holy Wars of Christianity and Islam*. Princeton: Princeton University Press, 1997.

Peters, Francis E. *Muhammad and the Origins of Islam*. Albany: State University of New York Press, 1994.

Peters, Rudolph. *Jihad in Medieval and Modern Islam: The Chapter on Jihad from Averroes' Legal Handbook and the Treatise "Koran and Fighting" by Shaykh al-Azhar and Mahmud Shaltut*. Leiden: Brill, 1977.

Peters, Ted. *God—The World's Future: Systematic Theology for a New Era*. 2nd ed. Minneapolis: Fortress Press, 2000.

Philips, Abu Ameenah Bilal. *Ad-Dajjaal: The Anti-Christ*. Alexandria, Va.: Sound-Knowledge Audio Publishers, 2001. [Audiotape.]

Pipes, Daniel. *In the Path of God: Islam and Political Power*. New York: Basic Books, 1983.

———. *Militant Islam Comes to America*. New York: Norton, 1983.

———. *The Rushdie Affair: The Novel, the Ayatollah, and the West*. New York: Carol Publishing Group, 1990.

Piscatori, James, ed. *Islamic Fundamentalism and the Gulf Crisis*. Chicago: Fundamentalism Project of the American Academy of Arts and Sciences, 1991.

Qaradawi, Yusuf. *Islamic Awakening between Rejection and Extremism*. 2nd rev. ed. Herndon, Va.: American Trust Publications and the International Institute of Islamic Thought, 1991.

Qush, Suleiman. *The Scientific Discoveries in Correlation to the Glorious Qur'an*. Doha, Qatar: Dar al-Thakafa; Manila: Islamic Da'wah Council of the Philippines, 1998.

Qutb, Sayyid. *Milestones*. Cedar Rapids, MI: Mother Mosque Foundation [Signposts], n.d.

———. *Social Justice in Islam*. Translated by John B. Hardie, revised by Hamid Algar. Oneonta, N.Y.: Islamic Publications International, 2000.

Race, Alan. *Christians and Religious Pluralism: Patterns in the Christian Theology of Religions*. Maryknoll, N.Y.: Orbis, 1982.

Rahman, Fazlur. *Islam*. 2nd ed. Chicago: University of Chicago Press, 1979.

———. *Islam and Modernity: Transformation of an Intellectual Tradition*. Chicago: University of Chicago Press, 1982.

———. *Major Themes of the Qur'an*. Minneapolis: Bibliotheca Islamica, 1980.

———. *Revival and Reform in Islam: A Study of Islamic Fundamentalism*. Oxford: Oneworld, 2000.

Rahner, Karl. *Foundations of Christian Faith: An Introduction to the Idea of Christianity*. New York: Seabury Press, 1978

Rajashekar, J. Paul, ed. *Religious Pluralism and Lutheran Theology*. Geneva: Lutheran World Federation, 1988.

Rajashekar, J. Paul, and H. S. Wilson. *Islam in Asia: Perspectives for Christian-Muslim Encounter.* Geneva: Lutheran World Federation, 1991.

Rashid, Ahmed. *Jihad: The Rise of Militant Islam in Central Asia.* New Haven: Yale University Press, 2002.

————. *Taliban: Militant Islam, Oil, and Fundamentalism in Central Asia.* New Haven: Yale University Press, 2000.

Richardson, Don. *Secrets of the Koran.* Ventura, Calif.: Regal Books, 2003.

Riddle, Peter, and Tony Street, eds. *Islam: Essays on Scripture, Thought, and Society: A Festschrift in Honour of Anthony H. Johns.* Leiden: Brill, 1997.

Ridgeon, Lloyd, ed. *Islamic Interpretations of Christianity.* Richmond, U. K.: Curzon, 2001.

Rippon, Andrew, ed. *The Qur'an: Formative Interpretation.* Brookfield, Vt.: Ashgate, 1999.

Robinson, George. *Essential Judaism: A Complete Guide to Beliefs, Customs and Rituals.* New York: Pocket Books, 2000.

Robinson, James, ed. *The Nag Hammadi Library in English.* Rev. ed. San Francisco: Harper and Row, 1988.

Robinson, Neal. *Christ in Islam and Christianity.* Albany: State University of New York Press, 1991.

Ruderman, David. *Between Cross and Crescent: Jewish Civilization from Mohammad to Spinoza.* 2 pts. Chantilly, Va.: Teaching Company, 2005.

Rumi, al-Din Jalal. *Discourses of Rumi.* Translated by A. J. Arberry. London: Routledge Curzon, 2004.

Saad-Ghorayeb. *Hizbu'llah: Politics and Religion.* London: Pluto Press, 2002.

Safi, Omar, ed. *Progressive Muslims on Justice, Gender, and Pluralism.* Oxford: Oneworld, 2003.

Said, Edward. *Orientalism.* New York: Vintage Books, 1985.

Sakr, Ahmad H. *Al-Jinn.* Lombard, Ill.: Foundation for Islamic Knowledge, 1994.

Salahi, M. A. *Muhammad: Man and Prophet.* Rockport, Ill.: Element, 1995.

Sanadiki, Khaled. *Legends and Narratives of Islam: The Biblical Personalities.* Chicago: Kazi Publications, 2000.

Sanders, E. P., A. I. Baumgartner, and Alan Mendelson, eds. *Jewish and Christian Self-Definition: Aspects of Judaism in the Greco-Roman Period.* Philadelphia: Fortress Press, 1991.

Saulat, Sarwat. *Maulana Maududi.* Karachi: International Islamic Publishers, 1984

Schulze, Reinhard. *A Modern History of the Islamic World.* New York: New York University Press, 2002.

Schweitzer, Albert. *The Quest of the Historical Jesus: A Critical Study of Its Progress from Reimarus to Wrede.* Baltimore, Md.: Johns Hopkins University Press, 1998.

Sell, Michael. *Approaching the Qur'an: The Early Revelations.* Ashland, Ore.: White Cloud Press, 1999.

Shanks, Hershel, ed. *Christianity and Rabbinic Judaism: A Parallel History of Their Origins and Early Development.* Washington, D.C.: Biblical Archaeology Society, 1992.

Sheerin, John, and John Hotchkin, eds. *John Paul II: Addresses and Homilies on Ecumenism, 1978–1980.* Washington, D.C.: United States Catholic Conference, 1980.

Sherif, Faruq. *A Guide to the Contents of the Qur'an.* Reading, U. K.: Garnet, 1995.

Sicard, Sigvard von, and Ingo Wulfhorst, eds. *Dialogue and Beyond: Christians and Muslims Together on the Way.* Geneva: Lutheran World Federation, 2003.

Smalley, Beryl. *The Study of the Bible in the Middle Ages.* Notre Dame, Ind.: University of Notre Dame Press, 1964.

Smith, Jane, and Yvonne Haddad. *The Islamic Understanding of Death and Resurrection.* Albany: State University of New York Press, 1981.

Smith, Wilfred Cantwell. *Patterns of Faith around the World.* Oxford: Oneworld, 1998.

Sobrino, Jon. *Jesus in Latin America.* Maryknoll, N.Y.: Orbis, 1988.

Spinoza, Baruch. *Theological-Political Treatises.* Reprint. Indianapolis: Hackett, 1998.

Stille, Alexander. "Scholars Are Quietly Offering New Theories of the Qur'an." *New York Times,* March 2, 2002.

Swidler, Leonard, ed. *Toward a Universal Theology of Religion.* Maryknoll, N.Y.: Orbis, 1987.

al-Tabari, Abu Ja'far Muhammad bin Jarir. *The History of al-Tabari.* Translated by Franz Rosenthal. Albany: State University of New York Press, 1989.

Taji-Farouki, Suha. *Modern Muslim Intellectuals and the Qur'an.* London: Oxford University Press, 2004.

Thompson, Bard. *Humanists and Reformers: A History of the Renaissance and Reformation.* Grand Rapids, Mich.: Eerdmans, 1996.

Timmerman, Kenneth R. *Preachers of Hate: Islam and the War on America.* New York: Crown Forum, 2003.

Treadgold, Warren. *A History of the Byzantine State and Society.* Stanford: Stanford University Press, 1997.

Tuchman, Barbara. *The Bible and the Sword: England and Palestine from the Bronze Age to Balfour.* New York: New York University Press, 1956.

United States Catholic Conference. *Catechism of the Catholic Church.* Vatican City: Libreria Editrice Vaticana, 1994.

Wadud, Amina. *Qur'an and Woman: Rereading the Sacred Text from a Woman's Perspective.* New York: Oxford University Press, 1999.

Wagner, Walter H. *After the Apostles: Christianity in the Second Century.* Minneapolis: Fortress Press, 1994.

————. *God Is Great: Toward Understanding Islam*. Bethlehem, Pa.: Moravian Church Press, 2004.

————. "Interpretations of Genesis 6:1–4 in Second-Century Christianity." *Journal of Religious History* 20, no. 2 (1996): 137–55.

————. "Journeying to God: Muhammad's Isra and Mi'raj." *Cithara* 36, no. 2 (1997): 20–29.

————. "Toward a Christian-Islamic Ecumenic Encounter." *Dialog: A Journal of Theology* 43, no. 3 (2004): 238–43.

Wagner, William. *How Islam Plans to Change the World*. Grand Rapids, Mich.: Kregal Publications, 2004.

Wansbrough, John E., with John Rippin. *Quranic Studies: Sources and Methods of Scriptural Interpretation*. Amherst, NY: Prometheus Books, [1977] 2004.

Watt, W. Montgomery. *Christian-Muslim Encounter: Perceptions and Misperceptions*. London: Routledge and Kegan Paul, 1991.

————. *Companion to the Qur'an*. Oxford: Oneworld, 1994.

————. *Islam: A Short History*. Oxford: Oneworld, 1999.

————. *Islam and Christianity Today: A Contribution to Dialogue*. London: Routledge and Kegan Paul, 1983.

————. *Islamic Philosophy and Theology*. Edinburgh: University of Edinburgh Press, 1985.

————. *Islamic Revelation in the Modern World*. London: Oxford University Press, 1968.

————. *Muhammad: Prophet and Statesman*. New York: Oxford University Press, 1964.

Webster's New World College Dictionary. 4th ed. Edited by Michael Agnes. Cleveland: Wiley, 2002.

Welch, Alford, ed. *Studies in Qur'an and Tafsir*. Special issue. *Journal of the American Academy of Religion* 47, no. 5 (December 1979).

Wessels, Anton. *Understanding the Qur'an*. London: SCM Press, 2000.

Wilken, Robert. *John Chrysostom and the Jews*. Berkeley: University of California Press, 1983.

Witherington III, Ben. *The Jesus Quest: The Third Search for the Jew of Nazareth*. 2nd ed. Downers Grove, Ill.: Intervarsity Press, 1997.

Yahya, Harun. *The End Times and the Mahdi*. Clarksville, Md.: Khatoons, 2003.

Yannoulatos, Anastasios. "Byzantine and Contemporary Greek Orthodox Approaches to Islam." *Journal of Ecumenical Studies* 33, no. 4 (1996): 512–28.

————. "Facing People of Other Faiths." *Greek Orthodox Theological Review* 18, nos. 3–4 (1993): 131–52.

Yusseff, M. A. *Gospel of Barnabas*. Lahore: Muslim Educational Trust, n.d.

Zakaria, Fareed. "Why They Hate Us: The Roots of Islamic Rage—And What We Can Do about It." *Newsweek,* October 15, 2001, pp. 22–40.

GENERAL INDEX

INDEX OF RELIGIOUS TEXTS